Effective Human Relations

Effective Human Relations

Interpersonal and Organizational Applications

ELEVENTH EDITION

BARRY L. REECE, EMERITUS
Virginia Polytechnic Institute and State University

RHONDA BRANDT

KAREN F. HOWIE
Northwestern Michigan College

Australia • Brazil • Japan • Korea • Mexico • Singapore • Spain • United Kingdom • United States

Effective Human Relations: Interpersonal and Organizational Applications, Eleventh Edition

Barry L. Reece, Rhonda Brandt, Karen F. Howie

Vice President of Editorial, Business: Jack W. Calhoun

Editor-in-Chief: Melissa Acuna

Senior Acquisitions Editor: Michele Rhoades

Senior Developmental Editor: Julia Chase

Senior Editorial Assistant: Ruth Belanger

Marketing Manager: Clinton Kernen

Senior Marketing Communications Manager: Jim Overly

Senior Content Project Manager: Kim Kusnerak

Production Technology Analyst: Emily Gross

Media Editor: Rob Ellington

Frontlist Buyer, Manufacturing: Arethea Thomas

Production Service: KnowledgeWorks Global Limited (KGL)

Compositor: KnowledgeWorks Global Limited (KGL)

Senior Art Director: Tippy McIntosh

Internal Designer: Patti Hudepohl

Cover Designer: Rokusek Design

Cover Image: Keren Su/China Span/Alamy

Rights Account Manager—Text: Mardell Glinski-Schultz

Rights Account Manager—Images: Deanna Ettinger

Photo Researcher: Linda Ellis

Library of Congress Control Number: 2009937999
ISBN-13: 978-0-538-74750-9
ISBN-10: 0-538-74750-1

South-Western Cengage Learning
5191 Natorp Boulevard
Mason, OH 45040
USA

Cengage Learning products are represented in Canada by Nelson Education, Ltd.

For your course and learning solutions, visit **www.cengage.com**
Purchase any of our products at your local college store or at our preferred online store **www.ichapters.com**

Printed in Canada
2 3 4 5 6 7 13 12 11 10

In memory of my daughter Colleen, 1964–2003
Barry L. Reece

To Annika, Alexander, and Diane Howie
Karen Kozlowski Howie

Brief Contents

Contents

About the Authors

Effective Human Relations: Interpersonal and Organizational Applications, eleventh edition, represents a compilation of many years of research by the authors. Their combined years of post-secondary teaching experience and on-site consulting with business, industry, and educational institutions provide the basis for their real world approach to human relations skill building. With their diverse backgrounds, they work together to consistently offer their readers up-to-date information and advice in this best-selling text.

BARRY L. REECE is Professor Emeritus at Virginia Polytechnic Institute and State University. He received his Ed.D. from the University of Nebraska. Dr. Reece has been actively involved in teaching, research, consulting, and designing training programs throughout his career. He has conducted more than 500 workshops and seminars devoted to leadership, human relations, communications, sales, customer service, and small business operations. He has received the Excellence in Teaching Award for classroom teaching at Virginia Tech and the Trainer of the Year Award presented by the Valleys of Virginia Chapter of the American Society for Training and Development. Dr. Reece has contributed to numerous journals and is author or co-author of 33 books. He has served as a consultant to Lowe's Companies, Inc., Wachovia Corporation, WLR Foods, Kinney Shoe Corporation, and numerous other profit and nonprofit organizations.

PROFESSOR KAREN F. HOWIE has 30 years of teaching experience at Northwestern Michigan College in Traverse City, Michigan, where she teaches interpersonal relations, professional communications, and customer service. She is currently teaching both face-to-face and online courses in interpersonal relations and customer service. Her international background includes extensive lecturing in Germany and presentations in Matazlan, Mexico, and Osaka, Japan. Besides coauthoring the eleventh edition of *Effective Human Relations,* she worked with a multinational committee at a symposium in Japan in 2000 where her article on "The Role of Faculty in a Learner-Centered Environment" was published in both Japanese and English.

Professor Howie is the Director of the Center for Instructional Excellence on campus and facilitates an international exchange program between the University of Cooperative Education in Lorreach, Germany, and NMC.

Highlights of her educational career include a Fulbright Scholarship to Russia in 2004 and her participation at St. Anne's College at the Oxford Round Table in Oxford, England, in 2009.

Rhonda Brandt: A Tribute

RHONDA BRANDT passed away on January 9, 2008, after a long, courageous battle with cancer. Ms. Brandt was born March 3, 1945, in Hampton, Iowa. After graduating from Hampton High School, she obtained a Bachelor of Arts degree in Business Education from the University of Northern Iowa. She began her teaching career as a faculty member at Hawkeye Community College in Waterloo, Iowa. Upon moving to Missouri in 1991, she obtained a Masters of Education degree from the University of Missouri. Over a period of several years, she served as Administrative Support Department chair at Springfield College and later taught business courses at Ozarks Technical Community College. As a human resource specialist, she conducted workshops and seminars for a wide range of clients across the nation. Ms. Brandt was an early adopter of online instruction and served as Executive Director of the International Association of Online Teachers. She developed numerous training programs in the area of interpersonal relations and co-authored 17 books. She will be remembered as a talented writer and teacher who set high standards for her students and herself. We will greatly miss her wit, charm, wisdom, and keen insights.

Preface

The importance of human relations can be summarized in one concise law of personal and organizational success: All work is done through relationships. The quality of our personal and professional relationships, in many ways, determines the quality of our lives.

Those who enter the work force today encounter a work/life landscape that is more complex and unpredictable than at any other time in history. The mastery of interpersonal relationship skills gives us the self-confidence needed to achieve success in our highly competitive workforce. Persons who have superb interpersonal skills are more likely to be hired and more likely to receive promotions. People skills become more important the higher you rise in the organization.

Effective Human Relations: Interpersonal and Organizational Applications, eleventh edition, continues to be one of the most practical and applied textbooks available. The revision process involved a review of over 1,000 articles that appeared in *Fast Company, Inc.* magazine, *The Wall Street Journal, Fortune, Harvard Business Review, Health & Spirituality,* and several other journals. The authors have also reviewed numerous best-selling books and research reports written by scholars who are searching for what is true, right, and lasting in the field of interpersonal relations.

Building on Previous Strengths

Effective Human Relations: Interpersonal and Organizational Applications, eleventh edition, continues to be one of the most widely adopted human relations texts available today. It has been successful because the authors continue to build on strengths that have been enthusiastically praised by instructors and students.

- The "**total person**" **approach** to human relations continues to be a dominant theme of this new edition. We continue to believe that human behavior at work and in our private lives is influenced by many interdependent traits such as emotional balance, self-awareness, integrity, self-esteem, physical fitness, and healthy spirituality. This approach focuses on those interpersonal relationship skills needed to be well-rounded and thoroughly prepared to handle a wide range of human relations problems and issues.
- This edition, like all previous editions, provides the reader with an in-depth presentation of the **seven major themes of effective human relations:** Communication, Self-Awareness, Self-Acceptance, Motivation, Trust, Self-Disclosure, and Conflict Resolution. These broad themes serve as the foundation for contemporary human relations courses and training programs.
- **Self-assessment and self-development opportunities** are strategically placed throughout the entire text. One of the few certainties in today's rapidly changing workplace is the realization that we must assume greater responsibility for developing and upgrading our own skills and competencies. In many cases, self-development begins with self-awareness. A deficit in self-awareness can be damaging to one's personal relationships and career success.

- A hallmark of this edition, and of all previous editions, is the use of many **real world examples** of human relations issues and practices. These examples build the reader's interest and promote understanding of major topics and concepts. Many of the organizations cited in the eleventh edition have been recognized by the authors of *The 100 Best Companies to Work For, The 100 Best Corporate Citizens, 100 Best Companies for Working Mothers,* and *America's 50 Best Companies for Minorities.* The eleventh edition also includes companies who have received the *Top Small Workplace Award* given by the *Wall Street Journal.*

Staying on the Cutting Edge—New to This Edition

The eleventh edition of *Effective Human Relations: Interpersonal and Organizational Applications* has been updated to reflect the growing importance of the human element in our service-oriented, information-saturated, global economy. It is a practical text designed to help students achieve the insight, knowledge, and relationship skills needed to deal with a wide range of people-related problems. Staying on the cutting edge requires improvements in every edition.

Major Changes and Improvements

These significant changes and improvements can be found in the eleventh edition:

- Every chapter features a new opening vignette.
- Every chapter includes a new Career Insight boxed insert that provides practical tips for job-hunters and career changers.
- There are 17 new Human Relations in Action boxed inserts.
- There are 26 new Total Person Insights.
- There are 16 new Internet Insight exercises.
- Twenty-two of the chapter cases are new.
- Coverage of generational differences has been expanded.
- Fifty-four new photo and cartoon images enhance the learning process.
- Several Critical Thinking and Skill Development exercises have been revised.
- Every chapter has been updated to include new real-world examples.

Chapter Organization

This book is divided into six parts. **Part 1, "Human Relations: The Key to Personal Growth and Career Success,"** provides a strong rationale for the study of human relations and reviews the historical development of this field. One important highlight of Chapter 1 is a detailed discussion of the major developments influencing behavior at work. This material helps students develop a new appreciation for the complex nature of human behavior in a work setting. The communication process—the basis for effective human relations—is explained from both an individual and organizational level in Chapter 2.

Part 2, "Career Success Begins with Knowing Yourself," reflects the basic fact that our effectiveness in dealing with others depends in large measure on our self-awareness and self-acceptance. We believe that by building high self-esteem and by learning to explore inner attitudes, motivations, and values, the reader will learn to be more sensitive to the way others think, feel, and act. Complete chapters are devoted to such topics as communication styles, building high self-esteem, personal values and ethical choices, attitude formation, and motivation.

Part 3, "Personal Strategies for Improving Human Relations," comprises four chapters that feature a variety of practical strategies that can be used to develop and maintain good relationships with coworkers, supervisors, and customers. Chapters on constructive self-disclosure, learning to achieve emotional control, building stronger relationships with positive energy, and developing a professional presence are featured in this part of the text.

In **Part 4, "If We All Work Together ...,"** the concepts of team building and conflict resolution are given detailed coverage. Because employers are increasingly organizing employees into teams, the chapter on team-building leadership strategies (Chapter 12) takes on major importance. The chapter on conflict resolution (Chapter 13) describes several basic conflict resolution strategies, discusses ways to deal with difficult people, and provides an introduction to the role of labor unions in today's work force.

Part 5, "Special Challenges in Human Relations," is designed to help the reader deal with some unique problem areas—coping with personal and work-related stress, working effectively in a diverse work force, and understanding the changing roles of men and women. The reader is offered many suggestions on ways to deal effectively with these modern-day challenges.

Part 6, "You Can Plan for Success," features the final chapter, which serves as a capstone for the entire text. This chapter offers suggestions on how to develop a life plan for effective human relations. Students will be introduced to a new definition of success and learn how to better cope with life's uncertainties and disappointments. This chapter also describes the nonfinancial resources that truly enrich a person's life.

Tools That Enhance the Teaching/Learning Process

The extensive supplements package accompanying the eleventh edition of *Effective Human Relations: Interpersonal and Organizational Applications* includes a variety of new and traditional tools that will aid both teaching and learning. The supplements emphasize learning by doing.

Student Support

Student Companion Website

The student companion website includes a five-question practice test, Flashcards, and a Glossary.

Student Premium Website

This robust website includes interactive games, quizzes, streaming videos, PowerPoint® slides, and more. This content is accessible via an optional printed access card. Standalone instant access is also available via iChapters.com.

Instructor Support

Instructor's Resource Manual

The Instructor's Resource Manual, found on the Instructor CD and protected instructor website, includes two parts. Part One contains, for each chapter, a Chapter Preview, Purpose and Perspective, Presentation Outline, Suggested Responses to

Critical Thinking and Skill Development Challenges, Answers to Try Your Hand exercises, and additional application exercises. Part Two contains Instructional Games.

Test Bank

The Test Bank contains 20 True/False, 20 Multiple Choice, 10 Completion, 10 Short Answer, and Short Case + 5 Multiple Choice questions. The word version of the Test Bank can be found on the Instructor CD and protected instructor website. The electronic version of the Test Bank, ExamView, is found on the Instructor CD. It allows instuctors to streamline assessment from start to finish with ExamView toolset in three seamless applications.

PowerPoint® Slides

These dynamic slides are available on the instructor companion website and Instructor CD. The instructor slides follow the structure of the chapter and facilitate in-class discussion of key concepts. Additional talking points and non-text material are included in the instructor version of the slides. The pared student version of the slides are available on the student premium website.

DVD

The video package consists of several segments that illustrate chapter concepts using examples from real-world companies. Teaching notes and suggested uses for the segments are included in the DVD Guide found on the Instructor CD and instructor website.

Instructor Companion Website

The instructor companion website includes electronic Instructor's Manual files, electronic Word Test Bank files, PowerPoint® slides, and a DVD Guide.

Instructor's Resource CD

This Instructor CD includes the Instructor's Resource Manual, ExamView, Test Bank Word files, DVD Guide, and PowerPoint® slides.

WebTutor for BB/WebCT

WebTutor is an interactive, web-based, teaching and learning resource that is specifically designed for your course. WebTutor gives the instructor a website specifically for his or her class, and this website contains pre-prepared material that reinforces the concepts discussed in the text. Notes, study sheets, a glossary, frequently asked questions about the content, and quiz questions are included in each chapter of the WebTutor program. The communication tools specific to the WebCT and BlackBoard products give instructors access to their students when they are not in class. Although course-specific material is created to complement the material in the text, the WebTutor materials are completely customizable by the instructor, so it's easy to add the syllabus, class notes, or assignments to the site.

The Search for Wisdom

The search for what is true, right, or lasting has become more difficult because we live in the midst of an information explosion. The Internet is an excellent

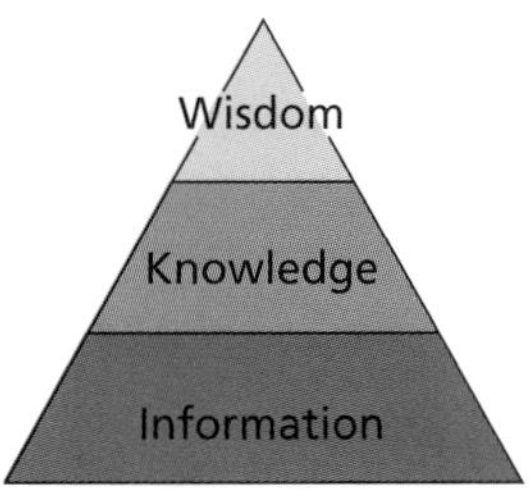

source of mass information, but it is seldom the source of wisdom. Television often reduces complicated ideas to a sound bite. Books continue to be one of the best sources of knowledge. Many new books, and several classics, were used as references for the eleventh edition of *Effective Human Relations: Interpersonal and Organizational Applications.* A sample of the books we used to prepare this edition follows:

How Full Is Your Bucket? by Tom Rath and Donald O. Clifton
A Whole New Mind by Daniel H. Pink
Now Discover Your Strengths by Marcus Buckingham and Donald O. Clifton
The Success Principles by Jack Canfield
The Leadership Challenge by James M. Kouzes and Barry Z. Posner
The Sedona Method by Hale Dwoskin
The Art of Happiness by the Dalai Lama and Howard C. Culter
Be Your Own Brand by David McNally and Karl D. Speak
Civility—Manners, Morals, and the Etiquette of Democracy by Stephen L. Carter
Complete Business Etiquette Handbook by Barbara Pachter and Majorie Brody
Creative Visualization by Shakti Gawain
Do What You Love … The Money will Follow by Marsha Sinetar
Emotional Intelligence by Daniel Goleman
The Speed of Trust by Stephen M. R. Covey
The Four Agreements by Don Miquel Ruiz
Getting to Yes by Roger Fisher and William Ury
How to Control Your Anxiety Before It Controls You by Albert Ellis
How to Win Friends and Influence People by Dale Carnegie
The Human Side of Enterprise by Douglas McGregor
I'm OK—You're OK by Thomas Harris
Minding the Body, Mending the Mind by Joan Borysenko
Multiculture Manners—New Rules of Etiquette for a Changing Society by Norine Dresser
The 100 Absolutely Unbreakable Laws of Business Success by Brian Tracy
1001 Ways to Reward Employees by Bob Nelson
The Power of 5 by Harold H. Bloomfield and Robert K. Cooper
Psycho-Cybernetics by Maxwell Maltz
Self-Matters: Creating Your Life from the Inside Out by Phillip C. McGraw
The 7 Habits of Highly Effective People by Stephen Covey
The 17 Essential Qualities of a Team Player by John C. Maxwell
The Carrot Principle by Adrian Gostick and Chester Elton
The Six Pillars of Self-Esteem by Nathaniel Branden
Spectacular Teamwork by Robert R. Blake, Jane Srygley Mouton, and Robert L. Allen
Working with Emotional Intelligence by Daniel Goleman
The Five Dysfunctions of a Team by Patrick Lencioni
Womenomics by Claire Shipman and Katty Kay
In Praise of Stay-at-Home Moms by Laura Schlessinger

Acknowledgments

Many people have contributed to *Effective Human Relations: Interpersonal and Organizational Applications.* Throughout the years, the text has been strengthened as a result of numerous helpful comments and recommendations. We extend special appreciation to the following reviewers and advisors who have provided valuable input for this and prior editions:

James Aldrich, *North Dakota State School of Science*

Thom Amnotte, *Eastern Maine Technical College*

Garland Ashbacker, *Kirkwood Community College*

Sue Avila, *South Hills Business School*

Shirley Banks, *Marshall University*

Rhonda Barry, *American Institute of Commerce*

C. Winston Borgen, *Sacramento Community College*

Jane Bowerman, *University of Oklahoma*

Jayne P. Bowers, *Central Carolina Technical College*

Charles Capps, *Sam Houston State University*

Lawrence Carter, *Jamestown Community College*

Cathy Chew, *Orange County Community College*

John P. Cicero, *Shasta College*

Anne C. Cowden, *California State University Sacramento*

Michael Dzik, *North Dakota State School of Science*

Jim Elias, *Muscatine Community College*

John Elias, *University of Missouri*

Patrick G. Ellsberg, *Lower Columbia College*

Marilee Feldman, *Kirkwood Community College*

Mike Fernsted, *Bryant and Stratton Business Institute*

Dave Fewins, *Neosho County Community College*

Dean Flowers, *Waukesha County Technical College*

Jill P. Gann, *Ann Arundel Community College*

M. Camille Garrett, *Tarrant County Junior College*

Roberta Greene, *Central Piedmont Community College*

Ralph Hall, *Community College of Southern Nevada*

Sally Hanna-Jones, *Hocking Technical College*

Daryl Hansen, *Metropolitan Community College*

Carolyn K. Hayes, *Polk Community College*

John J. Heinsius, *Modesto Junior College*

Stephen Hiatt, *Catawba College*

Jan Hickman, *Westwood College*

Larry Hill, *San Jacinto College—Central*

Bill Hurd, *Lowe's Companies, Inc.*

Thomas Jay, *Flathead Valley Community College*

Dorothy Jeanis, *Fresno City College*

Marlene Katz, *Canada College*

Robert Kegel, Jr., *Cypress College*

Karl N. Kelley, *North Central College*

Vance A. Kennedy, *College of Mateo*

Marianne Kozlowski, *Evergreen State College*

Kristina Leonard, *Westwood College*

Deborah Lineweaver, *New River Community College*

Thomas W. Lloyd, *Westmoreland County Community College*

Jerry Loomis, *Fox Valley Technical College*

Roger Lynch, *Inver Hills Community College*

Edward C. Mann, *The University of Southern Mississippi*

Paul Martin, *Aims Community College*

James K. McReynolds, *South Dakota School of Mines and Technology*

Russ Moorhead, *Des Moines Area Community College*

Marilyn Mueller, *Simpson College*

Erv J. Napier, *Kent State University*

Barbara Ollhoff, *Waukesha County Technical College*

Leonard L. Palumbo, *Northern Virginia Community College*

James Patton, *Mississippi State University*

C. Richard Paulson, *Mankato State University*

Naomi W. Peralta, *The Institute of Financial Education*

William Price, *Virginia Polytechnic Institute and State University*

Shirley Pritchett, *Northeast Texas Community College*

Linda Pulliam, *Pulliam Associates Chapel Hill, N.C.*

Erin Rea, *University of Michigan*

Lynne Reece, *Alternative Services*

Jack C. Reed, *University of Northern Iowa*

Lynn Richards, *Johnson County Community College*

Khaled Sartawi, *Fort Valley State University*

Robert Schaden, *Schoolcraft College*

Mary R. Shannon, *Wenatchie Valley College*

J. Douglas Shatto, *Muskingum Area Technical College*

Dan Smith, *Dept. Ohio Business College*

Kaischa Smith, *Northwestern Michigan College*

Marilee Smith, *Kirkwood Community College*

Camille Stallings, *Pima Community College*

Lori Stearns, *Minnesota West Community Technical College*

Cindy Stewart, *Des Moines Area Community College*

Rahmat O. Tavallali, *Wooster Business College*

Jane Tavlin, *Delgado Community College*

V. S. Thakur, *Community College of Rhode Island*

Linda Truesdale, *Midlands Technical College*

Wendy Bletz Turner, *New River Community College*

David Wang, *Gateway Technical College*

Marc Wayner, *Hocking Technical College*

Tom West, *Des Moines Area Community College*

Steven Whipple, *St. Cloud Technical College*

Burl Worley, *Allan Hancock College*

We would also like to thank Kaischa Smith of Northwestern Michigan College for her assistance in revising the test items and PowerPoint® slides and Paul Mallette at Colorado State for his work on the quizzes and student games.

Over 200 business organizations, government agencies, and nonprofit institutions provided us with the real-world examples that appear throughout the text. We are grateful to those organizations that allowed us to conduct interviews, observe workplace environments, and use special photographs and materials.

The partnership with Cengage Learning has been very rewarding. Several members of the staff have made important contributions to this project. Sincere appreciation is extended to Julia Chase, who has worked conscientiously on the text from the planning stage to completion of the book. We also offer sincere thanks to other key contributors: Michele Rhoades, Kim Kusnerak, Tippy McIntosh, Emily Gross, Linda Ellis, Deanna Ettinger, Mardell Glinski-Schultz, Sandee Milewski, Ruth Belanger, Rob Ellington, and Clint Kernen.

Barry L. Reece

Karen F. Howie

PART 1

Human Relations: The Key to Personal Growth and Career Success

Chapter 1
Introduction to Human Relations

Chapter 2
Improving Personal and Organizational Communications

CHAPTER 1

Introduction to Human Relations

CHAPTER PREVIEW

LEARNING OBJECTIVES

After studying Chapter 1, you will be able to

- Understand how the study of human relations will help you achieve career success and increased work/life balance.
- Explain the nature, purpose, and importance of human relations.
- Identify major developments in the workplace that have given new importance to human relations.
- Identify major forces influencing human behavior at work.
- Review the historical development of the human relations movement.
- Identify seven basic themes that serve as the foundation for effective human relations.

© Image Source/Getty Images

TIP OF THE ICEBERG

Thomas Moore's Dilemma

Thomas Moore, author of *Care of the Soul*, wasn't thinking too much about work-related issues. He was an author of several best-selling books and enjoyed success as a psychotherapist when he suddenly experienced a major work—life crisis. He discovered that much of the money he had earned from sales of his popular books had vanished into some economic black hole. He was forced to reinvent himself and his work.[1]

Faced with an economic crisis, Moore decided to write a new book, *A Life at Work*, that explored the confusion and anxiety many workers are experiencing during these complex times. While doing research for the new book, Moore encountered an unexpected source of insight. He read *Broken Music*, a penetrating and honest autobiography written by Sting, the talented rock musician. Sting's early work life included outdoor building construction, work as a bus conductor, and work as a civil servant. He eventually worked as a teacher in an elementary school. Sting felt his life was empty of challenge and vitality. None of these jobs offered him enough challenge, nor did they offer an outlet for his unbounded creativity. By paying attention to his deep and complex interior life and being more loyal to his dreams, Sting moved on to become one of the most successful singers in the history of rock music.[2]

Today's labor market is characterized by a great deal of uncertainty. The old *social* contract between employer and employee was based on the notion of lifetime employment. The new *social* contract emphasizes personal responsibility for self-development. Today's employers expect

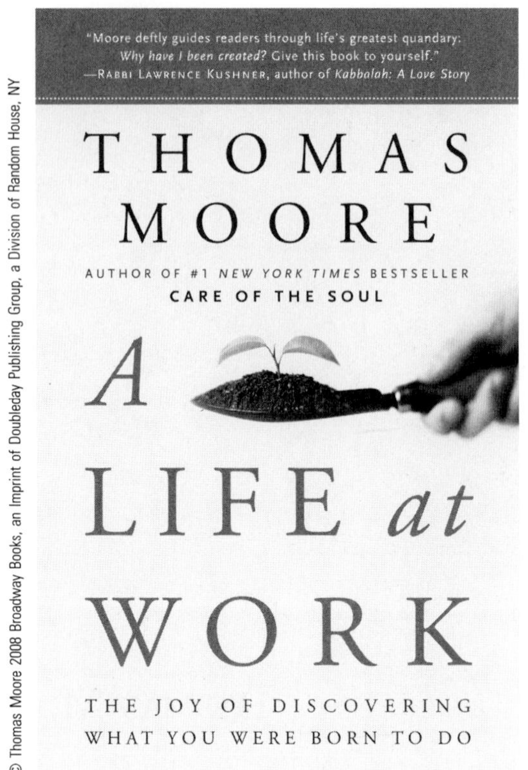

The author of *A Life at Work* encourages us to view the workplace as a laboratory where we can discover who we are and identify the type of work that gives meaning to our lives. It is a book about a search for life work—not just a job. Thomas Moore recognizes that many people are experiencing confusion and anxiety as they cope with issues at work and in their personal lives. He fully understands that unhappiness at work spills over into other areas of life.

employees to assume greater responsibility for increasing their value. Self-development is a major theme of this text.

The Nature, Purpose, and Importance of Human Relations

Each year *Fortune* magazine publishes a list of the 100 best companies to work for in America. The list always includes a variety of small and large companies representing such diverse industries as health care, retailing, finance, manufacturing, hospitality, and customer service. Job seekers study the list carefully because these are the companies where morale is high and relationships are characterized by a high level of trust and teamwork. These companies provide a strong foundation for employees to focus on their necessary self-development. America's best companies realize that all work is done through relationships. This chapter focuses on the nature of human relations, its development, and its importance to the achievement of individual and organizational goals.

Human Relations Defined

The term **human relations** in its broadest sense covers all types of interactions among people—their conflicts, cooperative efforts, and group relationships. It is the study of *why* our beliefs, attitudes, and behaviors sometimes cause relationship problems in our personal lives and in work-related situations. The study of human relations emphasizes the analysis of human behavior, prevention strategies, resolution of behavioral problems, and self-development.

Human Relations in the Age of Information

The restructuring of America from an industrial economy to an information economy has had a profound impact on human relationships. Living in an age in which the effective exchange of information is the *foundation* of most economic transactions means making major life adjustments.

Most of us will work with information instead of producing goods. Many people feel a sense of frustration because they must cope with a glut of information that arrives faster than they can process it. The age of information has spawned the information technology revolution, and many workers experience stress as they try to keep up with ever-changing technology.

Increased reliance on information technology often comes at a price—less human contact. Sources of connection away from work are also being trimmed. Unfortunately, a human-contact deficiency weakens the spirit, the mind, and the body.[3] To thrive, indeed to just survive, we need warm-hearted contact with other people.

The authors of *The Social Life of Information* describe another price we pay for living in the age of information. A great number of people are focusing on information so intently that they miss the very things that provide valuable balance and perspective. Neglecting the cues and clues that lie outside the tight focus on information can limit our effectiveness. Think about written proposals negotiated on the Internet and signed by electronic signature. Such transactions lack the essence of a face-to-face meeting: a firm handshake and a straight look in the eye. Today's knowledge worker needs to take more account of people and a little less of information.[4]

Major Developments That Give New Importance to Human Relations

Every organization depends on three essential factors: people, process, and technology. The first success factor is people.[5] Personal and interpersonal effectiveness set the stage for career success. Studies indicate that communication and interpersonal skills are highly rated by nearly all employers who are hiring new employees. They want to know how new hires will treat coworkers and customers, how they speak and listen at meetings, and how well they extend the minor courtesies that enhance relationships. Your people skills will often make the difference in how high you rise in the organization.[6]

Several important developments in the workplace have given new importance to human relations. Each of the following developments provides support for human relations in the workplace.

- *The labor market has become a place of churning dislocation caused by the heavy volume of mergers, acquisitions, business closings, bankruptcies, downsizings, and outsourcing of jobs to foreign countries.* Executives such as Alan Mulally often view downsizing as an important step toward profitability. As CEO of Boeing Corporation, he trimmed the workforce to 50,000 employees from

ROBERT ARIAIL/THE STATE

120,000. After accepting the CEO position at Ford Motor Company, he announced plans to close 14 factories and slash up to 34,000 jobs.[7] Restructuring efforts often result in low morale and mistrust of management. Employees who remain after a company reduces its ranks also suffer; they often feel demoralized, overworked, and fearful that in the next round of cuts they will be targeted.[8]

- *Changing work patterns create new opportunities and new challenges.* The Census Bureau reports that about 18 million Americans are self-employed. When enterprising persons are laid off by corporations, they increasingly become independent consultants, contractors, landscape gardeners, carpenters, and tax consultants. We are also seeing a strong demand for temporary workers in such diverse fields as medical services, banking, heavy manufacturing, and computers. Many temps land full-time jobs after proving themselves in temporary positions.[9]
- *Organizations are increasingly oriented toward service to clients, patients, and customers.* We live in a service economy where relationships are often more important than products. Restaurants, hospitals, banks, public utilities, colleges, airlines, and retail stores all must now gain and retain the patronage of their clients and customers. In any service-type firm, there are thousands of "moments of truth"—those critical incidents in which customers come into contact with the organization and form their impressions of its quality and service.

In the new economy, almost every source of organizational success—technology, financial structure, and competitive strategy—can be copied in an amazingly short period of time.[10] However, making customers the center of the company culture can take years.

- *Workplace incivility is increasingly a threat to employee relationships.* In this information-based, high-tech, speeded-up economy, we are witnessing an increase in workplace incivility. Rude behavior in the form of high-decibel cell phone conversations, use of profanity, or failure to display simple courtesies such as saying "thank you" can damage workplace relationships. Incivility is the ultimate career killer.
- *Many companies are organizing their workers into teams in which each employee plays a part.* Organizations eager to improve quality, improve job satisfaction, increase worker participation in decision making and problem solving, and improve customer service are turning to teams.

  Although some organizations have successfully harnessed the power of teams, others have encountered problems. One barrier to productivity is the employee who lacks the skills needed to be a team member. In making the transition to a team environment, team members need skills in group decision making, leadership, conflict resolution, and communications.[11]
- *Diversity has become a prominent characteristic of today's work force.* A number of trends have contributed to greater work force diversity. Throughout the past two decades, participation in the labor force by Asian Americans, African Americans, and Hispanics has increased; labor force participation by adult women has risen to a record 60 percent; the employment door for people with physical or mental impairments has opened wider; and larger numbers of young workers are working with members of the expanding 50-plus age group. Within this heterogeneous work force, we will find a multitude of values, expectations, and work habits. The major aspects of work force diversity are discussed in Chapters 15 and 16.

These developments represent trends that will no doubt continue for many years. Many other developments have also had an unsettling impact on the U.S. work force in recent years. In 2001, the economy was jarred by the collapse of several hundred dot.com companies. The World Trade Center terrorist attack on September 11, 2001, crippled the airline and aerospace industries. In 2002, public trust in the corporate establishment was shaken by a wave of corporate scandals that involved Enron, Tyco, Merrill Lynch, Arthur Anderson, WorldCom, and many other companies. In 2007, our economy slumped into a recession triggering a sharp rise in unemployment.

We live in a service economy where relationships are often more important than products.

It is safe to say that no line of work, organization, or industry will enjoy immunity from developments similar to these. Today's employees must be adaptable and flexible to achieve success within a climate of change and uncertainty.

The Challenge of Human Relations

To develop and apply the wide range of human skills needed in today's workplace can be extremely challenging. You will be working with clients, customers, patients, and other workers who vary greatly in age, work background, communications style, values, cultural background, gender, and work ethic.

Human relations are further complicated by the fact that we must manage three types of relationships (see Figure 1.1). The first relationship is the one with ourselves. Many people carry around a set of ideas and feelings about themselves that are quite negative and in most cases quite inaccurate. People who have negative feelings about their abilities and accomplishments and who engage in

HUMAN RELATIONS IN ACTION

Dartmouth Number One Again

The 2007 Wall Street Journal/Harris Interactive business school poll placed the Dartmouth College MBA program number one. The Hanover, New Hampshire, college has won this award on three previous occasions. MBA recruiters, who are participants in the poll, like students from Dartmouth for their collegiality and teamwork. Dartmouth students are considered impressive because of their humble attitudes, maturity, and strong work ethic. Relationship skills and the ability to work well across an organization are highly valued today.[12]

constant self-criticism must struggle to maintain a good relationship with themselves. The importance of high self-esteem is addressed in Chapter 4.

The second type of relationship we must learn to manage is the one-to-one relationships we face in our personal and work lives. People in the health-care field, sales, food service, and a host of other occupations face this challenge many times each day. In some cases, racial, age, or gender bias serves as a barrier to good human relations. Communication style bias, a topic that is discussed in Chapter 3, is another common barrier to effective one-to-one relationships.

The third challenge we face is the management of relationships with members of a group. As already noted, many workers are assigned to a team on either a full-time or a part-time basis. Lack of cooperation among team members can result in quality problems or a slowdown in production.

The Influence of the Behavioral Sciences

The field of human relations draws on the behavioral sciences—psychology, sociology, and anthropology. Basically, these sciences focus on the *why* of human behavior. Psychology attempts to find out why *individuals* act as they do, and sociology and anthropology concentrate primarily on *group* dynamics and social

FIGURE 1.1 Major Relationship Management Challenges

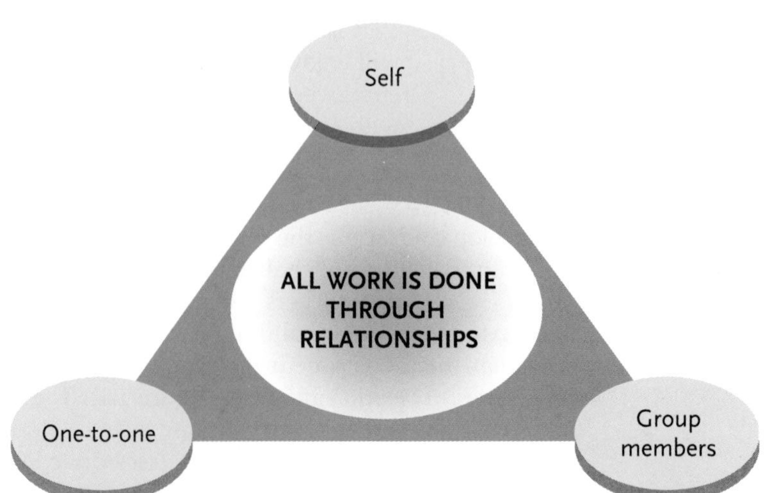

interaction. Human relations differs from the behavioral sciences in one important respect. Although also interested in the why of human behavior, human relations goes further and looks at what can be done to anticipate problems, resolve them, or even prevent them from happening. In other words, this field emphasizes knowledge that can be *applied* in practical ways to problems of interpersonal relations at work or in our personal life.

Human Relations and the "Total Person"

The material in this book focuses on human relations as the study of *how people satisfy both personal and work-related needs.* We believe, as do most authors in the field of interpersonal relations, that such human traits as physical fitness, emotional control, self-awareness, self-esteem, and values orientation are interdependent. Although some organizations may occasionally wish they could employ only a person's physical strength or creative powers, all that can be employed is the **total person**. A person's separate characteristics are part of a single system making up that whole person. Work life is not totally separate from home life, and emotional conditions are not separate from physical conditions. The quality of one's work, for example, is often related to physical fitness or one's ability to cope with the stress created by family problems.

Many organizations are beginning to recognize that when the whole person is improved, significant benefits accrue to the firm. These organizations are establishing employee-development programs that address the total person, not just the employee skills needed to perform the job. Gregg Appliances Inc., an appliance and electronics retail chain, offers employees education programs that help them cope with marital stresses.[13] International Business Machines has launched a program to combat childhood obesity among employees' children.[14] Some organizations offer lunchtime seminars on financial planning, parenting skills, and other topics.

Total Person Insight

DANIEL GOLEMAN
Author, *Working with Emotional Intelligence*

"The rules for work are changing, and we're all being judged, whether we know it or not, by a new yardstick—not just how smart we are and what technical skills we have, which employers see as givens, but increasingly by how well we handle ourselves and one another."[15]

The Need for a Supportive Environment

Some persons in leadership positions do not believe that total person development, job enrichment, motivation techniques, or career development strategies help increase productivity or strengthen worker commitment to the job. It is true that when such practices are tried without full commitment or without full management support, there is a good chance they will fail. Such failures often have a demoralizing effect on employees and management alike.

A basic assumption of this book is that human relations, when applied in a positive and supportive environment, can help individuals achieve greater personal satisfaction from their careers and help increase an organization's productivity and efficiency.

CRITICAL THINKING CHALLENGE:

Evaluate It

You are in the process of preparing a résumé that will be used in conjunction with several upcoming job interviews. Assume that you cannot include any past employment experience, training programs, degrees, awards, or community service. The only data you can put on your résumé are the interpersonal skills that you have developed. How would you select and document these critical transferable skills?[16]

The Forces Influencing Behavior at Work

A major purpose of this text is to increase your knowledge of factors that influence human behavior in a variety of work settings. An understanding of human behavior at work begins with a review of the six major forces that affect every employee, regardless of the size of the organization. As Figure 1.2 indicates, these are organizational culture, supervisory-management influence, work group influence, job influence, personal characteristics of the worker, and family influence.

FIGURE 1.2 Major Forces Influencing Worker Behavior

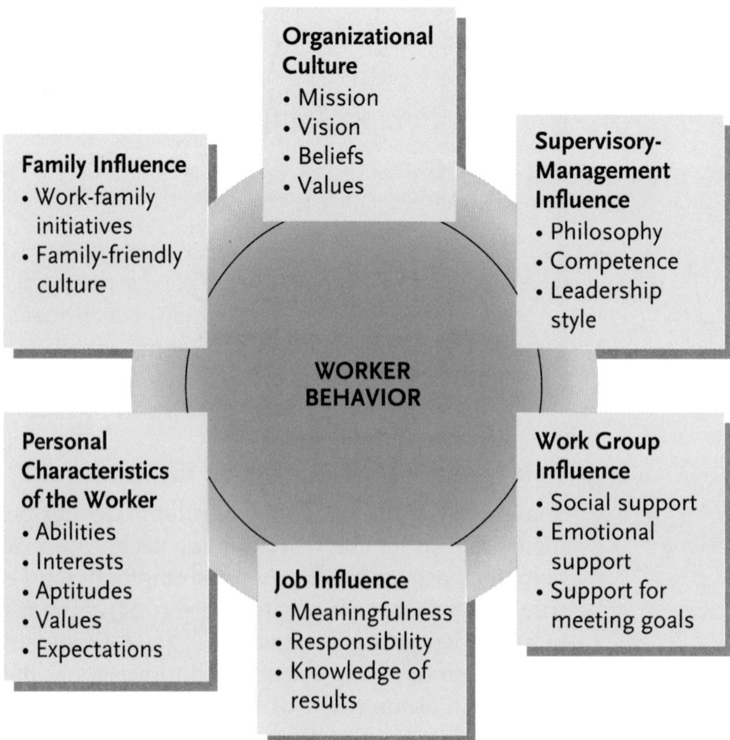

Organizational Culture

Every organization, whether a manufacturing plant, retail store, hospital, or government agency, has its own unique culture. The **organizational culture** is the collection of shared values, beliefs, rituals, stories, and myths that foster a feeling of community among organizational members.[17] The culture of an organization is, in most cases, the reflection of the deeply held values and behaviors of a small group of individuals. In a large organization, the chief executive officer (CEO) and a handful of senior executives will shape the culture. In a small company, the culture may flow from the values held by the founder.[18]

Enron Corporation, the second-largest company in U.S. history to file for bankruptcy, maintained a corporate culture that pushed everything to the limits: business practices, laws, and personal behavior. This culture drove Enron to dizzying growth, but it eventually collapsed under the weight of greed, deception, and corruption.[19]

By contrast, eBay, the auction website company, has developed a culture that emphasizes customer service and a loyal work force. The culture is based on two principles: "We believe people are basically good" and "We believe everyone has something to contribute."[20]

Many employees are fired or choose to quit their jobs because they are a poor fit with the corporate culture. It is a good idea to carefully study the organizational culture of a company before accepting employment there.

The workers at ATA Engineering Inc. don't just talk about the merits of teamwork. They help create a culture that nourishes a collegial and collaborative spirit. This ATA Engineering team has entered an Extreme Gravity Racing event.

Supervisory-Management Influence

Supervisory-management personnel are in a key position to influence employee behavior. It is no exaggeration to say that supervisors and managers are the spokespersons for the organization. Their philosophy, competence, and leadership style establish the organization's image in the eyes of employees. Each employee develops certain perceptions about the organization's concern for his or her welfare. These perceptions, in turn, influence such important factors as productivity, customer relations, safety consciousness, and loyalty to the firm.

> **_Total Person Insight_**
>
> Brian Tracy
> Author, *The Law of Integrity*
>
> *"Integrity lies at the very heart of leadership. Everything you do revolves around the person you are inside. The person you really are inside is always demonstrated by the things you do and say."*[21]

Work Group Influence

In recent years, behavioral scientists have devoted considerable research to determining the influence of group affiliation on the individual worker. This research has identified three functions of group membership. First, it can satisfy *social needs*. When employees feel more connected to their colleagues at work, they are generally more productive.[22] Many people find the hours spent at work enjoyable because coworkers provide needed social support. Second, the work group can provide the *emotional support* needed to deal with pressures and problems on or off the job. Finally, the group provides *assistance in solving problems* and *meeting goals*. A cohesive work group lends support and provides the resources we need to be productive workers.

"We spend most of our waking hours doing our jobs, thinking about work, and getting to and from our workplaces."

Job Influence

Work in modern societies does more than fulfill economic needs. When we find meaning and fulfillment in our jobs, we become more complete as human beings.[23] As one organizational consultant noted, work has taken center stage in the lives of most people: "We spend most of our waking hours doing our jobs, thinking about work, and getting to and from our workplaces. When we feel good about our work, we tend to feel good about our lives. When we find our work unsatisfying and unrewarding, we don't feel good."[24] Unfortunately, many people hold jobs that do not make them feel good. Many workers perceive their jobs to be meaningless and boring. Some workers experience frustration because they feel powerless to influence their working conditions.

Personal Characteristics of the Worker

Every worker brings to the job a combination of abilities, interests, aptitudes, values, and expectations. Worker behavior on the job is most frequently a reflection of how well the work environment accommodates the unique characteristics of each worker.

Identifying the ideal work environment for today's work force is difficult. A single parent may greatly value a flexible work schedule and child care. The recipient of a new business degree may seek a position with a new high-tech firm, hoping to make a lot of money in a hurry. Other workers may desire more leisure time, and some workers seek job security.

Coming into the workplace today is a new generation of workers with value systems and expectations about work that often differ from those of the previous generation. Today's better-educated and better-informed workers value identity and achievement. They also have a heightened sense of their rights.

Family Influence

A majority of undergraduates name balancing work and personal life as their top career goal.[25] Most people want time for family, friends, and leisure pursuits. However, finding employers who truly support work/life balance can be difficult, especially during a slowing economy.

The "New Economy" is a 24/7 economy. When businesses operate 24 hours a day, 7 days a week, the result is often a culture of relentless overwork. In many cases workers must live with on-call-all-the-time work schedules.

The number of dual-income families has doubled since 1950. Both parents have jobs in 63 percent of married-couple homes. When both partners are working long hours, it may be difficult to stay committed to a good life together. Marital distress often has a negative impact on organizational productivity.

Many organizations have found that family problems are often linked to employee problems such as tardiness, absenteeism, and turnover. The discovery has led many companies to develop work-family programs and policies that help employees juggle the demands of children, spouses, and elderly parents.[26]

The Development of the Human Relations Movement

The early attempts to improve productivity in manufacturing focused mainly on trying to improve such things as plant layout and mechanical processes. But, over time, there was more interest in redefining the nature of work and perceiving workers as complex human beings. This change reflected a shift in values from a concern with *things* to a greater concern for *people*. In this section, we briefly examine a few major developments that influenced the human relations movement.

The Impact of the Industrial Revolution

The Industrial Revolution marked a shift from home-based, handcrafted processes to large-scale factory production. Before the Industrial Revolution, most work was performed by individual craft workers or members of craft guilds. Generally, each worker saw a project through from start to finish. Skills such as tailoring, carpentry, and shoemaking took a long time to perfect and were often a source of pride to an individual or a community. Under this system, however, output was limited.

The Industrial Revolution had a profound effect on the nature of work and the role of the worker. Previously, an individual tailor could make only a few items of clothing in a week's time; factories could now make hundreds. However, the early industrial plants were not very efficient because there was very little uniformity in the way tasks were performed. It was this problem that set the stage for research by a man who changed work forever.

Taylor's Scientific Management

In 1874, Frederick W. Taylor obtained a job as an apprentice in a machine shop. He rose to the position of foreman, and, in this role, he became aware of the inefficiency and waste throughout the plant. In most cases, workers were left on their own to determine how to do their jobs. Taylor began to systematically study each job and break it down into its smallest movements. He discovered ways to reduce the number of motions and get rid of time-wasting efforts. Workers willing to follow Taylor's instruction found that their productivity increased.[27]

Frederick W. Taylor started the **scientific management** movement, and his ideas continue to influence the workplace today. Critics of Taylor's approach say that the specialized tasks workers perform often require manual skills but very little or no thinking.

> ***Total Person Insight***
>
> JAMES BAUGHMAN
> Director of Management Development, General Electric Co.
>
> *"You can only get so much more productivity out of reorganization and automation. Where you really get productivity leaps is in the minds and hearts of people."*[28]

Mayo's Hawthorne Studies

Harvard Business School Professor Elton Mayo and his colleagues accidentally discovered part of the answer to variations in worker performance while conducting research in the mid-1920s at the Hawthorne Western Electric plant, located near Chicago. Their original goal was to study the effect of illumination, ventilation, and fatigue on production workers in the plant. Their research, known as the **Hawthorne Studies**, became a sweeping investigation into the role of human relations in group and individual productivity. These studies also gave rise to the profession of industrial psychology by legitimizing the human factor as an element in business operations.[29]

After three years of experimenting with lighting and other physical aspects of work, Mayo made two important discoveries. First, all the attention focused on workers who participated in the research made them feel more important. For the first time, they were getting feedback on their job performance. In addition, test conditions allowed them greater freedom from supervisory control. Under these circumstances, morale and motivation increased and productivity rose.

Second, Mayo found that the interaction of workers on the job created a network of relationships called an **informal organization**. This organization exerted considerable influence on workers' performance.

Although some observers have criticized the Hawthorne studies for flawed research methodology, this research laid the foundation for the field of organizational behavior.[30]

From the Great Depression to the New Millennium

During the Great Depression, interest in human relations research waned as other ways of humanizing the workplace gained momentum. During that period, unions increased their militant campaigns to organize workers and force employers to pay attention to such issues as working conditions, higher pay, shorter hours, and protection for child laborers.

After World War II and during the years of postwar economic expansion, interest in the human relations field increased. Countless papers and research studies on worker efficiency, group dynamics, organization, and motivational methods were published. Douglas McGregor, in his classic book *The Human Side of Enterprise*, argued that how well an organization performs is directly proportional to its ability to tap human potential.[31] Abraham Maslow, a noted psychologist, devised a "hierarchy of needs," stating that people satisfied their needs in a particular order. Later Frederick Herzberg proposed an important theory of employee motivation based on satisfaction. Each theory had considerable influence on the study of motivation and is explored in detail in Chapter 7.

Since the 1950s, theories and concepts regarding human behavior have focused more and more on an understanding of human interaction. Eric Berne, in the 1960s, revolutionized the way people think about interpersonal communication when he introduced transactional analysis, with its "Parent-Adult-Child" model. At about the same time, Carl Rogers published his work on personality development, interpersonal communication, and group dynamics.

Peter Drucker, often described as the greatest management thinker and writer of all time, influenced organizational behavior for a period of 60 years. He originated the view of the corporation as a human community built on trust and respect for the worker. He made clear there is "No business without a customer," a simple concept that created greater support for customer services.[32]

HUMAN RELATIONS IN ACTION

Big-Book Blockbusters

Each year, between 4,000 and 5,000 new books claiming to be about business are published. Here is a list of five heavyweights:

- *The One Minute Manager* by Kenneth Blanchard and Spencer Johnson. (Published in 1982 and still making best-seller lists.)
- *Reengineering the Corporation* by Michael Hammer and James Champy. (A *Business Week* reviewer said, "May well be the best-written book for the managerial masses since *In Search of Excellence*.")
- *Built to Last* by Jim Collins. (According to *USA Today*, it's "one of the most eye-opening business studies since *In Search of Excellence*.")
- *In Search of Excellence* by Tom Peters and Robert Waterman. (Described by the *Wall Street Journal* as "one of those rare books on management that are both consistently thought provoking and fun to read.")
- *How to Win Friends and Influence People* by Dale Carnegie. (Published in 1936 and still a best seller.)[34]

There is no doubt that management consultants Tom Peters and Robert Waterman also influenced management thinking regarding the importance of people in organizations. Their best-selling book *In Search of Excellence*, published in 1982, describes eight attributes of excellence found in America's best-run companies. One of these attributes, "productivity through people," emphasizes that excellent companies treat the worker as the root source of quality and productivity. The editors of *Fast Company* magazine say that *In Search of Excellence* "fired the starting gun in the race to the New Economy."[33]

We have provided you with no more than a brief glimpse of selected developments in the human relations movement. Space does not permit a review of the hundreds of theorists and practitioners who have influenced human relations in the workplace. However, in the remaining chapters, we do introduce the views of other influential thinkers and authors.

Major Themes in Human Relations

It is not an exaggeration to describe communication as the "heart and soul" of human relations.

Seven broad themes emerge from the study of human relations. They are communication, self-awareness, self-acceptance, motivation, trust, self-disclosure, and conflict resolution. These themes reflect the current concern in human relations with the twin goals of (1) personal growth and development and (2) the achievement of organizational objectives. To some degree, these themes are interrelated (see Figure 1.3), and most are discussed in more than one chapter of this book.

Communication

It is not an exaggeration to describe communication as the "heart and soul" of human relations. **Communication** is the means by which we come to an understanding of ourselves and others. To grow and develop as persons, we must develop the awareness and the skills necessary to communicate effectively.

FIGURE 1.3 Major Themes in Human Relations

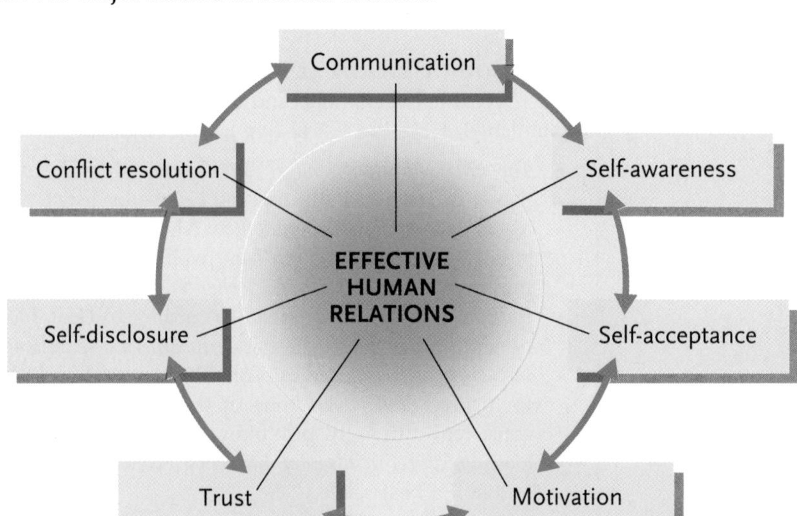

Communication is the *human* connection. That is why the subject is covered in more than one section of this book. In Chapter 2, we explore the fundamentals of both personal and organizational communication. It is these fundamentals that provide the foundation for all efforts to improve communication. Chapter 3 provides an introduction to communication styles and outlines several practical tips on how you can cope with communication style bias. Chapter 8 explains how constructive self-disclosure, an important form of personal communication, can be used to improve human relationships.

Self-Awareness

One of the most important ways to develop improved relationships with others is to develop a better understanding of ourselves. With increased **self-awareness** comes a greater understanding of how our behavior influences others. Stephen Covey, author of *The Seven Habits of Highly Effective People*, says that self-awareness enables us to stand apart and examine the way we "see" ourselves, as well as to see other people.[35]

The importance of self-awareness is being recognized by an increasing number of authors, trainers, and educators. Daniel Goleman, author of the best-selling book *Emotional Intelligence*, has given us new insights into the importance of self-awareness. Goleman says IQ accounts for only about 20 percent of a person's success in life. The rest, he says, you can credit to "emotional intelligence." Of all the elements that make up emotional intelligence, Goleman asserts, self-awareness is the most important. He notes that a deficit in self-awareness can be damaging to one's personal relationships and career.[36] Self-awareness is discussed in greater detail in the chapters that are featured in Part 2.

CAREER INSIGHT

Life Changing Meeting

Jim Collins, best-selling author, recalls a life-changing meeting with Peter Drucker. Collins says Drucker altered the direction of his life by focusing the discussion around one simple question: "What do you want to contribute?"

Self-Acceptance

The degree to which you like and accept yourself is the degree to which you can genuinely like and accept other people. **Self-acceptance** is the foundation of successful interaction with others. In a work setting, people with positive self-concepts tend to cope better with change, accept responsibility more readily, tolerate differences, and generally work well as team members. A negative self-concept, however, can create barriers to good interpersonal relations. Self-acceptance is crucial not only for building relationships with others but also for setting and achieving goals. The more you believe you can do, the more you are likely to accomplish. Chapter 4 explains why high self-esteem (complete self-acceptance) is essential for effective human relations. That chapter also helps you identify ways to achieve greater self-acceptance.

Motivation

Most people who engage in the study of **motivation** seek answers to two questions: "How do I motivate myself?" and "How do I motivate others?" If you are really committed to achieving peak performance, you must motivate yourself from within.[37] Inner drives for excellence can be very powerful. To motivate others, you need to understand time-proven, well-researched theories and well-established motivation strategies. Chapter 5 will help you identify the priorities and values that motivate you. Chapter 7 explores the complex nature of human motivation, particularly of self and others, and examines various motivation strategies. In Chapter 10, you will learn how incentives and various positive reinforcement methods serve as external motivators.

Trust

Trust is the building block of all successful relationships with coworkers, customers, family members, and friends. There is compelling evidence that low levels of trust in a work force can lead to reduced productivity, stifled innovation, high stress, and slow decision making.[38] When a lack of trust exists in an organization, a decline in the flow of information almost always results. Employees communicate less information to their supervisors, express opinions reluctantly, and avoid discussions. Cooperation, so necessary in a modern work setting, deteriorates. When a climate of trust is present, frank discussion of problems and a free exchange of ideas and information is more likely to take place. The concept of trust is discussed in Chapters 8 and 12.

Skill Development: Apply It

To achieve a better understanding of the major themes in human relations, complete the sentences below. Work quickly and don't worry too much about the ending. Sentence completion exercises can be powerful vehicles for self-discovery and personal growth.

To become more self accepting I need to...

To build a more trusting relationship with others, I need to...

My greatest strength in the area of communication is...

To grow in the area of self-awareness, I need to...

I am motivated to give my best when...

Self-Disclosure

Self-disclosure and trust are two halves of a whole. The more open you are with people, the more trust you build. The more trust there is in a relationship, the safer you feel to disclose who you are. Self-disclosure is also part of good communication and helps eliminate unnecessary guessing games. Managers who let their subordinates know what is expected of them help those employees fulfill their responsibilities. Chapter 8 emphasizes the need of individuals to verbalize the thoughts and feelings they carry within them and provides many practical suggestions on how to use constructive self-disclosure.

Conflict Resolution

Conflict in one form or another surfaces almost daily in the lives of many workers. You may experience conflict during a commute to work when a careless driver cuts you off at a freeway exit ramp. If your job includes supervisory-management responsibilities, you will spend a great deal of time in **conflict resolution**, attempting to resolve conflicts among members of your staff. As a team member, you may assume the role of mediator when other team members clash. Conflict also surfaces when working parents attempt to balance the demands of both work and family. Stressful conditions at home often interfere with work performance, and on-the-job pressures create or magnify problems at home.[39] The ability to anticipate or resolve conflict can be an invaluable skill. Although Chapter 13 deals specifically with the topic of conflict resolution, the chapters devoted to communication, achievement of emotional control, and team building provide many valuable suggestions on how conflict can be handled constructively.

Human Relations: Benefits to You

As previously noted, the work force is currently characterized by downsizing, mergers, buyouts, business closings, and other disruptive forces. We are seeing more emphasis on quality products and quality services. In addition, diversity

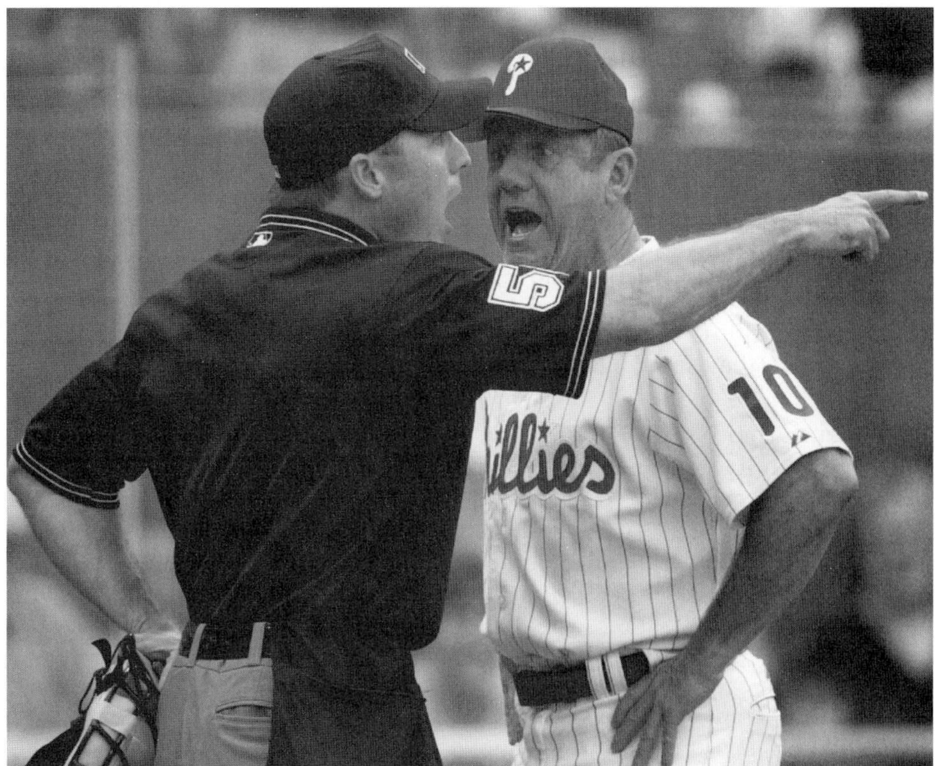

"Philadelphia Phillies' Manager Larry Bowa argues with home plate umpire Dan Iassogna (L) after being ejected during the seventh inning of interleague play against the Toronto Blue Jays in Philadelphia. Bowa was yelling from the dugout about a high strike in the Phillies' 4-2 loss to the Blue Jays."

has become a more prominent characteristic of today's work force. These conditions will very likely continue in the new millennium. One of the best ways to cope with these changes is to develop and apply the interpersonal skills needed for success in today's working world.

Many leaders think that courses in human relations are important because very few workers are responsible to themselves alone. These leaders point out that most jobs today are interdependent. If people in these jobs cannot work effectively as coworkers, the efficiency of the organization will suffer.

LOOKING BACK: REVIEWING THE CONCEPTS

- Understand how the study of human relations will help you achieve career success and increased work/life balance.

Human relations covers all types of interactions among people—their conflicts, cooperative efforts, and group relationships. The importance of interpersonal relations can be summarized in one concise law of personal and organizational success: All work is done through relationships. Employees are more productive when they have the ability to develop effective relationships with their supervisor, fellow workers, customers, and clients.

- Explain the nature, purpose, and importance of human relations.

The healthy functioning of any organization, large or small, depends on teamwork. Effective human relations are the very foundation of teamwork. Human relations, when applied in a positive and supportive environment, can help increase an organization's productivity and efficiency.

- Identify major developments in the workplace that have given new importance to human relations.

The restructuring of America from an industrial economy to an information economy has had profound implications for the study of human relations. Several major developments in the workplace have given new importance to this branch of learning. Some of these developments include churning dislocation in the labor market, changing work patterns, the need for higher service standards, increasing workplace incivility, greater reliance on team-based structures, and work force diversity.

- Identify major forces influencing human behavior at work.

A major purpose of this text is to increase understanding of major factors that influence human behavior in a variety of work settings. These include organizational culture, supervisory-management influence, work group influence, job influence, personal characteristics of worker, and family influence.

- Review the historical development of the human relations movement.

Early attempts to improve productivity in manufacturing focused on such things as plant layout and mechanical processes. With the passing of time, there was more interest in redefining the nature of work and perceiving workers as complex human beings. Two landmarks in the study of motivation and worker needs are Frederick Taylor's work in scientific management and Elton Mayo's Hawthorne studies. Later research by Douglas McGregor, Frederick Herzberg, Carl Rogers, Peter Drucker, and others contributed greatly to our understanding of how to achieve productivity through people.

- Identify seven basic themes that serve as the foundation for effective human relations.

Seven major themes emerge from a study of human relations: communication, self-awareness, self-acceptance, motivation, trust, self-disclosure, and conflict resolution. These themes reflect the current concern in human relations with personal growth and satisfaction of organization objectives.

ON THE JOB Q & A: SKILLS YOU CAN TAKE ANYWHERE

Q: The daily newspapers and television news shows are constantly reporting on mergers, business closings, and downsizing efforts. With so much uncertainty in the job market, how can I best prepare for a career?

A: You are already doing one thing that is very important—keeping an eye on labor market trends. During a period of rapid change and less job security, you must continuously study workplace trends and assess your career preparation. Louis S. Richman, in a *Fortune* magazine article entitled "How to Get Ahead in America," said, "Climbing in your career calls for being clear about your personal goals, learning how to add value, and developing skills you can take anywhere." Richard Bolles, author of the best-selling job-hunting book, *What Color Is Your Parachute?*, says you must do a systematic inventory of the transferable skills that you already possess, and then identify the skills that you still need to develop. Keep in mind that today's employers demand more, so be prepared to add value to the company from day one. Search for your employer's toughest problems and make yourself part of the solutions.

You have already developed some important transferable work skills in school. If you have worked on group projects, then you have no doubt developed skills in the areas of collaboration and conflict resolution.[40]

KEY TERMS

human relations 4
total person 9
organizational culture 11
scientific management 14
Hawthorne Studies 14
informal organization 14
communication 16
self-awareness 17
self-acceptance 17
motivation 18
trust 18
self-disclosure 18
conflict resolution 19

TRY YOUR HAND

1. Throughout this book you will be given many opportunities to engage in self-assessment activities. Self-assessment involves taking a careful look at the human relations skills you need to be well rounded and thoroughly prepared for success in your work life and fulfillment in your personal life. To assess your human relations skills, complete the Human Relations Abilities Assessment Form found on the website (www.cengage.com/management/reece). This assessment form will provide you with increased awareness of your strengths and a better understanding of the abilities you may want to improve. Each item offers an opportunity for goal setting to achieve personal development. Goal setting guidelines are described in Chapter 4.

2. In his book, *The Success Principles*, Jack Canfield describes 50 principles that will increase your confidence, help you tackle daily challenges, and teach you how to realize your ambitions. Number one on his list is "Take 100% responsibility for your life." This includes the quality of your relationships, your health and fitness, your income, your career success—everything! He says most of us have been conditioned to blame events outside of our lives for those parts of our lives we dislike. Reflect on your life up to this point and identify situations in which you

blamed someone or something else for your failure to achieve a goal or improve in some area. Do you see any situations in which you felt justified in blaming others or refused to take risks?[41]

3. Human relations and the *Total Person* concept are interwoven in the 17 chapters of this text. Progressive organizations recognize that most employees are striving to satisfy both personal and work related needs. They also recognize that employees display a wide range of interrelated human traits such as emotional control, values orientation, and self-awareness.
   a. Analyze the importance of creating an organizational culture that meets the needs of the *Total Person.*
   b. Many organizations that have been selected for *Fortune* magazine's list of 100 best companies to work for in America provide benefits that meet the needs of the total person. Brainstorm with classmates the benefits you will seek throughout your employment career.

INTERNET INSIGHTS

Companies featured in *Fortune's* list of the 100 best companies to work for in America are characterized by openness, fairness, camaraderie among employees, job security, opportunities for advancement, and sensitivity to work/family issues. These companies are concerned about the total person, not just the skills that help the company earn a profit. Here are some of the companies that have made the "best companies" list:

COMPANY	LOCATION	TYPE OF BUSINESS
NetApp	Sunnyvale, CA	Storage & Data Management
Zappos.com	Henderson, NV	E-Commerce Retailer
NuStar energy	San Antonio, TX	Pipeline Operator & Refinery
DreamWorks	Glendale, CA	Animation
Marriott International	Washington, DC	Hotel Chain
e-Bay	San Jose, CA	Online Auctioneer

Develop a profile of two of these companies by visiting their websites and reviewing the available information. Also, visit Hoover's Inc. (http://www.ab.hoovers.com), a resource that provides access to profiles of thousands of companies. Additional information on each of these companies may be found in *BusinessWeek, Forbes, Fortune,* and other business publications.

YOU PLAY THE ROLE

The college you attend offers career counseling, job-placement assistance, and help finding summer internships. You plan to meet with a career counselor and seek help finding a summer internship with a well-established company. You will be meeting with a class member who will assume the role of career counselor. The purpose of this meeting is to give the counselor some basic information about your career plans and the type of company you would like to work for. Before the meeting, prepare a written outline of information you plan to present during the meeting. Base your outline on your academic studies and your current employment interests. The outline should focus on the following areas:

- Define what type of work would be most meaningful.
- Describe what type of organizational culture would be most appealing to you.
- Identify what you find to be the basic rewards of work.

BELOW THE SURFACE:

In Search of Meaningful Work

At the beginning of this chapter, we described how Sting spent several years moving from one job to another, only to discover that each career path was empty of challenge. Some of these jobs provided job security, but none of them provided an outlet for his creative powers and musical talents. He could have spent his entire working life as a bus conductor or a civil servant, but he would have been a very unhappy person. In his memoir, *Broken Music,* we learn that his success as an artist (sales of nearly 100 million albums) was the result of risk taking. Some people are griped with the feeling they are getting nowhere at work but still can't move ahead. Some people in their fifties and sixties are still not sure who they are and what they are called to do.[42]

Some organizations will help you find rewarding work. Deloitte Development LLC (http://www.deloitte.com) provides a wide range of audit, tax, and financial services throughout the world. This large company (165,000 employees) offers increasingly customized career paths with great emphasis on coaching. Each of the major divisions with the company offers its own tailored mentoring effort. These mentoring programs are customized to fit an employee's development cycle.[43]

A great place to work need not be a large company. Many small businesses and nonprofits have created workplace environments and cultures that offer rewarding career paths. The *Wall Street Journal* identified the 15 top small workplaces. Companies such as Guerra DeBerry Coody (advertising and public relations) and NRG Systems (maker of wind measuring equipment) tend to let employees at all levels make key decisions. They constantly identify new ways to improve the employee experience and engage employees.[44]

QUESTIONS

1. Support your position for searching for an employer who will provide a healthy balance between work and personal life.
2. As you search for a rewarding job, differentiate your goals related to a work environment versus a paycheck.

CLOSING CASE:
Challenges in the New Economy

At the beginning of the new millennium, a growing number of social researchers, economists, and consultants tried to predict what the world of work would be like in the years ahead. We pay close attention to these and to even more recent forecasts because work is a central part of our identities. As one writer has noted, our working life—in a few short decades—adds up to life itself. Work can also be one of the major fulfillments in life. What will the New Economy be like from a worker's viewpoint? Here are three predictions:

- *In the New Economy, everyone is an entrepreneur.* This is the view expressed by Thomas Petzinger, Jr., author and former columnist for the *Wall Street Journal.* He reports on factories where employees handle customer service calls and create new ways to solve customer problems. At UPS, the drivers are the eyes and ears of the sales force. They help identify new customers and help solve customer service problems. Many bank tellers are actively involved in sales and service activities.[45] Today, the term *intrapreneur* is used to describe an employee who takes personal "hands-on responsibility" for developing ideas, products, or processes. To become an intrapreneur in a corporate setting often means using your creativity more often, taking some risks, and moving beyond your job description.[46]

- *The New Economy features the art of the relaunch.* How often will you change jobs during your lifetime? Five times? Ten? Fifteen? The New Economy offers more career options, more challenges, and more uncertainty. Chances are you will need to relaunch your career several times.
- *In the New Economy, getting a job may be easier than getting a life.* We have, in recent years, seen an increase in the standard of living. The price we pay for a bigger home, a nicer automobile, or a vacation in Italy is often a more demanding work life. Some people choose to work harder in order to acquire more "things." In some cases, corporate downsizing has left fewer people to do the same amount of work. Working more hours and working harder during those hours can result in greater stress, a breakdown in family life, and a decrease in leisure time.[47]

QUESTIONS

1. Would you feel comfortable assuming the duties of an entrepreneur within an existing company, or would you rather start your own business? Differentiate the strengths and weakness of both positions.
2. You are likely to relaunch yourself several times during the years ahead. Evaluate the prospect of several relaunches; does it seem frightening to you, or do you look forward to the challenge? Substantiate your position.
3. Assess what steps you would need to take to achieve a better work/life balance.

INTEGRATED RESOURCES

VIDEOS:

Allstate: In Good Hands

Organizational Structure at Green Mountain Coffee Roasters

CLASSROOM ACTIVITIES

Human Relations Abilities Assessment Questionnaire

IRM Application Exercise 1.1

IRM Application Exercise 1.2

IRM Application Exercise 1.3

IRM Application Exercise 1.4

Improving Personal and Organizational Communications

TIP OF THE ICEBERG

CHAPTER PREVIEW

LEARNING OBJECTIVES

After studying Chapter 2, you will be able to

- Understand the communication process.
- Identify and explain the filters that affect communication.
- Identify ways to improve personal communication, including developing listening skills.
- Understand how communications flow throughout an organization and how to improve the flow when necessary.
- Learn how to effectively communicate through technology.

The Age of Overload

Surviving 21st century living takes *focus* according to Maggie Jackson, *Boston Globe* columnist and author of *Distracted: The Erosion of Attention and the Coming Dark Age.* In the age of tech-savvy, hyper-mobility, split-focused, cyber-centric behaviors, more information is not necessarily more knowledge.[1]

In an age of overload, Jackson says we need to re-balance and concentrate on the powers of attention. The erosion of attention in society resonates with many students, educators, parents, workers, and bosses. In a knowledge economy where overload and instant stimulation is the norm, we need to strengthen our skills of focus and perception. When we focus on our high-tech innovations rather than face-to-face communication, we create a culture of isolation. Jackson says it is time we paid attention to each other and to our inner voices—it is time we relearn to think deeply by filtering out hyper-stimulation distractions.[2]

One-third of today's knowledge workers say they are so frequently interrupted and so consumed with multitasking that they have no time to think. In the spirit of Fredrick W. Taylor's scientific management, Jackson reports, researchers have found that workers "typically change tasks every three minutes" and "take about twenty-five minutes to return to an interrupted task...usually plugging into two other work projects in the interim." By one estimate "interruptions take up to 2.1 hours of an average worker's day and cost the U.S. economy $588 billion a year. In a hectic, multitasking world filled with information and distractions, Ms. Jackson

DISTRACTED

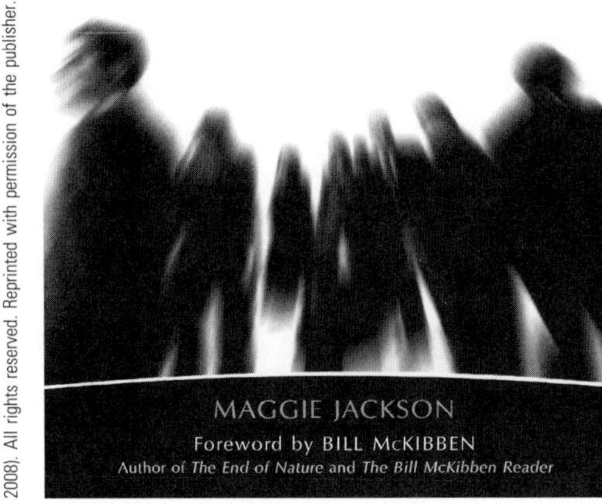

Maggie Jackson reminds us that more information flowing into our lives does not necessarily make us more knowledgeable. Many workers say frequent interruptions and the need to engage in multitasking rob them of time to think. The author of *Distracted: The Erosion of Attention and the Coming Dark Age* says we need to strengthen our skills of focus and perception.

suggests, "Self-discipline proves the key to the attention puzzle." Critical thinking, problem solving, reflection, and *focused* communications are critical to personal and career success.[3]

Communication in a High-Tech World

The new millennium has ushered in the age of information, led by rapid advances in technology-based communication. But technology without the involvement of people can create more problems than it solves. Developing new technology to move more information faster is critical to staying competitive in today's global marketplace. But the leaders of successful organizations realize that their primary goal continues to be creating an organizational culture that fosters teamwork, which involves effective communication among its workers so that they are motivated to do their best and thereby improve customer service.

Often individuals must wade through useless data to find the information they are seeking—and this data glut has become a serious issue in the workplace. Although the speed and volume of information have increased, the average person cannot process it any faster. A young narrator in a television commercial for Volkswagen expressed the feelings of many people:

> *I've got gigabytes, I've got megabytes, I'm voice-mailed. I'm e-mailed. I surf the Net. I'm on the Web. I am Cyber-Man. So how come I feel so out of touch?*[4]

As the speed and number of messages increase, workers often find themselves distracted and unable to concentrate. This often leads to a breakdown in communication, which can result in human relations problems that may be hard to fix once the damage is done.

The Communication Process

Most people take communication for granted. When they write, speak, or listen to others, they assume that the message given or received is being understood. In reality, messages are often misunderstood because they are incomplete or because different people interpret messages in different ways. The diversity of today's work force calls for a greater understanding of how to communicate effectively, through technology or face-to-face, with people from different cultures, countries, and lifestyles. Yet even though people and communication methods may be diverse, the basic communication process remains the same.

Impersonal Versus Interpersonal Communication

In a typical organization, the types of communication used to exchange information can be placed on a continuum ranging from "impersonal" on one end to "interpersonal" on the other.[5] **Impersonal communication** is a one-way process that transfers basic information such as instructions, policies, and financial data. Generally, organizations use this information-delivery process when they use electronic bulletin boards or memos as quick, easy ways to "get the word out." Their effectiveness is somewhat limited because there is little, if any, possibility for the person receiving the information to clarify vague or confusing information.

Interpersonal communication is the exchange of information between two or more people. Such words as *share, discuss, argue*, and *interact* refer to this form of two-way communication. Interpersonal communication can take place in meetings, over the phone, in face-to-face interviews, or even during classroom discussions between instructors and students. If interpersonal communication is to be effective, some type of **feedback**, or understood response, from the person receiving the information is necessary. When this exchange happens, those involved can determine whether the information has been understood in the way intended. This is one of the reasons that some managers still prefer person-to-person meetings and telephone calls instead of e-mail. The speed of technology can be invaluable when it comes to impersonal information giving, but it cannot replace the two-way, interpersonal communication process when feedback and discussion are necessary.

Sender—Message—Receiver—Feedback

Effective communication is a continuous loop that involves a sender, a message, a receiver, and feedback that clarifies the message.[7] To illustrate, suppose your

Total Person Insight

Kerry J. Sulkowicz
Founder, Boswell Group LLC

"The ability to converse should be a basic building block of organizations. Healthy conversations allow leaders to lead, followers to respond, negotiators to make deals, salespeople to sell, and researchers to develop ideas."[6]

friend phones from your neighborhood convenience store and asks for directions to your home. You give your friend the appropriate street names, intersections, and compass directions so that he can drive to your door without getting lost. When your friend repeats his understanding of your directions, you clarify any misunderstandings, and he drives directly to your home. A simplified diagram of this communication process would look like Figure 2.1.

Now suppose you are late for an appointment, and the plumber you had requested three days ago calls you from her cell phone and asks directions to your house. She explains that she has gotten lost in this neighborhood before, and it is obvious that English is her second language. The communication process becomes much more complicated, as shown in Figure 2.2. As your message travels from you to your plumber, it must pass through several "filters," each of which can alter the way your message is understood. Most communications flow through this complex process.

Communication Filters

Messages are sent—and feedback is received—through a variety of filters that can distort the intended message (see Figure 2.2). When people are influenced by one or more of these filters, their perception of the message may be totally different from what the sender was attempting to communicate. Both sender and receiver must be keenly aware of these possible distortions so that they can intercept any miscommunication.

Semantics

We often assume that the words we use mean the same things to others, but this assumption can create problems. **Semantics** is the study of the relationship between a word and its meaning(s). Words have associated meanings and usages. We can easily understand what words like *typewriter*, *computer*, or *envelope* mean. But more abstract terms, such as *job satisfaction*, *downsizing*, or *internal customers*, have less precise meanings and will be used and interpreted by different people in different ways.

A new crop of buzzwords usually surfaces every three to five years. Just about the time people understood the meaning of *rightsizing* and *downsizing*, the term *delayering* was introduced. The buzzword *unsiloing* was introduced to make a simple but important point: Managers should cooperate across departments and

FIGURE 2.1 Diagram of Simple Communication Process

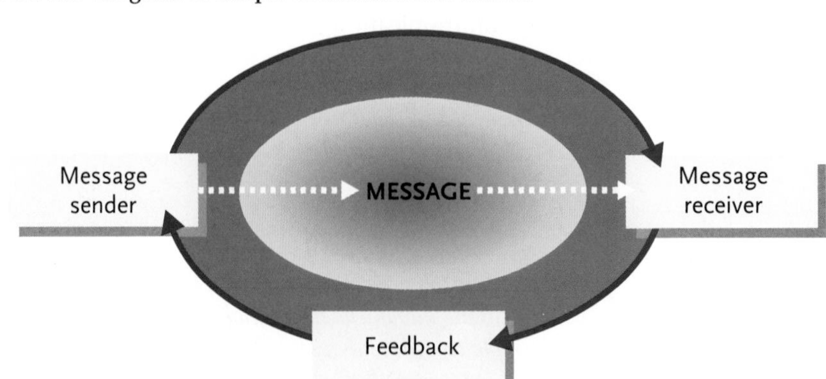

FIGURE 2.2 Diagram of More Complex Communication Process

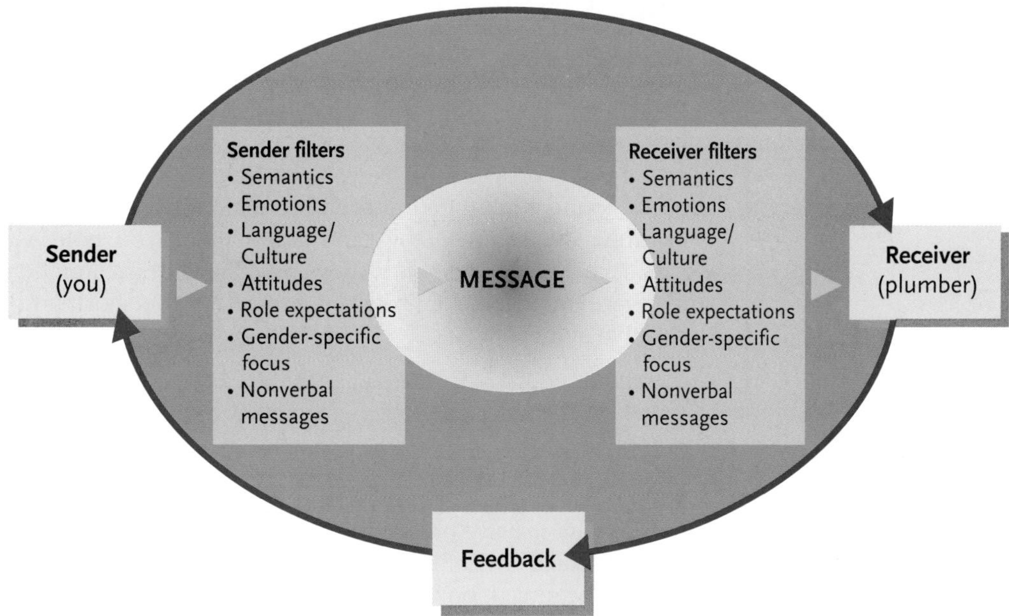

share resources. Sometimes buzzwords confuse or cover up what someone is actually saying.[8]

Young people who have communicated extensively via Internet chat rooms, blogs, and text messaging often assume that their jargon, or cyberlingo, will be understood by everyone. However, when cyberlingo is used in the mainstream of communication within organizations, it can be confusing to those who are unfamiliar with "words" such as FAQ (frequently asked questions), GMTA (great minds think alike), IMHO (in my humble opinion), and OTOH (on the other hand).[9] The impact of generational differences on interpersonal communications will be discussed in future chapters.

Language and Cultural Barriers

When organizations throughout the world connect to the Internet, the people within those organizations must be ready, willing, and able to communicate in a multilingual, multicultural working environment. Although English is the dominant language in the global marketplace, everyone must adjust his or her communication style to accommodate the needs of those whose first language is not English. Keep in mind how muddled a message might get when it is translated from one language to another in the mind of the receiver. To avoid the damage this filter might cause, avoid using industry-specific jargon, *short seller,* for example, or culture-specific slang such as *McMansion.*

The needs of a multicultural work force are getting more attention today because of globalization and employers' growing support for cultural diversity among their workers. The culture in which we are raised strongly influences our values, beliefs, expressions, and behaviors. It also influences the way we interpret the values, beliefs, expressions, and behaviors of others.

When the sender and receiver understand each other's cultural background, each should make the effort to adjust and improve his or her message

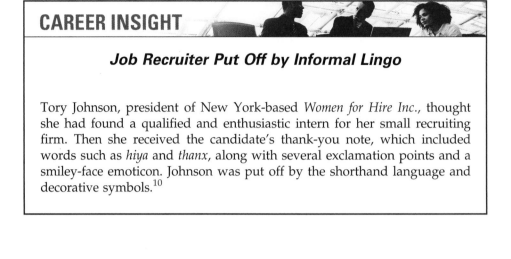

CAREER INSIGHT

Job Recruiter Put Off by Informal Lingo

Tory Johnson, president of New York-based *Women for Hire Inc.*, thought she had found a qualified and enthusiastic intern for her small recruiting firm. Then she received the candidate's thank-you note, which included words such as *hiya* and *thanx*, along with several exclamation points and a smiley-face emoticon. Johnson was put off by the shorthand language and decorative symbols.[10]

accordingly. For example, people living in the United States, Canada, Europe, Israel, or Australia usually prefer direct-approach communication; they tend to say more or less exactly what they mean. Their cultures value clarity, fluency, and brevity in communication. Many people from Asia, Arab countries, and much of Africa prefer a more indirect style of communication and therefore value harmony, subtlety, sensitivity, and tact more than brevity. They try hard to connect with their listeners.[11]

Emotions

Strong emotions can either prevent people from hearing what a speaker has to say or make them too susceptible to the speaker's point of view. If they become angry or allow themselves to be carried away by the speaker's eloquence, they may "think" with their emotions and make decisions or take action they regret later. They have shifted their attention from the content of the message to their feelings about it.

You may have had the experience of your spouse or parent angrily demanding to know why you forgot to run an errand. If you allow someone else's anger to trigger your own, the conversation may quickly deteriorate into an argument. The real issue—what happened and what is to be done about it—may be lost in a shouting match. Detaching yourself from another's feelings and responding to the content of the message is often difficult. It is hard to realize that another person's emotional response is more likely about fear or frustration than it is about you as an individual. Many jobs require that employees remain calm and courteous regardless of a customer's emotional state. Emotional control is discussed extensively in Chapter 9.

Attitudes

Attitudes can be a barrier to communication in much the same way as emotions. The receiver may have a negative attitude toward the sender's voice, accent, gestures, mannerisms, dress, or delivery. These negative attitudes create resistance to the message and can lead to a breakdown in communication. Perhaps the listener has an established attitude about the speaker's topic. For example, a person who is strongly opposed to abortion will most likely find it difficult to listen with objectivity to a prochoice speaker. Keep in mind, however, that an overly positive attitude can also be a barrier to communication. When biased in favor of the message, the listener may not effectively evaluate the speaker's information. More is said about the power of attitudes in Chapter 6.

Role Expectations

Role expectations influence how people expect themselves, and others, to act on the basis of the roles they play, such as boss, customer, or subordinate. These expectations can distort communication in two ways. First, if people identify others too closely with their roles, they may discount what the other person has to say: "It's just the boss again, saying the same old thing." A variation of this distortion occurs when we do not allow others to change their roles and take on new ones. This often happens to employees who are promoted from within the ranks of an organization to management positions. Others may still see "old Chuck" from accounting rather than the new department head.

Second, role expectations can affect good communication when people use their roles to alter the way they relate to others. This is often referred to as "position power." For example, managers may expect employees to accept what they say simply because of the authority invested in the position. Employees are not allowed to question the manager's decisions or make suggestions of their own, and communication becomes one-way information giving.

Gender-Specific Focus

Gender roles learned throughout childhood can influence the way men and women communicate. After all, boys and girls do grow up in different worlds, and they are conditioned to approach communication in different ways. Girls are often socialized as children to believe that talking holds relationships together. As adults, women use conversation to seek and give confirmation and support and to reach a consensus with others. Boys are often socialized to maintain their relationships primarily through their activities. As a result, men are more likely to perceive conversation as a form of competition during which they must negotiate to gain the upper hand and protect themselves from being put down.[12] Chapter 16, "The Changing Roles of Men and Women," discusses specific strategies you can use to communicate more effectively with those whose gender differs from your own.

Nonverbal Messages

When we attempt to communicate with another person, we use both verbal and nonverbal communication. **Nonverbal messages** are "messages without words" or "silent messages." These are the messages (other than spoken or written words) we communicate through facial expressions, voice tone, gestures, appearance, posture, and other nonverbal means. Research indicates that our nonverbal messages have much more impact than verbal messages. In fact, some researchers suggest that as much as 75 percent of our communication is nonverbal. This chapter limits its discussion to the form of nonverbal communication commonly referred to as "body language." Physical appearance, another powerful form of nonverbal communication, is discussed in Chapter 11.

Many of us could communicate more clearly, more accurately, and more credibly if we became more conscious of our body language. We can learn to

AFP/Getty Images

Say *Ni Hao* (Hello) to Home Depot employees who are preparing for work at a store located in Beijing. The world's largest home improvement retailer must embrace lots of cultural adaptation if it is to achieve success in China.

strengthen our communications by making sure our words and our body language are consistent. When our verbal and nonverbal messages match, we give the impression that we can be trusted and that what we are saying reflects what we truly believe. But when our body language contradicts our words, we are often unknowingly changing the message we are sending. If a manager says to an employee, "I am very interested in your problem," but then begins to look at her watch and fidget with objects on her desk, the employee will most likely believe the nonverbal rather than the verbal message.

Eyes transmit more information than any other part of the body.

You can improve your communication by monitoring the nonverbal messages you send through your eye contact, facial expressions, gestures, and personal space.

Eye Contact. Eyes transmit more information than any other part of the body. Because eye contact is so revealing, people generally observe some unwritten rules about looking at others. People who hold direct eye contact for only a few seconds, or avoid eye contact altogether, risk communicating indifference. However, a direct, prolonged stare between strangers is usually considered impolite, even potentially aggressive or hostile. Continuous eye contact is especially offensive in Asian and Latin American countries. As a general rule in North America, when you are communicating in a business setting, your eyes should meet the other person's about 60 to 70 percent of the time. This timing is an effective alternative to continuous eye contact.

HUMAN RELATIONS IN ACTION

Calling the Right Play

BusinessWeek magazine recognized Ace Hardware as one of the top ten Customer Service Champs in America. One employee at each store serves as the customer coordinator. When customer traffic is heavy, the coordinator talks to incoming shoppers, analyzes their body language, and decides if the person is a browser, a mission shopper with no time to spare, or someone gearing up for a project. Then, using an earpiece, the coordinator makes radio contact with the right employee who immediately approaches the customer and offers assistance.[13]

Facial Expressions. If you want to identify the inner feelings of another person, watch facial expressions closely. A frown or a smile will communicate a great deal. We have all encountered a "look of surprise" or a "look that could kill." Most of our observations are very accurate. However, facial expressions can be intentionally manipulated. When a person is truly happy, the muscles used for smiling are involuntarily controlled by the body's limbic system. When you force a smile, the cerebral cortex (under voluntary control) activates and the person appears to have a "fake" look when he or she smiles. That is why actors often recall a past emotional experience to produce the emotional state they want.[14] If we are able to accurately assess the facial expressions of others and draw conclusions accordingly, we can be sure that others are doing the same to us.

Gestures. Gestures send messages to people about how you are reacting to them and to the situation in which you find yourself. They often add an element that is perceived as a lively speaking style that keeps the attention of others. In some cultures, if you fail to gesture, you may be perceived as boring and stiff.[15] Be aware that some gestures that may be common in one culture may have dramatically different meaning to people from another culture. The examples in Figure 2.3 illustrate how the same gesture can have very different meanings.

Personal Space. Research conducted by Edward Hall provides evidence that people use the space around them to define relationships. It is possible to make others uncomfortable by standing too close to them or too far away from them. A customer may feel uncomfortable if a salesperson stands too close. A job applicant may feel uncomfortable if the interviewer maintains a distance of several feet. Hall identified four "zones" of comfortable distances that help us understand this nonverbal effect on others:[16]

1. *Intimate distance* includes touching to approximately 18 inches from another person. Most people will respond with defensiveness when strangers intrude into this territory.
2. *Personal distance* ranges from 18 inches to 4 feet. This distance is usually reserved for people we feel close to, such as spouses or close friends.
3. *Social distance* is 4 to 12 feet and is used for most business meetings and impersonal social gatherings. Business can be conducted with a minimum of emotional involvement.
4. *Public distance*, which usually involves one-way communication from a speaker to an audience, is 12 to 15 feet.

FIGURE 2.3 Same Sign, Different Meanings

OK SIGN
France: You're a zero;
Japan: Please give me coins;
Brazil: an obscene gesture;
Mediterranean countries: an obscene gesture.

THUMBS-UP
Australia: Up yours;
Germany: The number one;
Japan: The number five;
Saudi Arabia: I'm winning;
Ghana: An insult;
Malaysia: The thumb is used to point rather than the finger.

THUMB AND FOREFINGER
Most countries: money;
France: Something is perfect;
Mediterranean: a vulgar gesture.

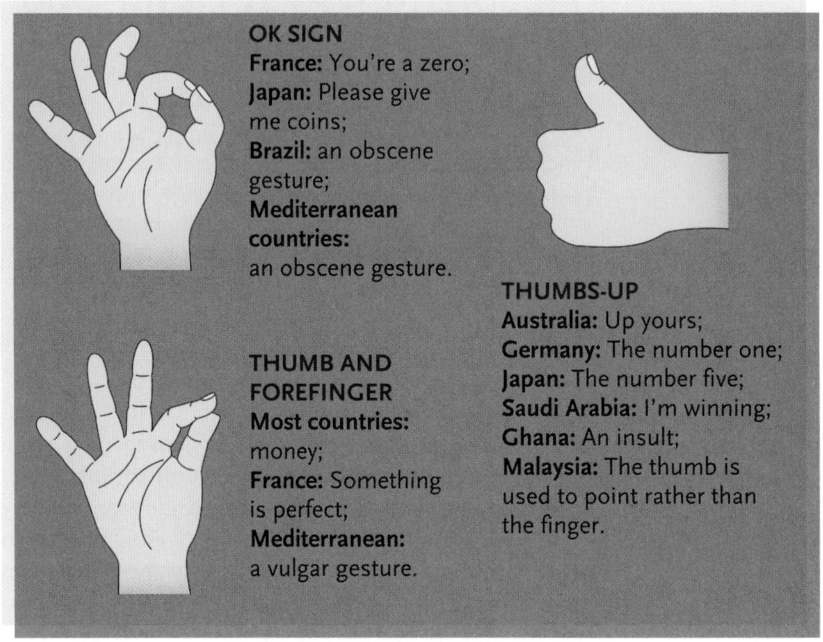

Source: "Same sign, different meanings" (graphic) by Sam Ward from USA Today, March 14, 1996, p. 7c. Reprinted by permission.

Hall's research involved the culture of only the United States and should prove helpful to those from other cultures who are attempting to communicate better with Americans. Americans should realize that the distances Hall describes may be different when they are attempting to effectively communicate with those from another culture. For example, Asians are accustomed to close contact. Watch for signals of discomfort, such as leg swinging, foot or finger tapping, and gaze aversion, caused by invading the other person's space.[17]

Who Is Responsible for Effective Communication?

The sender and the receiver share *equal* responsibility for effective communication. The communication loop, as shown in Figure 2.2, is not complete if the message the receiver hears, and acts upon, differs from the one the sender intended. When the sender accepts 100 percent of the responsibility for sending a clear, concise message, the communication process begins. But the receiver must also accept 100 percent of the responsibility for receiving the message as the sender intended. Ideally receivers should provide senders with enough feedback to ensure that an accurate message has passed through all the filters that might alter it.

How to Improve Personal Communication

Now that you understand the communication process and the various filters messages must pass through, you can begin to take the necessary steps to improve your own personal communication skills.

Skill Development: Evaluate It

As you build your human relations skills, it is very important to establish an acute sensitivity to the impact communication filters have on your interpersonal relationships at home and at work. Review Figure 2.2, and identify the communication filters that were in place during a recent face-to-face conversation, argument, or confrontation you had with another person. Did any of these filters interfere with your ability to send or receive the information being transmitted during the exchange? Evaluate how, if you were to repeat the interaction with this person, you could reduce the impact of these filters and thereby improve your ability to effectively communicate the messages you were sending and receiving.

Send Clear Messages

Send clear, concise messages with as little influence from filters as possible so that you can avoid being misunderstood. Miscommunication can easily be avoided if both parties follow these simple rules:

- *Use clear, concise language.* Avoid slang; jargon; or complex, industry-specific semantics that the receiver might not understand. Tailor your messages to your receivers by using words and concepts they understand.
- *Use repetition.* When possible, use parallel channels of communication. For example, by sending an e-mail and making a phone call, you not only gain the receiver's attention through dialogue but also make sure there is a written record in case specific details need to be recalled.
- *Use appropriate timing.* An important memo or e-mail may get no attention simply because it is competing with more pressing problems facing the receiver. When you need someone's cooperation, be acutely aware of his or her schedule and workload so that you can avoid causing any inconvenience or frustration. Timing the delivery of your message will help ensure that it is accepted and acted on.
- *Consider the receiver's preferences.* Some people prefer to receive information via e-mail, and others prefer telephone calls or face-to-face contact. Monitor and discover the preferences of those you communicate with on a regular basis, and adjust your communications with them accordingly.

Develop Effective Listening Skills

We may be born with the ability to hear, but we have to *learn how to listen.* We may think we are good listeners, but the truth is that most people don't listen at all. Too often we simply speak and then think about what we are going to say next, rather than concentrating on what the other person is trying to say.

At Hewlett Packard, employees take listening courses in which they listen, mirror back what they heard, and then elaborate on what it meant. Participants learn that two customers might say similar things, but their messages might have totally different meanings because they have had their own unique experiences that influence their messages. Two employees experiencing a similar frustration at work may take their concerns to management for corrective action. Yet each employee has a unique perspective on the problem, and both need to be heard before management can take effective, appropriate action.

Effective listening can often evoke creative, "out-of-the-box" ideas. An engineer at Hewlett Packard took his listening-skills training seriously and started "coffee talks" in his department every Friday afternoon to improve the listening skills among his coworkers. The resulting lively conversations generated new ideas that stimulated the creation of new products that led to millions of dollars in profits.[18]

Active listening is fueled by curiosity.

CAREER INSIGHT

Know When to Keep Your Mouth Shut

A recent college graduate wrote to Anne Fisher, career advice columnist for *Fortune* magazine, and asked: "I just graduated from Yale and am about to start my first real job, and I'm curious about something. If you had to pass along just one piece of advice on which to build a career, what would it be?" Anne answered, "I've always liked Albert Einstein's dictum: 'If A equals success, then the formula is A = X + Y + Z. X is work. Y is play. And Z is, keep your mouth shut.' Or as my dad used to say, 'Nobody ever learns anything while they're talking.' If you make it a habit to listen more than you speak, you can't go too far wrong."[19]

Active Listening. **Active listening** is fueled by curiosity and requires your complete concentration on what you are hearing, body language that exhibits your listening attitude, and feedback as to what you think the speaker is trying to tell you. In some cases, a simple statement such as "Please tell me more about that" will help you to become an active listener. Susan Scott, author of *Fierce Conversations*, offers this advice: "Dig for full understanding. Use paraphrasing and perception checks; don't be satisfied with what's on the surface."[20] When you become an active listener, you will make fewer mistakes, learn new information, and build stronger relationships.

If you would like to pursue additional resources to help you become a better listener, access the information available through the International Listening Association at *http://www.listen.org*. In addition, carefully examine Table 2.1, Active Listening Skills, and make every effort to implement its recommendations when you are interacting with others. You may be surprised by the impact you can make.

Critical Listening. To add depth to your active listening skills, consider honing your critical listening skills. **Critical listening** is the attempt to see the topic of discussion from the *speaker's* point of view and to consider how the speaker's perception of the situation may be different from your own. To improve your

TABLE 2.1 ACTIVE LISTENING SKILLS

1. *Develop a listening attitude.* Regard the speaker as worthy of your respect and attention. Drop your expectations as to what you are going to hear or would like to hear. Maintain good eye contact and lean slightly forward. Don't rush the speaker. Be patient and refrain from planning what to say in response until the speaker has finished talking.
2. *Give the speaker your full attention.* This is not easy because the messages you hear are often spoken at a much slower rate than you are able to absorb them. This allows your mind to roam. Your senses are constantly receiving extraneous information that may divert your attention. To stay focused, you may want to take notes, if it is appropriate to do so.
3. *Clarify by asking questions.* If something is not clear because the speaker has referred to a person or an event that you are not familiar with, ask him or her to back up and explain. If you want the speaker to expand on a particular point, ask open-ended questions such as "How do you feel about that?" or "Can you tell us some ways to improve?"
4. *Feed back your understanding of the speaker's message.* Paraphrase, in your own words, your understanding of what the speaker has just said: for example, *"Do you mean ... ?" "Am I right in assuming that we should ...?" "What I hear you saying is ..." or "In other words, we.... "*

ability to critically view new information, be sure to listen for evidence that challenges, as well as confirms, your own point of view. This is especially important when there is no opportunity for feedback, such as when you are viewing "tabloid" television, listening to network TV news "sound bites," or reading Internet blogs. Analyze the source of the information and determine its validity and credibility. Ask yourself, "Why have I been given this information? Is it relevant, or am I just being used to advance the agenda of another person or group?" Critical listening skills will help you avoid perpetuating erroneous information simply because you heard it through gossip, saw it on TV, or read it on an Internet blog.

All of the communications filters identified in Figure 2.2 tend to distort your ability and willingness to listen, so activating your critical thinking/listening skills will take some effort.

To help you in this skill development process, ask yourself the following questions:

- Does the speaker's reasoning make sense?
- What evidence is being offered to support the speaker's views?
- Do I know each point to be valid based on my own experience?
- Is each point based on a source that can be trusted?[21]

For some people, critical listening at a meeting is very difficult. They fear that if they sit in silence, everyone will assume they have nothing to say. It is fine just to listen and learn at a meeting. Quality of participation should matter more than quantity.[22]

Empathic Listening. Another dimension to becoming a better listener involves empathy, which means understanding another person's feelings. Many workers today face serious personal problems and feel the need to talk about them with

© James W. Porter/Corbis

This supervisor listens carefully to an employee who needs assistance. He will ask questions and use his active listening skills to acquire the information needed to help the employee with a work-related problem. Active listening is a skill that can be learned.

someone. They do not expect specific advice or guidance; they just want to spend some time with an empathic listener. Stephen Covey, the noted author and consultant, described **empathic listening** as listening with your ears, your eyes, and your heart.[23] If you want to practice empathic listening, adopt the following practices:

- *Avoid being judgmental.* Objectivity is the heart and soul of empathic listening. The person is communicating for emotional release and does not seek a specific response.
- *Acknowledge what is said.* You do not have to agree with what is being said, but you should let the person know you are able to understand his or her viewpoint.
- *Be patient.* If you are unable or unwilling to take the time to hear what the person has to say, say so immediately. Signs of impatience send a negative message to the person needing to talk.[24]

We live in a culture in which empathic listening is quite rare. Interrupting has become all too common as people rush to fill every gap in the conversation. Nevertheless, empathic listening is greatly valued by those with personal or work-related problems—people want to spend time with a good listener.[25]

CRITICAL THINKING CHALLENGE:

Analyze It

Each conversation we have with a coworker, a customer, or a significant other can enhance or weaken the relationship. A conversation that has the power to truly transform a relationship requires some silence. Yet, for most Americans, silence in a conversation is almost unendurable. Interrupting the other person or responding too quickly with little or no thought can weaken a relationship. Every important conversation requires moments of silence—time to reflect on what the other person has said and consider our response. During most conversations, do you use silence to improve communication? Analyze your response.[26]

Communications in Organizations

Strong teams depend on the effective exchange of information among all the team members so that they can reach their goals. Poor communication can create an atmosphere of mistrust. It is, therefore, critically important that every team member understands how to get his or her point across by using the appropriate communication channels within the organization's structure. They have a choice of the organization's formal communication channels or its informal "grapevine."

Formal Channels: Horizontal and Vertical

Most organizations establish a formal structure through which official information travels. **Horizontal channels** are used to move information among people on the same level of authority, such as all the store managers of a national retail clothing store chain, all department chairpersons within a college, or all the administrative assistants within an organization. **Vertical channels** move information up and down through all levels of authority within an organization. A message from the president of the organization will move down to the vice president(s), then to the manager(s), and then to the workers. Communicating down vertical channels is fairly routine. Communicating back up can be more difficult because top managers sometimes have the mistaken impression that their subordinates' messages are less important.

Messages sent through both horizontal and vertical channels can be delivered on the phone, electronically, in writing, or face to face. Many managers find that brief phone calls to their staff members are generally more effective than e-mails or memos because phone calls are quick and allow for immediate feedback. E-mail is quick and efficient and provides a permanent record of the exchange of information. Keep in mind that sensitive matters are best handled face to face.

When formal communication channels are working effectively, everyone authorized to initiate and receive companywide communications will receive the same information in a timely manner. If the level of trust among those sending and receiving the information is fairly high, these messages will usually be understood, believed, accepted, and acted on. If the level of trust is low, however, workers will tend to put more faith in rumors, even if such information conflicts with the formal message.

Informal Channel: The Grapevine

Messages passed through the horizontal and vertical channels can usually be tracked through linear paths, but the pathway of rumors may look more like a cobweb interwoven throughout the organizational chart. The **grapevine**, the informal communication channel, carries unofficial information and exists in every organization. It can have either positive or negative effects. Many times, the grapevine will clarify orders sent through the formal channels. At times, however, messages that move through the grapevine may be exaggerated, distorted, or completely inaccurate. These rumors develop quickly when at least two conditions exist in an organization: high degrees of anxiety and a great deal of uncertainty. To quell rumors, top management has to communicate in a timely and honest way.[27]

Rumors about individuals, or gossip, in the workplace can undermine morale, weaken authority, ruin reputations, and leave even the best teams decimated in its wake. It's no wonder gossip is often referred to as "verbal terrorism."[28] Unless you know for sure that the information is fact, never participate in gossip; always question the source. Once you are identified as a gossip, others will not trust you again. This can destroy all your efforts to build solid future relationships within that organization.

Modern Internet and communication technologies have vastly and instantly extended the reach of the grapevine. Workplace rumors and gossip now spread faster than ever. And e-mail messages and blogs leave an electronic trail that can be read by anyone.[29]

How to Improve Organizational Communication

Every effort should be made to encourage upward communication. **Upward communication**, the process of encouraging employees to share their feelings and ideas with their managers, is one of the most effective ways to improve organizational communication and is common among the best companies to work for in America. Employees with limited power are naturally very cautious about discussing mistakes, complaints, and failings with a more powerful person. However, when managers demonstrate the desire to listen to their subordinates, ideas, suggestions, and complaints begin to flow upward. Here are two examples of leaders who have taken steps to improve upward communication:

- Winnebago Industries, maker of recreational vehicles, uses a well-established suggestion system to obtain ideas from employees. More than 10,000 suggestions have come from employees since the program began in 1991.[30]
- Peter Brabeck, CEO of Nestlé, meets with 12 to 14 employees each month over lunch. Their bosses are not in attendance. He encourages the employees to talk frankly about their work and to ask questions.[31]

These organizations actively pursue ways to remove barriers that prevent open communication. They recognize that improving communications will inevitably help build trust among all employees, regardless of their position in the organization.

Communicating via Technology

The traditional memos, letters, phone calls, and face-to-face conversations seem to be the exception rather than the rule in today's high-tech communications environment. Many organizations now maintain **virtual offices**, networks of workers connected by the latest technology. These workers can "set up shop" wherever they are—at home, on an airplane, in a motel room—and communicate with coworkers via e-mail, cell phone, instant messaging, fax, or some other method. **Telecommuting**, an arrangement that allows employees to work from their homes, enables people scattered all over the world to stay connected.

The advantages of using these technology-based communication alternatives are obvious. Time efficiency is unsurpassed because people can transmit simple or detailed information across all time zones, and receivers can retrieve the information at their convenience. Cost effectiveness is unsurpassed because fiber optic and satellite transmissions cost the consumer virtually pennies compared with traditional transworld phone calls.

In all the frantic speed with which information now flows, many people forget that communication still must be carefully created before it is transmitted. Voice mail can be frustrating and time-consuming if it is not handled properly, and poorly written e-mails can leave the impression that the sender is either poorly educated or careless.

Voice Mail

Now that everyone is adjusting to the opportunities that immediate communication systems offer, nothing is more dismaying than playing phone tag (the exchange of several voice mails without successful transmission of the message). Whether you are on the sending or the receiving end, however, there are ways to avoid this counterproductive exercise in frustration.

When people call you and connect with your voice mail, be sure your recorded message includes your full name and when you will be retrieving your messages. If, for some reason, you will not be returning your calls for an extended time, edit your standard message to reflect this information so that your friends, customers, and colleagues will understand the delay and avoid repeated calls and duplicate messages. Forward your calls to another person's extension, if possible, or explain how the caller can reach a live person if the call is urgent. When you retrieve your messages, write down essential information, prioritize the messages in the order of importance, and return all of the calls as soon as possible.

When you are connected to another person's voice mail, slowly state your full name, *a brief explanation of what information or action you need from that person* (the component most often neglected), your phone number, and the best time to reach you. All four components are necessary to avoid phone tag. Then, if the receiver reaches your voice mail when calling back, he or she can simply leave you a voice message with the information you wanted. The communication loop is complete.

E-mail

E-mail takes careful planning and new writing skills. Those who read your e-mail will make judgments about your intelligence, competence, and attitude whether you want them to or not. Therefore, you need to carefully monitor not only what you write about but also how you word your messages.

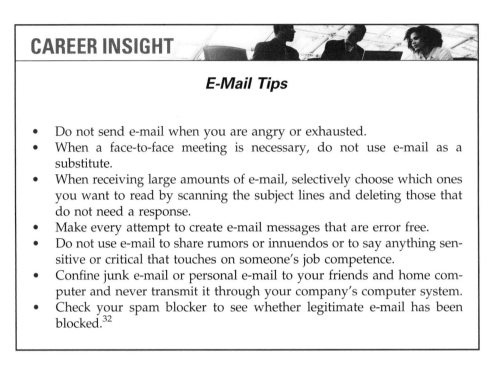

CAREER INSIGHT

E-Mail Tips

- Do not send e-mail when you are angry or exhausted.
- When a face-to-face meeting is necessary, do not use e-mail as a substitute.
- When receiving large amounts of e-mail, selectively choose which ones you want to read by scanning the subject lines and deleting those that do not need a response.
- Make every attempt to create e-mail messages that are error free.
- Do not use e-mail to share rumors or innuendos or to say anything sensitive or critical that touches on someone's job competence.
- Confine junk e-mail or personal e-mail to your friends and home computer and never transmit it through your company's computer system.
- Check your spam blocker to see whether legitimate e-mail has been blocked.[32]

Here are some guidelines to follow:

Know Your Company's Policies. Most organizations monitor their employees' e-mail carefully. Keep in mind that even deleted messages live on indefinitely in the company's hard drives and may resurface. E-mail that might be sexually offensive could be considered sexual harassment and have serious ramifications. Avoid sending personal e-mail messages on company time.

Create an Appropriate E-mail Address. Carefully design your e-mail address to give the impression you want to convey. Addresses such as Crazylady@_____.com or Buddyboy@______.com may be acceptable for personal e-mail but should never be used in a business setting. Your organization will generally have a specific format for your e-mail address that includes variations of your first and last names.

Use the* Subject: *Line. One of the best ways to set the stage for effective communications is to learn how to appropriately use the *Subject*: line available on all e-mail messages. It usually appears next to the sender's name on the receiver's screen. This brief introduction to your message will cue the receiver as to the probable content of your message. If your message is time-critical, add *Urgent* to the subject line, but be careful of overuse. When responding to another person's e-mail, be sure to forward the original subject line so that the receiver knows you are responding to his or her original request.

Compose Clear, Concise Messages. The authors of *Send,* a combination stylebook and etiquette manual for e-mail users, say their title is intended to be an acronym, guiding us to improved e-mail use. Messages should be **S**imple,

Effective, **N**ecessary, and aimed at getting something **D**one. A message written in simple conversational language takes less time to write and is more pleasant to read. Tell readers what action you want them to take.[33]

Watch Your Language. The biggest clue to your competence will be the words you use. Be sure they are all spelled correctly and that there are no typographical errors. E-mails filled with typing errors convey an attitude of disrespect toward the reader. Be sure that you have selected the appropriate word—when choosing, for example, from *there/their/they're; sight/site/cite; then/than; which/witch,* and so on. Do your verbs agree with their subjects? If your writing skills are limited, use software that includes grammar- and spelling-checkers.

Keep your messages brief by summarizing your main points, indicate the action or response you are seeking, and be sure you provide all the details the receiver needs. Be very careful about the *tone* of your messages. Remove any potentially offending words and phrasing from your documents. Some people feel that they have to use stronger language to get a message across because the receiver cannot "hear" them. If you use solid capital letters in your e-mail, though, readers may think you are shouting at them.[34]

Recognize E-mail Limitations. The missing element in e-mail and other electronic communication is *rapport,* that bonding state that is easier to establish in person or by phone. Facial expressions, tone of voice, and gestures—important social cues—are missing in e-mail.[35] Neither the sender nor the receiver can assume anything about the correspondent's frame of mind. Readers will not be able to tell if you are serious or being sarcastic, prying or simply curious, angry or merely frustrated. After creating your message, reread it as a stranger might. If words or phrases might be misconstrued, rewrite it so as to make clear *exactly* what you mean to say.

The Pursuit of Speed in Communication

Members of Generation Y often describe e-mail as "so last millennium." They still use e-mail at school or at work, but they prefer the instant gratification that comes with the use of instant messaging (IM), text messaging (TM), or Twitter.

Instant messaging is a form of real-time communication based on a typed text conveyed via computers connected over the Internet or some form of internal network. It is faster and more casual than e-mail. IM has been very popular among employees who are assigned to teams. A sales team, for example, may include employees from engineering, finance, sales, and marketing. These team members, often widely dispersed, can resolve customer issues quickly by getting real time input needed to move the sales process forward.[36]

Text messaging involves real-time communication based on typed text sent electronically via cell phone, PDA, pager, or other handheld device. This messaging option is extremely popular among Generation Ys who enjoy multitasking. Text messaging received national attention when presidential candidate Barack Obama said he would announce his vice-presidential running mate via text message.[37]

Twitter is a free social networking service that enables its users to send and read messages known as *tweets.* Tweets are text-based posts of up to 140 characters displayed on the author's profile page and delivered to subscribers who are

Pepper . . . And Salt

THE WALL STREET JOURNAL

"No homework for the first one who can show me how to use my new phone."

known as *followers.* Senders can restrict delivery to those in their circle of friends or allow open access.[38]

LOOKING BACK: REVIEWING THE CONCEPTS

- Understand the communication process.

The age of information has given us major advances in technology-based communication. However, successful communication in a work setting requires human involvement. The diversity of today's work force calls for a greater understanding of how to communicate effectively. Impersonal one-way communication methods can be used effectively to share basic facts, policies, and instructions. If feedback is necessary, rely on interpersonal communication that involves a two-way exchange. As noted in this chapter, two-way communication is often a complex process.

- Identify and explain the filters that affect communication.

Messages are sent—and feedback is received—through a variety of filters that often distort the messages. Figure 2.2 provides a summary of the most common filters that can challenge both senders and receivers of messages. For example, body language conveys information through eye contact, facial expressions, gestures, and the use of personal space. When you are influenced by one or more of these filters, the message you receive may be totally different from what the sender was attempting to communicate.

- Identify ways to improve personal communication, including developing listening skills.

The sender and the receiver share equal responsibility for effective communication. Therefore, both sender and receiver should take the necessary steps to improve their personal communication skills. Individuals can make their messages clearer by choosing words carefully, using repetition, timing the message correctly, and considering the receivers' preferences. Personal communication can also be improved by the use of active, critical, and empathic listening skills.

- Understand how communications flow throughout an organization and how to improve the flow when necessary.

Effective communication in organizations unifies group behavior, builds teamwork, and contributes to improved productivity. Formal communication channels can be vertical or horizontal. The grapevine uses an informal approach to rapidly transmit information, but rumors or gossip may have a negative effect if the information is untrue. Progressive organizations are constantly searching for ways to improve upward communication. They recognize that frontline employees are often in the best position to recommend ways to improve the organization.

- Learn how to effectively communicate through technology.

Memos, letters, phone calls, and face-to-face conversations have been replaced, in many situations, by technology-based communication alternatives. Virtual offices, networks of workers connected by the latest technology, are now quite common. These communication technologies are time efficient and cost-effective for organizations. However, the increase in the use of e-mail, instant messaging, text messaging, Twitter, voice mail, teleconferencing, and other high-tech communication methods often creates human relations problems. Employees often forget that communication must still be carefully created before it is transmitted.

ON THE JOB Q & A: STANDING OUT IN THE CROWD

Q: I have just been "released" from the job I held for 12 years because my company was bought out by our competitor. I am highly skilled, competent, and dependable, but it has been a long time since I have gone on a job interview, and I'm scared to death. How should I communicate my strengths and commitment to a prospective employer? What happens if I blow it?

A: Fear is your greatest enemy, so be confident that many employers want to know that you are available. Remember that no one wants to hire a "victim," so do not refer to your "release" or your previous employer in a negative way. Prepare a positive statement that explains why you are looking for a new opportunity. It should focus on your strengths rather than on why you were released: for example, "My computer skills far exceeded the needs of my company's new owner." Be aware that your degree, references, wardrobe, and handshake get you in the door, but that interviews today often include probing questions that test your ability to react and respond quickly. Most interviewers expect applicants to ask their own series of questions, such as: How does this position fit into the organizational structure? Why is the position vacant? What are the opportunities for advancement? If you want the job at the conclusion of the interview, ask for it! Be sure to send a follow up thank-you note or letter to the interviewer that reemphasizes your strengths. If you feel you blew it, contact the interviewer by phone or letter to correct misleading or misinterpreted information. This type of persistence will show that you sincerely want the job. If you don't get the job, consider the interview a great practice session and enter the next one with renewed confidence![39]

KEY TERMS

impersonal communication 27
interpersonal communication 27
feedback 27
semantics 28
nonverbal messages 31
active listening 36
critical listening 36
empathic listening 38
horizontal channels 39
vertical channels 39
grapevine 40
upward communication 40
virtual offices 40
telecommuting 41
instant messaging 43
text messaging 43
Twitter 43

TRY YOUR HAND

1. During the next week, study the listening habits of students in another class in which you are enrolled. Keep a journal of your observations by identifying the nonverbal behaviors you witness. Are there barriers to effective communication between the instructor and the student? How do you believe the students' nonverbal behaviors might affect the relationship between the instructor and the students?

2. Print out the most recent e-mails that you have sent or received and bring them to class. Analyze their effectiveness in terms of the e-mail tips in this chapter. Did the messages violate any of the tips? If so, which ones? How could these messages be improved?

3. Many times, we take the conversation away from others and make it our own. This practice not only wastes time, but is a major relationship killer. Here is how it works: At the beginning of the conversation, you tell the other person about a problem you are dealing with, and, before you finish the story, the other person says, "I know what you mean," and then describes a personal experience that may or may not have anything to do with your problem. Once the other person takes over the conversation, a valuable exchange of ideas is probably lost. During the next week, monitor your conversations with friends, family members, and coworkers. How often did the other person attempt to take the conversation away from you? How often did you attempt to take over the conversation?[40]

INTERNET INSIGHTS

1. Assume that you are currently employed by Toyota International in their Information Technology Department, which has offices in several countries around the globe. Next week, you will travel to Poland and Greece to check on the installation of new telecommunications equipment. Your manager told you that *most* of the people you will work with speak English. However, you want to be prepared to greet people and say "yes," "no," "thank you," and "goodbye" in the languages of the countries you will visit. Go to *http://www.travlang.com*, scroll down, and select "Foreign Languages for Travelers." Then follow the two steps for the language of your choice and click on the option "basic words." Select, record, and practice the appropriate words.

2. Now go to *http://www.kwintessential.co.uk/resources/country-profiles.html* and click on the

country that corresponds with the language you learned in the exercise above. Learn more about the country's social customs, such as rules and taboos of doing business, verbal and nonverbal communication techniques, decision-making techniques, and meeting, gift-giving, and dining etiquette. Discover the country's family values, religion, and expressive communication techniques. Write a brief report on your discoveries.

YOU PLAY THE ROLE

This role-play exercise is designed to enhance your awareness of the filters that can alter or aid a message between a sender and a receiver in the communication process. Review Figure 2.2 *Diagram of More Complex Communication Process* before you begin this activity. Select a partner and be prepared to discuss specific information about your present or past work situation. Assume the role of sender and share this information with the receiver. After your presentation, critique the communication process. Did your message match what the receiver understood? What filters led to parallel communication, and what filters led to distortion? After you have discussed the complexity of the communication process, change roles; you are now the receiver, and the receiver is the sender.

BELOW THE SURFACE:

The Erosion of Attention

At the beginning of this chapter, you were introduced to the multifaceted world of digital technology. Preference is given to gadgets and machines, personal relationships are conducted through e-mails, and text messaging and cell phones dominate our lives. According to Jackson, we have incredible freedom and mobility in our personal and work lives. The cost, or underside, is the nurturing of a culture of diffusion, fragmentation, and detachment. When she talks about a culture of isolation, despite supreme connectivity, most agree that we don't even know our neighbors. There are studies that show that the more ties you have, even in your core network, the less contact you have in all forms—visits, telephone calls, and, of course, letters. Few write letters or personal notes anymore. Contacts with your close ties—families and friends—diminish except for e-mail, which is faceless and a very thin form of communication. Jackson argues that the same thing is true of the way we work. She sees a need for improving critical thinking and problem-solving skills in the workplace.[41]

QUESTIONS

1. Analyze your work or school environment. Identify the distractions that you face on a daily basis and defend or reject their relevance to your ability to critically think, problem solve, and communicate effectively with others.
2. There is no simple solution to the distractions that we face in our personal and work lives. Jackson states that the solution to the issue is self-discipline. Many distractions are self-initiated. Do you support this premise? If so, justify and defend your position.
3. Is your life filled with too many distractions? If so, analyze what can be done to eliminate the stress and tension (distractions) and make room in your life for more meaningful communication. If not, record what have been the keys to your success.

CLOSING CASE: Communication Breakdown

Workers employed by Automatic Elevator, a Durham, North Carolina Company, performed routine maintenance on the elevators at two Duke University Health System hospitals. After the completion of their service, employees of Automatic Elevator emptied used petroleum-based hydraulic fluid into several empty detergent drums. Duke employees discovered the drums, assumed they were surplus stock, and returned them to the original vendor, Cardinal Health, a hospital-supply company. Employees at Cardinal Health failed to detect the contents of the detergent drums and delivered the drums to two Duke hospitals. Later, Duke University Health System administrators found that the used hydraulic fluid was piped into the instrument cleaning systems at both hospitals.

Duke administrators were slow to notify the nearly 3,700 surgical patients who may have had contact with the improperly cleaned surgical instruments. Many of these patients reported suffering infections, poor healing, achy joints, weight loss, and extreme fatigue during the months after their surgery. Some of these patients, feeling that Duke should have made more information available sooner, have hired lawyers.[42]

Soon after discovery of the problem, a crisis team gathered to determine how to handle the potentially devastating situation. Within one week, letters went out to all affected patients and their physicians apologizing for the mix-up and telling them that it should pose little risk to their health. They were invited to call a hotline to report any changes in their health. A website was created to offer them information about the effects of hydraulic fluid on the body. The goal of the crisis team was to balance the urgency of getting the information out with the need for accuracy.

During the months that followed the hydraulic fluid mix-ups, Duke commissioned a study, costing more than $2 million, to track the medical records of all patients at the time of exposure. The Duke study indicates that about 90 percent of the patients exposed to the fluid had no major clinical problems during the two years after the fluid mix-up. The remaining patients reported problems such as infections, weight loss, new malignancies, or autoimmune diseases.[43]

QUESTIONS

1. Analyze what filters were in place to block effective communication between the hospital administrators, medical staff, and affected patients.
2. Evaluate how the original problem could have been intercepted before it became a health care crisis.
3. Let's assume that you have been hired to study the series of mix-ups that involved personnel employed by Automatic Elevator, Cardinal Health, and Duke Hospitals; propose your recommendation that would prevent a reoccurrence of this costly crisis.

INTEGRATED RESOURCES

VIDEOS:

BP: Operation Village People
The Job Interview
Communicating Across Cultures at IDG
Alexander and Melinda: Performance Review

CLASSROOM ACTIVITIES

IRM Application Exercise 2.1
IRM Application Exercise 2.2
IRM Application Exercise 2.3

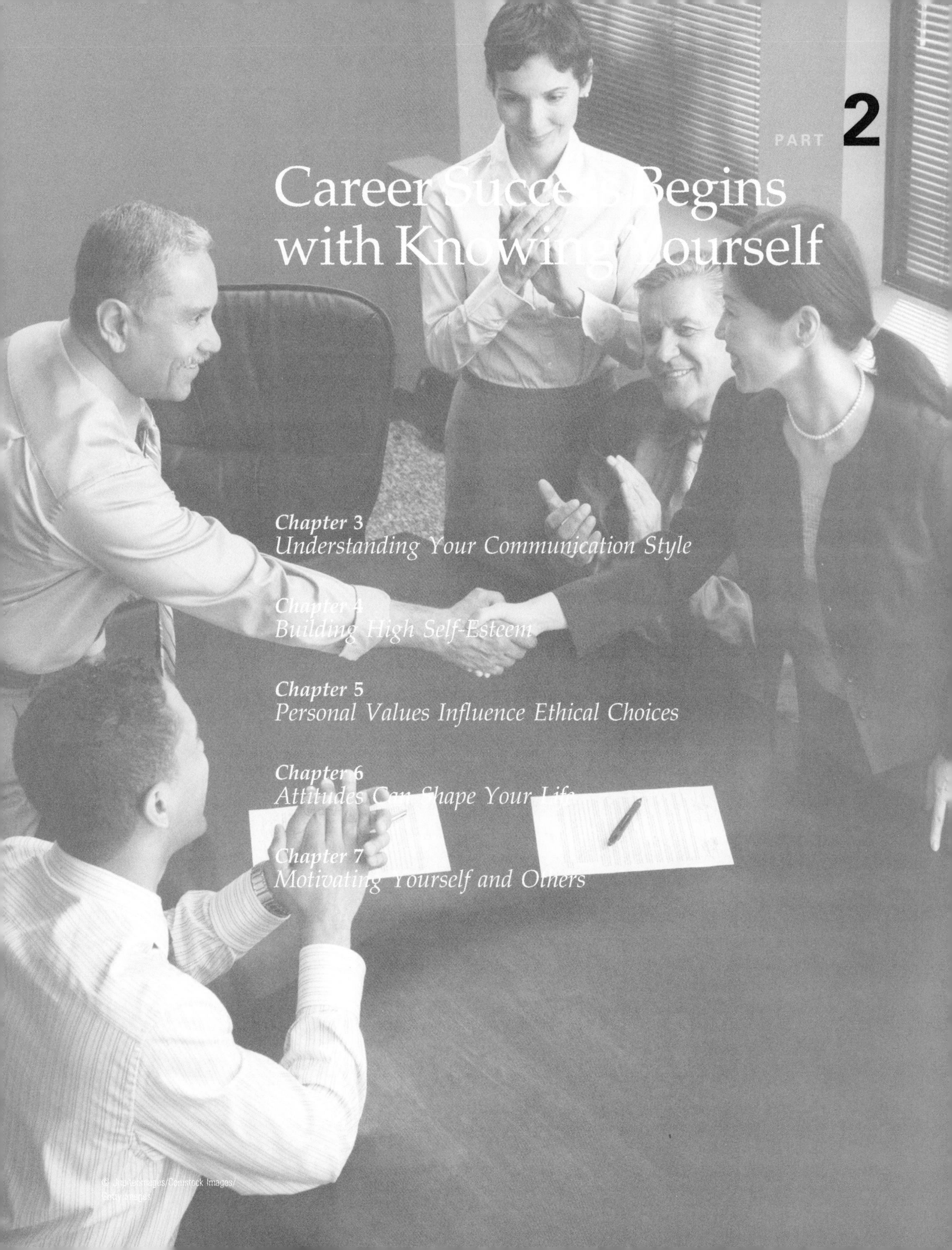

PART **2**

Career Success Begins with Knowing Yourself

Chapter 3
Understanding Your Communication Style

Chapter 4
Building High Self-Esteem

Chapter 5
Personal Values Influence Ethical Choices

Chapter 6
Attitudes Can Shape Your Life

Chapter 7
Motivating Yourself and Others

CHAPTER 3

Understanding Your Communication Style

TIP OF THE ICEBERG

CHAPTER PREVIEW

LEARNING OBJECTIVES

After studying Chapter 3, you will be able to

- Understand the concept of communication style and its effect on interpersonal relations.
- Discuss the major elements of the communication style model.
- Identify your preferred communication style.
- Improve communication with others through style flexing.

© Somos/Veer/Getty Images

Contrasting Communication Styles

Several years ago, Bill Gates, Chair and co-founder of Microsoft Corporation, turned over the reins of the company to his longtime Number 2, Chief Executive Steve Ballmer. It was a time to reflect on their undergraduate days at Harvard University. Both were math whizzes. Gates eventually dropped out of Harvard to form Microsoft, and Ballmer ended up teaching at the Stanford Business School. When Gates needed a tough-minded manager at his fledgling company, Ballmer was recruited. Ballmer built a sales and marketing organization to compete with IBM in large corporate accounts.

During the early years at Microsoft, Ballmer was known as an aggressive executive with little patience. His explosive temper was legendary, and he often put the fear of God into his staff members. As CEO, he was able to fortify Microsoft's position as an industry leader.[1]

Steve Ballmer displays the characteristics of the *Director* communication style, one of four styles we will discuss in this chapter. Bill Gates, by contrast, displays the characteristics of the *Reflective* communication style. Despite these differences, Ballmer and Gates formed a highly effective partnership.

Communication Styles: An Introduction

Have you ever wondered why it seems so difficult to talk with some people and so easy to talk with others? Can you recall a situation in which you met someone for the first time and immediately liked that person? Something about the

AP Photo/Lionel Cironneau

© David Lefranc/Kipa/Corbis

We form impressions of others by observing their behavior. Steve Ballmer, CEO of Microsoft Corporation, is a "take charge" kind of guy. He displays characteristics of the *Directive* style. Bill Gates, Chairman and co-founder of Microsoft, displays the characteristics of the *Reflective* communication style. He is described as a "thinker" who often seems preoccupied with other matters.

individual made you feel comfortable. You may have had this experience when you started a new job or began classes at a new school. A major goal of this chapter is to help you understand the impact your communication style has on the impression others form of you. This chapter also provides you with the information you will need to cope effectively in today's workplace, which is characterized by greater diversity and more emphasis on teamwork.

Communication Style Defined

The impressions that others form about us are based on what they observe us saying and doing. They have no way of knowing our innermost thoughts and feelings, so they make decisions about us based on what they see and hear.[2] The patterns of behavior that others can observe can be called **communication style**.

Each person has a unique communication style. By getting to know your style, you can achieve greater self-awareness and learn how to develop more effective interpersonal relations. Accurate self-knowledge is truly the starting point for effectiveness at work. It is also essential for managing the three key relationships described in Chapter 1: relationships with self, with another person, and with members of a group. If your career objective is to become a supervisor or manager, you will benefit by being more aware of your employees' communication styles. Job satisfaction and productivity increase when employees feel that their leaders understand their personal needs and take these into consideration.

Accurate self-knowledge is truly the starting point for effectiveness at work.

Communication-Style Bias

Your communication style is the "you" that is on display every day—the outer pattern of behavior that others see. If your style is very different from another person's, it may be difficult for the two of you to develop rapport. **Communication-style bias** is a state of mind that most of us experience from time to time.

Mirroring the Behavior of Others

Psychologists and sociologists use the term **mirroring** to describe a situation in which one person intentionally matches the body language of the individual they are meeting with. Mirroring is based on the premise that we are more likely to develop a kinship with those who are like ourselves. In many cases, subtle shifts in how you present yourself can increase the comfort level of the other person. If you participate in a job interview, observe key elements of the person's style. If the person speaks slowly and seems to deliberately select each word, consider slowing your own speech pattern. Your goal is not to manipulate the other person, nor mimic the person, but to avoid a situation where the other individual is distracted by differences.[3]

Fundamental Concepts Supporting Communication Styles

This may be your first introduction to communication styles. Therefore, let's begin by reviewing a few basic concepts that support the study of this dimension of human behavior.

1. *Individual differences exist and are important.* Length of eye contact, use of gestures, speech patterns, facial expressions, and the degree of assertiveness people project to others are some of the characteristics of a personal communication style. We can identify a person's unique communication style by carefully observing these patterns of behavior.[4]
2. *Individual style differences tend to be stable.* The basics of communication style theory were established by Swiss psychiatrist Carl Jung. In his classic book *Psychological Types,* he states that every individual develops a primary communication style that remains quite stable throughout life. Each person has a relatively distinctive way of responding to people and events.[5] Many psychologists now believe that people are born with a predisposition to prefer some behaviors (actions) over others.
3. *There is a limited number of styles.* Jung observed that people tend to fall into one of several behavior patterns when relating to the world around them. He describes four behavior styles: intuitor, thinker, feeler, and sensor.[6] Those in the same behavior category tend to display similar traits.
4. *A communication style is a way of thinking and behaving.* It is not an ability but instead a preferred way of using the abilities one has. This distinction is very important. An *ability* refers to how well someone can do something. A *style* refers to how someone likes to do something.[7]
5. *To create the most productive working relationships, it is necessary to get in sync with (mirror) the behavior patterns (communication style) of the people you work with.*[8] The ability to identify another person's communication style and to know how and when to adapt your own preferred style to it, can give you an important advantage in dealing with people. Learning to adapt your style

to fit the needs of another person is called "style flexing," a topic that is discussed later in this chapter.

> ***Total Person Insight***
>
> P. CHRISTOPHER EARLEY
> ELAINE MOSAKOWKI
> Authors, *Cultural Intelligence*
>
> *"An expanding global economy increases the odds that you may someday be given an overseas assignment. Even if you don't receive a global assignment, you will likely be working with foreign clients at some time during your career. The ability to mirror the gestures and mannerisms of people with cultural backgrounds different from your own indicates you understand one important component of* Cultural Intelligence."[9]

The Communication Style Model

This section introduces a model that encompasses four basic communication styles. This simple model is based on research studies conducted during the past 70 years and features two important dimensions of human behavior: dominance and sociability. As you study the communication style model, keep in mind that it describes your *preferences*, not your *skills* or *abilities*.

The Dominance Continuum

In study after study, those "differences that make a difference" in interpersonal relationships point to dominance as an important dimension of style. **Dominance** can be defined as the tendency to display a "take-charge" attitude. Every person falls somewhere on the **dominance continuum**, illustrated in Figure 3.1. David W. Johnson in his book *Reaching Out—Interpersonal Effectiveness and Self-Actualization* states that people tend to fall into two dominance categories: low or high.[10]

1. *Low dominance.* These people are characterized by a tendency to be cooperative and eager to assist others. They tend to be low in assertiveness and are more willing to be controlled by others.
2. *High dominance.* These people give advice freely and frequently initiate demands. They are more assertive and tend to seek control over others.

The first step in determining your most preferred communication style is to identify where you fall on the dominance continuum. Do you tend to be low or high on this scale? To answer this question, complete the dominance indicator form in Figure 3.2. Rate yourself on each scale by placing a checkmark at a point

FIGURE 3.1 Dominance Continuum

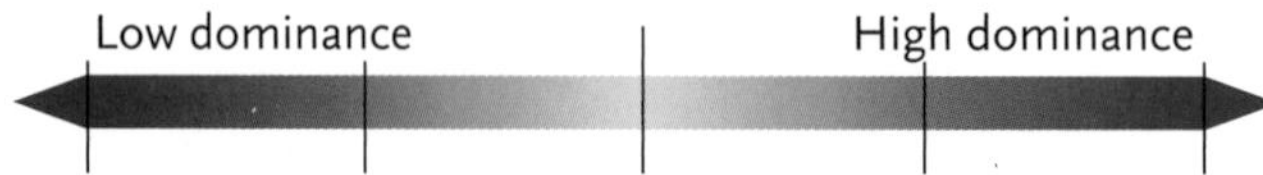

Source: From Manning, Gerald L.; Reece, Barry L., *Selling Today: Creating Customer Value*, 9th, © 2004. Reproduced by permission of Pearson Education, Inc., Upper Saddle River, New Jersey .

FIGURE 3.2 Dominance Indicator Form

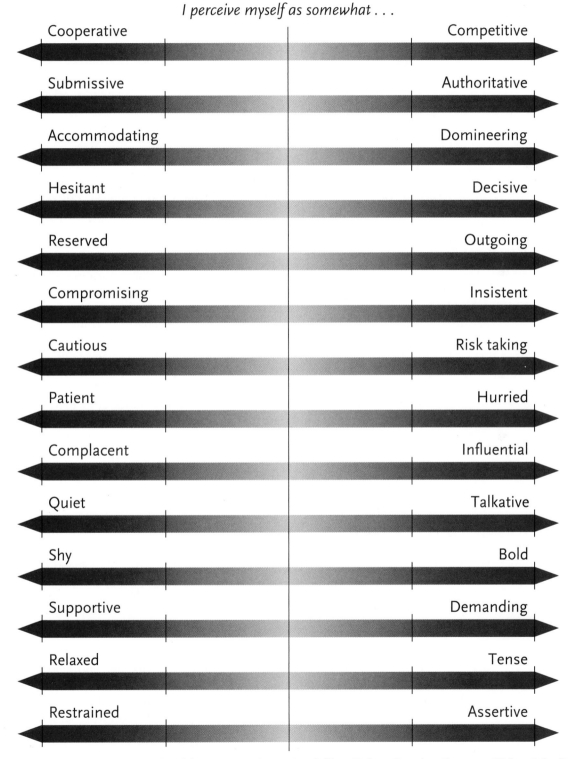

I perceive myself as somewhat . . .

Cooperative	Competitive
Submissive	Authoritative
Accommodating	Domineering
Hesitant	Decisive
Reserved	Outgoing
Compromising	Insistent
Cautious	Risk taking
Patient	Hurried
Complacent	Influential
Quiet	Talkative
Shy	Bold
Supportive	Demanding
Relaxed	Tense
Restrained	Assertive

Source: From Manning, Gerald L.; Reece, Barry L., *Selling Today: Creating Customer Value,* 9th, © 2004. Reproduced by permission of Pearson Education, Inc., Upper Saddle River, New Jersey .

along the continuum that represents how you perceive yourself. If most of your checkmarks fall to the right of center, you rank high in dominance. If most fall to the left of center, you rank low in dominance.

Another way to assess the dominance dimension is to ask four or five people who know you well to complete the dominance indicator form for you. Their assessment may provide a more accurate indication of where you fall on the continuum. Self-assessment alone is sometimes inaccurate because we often lack self-insight.[11] Once you have received the forms completed by others, try to determine whether a consistent pattern exists. (Note: It is best not to involve parents, spouses, or close relatives. Seek feedback from coworkers or classmates.)

Where Should You Be on the Dominance Continuum?

Is there any best place to be on the dominance continuum? Not really. Successful people can be found at all points along the continuum. Nevertheless, there are times when people need to act decisively to influence the adoption of their ideas and communicate their expectations clearly. This means that someone low in dominance may need to become more assertive temporarily to achieve an objective. New managers who are low in dominance must learn to influence others without being viewed as aggressive or insensitive. The American Management Association offers a course entitled "Assertiveness Training," which is designed for individuals who want to exercise a greater influence on others, get their suggestions across more effectively, and resolve conflict situations decisively yet diplomatically.[12]

People who are high in dominance must sometimes curb their desire to express strong opinions and initiate demands.

People who are high in dominance must sometimes curb their desire to express strong opinions and initiate demands. A person who is perceived as being extremely strong-willed and inflexible will have difficulty establishing a cooperative relationship with others.

CRITICAL THINKING CHALLENGE:

Analyze It

After you have determined your own place on the dominance scale, think about your closest coworkers and friends. Who is the most dominant in your circle? Who is the least dominant? Can you recall occasions when either low dominance or high dominance created a barrier to effective interpersonal relations?[13]

The Sociability Continuum

Have you ever met someone who was open and talkative and who seemed easy to get to know? An individual who is friendly and expresses feelings openly can be placed near the top of the **sociability continuum**.[14] The continuum is illustrated in Figure 3.3. **Sociability** can be defined as the tendency to seek and enjoy social relationships.

Sociability can also be thought of as a measure of whether you tend to control or express your feelings. Those high in sociability usually express their feelings freely, whereas people low on the continuum tend to control their feelings. The

FIGURE 3.3 Sociability Continuum

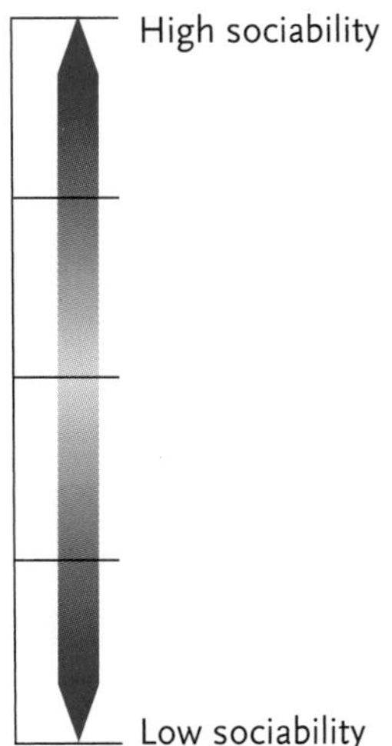

Source: From Manning, Gerald L.; Reece, Barry L., *Selling Today: Creating Customer Value*, 9th, © 2004. Reproduced by permission of Pearson Education, Inc., Upper Saddle River, New Jersey .

person who is classified as being high in sociability is open and talkative and likes personal associations. The person who is low in sociability is more reserved and formal in social relationships.

The second step in determining your most preferred communication style is to identify where you fall on the sociability continuum. To answer this question, complete the sociability indicator form shown in Figure 3.4. Rate yourself on each scale by placing a checkmark at a point along the continuum that represents the degree to which you feel you exhibit each of the characteristics. If most of your checkmarks fall to the right of center, you are high in sociability. If most fall to the left of center, you are low in sociability.

The sociability indicator form is not meant to be a precise instrument, but it will provide you with a general indication of where you fall on each of the scales. You may also want to make copies of the form and distribute them to friends or coworkers for completion. (Remember, it is advisable not to involve parents, spouses, or close relatives in this feedback exercise.)

Where Should You Be on the Sociability Continuum?

Where are successful people on the sociability continuum? Everywhere. There is no best place to be. People at all points along the continuum can achieve success in an organizational setting. Nevertheless, there are some commonsense guidelines that persons who fall at either end of the continuum are wise to follow.

A person who is low in sociability is more likely to display a no-nonsense attitude when dealing with other people. This person may be seen as impersonal and businesslike. Behavior that is too guarded and too reserved can be a barrier to effective communication. Such persons may be perceived as unconcerned about the feelings of others and interested only in getting the job done. Perceptions are critical in the business world, especially among customers. Even a hint of indifference can create a customer relations problem.

People who are high in sociability openly express their feelings, emotions, and impressions. They are perceived as being concerned with relationships and

FIGURE 3.4 Sociability Indicator Form

I perceive myself as somewhat . . .

Disciplined	Easygoing
Controlled	Expressive
Serious	Lighthearted
Methodical	Unstructured
Calculating	Spontaneous
Guarded	Open
Introverted	Extroverted
Aloof	Friendly
Formal	Casual
Reserved	Attention seeking
Cautious	Carefree
Conforming	Unconventional
Subdued	Dramatic
Restrained	Impulsive

Source: From Manning, Gerald L.; Reece, Barry L., *Selling Today: Creating Customer Value*, 9th, © 2004. Reproduced by permission of Pearson Education, Inc., Upper Saddle River, New Jersey .

CRITICAL THINKING CHALLENGE:

Analyze It

After you have determined your position on the sociability scale, think about your closest coworkers and friends. Who is the highest on the sociability indicator? Who is the lowest? Can you recall an occasion when high sociability or low sociability created a barrier to effective interpersonal relations?[15]

therefore are easy to get to know. At times, emotionally expressive people need to curb their natural exuberance. Too much informality can be a problem in some work relationships. The importance of adapting your style to accommodate the needs of others is discussed later in this chapter.

Four Basic Communication Styles

The dominance and sociability continua can be combined to form a rather simple model that will tell you more about your communication style (see Figure 3.5).

The **communication style model** will help you identify your most preferred style. Dominance is represented by the horizontal axis and sociability by the vertical axis. The model is divided into quadrants, each representing one of four communication styles: emotive, director, reflective, or supportive. As you review the descriptions of these styles, you will likely find one that is "most like you" and one or more that are "least like you."

Emotive Style. The upper-right-hand quadrant combines high sociability and high dominance. This is characteristic of the **emotive style** of communication (Figure 3.6).

You can easily form a mental picture of the emotive type by thinking about the phrases used earlier to describe high dominance and high sociability. A good example of the emotive type of person is comedian Jay Leno. Rosie O'Donnell also projects an outspoken, enthusiastic, and stimulating style. Rachael Ray, host of several Food Network cooking shows, displays the emotive style. She is animated, frequently laughs at herself, and seems to like an informal atmosphere. Larry King, popular talk-show host, and Jeff Bezos, CEO of Amazon.com, also project the emotive communication style.

FIGURE 3.5 When the dominance and sociability dimensions are combined, the framework for communication style classification is established.

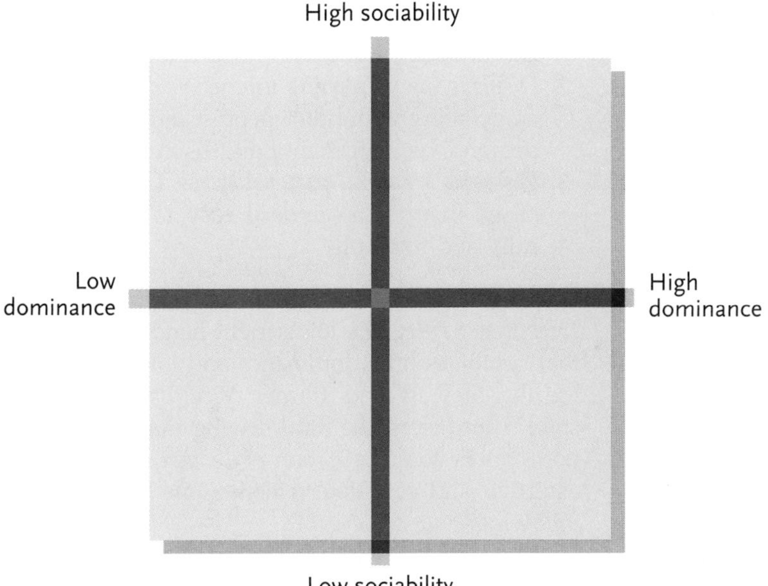

Source: From Manning, Gerald L.; Reece, Barry L., *Selling Today: Creating Customer Value*, 9th, © 2004. Reproduced by permission of Pearson Education, Inc., Upper Saddle River, New Jersey .

FIGURE 3.6 **The emotive style combines high sociability and high dominance.**

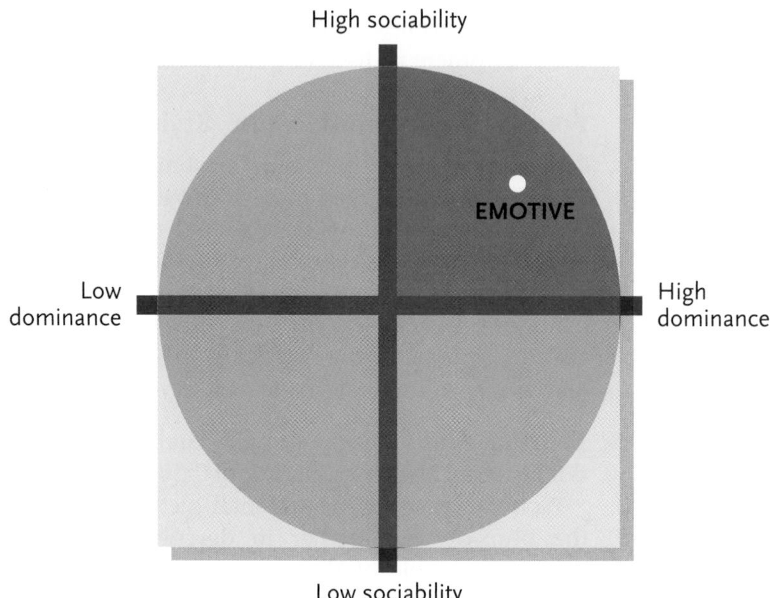

Source: From Manning, Gerald L.; Reece, Barry L., *Selling Today: Creating Customer Value*, 9th, © 2004. Reproduced by permission of Pearson Education, Inc., Upper Saddle River, New Jersey .

Here is a list of verbal and nonverbal clues that identify the emotive person:

1. *Displays spontaneous, uninhibited behavior.* The emotive person is more apt to talk rapidly, express views with enthusiasm, and use vigorous hand gestures. David Letterman and Jim Carrey fit this description.
2. *Displays the personality dimension described as extroversion.* Extroverts typically enjoy being with other people and tend to be active and upbeat. The emotive person likes informality and usually prefers to operate on a first-name basis.
3. *Possesses a natural persuasiveness.* Combining high dominance and high sociability, this person finds it easy to express his or her point of view dramatically and forcefully.

Director Style. The lower-right-hand quadrant represents a communication style that combines high dominance and low sociability—the **director style** (Figure 3.7). Martha Stewart and former Vice President Dick Cheney, project the director style. Tom Peters, the hard-driving management consultant, easily fits the description of this communication style. All these people have been described as frank, assertive, and very determined. Some behaviors displayed by directors include the following:

1. *Projects a serious attitude.* John McCain, recent Republican nominee for President, was described as the least emotive of the presidential candidates.[16]
2. *Expresses strong opinions.* With firm gestures and a tone of voice that communicates determination, the director projects the image of someone who wants to take control. Judge Judith Sheindlin of the *Judge Judy* television show displays this behavior.

FIGURE 3.7 The directive style combines high dominance and low sociability.

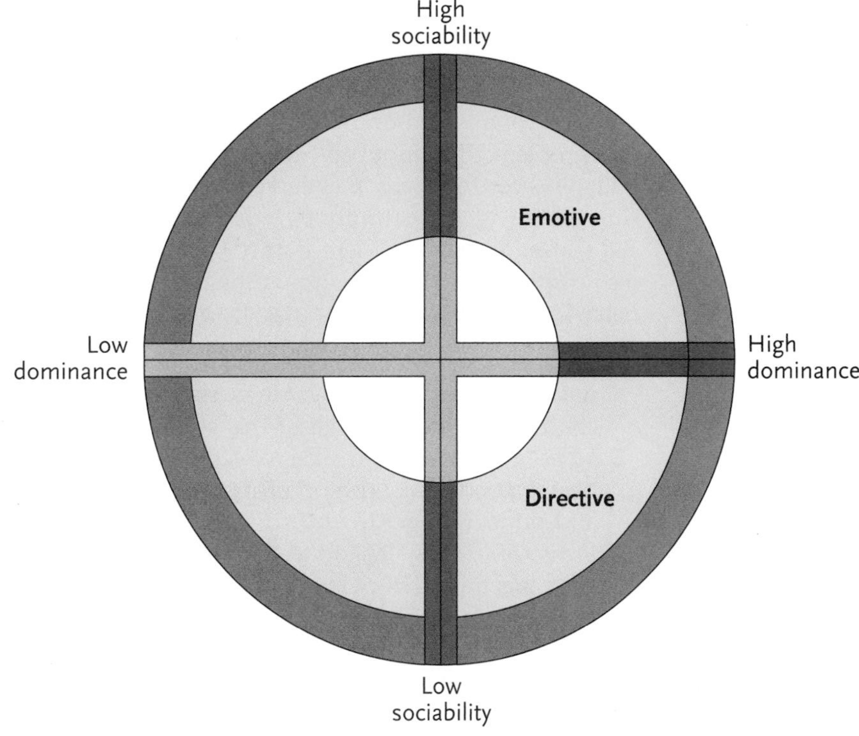

Source: From Manning, Gerald L.; Reece, Barry L., *Selling Today: Creating Customer Value*, 9th, © 2004. Reproduced by permission of Pearson Education, Inc., Upper Saddle River, New Jersey .

3. *May project indifference.* It is not easy for the director to communicate a warm, caring attitude. He or she does not find it easy to abandon the formal approach in dealing with people.

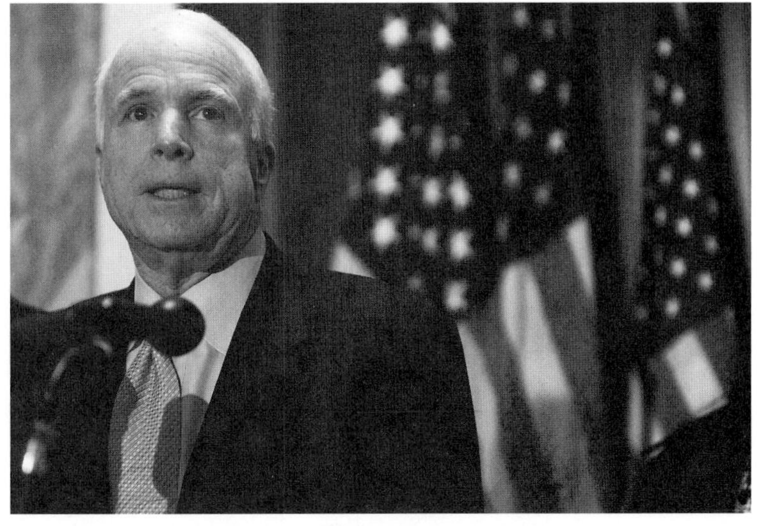

Alex Wong/Getty Images

Persons who display the *Directive* style, such as Senator John McCain, like to take charge and maintain control. People who display the *Directive* style are generally viewed as determined, serious, and somewhat impersonal.

Reflective Style. The lower-left-hand quadrant of the communication style model features a combination of low dominance and low sociability. This is the **reflective style** of communication (Figure 3.8).

The reflective person is usually quiet, enjoys spending time alone, and does not make decisions quickly. The late physicist Albert Einstein fits this description. He once commented on how he liked to spend idle hours: "When I have no special problem to occupy my mind, I love to reconstruct proofs of mathematical and physical theorems that have long been known to me. There is no goal in this, merely an opportunity to indulge in the pleasant occupation of thinking."[17] Bill Gates, former president Jimmy Carter, and Dr. Joyce Brothers (psychologist) also display the characteristics of the reflective communication style. Some of the behaviors characteristic of this style are as follows:

1. *Expresses opinions in a disciplined, deliberate manner.* The reflective person does not seem to be in a hurry. He or she expresses measured opinions. Emotional control is a common trait of this style.
2. *Seems to be preoccupied.* The reflective person is rather quiet and may often appear preoccupied with other matters. As a result, he or she may seem aloof and difficult to get to know.
3. *Prefers orderliness.* The reflective person prefers an orderly work environment. At a meeting, this person appreciates an agenda. A reflective person enjoys reviewing details and making decisions slowly.

Supportive Style. The upper-left-hand quadrant combines low dominance and high sociability—the **supportive style** of communication (Figure 3.9). People who possess this style tend to be cooperative, patient, and attentive.

FIGURE 3.8 The reflective style combines low dominance and low sociability.

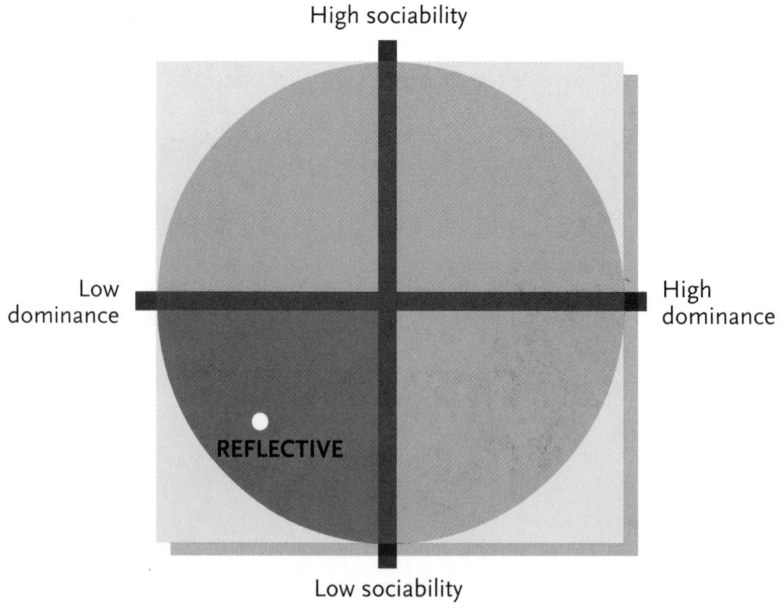

Source: From Manning, Gerald L.; Reece, Barry L., *Selling Today: Creating Customer Value*, 9th, © 2004. Reproduced by permission of Pearson Education, Inc., Upper Saddle River, New Jersey .

FIGURE 3.9 **The supportive style combines low dominance and high sociability.**

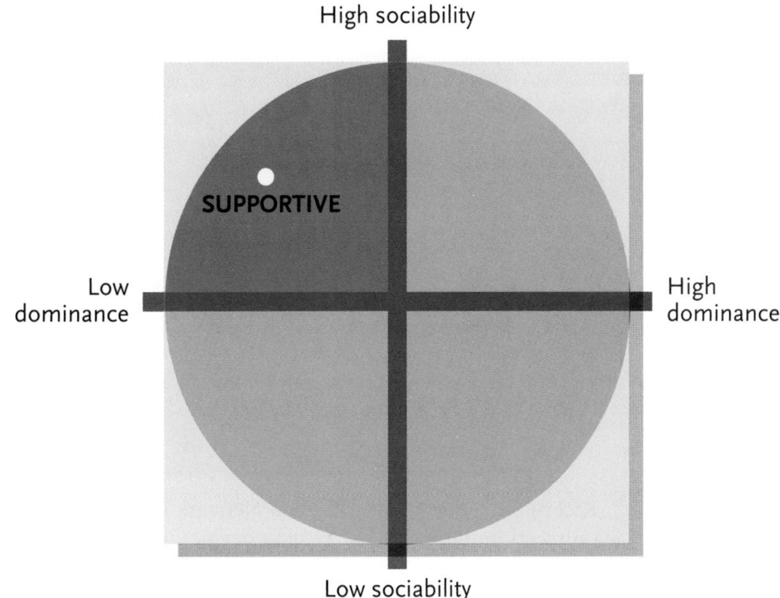

Source: From Manning, Gerald L.; Reece, Barry L., *Selling Today: Creating Customer Value*, 9th, © 2004. Reproduced by permission of Pearson Education, Inc., Upper Saddle River, New Jersey .

The supportive person is reserved and usually avoids attention-seeking behavior. Additional behaviors that commonly characterize the supportive style include the following:

1. *Listens attentively*. Good listeners have a unique advantage in many occupational settings. This is especially true of loan officers, sales personnel, and supervisors. The talent comes more naturally to the supportive person.
2. *Avoids the use of power*. Supportive persons are more likely to rely on friendly persuasion than power when dealing with people. They like to display warmth in their speech and written correspondence. Neil Armstrong, Apollo 11 crew member, and Julia Roberts, actress, display these behaviors.
3. *Makes and expresses decisions in a thoughtful, deliberate manner*. Supportive persons appear low-key in a decision-making role. Meryl Streep, Paul Simon, Meg Ryan, Kevin Costner, the late Princess Di, and Mary Tyler Moore all display characteristics of this style.

HUMAN RELATIONS IN ACTION

International Market for Four-Style Training

Although four-style programs were initially created and marketed in the United States, they have become a global phenomenon according to the staff at Wilson Learning Corporation. Wilson Learning conducts communication-style seminars throughout the world. Inscape Publishing, the company that developed the popular DiSC learning instrument over three decades ago, reports that more than 40 million people worldwide have completed DiSC four-dimension workshops.[18]

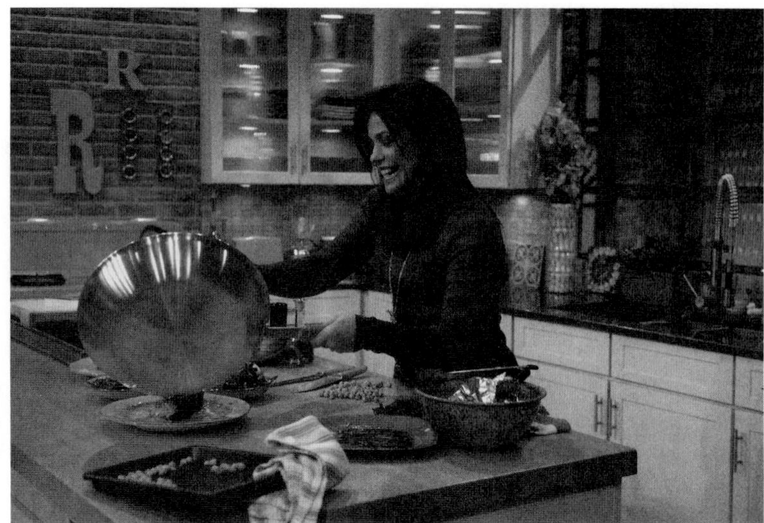

Brad Barket/Getty Images

Rachael Ray, host of several Food Network cooking shows, often expresses her views dramatically and impulsively. The *Emotive* person likes to create a social relationship quickly and usually feels more comfortable in an informal atmosphere.

Did you find one particular communication style that is most like yours? If your first attempt to identify your most preferred style was not successful, do not be discouraged. No one conforms completely to one style. You share some traits with other styles. Also, keep in mind that communication style is just one dimension of personality. As noted previously, your personality is made up of a broad array of psychological and behavioral characteristics. It is this unique pattern of characteristics that makes each person an individual. *Communication style* refers only to those behaviors that others can observe.

Did you discover a communication style that is least like yours? In many cases, we feel a sense of tension or discomfort when we have contact with persons who speak or act in ways that are at odds with our communication style. For example, the person with a need for orderliness and structure in daily work may feel tension when working closely with someone who is more spontaneous and unstructured.

Online Assessment of Your Communication Style

You can gain additional insight into your communication style by accessing the web address *www.cengage.com/management/reece* and clicking on the Online Assessment of Your Communication Style link. After completing the assessment, you will be provided with a profile indicating your most preferred communication style.

Variation within Your Communication Style

Communication styles also vary in intensity. For example, a person may be either moderately or strongly dominant. Note that the communication style model features zones that radiate outward from the center, as illustrated in Figure 3.10. These dimensions might be thought of as **intensity zones**.

Zone 1. People who fall within Zone 1 will display their unique behavioral characteristics with less intensity than people in Zone 2. This means that it may be more difficult to identify the preferred communication style of people in Zone 1.

FIGURE 3.10 Communication Style Intensity Zones

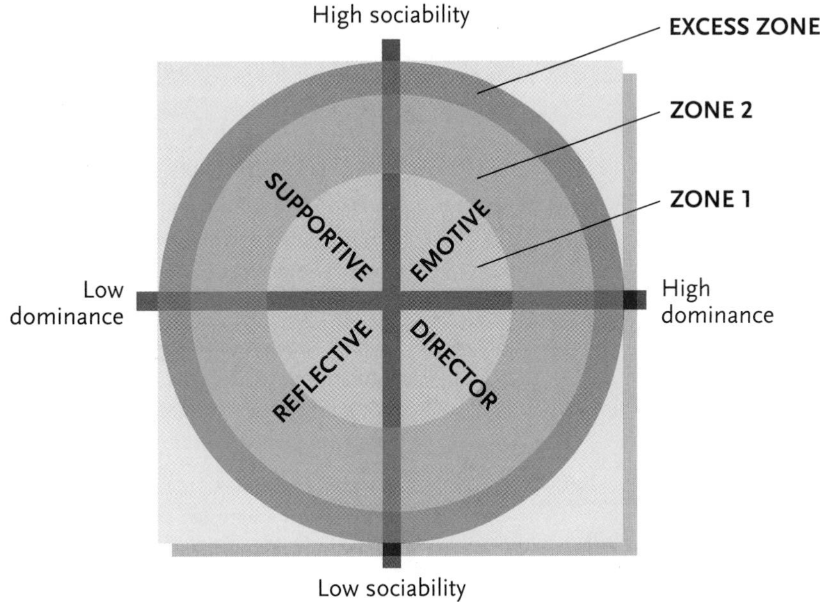

Source: From Manning, Gerald L.; Reece, Barry L., *Selling Today: Creating Customer Value*, 9th, © 2004. Reproduced by permission of Pearson Education, Inc., Upper Saddle River, New Jersey .

They will not be as obvious in their gestures, tone of voice, speech patterns, or emotional expressions. You may have trouble picking up the right clues to identify their communication style.

Zone 2. People who fall within Zone 2 will display their behavioral characteristics with greater intensity than those in Zone 1. For example, on the following dominance continuum, Sue, Mike, Harold, and Deborah each fall within a different zone.

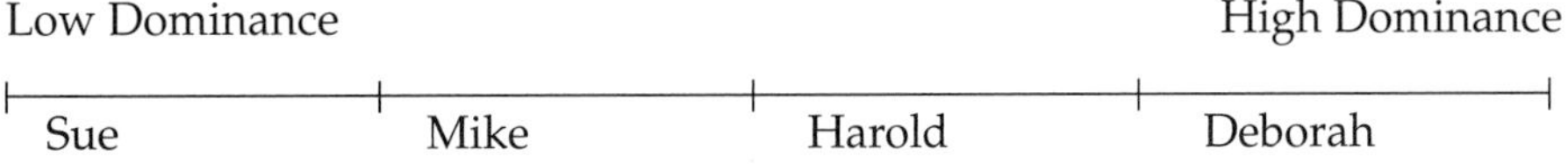

In terms of communication style identification, it is probably easier to distinguish between Sue and Deborah (who are in Zone 2) than between Mike and Harold (who are in Zone 1). Of course, the boundary line that separates Zone 1 from Zone 2 should not be viewed as a permanent barrier. It is important to understand that under certain conditions, people will abandon their preferred style temporarily.

You can sometimes observe this behavior change when a person is upset or angry. For example, Sue is a strong supporter of equal rights for women. At school she hears a male student say, "I think a woman's place is in the home." At that point, she may express her own views in the strongest possible terms. This forcefulness will require temporarily abandoning the comfort of her low dominance style to display assertive behavior.

Excess Zone. The **excess zone** is characterized by a high degree of intensity and rigidity. It can also be labeled the "danger" zone. When people occupy this zone, they become inflexible and display a lack of versatility (see Table 3.1). Extreme intensity in any quadrant is bound to interfere with good human relations.

TABLE 3.1 BEHAVIORS DISPLAYED IN THE EXCESS ZONE

Supportive Style	Attempts to win approval by agreeing with everyone Constantly seeks reassurance Refuses to take a strong stand Tends to apologize a great deal
Director Style	Is determined to come out on top Will not admit to being wrong Appears cold and unfeeling when dealing with others Tends to use dogmatic phrases such as "always," "never," or "you can't"
Emotive Style	Tends to express highly emotional opinions Is outspoken to the point of being offensive Seems unwilling to listen to the views of others Uses exaggerated gestures and facial expressions
Reflective Style	Tends to avoid making a decision Seems overly interested in detail Is very stiff and formal when dealing with others Seeks to achieve perfection

People often move into the excess zone when they are under stress or not feeling well. A person who feels threatened or insecure may also move into the excess zone. Even a temporary excursion into the excess zone should be avoided if at all possible. Inflexible and rigid communication styles are likely to lead to a breakdown in human relations.

Tips on Style Identification

To identify a person's communication style, focus your full attention on observable behavior. The best clues for identifying styles are nonverbal. Learn to be observant of people's gestures, posture, facial expressions, and the rapidity and loudness of their speech.[19] Animated facial expressions and high-volume, rapid speech are characteristic of the emotive communication style. Infrequent use of gestures, speaking in a steady monotone, and few facial expressions are characteristic of the reflective style. Of course, verbal messages will also be helpful. If a person tends to be blunt and to the point and makes strong statements, you are likely observing a director.

Inflexible and rigid communication styles are likely to lead to a breakdown in human relations.

We have noted that communication style is determined by where a person falls on the sociability continuum and the dominance continuum. Once you have identified as many verbal and nonverbal clues as possible, use this information to place the person on each continuum. Let's assume that the clues indicate that the person is low in dominance. This means you can automatically eliminate the emotive and director styles because both are characterized by high dominance. The next step is to place the person on the sociability continuum. If the clues indicate that the person is low in sociability, you automatically eliminate the supportive style. By the process of elimination, you conclude that this person is probably reflective. The authors of *People Styles at Work,* however, warn that your initial perception of another person's style should not be carved in stone. You should continue to collect new information and reassess your initial observations.[20]

Keep in mind that different situations bring out different behaviors. If you observe someone participating in a classroom discussion, then later observe the same person relaxing with friends at a local restaurant, you may witness two different behavioral patterns. Getting to know someone is hard work, and it's best not to look for shortcuts.[21]

HUMAN RELATIONS IN ACTION

Yeeeeaaahh

Many political observers believe that Howard Dean's presidential campaign was undone by one unscripted scream. After losing the Iowa Democratic caucus, he met with his dispirited supporters and promised the campaign would continue. After listing all the states he planned to visit in the weeks ahead, he ended the speech with an emotional promise: "And then we're going to Washington, DC, to take back the White House. Yeeeaaahh!" What followed was a near-saturation replay of that scream on cable, radio, and network television. On that cold night in Iowa, Dean created the impression that his passion had crossed over to anger. A move into the excess zone can have unexpected consequences.[22]

Versatility: The Third Dimension

Earlier in this chapter, we described two important dimensions of the communication style model: dominance and sociability. You will recall that these dimensions of human behavior are independent of each other. Now we are ready to discuss versatility, an important third dimension of human behavior.

Persons who can create and maintain interpersonal relations with others, regardless of their communication styles, are displaying versatility. **Versatility** can be defined as acting in ways that earn a social endorsement. Endorsement simply means other people's approval of our behavior. People give us their endorsement when they feel comfortable and non-defensive with us.[23]

The dimension of versatility is independent of style. This means that the emotive style is no more or less likely to be versatile than is the reflective style. Communication style remains relatively stable throughout life, whereas versatility is changeable.

Versatility is a trait we exhibit ourselves rather than elicit from others. Versatile people recognize that they can control their half of relationships and that it is easier to modify themselves than it is to modify others. The versatile person asks, "What can I do to make it easier for the other person to relate to me?"[24]

Research on versatility conducted by Wilson Learning Corporation indicates that the ability to adapt to another person's communication style greatly improves interpersonal relationships. People are divided nearly equally across the four communication styles, so we share our own style with only one out of four persons we have contact with. Once we develop and apply versatility skills, a greater number of people will feel comfortable and non-defensive in our presence.[25]

EMMANUEL DUNAND/Getty Images

Versatility is a trait displayed by President Barack Obama. He has the ability to adapt to another person's communication style quite easily. The dimension of versatility is independent of style.

Achieving Versatility through Style Flexing

Getting classified according to communication style doesn't mean you are "typecast" for life. You can always learn to strengthen areas of your most preferred communication style to get along better with others.[26] One way to broaden your personality is to engage in **style flexing**, which is the deliberate attempt to change or alter your style to meet the needs of another person. It is a temporary effort to act in harmony with the behavior of another person's communication style. Style flexing is communicating in a way that is more agreeable to persons of other styles. As noted earlier in this chapter, you can learn to adapt your style to accommodate others.

Total Person Insight

KERRY J. SULKOWICZ
Author, *The Corporate Shrink*

"The best etiquette strategy is one that adjusts on the fly, based on careful listening and empathizing with the other person."[27]

Style Flexing at Work. To illustrate how style flexing can be used in an organizational setting, let's take a look at a communication problem faced by Jeff Walker, buyer of sporting goods for a small chain of sporting goods stores. Jeff has a strong emotive communication style and usually gets along well with other emotive communicators. His immediate supervisor is Rhonda Greenbaum, a reflective person who tends to approach her work in an orderly, systematic manner. Jeff finds it difficult to curb his stimulating, promotional style and therefore is sometimes viewed as "unstable" by Ms. Greenbaum.

What might Jeff do to improve communication with his supervisor? Jeff is naturally an open, impulsive communicator. During meetings with a reflective person, he should appear less spontaneous, slow his rate of speech, and avoid the use of dramatic gestures. He should try to appear more reserved.

The reflective person admires orderliness, so Jeff should be sure he is well prepared. Before each meeting, he should develop a mental agenda of items that he wants to cover. At the beginning of the meeting he might say, "Ms. Greenbaum, there are three things I want to discuss." He would then describe each item concisely and present information slowly and systematically. This disciplined approach will be appreciated by the reflective supervisor.

How could Jeff's boss use style flexing to foster better communication? She could avoid appearing too stiff and formal. During meetings, the reflective person should try to avoid being "all business." (The emotive person does not object to small talk during meetings.) The reflective communicator might also be more informal about starting and ending meetings exactly on time, might allow the emotive person to depart from the agenda now and then, or might bring up an item spontaneously. The reflective person should try to share feelings and concerns more openly in the presence of an emotive person.

Strategies for Adapting Your Style

Once you have identified the dominant style of the other person, begin thinking of ways to flex your style to gain a social endorsement. Remember, you can control your half of the relationship. What can be done to meet the interpersonal needs of the other person? Here are a few general style adaptation strategies:

Flexing to the Emotive Style

- Take time to build a social as well as a business relationship. Leave time for relating and socializing.
- Display interest in the person's ideas, interests, and experiences.
- Do not place too much emphasis on details. Emotive people like fast-moving, inspirational verbal exchanges.
- Maintain a pace that is fast and somewhat spontaneous.

Flexing to the Director Style

- Be specific, brief, and to the point. Use time efficiently.
- Present the facts logically, and be prepared to provide specific answers to questions.
- Maintain a pace that is fast and decisive; project an image of strength and confidence.
- Messages (written or oral) should be short and to the point.

Flexing to the Reflective Style

- Appeal to the person's orderly, systematic approach to life. Be well organized.
- Approach this person in a straightforward, direct manner. Get down to business quickly.
- Be as accurate and realistic as possible when presenting information.
- Messages (written or oral) should be detailed and precise. The pace of verbal messages should be slow and systematic.

Flexing to the Supportive Style

- Show a sincere interest in the person. Take time to identify areas of common interest.
- Patiently draw out personal views and goals. Listen and be responsive to the person's needs.
- Present your views in a quiet, nonthreatening manner. Do not be pushy.
- Put a priority on relationship building and communication.

In those situations where you are attempting to win the support or cooperation of another person, look and listen for clues that identify the individual's preferred communication style. Once you are able to recognize and adjust to communication styles different from your own, gaining a social endorsement will be much easier.

HUMAN RELATIONS IN ACTION

Robert J. Nardelli Often Embraced the Excess Zone

As CEO of Home Depot Inc., Robert Nardelli's leadership style was often described as callous, arrogant, and heavy handed. Driven by a housing and home improvement boom, sales soared during the early years of his tenure. However, his hard-driving style provoked anger and frustration among his key constituencies: employees, customers, and shareholders. When the board could no longer embrace his leadership style, Nardelli was encouraged to resign. The CEO who always seemed comfortable in the excess zone was no longer welcome.[28]

Style Flexing: Pitfalls and Possibilities

Is style flexing just another way to manipulate others? The answer is yes if your approach is insincere and your only objective is to get something for yourself. The choice is yours. If your objective is to build an honest, constructive relationship, then style flexing can be a valuable and productive communication skill.

In an organizational setting, style flexing is especially critical when something important is at stake. Let's assume that you are head of a major department in a large hospital. Tomorrow you will meet with the hospital administrator and propose the purchase of new x-ray equipment that will cost a large amount of money. This is a good time to think about the administrator's communication style and consider your style-flexing strategies. Every decision is influenced by both reason and emotion, but the weight given to each of these elements during the decision-making process can vary from one person to another. Often we make the mistake of focusing too much attention on the content of our message and not enough on how to deliver that message.[29]

It is tempting to put a label on someone and then assume the label tells you everything you need to know about that person.

A Final Word of Caution

A discussion of communication styles would not be complete without a few words of caution. It is tempting to put a label on someone and then assume the label tells you everything you need to know about that person. In *The Name of*

CAREER INSIGHT

Tip of the Iceberg

An organizational consultant noticed something unusual during a visit to a large engineering firm. Most employees wore plastic name tags with large capitalized letters after their names: Sue Banson ENFP or Raymond Bloom INTJ. Every employee in the company had completed the Myers-Briggs personality inventory. Each employees' four-letter personality description was on display so coworkers could quickly understand their personality type. Good idea? This approach will create problems if employees assume the labels of any personality test tells them everything they need to know. The Myers-Briggs personality descriptor is just the tip of the iceberg.[30]

Your Game, Stuart Atkins says we should be careful not to use labels that make people feel boxed in, typecast, or judged. He says we should not classify *people;* we should classify their *strengths* and *preferences* to act one way or another under certain circumstances.[31] As noted in Chapter 1, the "total person" is made up of such interdependent traits as emotional control, values orientation, self-esteem, and self-awareness. To get acquainted with the whole person takes time and effort. Atkins makes this observation: "It requires much more effort to look beyond the label, to experience the person as a dynamic process, to look at the fine print on the box and carefully study the ingredients inside the package. We have been conditioned to trust the label and look no further."[32]

You must also be careful not to let the label you place on yourself become the justification for your own inflexible behavior. If you discover that your most preferred communication style is reflective and take the position that "others will simply have to get used to my need for careful analysis of data before making a decision," then you are not displaying the characteristics of a versatile person. Try not to let the label justify or reinforce why you are unable to communicate effectively with others.[33]

Strength/Weakness Paradox

As noted previously in this chapter, there is no "best" communication style. Each style has its unique strong points. Supportive people are admired for their easygoing, responsive style. Directors are respected for the thoroughness and determination they display. The stimulating, personable style of emotive persons can be very refreshing. And the emotional control and disciplined nature of reflective persons are almost universally admired.

Problems arise when people overextend or rely too much on the strengths of their style. The director who is too demanding may be viewed by others as "pushy." The supportive person may try too hard to please others and risk being viewed as "wishy-washy." An emotive person may be viewed as too excitable or not serious enough in a business setting. The reflective person who cannot seem to make a decision without mountains of information may be viewed as too cautious and inflexible. Some people rely too heavily on established strengths and fail to develop new skills that will increase their versatility.

To get along with people at all levels of an organization, you must be able to build rapport with those who are different from you. Customizing your communication style often requires learning *how to overcome your strengths*.[34]

LOOKING BACK: REVIEWING THE CONCEPTS

- Understand the concept of communication style and its effect on interpersonal relations.

Communication styles are our patterns of behaviors that are observable to others. Each of us has a distinctive way of responding to people and events. Communication style bias is likely to surface when you meet someone who displays a style distinctly different from your own.

- Discuss the major elements of the communication style model.

The communication style model is formed by combining two important dimensions of human behavior: dominance and sociability. Combinations of these two aspects create four communication styles —emotive, director, reflective, and supportive.

- Identify your preferred communication style.

With practice you can learn to identify your communication style. The starting point is to rate yourself on each scale (dominance and sociability) by placing a checkmark at a point along the continuum that represents how you perceive yourself. Completion of the dominance and sociability indicator forms will help you achieve greater awareness of your communication style. You may also want to ask others to complete these forms for you.

- Improve communication with others through style flexing.

A third dimension of human behavior—versatility—is important in dealing with communication styles that are different from your own. You can adjust your own style to meet the needs of others—a process called style flexing.

We must keep an open mind about people and be careful not to use labels that make them feel typecast or judged. Keeping an open mind requires more thought than pigeonholing does.

ON THE JOB Q & A: PERSONAL CALLS CREATE PROBLEMS

Q: The company I work for discourages personal phone calls during working hours. I am a single parent with two young children. How can I convince my supervisor that some personal calls are very important?

A: Placing personal phone calls during working hours is an issue that often divides employers and employees. From the employer's point of view, an employee who spends time on nonwork calls is wasting time, a valuable resource. Also, many organizations want to keep telephone lines clear for business calls. From your point of view, you need to know about changes in child-care arrangements, serious health concerns of family members, and similar problems. In fact, you will probably perform better knowing that family members are safe and secure. Explain to your supervisor that some personal calls will be inevitable. It is very important that you and your supervisor reach an agreement regarding this issue. When possible, make most of your personal calls during your lunch hour or during work breaks. Encourage friends to call you at home.

To improve communications with your supervisor, get acquainted with his or her communication style. Once you have identified this person's dominant style, use appropriate style-flexing strategies to gain a social endorsement.[35]

KEY TERMS

TRY YOUR HAND

1. Oprah Winfrey is one of America's most popular talk-show hosts. Consider the behaviors she displays on her show, and then complete the following exercises:
   a. On the dominance continuum, place a mark where you feel she belongs.
   b. On the sociability continuum, place a mark where you feel she belongs.
   c. On the basis of these two continua, determine Oprah Winfrey's communication style.
   d. In your opinion, does Oprah Winfrey display style flexibility?

2. To get some practice in identifying communication styles, watch two or three television shows and attempt to identify the style of individuals portrayed on the screen. To fully develop your skills of listening and observing, try this three-step approach:
   a. Cover the screen with a towel or newspaper and try to identify the style of one or two persons, using voice only.
   b. Turn down the volume, uncover the screen, and attempt to identify the style of the same persons, using visual messages only.
   c. Turn up the volume and make another attempt to identify the communication style of the persons portrayed on the screen. This time the identification process should be easier because you will be using sight and sound.

   These practice sessions will help you learn how to interpret the nonverbal messages that are helpful in identifying another person's communication style. When you select television shows, avoid situation comedies that often feature persons displaying exaggerated styles. You may want to watch a talk show or a news program that features interviews.

3. Self-awareness is very important. As we get to know ourselves, we can identify barriers to acceptance by others. Once you have identified your most preferred communication style, you have taken a big step in the direction of self-awareness. If you have not yet determined your most preferred communication style, take a few minutes to complete the dominance indicator form (Figure 3.2) and the sociability indicator form (Figure 3.4). Follow the instructions provided.

4. You have been given the opportunity to complete an online assessment of your communication style (see page 64). After completion of this assessment you were provided with a profile that indicates your most preferred communication style. In some work or social situations, you may find yourself exhibiting a communication style that is different than your preferred style. Reflect on a situation where you engaged in style flexing. What communication style did you display? Did the movement away from your most preferred style improve communication?

INTERNET INSIGHTS

1. The primary purpose of this chapter is to provide you with an introduction to communication styles and prepare you to apply the concepts presented here at work and in your personal life. You now have the foundation you need to continue your study. A great deal of information related to communication styles can be found on the Internet. Using your search engine, type in the following key words, and then review the resources available:
   - communication style
   - personality types
   - personality profile

2. Visit the following Web sites and review the popular communication style training programs offered by each company:

   Wilson Learning Worldwide
   http://www.wilsonlearning.com
   Inscape Publishing
   http://www.inscapepublishing.com

YOU PLAY THE ROLE

For the purpose of this role play, read the Closing Case: Style Flexing and assume the role of Eric Welch, who is described as a quiet, amiable person who displays the supportive communication style.

You will meet with Susan Perez, who has set up an appointment to inspect the property you represent. Before the role play, study the chapter material on style flexing and on how to communicate effectively with persons who display the director communication style. Prepare for the first 5–7 minutes of the meeting. How will you present yourself during the initial contact? What would be the best way to get the meeting off to a good start?

BELOW THE SURFACE:

Communication Styles at the Top

At the beginning of this chapter, you were introduced to Bill Gates, Chairman of Microsoft, and Steve Ballmer, CEO of Microsoft. Gates displays the reflective style and is impressed by detailed proposals that are supported by data. Joel Spolsky, former program manger at Microsoft says, "Bill Gates was amazingly technical, and he knew more about the details of his company's software than most of the people who worked on these details day in and day out."[36]

Gates recently ended full-time work at Microsoft to focus on philanthropy. He asked CEO Steve Ballmer to run the company. Ballmer displays the director communication style. He hopes to make the 100,000-employee corporation with 11 or 12 layers of management more agile. Ballmer feels that some of its groups need to work more closely together, with more "cohesion." During the early years, Ballmer displayed a domineering leadership style and was unwilling to delegate decision making. Today his leadership style is more diplomatic, and he is more willing to delegate authority.[37]

QUESTIONS

1. If Bill Gates and Steve Ballmer met for the first time, would any form of communication style bias surface? Predict what the initial reactions might be.

2. Let's assume you are a marketing representative for the Southwestern Region of the American Red Cross. You plan to schedule separate meetings with Gates and Ballmer to solicit major funding for residents of Louisiana, Mississippi, and Alabama, who lost almost everything during a series of tropical storms and hurricanes. How would you flex your own personal style to meet the interpersonal needs of each person?

CLOSING CASE: Style Flexing

Eric Welch has been employed at Grant Real Estate for almost two years. Before receiving his real estate license, he was a property manager with a large real estate agency in another community. During his first year with Grant, he was assigned to the residential property division and sold properties totaling $825,000. He then requested and received a transfer to the commercial division.

Three months ago, Eric obtained a commercial listing that consisted of 26 acres of land near a growing residential neighborhood. The land is zoned commercial and appears to be ideally suited for medium-size shopping center. Eric prepared a detailed prospectus and sent it to Susan Perez, president of Mondale Growth Corporation, a firm specializing in development of shopping centers. One week later he received a letter from Ms. Perez requesting more information. Shortly after receiving Eric's response, Ms. Perez called to set up an appointment to inspect the property. A time and date were finalized, and Eric agreed to meet her plane and conduct a tour of the property.

Eric is a quiet, amiable person who displays the *Supportive* communication style. Friends say that they like to spend time with him because he is a good listener.

QUESTIONS

1. If Ms. Perez displays the characteristics of the *Director* communication style, how should Eric conduct himself during the meeting? Be specific as you analyze those behaviors that would be admired by Ms. Perez.
2. If Ms. Perez wants to build rapport with Eric Welch, what behaviors should she display?
3. It is not a good idea to put a label on someone and then assume the label tells us everything about the person. As Eric attempts to build rapport with Ms Perez, what other personal characteristics should he try to identify?

INTEGRATED RESOURCES

CLASSROOM ACTIVITIES

IRM Application Exercise 3.1
IRM Application Exercise 3.2

CHAPTER 4

Building High Self-Esteem

TIP OF THE ICEBERG

CHAPTER PREVIEW

LEARNING OBJECTIVES

After studying Chapter 4, you will be able to

- Define self-esteem and discuss its impact on your life.
- Discuss how self-esteem is developed.
- Identify the characteristics of people with low and high self-esteem.
- Identify ways to increase your self-esteem.
- Understand the conditions organizations can create that will help workers increase their self-esteem.

Dare to Dream

Vickie Stringer, founder and CEO of Triple Crown Publications, wasn't from a broken home. She was raised in a middle-class Detroit neighborhood by her mother, a teacher and her father, an electrical engineer. During her freshman year in college, she met a drug dealer, fell in love, and dropped out of school. When Stringer got pregnant, her boyfriend abandoned her. After her son was born, she needed money. She was successful selling drugs until one of her customers turned out to be a police informant.

When she was released from a federal penitentiary after five years, she was a 29-year-old felon with no degree, résumé, legal work experience, money, or prospects. She knew she wanted her life to have meaning; however, the path was uncertain. She was free, but she felt that there was nothing waiting for her.[1] Fortunately, she had spent some of her free time in prison writing a novel. After the manuscript was rejected by 26 publishers, she decided to self-publish. Later her book, *Let That Be the Reason,* was published by UpStream Publications and sold more than 100,000 copies.

Motivated by the desire to become an entrepreneur, she founded a publishing company. Today Triple Crown Publications is the first name in "hip-hop-lit," a booming genre of raw, gritty urban fiction, sold everywhere from street corners to small African-American bookstores to Barnes & Noble. *Let That Be the Reason,* and her follow-up book, *Imagine,* were the entrepreneurial paths that transformed federal prisoner 63752-06, Vickie Stringer, into the owner of a $1.8 million publishing company.[2]

Courtesy of Vickie Stringer, Publisher, Triple Crown Publications

Within the walls of a sterile prison, Vickie Stringer began thinking about changing her life. She spent some of her free time writing a novel. After many rejections, the book was finally published and sold over 100,000 copies. The success of that book set the stage for developing her own publishing company.

Ball State University's Entrepreneurship Center named Vickie Stringer *2007 Entrepreneur of the Year.* The Entrepreneurship Center honors prominent entrepreneurs it defines as "individuals who tackle tough problems, work from the bottom up, and craft businesses that creatively solve the challenges of life." After receiving the Ball State University award, Ms. Stringer was asked what advice she would give to future entrepreneurs: "Be patient, allow room for growth, build your company on a strong accounting system, and as always, dare to dream."[3]

The Power of Self-Esteem

The importance of self-esteem as a guiding force in our lives cannot be overstated. Your self-esteem includes your feelings about your adequacy in the many roles you play in life—friend, brother or sister, daughter or son, employee or employer, a student leader, and so on. In this chapter, we will discuss how self-esteem is developed and identify ways to increase your self-esteem. This information will help you realize your full human potential, both individually and as a group member.

The importance of self-esteem as a guiding force in our lives cannot be overstated.

Self-Esteem = Self-Efficacy + Self-Respect

Nathaniel Branden, author of *The Six Pillars of Self-Esteem* and *Self-Esteem at Work,* has spent the past three decades studying the psychology of self-esteem. He states that the ultimate source of **self-esteem** can only be internal: It is the relationship between a person's self-efficacy and self-respect. **Self-efficacy** is the learned expectation of success. What we do or try to do is controlled by our perceptions or beliefs about our chances of success at a particular task or problem.

HUMAN RELATIONS IN ACTION

The Power of Strong Self-Efficacy

Over the years, many people we now know to be extremely intelligent and talented have had to develop a strong belief in themselves. If they had relied on others' opinions of their capabilities and potential, who knows where this world would be!

- **Walt Disney** was fired by a newspaper editor for lack of ideas. He went bankrupt several times before he built Disneyland.
- **Thomas Edison's** teacher said he was "too stupid to learn anything."
- **Fred Astaire** recalls the 1933 memo from the MGM casting director that stated, "Can't act. Can't sing. Slightly bald. Can dance a little."
- **Albert Einstein** did not speak until he was four years old and did not read until he was seven. His teacher described him as "mentally slow, unsociable, and adrift forever in foolish dreams."
- **Alan Jackson**, country-music superstar, was turned down by every Nashville label at least once. Some said he lacked "star quality."[4]

Your perception of your self-efficacy can influence which tasks you take on and which ones you avoid. Albert Bandura, a professor at Stanford University and one of the foremost self-efficacy researchers, views this component of self-esteem as a resilient belief in your own abilities. For example, an administrative assistant who masters a sophisticated computerized accounting system is more likely to tackle future complicated computer programs than is a person who feels computer illiterate and may not even try to figure out the new program, regardless of how well he or she *could* do it.[5]

Self-respect, the second component of self-esteem, is what you think and feel about yourself. Your judgment of your own value is a primary factor in achieving personal and career success. People who respect themselves tend to act in ways that confirm and reinforce this respect. People who lack self-respect may put up with verbal or physical abuse from others because they feel they are unworthy of praise and deserve the abuse. Nathaniel Branden believes that the healthier our self-esteem, the more inclined we are to treat others with respect, goodwill, and fairness, since we do not tend to perceive them as a threat, and since self-respect is the foundation of respect for others.[6]

Self-efficacy and self-respect are central themes of the definition of self-esteem adopted by the National Association for Self-Esteem (NASE). NASE defines self-esteem as, "The experience of being capable of meeting life's challenges and being worthy of happiness."[7] It is having the conviction that you are able to make appropriate choices and decisions.

Ethan Miller/Getty Images

To achieve stardom in the competitive world of country music, Alan Jackson had to overcome years of disappointment. His music was rejected by all of the major Nashville labels. Finally, his "star quality" was discovered.

The NASE definition of self-esteem helps us make the distinction between authentic (healthy) self-esteem and false (unhealthy) self-esteem. Authentic self-esteem is not expressed by self-glorification at the expense of others or by the attempt to diminish others so as to elevate oneself. Arrogance, boastfulness, and overestimation of your abilities are more likely to reflect inadequate self-esteem rather than, as it might appear, too much self-esteem.

How Self-Esteem Develops

To understand the development of self-esteem, it is helpful to examine how you form your self-concept. Your **self-concept** is the bundle of facts, opinions, beliefs, and perceptions about yourself that are present in your life every moment of every day.[8] The self-concept you have today reflects information you have received from others and life events that occurred throughout childhood, adolescence, and adulthood. You are *consciously* aware of some of the things you have been conditioned to believe about yourself. But many comments and events that have shaped your self-concept are processed at the *unconscious* level and continue to influence your judgments, feelings, and behaviors whether you are aware of them or not.[9]

"Just remember, son, it doesn't matter whether you win or lose—unless you want Daddy's love."

Childhood

Researchers in the field of **developmental psychology** are concerned with the course and causes of developmental changes over a person's lifetime. They pay close attention to genetic and environmental factors (nature versus nurture).[10] Although space does not permit a detailed discussion here of cognitive, social, and emotional development during early childhood, we can state with conviction that developmental experiences during the first few years of life are extremely important. For example, too little attention from nurturing parents and too much television viewing can hinder healthy childhood development.[11]

Because childhood events are retained in your brain, poor performance in school, abusive or uncaring parents, or a serious childhood accident can be defining experiences in your life. Messages from siblings, teachers, and various authority figures can have a lasting impact on your self-concept. Consider the father who repeatedly says, "Real men don't cry," or places undue emphasis on successful performance during contact sports. These childhood experiences can form the foundation for your level of self-esteem that emerges later in life.

Adolescence

The transition from childhood to adulthood can be a long and difficult period. At about age 11, children begin to describe themselves in terms of social relationships and personality traits. By the end of early adolescence, most youth are ready to develop a personal identity as a unique individual. Identity formation, the central task of adolescence, is usually more difficult for youth if their infancy and childhood has resulted in feelings of shame, guilt, and inferiority.[12]

As adolescents attempt to resolve questions about self-worth, sexuality, and independence, they may "try out" alternative identities.[13] Teens often turn to movies, music videos, and magazines for guidance and attempt to emulate the unrealistic body images and fashions that their peers deem worthwhile. Adolescence can last well into the 20s as each person attempts to develop his or her own unique identity.[14]

Parents, teachers, and employers can have a powerful effect on teenage self-esteem. When they offer encouragement, support, enthusiasm, and commendation for achievements, they enable teens to learn how to take healthy risks, tolerate frustration, and feel proud of their accomplishments.

Adulthood

When you reach adulthood, you are greatly influenced by a time-reinforced self-concept that has been molded by people and events from all your past experiences. You have been bombarded over the years with positive and negative messages from your family, friends, teachers, supervisors, and the media. You may compare yourself to others, as was so common in adolescence, or you may focus on your own inner sense of self-worth. Emmett Miller, a noted authority on self-esteem, says that as adults we tend to define ourselves in terms of the following items:[15]

The Things We Possess. Miller says this is the most primitive source of self-worth. If we define ourselves in terms of what we have, the result may be an effort to accumulate more and more material things to achieve a greater feeling of self-worth. The idea that we can compensate for self-doubt and insecurity with our checkbook is widely accepted in America.[16] People who define themselves in terms of what they have may have difficulty deciding "what is enough" and may spend their life in search of more material possessions.

What We Do for a Living. Miller points out that too often our self-worth and identity depend on something as arbitrary as a job title. Amy Saltzman, author of *Downshifting,* a book on ways to reinvent (or redefine) success, says, "We have allowed our professional identities to define us and control us."[17] She points out that we have looked to outside forces such as the corporation, the university, or the media to provide us with a script for leading a satisfying, worthwhile life.

Our Internal Value System and Emotional Makeup. Miller says this is the healthiest way for people to identify themselves:

> *If you don't give yourself credit for excellence in other areas of life, besides your job and material possessions, you've got nothing to keep your identity afloat during a job layoff or a troubled family relationship. People who are in touch with their real identity weather the storm better because they have a more varied and richer sense of themselves, owing to the importance they attach to their personal lives and activities.*[18]

As an adult, you will be constantly adjusting the level of your self-esteem as you cope with events at work and in your personal life. The loss of a job or being passed over for a promotion may trigger feelings of insecurity or depression. A messy divorce can leave you with feelings of self-doubt. An unexpected award may raise your spirits and make you feel better about yourself.

The Past Programs the Future

Phillip McGraw, better known as "Dr. Phil," has developed a one-sentence guide to understanding the importance of your self-concept: *The past reaches into the present, and programs the future, by your recollections and your internal rhetoric about what you perceived to have happened in your life.*[19] Past experiences and events, which McGraw describes as "defining moments," can influence your thinking for a lifetime and program your future. They get incorporated into your deepest understanding of who you are because they are often the focus of your internal dialogue—a process we call "self-talk." Later in this chapter, we will discuss how to avoid the influence of negative self-talk and build upon positive messages.

> ***Total Person Insight***
>
> DON MIGUEL RUIZ
> Author, *The Four Agreements*
>
> *"How many times do we pay for one mistake? The answer is thousands of times. The human is the only animal on earth that pays a thousand times for the same mistake. The rest of the animals pay once for every mistake they make. But not us. We have a powerful memory. We make a mistake, we judge ourselves, we find ourselves guilty, and punish ourselves… . Every time we remember, we judge ourselves again, we are guilty again, and we punish ourselves again, and again, and again."*[20]

Self-Esteem Influences Your Behavior

Your level of self-esteem can have a powerful impact on your behavior. Your sense of competence and resulting self-respect, the two components of self-esteem, stem from the belief that you are generally capable of producing the results in life that you want by making appropriate, constructive choices. This confidence makes you less vulnerable to the negative views of others, which then enables you to be more tolerant and respectful of others. People with healthy self-esteem tend to have a sense of personal worth that has been strengthened through various achievements and through accurate self-appraisal.[21]

When we rely too heavily on validation from external sources, we can lose control over our lives.

Characteristics of People with Low Self-Esteem

1. ***They tend to maintain an external locus of control.*** People who maintain an **external locus of control** believe that their life is almost totally controlled by outside forces and that they bear little personal responsibility for what happens to them.[22] When something goes wrong, they have a tendency to blame something or someone other than themselves. Even when they succeed, they tend to attribute their success to luck rather than to their own expertise and hard work. They continually rely on other people to make them feel good about themselves, and therefore need an ever-increasing dose of support from others to keep them going. When we rely too heavily on validation from external sources, we can lose control over our lives.[23]

2. ***They are more likely to participate in self-destructive behaviors.*** If you do not like yourself, there is no apparent reason to take care of yourself. Therefore, people with low self-esteem are more likely to drink too much, smoke too much, and eat too much. Some may develop an eating disorder such as bulimia or anorexia, often with devastating results.
3. ***They tend to exhibit poor human relations skills.*** Individuals with low self-esteem may have difficulty developing effective interpersonal skills. Workers with low self-esteem may reduce the efficiency and productivity of a group: They tend to exercise less initiative and hesitate to accept responsibility or make independent decisions, and are less likely to speak up in a group and criticize the group's approach.

CRITICAL THINKING CHALLENGE:

Synthesize It

Oprah Winfrey says, "Each of us arrives with all we need to feel valued and unique, but slowly that gets chipped away." She is correct, but some life experiences do cause us to increase the value we place on ourselves. After careful reflection on your childhood and adolescence, identify five events or people who had a significant impact (positive or negative) on your self-esteem. Think of these experiences as "defining moments" in your life.[24]

Characteristics of People with High Self-Esteem

1. ***They tend to maintain an internal locus of control.*** People who believe they are largely responsible for what happens to them maintain an **internal locus of control**. They make decisions for their own reasons based on their standards of what is right and wrong. They learn from their mistakes, but are not immobilized by them.
2. ***They are able to feel all dimensions of emotion without letting those emotions affect their behavior in a negative way.*** They realize emotions cannot be handled either by repressing them or by giving them free rein. Although you may not be able to stop feeling the emotions of anger, envy, and jealousy, you can control your thoughts and actions when you are under the influence of these strong emotions. It is okay to have anxious, scared, angry, or depressed feelings—as long as you don't let them stop you from doing what you have to do.[25]
3. ***They are less likely to take things personally.*** Don Miguel Ruiz, author of the best-selling book *The Four Agreements,* cautions us to avoid taking others' comments personally: "When you make it a strong habit not to take anything personally, you avoid many upsets in your life." He says that when you react strongly to gossip or strongly worded criticism ("You're so fat!"), you suffer for nothing. Ruiz notes that many of these messages come from people who are unable to respect you because they do not respect themselves.[26]
4. ***They are able to accept other people as unique, talented individuals.*** They learn to accept others for who they are and what they can do. Our multicultural work force makes this attitude especially important. Individuals who cannot tolerate other people who are "different" may find themselves out of a job. (See Chapter 15, "Valuing Workforce Diversity.") People with high self-esteem build mutual trust based on each individual's uniqueness.

5. ***They have a productive personality.*** They are optimistic in their approach to life and are capable of being creative, imaginative problem solvers. Because of this, they tend to be leaders and to be skillful in dealing with people. They have the ability to evaluate the dynamics of a relationship and adjust to the demands of the interaction. They are able to handle stress in a productive way by putting their problems and concerns into perspective and maintaining a balance of work and fun in their lives.[27]

Skill Development: Apply It

People with high self-esteem tend to associate with others who exhibit self-confidence and self-respect. Conversely, people with low self-esteem find comfort associating with people who share negative self-images. Can you identify these people in your circle of friends, classmates, and colleagues? Practice your people-reading skills by considering all those people in your life right now, and then mentally decide in which of the two categories they belong: low self-esteem or high self-esteem. What qualities do these people exhibit that helped you make your decisions? In order to build your own self-esteem, which of these people should you associate with more often?

How to Increase Your Self-Esteem

"The level of our self-esteem is not set once and for all in childhood," says Nathaniel Branden. It can grow throughout our lives or it can deteriorate.[28] Healthy self-esteem comes from realizing what qualities and skills you have that you can rely on and then making a plan to build those qualities and skills that you want in the future. The person you will be tomorrow has yet to be created. Your new, higher level of self-esteem will not happen overnight. Such a change is the result of a slow, steady evolution that begins with the desire to overcome low self-esteem.

Search for the Source of Low Self-Esteem

Many people live with deep personal doubts about themselves but have difficulty determining the source of those feelings. They even have difficulty finding the right words to describe those negative feelings. People with low self-esteem are less likely to see themselves with great clarity. The self-image they possess is like a reflection in a warped funhouse mirror; the image magnifies their weaknesses and minimizes their strengths. Increasing your self-esteem requires achieving a greater level of self-awareness and learning to accurately perceive your particular balance of strengths and weaknesses.[29]

To start this process, take time to list and carefully examine the defining moments in your life. Pay special attention to those that were decidedly negative, and try to determine how these moments have shaped your current self-concept. Next, make a list of the labels that others have used to describe you. Study the list carefully, and try to determine which ones you have internalized and accepted. Have these labels had a positive or negative influence on your concept of yourself? Phillip McGraw says, "If you are living to a label, you have molded for yourself a fictional self-concept with artificial boundaries."[30]

Identify and Accept Your Limitations

Become realistic about who you are and what you can and cannot do. Demanding perfection of yourself is unrealistic because no one is perfect. The past cannot be changed: Acknowledge your mistakes; learn from them; then move on.

Acting as an observer and detaching yourself from negative thoughts and actions can help you break the habit of rating yourself according to some scale of perfection and can enable you to substitute more positive and helpful thoughts. A good first step is learning to dislike a behavior you may indulge in, rather than condemning yourself.

Take Responsibility for Your Decisions

Psychologists have found that children who were encouraged to make their own decisions early in their lives have higher self-esteem than those who were kept dependent on their parents for a longer period of time. Making decisions helps you develop confidence in your own judgment and enables you to explore options. Take every opportunity you can to make decisions both in setting your goals and in devising ways to achieve them.

The attitude that you must be right all the time is a barrier to personal growth. With this attitude, you will avoid doing things that might result in mistakes. Much unhappiness comes from the widespread and regrettable belief that it is important to avoid making mistakes at all costs.[31] Taking risks that reach beyond what you already know how to do can often be fun and extremely rewarding.

> ***Total Person Insight***
>
> MARCUS BUCKINGHAM
> Author, *Go Put Your Strengths to Work*
>
> *"You will succeed in putting your strengths to work only if you believe that capitalizing on your strengths is the best way to compete."*[32]

Engage in Strength Building

During the past 30 years, the Gallup International Research and Education Center has researched the best way to maximize a person's potential. One of the most important findings can be summarized in a single sentence: Most organizations take their employees' strengths for granted and focus on minimizing their weaknesses. The research findings suggest that the best way to excel in a career is to maximize your strengths.[33]

The Gallup Organization research has been summarized in *Now, Discover Your Strengths* by Marcus Buckingham and Donald Clifton. The first step toward strength building is to discover your greatest talents. A **talent** is any naturally recurring pattern of thought, feeling, or behavior that can be productively applied. It is important to distinguish your natural talents from things you can learn. With practice, of course, we can all get a little better at doing most things. However, to reach consistent, near-perfect performances through practice alone is very difficult. Many successful salespeople have a talent for making new acquaintances and derive satisfaction from breaking the ice to make a connection with new people. They are intrigued with the unique qualities of each customer. They have a natural gift, enhanced through practice, for figuring out how to customize their sales presentation so it appeals to the unique needs of each customer. Without these talents, salespeople will struggle to achieve success.[34]

Strength building also requires the acquisition of knowledge and skill. As we prepare for a career, we must acquire certain factual knowledge. An accountant must know how to prepare a statement of cash flow. Nurses must know how to administer medications with precision. Skill, the application of knowledge, might be thought of as the "doing" part of strength building.[35]

Identifying Your Dominant Talents. Marcus Buckingham states that when we are not doing what we are truly good at, we are not living up to our greatest performance capabilities. He says that one effective way to identify your dominant talents is to step back and watch yourself as you try out different activities. Pay close attention to how you feel about these experiences. Take an elective course, volunteer to be chair of a committee, complete a summer internship, or accept a part-time job in an area that appeals to you. If you flourish in some activities, but wither in others, analyze why this happened.

Buckingham's research indicates that the best managers spend 80 percent of their time trying to amplify their employees' strengths.[36] Chances are, however, you will not be working for a boss who encourages strength building. So, be prepared to assume responsibility for identifying your natural talents and building your strengths.

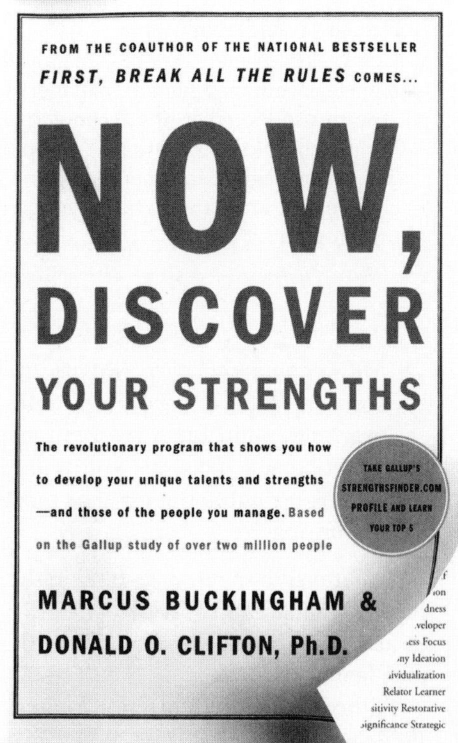

The authors of the bestselling book *Now, Discover Your Strengths* encourage us to identify our dominant talents. Get involved in a wide range of activities and then pay close attention to how you feel about these experiences.

Seek the Support and Guidance of Mentors

Chip Bell, author of *Managers as Mentors: Building Partnerships for Learning*, defines a **mentor** as "someone who helps someone else learn something the learner would otherwise have learned less well, more slowly, or not at all."[37] In most organizations, mentoring is carried out informally, but formal programs that systematically match mentors and protégés are common.

Most people who have had a mentoring experience say it was an effective development tool. However, many surveys indicate that only a small percentage of employees say they have had a mentor. In today's fast-paced work environment, where most people have a heavy workload, you must be willing to take the initiative and build a mentor relationship.[38] Warren Bennis, founding chairman of the Leadership Institute at the University of Southern California, states, "Being mentored isn't a passive game. It's nothing less than the ability to spot the handful of people who can make all the difference in your life."[39] Here are some tips to keep in mind.

1. ***Search for a mentor who has the qualities of a good coach.*** Mentors need to be accomplished in their own right, but success alone does not make someone a good mentor. Look for someone whom you would like to emulate, both in business savvy and in operating style. Be sure it is someone who is absolutely credible, a person you trust enough to talk with about touchy issues.[40]

HUMAN RELATIONS IN ACTION

Reverse Mentoring

Jack Welch, former CEO of General Electric, pioneered the concept of *reverse mentoring*. He encouraged his top managers to meet regularly with their workers and learn how to use the emerging technology. Today, many older workers (baby boomers) are turning to Generation Y employees to better understand the nuances of instant messaging, Internet blogs, and other forms of technology. Procter & Gamble and Deloitte and Touche have had considerable success with formal reverse mentoring programs.[41]

2. ***Market yourself to a prospective mentor.*** The best mentor for you may be someone who is very busy. Sell the benefits of a mentoring partnership. For example, point out that mentoring can be a mutually rewarding experience. Describe specific steps you will take to avoid wasting the time of a busy person. You might suggest that meetings be held during lunch or agree to online mentoring.[42]

An effective mentor is someone who will tell you things you may not want to hear but make you want to be better. A good mentor will support your attempts to accomplish goals and give you the confidence to rise above your inner doubts and fears.

Although mentors are not mandatory for success, they certainly help. Indeed, there will always be days when you feel nothing you do is right. Your mentor can help repair damaged self-esteem and encourage you to go on. With the power of another person's positive expectations reinforcing your own native abilities, it is hard to fail.

Many young workers have felt they know more than their bosses. The truth is, they often possess knowledge and skills that should be shared with senior managers. Alicia Blain, VP of information systems at Visa International, says she has learned a lot from younger employees such as Julio Delgado. Reverse mentoring is evolving as an informal way to learn skills.

Set Goals

Research points to a direct link between self-esteem and the achievement of personal and professional goals. People who set goals and successfully achieve them are able to achieve higher self-esteem. Why? Because setting goals enables you to take ownership of the future. Once you realize that just about every behavior is controllable, the possibilities for improving your self-esteem are endless. Self-change may be difficult, but it's not impossible.

The major principles that encompass goal setting are outlined in Table 4.1. Goal setting should be an integral part of your efforts to break old habits or form new ones. Before you attempt to set goals, engage in serious reflection. Make a list of the things you want to achieve, and then ask yourself this question: What goals are truly important to me? If you set goals that really excite you, desire will fuel your will to achieve them.[43]

Practice Guided Imagery

Guided imagery is one of the most creative and empowering methods for achieving your goals available today. It provides you with a way to harness the power of the mind and imagination to succeed at something. It can be used to help you relax, set goals (like losing weight), or prepare for a challenging opportunity such as interviewing for a new job. Some heart surgeons use guided imagery to calm their patients, which helps speed recovery. Wearing headphones, the patient hears carefully crafted, medically detailed messages that urge the person to relax and imagine themselves in a safe, comfortable place: "Feel the new strength flowing through you, through arteries that are wider and more open, more flexible with smoother surfaces than before."[44]

To **visualize** means to form a mental image of something. It refers to what you see in the mind's eye. Once you have formed a clear mental picture of what you

TABLE 4.1 GOAL-SETTING PRINCIPLES

Goal setting gives you the power to take control of the present and the future. Goals can help you break old habits or form new ones. You will need an assortment of goals that address the different needs of your life. The following goal-setting principles should be helpful.

1. *Spend time reflecting on the things you want to change in your life.* Take time to clarify your motivation and purpose. Set goals that are specific, measurable, and realistic. Unrealistic goals increase fear, and fear increases the probability of failure.
2. *Develop a goal-setting plan that includes the steps necessary to achieve the goal.* Put the goal and the steps in writing. Change requires structure. Identify all activities and materials you will need to achieve your goal. Review your plan daily—repetition increases the probability of success.
3. *Modify your environment by changing the stimuli around you.* If your goal is to lose five pounds during a one-month period, make a weight chart so you can monitor your progress. You may need to give up desserts and avoid restaurants that serve huge portions. Gather new information on effective weight loss techniques, and seek advice from others. This may involve finding a mentor or joining a support group.
4. *Monitor your behavior, and reward your progress.* Focus on small successes, because each little success builds your reservoir of self-esteem. Reinforcement from yourself and/or others is necessary for change. If the passion for change begins to subside, remind yourself why you want to achieve your goal. Be patient—it takes time to change your lifestyle.

want to accomplish, identify the steps needed to get there, and then mentally rehearse them. Rehearsal must be followed by *action* to further your goal. Rami Shapior, award winning author and teacher says, "It isn't enough to think differently, we must *be* different and *do* differently."[45]

Many athletes choreograph their performance in their imagination before competitions. Studies by the U.S. Olympic Training Center show that 94 percent of the coaches use mental rehearsal for training and competitions.[46] Artists rarely begin a work of art until they have an image of what it is they are going to create. Dancers physically and mentally rehearse their performances hundreds of times before ever stepping on stage. The same techniques can be used in the workplace.

Work-Related Visualization. Let's assume your team members have asked you to present a cost-saving plan to management. The entire team is counting on you. The visualization process should begin with identifying the steps you will take to get approval of the plan. What information will you present? What clothing will you wear? Will you use PowerPoint or some other visual presentation method? Will you use any printed documents? Once you have identified all important contingencies and strategies for success, visualize the actual presentation. See yourself walking into the room with your chin up, your shoulders straight, and your voice strong and confident. Picture yourself making appropriate eye contact with people in the room. The focus of your preparation should be on things within your control.

> ### *Total Person Insight*
>
> WILL SCHUTZ
> Author, *The Human Element*
>
> *"Once I accept that I determine my own life, everything is different. I accept my power. I am in control of my life."*[47]

Use Positive Self-Talk

Throughout most of your waking moments, you talk to yourself. **Self-talk** takes place in the privacy of your mind. It can be rational and productive, or it can be irrational and disruptive. When the focus of this internal conversation is on negative thoughts, you are usually less productive.[48] Some psychologists refer to these negative thoughts as your **inner critic**. The critic keeps a record of your failures but never reminds you of your strengths and accomplishments. A major step toward improving your self-esteem is to understand how to respond to the negative influence of your inner critic.[49]

Self-talk takes place in the privacy of your mind.

When your inner critic talks to you, ask yourself, "Who is this voice that is reminding me of my past failures?" (see Figure 4.1). The chances are it is not your current boss or spouse, but someone in your past such as a teacher, coach, harsh parent, or sibling. Recognize that this critical voice is probably no longer relevant and take the necessary steps to replace those negative messages with positive ones.[50] You can create effective, positive self-talk statements for each of your goals by using the following guidelines:

1. Be *specific* about the behavior you want to change. What do you want to do to increase your effectiveness? You should firmly believe that what you want is truly possible.
2. Begin each self-talk statement with a first-person pronoun, such as *I* or *my*. Use a present-tense verb, such as *am, have, feel, create, approve, do,* or *choose*. Don't say, "My ability to remember the names of other people *will* improve." Instead, focus on the present: "I *have* an excellent memory for the names of other people."
3. Describe the results you want to achieve. Be sure to phrase the statement as though you have already achieved what you want. Table 4.2 offers several general self-talk statements that might help you improve your self-esteem.[51]

FIGURE 4.1 The Self-Talk Endless Loop

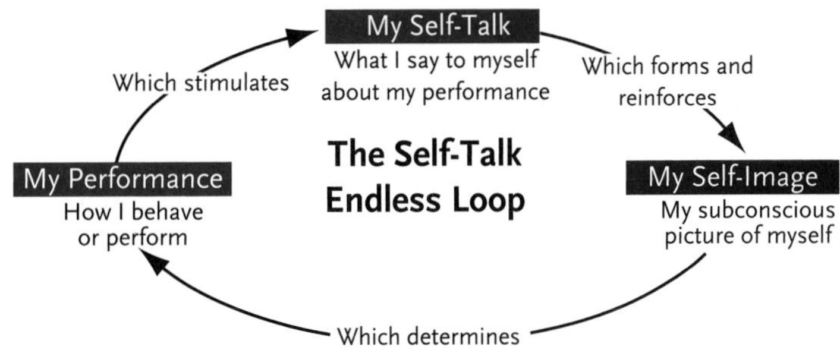

Source: From Jack Canfield, *The Success Principles: How to Get from Where You Are to Where You Want to Be*. Copyright © 2005. Reprinted by permission.

TABLE 4.2 CREATING SEMANTICALLY CORRECT SELF-TALK

WRONG	RIGHT
I can quit smoking.	I am in control of my habits.
I will lose twenty pounds.	I weigh a trim ________ pounds.
I won't worry anymore.	I am confident and optimistic.
Next time I won't be late.	I am prompt and efficient.
I will avoid negative self-talk.	I talk to myself, with all due respect.
I will not procrastinate.	I do it now.
I'm not going to let people walk all over me anymore.	I care enough to assert myself when necessary.

This last step is very important. You must focus on what you want, not on what you don't want. State your self-talk in a positive way. If you say "I will control my anger" the mind, which quickly creates visual images, focuses on anger. A better choice would be "I will be a more patient, accepting person." The words "patient" and "accepting" create positive images in the mind.

Jack Canfield, author of *Key to Living the Law of Attraction,* says we should avoid sending mixed signals to ourselves and those around us. When you are against something, you may actually be recreating it. So, instead of thinking "I don't want to be late," think "I want to be on time." When you create a self-talk statement, always keep your goal in mind.[52]

Keep in mind that positive self-talk that is truly effective consists of thoughts and messages that are realistic and truthful. It is rationally optimistic self-talk, not unfounded rah-rah hype. Positive internal dialogue should not be a litany of "feel good" mantras; it should be wholly consistent with your authentic self.[53]

Organizations Can Help

Although each of us ultimately is responsible for increasing or decreasing our own self-esteem, we can make that task easier or more difficult for others. We can either support or damage the self-efficacy and self-respect of the people we work with, just as they have that option in their interactions with us. Organizations are beginning to include self-esteem modules in their employee- and management-training programs.

When employees do not feel good about themselves, the result will often be poor job performance. This view is shared by many human resource professionals. Many organizations realize that low self-esteem affects their workers' ability to learn new skills, to be effective team members, and to be productive. Research has identified five factors that can enhance the self-esteem of employees in any organization (see Figure 4.2).[54]

- *Workers need to feel valuable.* A major source of worker satisfaction is the feeling that one is valued as a unique person. Self-esteem grows when an organization makes an effort to accommodate individual differences, to recognize individual accomplishments, and to help employees build their strengths.
- *Workers need to feel competent.* Earlier in this chapter, we noted that self-efficacy grows when people feel confident in their ability to perform

FIGURE 4.2 Factors That Enhance the Self-Esteem of Employees

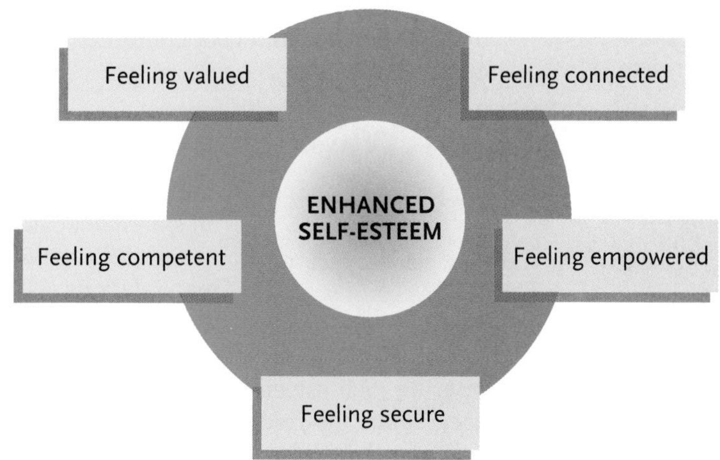

job-related tasks. One of the best ways organizations can build employee confidence is to involve employees in well-designed training programs.

- *Workers need to feel secure.* Employees are more likely to feel secure when they are well informed and know what is expected of them. Managers need to clarify their expectations and provide employees with frequent feedback regarding their performance.
- *Workers need to feel empowered.* Progressive organizations recognize that every employee has something to contribute to the organization and that limiting employees' contributions limits the organization's progress. When all employees are treated with respect and given the latitude for individual action within the defined limits of the organization, they are free to use their creativity and ingenuity to solve problems and make customers happy. Restrictions that suppress individuality can make people feel stunted and handicapped in the use of their personal skills, abilities, and resources.[55]
- *Workers need to feel connected.* People are likely to achieve high self-esteem when they feel their coworkers accept, appreciate, and respect

CAREER INSIGHT

One-Week Strength Building

Marcus Buckingham, author of *Go Put Your Strengths to Work*, encourages us to discover those activities at work that play to our strengths. To make this happen, he recommends a routine called the Strong Week Plan. Once each week, set aside 15 minutes to identify two specific actions to build your strengths. You might change your work schedule so you can use one of these strengths more. What new skill can you learn to leverage one of your strengths? To learn this new skill, what actions can you take? Are there articles you can read, classes you can take, or work assignments you can arrange?[56]

them. Many companies are fostering these feelings by placing greater emphasis on mentoring and teamwork. Team-building efforts help promote acceptance and cooperation.

LOOKING BACK: REVIEWING THE CONCEPTS

- Define self-esteem and discuss its impact on your life.

Self-esteem is a combination of self-respect and self-efficacy. If you have high self-esteem, you are more likely to feel competent and worthy. If you have low self-esteem, you are more likely to feel incompetent, unworthy, and insecure. Self-esteem reflects your feelings of adequacy about the roles you play, your personality traits, your physical appearance, your skills, and your abilities. High self-esteem is the powerful foundation for a successful personal and professional life.

- Discuss how self-esteem is developed.

A person begins acquiring and building self-esteem from birth. Parents, friends, associates, the media, and professional colleagues all influence the development of a person's self-esteem. Adolescents often depend on social relationships to define their value and may compare themselves to media personalities. Adults often define themselves in terms of their possessions, jobs, or internal values.

- Identify the characteristics of people with low and high self-esteem.

People with high self-esteem tend to maintain an internal locus of control, manage their emotions, rarely take things personally, accept other people as unique and talented, and have productive personalities. People with low self-esteem tend to maintain an external locus of control, are likely to participate in self-destructive behaviors, and exhibit poor human relations skills. They often rely on the opinions of others to establish their inner self-worth.

- Identify ways to increase your self-esteem.

To build high self-esteem, individuals must accept their limitations, take responsibility for their decisions, engage in strength building, identify their talents, and work with a mentor. Taking responsibility for your decisions and living with the consequences, positive or negative, can also help build self-esteem. Goal setting is an integral part of increasing one's self-esteem. Guided imagery and positive self-talk can help overcome the inner critic that often interferes with personal and professional success.

- Understand the conditions organizations can create that will help workers increase their self-esteem.

Many organizations now realize that they need to help build employees' self-esteem and are doing so by making workers feel valuable, competent, and secure. Employers are empowering their employees to use their creativity and ingenuity to solve problems and make customers happy, which allows workers to develop a sense of personal responsibility.

ON THE JOB Q & A: TIME TO DISCOVER YOUR STRENGTHS

Q: I realize that I am one of the fortunate many who are working for a company; however, I am fearful for my future. My goal is to stay employed. How can I sustain my current self-esteem under this pressure of uncertainty?

A: Obviously, your world, as you knew it, has changed. Many people are going through the same thing in today's ever-changing world of mergers, acquisitions, terminations, layoffs, and company closings. Nevertheless, it is important to maintain your self-esteem. You have a job; this would be an appropriate time to review your strengths. To learn more about how to discover or rekindle your strengths, read *Now, Discover Your Strengths* by Marcus Buckingham and Donald O. Clifton and *Go Put Your Strengths to*

Work by Marcus Buckingham. Take time to compile an inventory of transferable skills you have developed as an employee. Chances are you have talents and strengths that can be enhanced and applied with greater enthusiasm. Set some new goals and take pride in your past and current achievements. Remember there is no security in life, only opportunity.[57]

KEY TERMS

self-esteem 79
self-efficacy 79
self-respect 79
self-concept 80
developmental psychology 81
external locus of control 83
internal locus of control 84
talent 86
mentor 88
guided imagery 89
visualize 89
self-talk 91
inner critic 91

TRY YOUR HAND

1. Review Table 4.1, Goal-Setting Principles. Work through each of the four principles in light of something you would like to change in your world. It could be a physical characteristic, such as weight control or beginning an exercise regimen. It might be a component of your personality, such as becoming more confident or assertive. Perhaps you would like to reexamine your career goals. Whatever your choice, write out your plan for change then follow it through.
2. This chapter identified five characteristics of people with high self-esteem. Read each of the statements below and rate yourself with this scale: U = Usually; S = Sometimes.

	U	S
I maintain an internal locus of control.	☐	☐
I am able to feel all dimensions of emotions without letting these emotions affect my behavior in a negative way.	☐	☐
I do not take things personally.	☐	☐
I am able to accept other people as unique, talented individuals.	☐	☐
I feel I have a productive personality.	☐	☐

3. Draw a line down the center of a piece of paper and write HIGH Self-Esteem on top of the left column and LOW Self-Esteem on the top of the right column. In each column, record how your personal and professional interpersonal relationships might change if you maintained that level of self-esteem. Share your insights with your classmates.

INTERNET INSIGHTS

1. Building your self-esteem is often a do-it-to-yourself project. No one can wrap a package of self-esteem and give it to you for your birthday. If you, or someone you care about, needs more support in building this life-skill, visit the National Mental Health Information Center, http://mentalhealth.samhsa.gov/publications, and click on *Building Self-esteem—A Self-Help Guide* listed under "Publications." Go to the table of contents and click on *Things You Can Do Right Away—Every Day—to Raise Your Self-Esteem.* Select five activities you would recommend to someone who is experiencing low self-esteem.
2. This text attempts to help you understand how the concepts discussed in each chapter influence you as a total person, since it is difficult

to separate your personal and professional lives. It may appear that building your self-esteem is a personal issue, but it is important to understand how self-esteem can impact your chosen career. Regardless of your career focus, you will be connected to an organization of some kind. For example, nurses are part of a major organization, car mechanics can be part of a small business or a giant corporation, and even public school teachers work for an organization. To help you understand how your self-esteem can influence your business, visit *http://www.smallbusinessbible.org/developingyourselfesteem.html*. Click on the various topics within the Leadership and Development column at the top left of this site. Discover why organizations should be concerned about the self-esteem of their workers. Review this material not only as a potential employee, but also as a potential employer.

3. Many prospective entrepreneurs and small business owners are finding social networking important to the marketing of their products and others are turning to MicroMentor, a nonprofit that helps them find business mentors online. Visit *http://socialnetworking.com* and *http://micromentor.org* and review these virtual websites as potential resources for entrepreneurs and small business owners.

YOU PLAY THE ROLE

You have accepted a summer job with Neiman Marcus. Throughout the summer, you will replace sales staff who are on vacation. In addition to earning money to pay next fall's college tuition, you anticipate that this job will help you develop your customer service skills. To maximize the learning opportunities and explore another area within the company, you want to develop a mentor relationship with the assistant store manager. You have an appointment with her tomorrow. In this role-play situation, you will meet with a class member who will assume the role of the assistant store manager who is very busy and has scheduled the meeting to last no more than 15 minutes. During this short period of time, you will need to explain why you need a mentor and market yourself to this prospective mentor. Prior to the role-play activity, review the information on mentoring in this chapter.

BELOW THE SURFACE:

The Queen of "HIP-HOP-LIT"

At the beginning of this chapter you were introduced to Vickie Stringer, founder and CEO of Triple Crown Publications. When released from prison, she was a single mother and a felon with no formal education. She lived in a half-way house for several months before receiving permission to live with her young son. Ninety days before she was released from prison, she had an epiphany: God wanted her to tell her story. Six weeks later, she had a manuscript for *Let That Be the Reason.*[58]

She recalls that she always had hustling in her but in a negative way. After writing *Let That Be the Reason,* she turned hustling into something positive. After 26 rejections by publishing houses, Vicki decided to self-publish. She raised enough money to print 2,500 copies. Then she started hustling her product, one book at a time. One of the people she approached was owner of UpStream Publications, an African-American owned publishing house based in Brooklyn. UpStream agreed to publish *Let That Be the Reason,* which sold more than 100,000 copies as did her second book, *Imagine This.*[59] After achieving success as an author, Stringer decided to establish her own publishing company. Her company now represents nine writers with contracts valued at more than a million dollars.

Vickie Stringer feels she has received many blessings and now wants to help others. She has become a mentor to many aspiring writers. Stringer also conducts motivational seminars. In 2004, she founded the Valen Foundation, a non-profit organization named for her son. This organization helps reunite and restore bonds between children and their incarcerated parents.

QUESTIONS

1. Within the walls of a sterile prison Vickie Stringer began changing her life. Describe what mental processes were available to her in this environment.
2. Explain how the Self-Talk Endless Loop in Figure 4.1 can help individuals like Vickie Stringer.
3. When asked for advice for future entrepreneurs, Vickie Stringer said, "Be patient, allow room for growth, build your company on a strong accounting system, and as always, *dare to dream*." How does this philosophy relate to your career plans? Elaborate on your response.

CLOSING CASE: The Mentoring of Edward

Shoshana Zuboff likes to reflect on some of the special students she taught at the Harvard Business School. Some students, she recalls, "threw themselves at learning as if their lives depended on it." One of those students, Edward, had a troubled past. His parents split up when he was a small boy, and he was on his own much of the time because his mother needed to work. Edward and his mother lived in a neighborhood where drugs and gangs were common. By the sixth grade, he was a drug dealer, and later he ended up in a penitentiary. Then he had the good fortune to meet a judge who offered him two years in a drug-rehabilitation program in return for good behavior. After rehab, he got a job, enrolled in a community college, and made the dean's list several times. A counselor encouraged Edward to set his sights high, so he applied and was accepted to an Ivy League school, where he studied business and economics. This success led to his acceptance into the Harvard Business School, where he met Professor Zuboff.

Although Edward had accomplished a great deal since leaving the penitentiary, he felt a growing sense of shame over things he did not know. During one lecture, Professor Zuboff briefly mentioned the name of an author who had written about Auschwitz. After class, Edward asked, "What is Auschwitz?" Because of his disadvantaged childhood, he had missed out on many learning experiences that most students take for granted. To avoid giving away his deep-seated, inner secret, he mastered many defense strategies to protect his image amongst his peers. Professor Zuboff noted, "he was haunted by the sense of not knowing what he didn't know or how to learn it."

With help from this caring professor and her husband, who agreed to serve as his mentor, Edward began a program of study designed to fill in the gaps in his education. His self-esteem improved greatly as his program of self-improvement unfolded. Today Edward runs a successful consulting firm that focuses on leadership and emotional intelligence.[60]

QUESTIONS

1. Professor Zuboff says Edward was haunted by the sense of not knowing what he didn't know or how to learn it. Is it possible that many employees in today's labor force suffer from that same fear? Explain your answer.
2. Some people can benefit from multiple mentors. What other types of mentors, in addition to Professor Zubofff and her husband, might Edward find helpful?

INTEGRATED RESOURCES

CLASSROOM ACTIVITIES

IRM Application Exercise 4.1
IRM Application Exercise 4.2

CHAPTER 5

Personal Values Influence Ethical Choices

CHAPTER PREVIEW

LEARNING OBJECTIVES

After studying Chapter 5, you will be able to

- Explain the personal benefits of developing a strong sense of character.
- Understand how personal values are formed.
- Understand values conflicts and how to resolve them.
- Learn how to make the right ethical decisions based on your personal value system.
- Understand the danger of corporate crime and the steps being taken to eliminate it.

TIP OF THE ICEBERG

THE SOURCE OF DISHONEST HABITS

Are today's business schools preparing tomorrow's corporate criminals? This question was asked when Duke University's business school announced that 24 first-year MBA students were expelled, suspended, or awarded failing grades for cheating on a take-home examination in a required class. Students were told by the instructor to complete an open-book test individually, but several collaborated in groups. The professor was alerted to investigate after discovering similar answers. Some of the students who were found guilty of cheating said they did not understand Duke's honor code.[1]

The incident at Duke is not an isolated case. The Academy of Management reports that cheating on tests and written assignments is at an all-time high, and not just in MBA programs, but across the board—graduate and undergraduate students.[2] Dishonest habits often are formed in high school. The Josephson Institute reports that 64 percent of secondary students admitted to cheating on a test, and 36 percent used the Internet to plagiarize an assignment.

The new generation of workers are occupationally and educationally ambitious. They are coming of age at a time when our culture is placing a great deal of emphasis on self-gratification, the crossing of many moral boundaries, and the breaking of many social taboos. This chapter will help you understand how to make the right ethical decisions based on a value system that embraces honor and integrity. It will help you understand how your values are formed, how to clarify which values are important to you, and how to resolve human relations problems that result when your personal values conflict with others' values.

Adam Rountree/Getty Images

Top executives at WorldCom helped engineer the largest accounting fraud in corporate history. The victims of corporate crime include both investors and the employees who lost their jobs. As this protest notes, the outcome is often "Jobs lost, hopes crushed."

Character, Integrity, and Moral Development

Former U.S. senator Al Simpson said, "If you have character, that's all that matters; and if you don't have character, that's all that matters, too."[3] **Character** is composed of personal standards of behavior, including honesty, integrity, and moral strength. It is the main ingredient we seek in our leaders and the quality that earns us respect in the workplace. In *The Corrosion of Character*, author Richard Sennett says that we have seen a decline of character that can be traced to conditions that have grown out of our fast-paced, high-stress, information-driven economy.[4] He notes that many people are no longer connected to their past, to their neighbors, and to themselves.

Integrity is the basic ingredient of character that is exhibited when you achieve congruence between what you know, what you say, and what you do.[5] When your behavior is in tune with your professed standards and values—when you practice what you believe in—you have integrity. When you say one thing but do something else, you *lack* integrity.

How important is it to be viewed as a person with integrity and a strong sense of character in the eyes of your friends, family members, fellow workers, and leaders? When you look closely at the factors that contribute to warm friendships, strong marriages, successful careers, and successful organizations, you quickly come to the conclusion that character and integrity are critical.

You are not born with these qualities, so what can a person do to build his or her character? One approach, recommended by author Stephen Covey, is to keep your commitments. "As we make and keep commitments, even small commitments, we begin to establish an inner integrity that gives us the awareness of self-control and courage and strength to accept more of the responsibility for our own lives."[6] Covey says that when we make and keep promises to ourselves and others, we are developing an important habit. We cannot expect to maintain our integrity if we consistently fail to keep our commitments.

Total Person Insight

ROY CHITWOOD
President, Max Sacks International

"A person's true character can be judged by how he treats those who can do nothing for him."[7]

How Personal Values Are Formed

Hyrum Smith, author of *The 10 Natural Laws of Successful Time and Life Management*, says that certain natural laws govern personal productivity and fulfillment. One of these laws focuses on personal beliefs: Your behavior is a reflection of what you truly believe.[8] **Values** are the personal beliefs and preferences that influence your behavior. They are deep-seated in your personality. To discover what really motivates you, carefully examine what it is you value.

Table 5.1 details the values clarification process. These five steps can help you determine whether or not you truly value something. Many times you are not consciously aware of what is really driving your behavior because values exist

TABLE 5.1 A FIVE-PART VALUING PROCESS TO CLARIFY AND DEVELOP VALUES

THINKING
We live in a confusing world where making choices about how to live our lives can be difficult. Of major importance is developing critical thinking skills that help distinguish fact from opinion and supported from unsupported arguments. Learn to think for yourself. Question what you are told. Engage in higher-level thinking that involves analysis, synthesis, and evaluation.
FEELING
This dimension of the valuing process involves being open to your "gut level" feelings. If it doesn't "feel right," it probably isn't. Examine your distressful feelings such as anger, fear, or emotional hurt. Discover what you prize and cherish in life.
COMMUNICATING
Values are clarified through an ongoing process of interaction with others. Be an active listener and hear what others are really saying. Be constantly alert to communication filters such as emotions, body language, and positive and negative attitudes. Learn to send clear messages regarding your own beliefs.
CHOOSING
Your values must be freely selected with no outside pressure. In some situations, telling right from wrong is difficult. Therefore, you need to be well informed about alternatives and the consequences of various courses of action. Each choice you make reflects some aspect of your values system.
ACTING
Act repeatedly and consistently on your beliefs. One way to test whether something is of value to you is to ask yourself, "Do I find that this value is persistent throughout all aspects of my life?"

Source: Howard Kirschenbaum, *Advanced Values Clarification* (La Jolla, CA: University Associates, 1977).

Once you are aware of your value priorities, you are in a better position to place and initiate life-changing activities.

at different levels of awareness.[9] Unless you clarify your values, life events are likely to unfold in a haphazard manner. Once you are aware of your value priorities, you are in a better position to plan and initiate life-changing activities.

Identifying Your Core Values

Hyrum Smith says that everything starts with your **core values**, those values that you consistently rank higher than others. When you are able to identify your core values, you have a definite picture of the kind of person you want to be and the kind of life you want to have. Anne Mulcahy, CEO of Xerox Corporation and a mother of two sons, says she and her husband make decisions at home and work based on their core values: "Our kids are absolutely the center of our lives—and we never mess with that."[10] Maura FitzGerald, CFO of FitzGerald Communications, Inc., a public relations firm, asks all her employees to adhere to the "FitzGerald Family Values" before accepting a job with her company. All her workers carry with them a wallet-size card listing the organization's basic operating principles, one of which is, "Never compromise our integrity—this is our hallmark."[11]

We often need to reexamine our core values when searching for a job. Joanne Ciulla, author of *The Working Life,* says taking a job today is a matter of choosing among four core values: high salary, security, meaningful work, and lots of time off.[12] Needless to say, most jobs would require putting at least one of these values on the back burner.

Focus on Your Life's Purpose

Jack Canfield, Brian Tracy, and other authorities on the development of human potential emphasize how important it is to define your purpose in life. Canfield says, "Without purpose as the compass to guide you, your goals and action plans may not ultimately fulfill you." To get from where you are today to where you want to be, you have to know two things: where are you today and where you want to get to.[13] Once you have identified your core values, defining your purpose in life will be much easier.

CRITICAL THINKING CHALLENGE:

Analyze It

To create your future, look to the future, not the past. Find a quiet place, close your eyes, and create images of what the ideal life would look like if you could have it exactly the way you want it in each of the following categories:

- *The financial area of your life*: Where are you living? In what type of home? How much money do you have in savings and investments? What kind of car are you driving?
- *Your job or career*: Where are you working? What are you doing? What is your compensation?
- *Your personal relationships*: Are you closely connected to your family? Who are your friends?

Note: This visualization exercise can be expanded to include other important areas of your life such as physical and mental health, spirituality, and leisure time.[14]

Influences That Shape Your Values

As you engage in the values-clarification process, it helps to reflect on those things that have influenced your values, such as people and events of your generation, your family, religious groups, your education, the media, and people you admire.

Generational Influences. Generational influences are among the most powerful forces shaping our values. Generations follow observable historical patterns and thus offer a powerful tool for predicting future workforce attitudes.[15]

Table 5.2 provides a summary of some of the key events and people that have shaped the values of four generations: the Matures, the Baby Boomers, Generation X, and Generation Y, often called Millennials. Although workers of different ages want basically the same things—the opportunity for personal growth, respect, and a fair reward for work done well—they can have very different ideas about what these mean. An older baby boomer might believe that respect is due when someone spends many years on the job. To a Generation Xer, respect is expected when someone displays competence. Someone born during the early years of the baby-boom generation might be satisfied with feedback during annual or semiannual performance reviews. Generation Xers, as a group, have a need to see results almost daily and receive frequent feedback on their performance. Analyzing the traits of any large population can lead to unfair and unrealistic stereotyping, but generational differences shaped by sociological, political, and economic conditions can be traced to differences in values.[16] This important topic is discussed in several other chapters.

TABLE 5.2 PEOPLE AND EVENTS HAVE INFLUENCED THE FORMATION OF VALUES FOR FOUR GROUPS OF AMERICANS: MATURES, BABY BOOMERS, GENERATION X, AND GENERATION Y (SOMETIMES CALLED MILLENNIALS). THIS MEANS THAT TODAY'S WORK FORCE REPRESENTS THE BROADEST RANGE OF AGES AND VALUES IN AMERICAN HISTORY.

MATURES (BORN 1928–1945)	BABY BOOMERS (BORN 1946–1964)	GENERATION X (BORN 1965–1976)	GENERATION Y (BORN 1977–2005)	GENERATION ?
Eisenhower	Television	AIDS	Corporate downsizing	It's too early to label or generalize about this generation.
MacArthur	The Cold War	The Wellness movement	Ethics scandals	It will be formed by the way historical events and moods shape its members lives.*
The A-bomb	The space race	Watergate	Digital technology	
Dr. Spock	The Civil Rights Act	Glasnost	24/7 economy	
John Wayne	The pill	The Oklahoma City bombing	Jeff Bezos	
The Great Depression	The drug culture	MTV	9/11 terrorist attacks	
World War II	Gloria Steinem	The World Wide Web	Iraq War	
The New Deal	The Vietnam War	Information economy	Income gap	
	JFK and MLK assassinations	Work/Life balance concerns	Globalization	
			Personal downsizing	

*Views expressed by Neil Howe and William Strauss, authors of *Generations: The History of America's Future, 1584 to 2069* and *Fourth Turning: An American Prophecy.*

Your Family. Parents must assume many roles, none more important than moral teacher. In many families in contemporary society, one parent must assume full responsibility for shaping children's values. Some single parents—those overwhelmed with responsibility for career, family, and rebuilding their own personal lives—may lack the stability necessary for the formation of the six pillars of character. And in two-parent families, both parents may work outside the home and, at the end of the day, may lack the time or energy to intentionally direct the development of their children's values. The same may be true for families experiencing financial pressures or the strains associated with caring for elderly parents.[17]

Religious Groups. Many people learn their value priorities through religious training. This may be achieved through the accepted teachings of a church, through religious literature such as the Koran and the Bible, or through individuals in churches or synagogues who are positive role models. Some of the most powerful spiritual leaders do not have formal ties to a particular religion. John Templeton is one example. He is a successful investor and one of the greatest philanthropists of the modern age. Templeton says the only real wealth in our lives is spiritual wealth. Over the years, he has given more than $800 million to fund forgiveness, conflict-resolution, and character-building projects.[18]

Religious groups that want to define, instill, and perpetuate values may find an eager audience. Stephen Covey and other social observers say that many people are determinedly seeking spiritual and moral anchors in their lives and in their work. People who live in uncertain times seem to attach more importance to spirituality.[19] Healthy spirituality is discussed in Chapter 17.

Education. Many parents, concerned that their children are not learning enough about moral values and ethical behavior, want character education added to the curriculum. They are concerned about the constant barrage of messages children are getting about behavior in government and corporate America. The Fifth Annual Junior Achievement/Deloitte Teen Ethics Survey results indicate that parents have reason to worry. Thirty-eight percent of the teens surveyed believe it is sometimes necessary to cheat, plagiarize, or lie to succeed.[20]

Several nonprofit organizations have responded to the call for more character education in our public schools, colleges, and universities. The Josephson Institute of Ethics (*http://www.josephsoninstitute.org*) has formed the Character Counts Coalition, an alliance of organizations that addresses the issue of character development in educational institutions and organizations throughout the country. This coalition has developed a variety of grassroots training activities involving what it refers to as the "six pillars of character": trustworthiness, respect, responsibility, fairness, caring, and citizenship.[21]

The Institute for Global Ethics, or IGE (*http://www.globalethics.org*), is dedicated to promoting ethical action in a global context. The Center for Corporate Ethics, or CCE (*http://www.ethics-center.com*), is a division of the IGE. The CCE has developed tools, techniques, and training programs aimed at reducing the likelihood and risks of ethical lapses.

The Media. Some social critics say that if you are searching for signs of civilization gone rotten, you can simply tune into the loud and often amoral voices of mass entertainment on television, radio, and the Internet. They point out that viewers too often see people abusing and degrading other people without any significant consequences. Mainstream television, seen by a large number of young viewers, continues to feature a great deal of violence and antisocial behavior.

Is there a connection between violence in the media and violence in real life? The American Academy of Pediatrics and the American Psychiatric Association report that repeated exposure to violent imagery desensitizes children and increases the risk of violent behavior.[22] Research has also found a connection between heavy television viewing and depressed children. More research is needed to help us fully understand the extent of the influence of media on our culture's values.

People You Admire. In addition to being influenced by the media, you have probably also done some **modeling**—you have shaped your behavior to resemble that of people you admire and embraced the qualities those people demonstrate. The heroes and heroines you discover in childhood and adolescence help you form a "dominant value direction."[23] The influence of modeling is no less important in our adult life. Most employees look to their leaders for moral guidance. Unfortunately, there is a shortage of leaders who have a positive impact on ethical decision making. A survey found that less than half of employees in large organizations think their senior leadership is highly ethical.[24] In addition to role models at work, you may be influenced by religious leaders, sports figures, educators, and others whom you admire.

Avoiding Values Drift

Once you have examined the various influences on your values and have clarified what is important to you now that you are an adult (see Table 5.1), you also need to be aware of **values drift**, the slow erosion of your core values over time—those tiny changes that can steer you off course. When you observe lying, abuse, theft, or other forms of misconduct at work, or feel pressure to make ethical compromises, carefully and intentionally reflect on the values you hold dear and choose the appropriate ethical behavior that maintains your character and

Tony Anderson/Getty Images

Companies that focus on their employees' values, like allowing dogs in the workplace, are an example of the idea that if employees feel valued, they will be more committed to the organization.

integrity. Monitor your commitment to your values and make adjustments when necessary to get your life back on track.

A friend offers to take you to the movies. She says she will save a few dollars by buying senior tickets online. Neither of you is a senior. What do you do?[25] The person you are dating often picks you up in his mother's car, which has a handicap license plate. He usually parks in spaces reserved for handicap drivers. Do you say anything? The erosion of your core values can begin with decisions that may seem insignificant.

Total Person Insight

MICHAEL L. ESKEW
CEO, UPS Inc.

"The strategies change and the purpose changes, but the values never change."[26]

Values Conflicts

One of the major causes of conflict within an organization is the clash between the personal values of different people. There is no doubt about it; people are different. They have different family backgrounds, religious experiences, educations, role models, and media exposure. These differences can pop out anywhere and anytime people get together. Many observers suggest that organizations look for **values conflicts** when addressing such problems as declining quality, absenteeism, and poor customer service. The trouble may lay not so much in work schedules or production routines as in the mutual distrust and misunderstanding brought about by clashes in workers' and managers' value preferences. The late Peter Drucker, author of *The Practice of Management*, said, "Organizations are no longer built on force but on trust. The existence of trust between people does not mean that they like one another. It means that they understand one another. Taking responsibility for relationships is therefore an absolute necessity. It is a duty."[27]

Internal Values Conflicts

A person who is forced to choose between two or more strongly held values is experiencing an **internal values conflict**. Soon after the World Trade Center was attacked by terrorists, many people began to reexamine their values. Some decided to spend more time with family and friends, thinking that although overtime might be an opportunity to make more income, it was also an obstacle to maintaining a commitment to their family. Some workers also decided that their "work and spend" lifestyle no longer made sense. Before the terrorist attacks, a 28-year-old market research manager described herself as "very driven" and motivated to acquire things. Following September 11 she said, "Maybe I don't need all this stuff."[28]

A recent study of Generation Xers by Catalyst, a group that seeks to advance women in business, found that members of this group are seeking a well-rounded life. They are not frenetic job hoppers, as some social commentators maintain, but traditionalists at heart. They value company loyalty and are inclined to stay with their current company. Earning a great deal of money is not nearly as important to these Xers as having the opportunity to share companionship with family and friends. In fact, family is the value priority chosen most often by people of all generations.[29]

How you resolve internal values conflicts depends on your willingness to rank your core values in the order of their importance to you. Prioritizing your values will help you make decisions when life gets complicated and you have to make difficult choices. If one of your values is to be an outstanding parent and another is to maintain a healthy body, you should anticipate an internal values conflict when a busy schedule requires a choice between attending your daughter's soccer game and your weekly workout at the fitness center. However, when you rank which value is most important, the decision will be much easier.

Values Conflicts with Others

As we have noted, four distinct generations have come together in the workplace. Employees from each generation bring with them different experiences and expectations. Values conflicts are more likely in this environment. These conflicts require effective human relations skills.

How will you handle a tense situation where it is obvious your values conflict with those of a colleague? You may discover your supervisor is a racist, and you strongly support the civil rights of all people. One option is to become indignant and take steps to reduce contact with your supervisor. The problem with being indignant is that it burns your bridges with someone who can influence your growth and development within the organization. The opposite extreme would be to do nothing. But when we ignore unethical or immoral behavior, we compromise our integrity, and the problem is likely to continue and grow.[30] With a little reflection, you may be able to find a response somewhere between these two extremes. If your supervisor tells a joke that is demeaning to members of a minority group, consider meeting with her and explaining how uncomfortable these comments make you feel. When we confront others' lapses in character, we are strengthening our own integrity.

HUMAN RELATIONS IN ACTION

Ex-Cons Scare MBAs

Some business schools, eager to impress upon students the importance of ethical behavior, are hiring white-collar felons to speak to students. After completing his MBA, Walter Pavlo worked as a manager at MCI. He initiated a $6 million money-laundering scheme that earned him a two-year sentence in a federal prison. At the time he was paroled from prison, Pavlo was divorced, unemployed, and living with his parents. Since starting his one-man company, Etika, he has given 25 lectures at business schools across America.[31]

Personal Values and Ethical Choices

Ethics refers to principles that define behavior as right, good, and proper. Your ethics, or the code of ethics of your organization, does not always dictate a single moral course of action, but it does provide a means of evaluating and deciding among several options.[32] Ethics determines where you draw the line between right and wrong.

As competition in the global marketplace increases, moral and ethical issues can become cloudy. Although most organizations have adopted the point of view that "good ethics is good business," exceptions do exist. Some organizations encourage, or at least condone, unethical behaviors. Surveys show that many workers feel pressure to violate their ethical standards in order to meet business objectives.[33] Thus, you must develop your own *personal* code of ethics.

Every job you hold will present you with new ethical and moral dilemmas. And many of the ethical issues you encounter will be very difficult. Instead of selecting from two clear-cut options—one right, one wrong—you often face multiple options.[34]

> ### *Total Person Insight*
>
> **William J. Bennett**
> Author, *The Book of Virtues*
>
> *"If you want young people to take notions like right and wrong seriously, there is an indispensable condition: they must be in the presence of adults who take right and wrong seriously."*[35]

How to Make the Right Ethical Choices

Unethical acts by employees cost U.S. businesses billions of dollars each year. Employee theft and fraud represent two of the largest loss categories. For small businesses, preventing these losses can be an uphill struggle.[36] The following guidelines may help you avoid being part of this growing statistic.

Learn to Distinguish Between Right and Wrong. Although selecting the right path can be difficult, a great deal of help is available through books, magazine articles, and a multitude of online resources. Support may be as close as your employer's code of ethics, guidelines published by your professional organization, or advice provided by an experienced and trusted colleague at work. In some cases, you can determine the right path by *restraining* yourself from choosing the *wrong* path. For example:

- Just because you have the power to do something does not mean it is the proper thing to do.
- Just because you have the right to do something does not mean it is right to do.
- Just because you want to do something does not mean you should do it.
- Choose to do more than the law requires and less than the law allows.[37]

Don't Let Your Life Be Driven by the Desire for Immediate Gratification. Progress and prosperity have almost identical meanings to many people. They equate progress with the acquisition of material things. One explanation is that young business leaders entering the corporate world are under a great deal of pressure to show the trappings of success—a large house or an expensive car, for example.

Some people get trapped in a vicious cycle: They work more so that they can buy more consumer goods; then, as they buy more, they must work more. They fail to realize that the road to happiness is not paved with Rolex watches, Brooks Brothers suits, and a Lexus. Chapter 17 offers support for finding satisfaction through nonfinancial resources that make the biggest contribution to a fulfilling life.

Make Certain Your Values Are in Harmony with Those of Your Employer. You may find it easier to make the right ethical choices if your values are compatible with those of your employer. Many organizations have adopted a set of beliefs, customs, values, and practices that attract a certain type of employee (see Figure 5.1). Harmony between personal and organizational values usually leads to success for the individual as well as the organization. Enlightened companies realize that committed employees give them their competitive edge and are taking values seriously. They realize that reconciling corporate and employee values helps to cement the ethical environment within the organization. Before you select an organization in which to build your career, determine what the organization stands for, and then compare those values to your own priorities.[38]

Timberland, a New Hampshire-based company that sells outdoor-themed clothes, shoes, and accessories, does not choose between profits and passion. Employees get 40 hours paid leave every year to pursue volunteer projects. During one recent year, the company hosted 170 service projects in 27 countries, covering 45,000 volunteer hours of work. Jeffrey Swartz, CEO of Timberland Company, feels a culture that emphasizes service has helped develop a productive, efficient, and committed labor force.[39]

Total Person Insight

DAN RICE
CRAIG DREILINGER
Management Consultants, Authors, *Rights and Wrongs of Ethics Training*

"Nothing is more powerful for employees than seeing their managers behave according to their expressed values and standards; nothing is more devastating to the development of an ethical environment than a manager who violates the organization's ethical standards."[40]

Corporate Values and Ethical Choices

When organizations consistently make ethical decisions that are in the best interest of their stakeholders—employees, customers, stockholders, and the community—they are considered good corporate citizens because they are socially responsible. The list "The 100 Best Corporate Citizens" published by *Corporate Responsibility Officer* magazine reminds us that a company can be socially responsible and still achieve excellent earnings. In her *Business Week* article "A Conscience Doesn't Have to Make You Poor," Susan Scherreik interviewed stockholders who invest only in companies that are good corporate citizens.

FIGURE 5.1 For nearly 40 years, the Certified Medical Representatives Institute has been empowering pharmaceutical professionals. Graduates of this certification program are strongly encouraged to embrace the CMR Code of Conduct.

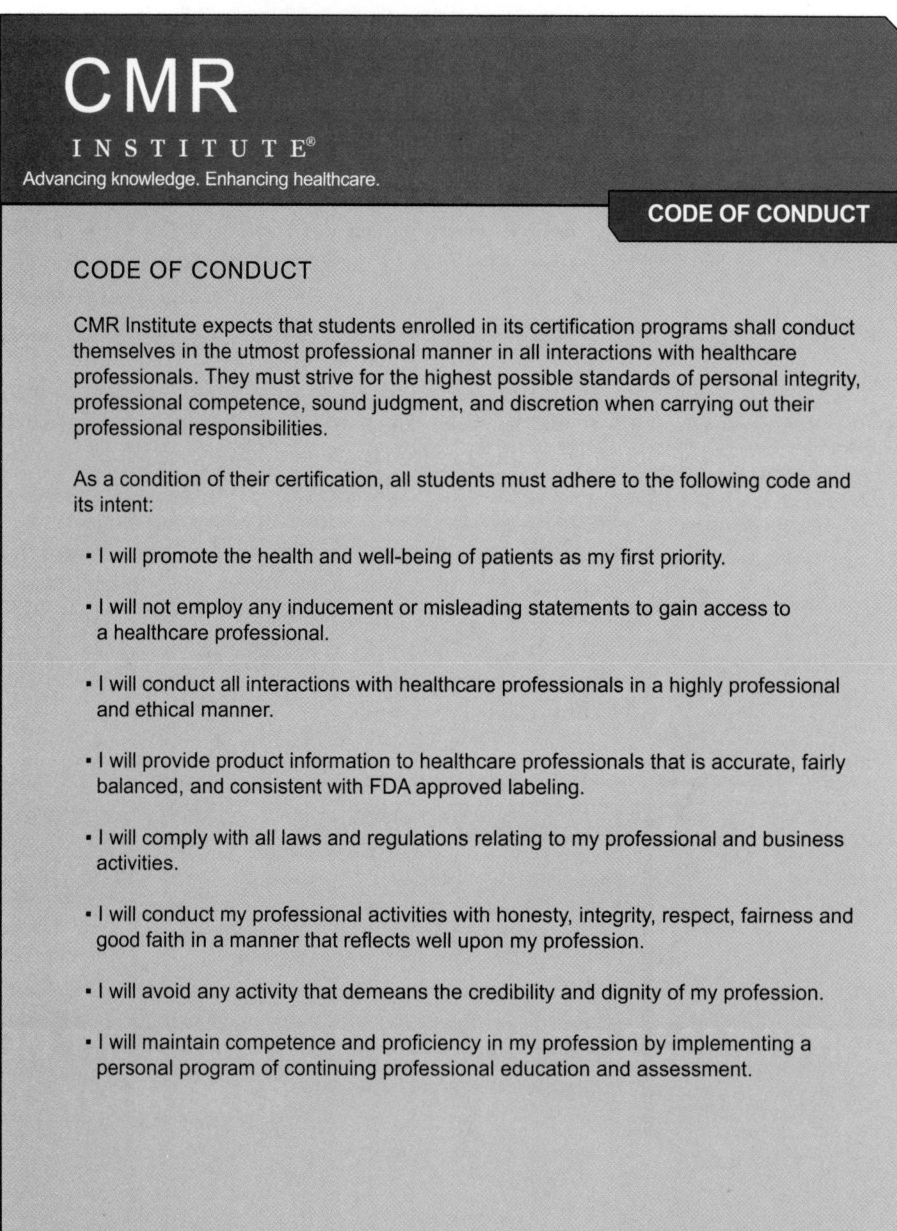

CMR

INSTITUTE®

Advancing knowledge. Enhancing healthcare.

CODE OF CONDUCT

CODE OF CONDUCT

CMR Institute expects that students enrolled in its certification programs shall conduct themselves in the utmost professional manner in all interactions with healthcare professionals. They must strive for the highest possible standards of personal integrity, professional competence, sound judgment, and discretion when carrying out their professional responsibilities.

As a condition of their certification, all students must adhere to the following code and its intent:

- I will promote the health and well-being of patients as my first priority.
- I will not employ any inducement or misleading statements to gain access to a healthcare professional.
- I will conduct all interactions with healthcare professionals in a highly professional and ethical manner.
- I will provide product information to healthcare professionals that is accurate, fairly balanced, and consistent with FDA approved labeling.
- I will comply with all laws and regulations relating to my professional and business activities.
- I will conduct my professional activities with honesty, integrity, respect, fairness and good faith in a manner that reflects well upon my profession.
- I will avoid any activity that demeans the credibility and dignity of my profession.
- I will maintain competence and proficiency in my profession by implementing a personal program of continuing professional education and assessment.

4423 Pheasant Ridge Road, Suite 100, Roanoke, VA 24014-5274 www.cmrinstitute.org | 800.328.2615

Source: http://www.cmrinstitute.org.

One stated, "I see the damage that many companies do to people's health and the environment by polluting or creating dangerous products. Investing in them makes no sense because these companies won't flourish in the long run."[41]

Corporate Crime

Many organizations have gotten into serious trouble by ignoring ethical principles. In recent years, the media have carried headlines concerning organizations involved in corporate crime. Executives employed by Enron, WorldCom, Adelphia Communications, Tyco International, and other corporations have spent time in prison for criminal acts. Many employees working for these firms lost their jobs and their retirement savings. Some stock holders saw their investments disappear.

Fortunately, bad behavior among corporate leaders is quite rare. The *Wall Street Journal* estimates that only a tiny fraction of the millions of businesspeople have been convicted of corporate crimes. The overwhelming number of businesses play by the rules.[42]

Leaders such as Jeffrey Immelt, CEO of General Electric, believe you can fuse high performance with high integrity. He realizes that employees at all levels of the company will be tempted to "make the numbers" by juggling accounts or cutting corners. From day one, he made a stirring call for performance with integrity. General Electric's 220 officers and 600 senior managers were told that failure to create the right culture would result in termination.[43]

Skill Development: Apply It

Practice making ethical choices based on your value priorities in the following scenarios.

- You are offered a great job, but you have to relocate to a distant city. Your family agrees that the decision is yours to make, but you know they do not want to move. What do you do?
- You have discovered that your boss lied on her résumé about her academic credentials. She is being considered for a new position in your organization, but you believe you are more qualified than she is. Will you tell the hiring panel about your boss's indiscretion?
- You are taking an online college class and have been offered the final exam from a student who printed a copy for you after taking the exam yesterday. The correct answers are not on the test copy. You are in danger of failing the class and losing your financial aid. Do you accept the document and use it to study for your exam?

Many business leaders say they have difficulty determining the right course of action in difficult "gray-area" situations. And even when the right ethical course of action is clear, competitive pressures sometimes lead well-intentioned managers astray.[44] Tom Chappell, author of *The Soul of a Business*, explains why organizations often have difficulty doing what is morally right and socially responsible: "It's harder to manage for ethical pursuits than it is to simply manage for profits."[45]

How to Prevent Corporate Crime

Establish and Support a Strong Code of Ethics. We have recently seen an increase in ethical initiatives that make ethics a part of core organizational values. **Codes of ethics**, written statements of what an organization expects in the way of ethical behavior, can give employees a clear indication of what behaviors are acceptable or improper.[46] An ethics code can be a powerful force in building a culture of honesty, but only if it is enforced without exception. The list of corporate values at Enron Corporation included respect, integrity, communication, and excellence. As events have shown, these values did not prevent unethical conduct at the highest levels of the company. Empty values statements create cynical and dispirited employees and undermine managerial credibility.[47]

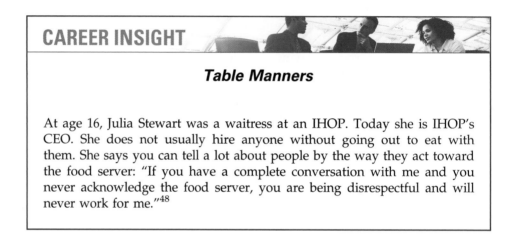

CAREER INSIGHT

Table Manners

At age 16, Julia Stewart was a waitress at an IHOP. Today she is IHOP's CEO. She does not usually hire anyone without going out to eat with them. She says you can tell a lot about people by the way they act toward the food server: "If you have a complete conversation with me and you never acknowledge the food server, you are being disrespectful and will never work for me."[48]

Hire with Care. Thomas Melohn, president of North American Tool & Die, Inc., located in San Leandro, California, says the key to operating a successful company is to first identify a guiding set of values and then "make sure you find people who have those values and can work together."[49] He says the hiring process should be given a very high priority. Melohn never hires any employee without checking references and conducting a lengthy job interview.

Some companies use integrity tests (also called honesty or character tests) to screen out dishonest people. Two standardized tests designed to measure honesty are the Reid Report (*http://www.reidlondonhouse.com*) and the newer Career Ethic Inventory (*http://www.careerethic.com*). These tests are helpful, but they are not a substitute for rigorous interviewing and reference checks. Résumés that include exaggerations or outright fabrications tell you a lot about the integrity of the applicants.[50]

Provide Ethics Training. Many ethical issues are complex and cannot be considered in black-and-white moral terms. The fact that an action is legal and does not violate a law does not necessarily make the action morally or ethically acceptable.[51] It is for these reasons that ethics training has become quite common. In some cases, the training involves little more than a careful study of the company ethics code and its implications for day-to-day decision making. In other cases, employees participate in in-depth discussions of complex ethical decisions.

Can colleges and universities teach ethics? In the wake of numerous corporate scandals, business schools have been criticized for producing graduates who are obsessed with making money, regardless of the ethical consequences. In response to this criticism, business schools are trying a host of new methods, including required ethics courses and honor codes. At Ohio University, the Fisher College of Business created a new honor code that students are required to sign. The code states, "Honesty and integrity are the foundation from which I will measure my actions."[52]

Develop Support for Whistleblowing. When you discover that your employer or a colleague is behaving illegally or unethically, you have three choices. You can keep quiet and keep working. You can decide that you can't be party to the situation and leave. Or you can report the situation in the hope of putting a stop to it. When you reveal wrongdoing within an organization to the public or to those in positions of authority, you are a **whistleblower**.

Total Person Insight

TERRY KABACHNICK, CEO
The Kabachnick Group, Inc.

"Like an individual, a company has a culture of values. What does the company reward? Where does it focus its efforts? What actions does it deem critical to its success?"[53]

FBI attorney Coleen Rowley wrote a memo to FBI director Robert Mueller claiming that the department ignored the pleas of the Minneapolis field office to investigate Zacarias Moussaoui, who was subsequently indicted as a September 11 co-conspirator. Cynthia Cooper informed WorldCom's board of directors that illegal accounting procedures covered up $3.8 billion in corporate losses. Enron vice president Sherron Watkins wrote a letter to Enron chairman Kenneth Lay alerting him to the illegal accounting procedures that misled stockholders about Enron's financial picture. All three of these women tried to keep their concerns "in house" by speaking the truth to executives in a position of power and not to the public. As details exploded in the media, these women were plunged into the public eye. *Time* magazine proclaimed them "Persons of the Year for 2002" and made them national celebrities.[54]

Disclosing wrong-doing can be a daunting experience. Your fellow colleagues may resent the disruption your revelations cause in their lives. They may be impressed with your integrity, but not everyone will be on your side in your struggle to do what is right and ethical. Your efforts may result in months or even years of emotional and financial turmoil. A survey conducted by the National Whistleblower Center in Washington, DC, showed that one-half of the whistleblowers were fired because of their actions. Most reported being unable to acquire new jobs because prospective employers perceived them as troublemakers. Others faced demotions or were placed in jobs with little impact or importance.[55]

Each individual must make his or her own decision as to whether the disturbing unethical offense is worth the personal cost. Table 5.3 lists four questions potential whistleblowers should ask themselves before taking action.

Values and Ethics in International Business

If the situation is complex on the domestic scene, values and ethical issues become even more complicated at the international level. American business firms are under great pressure to avoid doing business with overseas contractors that

Pat Sullivan/Associated Press

Sherron Watkins helped give corporate misconduct national attention. As an Enron vice president, she wrote a letter to Enron chairman Kenneth Lay alerting him to illegal accounting procedures. Later she would testify in the Enron fraud and conspiracy trial of Kenneth Lay. He was found guilty.

TABLE 5.3 WHISTLEBLOWER CHECKLIST

Experts say that people who are thinking about blowing the whistle on their company should ask themselves four important questions before doing so.

1. **Is this the only way?**
   Do not blow the whistle unless you have tried to correct the problem by reporting up the normal chain of command and gotten no results. Make sure your allegations are not minor complaints.
2. **Do I have the goods?**
   Gather documentary evidence that proves your case, and keep it in a safe place. Keep good notes, perhaps even a daily diary. Make sure you are seeing fraud, not merely incompetence or sloppiness.
3. **Why am I doing this?**
   Examine your motives. Do not act out of frustration or because you feel underappreciated or mistreated. Do not embellish your case, and do not violate any confidentiality agreements you may have.
4. **Am I ready?**
   Think through the impact on your family. Be prepared for unemployment and the possibility of being blacklisted in your profession. Last, but not least, consult a lawyer.

Source: Paula Dwyer and Dan Carney, with Amy Borrus and Lorraine Woellert in Washington and Christopher Palmeri in Los Angeles, "Year of the Whistleblower," *BusinessWeek*, December 16, 2002, pp. 107–108.

permit human rights violations such as child labor, low wages, and long hours in their factories. The 1977 Foreign Corrupt Practices Act and later amendments prohibits U.S. companies from using bribes or kickbacks to influence foreign officials, and many industrial nations have signed a multinational treaty outlawing corporate bribery. But monitoring illegal activities throughout the world is a difficult task. Doing business in the global marketplace continues to be an ethical minefield, with illegal demands for bribes, kickbacks, or special fees standing in the way of successful transactions. American businesses acknowledge that it is difficult to compete with organizations from other countries that are not bound by U.S. laws. However, according to the International Business Ethics Institute (*http://www.business-ethics.org*) there has been significant progress in the last few years.

Kevin Tan, the Shanghai director of the marketing research firm Frank, Small & Associates, believes U.S. companies have been a very positive role model for the rest of the business world. Although it is understood by many in the global business community that violations do occur, the question is often one of degree. Paul Jensen, a consultant working for U.S., European, and Japanese interests in China, suggests: "What every internal manager has to do is find what he's personally comfortable with. That's a combination of the company's standards and his personal standards."[56]

LOOKING BACK: REVIEWING THE CONCEPTS

- Explain the personal benefits of developing a strong sense of character.

A strong sense of character grows out of your personal standards of behavior. When you consistently behave in accordance with your values, you maintain your integrity.

- Understand how personal values are formed.

Your values are the personal importance you give to an object or idea. People's values serve as the foundation for their attitudes, preferences, opinions, and behaviors. Your core values are largely formed early in life, and are influenced by people and events in your life, your family, religious groups, your education, the media, and people you admire.

- Understand values conflicts and how to resolve them.

Internal values conflicts arise when you must choose between strongly held personal values. Value conflicts with others, often based on age, racial, religious, gender, or ethnic differences, require skilled intervention before they can be resolved.

- Learn how to make the right ethical decisions based on your personal value system.

Once you have clarified your personal values, your ethical decisions will be easier. You must learn to distinguish right from wrong, avoid the pursuit of immediate gratification, and choose an employer whose values you share. Shared values unify employees in an organization by providing guidelines for behavior and decisions.

- Understand the danger of corporate crime and the steps being taken to eliminate it.

Corporate values and ethics on both the domestic and the international levels are receiving increasing attention because of the devastating effect and expense of corporate crime. Many organizations are developing ethics codes to help guide employees' behavior, hiring only those individuals who share their corporate values, offering ethics training opportunities to all employees, and supporting whistleblowing. As multinational organizations increase in number, the individuals involved will need to consciously examine their values and ethical standards to deal effectively with differing values structures around the world.

ON THE JOB Q & A: EVALUATING YOUR VALUES

Q: I am a college student, and I need to find a job. I am on financial aid; however, it just barely covers my books, tuition, and college travel expenses. I read in the local paper that the area Chamber of Commerce is hiring. The ad specially states that they want someone with an accounting degree and accounting experience. I have neither; however, I have some bookkeeping experience, I interview well, and I think that once they meet me, they will see that I am intelligent and a fast self-study. Do you have any advice for me?

A: You are treading on unsafe ground that may affect a future career. If you pretend that you have an accounting degree and experience, your ethics are in question. What you state on your résumé and cover letter, reflect your character. Companies, especially in today's economic climate, are looking for employees with verifiable skill sets and integrity.

You asked for advice. Why don't you call the Chamber and ask if the HR Director would have time for an informational interview? You can share that you are a college student seeking future employment opportunities. This is the time that your intelligence, enthusiasm, and abilities can shine without misrepresenting yourself or your background. Remember, the Chamber is made up of numerous companies throughout your region. Ethical conduct in your approach will enhance opportunities for current and future career employment.

KEY TERMS

character 100
integrity 100
values 101
core values 102
modeling 105
values drift 105
values conflicts 106
internal values conflict 106
ethics 107
codes of ethics 111
whistleblower 113

TRY YOUR HAND

1. Guilt and loss of self-respect can result when you say or do things that conflict with what you believe. One way to feel better about yourself is to "clean up" your integrity. Make a list of what you are doing that you think is wrong. Once the list is complete, look it over and determine whether you can stop these behaviors. Consider making amends for things you have done in the past that you feel guilty about.[57]

2. You work for a company in which the HR director has been involved in unethical activities. You know that others are also aware of the situation; however, no one is willing to share the director's behavior with upper management. You do not want to be the whistleblower; however, you realize that guilt and loss of self-respect can result when you do or do not do things that conflict with what you believe. Discuss this situation with two or three classmates. Identify the pros and cons of becoming a whistleblower.

3. One of the great challenges in life is the clarification of our values. The five-part valuing process described in Table 5.1 can be very helpful as you attempt to identify your core values. Select one personal or professional value from the following list, and clarify this value by applying the five-step process:

   a. Respect the rights and privileges of people who may be in the minority because of race, gender, ethnicity, age, physical or mental abilities, or sexual orientation.

b. Conserve the assets of my employer.
c. Utilize leisure time to add balance to my life.
d. Maintain a healthy lifestyle.
e. Balance the demands of my work and personal life.

INTERNET INSIGHTS

1. Visit the website of *Business Ethics Magazine* at *http://www.business-ethics.com*. Listed are the 100 best corporate citizens who demonstrate corporate responsibility and excel at service. Select one or two best corporate citizens, and study the factors that contributed to their recognition.

2. The Center for Public Integrity (*http://www.publicintegrity.org*) offers investigative journalism on current events that are in the public interest. Visit the site and read about the issues that are detailed. Report to your classmates your reaction to any or all of the stories.

3. On the basis of your academic area of study or major, visit a website that defines the ethics of your academic pursuits. Take notes and report your findings to your class members.

YOU PLAY THE ROLE

You are currently employed by a pharmaceutical wholesaler that sells prescription drugs to hospitals in a three-county area. Each morning you help other employees fill orders that arrive via computer or the telephone. Once the orders are completed and loaded into delivery vans, you spend the rest of the day delivering products to hospitals. Although others help fill the orders, you are responsible for the accuracy of each order and for timely delivery. Rob Howard, a fellow employee, performs the same duties but delivers items to hospitals in a different territory. During the past two months, you have noticed that he sometimes makes poor ethical choices. For example, the company's reimbursement for lunch is a maximum of $8. Rob packs each day's lunch and never eats at a restaurant. At the end of each week, however, his reimbursement form claims the maximum amount for each meal. Once he bragged about earning an extra $40 each week for meals that were not purchased.

Rob owns a small landscaping business on the side and sometimes uses the company van to transport items to customers. Recently you drove by a Home Depot store and noticed him loading bags of mulch into the company van. At one point, you thought about talking with the supervisor about these ethical lapses but decided to talk with Rob first. Another class member will assume the role of Rob Howard. Try to convince him that some of these on-the-job activities are unethical.

BELOW THE SURFACE:

Employee Theft

As noted in the opening vignette, today's business schools may be contributing to corporate crime. The media often focuses on executives who are involved in accounting fraud, tax evasion, and other serious crimes. However, the fastest growing crime in the United States is employee theft. Recent surveys indicate that companies lose more than $50 billion annually as employees steal time, money, and supplies from their employers. Employee theft comes in a variety of forms.

- Employees who pilfer pens, scissors, tape, and other office supplies may begin to refer jokingly to the supply room as the "gift shop."
- Padding an expense account with an extra meal or exaggerated tips to servers and baggage handlers may provide enough extra income to pay for the extended child care necessary while an employee is on a business trip.
- A salesperson who is a single parent may tell the boss that a customer needs additional time so returning to the office will be delayed, when in reality the employee's child has a dental appointment.
- An employee's aging father "dies" each time the employee changes employers, thus gaining the employee the paid time off for bereavement leave.
- The person in charge of arrangements for various luncheons within an organization routinely overorders and takes the "extra" food home.

Theft of this nature is often rationalized as a perk of the job. Some employees may believe that they are underpaid and that they are entitled to these little extras. This larcenous sense of entitlement may come from disgruntled employees who feel they are not appreciated, so they take matters into their own hands. It is true that there are a lot of bad examples at the top of many organizations, and it may be easy to blame top executives for fostering a culture of dishonesty, but does that justify the lack of character and integrity of lower-level employees?[58]

QUESTIONS

1. Research indicates that employee misconduct tends to increase in companies where mergers, acquisitions, and restructurings are under way. Why do you think this happens?
2. If your boss is so demanding that you have to lie to protect family time, will you do it? For example, if you have to miss a staff meeting or refuse a business trip to fulfill the needs of your family, will you fabricate work-related or health reasons? Are there any alternatives to lying? Explain.
3. If you were the employer, how would you handle each of the instances above?

CLOSING CASE: Whistleblowers' Rights

The U.S. Congress passed the Sarbanes-Oxley law in 2002 to protect employees who blow the whistle on their employers' illegal actions. If the charges are confirmed, employers must reinstate employees who were fired for blowing the whistle, plus pay their back wages and their legal fees. However, the employee has the burden of proof, not the employer. The law is enforced by Occupational Safety and Health Administration (OSHA), a division within the Department of Labor, but OSHA does not have subpoena power and therefore cannot force companies to turn over documents, require witnesses to testify, or place anyone under oath. The majority of these cases have been dismissed or withdrawn by the complainant.[59]

However, the Civil War era False Claims Act, including its qui tam (whistleblower) provisions, remains legally solid. It was initially enacted at the urging of President

Lincoln in 1863 in response to reports of widespread fraud by Civil War profiteers. Under this law, citizens with knowledge of fraud against the government were encouraged to come forward by authorizing them to file a civil suit in the name of the government and by rewarding them with a percentage of the recovery. Private citizens who bring suits under the act can receive up to 30 percent of the recovery. Because it takes a great deal of courage for any employee to risk his or her career to serve the public interest, those individuals who step forward with their evidence should be celebrated and rewarded.

- Three private citizens filed suit on behalf of the U.S. government against Schering-Plough, which offered kickbacks to Cigna, one of the nation's largest health insurers. The kickbacks, in effect, lowered the price that Cigna subscribers paid for Claritin to below the price the U.S. government paid for the same drug for its Medicaid patients, a blatant violation of Medicaid rules that require that the government receive the lowest price. Schering-Plough paid $346 million to settle charges, and the three complainants and their attorneys received $31.7 million.
- Dr. Joseph Gerstein was the medical director of the Tuft's University health plan when he was offered a $40,000 unrestricted grant by TAP Pharmaceuticals if he would keep the company's prostate cancer drug, Lupron, on the HMO's list of preferred drugs. Outraged by TAP's attempts to bribe him, Dr. Gerstein filed suit to try to stop the corruption. In the end, TAP Pharmaceuticals settled his case and another related whistleblower lawsuit, for a total of $875 million. Dr. Gerstein split his portion of the reward with Tufts and a science-literacy fund in Roxbury, Massachusetts.
- Brett Roby was a quality-control engineer at Soeca, the contractor that made gears for Boeing's Chinook heavy-lift transport helicopters used by the U.S. Army. Because of defects in the casting of the metal used in the gears, several helicopters crashed, and 15 soldiers and 2 Boeing engineers were killed. Although Speco and Boeing were told about the defects, both companies ignored the warnings. Boeing settled the case for $54 million plus attorney fees, and the U.S. Army replaced the defective gears in the helicopters. Mr. Roby said, "My primary goal in this litigation was to ensure the safety of the men and women who fly in these aircraft."[60]

QUESTIONS

1. In the bright light of hindsight, most of us would probably say we would blow the whistle on these instances had we been a witness to them, especially because there was so much money involved. But in reality, if you had to keep your job to feed your family, would you really step forward with your allegations, knowing that the legal process would take years?
2. What steps do you believe the government should take to reinforce the viability of the Sarbanes-Oxley Law?
3. Most employees do not disclose the fraud and corruption they observe in the workplace, and, therefore, criminal and immoral behaviors continue to flourish. Who or what can intercept this lack of moral fortitude?
4. The moral dilemmas you will face during your career may not be of the magnitude of those presented in this case, but may very well resemble those presented in Below the Surface: Employee Theft. If you were to make your ethical decisions on the basis of your value priorities, how would your interpersonal relationships be affected? List the positives and the negatives.

INTEGRATED RESOURCES

VIDEO:

The Whistleblower vs. the Non-Profit

CLASSROOM ACTIVITIES

IRM Application Exercise 5.1

IRM Application Exercise 5.2

CHAPTER 6

Attitudes Can Shape Your Life

CHAPTER PREVIEW

LEARNING OBJECTIVES

After studying Chapter 6, you will be able to

- Understand the impact of employee attitudes on the success of individuals as well as organizations.
- List and explain the ways people acquire attitudes.
- Describe attitudes that employers value.
- Learn how to change your attitudes.
- Learn how to help others change their attitudes.
- Understand what adjustments organizations are making to develop positive employee attitudes.

TIP OF THE ICEBERG

Stew Leonards's Culture

Stew Leonard's, a highly profitable four-store supermarket in Connecticut and New York, has a lot to be proud of. Year after year the company has been named one of the "100 Best Companies to Work For" by *Fortune* magazine. Managed by the Leonard family, the company has developed a distinctive culture that emphasizes teamwork and devotion to customer service. Each store has created a "Disneyland" theme complete with costumed characters, scheduled entertainment, a petting zoo, and other features that entertain customers while they shop.

Shortly after opening his first store, Stew Leonard adopted two basic store policies, which were chiseled into a 6,000-pound rock next to the front door of his store. The simple message reads:

Rule 1—**THE CUSTOMER IS ALWAYS RIGHT!**

Rule 2—**IF THE CUSTOMER IS EVER WRONG, RE-READ RULE 1.**

The Leonard family understands that losing a customer means more than losing a single sale. It means losing the entire stream of purchases that the customer would make over a lifetime of patronage. The management staff at Stew Leonard's estimates that when an unhappy customer switches to another supermarket, the store has lost $50,000 in revenue.[1]

The beneficial impact of individual and organizational attitudes is not always easy to measure. However, the correlation between positive attitudes and high performance, low turnover, and increased productivity exists in most organization.

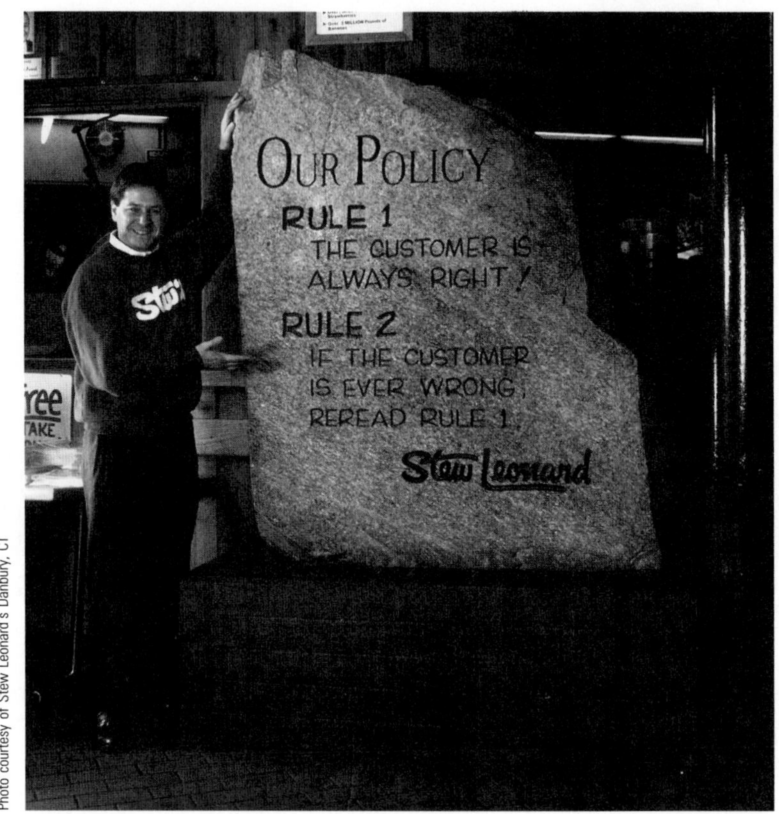

Photo courtesy of Stew Leonard's Danbury, CT

Stew Leonard's four-store supermarket company has achieved success by embracing a basic customer retention policy: Rule #1 The customer is always right. Rule #2 If the customer is ever wrong, reread Rule #1. The company works hard to shape the attitudes of its employees.

The Importance of Employee Attitudes

Attitudes are thoughts that you have accepted as true and that lead you to think, feel, or act positively or negatively toward a person, idea, or event. They represent an *emotional readiness* to behave in a particular manner. You are not born with these thoughts—you learn them. During childhood modeling and other forms of social learning are especially important.[2] Therefore, it is reasonable to conclude that you can learn new attitudes and/or change old ones.

Your values, those beliefs, and preferences you feel are important serve as a foundation for your attitudes. For example, if you believe your religion is important, you may form negative attitudes toward those people and activities that restrict your religious practices (working on Sunday for example) and positive attitudes toward those who support your convictions. Your attitudes, in turn, serve as a motivation for your behavior (see Figure 6.1). Therefore, when someone attempts to interfere with your right to practice your religion, you might become angry and retaliate. However, you also have the freedom to choose another response. Perhaps another value comes into play—peace—and it seems more important than "defending" oneself. Therefore, instead of retaliating, you decide to just ignore the interference. The most amazing things

FIGURE 6.1 The Relationship Among Core Values, Attitudes, and Behaviors

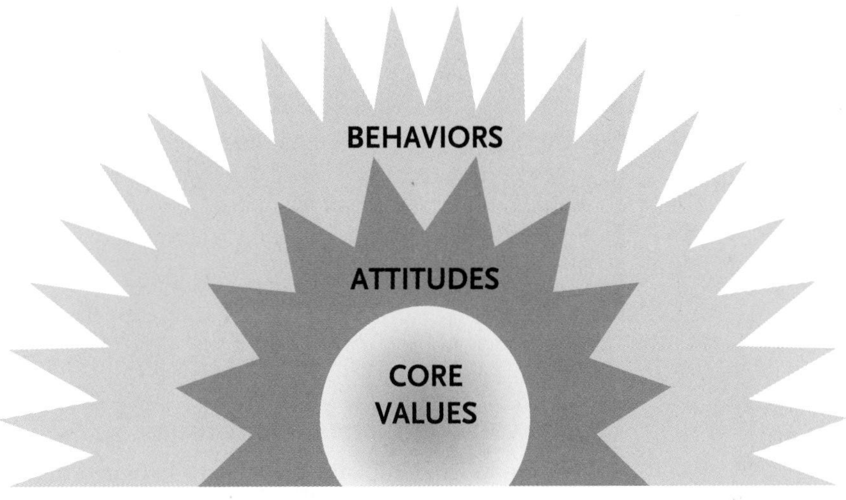

can happen once you realize that you can choose which attitude you will act upon.

Core Values Revisited

In Chapter 5, we described *core values* as those values that one consistently ranks higher than others. You were introduced to a five-part valuing process that will help you clarify and develop your values (see Table 5.1). Each of us lives our life according to a unique set of *core values.* They are fundamental building blocks of your personality. Examples may include honesty, financial security, healthy spirituality, generosity, or maintaining good health. They represent the clearest answers you can give to these questions[3]:

- What are the highest priorities in my life?
- Of these priorities, which do I value most?

Clarifying and developing values is a process that is available throughout our lives. We are constantly choosing from alternatives and considering the consequences of these alternatives. Stew Leonard experienced a change of attitude shortly after the store opened. He was standing at the entrance of the store when a customer came up and said in an angry voice, "This eggnog is sour." He took the half-gallon carton, opened it, and tasted it. He then looked the customer in the eye and said, "You're wrong; it's perfect." And to prove he was right, he added, "We sold over 300 half-gallons of eggnog this week, and you're the only one who complained." The angry customer demanded her money back and said, "I'm never coming back to this store again!"

That evening Leonard reflected on the incident and came to the conclusion that he had made a terrible mistake. He decided that the success of his small store would depend on outstanding service that would generate repeat business.[4] Today Stew Leonard has one of the highest percentage of repeat business in the supermarket industry.

Total Person Insight

Price Pritchett
Chairman, EPS Solutions

"The biggest career challenges these days are perceptual ... psychological. *Not technical. Not even skills-based. The major adjustments we need to make are mental. For example, how we frame things at work. The way we process events in our head. Our attitudes and outlook about how our jobs and organizations now have to operate."*[5]

The Powerful Influence of Attitudes

One of the most significant differences between high and low achievers is choice of attitude. People who go through life with a positive attitude are more likely to achieve their personal and professional goals. People who filter their daily experiences through a negative attitude find it difficult to achieve contentment or satisfaction in any aspect of their lives. Jack Welch, the former chairman and CEO of General Electric, believes that an organization needs people with "positive energy" and needs to get rid of those people who inject the workforce with "negative energy"—even if they are high performers.[6]

Attitudes represent a powerful force in any organization. An attitude of trust, for example, can pave the way for improved communication and greater cooperation between an employee and a supervisor. But when trust is absent, a manager's sincere attempts to improve something may be met with resistance. These same actions by management, filtered through attitudes of trust and hope, may result in improved worker morale.

The Age of Information Mandates Attitude Changes

During the early stages of the information age, many of the best jobs were filled by people who were proficient at reasoning, logical thinking, and analysis. However, as the information age unfolded and the global economy heated up, organizations discovered that it often takes more than quick and accurate information communicated through advanced technology to retain their clients and customers. In many cases, two competing firms, such as banks, may offer customers the same products at the same prices and use the same information technology. The competitive advantage is achieved through superior customer service provided by well-trained employees with effective interpersonal skills.

Daniel Pink, author of *A Whole New Mind*, says we are moving from the information age to the conceptual age. He predicts that one of the major players in the conceptual age will be the **empathizer**. Empathizers have the ability to imagine themselves in someone else's position and understand what that person is feeling. They are able to understand the subtleties of human interaction.[7] For example, several medical schools have come to the conclusion that empathy is a key element of compassionate medical care. Medical school students at Harvard, Columbia, and Dartmouth are learning that an important part of health-care diagnosis is contained in the patient's story. They are trained how to identify the subtle details of a patient's condition through caring, compassionate attitudes.[8]

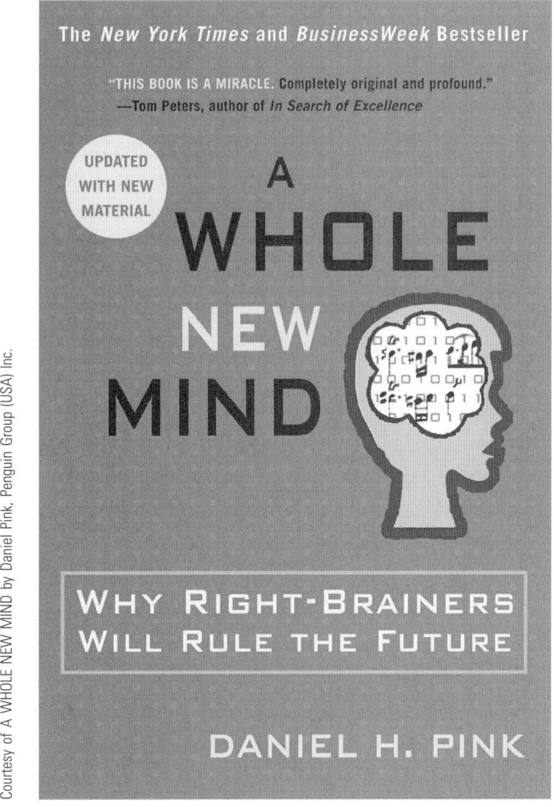

Courtesy of A WHOLE NEW MIND by Daniel Pink, Penguin Group (USA) Inc.

Daniel H. Pink, author of *A Whole New Mind,* predicts that one of the major players in the New Conceptual Age will be the empathizer. These workers have the ability to imagine themselves in someone else's position and understand what that person is feeling.

Technology, in its many forms, will continue to make a major contribution to the workplace. However, we must seek a better balance between "high tech" and "high touch." Leadership, for example, is about empathy. It is about having the ability to relate to and connect with people. Pink states: "Empathy builds self-awareness, bonds parent to child, allows us to work together, and provides the scaffolding for our morality."[9]

How Attitudes Are Formed

Throughout life, you are constantly making decisions and judgments that help form your attitudes. These attitude-shaping decisions are often based on behaviors your childhood authority figures told you were right or wrong, behaviors for which you were rewarded or punished. The role models you select and the various environmental and organizational cultures you embrace also shape your attitudes.

Socialization

The process through which people are integrated into a society by exposure to the actions and opinions of others is called **socialization**.[10] As a child, you interacted with your parents, family, teachers, and friends. Children often feel that statements made by these authority figures are the "proper" things to believe.

Peer and Reference Groups

Kurt Mortensen, author of *Maximum Influence—The 12 Universal Laws of Power Persuasion*, says we tend to change our perceptions, opinions, and behaviors in ways that are consistent with group norms. He states that people want to be liked by others and feel connected.[11] As children reach adolescence and begin to break away psychologically from their parents, the **peer group** (people their own age) can have a powerful influence on attitude formation. With the passing of years, reference groups replace peer groups as sources of attitude formation in young adults. A **reference group** consists of several people who share a common interest. Sales and Marketing Executives International would serve as a reference group for persons employed in sales and marketing.

Media Influence

Every day, we are subjected to several means of mass communication such as newspapers, magazines, radio, television, and the Internet. Nearly $100 billion is spent on such advertising alone in the United States each year. This is just one example of how profit and nonprofit organizations are trying to change our attitudes.[12] These messages focus on the importance of recycling, safe driving, exercise, eating habits, and numerous other topics.

Rewards and Punishment

Attitude formation is often related to rewards and punishment. People in authority generally encourage certain attitudes and discourage others. Naturally, individuals tend to develop attitudes that minimize punishments and maximize rewards. A child who is praised for sharing toys with playmates is more likely to develop positive attitudes toward caring about other people's needs. As an adult, you will discover that your employers will continue to attempt to shape your attitudes through rewards and punishment at work. Many organizations are rewarding employees who take steps to stay healthy, avoid accidents, increase sales, or reduce expenses.

HUMAN RELATIONS IN ACTION

Employee Empathy Valued at Fairmont

Customer satisfaction surveys conducted by Fairmont Hotels found that empathy is a highly valued employee attribute. The company then began screening for empathy as a personality trait during interviews. Fairmont also created an orientation program to help employees understand what it feels like to be a guest.[13]

Role Model Identification

Most young people would like to have more influence, status, and popularity. These goals are often achieved through identification with an authority figure or a role model. A **role model** is that person you most admire or are likely to emulate. As you might expect, role models can exert considerable influence—for better or for worse—on developing attitudes.

In most organizations, supervisory and management personnel can have the greatest impact on employee attitudes. The new dental hygienist and the recently hired auto mechanic want help adjusting to their jobs. They watch their supervisors' attitudes toward safety, cost control, accuracy, grooming, and customer relations and tend to emulate the behavior of these role models. Employees pay more attention to what their supervisors *do* than to what they *say*.

Cultural Influences

Our attitudes are influenced by the culture that surrounds us. **Culture** is the sum total of knowledge, beliefs, values, objects, and ethnic customs that we use to adapt to our environment. It includes tangible items, such as foods, clothing, and furniture, as well as intangible concepts, such as education and laws.[14]

Role models can exert considerable influence—for better or for worse—on developing attitudes.

Today's organizations are striving to create corporate cultures that attract and keep productive workers in these volatile times. When employees feel comfortable in their work environment, they tend to stay.

HUMAN RELATIONS IN ACTION

Attitudes Shape Starbucks Policies

The person who created an American institution—Starbucks—is a modern-day Horatio Alger. Howard Schultz grew up on some of Brooklyn's meaner streets and lived in a cramped apartment in a public housing project. Throughout his youth, he experienced things that shaped the attitudes he would later bring to Starbucks. He recalls coming home one day to find his father lying on the couch with a broken ankle. His father couldn't work, so he lost his job. Because the family had no medical benefits, its tight finances became even tighter. Recalling that early life experience, Schultz said, "I will never forget that episode; I never want that to happen to our employees." That is why thousands of part-time Starbucks workers have medical benefits.[15]

The company that sweats together stays together. That is the belief held by Greg Wittstock, CEO of Aquascape, a multi-million dollar pond-supply company based in St. Charles, Illinois. Several years ago, some employees said that they would like the company to build a soccer field. The company was expanding, so Wittstock decided to build a new home for Aquascape. He decreed that about 20 percent of the new headquarters would be dedicated to "fun stuff." He built a racquetball court, an indoor soccer field, a batting cage, a hot tub, and numerous other places of merriment. Greg Wittstock believes that happy workers are productive workers.[16]

Customers who stay at one of the Four Seasons Hotels know they will be treated like a VIP. The chain, with hotels in Europe, Middle East, Africa, Asia, and the Americas, has built a reputation on consistent high-touch service for every guest. And top management realizes that excellent customer service is not something you can dictate as a policy. It comes from the culture. New employees are carefully screened and then enrolled in a three-month training regimen that helps employees learn how to anticipate guest behavior and then fulfill their needs. Four Seasons has made the *Fortune* list of "100 Best Companies to Work For" ten years in a row.[17]

CRITICAL THINKING CHALLENGE:

Analyze It

Identify at least one strong attitude you have for or against an event, a person, or a thing. How did you acquire this attitude? Is it shared by any particular group of people? Do you spend time with these people? Now think of an attitude that a friend or coworker holds but that you strongly disagree with. What factors do you believe contributed to the formation of this person's attitude?

Attitudes Valued by Employers

Many organizations have discovered the link between workers' attitudes and profitability. This discovery has led to major changes in the hiring process. Employers today are less likely to assume that applicants' technical abilities are the best indicators of their future performance. They have discovered that the lack of technical skills is not the primary reason why most new hires fail to meet expectations. It is their lack of interpersonal skills that counts.[18]

Whether you are looking for your first career position, anticipating a career change, or being retrained for new opportunities, you may find the following discussion helpful concerning what attitudes employers want in their employees.

Basic Interpersonal Skills

In this information-based, high-tech, speeded-up economy, we are witnessing an increase in workplace incivility. Rude behavior in the form of high-decibel cell-phone conversations, use of profanity, or failure to display simple courtesies such as saying "thank you" can damage workplace relationships. As we note in Chapter 11, incivility is the ultimate career killer.

Self-Motivation

People who are self-motivated are inclined to set their own goals and monitor their own progress toward those goals. Their attitude is "I am responsible for this job." They do not need a supervisor hovering around them making sure they are on task and accomplishing what they are supposed to be doing. Many find ways to administer their own rewards after they achieve their goals. Employers often retain and promote those employees who take the initiative to make their own decisions, find better ways of doing their jobs, read professional publications to learn new things, and monitor the media for advances in technology.

People who are self-motivated are inclined to set their own goals and monitor their own progress toward those goals.

Openness to Change

In the age of information, the biggest challenge for many workers is adjusting to the rapidly accelerating rate of change. Some resistance to change is normal merely because it may alter your daily routine. However, you will get into trouble if you choose the following three attitudes[19]:

1. *Stubbornness.* Some workers refuse to be influenced by someone else's point of view. They also find fault with every new change.
2. *Arrogance.* Employees who reject advice or who give the impression that they do not want retraining or other forms of assistance send the wrong message to their employer.
3. *Inflexibility.* Displaying a closed mind to new ideas and practices can only undermine your career advancement opportunities.

Team Spirit

In sports, the person who is a "team player" receives a great deal of praise and recognition. A team player is someone who is willing to step out of the spotlight, give up a little personal glory, and help the team achieve a victory. Team players are no less important in organizations. Employers are increasingly organizing employees into teams (health teams, sales teams, product development teams) that build products, solve problems, and make decisions. Chapter 12 contains some tips on how to become a respected team member.

Health Consciousness

The ever-growing cost of health care is one of the most serious problems facing companies today. Many organizations are promoting wellness programs for all employees as a way to keep costs in line. These programs include tips on healthy eating, physical-fitness exercises, and stress-management practices, as well as other forms of assistance that contribute to a healthy lifestyle. Employees who actively participate in these programs frequently take fewer sick days, file fewer medical claims, and bring a greater level of energy to work. Some companies even give cash awards to employees who lose weight, quit smoking, or lower their cholesterol levels. Chapters 14 and 17 discuss health and wellness in greater detail.

Appreciation of Coworker Diversity

To value diversity in the work setting means to make full use of the ideas, talents, experiences, and perspectives of all employees at all levels within the organization. People who differ from each other often add richness to the organization. An old adage states: If we both think alike, one of us may not be necessary.

Development and utilization of a talented, diverse work force can be a key to success in a period of fierce global competition. Women and people of color make up a large majority of the new multicultural, global work force. Many people, however, carry prejudiced attitudes against those who differ from them. They tend to "prejudge" others' value based on the color of their skin, gender, age, religious preference, lifestyle, political affiliation, or economic status. Although deeply held prejudices that often result in inappropriate workplace behaviors are difficult to change, employers are demanding these changes. Chapter 15 contains specific guidance on how to develop positive attitudes toward joining a diverse work force.

Honesty

Honesty and truthfulness are qualities all employers are searching for in their employees. This is because relationships depend on trust. An honest employee's attitude is "I owe my employer and coworkers the truth." If you cannot be honest with your employer, customers, fellow workers, and friends, they cannot trust you, and strong relationships will be impossible.

How to Change Attitudes

If you are having difficulty working with other team members, if you believe you were overlooked for a promotion you should have had, or if you go home from work depressed and a little angry at the world, you can almost always be sure you need an attitude adjustment. Unfortunately, people do not easily adopt new attitudes or discard old ones. It is difficult to break the attachment to emotionally laden beliefs. Yet attitudes *can* be changed. There may be times when you absolutely hate a job, but you can still develop a positive attitude toward it as a steppingstone to another job you actually do want. There will be times, as well, when you will need to help colleagues change their attitudes so that you can work with them more effectively. And, of course, when events, such as a layoff, are beyond your control, you can accept this fact and move on. It is often said that life is 10 percent what happens to you and 90 percent how you react to it. Knowing how to change attitudes in yourself and others can be essential to effective interpersonal relations—and your success—in life.

It is often said that life is 10 percent what happens to you and 90 percent how you react to it.

Changing Your Own Attitude

You are constantly placed in new situations with people from different backgrounds and cultures. Each time you go to a new school, take a new job, get a promotion, or move to a different neighborhood, you may need to alter your attitudes to cope effectively with the change. The following attitudes will help you achieve positive results in today's world.

Choose Happiness. In his best-selling book *The Art of Happiness*, the Dalai Lama presents happiness as the foundation of all other attitudes. He suggests that the pursuit of happiness is the purpose of our existence. Survey after survey has shown that unhappy people tend to be self-focused, socially withdrawn, and even antagonistic. Happy people, in contrast, are generally found to be more sociable, flexible, and creative and are able to tolerate life's daily frustrations more easily than unhappy people.[20] Tal Ben-Shahar, Harvard University professor and author of *Happier*, sees a strong link between happiness and success[21]: "All else being equal, happy people have better relationships, are more likely to thrive at work, and also live better and longer."

HUMAN RELATIONS IN ACTION

Who Moved My Cheese?

Several years ago, Spencer Johnson wrote *Who Moved My Cheese?* In this small book, which has been on the bestseller list for more than seven years, Johnson introduces the reader to a fable on how to cope positively with change. He recognizes that change is a basic fact of life, so learning to cope with it is an important life strategy. Johnson's most important message is that instead of seeing change as the end of something, you need to learn to see it as a beginning. Breaking through your fear of change is a very important attitude shift in our fluid, ever changing working world.[22]

So, if achieving happiness is truly an important goal, what can we do to achieve it? Here are some important tips:

- *What we choose to focus on largely determines our level of happiness.* The potential for happiness may be all around us, but it may go unnoticed.[23] Let's assume that you are earning an adequate income, but you want to earn more money. Chances are that having more money will not bring greater happiness. It may be time to stop and answer the question: What gives me pleasure? What do I enjoy doing? If earning more money means working longer hours, you may be unable to do things (spend time with family, enjoy more leisure time) that you truly enjoy and that bring you happiness.

- *Mentally reframe events or activities that create unhappiness.* Ralph Waldo Emerson once said, "To different minds, the same world is a hell, and a heaven."[24] Beth Zimmerman, a successful entrepreneur, was not comfortable selling strategic planning services. However, without these sales, her business would fail. She viewed selling as *pushing or peddling products.* Then Zimmerman mentally reframed the personal selling process: "Instead of selling, I think of it as listening to the challenges that my customers face and providing them with a way to help solve them."[25] Once she saw herself as a *consultant* and not a *peddler,* she began to enjoy sales.
- *Seek happiness in relationships.* Two leading positive psychologists studied "very happy people" and compared them with those who were less happy. The only external factor that distinguished the two groups was the presence of "rich and satisfying social relationships." We need to share events, thoughts, and feelings in our lives with friends.[26] Have you stopped speaking to a former friend or family member? Do you avoid resolving problems with coworkers or your boss? Are you spending enough time with those who are closest to you?

Embrace Optimism. Optimistic thoughts give rise to positive attitudes and effective interpersonal relationships. When you are an optimist, your coworkers, managers, and—perhaps most important—your customers feel your energy and vitality and tend to mirror your behavior.

It does not take long to identify people with an optimistic outlook. Optimists are more likely to bounce back after a demotion, layoff, or some other disappointment. According to Martin Seligman, professor of psychology at the University of Pennsylvania and author of *Learned Optimism,* optimists are more likely to view problems as merely temporary setbacks on their road to achieving their goals. They focus on their potential success rather than on their failures.[27]

Total Person Insight

HIS HOLINESS THE DALAI LAMA
HOWARD C. CUTLER
Coauthors, *The Art of Happiness*

"We don't need more money, we don't need greater success or fame, we don't need the perfect body or even the perfect mate—right now, at this very moment, we have a mind, which is all the basic equipment we need to achieve complete happiness."[28]

Pessimists, in contrast, tend to believe bad events will last a long time, will undermine everything they do, and are their own fault. A pessimistic pattern of thinking can have unfortunate consequences. Pessimists give up more easily when faced with a challenge, are less likely to take personal control of their life, and are more likely to take personal blame for their misfortune.[29] Often pessimism leads to **cynicism**, which is a mistrusting attitude regarding the motives of people. When you are cynical, you are constantly on guard against the "misbehavior" of others.[30] If you begin to think that everyone is screwing up, acting inconsiderately, or otherwise behaving inappropriately, cynicism has taken control of your thought process, and it is time to change.

If you feel the need to become a more optimistic person, you can spend more time visualizing yourself succeeding, a process that is discussed in Chapter 4. Monitor your self-talk and discover whether or not you are focusing on the negative aspects of the problems and disappointments in your life, or if you are looking at them as learning experiences that will eventually lead you toward your personal and professional goals. Try to avoid having too much contact with pessimists, and refuse to be drawn into a group of negative thinkers who see only problems, not solutions. Attitudes can be contagious.

CAREER INSIGHT

Quitting During a Bad Economy

You may hate your job, but quitting during a bad economy may be a mistake. In a bad work situation, find an ally, an "anchor person," with whom to discuss coping strategies. Take the focus off your own misery by helping someone else who may be even more distressed.[31]

Think for Yourself. One of the major deterrents to controlling your own attitude is the power of "group think," which surfaces when everyone shares the same opinion. Individuals can lose their desire and ability to think for themselves as they strive to be accepted by team members, committee members, or coworkers in the same department. You are less likely to be drawn into group think if you understand that there are two overlapping relationships among coworkers. *Personal relationships* develop as you bond with your coworkers. When you share common interests and feel comfortable talking with someone, the bonds of friendship may grow very strong. You form small, intense groups. But there still exists the larger group—the organization. Within this setting, *professional relationships* exist for just one purpose: to get the job done.[32] Having two kinds of relationships with the same people can be confusing.

Let's assume you are a member of a project team working on a software application. The deadline for completion is rapidly approaching, yet the team still needs to conduct one more reliability test. At a team meeting, one person suggests that the final test is not needed because the new product has passed all previous tests, and that it's time to turn the product over to marketing. Another member of the team, a close friend of yours, enthusiastically supports this recommendation. You have serious concerns about taking this shortcut but hesitate to take a position that conflicts with that of your friend. What should you do? In a professional relationship, your commitment to the organization takes precedence—unless, of course, it is asking you to do something morally wrong.[33]

Keep an Open Mind. We often make decisions and then refuse to consider any other point of view that might lead us to question our beliefs. Many times, our attitudes persist even in the presence of overwhelming evidence to the contrary. If you have been raised in a family or community that supports racist views, it may seem foreign to you when your colleagues at work openly accept and enjoy healthy relationships with people whose ethnicity is different from your own. Exposing yourself to new information and experiences beyond what you have been socialized to believe can be a valuable growth experience.

In his book, *The 100 Absolutely Unbreakable Laws of Business Success*, Brian Tracy suggests reflecting on the "Law of Flexibility." He said "You are only as free in life as the number of well-developed options you have available to you." The more thoroughly you open your mind to the options available to you, the more freedom you have.[34] This flexibility to see beyond what you thought was true and examine others' perspectives could be one of the most powerful tools you have to inspire the rest of your life.

Helping Others Change Their Attitudes

As the Serenity Prayer (Figure 6.2) expresses, you have a choice whether to accept circumstances or try to change them. Sometimes we *can* do more than just change our attitude—perhaps we can change a condition over which we have no absolute control but which we might be able to influence. For example, at some point you may want to help another person change his or her attitude about something. If you try to beg, plead, intimidate, or even threaten him or her into thinking differently, you probably will get nowhere. This process is similar to attempting to push a piece of yarn across the top of a table. When you *push* the yarn in the direction you want it to go, it gets all bent out of shape. However, when you gently *pull* the yarn with your fingertips, it follows you wherever you want it to go. Two powerful techniques can help you pull people in the direction you want them to go:

1. Change the *conditions* that precede the behavior.
2. Change the *consequences* that follow the behavior.

Change the Conditions

If you want people to change their attitudes, identify the behaviors that represent the poor attitudes and alter the conditions that *precede* the behavior. Consider the following situation.

FIGURE 6.2 Serenity Prayer

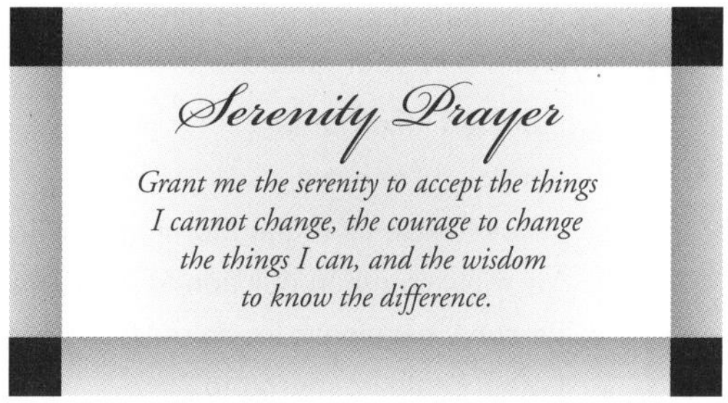

Serenity Prayer
Grant me the serenity to accept the things
I cannot change, the courage to change
the things I can, and the wisdom
to know the difference.

Source: "Serenity Prayer" by Dr. Reinhold Niebuhr.

A new employee in a retail store is having a problem adjusting to her job. The manager needed her on the sales floor as soon as possible, so he rushed through her job training procedures without taking time to answer her questions. Now she finds there are many customers' questions she cannot answer, and she has trouble operating the computerized cash register. She wants to quit, and her negative attitudes are affecting her job performance and the way she handles her customers.

The manager could easily have prevented this employee's negative attitudes by answering all her questions *before* she was placed on the sales floor. Perhaps he could have asked an experienced salesperson to stay with her as she helped her first few customers. Above all, he could have displayed a caring, supportive attitude toward her.

Change the Consequences

Another way to help other people change their attitudes is to alter what happens *after* they exhibit the behavior you are attempting to change. A simple rule applies: When an experience is followed by positive consequences, the person is likely to repeat the behavior. When an experience is followed by negative consequences, the person is more likely stop the behavior. For example, if you are a supervisor, and several of your employees are consistently late for work, you might provide some form of negative consequence each time they are tardy, such as a verbal reprimand or reduced pay. Keep in mind, however, that we tend to focus attention on the people who exhibit disruptive attitudes and to ignore the employees exhibiting the attitudes we want to encourage. Saying "Thank you for being here on time. I really appreciate your commitment" can be an extremely effective reward for those who arrive at work on time. Behaviors rewarded will be repeated.

An attitude is nothing more than a personal thought process. We cannot control the thinking that takes place in someone else's mind, but we can sometimes influence it. And sometimes we can't do that either, so we have to set certain rules of behavior. Some organizations have come to the conclusion that behavior that offends or threatens others must stop. It may be impossible to stop someone from thinking prejudicial thoughts, but you can establish a zero tolerance policy regarding acts that demean or threaten others.[35]

Skill Development: Apply It

An important step in changing your attitudes is understanding them. To practice the skill of monitoring your current thought patterns, add four or five different endings to each of the following incomplete sentences. Work as rapidly as possible, and don't worry about whether the ending is reasonable or significant; the object is to build awareness of your attitudes toward your life.[36]

I am very thankful for...

I am glad I'm not...

When I wake up in the morning, my first thoughts are...

My most common reaction to an annoying situation is...

Personal happiness to me means...

I often compare myself to...

Organizations' Efforts Toward Improving Employees' Attitudes

Most companies realize that an employee's attitude and performance cannot be separated. When employees have negative attitudes about their work, their job performance and productivity suffer. When Thomas Kuwatsch, vice president of the German information technology company Nutzwerk, discovered that employees' whining was cutting into productivity and costing the company an average of $17,600 a year, he formed the "two moans and you're out" policy. A clause in employees' contracts requires them to be in a good mood to keep their jobs. Everyone can complain, but employees must present a solution or better idea to overcome the problem they are complaining about.[37]

When employees have positive attitudes, job performance and productivity are likely to improve. One CEO of a software company has stated, "The way you get superior performance is to get people's passionate loyalty and belief. That means being flexible and giving your people what they need to do a great job."[38]

People who are asked what they most want from their job typically cite mutual respect among coworkers, interesting work, recognition for work well done, the chance to develop skills, and so forth. Of course, workers expect the pay to be competitive, but they want so much more. The late Peter Drucker said, "To make a living is not enough. Work also has to make a life."[39] Organizations are finding creative ways to influence worker attitudes. The following companies made *Fortune* magazine's list of the 100 best companies to work for.[40]

Throughout the world, NetApp, a data storage company, has received many "Best Companies" awards. The company ranked #1 on *Fortune* magazine's 2009 list of "100 Best Companies to Work For." NetApp maintains a culture defined by such core values as trust and integrity, effective leadership, teamwork, and fairness. Employees are encouraged to enjoy miniature golf, volleyball, or some other activity available on the campus.

- Plante & Moran is an accounting firm with a human touch and a sense of humor. The company describes itself as "relatively jerk-free." Full-time employees get at least four weeks of paid vacation. Employees are encouraged to bond.
- Baptist Health South Florida is a hospital that the competition tries to imitate. Top management maintains close contact with all employees, and employee-led initiatives have resulted in low turnover among registered nurses. Periodic open-forum meetings give employees a chance to voice concerns or make suggestions. Three child-care centers are popular.
- Adobe Systems, a successful Silicon Valley firm, strives to generate camaraderie among its employees. It schedules frequent all-hands meetings, job rotations, and employee councils feed management with ideas. Perks include a fitness center with trainer, seasonal farmers' market, and basketball court.

What do these organizations have in common? Each has given thought to the attitudes that are important for a healthy work environment and has taken steps to shape these attitudes. Many organizations are attempting to improve employee attitudes and productivity by enhancing the quality of their employees' work life.

A Final Word

Viktor Frankl, a survivor of the Auschwitz concentration camp and author of *Man's Search for Meaning*, said, "The last of the human freedoms is to choose one's attitude in any given set of circumstances." Changing an attitude can be a challenge, but the process can also be an important step toward your continued growth and success.

LOOKING BACK: REVIEWING THE CONCEPTS

- **Understand the impact of employee attitudes on the success of individuals as well as organizations.**

Attitudes represent a powerful force in every organization. Employees' attitudes and performance cannot be separated. When employees display a positive attitude toward their work and coworkers, teamwork and productivity improve. When employees display a caring attitude toward their customers, the business is likely to enjoy a high degree of customer loyalty and repeat business. When employees display a serious attitude toward safety rules and regulations, fewer accidents are likely to occur.

- **List and explain the ways people acquire attitudes.**

People acquire attitudes through early childhood socialization, peer and reference groups, rewards and punishment, role model identification, and cultural influences. However, attitudes are not set in stone. You always have the power to choose your attitude toward any situation.

- **Describe attitudes that employers value.**

Employers hire and attempt to retain employees who have basic interpersonal skills, are self-motivated, accept change, are team players, are concerned about their health, value coworker diversity, and are honest.

- **Learn how to change your attitudes:**

You can decide to change your attitudes by choosing to be happy, becoming an optimist, thinking for yourself without undue pressure from others, and keeping an open mind.

- **Learn how to help others change their attitudes.**

You can help others change their attitudes by altering the conditions that lead to negative behaviors, such as by providing effective training so that the employee's job performance and personal satisfaction improve. You can also alter the consequences following people's behavior by providing positive consequences, if you want them to have a positive attitude toward their behavior and repeat it, and negative consequences, to deter them from participating in that behavior again.

- Understand what adjustments organizations are making to develop positive employee attitudes.

Employers realize that money alone will not make employees happy. Organizations are taking steps to improve employee attitudes by enhancing the quality of their work life.

ON THE JOB Q & A: JUMPING TO A NEW EMPLOYER

Q: Two years ago, I left a job I loved when the executives of an exciting new company offered me a position that seemed to have tremendous potential. I gave my two weeks' notice and jumped to the new employer. I worked day and night to help the new company be successful and enhance my climb to the top of it. Last week, I was informed that it is declaring bankruptcy next month. I am choosing how I react to this devastating news and am trying not to panic, but I need advice on how to approach my former employer about returning to my old position. I still see some of my former colleagues socially, and they believe that there might be an opportunity to return to my old job. What can I do to enhance my chances at reentry?

A: You are not alone! Many workers grab new job opportunities when they believe the grass might be greener on the other side, only to discover they were better off in the first location. You were smart when you offered two weeks' notice before leaving your position. This considerate attitude toward your colleagues and customers will speak well for you during your reentry attempt. Determine what new skills you learned with the new organization and how those skills might be transferred to your former employer. Did you learn to effectively handle multiple priorities simultaneously, work faster, or take more risks? Point out why this new knowledge makes you even more valuable to your former employer. Who knows, they may reinstate you in a higher position than before!

Keep in mind that returning to your previous employer may not be your only choice. You could choose to look at this forced change as an opportunity to explore options you never considered before. Are there other employers in your field that might consider your experience an asset? Are your skills transferable to another career path? Keep an open mind as you examine your future.[41]

KEY TERMS

attitudes 122
empathizer 124
socialization 125
peer group 126
reference group 126
role model 126
culture 127
cynicism 132

TRY YOUR HAND

1. Describe your attitudes concerning

   a. a teamwork environment
   b. health and wellness
   c. life and work
   d. learning new skills

   How do these attitudes affect you on a daily basis? Do you feel you have a positive attitude in most situations? Can you think of someone you have frequent contact with who displays negative attitudes toward these items? How might you change this person's attitudes?

2. Identify an attitude held by a friend, coworker, or spouse that you would like to see changed. Do any conditions that precede this person's behavior fall under your control? If so, how could you change those conditions so the person might change his or her attitude? What positive consequences might you offer when the person behaves the way you want? What negative consequences might you impose when the person participates in the behavior you are attempting to stop?

3. For a period of one week, keep a diary or log of positive and negative events. Positive events might include the successful completion of a project, a compliment from a coworker, or just finding time for some leisure activities. Negative events might include forgetting an appointment, criticism from your boss, or simply looking in the mirror and seeing something you don't like. An unpleasant news story might also qualify as a negative event. At the end of one week, review your entries and determine what type of pattern exists. Also, reflect on the impact of these events. Did you quickly bounce back from the negative events, or did you dwell on them all week? Tal Ben-Shahar, a leader in the field of positive psychology, says the potential for happiness is all around us, but may go unnoticed. During the past week did you fail to recognize any sources of pleasure and meaning?

INTERNET INSIGHTS

An economic culture of layoffs and terminations is a time to reassess career goals, to avoid unnecessary fear or uncertainty, and to spend some time developing a career change plan. This is an excellent time to explore interests and passions. Call this your *fun employment* time. Visit *http://www.jobhuntersbible.com*, the official site for *What Color Is Your Parachute?* This best selling book is a favorite among many job hunters and career changers. Another career site would be *http://www.maggiemistal.com*. After you visit the sites, reflect and record basic steps that will guide a future career change process.

YOU PLAY THE ROLE

In this role-play exercise, you will be attempting to mentor a coworker who is a chronic underachiever. She has a great deal of potential, but she does things at work that result in self-sabotage. For example, she tends to procrastinate and often misses deadlines. When she does complete a project, her approach is to get by with the least amount of effort. When things don't go well at work, she tends to blame others. You will meet with another member of your class who will assume the role of your coworker. As a mentor, think about things you might say or do that would help your coworker develop the attitudes that employers value today.

BELOW THE SURFACE:

Stew Leonard's Regional Marketing Phenomenon

Stew Leonard's, introduced at the beginning of this chapter, has combined the atmosphere of a theme park with the business principles of a big box store. Entertaining shopping diversions include a petting zoo, robotic singing milk cartons, and employees who are sometimes dressed as farm animals.[42]

Roy Snider is the chain's official pep rally cheerleader. His title is Director of Wow, and he is responsible for boosting employee morale and building team spirit. Stop at Stew Leonard's, and you might see Snider dancing with a customer or singing happy birthday to an employee.[43]

Most of the customers who visit Stew Leonard's are repeat customers. The Leonard family maintains a distinctive corporate culture with an emphasis on teamwork and a strong devotion to customer satisfaction. Losing a customer means more than losing a single sale. It means losing the entire stream of purchases that the customer would make over a lifetime of patronage. Stew Leonard says he sees $50,000 flying out of his store every time he sees a sulking customer. The loss can be much greater if an unhappy customer shares a bad experience with other customers or potential customers.[44]

Year after year, Stew Leonard's is named to the "100 Best Companies to Work For" list published by *Fortune* magazine. The most recent award, given in 2009, provides an example of how the company pays attention to the needs of its employees. During the recent crippling economic downturn, the supermarket's founders staged a "road show" at each store location to assure employees that their jobs and benefits were safe.[45]

QUESTIONS

1. The first Stew Leonard's retail grocery was established in 1969. Do you think the culture established and nurtured at this successful firm could be adopted by other retail grocery stores? Explain your answer.
2. Do you think it is realistic to attempt to encourage a lifetime of customer patronage in today's uncertain business climate? Elaborate on your response.
3. Would you like to work at a Stew Leonard's retail store? Develop your rationale for employment or nonemployment.

CLOSING CASE:
An A-Mazing Way to Deal with Change

The new millennium was ushered in by a series of corporate scandals involving Enron, WorldCom, Tyco, and other large companies. In many cases, investors in these companies lost large amounts of money, and employees lost all or part of their pension funds. Also, several large companies have declared bankruptcy. United Airlines and U.S. Airways provide just two examples. Most of these firms' employees had defined-benefit pension plans that guaranteed payments to retirees based on a specific formula. When it became obvious that these organizations could no longer pay out these enormous sums of money in light of

(continued)

their financial woes, many handed off their pension obligations to the Pension Benefit Guaranty Corporation, the federal agency that was established to protect these individuals from losing their promised retirement funds. Now, this agency has a deficit of more than $23 billion and faces an even larger deficit as more and more companies bail out of their pension fund obligations. Some organizations have seen the writing on the wall and have taken action to reduce or eliminate employees' pension funds so that they can remain competitive with organizations that do not offer such generous pensions.

When a company enters bankruptcy or goes out of business, employees usually lose their health-care benefits. The loss of health-care benefits and the loss of pension funds place an enormous burden on employees who no longer have jobs. Needless to say, most of these employees are feeling a deep sense of frustration and anger.

These employee attitudes are contagious. Workers in companies that have not yet been hit with such troubles face the fear that their organization is next. Perhaps they could benefit by reading the simple parable presented in Spencer Johnson's book *Who Moved My Cheese? An A-Mazing Way to Deal with Change in Your Work and in Your Life.* The four characters in the book, Sniff and Scurry (two little mice) and Hem and Haw (two little people the size of mice), live in a maze with lots of paths leading nowhere and some leading to rooms filled with cheese that could keep them happy for the rest of their lives. Each of the characters has a unique way of handling the depletion of their cheese supply in Cheese Station C. All four were initially very comfortable thinking that their cheese would always be there. Sniff and Scurry noticed that the cheese was rapidly diminishing and risked exploring the maze to discover a new source for their happiness. Hem and Haw kept doing their daily routine over and over again, thinking the situation would improve. They did not acknowledge what was happening around them, and when the cheese was gone, they demanded compensation, declaring that the problem was not their fault. They waited for someone else to replace the cheese and continue to provide their security. They considered going out into the maze but were afraid they could never find another source of cheese.[46]

QUESTIONS

1. *Who Moved My Cheese?* is the all-time best-selling book in Amazon.com's history and is printed in 42 languages. Analyze why organizations around the world would buy millions of these books for their employees.
2. The book encourages readers to pay attention to what is happening around them, anticipate change, and look at the opportunities that exist outside their comfort zones. How does this reflect on those workers losing their pension funds?
3. One of the book's most powerful questions is "What would you do if you were not afraid?" As you look to your future and grasp the attitudes Spencer Johnson suggests, share your answer to that question with your classmates.

INTEGRATED RESOURCES

VIDEO:

The Job Interview

CLASSROOM ACTIVITIES

IRM Application Exercise 6.1
IRM Application Exercise 6.2
IRM Application Exercise 6.3
IRM Application Exercise 6.4

CHAPTER 7

Motivating Yourself and Others

TIP OF THE ICEBERG

CHAPTER PREVIEW

LEARNING OBJECTIVES

After studying Chapter 7, you will be able to

- Understand the complex nature of motivation.
- Describe five of the most influential theories of motivation.
- List and describe contemporary motivation strategies.
- Identify motivating factors important to individuals from different generations.
- Describe selected self-motivation strategies.

MOTIVATION OF MICHAEL PHELPS

All eyes were on Michael Phelps at the Beijing Olympics. Could he win a gold medal in all eight events that he entered? Anything less than eight gold medals would be a disappointment for Phelps and his many fans. He won gold medals in the first six events, and then had a very close victory in the 100-meter butterfly event. The margin of victory was one-hundredth of a second. In the final event of the Beijing Olympics swimming competition, the 4 × 100 meter relay, he left the blocks with his team in third place but gave the lead to the final team member who closed out the victory.[1]

Early in his life, Phelps was diagnosed with Attention–Deficit Hyperactivity Disorder (ADHD). He started swimming at age seven, partly because of the influence of his sisters, who were good swimmers, and partly to provide an outlet for his energy. He steadily improved as a swimmer and qualified for the 2000 Summer Olympics at age 15.[2]

Since age 11, Phelps has been coached by Bob Bowman. Bowman says the key to Phelps' success is his single-mindedness—the ability to shut out distractions and stay focused on winning the race. Of course, he is also highly motivated to maintain an active training regimen, which includes swimming nearly 50 miles a week.[3]

What motivated Michael Phelps to perform so well? Questions about what motivates anyone are not easily answered because everyone's needs differ so much. This chapter will help you gain some useful insight

Bob Thomas/Getty Images

Michael Phelps has won 14 career gold medals and holds seven world records in swimming. Chances are, he will continue to win Olympic gold medals in the years ahead because he is highly motivated to be the best swimmer in the world. When Phelps is swimming in competition, he has the ability to shut out distractions and stay focused on winning.

into understanding how your needs motivate you to take action and learn how to identify the needs of others.

The Complex Nature of Motivation

People are motivated by many different kinds of needs. They have basic needs for food, clothing, and shelter, but they also need acceptance, recognition, and self-esteem. Each individual experiences these needs in different ways and to varying degrees. To complicate matters more, people are motivated by different needs at different times in their lives. Adults, like children and adolescents, continue to develop and change in significant ways throughout life.

Motivation Defined

People interact with each other in a variety of ways because they are driven by a variety of forces. **Motivation**, derived from the Latin word *movere,* meaning "to move," can be defined as the influences that account for the initiation, direction, intensity, and persistence of behavior. The study of motivation is complicated by the fact that the number of possible motives for human behavior seems endless. *Emotional* factors such as fear, anger, and love are some sources of motivation. Others may stem from *social* factors that are influenced by parents, teachers, friends, and television. And then there are the basic *biological* factors such as our need for food, water, or sleep.[4]

Total Person Insight

Jack Canfield
Author, *Key to Living the Law of Attraction*

"Remember that all *things are possible. Don't limit or censor your visions for the future. You must believe in yourself and believe that you are worthy."*[5]

Although the major focus of this chapter will be motivation in a work setting, it is important to realize that some people find meaning through the obsessions that consume their leisure time. To earn a living, Henry Sakaida helps operate a wholesale nursery in Rosemead, California, but his passion is World War II aviation history. For the past 20 years, he has arranged healing meetings between Japanese and American pilots who once shot at each other over the Pacific.[6] Tatsuo and Yukiko Ono operate a small business in Japan, but they get their greatest satisfaction from following the band The Rolling Stones. They have attended about 300 Stones concerts held at major cities around the world.[7]

In a work setting, it is motivated employees who get the work done. Without them, most organizations would falter. Motivation is two dimensional; it can be internal or external.

Internal motivation comes from the satisfaction that occurs when work is meaningful and gives us a sense of purpose. Psychologist Frederick Herzberg has said that motivation comes from an internal stimulus resulting from job content, that is, what a worker actually does all day long. He suggests that organizations motivate their employees by enriching jobs so that workers are challenged, have an opportunity for achievement, and can experience personal growth.[8] These intrinsic rewards motivate some people more than money, trophies for outstanding performance, or other similar external rewards.

External motivation is an action taken by another person. It usually involves the anticipation of a reward of some kind. Typical external rewards in a work setting include money, feedback regarding performance, and awards. Some organizations are using **incentives** to encourage workers to develop good work habits and to repeat behavior that is beneficial to themselves and the organization. An incentive can take the form of additional money, time off from work, or some other type of reward. Generation Y workers, the Millennial generation, desire frequent and candid performance feedback and recognition for accomplishments.[9]

External rewards are rarely enough to motivate people on a continuing basis.

External rewards are rarely enough to motivate people on a continuing basis. Ideally, an organization will provide an appropriate number of external rewards while permitting employees to experience the ongoing, internal satisfaction that comes from meaningful work.

The Motivation to Satisfy Basic Desires

Steven Reiss, professor of psychology and psychiatry at Ohio State University, conducted a major study to determine what *really* drives human behavior. He asked 6,000 people from many stations in life which values were most

FIGURE 7.1 The Sixteen Basic Desires in the Reiss Profile (Order of Presentation Not Significant)

DESIRE	DEFINITION
CURIOSITY	The desire for knowledge
ACCEPTANCE	The desire for inclusion
ORDER	The desire for organization
PHYSICAL ACTIVITY	The desire for exercise of muscles
HONOR	The desire to be loyal to one's parents and heritage
POWER	The desire to influence others
INDEPENDENCE	The desire for self-reliance
SOCIAL CONTACT	The desire for companionship
FAMILY	The desire to raise one's own children
STATUS	The desire for social standing
IDEALISM	The desire for social justice
VENGEANCE	The desire to get even
ROMANCE	The desire for sex and beauty
EATING	The desire to consume food
SAVING	The desire to collect things
TRANQUILITY	The desire for emotional calm

Source: Steven Reiss, *Who Am I?* (New York:: Berkley Books, 2000), pp. 17-18.

significant in motivating their behavior and in contributing to their sense of happiness.[10]

The results of his research showed that nearly everything we experience as meaningful can be traced to one of sixteen basic desires or to some combination of these desires (see Figure 7.1). Each of us has a different combination of the sixteen desires, a mix that can change with time and circumstances. The challenge is to determine which ones (the fundamental values) are most important, and then live your life accordingly. You do not need to satisfy all sixteen desires, only the five or six that are the most important to you.

Reiss and his research team found that most people cannot find *enduring* happiness by aiming to have more fun or pleasure. People who focus primarily on "feel-good" happiness (partying, drinking, etc.) discover that this source of satisfaction rarely lasts more than a few hours. It is "value-based" happiness that gives life meaning over the long run.[11]

Characteristics of Motives

Motives have been described as the "why" of human behavior. An understanding of the following five characteristics of motives can be helpful as you seek to understand the complex nature of motivation.[12]

Motives Are Individualistic. People have different needs. What satisfies one person's needs, therefore, may not satisfy another's. This variation in individual motives often leads to a breakdown in human relationships, unless individuals take the time to understand the motives of others.

CRITICAL THINKING CHALLENGE:

Analyze It

In Chapter 5, you were encouraged to identify and reflect on the values that are important in your life. Return to Table 5.1, and review the five-part values clarification process. Now examine each of the 16 basic desires in Figure 7.1 and identify five or six that seem most important to you. Then apply the five-part valuing process to each of these desires. Do they accurately reflect factors that would motivate you at this point in your life? How might your desires change in the future?

Motives Change. As noted at the beginning of this chapter, motives change throughout our lives. What motivates us early in our careers may not motivate us later on.

Motives May Be Unconscious. In many cases, we are not fully aware of the inner needs and drives that influence our behavior. The desire to win the "Employee of the Month" award may be triggered by unconscious feelings of inadequacy or the desire for increased recognition.

Motives Are Often Inferred. We can observe the behavior of another person, but we can only infer (draw conclusions about) what motives have caused that behavior. The motives underlying our own behavior and others' behavior are often difficult to understand.

Motives Are Hierarchical. Motives for behavior vary in levels of importance. When contradictory motives exist, the more important motive usually guides behavior. Workers often leave jobs that are secure to satisfy the need for work that is more challenging and rewarding.

Influential Motivational Theories

The work of various psychologists and social scientists has added greatly to the knowledge of what motivates people and how motivation works. The basic problem, as many leaders admit, is knowing how to apply that knowledge in the workplace. Although many theories of motivation have emerged over the years, we will discuss five of the most influential.

HUMAN RELATIONS IN ACTION

Teen Tops Everest

At Age 18, Samantha Larson became the youngest American to scale the summit of Mount Everest. She fulfilled the dream of her lifetime. Samantha has now climbed all of the elusive "Seven Summits," the highest mountains on each continent. She has joined a very exclusive club.[13]

Maslow's Hierarchy of Needs

According to Abraham Maslow, a noted psychologist, people tend to satisfy their needs in a particular order—a theory he calls the **hierarchy of needs**. Maslow's theory rests on three assumptions: (1) people have a number of needs that require some measure of satisfaction; (2) only unsatisfied needs motivate behavior; and (3) the needs of people are arranged in a hierarchy of prepotency, which means that as each lower-level need is satisfied, the need at the next level demands attention.[14] Basically, human beings are motivated to satisfy physiological needs first (food, clothing, shelter); then the need for safety and security; then social needs; then esteem needs; and, finally, self-actualization needs, or the need to realize their potential. Maslow's theory is illustrated in Figure 7.2.

Physiological Needs. The needs for food, clothing, sleep, and shelter, or physiological needs, were described by Maslow as survival or lower-order needs. When the economy is strong and most people have jobs, these basic needs rarely dominate because they are reasonably well satisfied. But, needless to say, people who cannot ensure their own and their family's survival, or who are homeless, place these basic needs at the top of their priority list.

Safety and Security Needs. Most people want order, predictability, and freedom from physical harm in their personal and professional lives and will be motivated to achieve these safety needs once their basic physiological needs are satisfied. At this level of the hierarchy, job security is very important.

FIGURE 7.2 Maslow's Hierarchy of Needs

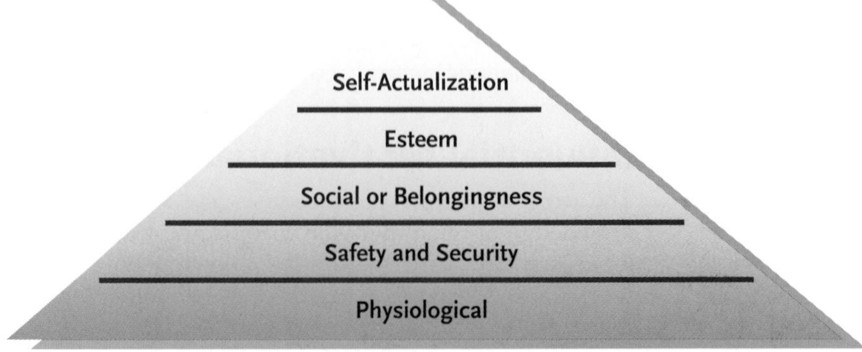

Social or Belongingness Needs. Whereas the first two types of needs deal with aspects of physical safety and survival, social or belongingness needs deal with emotional and mental well-being. Research has shown that needs for affection, for a sense of belonging, and for identification with a group are powerful. There are two major aspects of the need to belong: frequent, positive interactions with the same people and a framework of stable, long-term caring and concern.[15]

Esteem Needs. People need respect and recognition from others as well as an inner sense of achievement and self-worth. Promotions, honors, and awards from outside sources tend to satisfy this need. Several esteem-building initiatives that build self-respect and self-confidence are discussed in Chapters 4 and 10.

Self-Actualization Needs. Maslow defined *self-actualization* as a need for self-fulfillment, a full tapping of one's potential. It is the need to "be all that you can be," to have mastery over what you are doing. Self-actualization is people fulfilling their potential or realizing their fullest capacities as human beings (see Table 7.1).

It is worth noting that Maslow's list of higher-level needs has been criticized because it does not specifically address some needs of the new generation of workers, such as the need for leisure time and the opportunity for self-actualization

TABLE 7.1 WAYS OF SATISFYING INDIVIDUAL NEEDS IN THE WORK SITUATION

NEED	ORGANIZATIONAL CONDITIONS
Physiological	Pay Breakfast or lunch programs Company services
Safety and security	Company benefits plans Pensions Seniority Pay
Social or belongingness	Coffee breaks Sports teams Company picnics and social events Work teams
Esteem	Recognition of work well done Responsibility Pay (as symbol of status) Prestigious office location and furnishings
Self-actualization	Challenge Autonomy

Source: Adapted from Judith Gordon, *A Diagnostic Approach to Organizational Behavior*, 3d ed. (Boston: Allyn & Bacon, 1991), p. 144.

through family relationships. However, it teaches us one important lesson: A need that is satisfied will usually not motivate an individual. If you have food and shelter, you will likely focus on safety and security needs. Maslow's work is considered a classic in the field of management theory, and his original works have been republished in the book *Maslow on Management*.

Herzberg's Motivation-Maintenance (Two-Factor) Theory

Psychologist Frederick Herzberg proposes another motivation theory called the **motivation-maintenance theory**.[16] **Maintenance factors** represent the basic things people consider essential to any job, such as salaries, fringe benefits, working conditions, social relationships, supervision, and organizational policies and administration. We often take such things for granted as part of the job. These basic maintenance factors *do not* act as motivators, according to Herzberg; but if any of them is absent, the organizational climate that results can hurt employee morale and lower worker productivity. Health insurance, for example, generally does not motivate employees to be more productive, but the loss of it can cause workers to look for employment in another organization that provides the desired coverage.

Motivational factors are those elements that go above and beyond the basic maintenance factors. They include opportunities for recognition, advancement, or more responsibility. When these are present, they tend to motivate employees to improve their productivity. The workers may seek out new and creative ways to accomplish their organizations' goals as well as their personal goals. Herzberg's list of motivational factors parallels, to some degree, Maslow's hierarchy of needs (see Table 7.2).

Herzberg theorized that if employees' motivational factors are not met, they may begin to ask for more maintenance factors, such as increased salaries and fringe benefits, better working conditions, or more liberal company policies regarding sick leave or vacation time. Critics of Herzberg's theory have pointed

TABLE 7.2 COMPARISON OF THE MASLOW AND HERZBERG THEORIES

	MASLOW	HERZBERG
Motivational factors	Self-actualization	Work itself
		Achievement
		Responsibility
	Esteem needs	Recognition
		Advancement
		Status
Maintenance factors	Social or belongingness needs	Social network
		Supervision
	Safety and security needs	Company policy and administration
	Physiological needs	Job security
		Working conditions
		Salary

out that he assumes that most, if not all, individuals are motivated only by higher-order needs such as recognition or increased responsibility, and that they seek jobs that are challenging and meaningful. His theory does not acknowledge that some people may prefer more routine, predictable work and may be motivated more by the security of a regular paycheck (a maintenance factor) than by the prospect of advancement. Nonetheless, Herzberg made an important contribution to motivation theory by emphasizing the importance of enriched work.

The Expectancy Theory

The **expectancy theory** is based on the assumption that motivational strength is determined by whether or not you *believe* you can be successful at a task. (This theory is an expansion of the self-efficacy concept detailed in Chapter 4.) If you really want something and believe that the probability of your success is high, then your motivation increases. *Perception* is an important element of this theory. Research conducted at the University of Kansas found a link between expectations and achievement in college. Students who wanted to complete college and believed they were capable of doing so earned higher grades and were less likely to drop out. In fact, aspirations combined with expectations predicted achievement better than standardized test scores.[17] This somewhat-mysterious connection between what you expect in life and what you actually achieve is sometimes referred to as the **self-fulfilling prophecy**: If you can conceive it and believe it, you can achieve it.

McGregor's Theory X/Theory Y

Douglas McGregor, author of the classic book *The Human Side of Enterprise*, suggests that managers who are placed in charge of motivating their workers are essentially divided into two groups. Theory X managers maintain a pessimistic attitude toward their workers' potential. These managers believe that workers are basically lazy and have to be goaded into doing things with incentives such as pay or with punishment, that they have little or no ambition, that they prefer to avoid responsibility, and that they do only as much work as they have to keep their jobs. Theory Y managers, on the other hand, maintain an optimistic view of workers' ambition. These managers believe that their subordinates are serious workers who want to work and do their best, are capable of self-direction, and can learn to both accept and seek responsibility if they are committed to the objectives of the organization. Often the expectancy theory kicks in and workers perform to their managers' pessimistic or optimistic expectations.

The Goal-Setting Theory

Successful people and successful organizations have one thing in common: They share the power of purpose. The more you focus on achieving a desired outcome, the greater your likelihood of success.[18] Your goals play a key role in bringing purpose to your life.

Motivation researchers indicate that goals tend to motivate people in four ways (see Figure 7.3). First, goals provide the power of purpose by directing your attention to a specific target. Second, they encourage you to make the effort to achieve something difficult. Third, reaching a goal requires sustained effort and therefore encourages persistence. Fourth, having a goal forces you to bridge the gap between the dream and the reality; it fosters your creating a plan of action filled with strategies that will get you where you want to go.[19]

FIGURE 7.3 A Model of How Goals Can Improve Performance

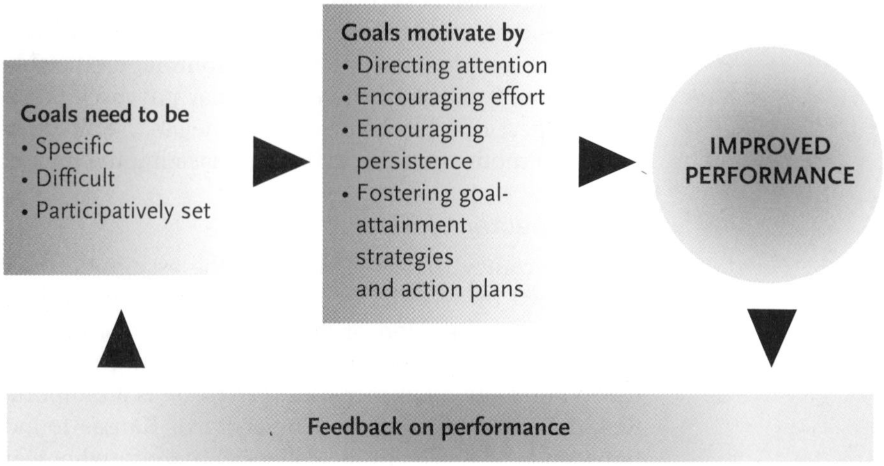

Source: Robert Kreitner, *Management*, 9th edition (Boston: Houghton Mifflin Company, 2004). Reprinted by permission of The Houghton Mifflin company.

If your goal is easy to achieve and requires little effort, it may not serve as a motivator. Goals need to be difficult enough to challenge you but not impossible to reach. Goal setting is an excellent self-motivation strategy. Take a moment and review the goal-setting principles listed in Table 4.1.

Contemporary Employee Motivation Strategies

A healthy, mutually supportive relationship based on trust, openness, and respect can create a work climate in which employees want to give more of themselves. However, creating this type of organizational culture in the age of information may not be easy. How do you motivate employees who work from virtual offices? How do organizations experiencing major upheavals keep their employees' trust? The answers may have been provided by Jeffrey Pfeffer, a Stanford professor who has reported a strong connection between people-centered practices and an organization's greater profits and lower employee turnover. Organizations that recognize human wants, needs, passions, and aspirations and put people first understand that many of the following motivation strategies have merit even during times of great uncertainty.[20]

Motivation Through Job Design

Today's workers place a high value on jobs that provide rewards such as a sense of achievement, challenge, variety, and personal growth. It is possible to redesign existing jobs so they will have characteristics or outcomes that are intrinsically satisfying to employees. There are at least three design options.[21]

Job Rotation. **Job rotation** allows workers to move through a variety of jobs in a predefined way over a period of time. For example, a worker might attach a wheel assembly one week, inspect it the next, organize the parts for assembly

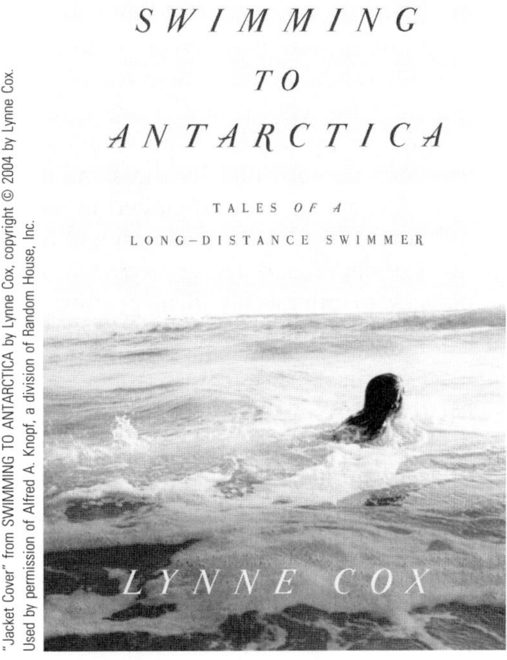

At the age of 14, Lynne Cox tackled her first open water swim, three miles in the rough Pacific ocean of the California coast. After that successful swim, she set more challenging goals that required greater strength and stamina.

during the third week, then return to the original assembly job the fourth week and begin the rotation again.

Job Enlargement. **Job enlargement** means expanding an employee's duties or responsibilities. When a job becomes stale, motivation can often be increased by encouraging employees to learn new skills or take on new responsibilities. In a bank setting, for example, a teller might develop expertise in the area of loan services or opening new accounts.

Job Enrichment. **Job enrichment** is an attempt to make jobs more desirable or satisfying, thereby triggering internal motivation. One approach assigns new and more difficult tasks to employees; another grants them additional authority. The Ritz-Carlton Hotel Co. has used this job-enrichment strategy to improve customer service. When a customer has a problem, employees are encouraged to find a solution immediately. They have the discretion to spend up to $2,000 to fix a problem.[22]

Job rotation, job enlargement, and job enrichment appeal to Generation Y workers, who often do not value work for only external rewards. These workers are more apt to view work as a valuable learning experience that helps them build a strong résumé.[23]

Motivation Through Incentives

Incentives are often used to improve quality, reduce accidents, increase sales, improve attendance, and speed up production. They often focus on improving behaviors that will cut expenses and improve customer satisfaction. J.A. Frate Inc., a regional trucking company based in Illinois, tries hard to make sure its drivers feel valued and want to stay with the company. Drivers who show special effort are given recognition and prizes. The recognition plan is based on a point system. Points can be earned for delivery of undamaged freight, carefully prepared log books, and on-time delivery of freight. Points can be redeemed for gift certificates.[24] We are seeing new incentive plans that erase the idea that everyone is motivated by the same thing—a "one-size-fits-all" approach. Incentives and rewards are discussed in more detail in Chapter 10.

Many companies are experimenting with programs that reward the development of new ideas. These programs, known as **intrapreneurship**, encourage employees to pursue an idea, product, or process, with the company providing encouragement and support.

Motivation Through Learning Opportunities

Learning opportunities, both on and off the job, can be a strong motivational force. Employees realize that education and training are critical to individual growth and opportunity. Yuri Kouzmov, director of Web technologies at World Golf Tour, sees working for this company as an "investment" in his career. He is given the opportunity to learn a lot beyond his assigned duties. As an employee in a small company, he has private access to a senior manager at any point.[25]

Many companies are using advanced communications technology to deliver instruction. Some organizations provide tuition reimbursement for online courses offered by colleges and universities across the country.

"My client wants a fifty-per-cent salary boost, a bonus guarantee, and a snappy choreographed victory dance he can do after he makes a touchdown."

Motivation Through Empowerment

Empowerment refers to those policies that share information, authority, and responsibility with the lowest ranks of the organization. When employees are empowered to make decisions for the good of the organization, they experience feelings of pride, self-expression, and ownership.

TechTarget, a Needham, Massachusetts, interactive media company, has embraced empowerment to a high degree. All of its 210 employees are free to set their own work schedules. There are no set policies mandating working hours or specifying the number of sick, personal, or vacation days. Managers set quarterly goals and timetables, but employees determine how to achieve them. In exchange for the flexibility, employees are expected to stay in contact with their managers. Greg Strakosch, founder and CEO, says the company's "open-leave" policy is credited with attracting and keeping a very talented and dedicated workforce.[26]

Although empowerment efforts are growing in popularity, this motivational strategy should not be viewed as a quick fix. Empowerment requires a long-term commitment of human and financial resources from top management down.

Motivation Through Others' Expectations

Earlier in this chapter, you were introduced to the power of your own self-fulfilling prophecy: You will probably get whatever it is you expect. But there is another aspect of the expectancy theory: the power *others'* expectations can have on your motivation.

Research has confirmed that people tend to act in ways that are consistent with what others expect of them. In the classic study *Pygmalion in the Classroom*, Harvard University professors Robert Rosenthal and J. Sterling Livingston described the significant effect of teachers' expectations on students. They discovered that when teachers had high expectations for certain students who they believed had excellent intellectual ability and learning capacity, those students learned at a faster rate than others in the same group—even though the teachers did not consciously treat the higher-achieving students differently. These teachers had unintentionally communicated their high expectations to the students they *thought* possessed strong intellectual abilities.

The source of low expectations in the workplace is often a boss who perceives an employee as a weak performer and then treats the employee differently than high performers. The employee who thinks he or she is a weak performer in the eyes of the boss will often perform down to expectations.[27]

Motivating the Generations

In Chapter 5, we discussed the variety of historical events that influence the values of various generations (see Table 5.2). It is interesting to discover how those values translate into motivational factors for people in those same generation categories. This information may be helpful in discovering your own motivators, but gaining a greater understanding of these population segments may also be helpful as you learn how to motivate others in your personal and professional life. Figure 7.4 provides a brief summary of motivational factors for each generation.

FIGURE 7.4 Motivational Factors for the Generations

MATURES Born between **1928** and **1945**	• They are often referred to as *loyalists*. • They want to build a legacy, both professionally and personally. • They want to be a part of the company's future. • Their view of feedback: No news is good news. • Rewards that are meaningful to them: The satisfaction of a job well done. • Their motivators: Money, public recognition, leadership opportunities, organizational loyalty, responsibility, accomplishment, control.
BABY BOOMERS Born between **1946** and **1964**	• They are often referred to as the *optimists*. • They want to build an outstanding career. • They want to move up within the company and gain personal and financial responsibilities. • Their view of feedback: Performance review once a year, with a lot of documentation. • Rewards that are meaningful to them: Money, title, recognition, the corner office. • Their motivators: More money, public recognition, desire for subordinates, loyalty to self, promotion, peer recognition, control.
GENERATION X Born between **1965** and **1976**	• They are often referred to as the *skeptics*. • They want to build a portable career. • They want to know exactly what they will be doing and whether they are on the right career path. • Their view of feedback: They want frequent comments on how they are doing. • Rewards that are meaningful to them: Freedom. • Their motivators: Doing good, meeting organizational goals, recognition from the boss, bonuses, and stock options.
GENERATION Y Born between **1977** and **2005**	• They are often referred to as the *realists*. • They want to build a multifaceted career. • They want help seeing the future and the role they will play in it. • Their view of feedback: Whenever they want it, at the push of a button. • Rewards that are meaningful to them: Work that has meaning for them. • Their motivators: Time off, meeting personal goals, recognition from the boss, skills training, stock options, mentoring.

Source: Adapted from Peggy Blake Gleeson, "Managing and Motivating the Generations: Implications for the Student and the Employee." [cited on 28 December 2005]. Available from http://www.uwsp.edu/education/facets/links_resource/4413.pdf; INTERNET; "Motivating Generation Y," *Management Issue News* [cited on 28 December 2005]. Available from http://www.management-issues.com; INTERNET.

Learning about the various generations helps you individualize your interactions with them, regardless of your generation. Whether you are a member of one of the older generations or of the younger generations, the majority of the work force of the future will include Generation X and Y workers. If you are one of them, manage them, or are managed by them, it will be critical to your

Jenny Ice, employed in the Washington office of Ernst & Young LLC, spent 12 weeks in Buenos Aires as a paid volunteer. She provided free accounting services to a small publishing firm. Ms. Ice remained on the company payroll during the time she was gone, and her job as a business advisory services manager was waiting for her when she got back. She describes the experience as among "the best three months of her life."

career to adjust your human relations skills accordingly. Some generalizations may be helpful[28]:

- They are more comfortable with diversity.
- They seek opportunities for team collaboration and knowledge sharing.
- They prefer to work with the newest technology.
- They expect rewards based on productivity, not hours at their desk.
- They prefer frequent feedback. Coach them, don't lecture them.
- They are more comfortable with limited bureaucracy. Do not burden them with corporate policies and excessive meetings.

Skill Development: Apply It

Identify at least one friend or family member from each of the generations discussed previously. Visualize them working for you as you enter a major project with a budget that allows no extra compensation for the additional work you will expect of them. List the ways you would motivate them to put forth their full efforts. Now, interview each of the people you identified and confirm whether your motivational techniques would work. Be prepared to share insights with your classmates.

Self-Motivation Strategies

The material presented in this chapter explains how, why, when, and where motivation strategies work, and we have identified many organizations that do all they can to motivate their employees to stay on the job and to improve their productivity. However, let's face it—some organizations just don't care if you are motivated or not, as long as you get your job done. If you are satisfied with your life and work, that's great! If you are yearning for a more exciting professional and/or personal life, guess what? It's up to you! The following self-motivation strategies can help you achieve your potential.

Nurture a Gritty Nature

What factors will contribute most to your future success? A series of recent studies indicate that the quality of **grit**, in the form of hard work and determination, is a major indicator of success. Intelligence accounts for only a fraction of the success formula. Grit has value for people at all levels of ability.[29]

Research conducted by University of Pennsylvania faculty members found that grit is the premier attribute for surviving the grueling first summer of training at West Point. Gritty people tend to be highly self-disciplined and focused on goal achievement. They also bring passion to their tasks. Lance Armstrong entered his first distance running race at age ten. He won, and within three years, he was winning swim meets and other forms of athletic competition. In his autobiography, *It's Not About the Bike*, he says, "If it was a suffer-fest, I was good at it."[30]

How do you nurture grit? Self-discipline, an important part of grit, can be achieved by refraining from doing something. M. Scott Peck, author of the best-selling book *The Road Less Traveled*, told his readers that delaying gratification was "the only decent way to live." Early in life, we are encouraged (or required by our parents) to complete our homework before watching television. Later in life, we have to make hard decisions on our own and become self-disciplined. Should I stay with my diet or throw in the towel? Should I stay home and study for an exam or go drinking with friends? Should I add to my credit-card debt or refrain from buying that wide screen television? With a measure of self-discipline, we can learn to schedule the pain first (using Peck's words) and enjoy the pleasure later.[31]

Go Outside Your Comfort Zone. Many people do not achieve their full potential because they are afraid to venture outside their "comfort zone." These individuals often earn less than they deserve, exert little effort to win a promotion to a more challenging position, and refuse assignments that might enhance their career. Some people stay in their comfort zone because they fear success. If someone says, "You can never do this," or, "It's never been done," consider accepting the challenge implicit in these statements.

Strive for Balance. Self-motivation often decreases when we no longer have a sense of balance in our lives. To achieve balance between your work and personal life, take time to reflect on what is most important to you, and then try to make the necessary adjustments. Employees at Miller & Associates, a Dallas wholesaler

Self-motivation often decreases when we no longer have a sense of balance in our lives.

of kitchen equipment, complete annual "life-purpose" statements. Each person records the ten most satisfying experiences in his or her life, making note of those that carry special meaning. When David Rogers, a salesperson, finished his "life-purpose" statements, he realized that he wasn't taking time to do some of the things he most valued. He said, "I was so weighted toward work that it was getting in the way of work." Once he cut back on his hours, freeing up time for his social life, his sales actually increased.[32]

CAREER INSIGHT

Invisible Work

In the information age, it can be harder to find gratification from work that is largely invisible. Work is harder to measure, so it's more difficult to measure success; a lot of work gets done in teams, so it is difficult to pinpoint individual productivity. Many workers today must rely on themselves to know if they are doing worthwhile work.

Take Action. If you are feeling bored or trapped in a dead-end job, you can enhance your self-motivation by taking responsibility for the situation you are in and then taking action to improve it. Taking personal responsibility for your current situation is not easy because change can be threatening. Don't just wait and hope that things get better. Do something!

- Instead of waiting to see what will happen, volunteer for a project or make a request.
- Have lunch with the person in your organization who is doing work that you find intriguing.
- Talk to your boss about the things you want to do.
- Follow up on an idea you have had for a long time.
- Read a book, attend a conference, or do something else that will help you grow and learn.[33]

LOOKING BACK: REVIEWING THE CONCEPTS

- Understand the complex nature of motivation.

Motivation is a major component of human relations training because it provides a framework for understanding why people do the things they do. Internal motivation occurs when the task or duty performed is in itself a reward. External motivation is initiated by another person and usually is based on rewards or other forms of reinforcement for a job well done.

Motives are individualistic and can change over the years. In many cases, people are not aware of the factors that motivate their behaviors. Because there is no valid measure of a person's motives, motives can only be inferred. Motives vary in strength and importance and are therefore hierarchical.

- Describe five of the most influential theories of motivation.

Maslow's hierarchy of needs theory states that physiological needs will come first, followed by safety and security, social, esteem, and then self-actualization needs. According to Maslow, although any need can be a motivator, only higher-order needs will motivate people over the long run.

Herzberg's motivation-maintenance theory contends that when motivational factors such as responsibility, recognition, and opportunity for advancement are not present, employees will demand improvement in maintenance factors such as higher salaries, more benefits, and better working conditions.

Expectancy theory is based on the assumption that personal expectations, as well as the expectations of others, have a powerful influence on a person's motivation. These expectations can become self-fulfilling prophecies. Managers can motivate employees by expressing belief in their abilities and talents.

McGregor's Theory X/Theory Y suggests that managers use two distinct motivational strategies when they attempt to motivate workers toward the goals of the organization. Theory X managers believe that people do not really want to work so they must be pushed, closely supervised, and prodded into doing things. Theory Y managers believe that people want to work and are willing to accept and seek responsibility if they are rewarded for doing so.

Goal-setting theory suggests that people become more focused and persistent if they establish specific, realistic goals in cooperation with their supervisors.

- List and describe contemporary motivation strategies.

Contemporary organizations attempt to motivate their employees through positive expectations and job design modifications such as job rotation, job enlargement, and job enrichment. They are also discovering the effects of various incentives, intrapreneurship opportunities, additional training, and empowerment.

- Identify motivating factors important to individuals from different generations.

There are specific strategies that can be used to motivate workers from various age brackets such as the Matures, the Baby Boomers, Generation X, and Generation Y. Once you understand their motivating factors, you can individualize your interactions with them and enhance your interpersonal relations skills, regardless of your age.

- Describe selected self-motivation strategies.

People must make their own plans to keep themselves motivated. They can nurture their grit, move beyond their comfort zone, strive for balance between their professional and personal lives, and take action.

ON THE JOB Q & A: SELLING TELECOMMUTING TO YOUR BOSS

Q: I love what I do, but I hate where I work. My workplace is very old, has no windows, and is very depressing. Besides, the two-hour commute is killing me! I've been with the company almost six months, and I hate to leave because the money and benefits are great, but I believe I can do my work from my home. When I asked my supervisor if she would consider allowing me to telecommute, she said her company tried that several years ago and it just didn't work.

A: For decades, managers have relied on the ability to walk past an employee's work area and *see* that the job is being done. Happily, that tradition has changed. Many managers have discovered that telecommuters are no more difficult to manage than in-house workers. Conduct your own research on the success of other organizations' telecommuting programs and learn about the sophisticated technology that will enhance your ability to fulfill your responsibilities to the organization. Succinctly present your findings to your supervisor. Remember to keep *her* needs in mind, not just yours. Employers know how difficult it can be to find and keep good workers, and they know that a happy worker is a productive worker. Suggest a 90-day trial period. If you or your employer is not satisfied with the arrangement, discontinue it. If you like the telecommuting arrangement and disagree with the decision to bring you back on site, take your skills elsewhere to an environment that will motivate you to do your best work.[34]

KEY TERMS

motivation 142
internal motivation 143
external motivation 143
incentives 143
hierarchy of needs 146
motivation-maintenance theory 148
maintenance factors 148
motivational factors 148
expectancy theory 149
self-fulfilling prophecy 149
job rotation 150
job enlargement 151
job enrichment 151
intrapreneurship 152
empowerment 153
grit 156

TRY YOUR HAND

1. How much grit have you got? On a scale of one to five, rate how well the following statements describe you. In the first section, a five is *strongly agree* and a one is *strongly disagree*. In the second section, the scoring is reversed: One is *strongly agree* and five is *strongly disagree*. Total your score and divide the total by six. If you score over 3.5, consider yourself gritty.[35]

	STRONGLY AGREE	AGREE	MODERATELY AGREE	DISAGREE	STRONGLY DISAGREE
I'm a hard worker.	5	4	3	2	1
Setbacks don't deter me.	5	4	3	2	1
I am now working on a project that may take years to finish.	5	4	3	2	1
I get interested in new pursuits every few months	1	2	3.	4	5
People often tell me that I don't perform to my potential.	1	2	3	4	5
New ideas and new projects sometimes distract me from previous ones.	1	2	3	4	5

2. Prepare a list of all the things you wanted to accomplish during the past year but didn't. Think of activities, responsibilities, and commitments, as well as personal and professional goals. Without making excuses for your behavior, or blaming others, identify self-motivating strategies discussed in this chapter that you can implement to improve your chances of completing those tasks successfully.

3. Are you frustrated with any aspect of your personal or professional life right now? Write down a major frustration on a piece of paper, but do not put your name on it. Form a group of four or five class members who have completed the same task. Pass each other's papers randomly from group member to group member, until your instructor says stop. One at a time, each group member can describe his or

her ideas on how to overcome the frustration identified on the paper he or she is holding. At the conclusion of this exercise, describe how this "outsider's" viewpoint of your situation has influenced your thinking.

INTERNET INSIGHTS

1. Visit *http://www.betterworkplacenow.com* and review the material presented. Click on the "Ideas and Insights" tab. Which comments mean the most to you? Why?

2. Visit Great Place to Work Inc. (*http://www.greatplacetowork.com*) and read the mission of the creators of this site. Then click on the various tabs at the top of the site. What factors make an organization a "great place to work?" Click on the "Best Companies List" and review the organizations that make up the list for the past year. Would you like to pursue job opportunities in one or more of the best places to work? If your answer is yes, explain your plan of action to get a job there. If your answer is no, why not? If location is an issue, what factors are holding you back from relocating?

YOU PLAY THE ROLE

You just graduated from a prestigious college with your accounting degree and have accepted a job with a large financial institution that has tremendous career potential. You love your work but hate your job because of Marilyn, your immediate supervisor. Marilyn is highly educated, knows everything there is to know about all of the organization's products and services, but seems to know little about how to manage people. Marilyn is about 20 years older than you are and sincerely believes that you can meet your weekly and monthly goals without any feedback as to how well you are doing. Your daily routine is highly restrictive, with two 15-minute breaks and a 30-minute lunch break that must be taken at specific points on the clock. Because you are new to the organization, you feel insecure and need positive reinforcement. You are losing your self-confidence and considering quitting, but your professional goal is to build a career within this organization. Meet with one of your classmates who will play the role of Marilyn, and discuss your concerns about the lack of feedback. Also, discuss how the organization can make better use of your knowledge, skills, and abilities, which will, in turn, make Marilyn (and you) look good to the executives in charge of promotions and enhance the company's bottom line.

BELOW THE SURFACE:

Awakening the Driving Force Within

At the beginning of this chapter, we described the exceptional accomplishments of Michael Phelps at the Beijing Olympics. After many years of daily training, he won eight gold medals. His motivation to become a good swimmer was present early in life. He started swimming at age seven.

At the early age of 9, Lynne Cox began training to become a long-distance swimmer. At age 12, she tackled her first open-water swim, three miles in the rough Pacific Ocean off the coast of California. At the age of 15, she swam across the English Channel in record time. After each successful swim, she set more challenging goals, such as swimming across Alaska's Glacier Bay. This event helped prepare her for her big dream—a swim from Alaska to the Soviet Union across the Bering Strait. This challenging swim is described in the book *Swimming to Antarctica*.[36]

Lance Armstrong provides another example of strong individual motivation. In 1998, he returned to cycling after almost losing his life to cancer. His goal was to dominate the famous Tour de France. This event requires immense physical endurance. Cyclists compete in the 2,000-mile race for over three weeks and spend nearly 90 hours on the bike. Armstrong has won this event seven times.[37]

QUESTIONS

1. This chapter reveals that a person's *needs* serve as motivators toward achieving challenging goals. Analyze what you believe drives persons like Phelps, Cox, and Armstrong to achieve these extremes.
2. Your goals play a key role in bringing purpose and direction to your life. Identify the short-term goals that are currently influencing your behavior. What long-term goals do you hope to achieve in the future?

CLOSING CASE: Can Personal Tales of Adversity Fire Up the Staff?

Many companies schedule annual meetings to give employees an update on the current status of the organization and involve them in developing plans for the future. At a one-week retreat for 300 Cisco Systems Inc. finance managers, the first order of business was a series of strategy sessions. This was followed by some team building activities. Then came a visit by a blind man.

In an after-lunch speech, Erik Weihenmayer described his bitterness as a teenager over losing his sight. He explained how he channeled his anger into rock climbing and dreamed of climbing Mount Everest. After some brief introductory comments, managers of the computer-networking company watched a video that showed Mr. Weihenmayer picking his way past deep crevasses until he reached the top of Mount Everest. Near the end of his presentation, he told the audience it is possible to use adversity to propel you forward.[38]

Several years ago, Plug Power Inc., an alternative energy company, was facing serious economic problems. The company was an energy success story in 2000, with stock briefly trading at $150 a share. A few years later, the company's shares had declined to single digit levels. Roger Saillant, CEO, decided Plug Power employees needed to hear an inspirational speaker. He spent $5,000 to bring Trisha Meili to its corporate office in Latham, New York. In 1989, Meili was assaulted in Central Park and left for dead. After a long recovery, she published her memoirs and began her speaking career. She tells her audiences about learning to walk again after spending months in a coma. She had been in a near-death state but was able to make a recovery. Saillant says she struck a chord with Plug Power employees who were working hard to keep the company alive.[39]

Today, organizations are spending hundreds of millions a year on speakers. These speaker lists include Mia Hamm (U.S. Women's Gold Medal Soccer Team), Greg Gadson (decorated U.S. Army Commander), Erin Brockovich (whistleblower), and many others.

QUESTIONS

1. Many inspirational speakers attempt to take the audience on an emotional journey. They try to erase cynicism and complacency and get employees fired up about their jobs. Do you think organizations should rely on inspirational speakers to build passion among their workers during challenging times? Discuss your answer.
2. Let's assume your company has spent a large sum of money to bring in Lance Armstrong. He makes an enthusiastic presentation and receives a standing ovation. Define what steps your company would need to take to ensure that this enthusiasm transfers back on the job during the weeks and months ahead. Be specific as you describe your recommendations.

Note: To learn more about available speakers, visit Leading Authorities Speakers Bureau at *http://www.leadingauthorities.com* and Brooks International at *http://www.brooksinternational.com.*

INTEGRATED RESOURCES

VIDEOS:

Motivating Employees: Empowered and Appreciated
Alternative Work Arrangements at Hewlett-Packard

CLASSROOM ACTIVITIES

IRM Application Exercise 7.1
IRM Application Exercise 7.2

PART 3

Personal Strategies for Improving Human Relations

Chapter 8
Improving Interpersonal Relations with Constructive Self-Disclosure

Chapter 9
Achieving Emotional Balance in a Chaotic World

Chapter 10
Building Stronger Relationships with Positive Energy

Chapter 11
Developing a Professional Presence

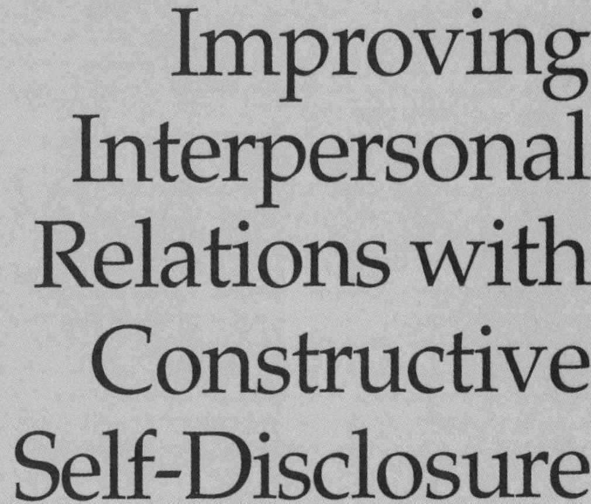

CHAPTER 8

Improving Interpersonal Relations with Constructive Self-Disclosure

CHAPTER PREVIEW

LEARNING OBJECTIVES

After studying Chapter 8, you will be able to

- Explain how constructive self-disclosure contributes to improved interpersonal relationships and teamwork.
- Understand the specific benefits you can gain from self-disclosure.
- Identify and explain the major elements of the Johari Window model.
- Explain the criteria for appropriate self-disclosure.
- Understand the barriers to constructive self-disclosure.
- Apply your knowledge and practice constructive self-disclosure.

© Medioimages/Photodisc/Getty Images

TIP OF THE ICEBERG

Pride Goes before a Fall

Pride that borders on arrogance or conceit can be a major barrier to good interpersonal relations. Jim Teeters learned this lesson the hard way. He accepted a part-time job teaching a beginning-level sociology course at a local community college. In his mind, this teaching assignment was a "step down" from his previous college teaching position. He approached his class with a smug attitude, thinking that these local students were no match for the bright students he was used to teaching.

The class meetings were going well until he started teaching a lesson on the statistical aspects of social research. Suddenly, he felt confused and started rambling. Student expressions turned from interest to confusion. Teeters was not sure how to proceed, so he instructed students to get into their assigned study groups and discuss the material he had just covered. He quickly walked to a nearby restroom and scooped handfuls of water into his dry mouth.

During the weekend, he reflected on the relationship he had established with his students. He was awash with shame and thought about quitting his teaching job. During church services on Sunday, Teeters began crying. The healing process started on that Sunday morning.

At the next meeting with his students he showed a video entitled, *Hello, I Need to Tell You Something.* As the video ended, he said to his students, "Hello, I need to tell you something." Teeters then told them the whole story. He admitted that he had failed to put his students' learning in front of his own need for recognition: "The class not only forgave me, but they also thanked

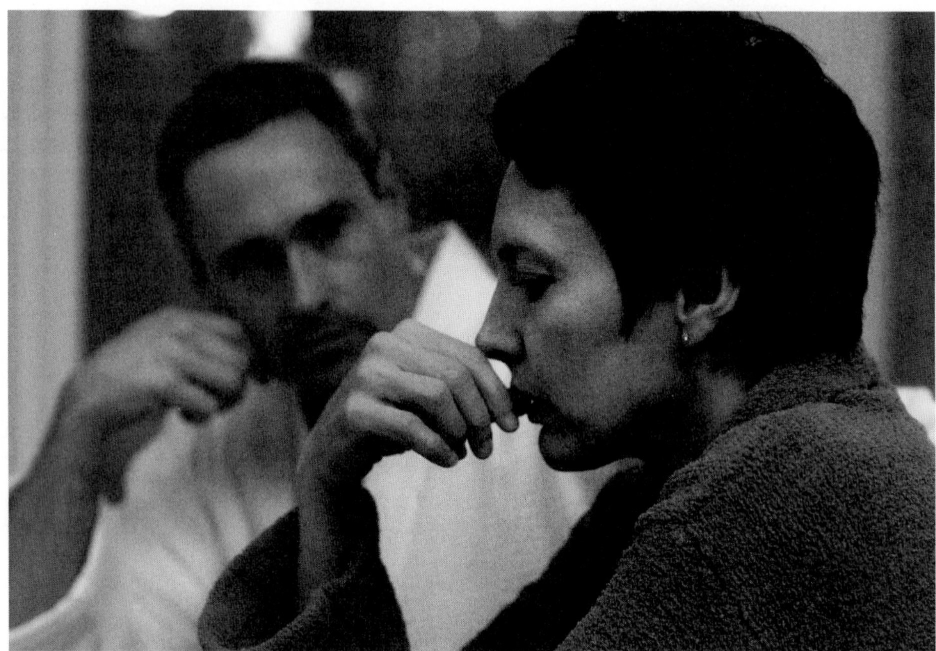
David Burch/Getty Images

Revealing one's thoughts, feelings, and needs to another person involves some risk, but the benefits of stronger, healthier relationships with others makes self-disclosure an important process on and off the job.

me for teaching them a wonderful lesson through my self-disclosure. They had never known a professor who was willing to be so 'real' with them."[1]

Self-disclosure, when it comes from the heart, can deepen relationships at home and at work. However, this form of communication can be difficult. Expressing personal thoughts and feelings to a coworker, friend, or family member is often very challenging.

Self-Disclosure: An Introduction

As a general rule, relationships grow stronger when people are willing to reveal more about themselves and their work experiences. It is a surprising but true fact of life that two people can work together for many years and never really get to know each other. In many organizations, the culture encourages employees to hide their true feelings. The result is often a weakening of the communication process. Self-disclosure can lead to a more open and supportive environment in the workplace.

In some cases, self-disclosure takes the form of an apology or of granting forgiveness to someone who apologizes to you. If you are a supervisor or manager, self-disclosure may take the form of constructive criticism of an employee whose performance is unsatisfactory. This chapter focuses on constructive self-disclosure and on conditions that encourage appropriate self-disclosure in a work setting.

Self-Disclosure Defined

Self-disclosure is the process of letting another person know what you think, feel, or want. It is one of the important ways you let yourself be known by others. Self-disclosure can improve interpersonal communication, resolve conflict, and strengthen interpersonal relationships.

It is important to note the difference between self-disclosure and self-description. **Self-description** involves disclosure of nonthreatening information, such as your age, your favorite food, or where you went to school. This is information that others could acquire in some way other than by your telling them. Self-disclosure, by contrast, often involves some degree of risk. When you practice self-disclosure, you reveal private, personal information that cannot be acquired from another source. Examples include your feelings about being a member of a minority group, job satisfaction, and new policies and procedures.

The importance of self-disclosure, in contrast to self-description, is shown by the following situation. You work at a distribution center and are extremely conscious of safety. You take every precaution to avoid work-related accidents. But another employee has a much more casual attitude toward safety rules and often "forgets" to observe the proper procedures, endangering you and other workers. You can choose to disclose your feelings to this person or stay silent. Either way, your decision has consequences.

Benefits Gained from Self-Disclosure

Before we discuss self-disclosure in more detail, let us examine four basic benefits you gain from openly sharing what you think, feel, or want.

1. *Increased accuracy in communication.* Self-disclosure often takes the guesswork out of the communication process. No one is a mind reader; if people conceal how they really feel, it is difficult for others to know how to respond to them appropriately. People who are frustrated by a heavy workload and loss of balance in their life, but mask their true feelings, may never see the problem resolved. The person who is in a position to solve this problem may be oblivious to what's important to you—unless you spell it out.

Self-disclosure often takes the guesswork out of the communication process.

Total Person Insight

Marshall Goldsmith
Author, *What Got You Here Won't Get You There*

"If you look back at tattered relationships in your life, I suspect many began to fray at the moment when one person couldn't summon the emotional intelligence to say: 'I'm sorry.' People who can't apologize at work may well be wearing a T-shirt that says: 'I don't care about you.'"[2]

2. *Reduction of stress.* Sidney Jourard, a noted psychologist who wrote extensively about self-disclosure, states that too much emphasis on privacy and concealment of feelings creates stress within an individual. Too many people keep their thoughts and feelings bottled-up inside, which can result in considerable inner tension. When stress indicators such as blood pressure,

perspiration, and breathing increase, our immune function declines. The amount of stress that builds within us depends on what aspects of ourselves we choose to conceal. If you compulsively think about a painful human relations problem but conceal your thoughts and feelings, the consequence will likely be more stress in your life.[3]

Your supervisor asks you to work late to help complete a project your coworkers fumbled. You must put in overtime without extra pay and with little appreciation. If you do your usual good job, there is a good chance you will get more worked dumped on you. Do you discuss the problem with your boss or simply hide your feelings of bitterness?[4]

3. *Increased self-awareness*. Chapter 1 stated that self-awareness is one of the major components of emotional intelligence at work. Daniel Goleman, author of *Working with Emotional Intelligence*, defines **self-awareness** as the ability to recognize and understand your moods, emotions, and drives, as well as their effect on others.[5] Self-awareness is the foundation on which self-development is built. To plan an effective change in yourself, you must be in touch with how you behave, the factors that influence your behavior, and how your behavior affects others. A young Asian associate at a financial services firm learned from her supervisor that she was perceived as not being assertive enough in her dealings with clients. As she reflected on this feedback and listened to views expressed by her female peers, the associate became aware of how her cultural background influenced her communication with clients. This feedback motivated her to modify her communication style.[6]

   The quality of feedback from others depends to a large degree on how much you practice self-disclosure. The sharing of thoughts and feelings with others often sets the stage for meaningful feedback (see Figure 8.1).

4. *Stronger relationships*. Another reward from self-disclosure is the strengthening of interpersonal relationships. When two people engage in an open, authentic dialogue, they often develop a high regard for each other's views. Often they discover they share common interests and concerns, and these serve as a foundation for a deeper relationship.

   In too many organizations, workers feel they must be careful about what they say and to whom they say it. David Stewart, organizational consultant, says people long for a work environment in which they can say what is on their mind in an honest and straightforward manner. They yearn for an authentic kind of interaction with their boss and coworkers.[7]

5. *Increased authenticity*. "People trust you when you are genuine and authentic, not a replica of someone else." These words of wisdom come to us from Bill

FIGURE 8.1 **Self-Disclosure/Feedback/Self-Awareness Cycle**

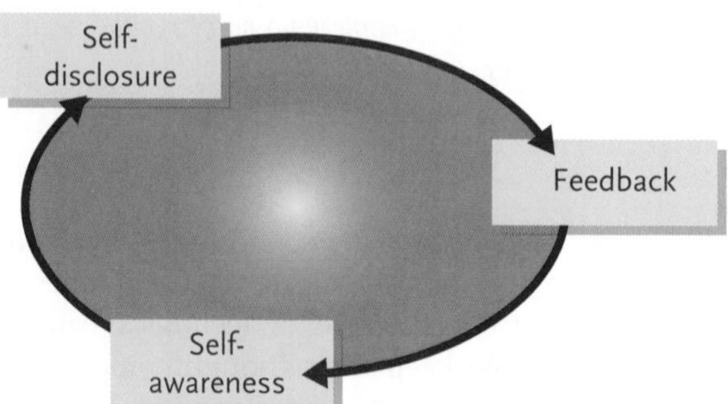

George, noted author and consultant in the area of authentic leadership.[8] Jack Welch, a highly successful CEO at General Electric for many years, says the most powerful thing you can do to get ahead is to be real[9]: "Think of authenticity as your foundation, your center, and don't let any organization try to wring it out of you, subtly or otherwise."

Authenticity has been defined as the unimpeded operation of one's true or core self in one's daily interactions with others. It requires acting in ways congruent with your own values and needs. Authenticity is necessary for close relationships because intimacy cannot develop without openness and honesty.[10]

CRITICAL THINKING CHALLENGE:

Evaluate It

Throughout life there are occasions when we feel great frustration over an incident and some type of self-disclosure is an option for improving the situation. Reflect on some frustrating personal or work-related events that occurred in the past. Did you use self-disclosure to achieve some degree of personal satisfaction? If so, were your efforts successful or unsuccessful?

The Johari Window: A Model for Self-Understanding

The first step in understanding the process of self-disclosure is to look at the **Johari Window**, illustrated in Figure 8.2. The word *Johari* is a combination of the first names of the model's originators: Joseph Luft and Harry Ingham. This

FIGURE 8.2 Johari Window

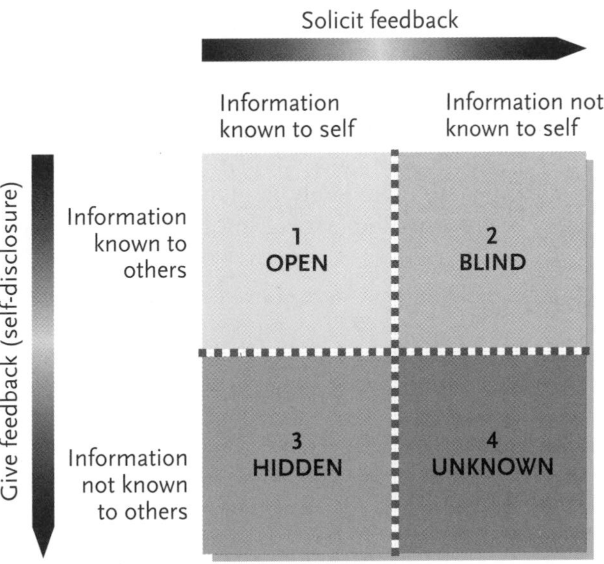

Source: From Joseph Luft, *Group Processes: An Introduction to Group Dynamics*. Copyright © 1984. Reprinted by permission of The McGraw-Hill Companies.

communication model takes into consideration that there is some information you know about yourself and other information you are not yet aware of. In addition, there is some information that others know about you and some they are not aware of. Your willingness or unwillingness to engage in self-disclosure, as well as to listen to feedback from others, has a great deal to do with your understanding of yourself and with others' understanding of you.[11]

The Four Panes of the Johari Window

The Johari Window identifies four kinds of information about you that affect your communication with others. Think of the entire model as representing your total self as you relate to others. The Johari Window is divided into four panes, or areas, labeled (1) open, (2) blind, (3) hidden, and (4) unknown.[12]

Open Area. The **open area** of the Johari Window represents your "public" or "awareness" area. This section contains information about you that both you and others know and includes information that you do not mind admitting about yourself. As your relationship with another person matures, the open pane gets bigger, reflecting your desire to be known.

The open pane is generally viewed as the part of the relationship that influences effective interpersonal relations. Therefore, a productive interpersonal relationship is related to the amount of mutually held information. Building a relationship with another person involves working to enlarge the open area. As self-awareness and sharing of information and feelings increase, the open pane becomes larger.

Blind Area. The **blind area** consists of information about yourself that others know but you are not aware of. Others may see you as aloof and stuffy, whereas you view yourself as open and friendly. Or you may view your performance at work as mediocre, and others see it as above average. You may consider your dress and grooming practices appropriate for work, but others feel your appearance is not suitable for such a setting. Information in the blind area is acquired when you learn about people's perceptions of you.

Building a relationship and improving interpersonal effectiveness often involve working to enlarge the open pane and reduce the size of the blind pane. This can be achieved as you become more self-disclosing and thereby encourage others to disclose more of their thoughts and feelings to you (see Figure 8.1). People are more likely to give feedback to a person who is open and willing to share appropriate personal information with them.

> ## *Total Person Insight*
>
> THOMAS MOORE
> Author, *A Life's Work*
>
> *"As long as you sit on your power to forgive, you suppress your joy in life."*[13]

Hidden Area. The **hidden area** contains information about you that you know but others do not. This pane is made up of all those private feelings, needs, and past experiences that you prefer to keep to yourself. These could be incidents that occurred early in life or past work-related experiences you would rather not share.

Sometimes people spend too much effort building a wall of separation between their inner and outer lives. They conceal too much private information, leading others to ask, "Is this person the same on the inside as he presents himself on the outside?" If we perceive in others—or they in us—a lack of *authenticity*, human relations problems are more likely to occur. It's very difficult to mask who we are because the people we work with are usually adept at discerning our thoughts, values, and beliefs.[14]

Unknown Area. The **unknown area** of the Johari Window is made up of things unknown to you and others. Because you, and others, can never be known completely, this area never completely disappears. The unknown may represent such factors as unrecognized talents, unconscious motives, or early childhood memories that influence your behavior but are not fully understood. Many people have abilities that remain unexplored throughout their lives. A person capable of rising to the position of department manager may remain a receptionist throughout his or her career because the potential for advancement is unrecognized. You may possess the talent to become an artist or musician but never discover it.

The Importance of Self-Awareness

Marshall Goldsmith, one of America's preeminent executive coaches, was hired to work with a very successful employee who treated direct reports and colleagues like "gravel in a driveway." Goldsmith says, "They were the pebbles; he was the SUV." Although this person was delivering outstanding results for the company, he was offending many of the employees he worked with. During the first meeting with Mike (not his real name), Goldsmith asked, "How do you treat people at home?" Mike insisted he was a great husband and father. He said, "I'm a warrior on Wall Street but a pussycat at home." Goldsmith suggested they call his wife and ask her how she viewed his behavior at home. When she finally stopped laughing at her husband's assessment, she confirmed that Mike was a jerk at home, too. His two sons also agreed with their mother. Once Mike realized how he was perceived by family members and coworkers, he made a commitment to change. Within a year his treatment-of-people scores on a standardized instrument improved dramatically—and so did his income.[15]

Some of the unknown information that is below the surface of awareness can be made public with the aid of open communication. Input from others (teachers, mentors, or supervisors) can reduce the size of the unknown pane and increase the size of the open area.

The four panes of the Johari Window are interrelated. As you change the size of one pane, others are affected. At the beginning of a relationship, the open area is likely to be somewhat small. When you start a new job, for example, your relationship with your supervisor and other workers may involve a minimum of open communication. As time passes and you develop a more open relationship with coworkers, the open area should grow larger.

Self-Disclosure/Feedback Styles

Our relationship with others is influenced by two communication processes over which we have control. We can consciously make an effort to self-disclose our thoughts, ideas, and feelings when such action would improve the relationship. And we can also act to increase the amount of feedback from others. Figure 8.3a represents a self-disclosure/feedback style that reflects minimum use of self-disclosure and feedback processes. This style represents an impersonal approach

FIGURE 8.3 Johari Window at the Beginning of a Relationship (a) and After a Closer Relationship Has Developed (b)

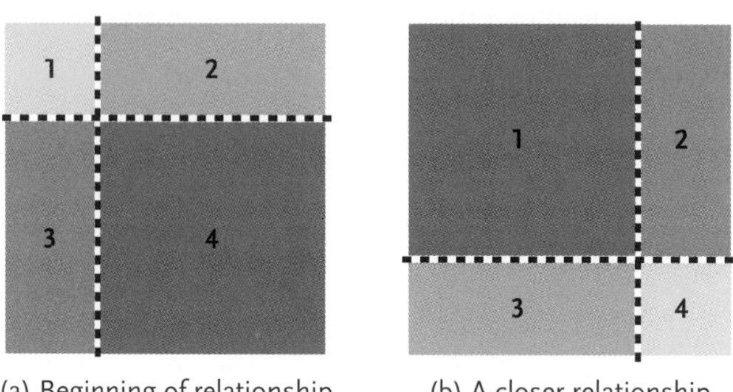

(a) Beginning of relationship (b) A closer relationship

Source: From Joseph Luft, *Group Processes: An Introduction to Group Dynamics.*

to interpersonal relations, one that involves minimal sharing of information. Figure 8.3b represents a self-disclosure/feedback style that reflects considerable use of self-disclosure and feedback. Candor, openness, and mutual respect are characteristics of this style.

You can take positive steps to develop a larger open window (Figure 8.3b) by displaying a receptive attitude when others attempt to give you feedback. Openness to feedback from supervisors and coworkers, as opposed to defensiveness, is an important key to success in the workplace. If you become defensive, this behavior is likely to cut off the flow of information you need to be more effective in your job. You can also actively solicit feedback from your supervisor and coworkers so that they will feel comfortable in giving it to you.

360-Degree Feedback. Many organizations are using an assessment strategy known as **360-degree feedback**. With this approach, employees are rated by persons who have had opportunities to observe their performance. The person who completes the feedback form may be the immediate boss, coworkers, team members, and, in some cases, even customers, clients, or patients. The feedback is generally anonymous and often provides valuable insights regarding a worker's talents and shortcomings.

Although 360-degree feedback programs are often successful, some poorly planned and implemented programs have resulted in heightened tensions and low morale. Some rating forms look too much like a report card. The multi-rater instrument should give raters an opportunity to designate the areas most in need of development. In an ideal situation, the person being reviewed will receive a feedback-summary report and help developing a plan for growth in areas that need improvement.[16]

What are some characteristics that might be included in a 360-degree evaluation form? Here are a few examples:[17]

Gratitude: Expresses thanks and gratitude genuinely.

Listening: Listens well to others before speaking.

Unity: Accepts others and works in harmony with a team.

Attention: Pays careful attention in all situations.

Appropriate Self-Disclosure

At the beginning of this chapter, we stated that the primary goal of self-disclosure should be to build stronger relations. Self-disclosure is also a condition for emotional health, according to Sidney Jourard. These goals (strong relationships and good emotional health) can be achieved if you learn how to disclose in constructive ways. Appropriate self-disclosure is a skill that anyone can learn. However, developing this skill often means changing attitudes and behaviors that have taken shape over a lifetime.

In the search for criteria for developing appropriate self-disclosure, many factors must be considered. How much information should be disclosed? How intimate should the information be? Who is the most appropriate person with whom to share information? Under what conditions should the disclosures be made? In this section, we examine several criteria that will help you develop your self-disclosure skills.

Use Self-Disclosure to Repair Damaged Relationships

Many relationships at work and in our personal life are unnecessarily strained. The strain often exists because people refuse to talk about real or imagined problems. Self-disclosure can be an excellent method of repairing a damaged relationship.

Throughout your career, you will encounter countless workplace defeats. Your boss said she would love to give you a salary increase but didn't have the authority to approve raises. Later, you find out that she lied. You miss a team meeting because of an illness. Later, you find out that a team member was highly

Many people personalize their work area with art, family pictures, awards, and other items. These things often tell us what is important to that person. Ken Viselman, chairman of Itsy Bitsy Entertainment in New York, displays many artifacts in his office. He states that, "Behind every object in my office is a story and a bit of my life."

critical of your work on an important project. Do you confront the foe or suffer in silence?

Most of us revisit the problem numerous times. The process of replaying the incident over and over in our mind is referred to in psychology circles as **rumination**. Some people are inclined to fester in a cycle of anger that results in stress, lost sleep, and loss of concentration.[18]

There will be times when something you say or something you do is highly offensive to someone else. What steps will you take to repair the damaged relationship?

Total Person Insight

Beverly Engel
Author, *The Art of Apologizing*

"Almost like magic, apology has the power to repair harm, mend relationships, soothe wounds, and heal broken hearts."[19]

The Art of Apologizing. If your actions have caused hurt feelings, anger, or deep-seated ill will, an apology is in order. A sincere apology can have a tremendous amount of healing power for both the receiver and the giver. In addition, it can set the stage for improved communications in the future. Many people avoid apologizing because they feel awkward about admitting they were wrong. If you decide to apologize to someone, the best approach is to meet with the injured party in private and own up to the wrongdoing. Do not rely on an e-mail message for an important apology. In a private setting, feelings can be exchanged with relative comfort. An effective apology will communicate the three Rs: Regret, Responsibility, and Remedy.[20]

Even in cases where your intention was not to upset or hurt someone, the apology must come from your heart.

- *Regret.* The regret that you feel must be communicated sincerely. Even in cases where your intention was not to upset or hurt someone, the apology must come from your heart.
- *Responsibility.* Do not make excuses or blame others for what you did. Don't say, "I'm sorry about what happened, but you shouldn't have..." You must accept total responsibility for your actions.
- *Remedy.* A meaningful apology should include a commitment that you will not repeat the behavior. It might also include an offer of restitution.

The Art of Forgiveness. If someone you work with, a friend, or a family member, offers a sincere apology, be quick to forgive. Forgiveness is almost never easy, especially when you feel you have been wronged. But forgiveness is the only way to break the bonds of blame and bitterness. To forgive means to give up resentment and anger. D. Patrick Miller, author of *A Little Book of Forgiveness,* says: "To carry an anger against anyone is to poison your own heart, administering more toxin every time you replay in your mind the injury done to you." He also says forgiveness provides healing and liberates your energy and your creativity.[21]

When you convey an apology to someone or forgive another person, remember that you reveal a great deal through nonverbal messages. The emotion in your voice, as well as your eye contact, gestures, and body posture, will communicate a great deal about your inner thoughts.

Present Constructive Criticism with Care

Constructive criticism is a form of self-disclosure that helps another person look at his or her own behavior without putting that individual on the defensive. Constructive criticism is not the same as blaming. Blaming people for mistakes will seldom improve the situation.

Many people are very sensitive and are easily upset when they receive criticism. However, giving criticism effectively is a skill that can be mastered through learning and practice. Here are two effective methods for giving constructive criticism. First, avoid starting your message with "You," such as "You didn't complete your monthly inventory report" or "You never take our customer service policies seriously." For better results, replace "You-statements" with "I-statements." Say, "I am concerned that you have not completed your monthly inventory report." Another way to avoid defensiveness is to request a specific change in the future instead of pointing out something negative in the past. Instead of saying, "You did not have authorization to order office supplies," try saying, "In the future, please obtain authorization before ordering office supplies."[22]

CAREER INSIGHT

The Dangers of Over Sharing

Many nervous job seekers blabber endlessly about irrelevant information. They create a poor impression and cut short the hiring manager's time for further questions. "Oversharing in an interview is the most dangerous thing you can do," says Anne Stevens, a managing partner at ClearRock, a Boston executive-coaching firm.[23]

Discuss Disturbing Situations as They Happen

You should share reactions to a work-related problem or issue as soon after the incident as possible. It is often difficult to recapture a feeling once it has passed, and you may distort the incident if you let too much time go by. Your memory is not infallible. The person who erred is also likely to forget details about the situation.

If something really bothers you, do not delay expressing your feelings. Clear the air as soon as possible so you can enjoy greater peace of mind. Some people maintain the burden of hurt feelings and resentment for days, weeks, or even years. The avoidance of self-disclosure usually has a negative effect on a person's mental and physical health as well as on-the-job performance.

"Let's offer an apology, but without expressing contrition, regret or responsibility."

Accurately Describe Your Feelings and Emotions

It has been said that one of the most important outcomes of self-disclosure is the possibility for others to become acquainted with the "real" you. When you accurately describe your feelings and emotions, others get to know you better. This kind of honesty takes courage because of the risk involved. When you tell another person how you feel, you are putting a great amount of faith in that person. You are trusting the other person not to ridicule or embarrass you for the feelings you express.[24]

> Experiencing feelings and emotions is a part of being human.

Too often, people view verbalizing feelings and emotions in a work setting as inappropriate. However, emotions are an integral part of human behavior. People should not be expected to turn off their feelings the moment they arrive at work. Experiencing feelings and emotions is a part of being human. If we don't know each other, we can't be close to each other.[25]

What is the best way to report emotions and feelings? Some examples may be helpful. Let's suppose you expected to be chosen to supervise an important project, but the assignment was given to another worker. At a meeting with your boss, you might make the following statement: "For several weeks I've been looking forward to heading up this project. I guess I didn't realize that anyone else was being considered. Can you tell me why I was not given this assignment?"

Or suppose a coworker constantly borrows equipment and supplies but usually fails to return them. You might say: "Thanks for taking a few minutes to meet with me. I'm the type of person who likes to keep busy, but lately I've spent a lot of time retrieving tools and supplies you've borrowed. I've experienced a great deal of frustration and decided I should tell you how I feel."

As you report your feelings, be sure the other person realizes that your feelings are temporary and capable of change. You might say, "At this point I feel very frustrated, but I am sure we can solve the problem." Expressing anger can be especially difficult. This special challenge is discussed in Chapter 9.

Select the Right Time and Place

Remarks that otherwise might be offered and accepted in a positive way can be rendered ineffective not because of what we say but because of when and where we say it. When possible, select a time when you feel the other person is not preoccupied and will be able to give you his or her full attention. Also, select a setting free of distractions. Telephone calls or unannounced visitors can ruin an opportunity for meaningful dialogue. If there is no suitable place at work to hold the discussion, consider meeting the person for lunch away from work or talking with the person after work at some appropriate location. If necessary, make an appointment with the person to ensure that time is reserved for your meeting.

HUMAN RELATIONS IN ACTION

Sharing Feelings in the Workplace

James Farley guided Toyota's marketing efforts in the United States before becoming the marketing czar at Ford Motor Company. Ford was trying to move away from gas-guzzling SUVs and sell more fuel-efficient sedans and small cars. Ford's marketing program needed a major overhaul, and Farley seemed up to the challenge. Upon arrival at Ford Motor Company, Farley scheduled a meeting with several hundred staffers. He knew that many of these employees were not optimistic regarding Ford's future. At the meeting, Farley talked about Ford's plan to develop one global brand and the need for better communication between departments that could achieve that goal. To show that he felt people's pain, he discussed the deaths of his premature twins and of his cousin, former *Saturday Night Live* star Chris Farley. James Farley's self-disclosure of personal trials was surprising to many of the staffers who were accustomed to Ford's conservative culture.[26]

Avoid Overwhelming Others with Your Self-Disclosure

Although you should be open, do not go too far too fast. Many strong relationships are built slowly. The abrupt disclosure of highly emotional or intimate information may actually distance you from the other person, who may find your behavior inappropriate. Unrestricted "truth" can create a great deal of anxiety, particularly in an organization where people must work closely together. Dr. Joyce Brothers says we must balance the inclination to be open and honest with the need to be protective of each other's feelings. Disclosure in such areas as mental illness, domestic violence, fertility problems, or drug abuse is usually off limits at work. To be safe, it is also best to avoid expressing strong political or religious beliefs.[27]

Be careful what you disclose in online networking sites. When employers are down to a short list of candidates, they may check Facebook or MySpace to see what kind of public image you have created. Posting inappropriate photos, making bizarre statements regarding a company you worked for in the past, or chronicling your behavior at some wild party may create the image of someone who is not very mature.[28]

Barriers to Self-Disclosure in an Organizational Setting

At this point, you might be thinking, "If self-disclosure is such a positive force in building stronger human relationships, why do people avoid it so often? Why do so many people conceal their thoughts and feelings? Why are candor and openness so uncommon in many organizations?" To answer these questions, let's examine some of the barriers that prevent people from self-disclosing.

Lack of Trust

Trust is an element of both character (which includes integrity) and competence. Although trust is intangible, it is at the core of all meaningful relationships. Low-trust relationships can be very frustrating when you are attempting to get things done in a timely fashion. It often takes a disproportionate amount of time and energy to reach agreements and execute projects when trust is absent.[29]

> ***Total Person Insight***
>
> Jack Welch
> Suzy Welch
> Columnists, *BusinessWeek*
>
> *"...you just cannot work long with people you don't trust, because trust is the foundation for everything good that happens in organizations, like candor, collaboration, feedback, debate, and creativity."*[30]

Trust is a complex emotion that combines three components: caring, competency, and commitment. Consider the relationship between a doctor and his or her patient. Trust builds when the patient decides that the doctor is competent (capable of diagnosing the health problem), caring (concerned about the patient's health), and committed (willing to find a solution to the medical problem).[31] Trust between a salesperson and a customer is built upon the same three components. Customers want to do business with a salesperson who can accurately diagnose their needs, prescribe the right product, and provide excellent service after the sale.

When the trust level in an organization is low, the consequences are a culture of insecurity, high employee-turnover, marginal loyalty, and often, damaged customer relations.[32] Unfortunately, in a work environment characterized by rapid change and uncertainty caused by frequent layoffs, trust has greatly declined in many organizations. The recent wave of business scandals and a nationwide financial crisis have also undermined employee trust at many companies.

Lack of trust is the most common—and the most serious—barrier to self-disclosure. Without trust, people usually fear revealing their thoughts and feelings because the perceived risks of self-disclosure are too high. When trust is present, people no longer feel as vulnerable in the presence of another person, and communication flows more freely.[33]

Jack Gibb, in his book *Trust: A New View of Personal and Organizational Development*, points out that the trust level is the thermometer of individual and group health. When trust is present, people function naturally and openly. Without it, they devote their energies to masking their true feelings, hiding thoughts, and avoiding opportunities for personal growth.[34]

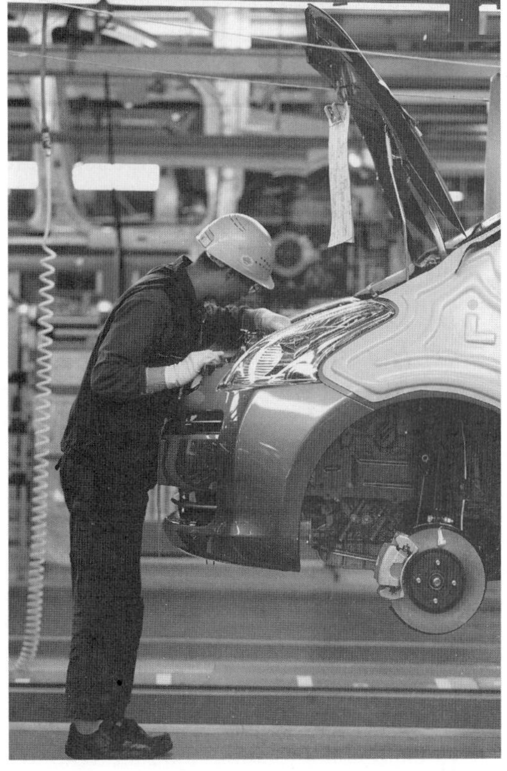
Junko Kimura/Getty Images

Toyota Motor Corporation trusts ordinary workers to run its production lines better. The company respects the problem-solving skills of every employee.

Many people spend part of their time building trust and part of their time destroying trust. Table 8.1 compares behaviors that build trust with behaviors that destroy it. Essentially, the way to build trust is to be trustworthy all the time.

Role Relationships versus Interpersonal Relationships

Self-disclosure is more likely to take place within an organization when people feel comfortable stepping outside their assigned roles and displaying openness and tolerance for the feelings of others. In our society, role expectations are often clearly specified for people engaged in various occupations. For example, some people see the supervisor's role as an impersonal one. Supervisors are supposed to enforce policies, maintain high production, and avoid getting too close to the people they supervise. The advice given to some new supervisors is "Don't try to

TABLE 8.1 HOW TRUST CAN BE BUILT AND DESTROYED

BUILDING TRUST	DESTROYING TRUST
• Openly share information.	• Withhold information.
• Admit your mistakes.	• Cover up mistakes.
• Network with coworkers.	• Keep your distance from coworkers.
• Display competence.	• Display incompetence.
• Be honest all the time.	• Be honest only some of the time.
• Be clear in your convictions.	• Avoid commitment.
• Be true to your values.	• Ignore your values.

be a nice guy, or people will take advantage of you." Yet often the most effective supervisors are those who are approachable, display a sense of humor, and take time to listen to employee problems.

Some newly appointed supervisors may deliberately try to build barriers between themselves and subordinates. They draw a sharp distinction between **role relationships** and **interpersonal relationships**. They are too impersonal and aloof, thinking that this is appropriate "role" behavior. Employees usually respond to these actions by becoming defensive or less trusting.

Roles are inescapable, but they need not contribute to the depersonalization of relationships. Each role is played by a person. Others should be able to get to know that person, regardless of the role the individual has been assigned.

Skill Development: Apply It

You have worked in the graphic design department for almost five years. About six months ago, your boss, who had been your mentor, retired and was replaced by someone who has very poor interpersonal relationship skills. Often, his attempts at communication with staff members tend to create a negative emotional wake. He frequently says, "If I were you . . ." or "You don't get it," accompanied by negative facial expressions. Sometimes he exaggerates by saying, "You always do this" or "Never once have you . . ." You have decided to meet with him and describe how uncomfortable you feel when he talks to you in such a demeaning way. On a piece of paper, write your opening statement, which should include examples of the behavior or situation you want to change. Be sure to describe the emotions that surface when he says something inappropriate. Once the statement is completed, practice saying it out loud.[35]

Practice Self-Disclosure

Many people carry around an assortment of hurt feelings, angry thoughts, and frustrations that drains them of the energy they need to cope with life's daily struggles. Although self-disclosure provides a way to get rid of this burden, some people continue through life imprisoned by negative thoughts and feelings. If you avoid disclosing your thoughts and feelings, you make it harder for others to know the real you. You will recall from the beginning of this chapter that self-disclosure involves revealing personal information that cannot be acquired from other sources. This type of information can often improve the quality of your relationships with others.

Could you benefit by telling others more about your thoughts, wants, feelings, and beliefs? To answer this question, complete Figure 8.4, which will give you an indication of your self-disclosure style. If you tend to agree with most of these items, consider making a conscientious effort to do more self-disclosing.

Becoming a more open person is not difficult if you are willing to practice.

Becoming a more open person is not difficult if you are willing to practice. If you want to improve in this area, begin by taking small steps. You might want to start with a nonthreatening confrontation with a friend or neighbor.

FIGURE 8.4 Self-Disclosure Indicator

Instructions: Read each statement and then place a checkmark (✔) in the appropriate space.

	YES	NO
1. In most cases, I avoid sharing personal thoughts and feelings with others.		
2. My relationships with others tend to be quite formal.		
3. I would not be comfortable discussing personal problems at work.		
4. I tend to avoid discussing my concerns even when feelings of frustration build inside me.		
5. I tend to avoid giving praise or criticism to others.		
6. I tend to believe that familiarity breeds contempt.		
7. I find it difficult to apologize.		
8. I find it difficult to forgive the wrongdoer.		

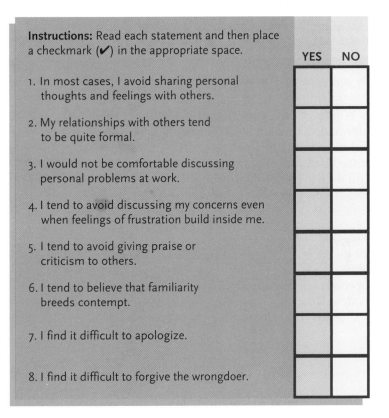

Pick someone with whom you have had a recent minor problem. Tell this person as honestly as possible how you feel about the issue or problem. Keep in mind that your objective is not simply to relate something that is bothering you, but also to develop a stronger relationship with this person.

As you gain confidence, move to more challenging encounters. Maybe you feel your work is not appreciated by your employer. Why not tell this person how you feel? If you are a supervisor and one of the people you supervise seems to be taking advantage of you, why not talk to this person openly about your thoughts? With practice you will begin to feel comfortable with self-disclosure, and you will find it rewarding to get your feelings out in the open. As you become a more open person, the people you contact will be more likely to open up and share more thoughts, ideas, and feelings with you. Everyone wins!

LOOKING BACK: REVIEWING THE CONCEPTS

- Explain how constructive self-disclosure contributes to improved interpersonal relationships and teamwork.

Open communication is an important key to personal growth and job satisfaction. Self-disclosure—the process of letting another person know what you think, feel, or want—improves communication. Most people want and need opportunities for meaningful dialogue with coworkers and the person who supervises their work.

- Understand the specific benefits you can gain from self-disclosure.

Constructive self-disclosure can pave the way for increased accuracy in communication, reduction of stress, increased self-awareness, stronger interpersonal relationships, and increased authenticity.

- Identify and explain the major elements of the Johari Window model.

The Johari Window helps you conceptualize four kinds of information areas involved in communication: The open area, what you and others know about you; the blind area, what others know about you that you do not know about yourself; the hidden area, what you know but others do not; and the unknown area, what neither you nor others know.

- Explain the criteria for appropriate self-disclosure.

Always approach self-disclosure with the desire to improve your relationship with the other person. Describe your feelings and emotions accurately, and avoid making judgments about the other person. Use self-disclosure to repair damaged relationships. It is helpful to understand the art of apologizing and the art of forgiveness.

- Understand the barriers to constructive self-disclosure.

A climate of trust serves as a foundation for self-disclosure. In the absence of trust, people usually avoid revealing their thoughts and feelings to others. Self-disclosure is more likely to take place within an organization when people feel comfortable stepping outside their assigned roles and displaying sensitivity to the feelings of others.

- Apply your knowledge and practice constructive self-disclosure.

As with learning any new skill, you can improve your ability to disclose your thoughts and feelings by starting with less threatening disclosures and proceeding slowly to more challenging situations.

ON THE JOB Q & A: IMPROVING THE SELF-EVALUATION PROCESS

Q: I am nearing my first employment anniversary, and my supervisor will soon complete my first performance appraisal. Before meeting with my boss, I will be completing a self-evaluation form. She gave me a copy of the form and said, "Be as objective as possible." Well, I am not sure how to approach this assignment. Can you give me some guidance?

A: In an ideal situation, you would have been given feedback on your performance throughout the past year. Effective supervisors document strengths and problem areas over time rather than "save them up" for the annual performance evaluation. Before completing the self-evaluation, reflect on your accomplishments for the time you have been employed. You should also review your job description. One of the best ways to approach self-evaluation is to prepare a three-part report. Part one includes major activities that consume most of your time. Part two includes a description of major accomplishments. The third part of your report might be a list of "discussion" topics, such as your ideas for improving the way work gets done. Use your self-evaluation as an opportunity to improve communication with your boss. Once you decide what approach you want to use, meet briefly with your supervisor and make sure she is comfortable with your plan.[36]

KEY TERMS

self-disclosure 166
self-description 167
self-awareness 168
authenticity 169
Johari Window 169
open area 170
blind area 170
hidden area 170
unknown area 171
360-degree feedback 172
rumination 174
constructive criticism 175
trust 178
role relationships 180
interpersonal relationships 180

TRY YOUR HAND

1. To learn more about your approach to self-disclosure, complete each of the following sentences. Once you have completed them all, reflect on your written responses. Can you identify any changes in your approach to self-disclosure that would improve communications with others? Are there any self-disclosure skills that you need to practice?
   a. "For me, the major barrier to self-disclosure is …"
   b. "To establish a more mutually trusting relationship with others, I need to …"
   c. "In order to receive more feedback from others, I need to …"
   d. "In situations where I should apologize for something or voice forgiveness, I tend to …"

2. On Friday afternoon, a coworker visits your office and requests a favor. She wants you to review a proposal she will give to her boss on Monday morning at 10:00 a.m. You agree to study the proposal sometime over the weekend and give her feedback on Monday before her meeting. You put a photocopy of the proposal in your briefcase and take it home. Over the weekend, you get busy and forget to review the proposal. In fact, you are so busy that you never open your briefcase. On Monday morning you make a call on a customer before reporting to the office. While sitting in the customer's office, you open your briefcase and see the report. It is too late to study the report and give feedback to your coworker. Which of the following actions would you take?
   a. Try to forget the incident and avoid feeling guilty. After all, you did not intentionally avoid your obligation.
   b. Call the person's boss and explain the circumstances. Confess that you simply forgot to read the report.
   c. Meet with your coworker as soon as possible and offer a sincere apology for failing to read the report and provide the feedback.

   Provide a rationale for your choice.

3. Constructive self-disclosure is based on a foundation of trust. When the trust level is low, open and honest communication is unlikely to occur. We inspire trust by what we say and what we do. Some behaviors that inspire trust are listed below. Rate yourself with this scale: U = Usually; S = Sometimes; I = Infrequently. After you finish the self-assessment, reflect on your ability to inspire trust, and think about ways to improve yourself in this area.

	U	S	I
I disclose my thoughts and feelings when appropriate.	☐	☐	☐
I admit my mistakes.	☐	☐	☐
Others know that I keep confidences.	☐	☐	☐
I keep my promises and commitments.	☐	☐	☐
I avoid distortion of information when communicating with others.	☐	☐	☐

INTERNET INSIGHTS

1. Do you *text*, *twitter*, or *blog*? Have you been invited to join someone's *Facebook* or a *chat room*? If so, you are among millions who use technology as a vehicle for communication. These technology tools allow for anonymity as well as self-disclosure. Assess why one has difficulty

communicating face-to-face, however, will readily self-disclose on Facebook, MySpace, or in a chat room. Appraise the impact of technology on work-related communication.

2. What is the best way for a supervisor to get feedback on his or her performance? One approach is to gather your staff in a meeting room and ask, "Who loves me? Show of hands!" To obtain truly anonymous feedback on your performance, the Internet is a good bet. Several companies offer web-based 360-degree review services. Visit the online clearinghouse HR Guide (*http://www.hr-guide.com*) and review the available resources for 360-degree feedback. Prepare a brief summary of your findings.

YOU PLAY THE ROLE

To prepare for this role-play activity, review the second exercise in this chapter's Try Your Hand. You have decided to take action c, which involves a sincere apology. For the purpose of this role play, you will assume the role of Taite Edwardson. The coworker who requested your help is Tyler Johnson. In order to be well prepared for the role play, read the text material that describes the use of self-disclosure to repair damaged relationships. Keep in mind that when you apologize to someone, you reveal a great deal through nonverbal messages. The emotion in your voice, as well as your eye contact, gestures, and body posture, will communicate a great deal about your inner thoughts.

BELOW THE SURFACE:

Achieving Self-Awareness

At the beginning of this chapter, we described how Jim Teeters struggled to overcome problems related to the powerful influence of pride in his life. He felt superior to students enrolled in one of his classes at a local community college. His smug attitude was quickly altered when he discovered that he was unable to clarify the statistical aspects of social research. After this emotional experience, Teeters was ready to accept the Hebrew proverb, "Pride goes before a fall." His life was changed for the better after meeting with his students and self-disclosing his thoughts and feelings.

Increased self-awareness is an important key to achieving authenticity. We have defined self-awareness as the ability to recognize and understand your moods, emotions, and drives, as well as their effect on others. Jim Teeters discovered that pride can be a negative emotion, especially when he felt superior to others. In the classroom, he was not acting in ways congruent with his values and needs.

Authenticity requires making conscious, informed choices based on accurate self-knowledge. Benoit Vincent manages 100-plus engineers and other staff members who report to him in his role as chief technical officer at Taylor Made–Adidas Golf (TMaG). TMaG is a golf equipment and accessories company located in California. At staff meetings, he often whizzed through finely detailed technical information, ignoring the puzzled expressions of staff members. He was viewed by many employees as cynical, abrasive, and insensitive. Employee turnover was high. Then things started to change.

Benoit Vincent was one of several managers at TMaG who enrolled in a carefully designed one-on-one workplace coaching program. The starting point was the completion of the Myers-Briggs Type Indicator (MBTI) and Hogan Personal Inventory. Information generated by these instruments helped Vincent better understand his shortcomings, strengths, temperament, and preferences. He and his coach began meeting to discuss ways to improve his managerial soft skills. He read *Crucial Conversations* to discover how to communicate best when it matters most.[37]

Vincent and other TMaG managers learned how to master crucial conversations with the aid of dialogue. This is the free flow of meaning between two or more people. A crucial conversation is one which gets all relevant information from themselves and others into the open.[38]

QUESTIONS

1. It has been said that authenticity is correlated with many aspects of psychological well-being such as improving self-esteem and coping skills. How does increased self-awareness help us grow in these important areas?
2. Benoit Vincent was able to become a more effective manager after completion of certain personality profile instruments (the MBTI for example), participating in a series of one-on-one workplace coaching sessions, and learning how to conduct coaching sessions that emphasize dialogue—the free flow of meaning between two or more people. Would you recommend this type of management development program to organizations—large and small? Explain your answers.
3. Do you think Benoit Vincent would have benefited from involvement in a 360-degree multi-rater assessment program? Explain your answer.

CLOSING CASE: The Importance of Building Trust

Within the past few years, we have seen greater recognition that trust is the core of all meaningful relationships. Stephen M.R. Covey, author of *The Speed of Trust,* says that trust is the one thing that changes everything. It is the one thing, that if removed, will destroy the most successful business, the most influential leadership, the greatest friendship, the strongest character, and the deepest love.[39]

Why did Covey include the word "speed" in the title of his book? He says that trust always affects two outcomes—speed and cost. When trust goes down, speed will also go down and costs will go up. Consider the influence of trust in personal selling. When the customer and the salesperson trust each other, they will usually find ways to form a productive relationship and buying decisions will be made without delay. If the trust level is low, the customer will likely be slow to make a buying decision. The response to the salesperson's proposal may be, "I need a little more time to think about your proposal."[40]

Trust is a critical dimension of every productive team. Patrick Lencioni, author of *The Five Dysfunctions of a Team,* says the *absence of trust* is a major threat to team cohesiveness and productivity:

> *This occurs when team members are reluctant to be vulnerable with one another and are unwilling to admit their mistakes, weaknesses or need for help. Without a certain comfort level among team members, a foundation of trust is impossible.*[41]

The ideal team environment encourages every member to engage in open debate about key issues. When team members do not openly air their opinions, inferior decisions are the result.[42]

(continued)

Many teams are characterized by great diversity. This is especially true of cross-functional teams staffed by a mix of specialists who represent different departments and job levels. Diverse teams are more likely to become dysfunctional because diverse membership can create communication problems. Jeffrey Polzer, Harvard professor, has examined the fit among team members and how to optimize it. He defines "fit" as interpersonal congruence. This is "...the degree to which members' appraisals of one another are similar to their self-assessments on dimensions relevant to team functioning."[43] For example, if a team member sees himself as someone who is willing to share the credit for team success, do others see him the same way? Polzer's research has shown that high congruence improves the performance of diverse teams.

QUESTIONS

1. Stephen M.R. Covey, author of *The Speed of Trust*, says that every employee in the organization should assume responsibility for building trust. Do you agree? Is this a realistic expectation? Explain.
2. Let's assume you are a member of a productive team that has received considerable praise from top management. You learn that one member of the team has met with the manager who organized the team and taken credit for the team's success. You fear that this individual's behavior will damage the team's future productivity. What should you do to correct this problem?
3. Jeffrey T. Polzer has stated that sharing self-assessments and appraisals of one another through 360-degree feedback can help team members achieve interpersonal congruence. Do you agree with his recommendation? What steps can be taken to be sure the team members are prepared for this type of intervention?

INTEGRATED RESOURCES

CLASSROOM ACTIVITIES

IRM Application Exercise 8.1
IRM Application Exercise 8.2
IRM Application Exercise 8.3

CHAPTER 9

Achieving Emotional Balance in a Chaotic World

TIP OF THE ICEBERG

CHAPTER PREVIEW

LEARNING OBJECTIVES

After studying Chapter 9, you will be able to

- Describe how emotions influence our thinking and behavior.
- Explain the critical role of emotions in the workplace.
- Describe the major factors that influence our emotional development.
- Learn how to address your anger and the anger of others.
- Understand the factors that contribute to workplace violence.
- Identify and explain the most common emotional styles.
- Describe strategies for achieving emotional control.

Hiring a Hospitalitarian

If you travel the nation in search of a great meal, you will likely consult the Zagat restaurant survey. Zagat publishes guides that include reviews of restaurants in more than 70 cities. Zagat's survey of New York's "most popular" restaurants includes several owned by Danny Miller—Union Square Café and Gramercy Tavern, for example. In a city where competition for high Zagat ratings is practically a blood sport, how do these restaurants achieve such high ratings year after year? Danny Meyer says it's not the food that keeps guests coming back, it's the power of hospitality.[1]

Restaurant managers employed by Danny Meyer learn how to hire for a certain emotional skill set that yields what is called a *hospitalitarian.* Some of the most important emotional qualities include a natural warmth, optimism, empathy, and work ethic. Integrity and self-awareness are also important qualities. Meyer believes that these qualities are important in any service-type business: "The companies that are going to prevail realize it's the quality of the emotional experience that sets them apart."[2]

As noted in Chapter 1, our labor force is increasingly geared toward service to clients, patients, and customers. In a service economy, relationships are usually more important than products. Several national training and development organizations are offering educational programs that help workers achieve emotional balance. Fred Pryor Seminars offers *Managing Emotions Under Pressure* and the American Management Association offers *Managing Emotions in the Workplace.*

Danny Meyer has established several successful restaurants in New York City. When hiring employees he looks for certain emotional qualities such as a natural warmth, optimism, and empathy. Meyer says it is the power of hospitality that keeps customers coming back.

Emotions—An Introduction

An **emotion** is a temporary experience with either positive or negative qualities. Emotional experiences tend to alter the thought processes by directing attention toward some things and away from others. Emotions energize our thoughts and behaviors.[3] Anger, fear, love, joy, jealousy, grief, and other emotions can influence our behavior at work and in our personal world. To the extent that we can become more aware of our emotions and assess their influence on our daily lives, we have the opportunity to achieve a new level of self-understanding.

Throughout each day, our feelings are activated by a variety of events (see Figure 9.1). You might feel a sense of joy after learning that a coworker has just given birth to a new baby. You might feel overpowering grief after learning that your supervisor was killed in an auto accident. Angry feelings may surface when

FIGURE 9.1 Behavior Is Influenced by Activating Events

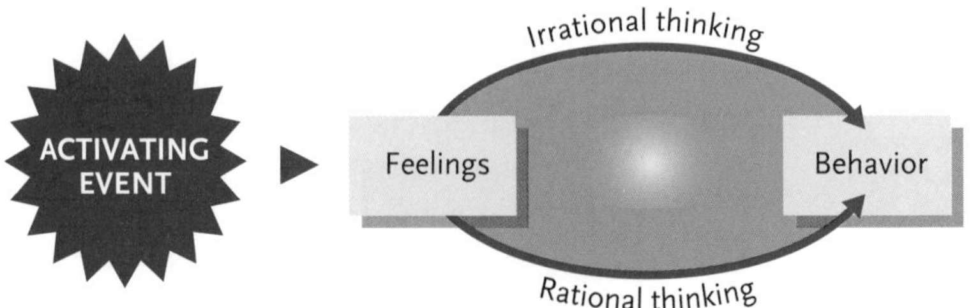

you discover that someone borrowed a tool without your permission. Once your feelings have been activated, your mind interprets the event. In some cases, the feelings trigger irrational thinking: "No one who works here can be trusted!" In other cases, you may engage in a rational thinking process: "Perhaps the person who borrowed the tool needed it to help a customer with an emergency repair." The important point to remember is that we can choose how we behave. We can gain control over our emotions.

Achieving Emotional Balance—A Daily Challenge

The need to discover ways to achieve emotional balance has never been greater, thanks to the pace of modern life. To be successful in these complex times, we need to be able to think and feel simultaneously. People make choices dictated primarily by either their heads (reason) or their hearts (feelings). The thinking function helps us see issues logically; the feeling function helps us be caring and human.[4] Many organizations are spawning fear, confusion, anger, and sadness because their leaders lack emotional balance.

The basic emotions that drive us—such as fear, love, grief, greed, joy, and anger—have scarcely changed over the years. However, we are now seeing enormous differences in the expression of emotions. Today, people are much more likely to engage in aggressive driving, misbehave at public events, or become abusive when they are unhappy with service. In the workplace, many people experience emotional pain because of disagreeable bosses or uncooperative team members.

Emotional Intelligence

Daniel Goleman, author of several popular books on emotional intelligence (EQ), challenges the traditional view of the relationship between IQ and success. He says there are widespread exceptions to the rule that IQ predicts success: "At best, IQ contributes about 20 percent to the factors that determine life success, which leaves 80 percent to other forces." **Emotional intelligence** can be described as the ability to monitor and control one's emotions and behavior at work and in social settings. Whereas standard intelligence (IQ) deals with thinking and reasoning, EQ deals more broadly with building social relationships and controlling one's emotions. Several studies indicate that EQ can be increased through a combination of awareness and training.[5] The focus of Goleman's research is the human characteristics that make up what he describes as *emotional-competence.* The emotional-competence framework is made up of two dimensions.[6]

Personal Competence. This term refers to the competencies that determine how we achieve and maintain emotional balance. The essential component of emotional intelligence is self-awareness, the ability to read one's own emotions and hence be better equipped to assess one's level of emotional maturity. Personal competence involves keeping disruptive emotions and impulses in check.

Social Competence. This refers to the competencies that determine how we handle relationships. Sensing others' thoughts, feelings and intentions; listening openly and sending convincing messages; and negotiating and resolving disagreements represent some of the competencies in this category.

Although IQ tends to be stable throughout life, emotional competence is learnable and can increase throughout our life span. For example, we can learn to manage the thoughts that influence our behavior. Our minds are capable of producing outrageously irrational mental images. We have the option of reacting to those images with irrational or rational thinking.

Emotional Expression

We sometimes suffer from a lack of emotional balance because we learn to inhibit the expression of certain emotions and to overemphasize the expression of others. Some families, for example, discourage the expression of love and affection. Some people are taught from an early age to avoid expressing anger. Others learn that a public display of grief (crying, for example) is a sign of weakness. If as a child you were strongly encouraged to avoid the expression of anger, fear, love, or some other emotion, you may repress or block these feelings as an adult.[7]

Emotional imbalance also develops if we become fixated on a single emotion. The high incidence of violent crime in America has motivated some people to become almost totally infused with the emotion of fear. To focus on one emotion to the exclusion of others creates a serious imbalance within us.

The Emotional Factor at Work

Emotions play a critical role in the success of every organization, yet many people in key decision-making positions—leaders with outstanding technical skills—fail to understand the important role emotions play in a work setting. In part, the problem can be traced to leadership training that emphasizes that "doing business" is a purely rational or logical process. Some leaders learn to value only those things that can be arranged, analyzed, and defined. One consultant put the problem into proper perspective when he said, "We are still trying to do business as if it requires only a meeting of the minds instead of a meeting of the hearts."[8]

> ***Total Person Insight***
>
> **Joan Borysenko**
> Author, *Inner Peace for Busy People*
>
> *"One moment I had been peaceful, expansive and present, thoroughly enjoying life; the next moment I was feeling deprived, crabby, and stressed. Nothing had changed except my thoughts, but that's where we live the majority of our lives."*[9]

Tim Sanders, former chief solutions officer at Yahoo! says, "How we are perceived as human beings is becoming increasingly important in the new economy." He notes that compassion is an important key to long-term personal success. This is the human ability to reach out with warmth through eye contact, physical touch, or words. It is a quality machines can never possess.[10]

Relationship Strategy

Emotional undercurrents are present in almost every area of every organization. Most banks, hospitals, retail firms, hotels, and restaurants realize that they need a relationship strategy—a plan for establishing, building, and maintaining quality relationships with customers. Cosco Systems, for example, measures itself by

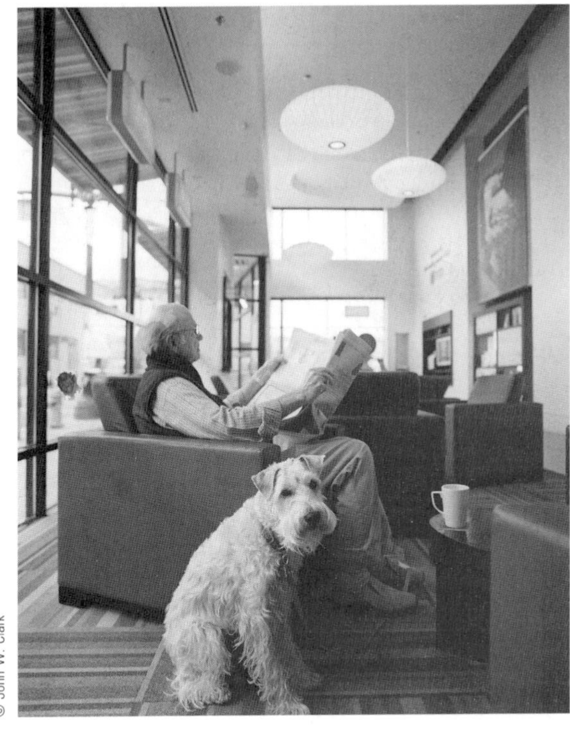
© John W. Clark

At Umpqua Bank, every element of the culture is focused on great customer service. Here we see a customer and his friend relaxing at an Umpqua Bank branch in Portland, Oregon.

the quality of its relationships with customers. Salespeople achieve their bonuses based in large part on customer satisfaction instead of on gross sales or profit.[11]

Front-line employees, those persons responsible for delivering quality service and building relationships, engage in "emotional labor," and those who have frequent contact with the public often find the work very stressful.[12] *Emotional labor*, which taxes the mind, is often more difficult to handle than physical labor, which strains the body. For this reason, front-line employees need the support of leaders who are both caring and competent.

Emotional labor, which taxes the mind, is often more difficult to handle than physical labor, which strains the body.

Toxic Emotions

Peter Frost, author of *Toxic Emotions at Work*, notes that many organizations and their leaders generate emotional pain, which is a form of *toxicity*. Some toxicity can demoralize employees, damage performances, and ultimately contaminate the health of the organization.[13] Worker humiliation is a common toxin in the workplace; lack of recognition for work well done is another.

Toxicity often creates the kind of pain that shows up in worker's diminished sense of self-worth. One or more workers who are depressed or angry can poison team or department morale. How people feel can rub off on others. If the boss is feeling optimistic and enthusiastic, these feelings are often transmitted to staff members.[14] Later in this chapter we will discuss how toxicity creates worker anger.

CRITICAL THINKING CHALLENGE:

Analyze It

Emotional undercurrents are present in almost every area of work and every aspect of our personal lives. Recall a situation at work or at school when the leadership displayed emotional blindness. What are some of the reasons the important role of emotions was not taken into consideration?

Factors That Influence Our Emotional Development

The starting point in achieving greater emotional control is to determine the source of emotional difficulties. Why do we sometimes display indifference when the expression of compassion would be more appropriate? Why is it so easy to put down a friend or coworker and so hard to recognize that person's accomplishments? Why do we sometimes worry about events that will never happen? To answer these and other questions, it is necessary to study the factors that influence our emotional development.

Temperament

Temperament refers to a person's individual style of expressing needs and emotions; it is biological and genetically based. It reflects heredity's contribution to the beginning of an individual's personality.[15] Researchers have found that certain temperamental characteristics are apparent in children at birth and remain somewhat stable over time. For example, the traits associated with extroversion and introversion (see Chapter 3) can be observed when a baby is born. Of course, many events take place between infancy and adulthood to alter or shape a person's temperament. Personality at every age reflects the interplay of temperament and of environmental influences, such as parenting.[16]

Within the field of psychology, the area of *instinct theory* has been given a great deal of attention. This theory presents the view that emotion is something that is influenced by automatic, involuntary, and unlearned responses.[17] For example, the potential for fear is wired into our brains. During the recent economic recession a *Wall Street Journal* article featured the following headline: "Job Losses Are Worst Since '74." Merely reading these words can instantly trigger one of the fear centers in your brain and increase your pulse, blood pressure, and tension in your muscles.[18]

Unconscious Influences

The **unconscious mind** is a vast storehouse of forgotten memories, desires, ideas, and frustrations, according to William Menninger, founder of the famed Menninger Foundation.[19] He noted that the unconscious mind can have a great influence on behavior. It contains memories of past *experiences* as well as memories of *feelings* associated with past experiences. The unconscious is active, continuously influencing conscious decision-making processes.

Although people cannot remember many of the important events of the early years of their lives, these incidents do influence their behavior as adults. Joan Borysenko offers this example:

Inside me there is a seven-year-old who is still hurting from her humiliation at summer camp. Her anguish is reawakened every time I find myself in the presence of an authority figure who acts in a controlling manner. At those moments, my intellect is prone to desert me, and I am liable to break down and cry with the same desolation and helplessness I felt when I was seven.[20]

This example reminds us that childhood wounds can cause us to experience emotions out of proportion to a current situation. Also, we often relive the experience in a context very different from the one we experienced as a child.

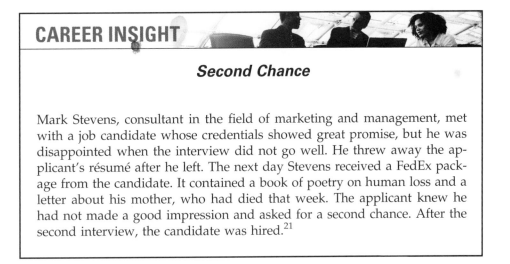

CAREER INSIGHT

Second Chance

Mark Stevens, consultant in the field of marketing and management, met with a job candidate whose credentials showed great promise, but he was disappointed when the interview did not go well. He threw away the applicant's résumé after he left. The next day Stevens received a FedEx package from the candidate. It contained a book of poetry on human loss and a letter about his mother, who had died that week. The applicant knew he had not made a good impression and asked for a second chance. After the second interview, the candidate was hired.[21]

Transactional Analysis. A promising breakthrough in understanding the influence of the unconscious came many years ago with the development of the **Transactional Analysis** (TA) theory by Eric Berne.[22] After years of study, Berne concluded that, from the day of birth, the brain acts like a two-track stereo tape-recorder. One track records events, and the other records the feelings associated with those events.

To illustrate how feelings associated with early childhood experiences can surface later in life, picture in your mind's eye a three-year-old walking around his mother's sewing room. He picks up a pair of sharp scissors and begins walking toward the staircase. The mother spots the child and cries, "Tommy, drop those scissors! Do you want to kill yourself?" Tommy's tape recorder records both the event (walking with scissors) and the emotions (fear and guilt). Ten years later, Tommy is taking an art class and his teacher says, "Tommy, bring me a pair of scissors." As he begins to walk across the room, his mind is flooded by the feelings of fear and guilt attached to that earlier childhood event.

The practical applications of TA were discussed in such books as *I'm OK—You're OK,* written by Thomas Harris; *Staying OK,* by Amy Bjork Harris and Thomas Harris; and *Born to Win,* by Muriel James and Dorothy Jongeward. TA concepts have been incorporated into many corporate training programs.

Cultural Intelligence

Culture can be defined as the accumulation of values, rules of behavior, forms of expression, religious beliefs, and the like, for a group of people who share a common language and environment. Culture helps shape just about every aspect of our behavior and our mental processes. Culture is frequently associated with a particular country; but actually, most countries are multicultural. African Americans, Hispanic Americans, Asian Americans, and American Indians represent a few of the subcultures within the United States.[23] Companies also have cultures. Persons who join a new company will often spend several weeks deciphering its cultural code.

The ability to interpret human actions, gestures, and speech patterns in a foreign culture is called **cultural intelligence** or (CQ). A person with a high CQ quickly analyzes an unfamiliar cultural situation and then responds appropriately.[24] The merits of CQ are highlighted in the movie *Outsourced.* A call center based in the United States is outsourced to India. The U.S. manager, Todd Anderson, is sent to Mumbai to train his successor. Serious cultural clashes soon arise as Anderson tries to explain American business practices to befuddled new employees.[25] Management professors P. Christopher Earley and Elaine Mosakowski have studied more than 2,000 managers in 60 countries. They have identified three sources of cultural intelligence.[26]

Head. Before visiting India, Todd Anderson should have learned as much as possible about the host country's customs, religion, politics, morals, social structure, food, table manners, and the roles of men and women. He should have been more open-minded and willing to suspend judgment—to think before acting.

Body. You can win the respect of foreign hosts, guests, or colleagues by showing you understand their culture. The way you shake hands, order coffee, or accept a gift, can demonstrate, to some degree, you have already entered their world. Talking business over lunch is a common practice in the United States, but it would be offensive in some countries. Research conducted at the University of Michigan found that job candidates who adopted some of the mannerisms of recruiters with cultural backgrounds different than their own were more likely to receive an offer.[27]

Heart. Adapting to a new culture is much easier when you have confidence in yourself. In Chapter 4, we introduced *self-efficacy*, the belief that you can achieve what you set out to do. A major source of *self-efficacy* is the experience of mastery in your area of specialization. Past successes give us the confidence and motivation needed to increase our cultural intelligence. Our head, body, and heart can work together to help us act appropriately in new cultures or among people with unfamiliar backgrounds.

Coping with Your Anger and the Anger of Others

Anger may be defined as the thoughts, feelings, physical reactions, and actions that result from unacceptable behavior by others. Anger is almost always a response to *perceived* injustice, and may dissolve with a deeper understanding of the cause. Some people have a genetic predisposition to anger. Learning to effectively deal with anger (anger management) is a key component of any healthy lifestyle.[28]

Anger is almost always a response to *perceived* injustice.

Managing Your Anger

Learning to address their own anger and the anger of other people is one of the most sophisticated and mature skills people are ever required to learn. Intense anger takes control of people and distorts their perceptions, which is why angry people often make poor decisions.[29]

Dr. Art Ulene, author of *Really Fit Really Fast*, says the first step in anger management is to monitor your anger. How often do you get angry each day? What are the causes of irritation in your life? How upsetting is each episode of anger? How well do you manage each episode? Ulene suggests using a diary or journal to record this information. This self-monitoring activity will help you determine the impact of anger in your life. Record not only the source of the irritation, but the feelings that surfaced when you became angry. Also record the behaviors you displayed when angry. Ulene says that people who monitor their behavior carefully see positive results: "Without even trying, their behavior begins to change in ways that are usually desirable."[30]

Intense anger often takes the form of rage. In addition to road rage, air rage, and customer rage, we are witnessing more incidents of "workplace rage." Workplace rage can take the form of yelling, verbal abuse, and physical violence. It is more likely to occur when workers are stressed by long hours, unrealistic deadlines, cramped quarters, excessive e-mail, lack of recognition, bullying incidents, or some combination of these factors.

Effective Ways to Express Your Anger

Buddha said, "You will not be punished for your anger, you will be punished by your anger." Buddhist teachings tell us that patience is the best antidote to aggression.[31] Intense anger that is suppressed will linger and become a disruptive force in your life unless you can find a positive way to get rid of it. Expressing feelings of anger can be therapeutic, but many people are unsure about the best way to self-disclose this emotion. To express anger in ways that will improve the chances that the other person will receive and respond to your message, consider these suggestions:

1. *Avoid reacting in a manner that could be seen as emotionally unstable.* If others see you as reacting irrationally, you will lose your ability to influence them. Jared Sandberg, writing in the *Wall Street Journal*, describes a major sale that faltered when only half the order arrived. When the bad news was delivered by the receiving clerk, the salesperson lost his temper and told the clerk, "I will ruin your life." He then threw the clerk against the wall and kicked his own cubicle wall, which in turn collapsed onto his neighbor's cubicle wall.[32] Lesson learned: Don't shoot the messenger.
2. *Do not make accusations or attempt to fix blame.* It would be acceptable to begin the conversation by saying, "I felt humiliated at the staff meeting this morning." It would not be appropriate to say, "Your comments at the morning staff meeting were mean spirited and made me feel humiliated." The latter statement invites a defensive response.[33]
3. *Express your feelings in a timely manner.* The intensity of anger can actually increase with time. Also, important information needed by you or the person who provoked your anger may be forgotten or distorted with the passing of time.
4. *Be specific as you describe the factors that triggered your anger, and be clear about the resolution you are seeking.* The direct approach, in most cases, works best.

In some cases, the person who triggers your anger may be someone you cannot confront without placing your job in jeopardy. For example, one of your best customers may constantly complain about the service he receives. You know he

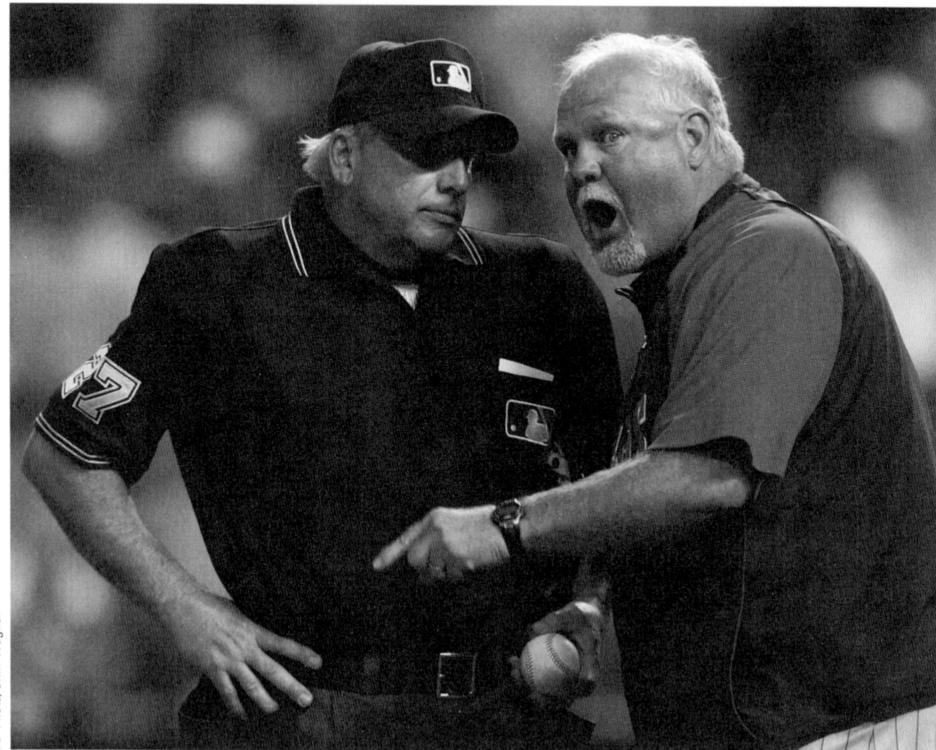

AP Photo/Orlin Wagner

Minnesota Twins manager Ron Gardenhire is arguing a call at home plate. The umpire, Larry Vanover, appears to be losing patience. This emotional exchange took place during a game with the Kansas City Royals.

receives outstanding service, and you feel anger building inside you each time he complains. But any display of anger may result in loss of his business.

> ### *Total Person Insight*
>
> **Pema Chodron**
> Author and Buddhist Teacher
>
> *"We can suppress anger or act it out, either way making things worse for ourselves and others. Or we can practice patience: wait, experience the anger and investigate its nature."*[34]

How to Handle Other People's Anger

Dealing with other people's anger may be the most difficult human relations challenge we face. The following skills can be learned and applied to any situation where anger threatens to damage a relationship.

1. *Recognize and accept the other person's anger.* The simple recognition of the intense feelings of someone who is angry does a lot to defuse the situation. In a calm voice you might say, "I can see that you are very angry. I was out of line when I criticized your work at the team meeting."
2. *Encourage the angry person to vent his or her feelings.* By asking questions and listening carefully to the response, you can encourage the person to discuss

the cause of the anger openly. Try using an open-ended question to encourage self-disclosure: "What have I done to upset you?" or "Can you tell me why you are so angry?"

3. *Do not respond to an angry person with your own anger.* To express your own anger or become defensive will only create another barrier to emotional healing. When you respond to the angry person, keep your voice tone soft. Keep in mind the old biblical injunction, "A soft answer turns away wrath."[35]
4. *Give the angry person feedback.* After venting feelings and discussing specific details, the angry person will expect a response. Briefly paraphrase what seems to be the major concern of the angry person and express a desire to find ways to solve the problem. If you are at fault, accept the blame for your actions and express a sincere apology.

Violence in the Workplace

Any discussion of workplace violence is likely to bring to mind a lone employee walking into the office or plant and shooting coworkers or supervisors. These are the images most often presented by the media. The Workplace Violence Research Institute has developed a definition of **workplace violence** that may be more appropriate for today's work environment:

> *Any act against an employee that creates a hostile work environment and negatively affects the employee, either physically or psychologically. These acts include all types of physical or verbal assaults, threats, coercion, intimidation, and all forms of harassment.*[36]

Violence in the workplace is often triggered by loss of a job, conflict between the employee and management, or a personal tragedy, such as divorce or separation. Michele Coleman Mages, Senior Vice President at Pitney Bowes, a mail and management—document company, says, "People bring all sorts of demons to work—from problems with spouses and kids to bipolar disease—that they shouldn't think they can solve on their own."[37]

Employee Sabotage

Employee sabotage is a problem that is causing nightmares throughout corporate America. It is often described as employee misconduct tinged with an edge of revenge. Employee sabotage may involve deliberate nonperformance, financial fraud, slander, destruction of equipment, arson, or some other act that damages the organization or the careers of people within the organization. Computer crimes have become a common form of sabotage. Computer sabotage by ex-workers is increasing.[38]

Sabotage is committed most often by employees who have unresolved grievances, want to advance by making others look less qualified, or want to get even for real or imagined mistreatment. Today, many employees are acting out their anger, rather than discussing it.[39]

Preventing Workplace Violence

Incidents of workplace violence cost employers and others several billion dollars each year. This figure does not, of course, reflect the human suffering caused by acts of violence. Although violence cannot be eliminated, some steps can help curb violent behavior in the workplace.

1. *Use hiring procedures that screen out unstable persons.* In-depth interviews, drug testing, and background checks can help identify signs of a troubled past.

2. *Develop a strategy for responding to incidents before they actually occur.* Establish policies that make it clear that workplace violence incidents will not be tolerated. Every organization should establish a strong expectation of workplace civility. After an employee at Lockheed Martin's airplane-parts plant shot six coworkers to death, they formed a task force on workplace violence. One outcome of this action is a zero-tolerance policy (violators can be fired) for hostile or intimidating speech or actions.[40]
3. *When employees are demoted, fired, or laid off, do it in a way that does not demoralize the employee.* When Intel reduced its workforce by 10,500, it used a highly structured process. Intel spokesman Chuck Mulloy says, "The key to making it work is very clear communications, what's going to happen and when."[41]
4. *Provide out-placement services for laid-off or terminated employees.* These services may include development of job-search skills, retraining, or, in cases where the employee is displaying signs of aggression, counseling.
5. *Establish a systematic way to deal with disgruntled employees.* This might involve providing a forum for employees who feel they have been treated unfairly.
6. *Provide supervisors and managers with training that will help them prevent workplace violence and deal effectively with violence if it does occur.* Workplace violence is a growing problem in America, but it is not a problem without solutions. As the workplace gets leaner, it need not become meaner.

As the workplace gets leaner, it need not become meaner.

Emotional Styles

A good starting point for achieving emotional control is to examine your current emotional style. How do you deal with emotions? Your style started taking shape before birth and evolved over a period of many years. As an adult, you are likely to favor one of four different emotional styles when confronted with events that trigger your emotions.

Suppressing Your Emotions

Some people have learned to suppress their feelings as much as possible. They have developed intellectual strategies that enable them to avoid dealing directly with emotional reactions to a situation. In response to the loss of a loved one, a person may avoid the experience of grief and mourning by taking on new responsibilities at work. This is not, of course, a healthy way to deal with grief.

Hale Dwoskin, author of *The Sedona Method*, says suppression is "keeping a lid on our emotions, pushing them back down, denying them, repressing them, and pretending they don't exist."[42] He says habitual suppression is unhealthy and unproductive. Dwoskin says an alternative to inappropriate suppression and expression is releasing emotions, an approach he calls the Sedona Method (see Figure 9.2).

To continually suppress feelings, hide fears, swallow annoyances, and avoid displaying anger is not healthy. If suppressing your feelings becomes a habit, you create opportunities for mental and physical health problems to develop.

Capitulating to Your Emotions

People who display this emotional style see themselves as the helpless victims of feelings over which they have no control. By responding to emotion in this

FIGURE 9.2 The Sedona Method

Hale Dwoskin, author of *The Sedona Method* and CEO of Sedona Training Associates *(http://www.sedonapress.com)*, developed a unique program for making positive changes in your life. He encourages everyone to let go of or release their unwanted emotions. A brief introduction to the process of releasing follows.

Step 1: Focus on an issue you would like to feel better about. You may be experiencing guilt or fear. Allow yourself to feel whatever you are feeling at this moment.

Step 2: Ask yourself one of the following questions:

- Could I let this feeling go?
- Could I allow this feeling to be here?
- Could I welcome this feeling?

Each of these questions points you to the experience of letting go.

Step 3: Ask yourself this basic question: Would I? Am I willing to let go?

Step 4: Ask yourself this simpler question: When?

Dwoskin suggests repeating these four steps as often as needed to feel free of a particular feeling.

Source: Hale Dwoskin, *The Sedona Method* (Sedona, AZ: Sedona Press, 2003), pp. 36–44.

manner, one can assign responsibility for the "problem" to external causes, such as other people or unavoidable events. For example, Paula, a busy office manager, is frustrated because her brother-in-law and his wife frequently show up unannounced on weekends and expect a big meal. Paula has a tight schedule during the week, and she looks forward to quiet weekends with her family. She is aware of the anger that builds within her but tends to blame others (family members) for these feelings. Paula would rather endure feelings of helplessness than find a positive solution to this problem. People who capitulate to their emotions are often overly concerned about the attitudes and opinions of others.[43]

Overexpressing Your Emotions

In a work setting, we need to be seen as responsible and predictable. One of the quickest ways to lose the respect and confidence of the people you work with is to frequently display a lack of emotional control. Frequent use of foul and vulgar language, flared tempers, raised voices, and teary eyes are still regarded as unacceptable behavior by most coworkers and supervisors.

One acceptable way to cope with fear, anger, grief, or jealousy is to sit down with pen and paper and write a letter to the person who triggered these emotions. Don't worry about grammar, spelling, or punctuation—just put all your thoughts on paper. Write until you have nothing more to say. Then destroy the letter. Once you let go of your toxic feelings, you will be ready to deal constructively with whatever caused you to become upset.[44] Another approach is to express your feelings through daily journal entries. Studies indicate that a significant emotional uplift and healing effect can result from spending as little as five to ten minutes a day writing about whatever issues or problems are getting you down.[45]

Accommodating Your Emotions

At the beginning of this chapter, we said an emotion can be thought of as a feeling that influences our thinking and behavior. Accommodation means you are willing to recognize, accept, and experience emotions and to attempt to react in ways appropriate to the situation. This style achieves an integration of one's feelings and the thinking process. People who display the accommodation style have adopted the "think before you act" point of view. It would be normal to feel defensive or angry during a negative performance review by your boss. However, career coaches advise against acting on these emotions. They suggest taking a day or two to digest the feedback and create an appropriate response.[46]

Do we always rely on just one of these four emotional styles? Of course not. Your response to news that a coworker is getting a divorce may be very different from your response to a demeaning comment made by your boss. You may have found appropriate ways to deal with your grief but have not yet learned to cope with the fear of making a team presentation. Dealing with our emotions is a very complex process.

 **Skill Development: Apply It**

Anger builds when we perceive an injustice. Take time to remember a few occasions when someone's behavior triggered a torrent of anger in you. With pen and paper (not your computer), start writing about the reasons for your anger. Keep writing until your feelings become more focused and the reasons for your anger more clear. Keep writing until the anger is fully voiced.

Gender Differences in Emotional Style

Male attitudes toward female ambitions in the workplace have changed over the years. Most men assume they will compete with smart, ambitious women. However, in the area of emotional control, women are often judged by a different standard than men. Research reported in *Psychological Science* indicates that when women display anger in a work setting, they are more likely to be viewed as out of control and incompetent. Men who display anger at work are more likely to be viewed as authoritative and in control. Debra Condren, author of *Ambition Is Not a Dirty Word*, says women can avoid the anger penalty by staying calm at work and using humor to disarm a foe.[47] A good relation does not require both people to have the same emotional style, but it does require each person to respect the other person's style.[48] Gender roles in the workplace will be discussed in more depth in Chapter 16.

Strategies for Achieving Emotional Control

Each day, we wake up with a certain amount of mental, emotional, and physical energy that we can spend throughout the day. If we allow toxic thoughts and

"Still won't start?"

unpleasant feelings to deplete our energy, we have no energy to change our life or to give to others.[49] Our emotions do have an impact on our health. The link between emotions and health is quite strong for negative feelings that are associated with anger, anxiety, and depression.[50] We can learn to discipline the mind and banish afflicting thoughts that create needless frustration, waste energy, and deplete our immune system. In this, the final part of the chapter, we share with you some practical suggestions for achieving greater control of the emotions that affect your life.

Identifying Your Emotional Patterns

We could often predict or anticipate our response to various emotions if we would take the time to study our emotional patterns—to take a running inventory of circumstances that touch off jealousy, fear, anger, or some other emotion. Journal entries can help you discover emotional patterns. Record not only your conscious feelings, such as anxiety or guilt, but feelings in your body, such as a knot in your stomach or muscle tension.

Becoming a skilled observer of your own emotions is one of the best ways to achieve greater emotional control.

If you don't feel comfortable with journal writing, consider setting aside some quiet time to reflect on your emotional patterns. A period of quiet reflection will help you focus your thoughts and impressions. Becoming a skilled observer of your own emotions is one of the best ways to achieve greater emotional control.

TABLE 9.1 CHARTING YOUR EMOTIONAL LANDSCAPE

TIME	CIRCUMSTANCE	EMOTION
6:00 a.m.	Alarm goes off. Mind is flooded by thoughts of all the things that must be done during the day.	Anxiety
7:10 a.m.	Depart for work. Heavy traffic interferes with plan to arrive at work early.	Anger and helplessness
8:00 a.m.	Thirty-minute staff meeting scheduled by the boss lasts fifty minutes. No agenda is provided. Entire meeting seems a waste of time.	Anger and frustration
9:35 a.m.	Finally start work on creative project.	Contentment
10:15 a.m.	Progress on project interrupted when co-worker enters office, sits down, and starts sharing gossip about another coworker.	Anger and resentment
11:20 a.m.	Progress is made on creative project.	Contentment
1:45 p.m.	Creative project is complete and ready for review.	Joy and contentment
2:50 p.m.	Give project to boss for review. She says she will not be able to provide any feedback until morning. This delay will cause scheduling problems.	Frustration
4:00 p.m.	Attend health insurance update seminar sponsored by human resources department. No major changes are discussed.	Boredom
5:40 p.m.	Give up on a search for a missing document, turn off computer, and walk to parking lot.	Relief and fatigue

In addition to journal writing and quiet reflection, there is one more way to discover emotional patterns. At the end of the day, construct a chart of your emotional landscape. Make a chart (see Table 9.1) of the range of emotions you experienced and expressed during the day.[51] Your first entry might be "I woke up at 6:00 a.m. and immediately felt _____." The final entry might be "I left the office at 5:30 p.m. with a feeling of _____." What emotions surfaced throughout your workday? Resentment? Creative joy? Anxiety? Boredom? Contentment? Anger? Reflect on the completed chart and try to determine which patterns need to be changed. For example, you might discover that driving in heavy traffic is a major energy drain. Repeat this process over a period of several days in order to identify your unique emotional patterns.

Fine-Tuning Your Emotional Style

Once you have completed the process of self-examination and have identified some emotional patterns you want to change, it is time to consider ways to fine-tune your emotional style. Bringing about discipline within your mind can help you live a fuller, more satisfying life. Here are four things you can begin doing today.

Total Person Insight

GERARD EGAN
Author, *You and Me*

"It's unfortunate that we're never really taught how to show emotion in ways that help our relationships. Instead, we're usually told what we should not do. However, too little emotion can make our lives seem empty and boring, while too much emotion, poorly expressed, fills our interpersonal lives with conflict and grief. Within reason, some kind of balance in the expression of emotion seems to be called for."[52]

- *Take responsibility for your emotions.* How you view your emotional difficulties will have a major influence on how you deal with them. If your frustration is triggered by thoughts such as "I can never make my boss happy" or "Things always go wrong in my life," you may never achieve a comfortable emotional state. By shifting the blame to other people and events, you cannot achieve emotional control.
- *Put your problems into proper perspective.* Why do some people seem to be at peace most of the time, while others seem to be in a perpetual state of anxiety? People who engage in unproductive obsessing (irrational thinking) are unable or unwilling to look at problems realistically and practically, and they view each disappointment as a major catastrophe. To avoid needless misery, anxiety, and emotional upsets, use an "emotional thermometer" with a scale of 0 to 100. Zero means that everything is going well, and 100 denotes something life-threatening or truly catastrophic. Whenever you feel upset, ask yourself to come up with a logical number on the emotional thermometer. If a problem surfaces that is merely troublesome but not terrible, and you give it 60 points, you are no-doubt overreacting. This mental exercise will help you avoid mislabeling a problem and feeling upset as a result.[53]
- *Take steps to move beyond toxic emotions such as envy, anger, jealousy, or hatred.* Some people are upset about things that happened many years ago. Some even nurse grudges against people who have been dead for years. The sad thing is that the negative feelings remain long after we can achieve any positive learning from them.[54] Studies of divorce, for example, indicate that anger and bitterness can linger a long time. Distress seems to peak one year after the divorce, and many people report that it takes at least two years to move past the anger.[55] When negative emotions dominate one's life, whatever the reason, therapy or counseling may provide relief. Learning to release unwanted patterns of behavior is very important.
- *Give your feelings some exercise.* Several prominent authors in the field of human relations have emphasized the importance of giving our feelings some exercise. Leo Buscaglia, author of *Loving Each Other*, says, "Exercise feelings. Feelings have meaning only as they are expressed in action."[56] Sam Keen, author of *Fire in the Belly*, said, "Make a habit of identifying your feelings and expressing them in some appropriate way."[57] If you have offended someone, how about sending that person a note expressing regret? If someone you work with has given extra effort, why not praise that person's work? Make a decision to cultivate positive mental states, such as kindness and compassion. A sincere feeling of empathy, for example, will deepen your connection to others.

Every day of our personal and work life, we face some difficult decisions. One option is to only take actions that feel good at the moment. In some cases, this means ignoring the feelings of customers, patients, coworkers, and supervisors. Another option is to behave in a manner that is acceptable to the people around you. If you choose this option, you will have to make some sacrifices. You may have to be warm and generous when the feelings inside you say, "Be cold and selfish." You may have to avoid an argument when your feelings are insisting, "I'm right and the other person is wrong!" To achieve a positive emotional state often requires restructuring our ways of feeling, thinking, and behaving.

LOOKING BACK: REVIEWING THE CONCEPTS

- Describe how emotions influence our thinking and behavior.

We carry inside us a vast array of emotions that can help us cope with our environment. An emotion can be thought of as a feeling that influences our thinking and behavior. Feelings are activated by a variety of events. Angry feelings may surface when another employee borrows something without your permission. Feelings of grief will very likely follow the loss of a close friend. The need to discover ways to achieve emotional balance has never been greater. We sometimes suffer from a lack of emotional balance because we learn to inhibit the expression of certain emotions and to overemphasize the expression of others.

- Explain the critical role of emotions in the workplace.

Emotions play a critical role in the success of every organization. Emotional undercurrents are present in almost every area of the organization, and they influence employee morale, customer loyalty, and productivity.

- Describe the major factors that influence our emotional development.

Our emotional development is influenced by temperament (the biological shaper of personality), our unconscious mind, and cultural intelligence. These influences contribute to the development of our emotional intelligence. Throughout the long process of emotional development, we learn different ways to express our emotions.

- Learn how to address your anger and the anger of others.

Appropriate expressions of anger contribute to improved interpersonal relations, help us reduce anxiety, and give us an outlet for unhealthy stress. We must also learn how to handle other people's anger. It takes a great deal of effort to learn how to deal with our own anger and the anger of others.

- Understand the factors that contribute to workplace violence.

Workplace violence encompasses a wide range of activities, including homicides, hostile remarks, physical assaults, and sabotage directed toward the employer or other workers. Although violence cannot be eliminated, steps can be taken to curb violent employee behavior in the workplace.

- Identify and explain the most common emotional styles.

To achieve emotional balance, we need to start with an examination of our current emotional style. When confronted by strong feelings, we are likely to display one of four different emotional styles: suppressing emotions, capitulating to them, overexpressing them, or accommodating them. Researchers suggest that there are gender differences in emotional style.

- Describe strategies for achieving emotional control.

Emotional control is an important dimension of emotional style. The starting point in developing emotional control is to identify your current emotional patterns. One way to do this is to record your anger experiences in a diary or journal. Additional ways to identify emotional patterns include setting aside time for quiet reflection and developing a chart of your emotional landscape.

ON THE JOB Q & A: COPING WITH IRRATIONAL FEAR

Q: When I started working for this company, I was never put in a situation where it was necessary to make presentations to others. After receiving a promotion to department head, I was expected to make monthly reports to my staff. I never feel comfortable in the role of group presenter. Hours before the monthly meeting, I start feeling tense, and by the time the meeting begins, I am gripped by fear. Two weeks ago, my boss asked me to make a presentation to senior management. Shortly before the meeting, I started experiencing chest pain, sweating, and trembling. I told my boss I was sick and went home. Why am I so frightened of speaking to a group? Should I seek professional help?

A: It appears that you may have developed a social phobia. Social phobias are fears of situations in which the person can be watched by others. Phobias of various types are quite common—they currently afflict more than 11 million Americans. The potential for fear is wired into our brains, so reasonable concern about group presentations is natural. When a fear escalates beyond reason, it is described as a phobia.

Your problem could be serious, and you might consider seeking help from a qualified therapist. Psychotherapy can result in greater self-understanding and self-expression. Throughout the treatment, you will learn new ways to cope with your problem. It is encouraging to note that about 80 percent of psychotherapy patients benefit from treatment.[58]

KEY TERMS

emotion 188
emotional intelligence 189
temperament 192
unconscious mind 192
Transactional Analysis 193
culture 193
cultural intelligence 194
anger 194
workplace violence 197

TRY YOUR HAND

1. Recall the last time you were angry at another person or were a victim of a situation that made you angry. For example, someone you trusted divulged some personal information about your family history or accused you of an unethical practice at work. Then answer the following questions:

   a. Did you express your anger verbally? Physically?
   b. Did you suppress any of your anger? Explain.
   c. What results did you experience from the way you handled this situation? Describe both positive and negative results.
   d. If you could relive the situation, would you do anything differently? Explain.

2. To learn more about the way you handle anger, record your anger responses in a journal for a period of five days. When anger surfaces, record as many details as possible. What triggered your anger? How intense was the anger? How long did your angry feelings last? Did you express them to anyone? At the end of the five days, study your entries and try to determine whether any patterns exist. If you find this activity helpful, consider keeping a journal for a longer period of time.

3. To learn more about how emotions influence your thinking and behavior, complete each of the following sentences. Once you have completed them all, reflect on your written responses.

Can you identify any changes you would like to make in your emotional style?

a. "When someone accuses me of a wrongdoing, I usually ..."
b. "When I feel frustrated, my response is ..."
c. "When I am fearful, I ..."
d. "My response to a lack of recognition is ..."
e. "When I am disappointed, my response is to ..."

INTERNET INSIGHTS

1. Many people have an anger-management problem. Although anger is a natural human emotion, the mismanagement of anger can result in serious interpersonal-relations problems. Help with anger management is as close as your computer. The American Psychological Association has a webpage on "Controlling Anger—Before It Controls You." The address is *http://www.apa.org/pubinfo/anger.html*. Visit this site, and prepare a written summary of the information presented. If you wish to study anger management in greater detail, visit *http://www.angermgt.com*.

2. As noted in this chapter, several national training and developmental organizations offer seminars that help workers achieve emotional balance. The American Management Association offers a seminar entitled *Managing Emotions in the Workplace: Strategies for Success*. Access *http://www.amanet.org* and click on Seminars/Communication Skills. Then click on the seminar title. Review the seminar topic outline and prepare a brief critique. Would you recommend this seminar to persons who are working in a stressful work environment? Do you think this seminar fee is reasonable?

YOU PLAY THE ROLE

You are currently manager of a bank branch that employs 26 people. About three weeks ago, you learned that one of your employees, Wesla Perez, needed time off to spend with a parent who was very ill. You approved the time off without hesitation. Soon, you learned that the parent (mother) had died. On Monday morning Wesla will return to work. You plan to meet with Wesla and express your condolences. In this role-play exercise, a member of your class will play the role of Wesla Perez. The name you will use during the role-play is Evony Hillison.

BELOW THE SURFACE:

Enlightened Hospitality

This chapter opens with an introduction to restaurants owned by Danny Meyer. At age 27, with little experience, he opened what would become one of New York City's most popular restaurants—Union Square Café. Today, Meyer is the CEO of one of the world's most successful restaurant organizations. He has established 11 unique dining establishments. In a very competitive area of commerce, he has consistently beaten the odds. *Zagat Survey* of restaurants gives Meyer properties very high marks.[59]

In his book *Setting the Table: The Transforming Power of Hospitality in Business,* we learn the "secrets" of his success. His winning recipe is described as "enlightened hospitality." This innovative philosophy emphasizes putting the power of hospitality in the hands of the people who work for you. Meyer says it is not the food that keeps people coming back—it's the service provided by employees who have certain emotional skills: surround yourself with people whose emotional intelligence quotient is as high as, or higher than, their IQ.

How do you deliver to customers a dining experience that makes them feel good? Meyer's philosophy is based on these insights:[60]

- Hospitality is present when something happens for you. It is absent when something happens to you. These two simple concepts—*for* and *to*—express it all.
- Shared ownership develops when guests talk about a restaurant as if it's *theirs.* That sense of affiliation builds trust and invariably leads to repeat business.
- Err on the side of generosity: You get more by first giving more.

QUESTIONS

1. Danny Meyer believes that his philosophy of customer service is applicable to any business or organization. Do you agree? Explain.
2. All of the managers working for Danny Meyer are encouraged to hire employees that display natural warmth, optimism, empathy, a strong work ethic, and integrity. What interview methods would help a manager identify these human traits?
3. Danny Meyer encourages his employees to err on the side of generosity. How can members of the wait staff display generosity when serving customers?

CLOSING CASE: Is Romancing a Colleague Okay?

Romance at work has become more common in recent years, but some relationships do have unintended consequences. Harry Stonecipher, Boeing Company's former president and CEO, lost his job when the board of directors learned (from an anonymous message) about his consensual extramarital affair with a female executive. Consensual romances at work are not unlawful and are tolerated far more today than they were in the past. So why did Stonecipher lose his job? Boeing's code of conduct prohibits behavior that may embarrass the company.

Today, men and women often work alongside each other in almost equal numbers, sharing long hours and job pressures. Although romance at work is more acceptable today, it is still viewed as a major productivity disrupter by many consultants, human-resource professionals, and executives. The president of a consulting business tells of a female employee in her office who broke off a relationship with a fellow worker. The spurned man began stalking the woman, who discussed her fears and anger openly with other employees. They, in turn, spent time on the job trying to advise and comfort her. Other critics of romance at work say companies should be concerned when relationships create conflicts of interest and lower job performance. The use of pet names, kissing, and hand-holding can be distracting to other workers.

Although critics of romance at work make some valid points, the truth is corporate America is getting more comfortable with love in the workplace. In fact, 67 percent of the respondents to a 2003 survey on romance at work by the American Management Association said they approved of dating by coworkers. Dennis Powers, author of *The Office Romance*, feels that companies need to lighten up in their attitudes about romance at work. He says that most of these romances have no detrimental effect on the workplace or on workers. However, he does feel that supervisors need to know how to ease conflict when a failed romance invades the workplace.[61]

QUESTIONS

1. Is an office romance likely to affect the productivity of the two workers involved? Is it likely to affect the people who work with them?
2. Should organizations establish policies that prevent dating a coworker? A supervisor? Explain your answer.
3. Can you think of a situation where employment of married couples would create problems for a firm? Explain your answer.

INTEGRATED RESOURCES

VIDEO:

Alex and Melinda: Performance Review

CLASSROOM ACTIVITIES

IRM Application Exercise 9.1
IRM Application Exercise 9.2
IRM Application Exercise 9.3

CHAPTER 10
Building Stronger Relationships with Positive Energy

TIP OF THE ICEBERG

CHAPTER PREVIEW

LEARNING OBJECTIVES

After studying Chapter 10, you will be able to

- Describe how positive energy contributes to improved interpersonal relationships.
- Create awareness of the strong need people have for encouragement and positive feedback.
- Understand how to use positive reinforcement to improve relationships and reward behavior.
- Describe the major barriers to the use of positive reinforcement.
- Explain how to reward individual and team performance.

© Anderson Ross/Blend Images/Getty Images

Top Small Workplaces

The search for a great place to work often focuses on large companies such as American Express, Procter & Gamble, or FedEx. But many small businesses and nonprofits have developed workplace environments and cultures that rival—or even outshine—the big companies. Each year, the *Wall Street Journal*, in partnership with Winning Workplaces, selects 15 small and midsize companies that have built exemplary workplaces (*http://www.winningworkplaces.org*).

New Belgium Brewing Company, based in Fort Collins, Colorado, is a recent recipient of the Top Small Workplace award. The company was founded by a husband and wife team that wanted to minimize the company's footprint on the planet. They have created a workplace where employees enthusiastically support the company's environmental cause. The company gives employees many ways to be environmentally conscious at work and in their free time. Each New Belgium employee is given a cruiser bicycle after one year of employment and is encouraged to commute by bike. An on-site recycling center allows employees to recycle a variety of items.

An employee ownership plan encourages employees to become more engaged. Employees own about 32 percent of New Belgium through a stock-ownership plan. The company has embraced open-book management practices that include monthly meetings where employees review the company's financial statements.

Courtesy of New Belgium Brewing, Fort Collins, CO

The owners of New Belgium Brewing focus their attention on two important goals: crafting Fat Tire and other excellent beers and developing an exemplary workplace. The company recognizes employees in a variety of ways. After one year of employment, employees receive a new bicycle. After five years, employees receive an all expense paid trip to Belgium.

In recent years, the company has expanded outside of the Fort Collins "mother ship" location. To encourage the feel of a close-knit community, New Belgium holds monthly videoconference meetings for all employees. These meetings keep employees up to date on new developments and provide an opportunity for input.[1]

Recipients of the Top Small Workplaces award have several things in common. These firms create an environment where employees enjoy coming to work and feel appreciated. They realize that when you put the employee first, the customer wins. Worker contentment is an important key to excellence in customer service. The founders create a culture (see Figure 10.1) that emphasizes cooperation, information sharing, and mutual respect.

This chapter discusses the impact of positive energy on both individual and group behavior. **Energy** can be defined as the capacity for work, or the force that helps us do things with vitality and intensity. The chapter examines the importance of encouragement, the power of positive feedback, various types of positive reinforcement, and the reasons why many people have difficulty expressing positive thoughts and feelings. A section of the chapter is devoted to awards and incentive programs that a variety of organizations use.

FIGURE 10.1 Top Small Workplaces Culture

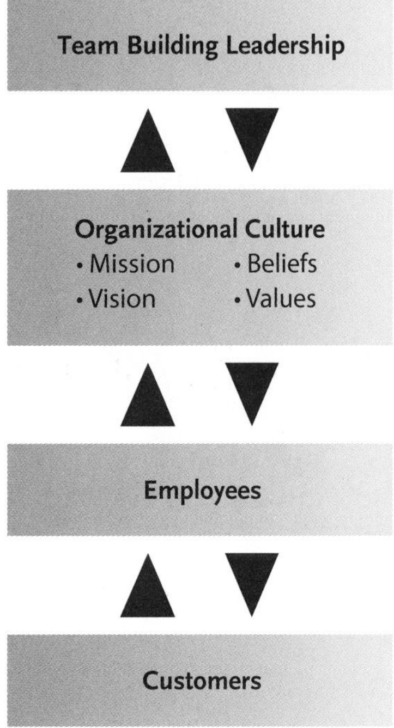

How Positive Energy Contributes to Improved Interpersonal Relationships

Throughout recent periods of great uncertainty and turbulence, negative energy became a powerful force. Many people went to work everyday wondering if they would be the next victim of a merger, buyout, downsizing effort, or business closing. Some wondered if they would be able to cope with rapid technological changes. Stressful working conditions caused by rising productivity demands and long hours can also be the source of negative energy. In a negative, stressful work climate, these pressures often result in physical fatigue, decreased optimism, and lower morale. A positive work climate is more likely to instill workers with positive energy, which results in greater strength of will, increased optimism, and higher employee productivity.

It is positive energy that helps us cope with disappointments, uncertainty, and work that is physically and mentally demanding.

It is positive energy that helps us cope with disappointments, uncertainty, and work that is physically and mentally demanding. In the presence of positive energy, people feel uplifted, encouraged, and empowered. Positive energy helps us remain balanced in a work environment that is increasingly characterized by change and uncertainty.

"THEY SAVE ALL OF THEIR ENERGY FOR QUITTING TIME."

Energy: An Important Force in Our Lives

Judith Orloff, author of *Positive Energy* and pioneer in the field of energy psychiatry, says *energy* is a term with many intriguing dimensions. In basic terms, it is the "get-up-and-go," the stamina that gets you through the day. Energy comes to us from food, exercise, sleep, and subtle forces that penetrate and surround our bodies. Envision energy as having one of two qualities: either positive or negative. Positive energy is supportive, loving, and nurturing. Negative energy is fearful, judgmental, and depleting. How you respond to people and places determines, to a large degree, your energy level. Dr. Orloff makes an interesting observation regarding the impact of relationships on our energy level: "Each millisecond of our relationships is governed by a give and take of energy. Some people make us more electric or at ease. Others suck the life right out of us."[2]

Actions and Events That Create Positive Energy

In the age of information, organizations need to discover creative ways to generate positive energy. Progressive companies, such as New Belgium Brewing, find ways to frequently encourage, recognize, and reward employees. Consider the following examples:

- At the end of 2007, US Airways was ranked *last* in on-time reliability among major airlines. During the early months of 2008, the company rallied its workforce to focus on one goal—getting planes pushed back from the gate on time. The result was a move to first place in on-time performance. The company made several procedural and equipment changes and began offering financial incentives to workers for better service. The rallying cry at US Airways was D-zero—every departure at or before its scheduled time.[3]

HUMAN RELATIONS IN ACTION

Most Important Pop Quiz Question

Justine Willis Toms, editor of *New Dimensions* magazine, feels we need to personalize the places where we live, work, study, and shop. One way to accomplish this is by getting to know the people who provide us with services. To make her point, she describes a student's experience in nursing school. The instructor gave the class a pop quiz, and the last question was "What is the first name of the woman who cleans our building?" The student didn't know, so she handed in the quiz with the last question unanswered.

Before the class ended, one student asked if the last question would count toward the quiz grade. The teacher said, "absolutely," and then provided a rationale: "In your careers you will meet many people. All are significant. They deserve your attention and care, even if all you do is smile and say hello."[4]

- Some companies are obsessed with the desire to keep their shareholders happy. At Container Store, a 39-store retail chain, the emphasis is placed on taking care of employees. Kip Tindell, CEO of Container Store, says, "If you take care of your employees, they'll take care of your customers—and that will take care of your shareholders." Sales staff receive 241 hours of training; the industry average is 8. Health-care coverage is offered to part-timers. Employees with children can work a special schedule: 9 a.m. to 2:00 p.m.[5]

This is a very small sample of actions and events that can generate positive energy. Throughout the remainder of this chapter, we will discuss how basic courtesy, positive written communication, encouragement, and various forms of positive reinforcement can be used to "accentuate the positive."

Our Need for Positive Experiences

How strong is the need for positive experiences in our lives? Psychologist William James believed that the craving to be appreciated is a basic principle of human nature. Mark Twain, the noted author, answered the question by saying he could live for three weeks on a compliment. Twain was willing to admit openly what most people feel inside. Many of us have a deep desire for personal recognition in one form or another, but we almost never verbalize these thoughts.

Psychologist William James believed that the craving to be appreciated is a basic principle of human nature.

Few people have the strength of ego to maintain high self-esteem without encouragement and positive feedback from others. We are often not certain that we have performed well until some other person tells us. Kenneth Blanchard and Spencer Johnson, authors of *The One Minute Manager,* stress the importance of "catching people doing things right" and engaging in "one minute praisings."[6] Without positive experiences, we often suffer from an energy deficit.

Support from Maslow

The hierarchy of needs developed by Abraham Maslow (discussed in Chapter 7) provides additional support for positive experiences. In part, the need for security (a second-level need) is satisfied by positive feedback from a supervisor, manager, coworker, or friend. You are likely to feel more secure when someone recognizes your accomplishments. A feeling of belonging (a third-level need) can be satisfied by actions that communicate the message, "You are part of the team." Maslow states that as each lower-level need is satisfied, the need at the next level demands attention. It would seem to be almost impossible to satisfy the esteem needs (fourth level) without positive feedback and reinforcement. A person's level of self-esteem may diminish in a work environment where accomplishments receive little or no recognition.

Support from Skinner

The research of B. F. Skinner at Harvard University has contributed to our understanding of reinforcement as a factor influencing the behavior of people in a work setting. Skinner maintained that any living organism will tend to repeat a particular behavior if that behavior is accompanied or followed by a reinforcer. A **reinforcer** is any stimulus that follows a response and increases the probability that the response will occur again.[7]

Support from Berne

In Chapter 9, you were given a brief introduction to Transactional Analysis (TA), a theory of communication developed by Eric Berne. TA is a simplified explanation of how people communicate. Berne's research also provided evidence that most people have a strong need for recognition, or "strokes."

The word *stroking* is used to describe the various forms of recognition one person gives to another. Strokes help satisfy the need to be appreciated. A **physical stroke** may be a pat on the back or a smile that communicates approval. **Verbal strokes** include words of praise and expressions of gratitude.

Berne said that stroking is necessary for physical and mental health. He believed, as do others, that infants who are deprived of physical strokes (hugs, caresses, and kisses) begin to lose their will to live. As people grow into adulthood, they are willing to substitute verbal stroking for physical stroking. Adults still need and want physical stroking, but they will settle for words of praise, positive feedback, awards, and other forms of recognition.

HUMAN RELATIONS IN ACTION

New Vacuum Sweepers Boost Morale

Anita Lum, a housekeeper at the Hotel Carlton in San Francisco, says you can tell a lot about management by the vacuum she uses. Former Carlton management did not replace aging vacuums despite complaints from the staff. When a new manager arrived, he purchased a new vacuum for each of the 15 housekeepers—and replaces them every year. Ms. Lum feels the new management cares more about the workers: "They try to do what we say." The Carlton hotel has one of the lowest employee turnover rates in the hotel industry.[8]

Monty Rakusen/Getty Images

Nearly all workers appreciate recognition for their accomplishments. They respond positively to notes, letters, gifts, awards, and comments that express appreciation.

Positive Reinforcement—Creating Positive Energy

In recent years, researchers have quantified the cost of negativity in the workplace, and the results are quite shocking. Negative, or "actively disengaged," workers cost the U.S. economy between $250 and $300 billion a year according to the Gallup International Research and Education Center. The costs associated with negativity are even higher when you add on the expenses associated with employee turnover, absenteeism, fraud, and workplace injuries.[9] The good news is that organizations such as New Belgium Brewing Company, US Airways, and Container Store have found ways to neutralize and even reverse damaging negativity.

A brief book entitled *How Full Is Your Bucket?* (*http://www.bucketbook.com*), written by Gallup Practice Leaders Tom Rath and Donald Clifton, provides a simple yet compelling strategy for reducing negativity in the workplace. After more than 50 years of comprehensive psychological and workplace research, they were inspired to develop the Theory of the Dipper and the Bucket (see Figure 10.2). According to Rath and Clifton, each of us has an invisible bucket. It is constantly being emptied or filled, depending on what others say or do to us. When our bucket is full, we feel great. A full bucket increases our positive emotions and renews our energy. When it is empty, we feel awful. There are a lot of empty buckets in today's work force. Survey after survey has found that more than half of the workers in America say they do not feel appreciated in their current jobs.[10]

Each of us also has an invisible dipper. We can use that dipper to fill other people's buckets or our own bucket. When we use that dipper to dip from another person's bucket, we diminish that person and ourselves.

FIGURE 10.2 How Full Is Your Bucket?

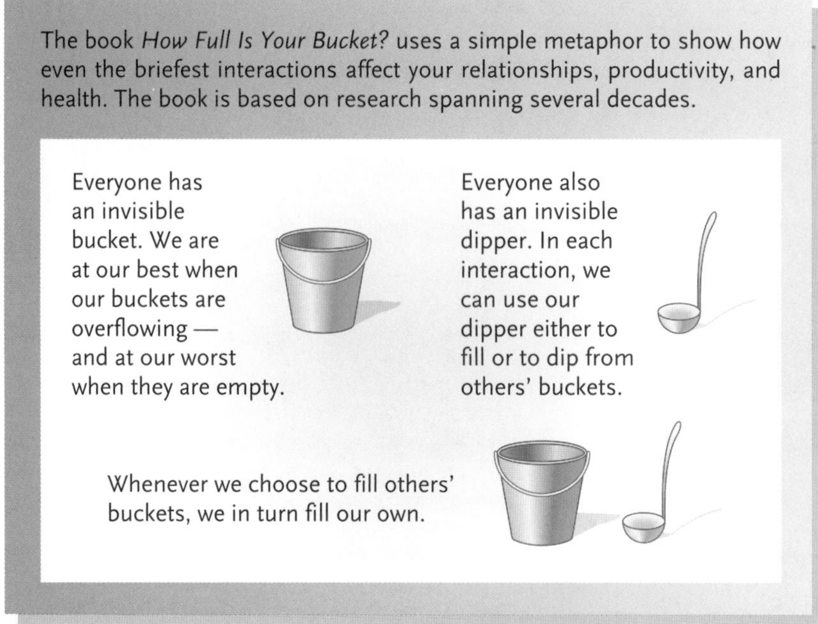

The book *How Full Is Your Bucket?* uses a simple metaphor to show how even the briefest interactions affect your relationships, productivity, and health. The book is based on research spanning several decades.
Everyone has an invisible bucket. We are at our best when our buckets are overflowing — and at our worst when they are empty.
Everyone also has an invisible dipper. In each interaction, we can use our dipper either to fill or to dip from others' buckets.
Whenever we choose to fill others' buckets, we in turn fill our own.

Source: Tom Rath and Donald O. Clifton, *How Full Is Your Bucket?* (New York: Gallop Press, 2004), p. 25.

Positive Reinforcement Defined

The goal of **positive reinforcement** is to encourage productive behaviors. At PaeTec Communications, located near Rochester, New York, everything revolves around respect for the employee. Arunas Chesonis, CEO, sets an example for every employee by sharing financial information, acquisition plans, profits, and other information usually discussed only in the boardroom. He answers e-mails from every employee and expects everyone else to do the same. He rewards information sharing with personal thank-you notes, e-mails, and visits. This pattern is followed in other important areas such as customer service and honoring family life.[11]

Positive reinforcement has never been more important than it is today. Large numbers of workers at all levels of organizations encounter energy-draining experiences at work and in their personal lives. Positive energy is an important form of life enrichment. As we will see in the remaining pages of this chapter, positive reinforcement is an easy to use, inexpensive, and effective way to generate positive energy in the workplace.[12]

CRITICAL THINKING CHALLENGE:

Analyze It

Throughout life we form habits that can have a major impact on our ability to develop positive relationships with others. Take a few minutes and reflect on the dipper and bucket metaphor. Do you find it easy or difficult to fill someone else's bucket? Your own bucket? Do you frequently dip from others' buckets?[13]

The Power of Recognition

Generation Y workers (Millennials) do not want to wait for the annual performance review for recognition. Ron Alsop, author of *The Trophy Kids Grow Up: How the Millennial Generation Is Shaking Up the Workplace,* notes that many Millennials grew up receiving a great deal of affirmation and positive reinforcement. Now, they come into the workplace needy for more.[14] For this generation, frequent feedback is vital and often more important than salary or a company's name recognition.

Giving recognition is one of the easiest and most powerful ways to make an employee feel important and needed. When handled correctly, recognition can be an effective reinforcement strategy that ensures repetition of desired behaviors. The authors of *The One Minute Manager,* a book that has sold more than 12 million copies, point out that recognition in the form of praise need not take a great deal of time. The key is to pay attention to what others are doing and try not to miss an opportunity to use praise to generate positive energy. Table 10.1 provides some excellent tips on planning and delivering praise.

Courtesy Can Be Contagious

The poet Alfred Tennyson once said, "The greater the man, the greater the courtesy." Courtesy means being considerate of others in small ways, showing respect for what others revere, and treating everyone, regardless of position, with consideration. In today's fast-paced world, the impact of courtesy can easily be overlooked. Rudeness flourishes in our society, so it is not surprising that common courtesies are sometimes forgotten. Someone arrives late for an important meeting but does not see the need to apologize or even explain why he is late. You schedule an important meeting with your team, and suddenly a member is talking to a friend on her cell phone. These behaviors create negative energy.

TABLE 10.1 ONE-MINUTE PRAISINGS

The one-minute praising works well, say authors Kenneth Blanchard and Spencer Johnson, when you:

1. Tell people up front that you are going to let them know how they are doing.
2. Praise people immediately.
3. Tell them what they did right—be specific.
4. Tell them how good you feel about what they did right and how it helps the organization and others who work there.
5. Stop for a moment of silence to let them feel how good you feel.
6. Encourage them to do more of the same.
7. Shake hands or touch people in a way that makes it clear that you support their success in the organization.

Source: "One Minute Praisings" from *The One Minute Manager* by Kenneth Blanchard and Spencer Johnson. 1981, 1982 by Blanchard Family Partnership and Candle Communications Corp., Inc. Reprinted by permission of HarperCollins Publishers, Inc.

FIGURE 10.3 Post Job Interview Letter

Infra-Dynamics, Inc.

Binghamton Houston Palo Alto

October 20, 2010

Ms. Pam Jarrett, CEO
Resource Alliance, Inc.
126 James River Avenue
Binghamton, NY 13901

Dear Ms. Jarrett:

Thank you for taking the time to interview me for your upcoming opening in account development. I enjoyed meeting you and learning more about your successful firm. Based on our discussion, I'm sure I possess the qualifications you seek.

As noted during our meeting, I managed the advertising department for the University of North Carolina student newspaper, print and on-line editions, over a two-year period. In the area of account development, my goal was to build long-term partnerships with our customers. I learned the importance of creating value during each contact with the customer. This was accomplished by always having the client's best interests at heart.

Please tell your secretary I appreciate her help in scheduling the interview. If a second interview is planned, please contact me at 643-292-9230 (cell).

Sincerely,

Paul L. Mason

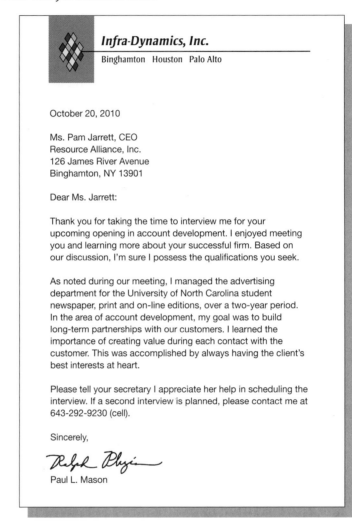

The Power of Gratitude. Gratitude is one of those human qualities that benefits the giver and the receiver. Grateful people experience higher levels of positive emotions such as joy, enthusiasm, happiness, and optimism. The practice of gratitude protects us from destructive impulses such as envy, resentment, and bitterness. One way to develop positive energy is to keep a "gratitude journal." Each day, write down three to five things for which you are grateful.[15]

Take time to notice small gestures of goodwill and learn to thank the givers of such gifts. Write thank-you notes frequently. Linda Kaplan, author of *The Power of Nice*, says, "In business, being nice has been underrated."[16]

Most job seekers know they should express their gratitude in writing following a job interview. A carefully prepared thank you note (see Figure 10.3) provides a great opportunity to gain a competitive edge in today's job market. A thoughtful follow-up letter goes beyond a simple thank you:[17]

- Link your skills to solving specific workplace problems you learned about during the interview.

- Describe relevant achievements and potential contributions beyond those you described in person.
- Revisit any important issue you may not have handled well during the interview.

Active Listening

As discussed in Chapter 2, everyone feels a sense of personal value when speaking with a good listener. Active listening can be a powerful reinforcer. Active listening is the process of sending back to the speaker what you as a listener think the speaker meant in terms of both content and feelings.

People long for more authentic interactions with coworkers or bosses who are good listeners. *Dialogue,* as a specific practice, is being implemented in a number of progressive organizations. A *dialogue group* is a meeting where all participants agree to be especially aware of what they say, how well they listen, and how well they give feedback to others. This training activity is designed to promote self-reflection and increased self-awareness.[18]

Pride as a Source of Positive Energy

Pride is the emotional high that follows performance and success. This definition was developed by Jon Katzenbach, author of *Why Pride Matters More Than Money.* He notes that the power of pride is obvious when you observe the high-performing work forces at Southwest Airlines, Marriott, the U.S. Marine Corps, and Microsoft. "Pride is a natural by-product of the successes of those organizations," says Katzenbach.[19]

Southwest Airlines Company was founded by Herb Kelleher (now retired). Over the years, he developed a culture that other airlines envy. By almost every measure of efficiency in the airline industry, Southwest is at the top of the charts. Kelleher's dedication to his employees was a major reason for the success of this company. Gary Kelly, the current CEO, is working hard to maintain the fun-loving, family-like feel among the 34,000-plus Southwest employees.[20]

Katzenbach notes that pride-builders can be found at all levels of the organization. They often get involved in the everyday problems of their employees. Roy Pelaez leads a work force of 426 people who clean airplanes for Delta Airlines and Southwest Airlines. Many of his staff are recent immigrants, so he brought in an English-language teacher to tutor employees twice a week on their own time. He scheduled Friday citizenship classes to help employees become U.S. citizens. To help single mothers, Pelaez arranged for certified babysitters subsidized by government programs.[21]

Barriers to Positive Reinforcement

The material in this chapter is based on two indisputable facts about human nature. First, people want to know how well they are doing and if their efforts are satisfactory. Second, they appreciate recognition for their accomplishments. Performance feedback, encouragement, and positive reinforcement can satisfy these important human needs. People often say they prefer negative feedback to no feedback at all. "Don't leave me in the dark" is a common plea (spoken or unspoken) of most people.

Skill Development: Apply It

Chances are you owe somebody a thank-you note. Think about the events of the past six months. Has someone given time and effort to assist you with a problem? Make a list of at least three people who deserve a thank-you note. Pick one, handwrite that person a note of appreciation, and mail it today.

Preoccupation with the Self

One of the major obstacles to providing positive reinforcement is preoccupation with the self. The term **narcissism** is often used to describe this human condition. Narcissism is a Freudian term alluding to the mythical youth who wore himself out trying to kiss his own reflection in a pool of water.

> If you want attention and appreciation, you must learn to give attention and appreciation.

Deepak Chopra, author of *The Seven Spiritual Laws of Success,* encourages everyone to practice the "Law of Giving." This law states that you must give in order to receive. If you want attention and appreciation, you must learn to give attention and appreciation. If you want joy in your life, you must give joy to others. He says the easiest way to get what you want is to help others get what they want.[22]

The publication of *Random Acts of Kindness* and many people's acceptance of its central theme may have signaled a movement away from self-preoccupation. Random acts of kindness are those little things that we do for others without receiving payback. They involve giving freely, purely, for no reason.[23] Here are some examples from the book:

- Send a letter to a teacher you once had letting him or her know about the difference he or she made in your life.
- Write a card thanking a service provider for his or her care and leave it with your tip.

Total Person Insight

Malcolm Boyd
Episcopal Priest; Author, *Volunteering Thanks*

"Feeling grateful is good for us. Gratitude is the opposite of the qualities of self-centeredness, indifference, and arrogance. Expressing gratitude affords each of us unique opportunities to reach out in love and share happiness. Saying thank you is a very positive thing to do."[24]

Misconceptions About Positive Reinforcement

Some people fail to use positive reinforcement because they have misconceptions about this human relations strategy. One misconception is that people will respond to positive feedback by demanding tangible evidence of appreciation. "Tell people they are doing a good job, and they will ask for a raise" seems to be the attitude of some managers. Actually, just the opposite response will surface more often than not. In the absence of intangible rewards (such as praise), workers may demand greater tangible rewards.

A few managers seem to feel they will lose some of their power or control if they praise workers. Yet, if managers rely on power alone to get the job done, any success they achieve will no doubt be short-lived.

The "Too Busy" Syndrome

Ken Blanchard says, "We're often too busy or too stressed to remember that the recognition we crave, others crave as well."[25] When you are under a great deal of pressure to get your work done, and you are struggling to achieve some degree of work/life balance, it is easy to postpone sending a thank-you note or contacting someone simply for the purpose of saying "Thank you."

The key to solving this problem is planning. A consciously planned positive reinforcement program will ensure that recognition for work well done is not overlooked. One approach might be to set aside a few minutes each day to work on performance feedback and positive reinforcement activities (see Table 10.1).

Failing to Identify Commendable Actions

There are numerous opportunities to recognize the people you work with. By exercising just a little creativity, you can discover many actions that deserve to be commended.

Assume you are the manager of a large auto dealership. One of the key people within your organization is the service manager. This person schedules work to be performed on customers' cars, handles customer complaints, supervises the technicians, and performs a host of other duties. If you want to give your service manager performance feedback and positive recognition, what types of behavior can you praise? Table 10.2 lists some examples.

Not Knowing What to Say or Do

Bob Nelson, author of *1001 Ways to Reward Employees,* reminds us that we can provide encouragement, praise, recognition, and rewards in a variety of ways. He encourages us to use thoughtful, personal kinds of recognition that signify true appreciation.[26] Many words and phrases can communicate approval. Here are several examples:

- "Good thinking!"
- "Thank you."
- "Excellent idea."
- "Keep up the good work."

Rich DeVos, cofounder of Amway Global Corporation, says there are several phrases that can be used every day to enrich your life and the lives of other people. Here are some of his favorites:[27]

- "I'm wrong."
- "I need you."
- "I'm sorry."
- "I'm proud of you."

TABLE 10.2 JOB PERFORMANCE BEHAVIORS TO BE REINFORCED

1. Performance Related to Interpersonal Relations
   a. Demonstrates empathy for customer needs and problems
   b. Is able to handle customer complaints effectively
   c. Is able to keep all employees well informed
   d. Cooperates with supervisory personnel in other departments
   e. Recognizes the accomplishments of employees
   f. Exhibits effective supervision of employees
2. Personal Characteristics
   a. Is honest in dealings with people throughout the organization
   b. Is punctual
   c. Does not violate policies and procedures
   d. Maintains emotional stability
   e. Maintains a neat appearance
   f. Is alert to new ways to do the job better
3. Management Skills
   a. Avoids waste in the use of supplies and materials
   b. Maintains accurate records
   c. Spends time on short- and long-range planning
   d. Takes steps to prevent accidents
   e. Delegates authority and responsibility
   f. Maintains quality-control standards

And you can give recognition to others through some type of action. Here are some activities that show approval:

- Sending an employee to a workshop or seminar that covers a topic he or she is interested in
- Asking for advice
- Asking someone to demonstrate the correct performance or procedure for others
- Recognizing someone's work at a staff meeting

Rewarding Individual and Team Performance

In recent years, we have seen expanded use of positive reinforcement strategies in the workplace. In the past, we viewed positive reinforcement as the responsibility of supervisors and managers. This view was much too narrow. As shown in Figure 10.4, everyone in the organization has opportunities to recognize the accomplishments of others. Persons in supervisory and management positions can benefit from positive reinforcement initiated by subordinates.

Employees can also be encouraged to recognize the accomplishments of coworkers. In some cases, praise from a respected colleague is more important than praise from the boss. This is especially true when employees work together on a team.

FIGURE 10.4 Shared Responsibilities for Positive Reinforcement

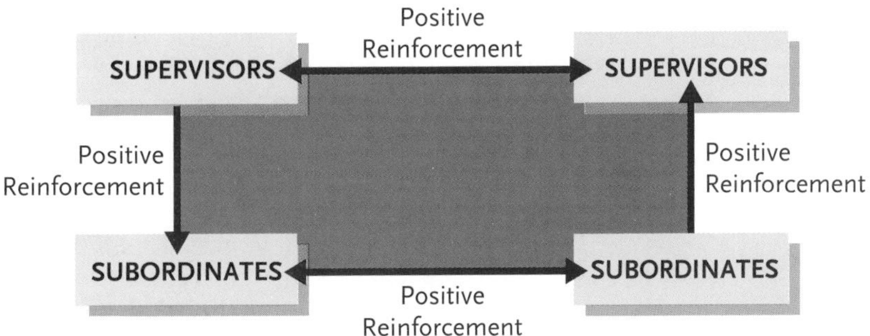

The concept of teamwork and the growing popularity of various types of teams are changing the way companies structure their reward systems. If a work force is reorganized into self-directed work teams (discussed in Chapter 12), it makes sense to consider various types of team recognition plans. Such plans often emphasize the recognition of group performance rather than the recognition of individual performance.

Incentive Programs

Every year, organizations spend billions of dollars for incentives and awards given to their employees. This money is spent on televisions, vacation trips, rings, plaques, pins, certificates, stock options, merit pay, cash bonuses, and a host of other items. An **incentive program** is a planned activity designed to motivate employees to achieve an organizational objective.[28]

One of the most widespread developments in recent years has been the introduction of innovative incentive plans that reward increased productivity, improved quality, improved customer service, lower operating costs, or some combination of these factors. These plans include cash and noncash awards. The most common noncash awards include merchandise, travel opportunities, and recognition in the form of a plaque, trophy, pin, or letter of commendation. As noted previously, New Belgium Brewing Company gives each employee a new bicycle after one year of employment. After five years of employment, each worker gets a one-week complimentary trip to Belgium to learn about Belgian beer culture.[29]

Although the vast majority of U.S. companies use some type of incentive program, many do not achieve positive results. It is possible to design programs that provide benefits to the organization and the individual employee, but care must be taken during the planning stage. Here are a few incentive plan fundamentals:

- *Do not assume that financial rewards provide the most powerful incentive.* Stephen J. Dubner, coauthor of the best selling book *Freakonomics,* says social and moral incentives are often more powerful.[30] An employee who is working excessive work hours may value more time with family, socializing, and recreation. Rewards must satisfy individual needs.
- *Avoid incentives that might foster unethical behavior.* Some retail companies encourage sales personnel to push extended warranties—a high-profit item that many customers don't want or need. In some cases these sales become the

basis for measuring employee performance. Employees who don't meet established incentive goals may lose their job.[31]

- *Always field test incentive plans.* Several questions need to be answered: Is the plan easy to administer? Will employees support the plan? Employee input during the planning stage is very important.[32]

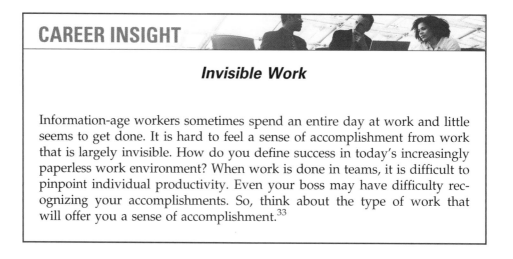

CAREER INSIGHT

Invisible Work

Information-age workers sometimes spend an entire day at work and little seems to get done. It is hard to feel a sense of accomplishment from work that is largely invisible. How do you define success in today's increasingly paperless work environment? When work is done in teams, it is difficult to pinpoint individual productivity. Even your boss may have difficulty recognizing your accomplishments. So, think about the type of work that will offer you a sense of accomplishment.[33]

Reexamining Our Ideas About Productivity

We need to continuously reexamine our ideas about what actions and events increase employee productivity. Many firms take the position that if employees work more hours, they will be more productive. Therefore, overtime pay is used to reward some employees who work extra hours. Critics of this approach say that employees perform optimally for six or seven hours, but then the fatigue factor surfaces. Critics of overtime (voluntary and required) also point out the need for employees to have a life outside work.[34]

Will the employee who is rewarded for working faster be more productive? Critics of this approach note that slower, intuitive thinking is often more effective in solving problems. Also, they note that a greater number of complex, creative ideas result from a slower thought process.[35]

As a nation, we have progressed from a society of farmers, to a society of factory workers, to a society of knowledge workers. And now, according to Daniel Pink, author of *A Whole New Mind,* we are progressing yet again—to a society of creators and empathizers. He says the information age is giving way to a new world in which creative abilities and high touch abilities mark the fault line between who gets ahead and who falls behind.[36] What type of organizational culture will bring out the best in these future employees?

The Critical Importance of Environment

Positive energy flourishes in a supportive environment. Within the organization, there should be respect for each person, regardless of job title, duties performed, or earnings. The prevailing climate within the organization should also be positive. People must feel good about the organization, its leadership, and other employees. Positive energy comes naturally in a positive work environment. But positive energy will almost never flourish in a negative work environment.

LOOKING BACK: REVIEWING THE CONCEPTS

- Describe how positive energy contributes to improved interpersonal relationships.

Positive energy can have a major influence on employee morale and productivity. Encouragement, positive feedback, and other types of practices that create positive energy are important factors in improving interpersonal relationships.

- Create awareness of the strong need people have for encouragement and positive feedback.

People usually feel good when their accomplishments are recognized and become upset when they are ignored. Positive reinforcement, when used correctly to reward accomplishments, is a powerful motivator. Everyone needs to receive personal recognition for work done well.

- Understand how to use positive reinforcement to improve relationships and reward behavior.

Although many studies indicate that recognition of their accomplishments is important to employees, often more so than monetary rewards and job security, many people seem unable or unwilling to reward a job well done. Praise, pride, courtesy, active listening, written thank-you notes, incentives, and awards can be used to instill positive energy.

- Describe the major barriers to the use of positive reinforcement.

Preoccupation with self is a major obstacle to providing reinforcement to others. Self-centered persons are likely to overlook the accomplishments of others. Some people say a busy schedule does not allow them time to give recognition to others, and some people have difficulty identifying commendable actions. These and other barriers tend to minimize the use of positive reinforcement.

- Explain how to reward individual and team performance.

Individual and team performance are often rewarded through the use of incentive programs. Some of the most common incentive programs involving cash payments are gain sharing, profit sharing, production incentives, pay for knowledge, and suggestion programs. Employee stock options have also been popular in recent years.

ON THE JOB Q & A: IS "KISSING UP" ACCEPTABLE?

Q: Is "kissing up" to the boss an acceptable behavior today? I have heard that this practice can make a difference in today's competitive workplace.

A: Performance is what matters most, but it would be a mistake to disregard the impact of flattery on your boss. Complimenting your supervisor on how he or she conducted a business meeting or solved a major problem may enhance your career. Employees with good people skills—which include building rapport with the boss—are the ones most likely to advance. The primary rule to follow when praising your boss is *do not fake it.* Do not give a compliment unless you genuinely believe it is deserved. To offer endless, insincere flattery will backfire. And do not forget to praise the accomplishments of your coworkers. The people you work with can often help or hinder your move up the ladder.[37]

KEY TERMS

energy 210
reinforcer 214
physical stroke 214
verbal strokes 214
positive reinforcement 216
pride 219
narcissism 220
incentive program 223

TRY YOUR HAND

1. Your company is considering adopting a tobacco-free employee hiring practice. As the Director of Human Resources, you have been charged to research the legality of this proposal and provide examples of companies/industries who engage in this practice. Your charge also includes drafting a smoking cessation program for employees who currently smoke. Creating a tobacco-free work environment is a health and economic issue that the CEO would like to see implemented. Make sure that you appraise the advantages and disadvantages of these proposals.

2. Organizations are continually searching for ways to reward various employee behaviors. Pretend you are currently working at an upscale retail clothing store and the manager asks you to help her design an incentive plan that would result in improved sales of clothing and accessories. She asks you to review and comment on the following options:
   - **a.** Employee-of-the-month awards for highest sales. (A special plaque would be used to recognize each monthly winner.)
   - **b.** Commission on sales. All employees would be given a 5 percent commission on all sales. Each salesperson would receive an hourly wage plus the commission.
   - **c.** Time off. Employees who achieve sales goals established by management could earn up to four hours of paid time off each week.
   - **d.** Prizes. Employees who achieve weekly sales goals established by management would be eligible for prizes such as sports or theater tickets, dinner at a nice restaurant, gift certificates, or merchandise sold by the store.

   Rank these four options by assigning "1" to your first choice, "2" to your second choice, "3" to your third choice, and "4" to your fourth choice. Provide a written rationale for your first choice.

3. The authors of *Random Acts of Kindness* tell us that the little things we do for others can have big payoffs. These acts give us an outward focus that helps us move away from self-preoccupation. Plan and initiate at least two acts of kindness during the next week, and then reflect on the experience. What impact did the act have on the other person? How did you feel about this experience?

INTERNET INSIGHTS

Much discussion has ensued regarding the effectiveness of incentives and awards designed to motivate employees. Visit the following websites *http://www.carrots.com* and *http://www.winningworkplaces.org* and assess whether the rewards of recognizing a job well done makes a difference in employee performance and morale. Prepare a written summary of findings.

YOU PLAY THE ROLE

Peggy Klaus, author of *Brag! The Art of Tooting Your Own Horn Without Blowing It,* says, "You have to let the people above you know what you are doing, what skills you're developing, which goals you're achieving." She says, "Don't make them guess." Self-promotion has become more important today because many careers are being buffeted by downsizing, mergers, and business closings. For the purpose of this role play, assume the role of Britten Higgins, a full-time employee in the computer electronics department of Best Buy. You have heard rumors that your department manager may be promoted. You hope to move up within the Best Buy organization, and advancing to department head would be an important first step. You have decided to meet with your manager and discuss two things: (1) your interest in becoming department head and (2) your accomplishments and the steps you have taken to prepare for advancement. Feel free to ad-lib the information you present during the role play.[38]

BELOW THE SURFACE:

Developing Positive Energy at Winning Workplaces

If you are looking for a great place to work, do consider one of the companies that has received a Top Small Workplace award. As noted at the beginning of this chapter, each year the *Wall Street Journal*, in partnership with Winning Workplaces, selects 15 small and midsize companies that have built exemplary workplaces (*http://www.winningworkplaces.org*). These employers understand the power of positive energy. Consider these two examples:

- Decagon Devices Inc. is a family-run business based in Pullman, Washington. The maker of scientific instruments and sensors takes steps to make sure all employees—actual kinfolk or not—feel like family. The company divides up 20 percent of pretax profit among employees each quarter and gives all employees a year-end bonus. Each Wednesday, some employees take turns bringing home-cooked meals to work for coworkers. Then all of the workers eat lunch together. These noon luncheons provide management with an opportunity to present news about the company. The office has a ping-pong table and slot-car track. Space is provided for employees who want to play soccer during their breaks. The company pays 100 percent of the premium for employees and dependents' health-insurance coverage. One of the judges for Top Small Workplaces rated the culture at Decagon Devices Inc. as the highest of any firm he had studied.[39]
- Paducah Bank & Trust Company works hard to instill an ownership mentality among its employees. They currently own about 23 percent of this Kentucky-based bank through a stock-ownership plan. Every morning, each department holds a short "Owners Meeting" to discuss bank events and how to improve customer service. These meetings provide an opportunity to celebrate employee birthdays and other milestones.

  The bank invests considerable time and money on training and development programs. The bank encourages employees to participate in its leadership-development program. Kerri Brotherson joined the bank in 2000 as a teller. Today, three promotions later, she is a commercial loan officer. The bank wants every employee to feel valuable to the company.[40]

QUESTIONS

1. Carefully review the employee development practices initiated by managers at Decagon Devices Inc. and Paducah Bank & Trust Company. Determine which of these practices would be most appealing to you. Why?
2. Many of the Top Small Workplace managers report that they invest more in training, recognition awards, and incentive programs than competing firms. They say these investments result in reduced employee expenses in other areas. Analyze some of the expenses that might be reduced as a result of these investments.

CLOSING CASE:
The Role of Pride in Building High Morale

Paetec Communications wants its employees to engage in exceptional efforts to make customers happy. Arunas Chesonis, CEO of Paetec, realizes that high morale among his employees is an important key to good customer service. He wants each employee to feel a sense of pride in the company, so he makes every effort to recognize work done well. Rewards range from a personal note to a cruise vacation.

Jon R. Katzenbach, author of *Why Pride Matters More Than Money,* says employee pride is what drives high-performing organizations like Southwest Airlines, SAS Institute, the U.S. Marine Corps, and the Container Store. He offers the following tool kit for those who want to become effective pride builders:

- *Personalize the workplace.* This means get involved in the everyday problems of your employees. Managers at some Marriott hotels work with employees from several different countries. These workers often need help learning the English language, preparing to become American citizens, and finding affordable child-care services. Marriott realizes that any problem that affects employees will eventually affect their on-the-job performance.
- *Always have your compass set on pride, not money.* There is no doubt that financial rewards can help an organization attract and retain good people. However, monetary incentives motivate only a narrow set of behaviors and place an emphasis on self-interest that may not be in the best interests of the company. In recent years, monetary rewards have proven to be a risky source of motivation. Compensation programs can be manipulated by clever employees to their advantage.
- *Localize as much as possible.* "Don't wait for your organization or its leaders to instill pride," says Katzenbach. The best pride builders are quick to spot and recognize the small achievements that will instill pride in their people.
- *Make your messages simple and direct.* A pride building program should not be built on needless complexity. In some cases, a good story about an employee who went the extra mile to help a customer solve a problem can stir up feelings of pride.[41]

QUESTIONS

1. Some human resource department employees voice concerns when supervisors or team leaders get involved with the everyday problems of their workers. Discuss your thoughts regarding this issue.
2. Some leaders in business and industry say that worker pride is the byproduct of achievement. What are your thoughts? What factors constitute achievement at your local McDonald's restaurant? Your local community hospital?
3. Do you agree that pride building can be localized throughout the organization?

INTEGRATED RESOURCES

VIDEO:

Motivating Employees: Empowered and Appreciated

CLASSROOM ACTIVITIES

IRM Application Exercise 10.1
IRM Application Exercise 10.2
IRM Application Exercise 10.3

Developing a Professional Presence

TIP OF THE ICEBERG

CHAPTER PREVIEW

LEARNING OBJECTIVES

After studying Chapter 11, you will be able to

- Explain the importance of professional presence.
- Understand the importance of a favorable first impression.
- Define *image* and describe the factors that form the image you project to others.
- List and discuss factors that influence your choice of clothing for work.
- Understand how workplace etiquette contributes to improved interpersonal relations.

© Noel Hendrickson/Photographer's Choice RF/Getty Images

Personal Brand Development

What? Pay a personal-branding consultant $10,000 to help develop my personal brand? Some high-end job hunters feel the need for "expert" advice in this area. They note that in today's crowded job market it is getting harder to stand out from the crowd.[1] These job seekers are taking a page from the marketing plans developed by Harley-Davidson motorcycles, Apple computers, Craftsman tools, and numerous other products and services.

Some brands have cultivated a cult following. BMW motorcycles have a loyal following of riders who feel these bikes are superior in quality, performance, and design. A brand is more than a product. The best brands have achieved *brand personality*, a specific mix of human traits that build an emotional connection with the consumer.[2]

Branding can play a crucial role in your success. The authors of *Be Your Own Brand: A Breakthrough Formula for Standing Out from the Crowd* say branding can have a significant impact on your relationships, career, and life. Developing a strong personal brand involves all the little ways you express what you believe and how you present yourself to others. This chapter presents an abundance of brand development information.[3]

Professional Presence—An Introduction

There are many personal and professional benefits to be gained from a study of the concepts in this chapter. You will acquire new insights regarding ways to communicate positive impressions during job interviews, business contacts, and social contacts made away from work. You will also learn how to shape an

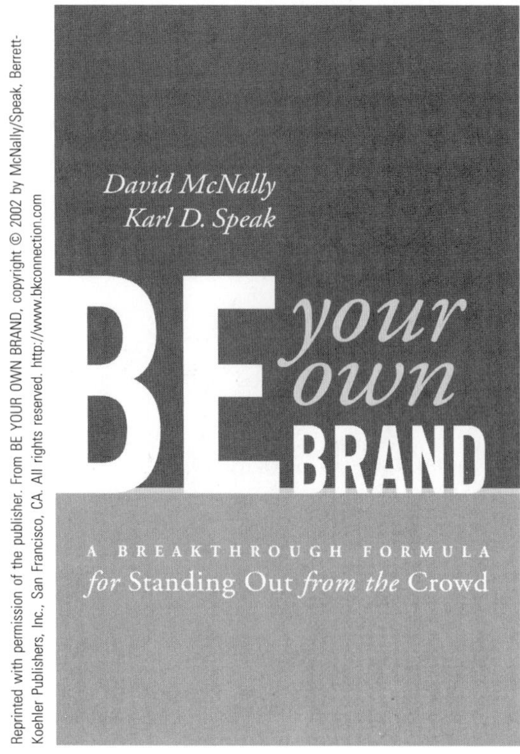

A personal brand and a business brand have a lot in common. The authors of *Be Your Own Brand* say both brands need to be distinctive, relevant, and consistent. Your personal brand should include a mix of human traits that help you stand out from the crowd.

image that will help you achieve your fullest potential in the career of your choice. Image is a major component of brand development.

This is not a chapter about ways to make positive impressions with superficial behavior and quick-fix techniques. We do not discuss the "power look" or the "power lunch." The material in this chapter will not help you become a more entertaining conversationalist or win new customers by pretending to be interested in their hobbies or families. Stephen Covey, author of *The Seven Habits of Highly Effective People*, says that the ability to build effective, long-term relationships is based on character strength and not quick-fix techniques. He notes that outward attitude and behavior changes do very little good in the long run *unless* they are based on solid principles governing human effectiveness. These principles include service (making a contribution), integrity and honesty (which serve as a foundation of trust), human dignity (every person has worth), and fairness.[4]

Professional Presence—A Definition

We are indebted to Susan Bixler, author of *Professional Presence*, for giving us a better understanding of what it means to possess professional presence. **Professional presence** is a dynamic blend of poise, self-confidence, control, and style that empowers us to be able to command respect in any situation.[5] Once acquired, it permits us to project a confidence that others can quickly perceive the first time they meet us. Obviously, to *project* this confidence, you need to *feel* confident.

Photo by Jason Kirk/Getty Images

Harley-Davidson has thrived by creating a strong brand image that appeals to baby boomers. Jay Leno says big Harleys will always be seen as older guys' bikes. Today, Harley-Davidson realizes that women are a growing segment of the market. The challenge is meeting the needs of smaller, less muscular riders, but avoiding creating brand confusion.

Bixler points out that, in many cases, the credentials we present during a job interview, or when we are being considered for a promotion, are not very different from those of other persons being considered. It is our professional presence that permits us to rise above the crowd.

The Importance of Making a Good First Impression

As organizations experience increased competition for clients, patients, or customers, they are giving new attention to the old adage "First impressions are lasting ones." Research indicates that initial impressions do indeed tend to linger. Therefore, a positive first impression can be thought of as the first step in building a long-term relationship.

Ann Demarais and Valerie White, authors of *First Impressions* (*http://www.firstimpressionsconsulting.com*), say the secret to a good first impression is "social generosity"—helping others feel good about themselves. This requires shifting your focus from your own feelings to making others feel good. When you meet someone for the first time, you need to put others' needs and feelings before your own.[6]

The development of professional presence begins with a full appreciation of the power of first impressions.

The Primacy Effect

The development of professional presence begins with a full appreciation of the power of first impressions. The tendency to form and retain impressions quickly at the time of an initial meeting illustrates what social psychologists call a **primacy effect** in the way people perceive one another. The general principle is that initial information tends to carry more weight than information received later. First impressions establish the mental framework within which a person is viewed, and information acquired later is often ignored or reinterpreted to coincide with this framework.[7]

Demarais and White note that in a first impression, others see only a very small sample of you, a tiny percentage of your life. But to them, that small sample represents 100 percent of what they know of you. And they will weigh initial information much more heavily than later information.[8]

The First Few Seconds

Malcolm Gladwell *(http://www.gladwell.com)*, a best-selling author, learned a great deal about the power of first impressions a few years ago when he let his close-cropped hair grow wild. His life changed immediately. He got far more speeding tickets and was routinely pulled out of airport security lines for special attention. People he met knew nothing about him except that he had shaggy hair, but they were ready to think the worst.[9]

Malcolm Gladwell, author of the best selling book *Blink: The Power of Thinking Without Thinking*, discovered that wearing long, shaggy hair has consequences. Some people who knew nothing about him were ready to think the worst.

Gladwell was inspired to try to understand what happens beneath the surface of rapidly made decisions. His findings later appeared in *Blink: The Power of Thinking Without Thinking*. He says most of us would like to think our decision making is the result of rational deliberation, but in reality, most decisions are made subconsciously in a split second.[10]

Total Person Insight

JUDITH SILLS
Clinical Psychologist

"At its heart, branding addresses a hard professional reality: For a successful long-term career, do not look to your company or industry to take care of you. As in every other arena of life, you must take care of yourself. A well-built brand will be your life raft."[11]

Most people assess another person very quickly and then settle on a general perception of that individual. Research conducted at Carleton University in Ottawa indicates that people are registering like and dislikes in as little as 1/20th of a second.[12] It is very difficult for us to reverse that first impression. Paula rushed into a restaurant for a quick lunch—she had to get back to her office for a 1:30 p.m. appointment. At the entrance of the main dining area was a sign reading "Please Wait to Be Seated." A few feet away, the hostess was discussing a popular movie with one of the waitresses. The hostess made eye contact with Paula but continued to visit with the waitress. In this situation, Paula immediately formed a negative impression of the hostess, even though no words were exchanged. She quickly left the restaurant. Unfortunately, the hostess may not have been fully aware of the negative impression she communicated to the customer.

CRITICAL THINKING CHALLENGE:

Analyze It

The authors of *First Impressions* say that making a good first impression means making the person you meet feel positive toward you. When you have contact with someone, do you think about how the other person is feeling during the initial contact, or do you stay focused on yourself? What can you do to make someone feel positively about you?[13]

Assumptions versus Facts

The impression you form of another person during the initial contact is made up of both assumptions and facts. Most people tend to rely more heavily on **assumptions** during the initial meeting. If a job applicant sits slumped in the chair, head bowed, and shoulders slack, you might assume the person is not very interested in the position. If the postal clerk fails to make eye contact during the transaction and does not express appreciation for your purchase, you may assume this person treats everyone with indifference. Needless to say, the impression you form of another person during the initial contact can be misleading. The briefer the encounter with a new acquaintance, the greater the chance that misinformation will enter into your perception of the other person. The authors of a popular book on first impressions state that "depending on assumptions is a one-way ticket to big surprises and perhaps disappointments."[14]

Cultural Influence

Cultural influences, often formed during the early years of our life, lead us to have impressions of some people even before we meet them. People often develop stereotypes of entire groups. Although differences between cultures are often subtle, they can lead to uncomfortable situations. We need to realize that the Korean shopkeeper is being polite, not hostile, when he puts change on the counter and not in your hand. Some Asian students do not speak up in class out of respect for the teacher, not boredom.[15]

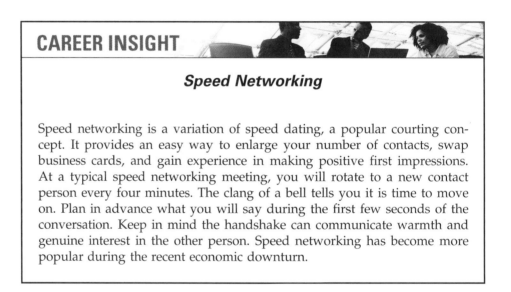

Speed Networking

Speed networking is a variation of speed dating, a popular courting concept. It provides an easy way to enlarge your number of contacts, swap business cards, and gain experience in making positive first impressions. At a typical speed networking meeting, you will rotate to a new contact person every four minutes. The clang of a bell tells you it is time to move on. Plan in advance what you will say during the first few seconds of the conversation. Keep in mind the handshake can communicate warmth and genuine interest in the other person. Speed networking has become more popular during the recent economic downturn.

Norine Dresser, author of *Multiculture Manners—Essential Rules of Etiquette for the 21st Century*, notes that it is becoming more difficult for organizations to develop policies that do not offend one ethnic group or another. She argues that it is the collective duty of the mainstream to learn the customs and practices of established minority groups.[16]

The Image You Project

Image is a term used to describe how other people feel about you. In every business or social setting, your behaviors and appearance communicate a mental picture that others observe and remember. This picture determines how they react to you. Think of image as a tool that can reveal your inherent qualities, your competence, your attitude, and your leadership potential. If you wish to communicate your professional capabilities and create your own brand, begin by investing the time and energy needed to refine and enhance your personal image.

FIGURE 11.1 Major Factors That Form Your Image

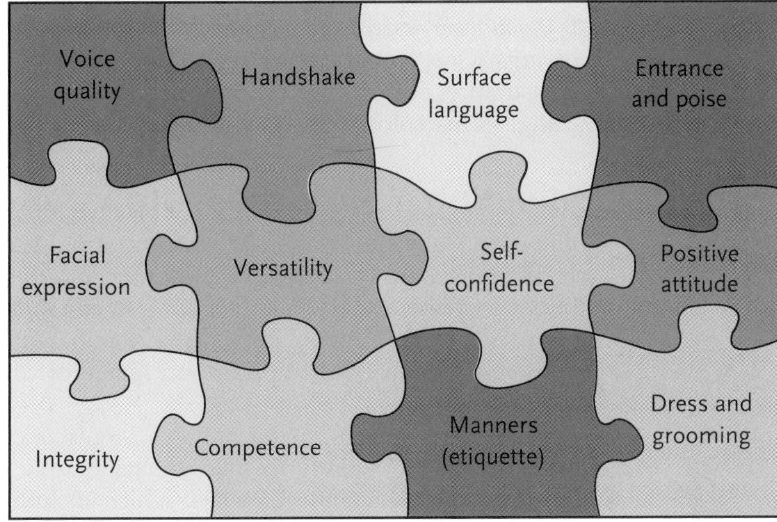

In many respects, the image you project is very much like a picture puzzle, as illustrated in Figure 11.1. It is formed by a variety of factors, including manners, self-confidence, voice quality, versatility (see Chapter 3), integrity (see Chapter 5), entrance and poise, facial expression, surface language, competence, positive attitude, and handshake. Each of these image-shaping components is under your control, though some are harder to develop than others. As you reflect on the image you want to project, remember that a strong personal brand is built from the inside out.

Surface Language

As noted earlier, we base opinions about other people on both facts and assumptions. Unfortunately, assumptions often carry a great deal of weight. Many of the assumptions we develop regarding other people are based on **surface language**, a pattern of immediate impressions conveyed by what we *see*—in other words, by appearance. The clothing you wear, your hairstyle, the fragrances you use, and the jewelry you display all combine to make a statement about you to others.

> A good rule to follow is to dress for the job you want, not the job you have.

According to many writers familiar with image formation, clothing is particularly important. Although a more relaxed dress code has evolved in some employment areas, people judge your appearance long before they judge your talents. It would be a mistake not to take your career wardrobe seriously. When making career wardrobe decisions keep in mind these basic guidelines:[17]

1. *If you want the job, you have to look the part.* Establish personal dress and grooming standards appropriate for the organization where you wish to work. Before you apply for a job, try to find out what the workers there are wearing.
2. *If you want the promotion, you have to look promotable.* A good rule to follow is to dress for the job you want, not the job you have. If you are currently a

bank teller and want to become a branch manager, identify the successful branch managers and emulate their manner of dress.

3. *If you want respect, you have to dress as well as, or better than, your industry standards.* One would expect to find conservative dress standards in banking, insurance, accounting, and law, and more casual dress standards in advertising, sports entertainment, and agriculture.

Selecting Your Career Apparel

Millions of American workers wear a uniform especially designed for a particular job. The judges on the U.S. Supreme Court and the technicians at the local Midas Muffler and Brake shop have one thing in common—both groups wear a special uniform to work. Companies that have initiated extensive career apparel programs rely on uniforms to project an image of consistent quality, good service, and uniqueness.

Enterprise Rent-A-Car, the nation's largest recruiter of college students, requires its 52,000 workers to follow conservative dress and grooming policies. Men, for example, follow 26 rules, which include no beards (unless medically necessary) and dress shirts with coordinated ties. Female employees follow 30 dress code guidelines, including one for skirt length (skirts must not be shorter than two inches above the knee) and one for mandatory stockings. Why does Enterprise choreograph how its employees look? The company maintains that its personal appearance and grooming standards give it a marketing advantage.[18]

The uniforms worn by United Parcel Service (UPS) employees, airport security workers (TSA), and the employees at your local restaurant might be classified as special-design **career apparel**. In addition to special-design uniforms, there is another type of career apparel, somewhat less predictable, worn by large numbers of people in the labor force. Here are two examples:

- A male bank loan officer would be appropriately dressed in a tailored gray or blue suit, white shirt, and tie. This same person dressed in a colorful blazer, sport shirt (without collar), and plaid slacks would be seen as too casual in most bank settings.
- A technician employed by an auto dealership that sells new luxury cars would be appropriately dressed in a matching gray, tan, or blue shirt and pants. The technician would be inappropriately dressed in jeans and a T-shirt.

Many organizations seek advice about career apparel from image consultants who have received certification from the Association of Image Consultants International (*http://www.aici.org*) or Global Protocol, Inc. (*http://www.globalprotocol.com*). The demand for etiquette and protocol consultants has increased in recent years.[19]

Wardrobe Engineering

The term **wardrobe engineering** was first used by John Molloy, author of *Dress for Success*, to describe how clothing and accessories can be used to create a certain image. This concept was later refined by several other noted image consultants in hundreds of books and articles on dress and grooming. Although these authors are not in complete agreement on every aspect of dress, they do agree on the four basic points presented in Table 11.1. Use this information as a guide and do not give in to blind conformity. As noted by one consultant, "Effective packaging is an individual matter based on the person's circumstances, age, weight, height, coloring, and objectives."[20]

TABLE 11.1 FACTORS INFLUENCING YOUR CHOICE OF CLOTHING FOR WORK

Dress codes are undergoing changes, and this complicates the selection of clothing for work. Use the four factors described here for guidance.

1. *Products and services offered.* In some cases, the organization's products and services more or less dictate a certain type of dress. For example, a receptionist employed by a well-established law firm is likely to wear clothing that is conservative, modest, and in good taste. These same dress standards would apply to a pharmaceutical sales representative who calls on medical doctors.
2. *Type of person served.* Research indicates that first impressions created by dress and grooming are greatly influenced by unconscious expectations. Throughout life, we become acquainted with real estate salespeople, nurses, police officers, and others employed in a wide range of occupations. We form mental images of the apparel common to each of these occupations. When we encounter someone whose appearance does not conform to our past experiences, we often feel uncomfortable.
3. *Desired image projected by the organization.* Some companies establish dress codes that help shape the image they project to the public. Walt Disney Company, for example, maintains a strict dress and grooming code for all its theme-park employees. They are considered "cast members" and must adhere to dress and grooming standards that complement the image projected by Disney theme parks.
4. *Geographic region.* Dress in the South and Southwest tends to be more casual than dress in the Northeast. Climate is another factor that influences the clothing people wear at work. Important regional variations in dress codes remain in place for men and women. Dress in the Midwest, South, and Southwest tends to be more casual than dress in the Northeast. Climate is another factor that influences the clothing people wear at work.

The Business Casual Look

The term **business casual** is used to describe the movement toward dress standards that emphasize greater comfort and individuality. Business casual is clothing that allows you to feel comfortable at work but looks neat and professional. It usually means slacks, khaki pants, collared long-sleeved shirts and blouses, and shoes with socks or hosiery. It usually does not include tattered, frayed, or wrinkled jeans; T-shirts with logos; sneakers or sandals; tank tops; sweat pants; ultra-short skirts; or garish print sport shirts.[21]

Some companies are relaxing dress codes and allowing workers to dress casually. Although no precise definition of business casual exists, the following casual-dress guidelines are typical.

1. *Wear dressier business clothing when meeting with customers or clients.* You should avoid creating inconsistencies between your message and your appearance.
2. *Respect the boundary between work and leisure clothing.* Victoria's Secret once sold body-hugging spandex tube tops as "workplace wear." Anne Fisher of *Fortune* magazine's "Ask Annie" career advice column says, "As a rule, people should avoid wearing anything that shows so much skin that it distracts other people from their work." Body piercings, tattoos, three-day stubble, no socks, micro-mini skirts, or flip-flops can also be distracting.
3. *Wear clothing that is clean and neat and that fits well.* Casual dress codes tend to emphasize the importance of this guideline.

4. *Business casual attire is closely watched in a work setting.* Managers often assume they are seeing the real person. Christina Binkley, writing in the *Wall Street Journal*, says "Business casual—all business, never casual."[22]

Do not let "dress-down" influences rob you of common sense. You don't get a second chance to make a good first impression, so select your casual clothing with care. If you have to ask yourself, "Is this clothing acceptable?" you probably shouldn't wear it to work.

Helping Gen Y Navigate the Workplace. Generation Yers may not see the connection between professional appearance and career success. Many have grown up in an environment that was very casual. Let them know that dressing better can build credibility with their boss and customers.[23]

Your Facial Expression

After your overall appearance, your face is the most visible part of you. Facial expressions are the cues most people rely on in initial interactions. They provide the clues by which others read your mood and personality.

Facial expressions are the cues most people rely on in initial interactions.

Studies conducted in nonverbal communication show that facial expressions strongly influence people's reactions to each other. The expression on your face can quickly trigger a positive or negative reaction from those you meet. How you rate in the "good-looks" department is not nearly as important as your ability to communicate positive impressions with a pleasant smile and eye contact.

If you want to identify the inner feelings of another person, watch the individual's facial expressions closely. A frown may tell you "something is wrong." A pleasant smile generally communicates "things are OK." Everyone has encountered a "look of surprise" or a "look that could kill." These facial expressions usually reflect inner emotions more accurately than words. The smile is the most recognizable signal in the world. People everywhere tend to trust a smiling face.[24]

Your Entrance and Poise

The way you enter someone's office or a business meeting can influence the image you project, says Susan Bixler. She notes that "your entrance and the way you carry yourself will set the stage for everything that comes afterward."[25] A nervous or apologetic entrance may ruin your chances of getting a job, closing a sale, or getting the raise you have earned. If you feel apprehensive, try not to let it show in your body language. Hold your head up, avoid slumping forward, and try to project self-assurance. To get off to the right start and make a favorable impression, follow these words of advice from Bixler: "The person who has confidence in himself or herself indicates this by a strong stride, a friendly smile, good posture, and a genuine sense of energy. This is a very effective way to set the stage for a productive meeting. When you ask for respect visually, you get it."[26] Bixler says the key to making a successful entrance is simply believing—and projecting—that you have a reason to be there and have something important to present or discuss.

Your Voice Quality and Speech Habits

The tone of your voice, the rate of speed at which you speak (tempo), the volume of your speech, your ability to pronounce words clearly (diction), and your

"Quick! Remind me—are they handshakers, huggers, single kissers, or kissers on both cheeks?"

speech habits contribute greatly to the image you project. Consider these real-world examples:

- Regina Tell, court reporter at a liability trial involving Merck & Company's painkiller Vioxx, said the rapid speech patterns of the attorneys was "killing her." She reported that they spoke at a rate of more than 300 words a minute, or more than 100 words a minute faster than average people speak.[27]
- Kristy Pinand, a youthful-looking 23-year-old, routinely used "teen speak" when talking to colleagues and clients. Words such as "cool" and "like" were frequently part of her speech pattern. With feedback from her supervisor, she was able to correct the problem.[28]
- A senior project manager at a major financial-service company was surprised when his boss blamed his thick Brooklyn accent for his stalled advancement in the company. Despite his MBA, the project manager was speaking too fast and skipping many consonants. His frequent use of "deez" and "doze" created the impression that he was poorly educated and inarticulate.[29]

A conscious effort to improve your voice begins with awareness. A tape or video recording of your conversations will help you identify problem areas. If you hear a voice that is too monotone, too nasal, too high-pitched, too weak, too insincere, or too loud, you can target the problem for improvement.

Your Handshake

When two people first meet, a handshake is usually the only physical contact between them. A handshake is a friendly and professional way to greet someone or to take leave, regardless of gender. The handshake can communicate warmth, genuine concern for the other person, and strength. It can also communicate aloofness, indifference, and weakness. The message you send the other party through your handshake depends on a combination of the following factors:

1. *Degree of firmness.* Generally speaking, a firm (but not viselike) grip communicates a caring attitude, whereas a weak grip communicates indifference.
2. *Degree of dryness of hands.* A moist, clammy palm is unpleasant to feel and can communicate the impression that you are nervous. People who have this problem often remove the moisture with a clean handkerchief.
3. *Duration of grip.* There are no specific guidelines for the ideal duration of a grip. Nevertheless, by extending the handshake just a little, you can often communicate a greater degree of interest in and concern for the other person.
4. *Depth of interlock.* A full, deep grip is more likely to convey friendship to the other person. Position your hand to make complete contact with the other person's hand. Once you have connected, close your thumb over the back of the other person's hand and give a slight squeeze.[30]
5. *Eye contact during handshake.* Visual communication, eye contact and a smile, can increase the positive impact of your handshake.[31]

Throughout your career, you will likely meet people from many ethnic backgrounds. Each may have a ritual, which might include bowing, kissing, hugging, or giving a "high five." In Jamaica, for example, approval of someone or someone's idea may involve hitting fists.[32]

Skill Development: Apply It

Four years ago, you completed a two-year culinary arts program at Northwestern Michigan College. Soon after graduation, you assumed the duties of Sous chef at a local country club. One of the primary duties was to plan the luncheon menu. Today, you are preparing to open a small restaurant that will focus on fresh, organic, high-quality breakfast and lunch meals. The restaurant will be located in a financial district and cater mostly to employees who work for various financial services firms. Using information presented in Table 11.1 and other material in this chapter, prepare a dress and grooming code for the wait staff.

Etiquette for a Changing World

Why are so many guides to etiquette crowding bookstore shelves? And why are many organizations hiring consultants to conduct classes on etiquette guidelines? One reason is that we need advice on how to avoid annoying other people, and what to do if they annoy us. In today's fast-paced, often tense, work environment, we have to work a little harder to maintain a climate of fairness, kindness, and mutual respect.[33]

HUMAN RELATIONS IN ACTION

Handyman Etiquette

Andy Bell, founder of Handyman Matters Franchising Corporation, manages 100 franchises in 37 states. He has implemented strict initial contact guidelines for all of his technicians. Technicians must take two steps back after ringing a doorbell and wear a clean, neat uniform (collared shirt and slacks) with identifying logo. When the homeowner comes to the door, the technician immediately presents a business card. Handyman technicians receive training in all areas of in-home conduct.[34]

Etiquette (sometimes called *manners* or *protocol*) is a set of traditions based on kindness, efficiency, and logic.[35] Letitia Baldrige, author and etiquette consultant, says, "It's consideration and kindness and thinking about somebody other than oneself."[36] Sometimes we need new etiquette guidelines to deal with our changing world. Today, smoking at work is usually prohibited or restricted to a certain area. Meetings often begin with the announcement "Please silence your cell phones and beepers." And the nearly universal use of e-mail has spawned hundreds of articles on e-mail etiquette (see Chapter 2). A diverse work force has created many new challenges in the area of protocol.

Although it is not possible to do a complete review of the rules of etiquette, we will discuss those that are particularly important in an organizational setting.

Dining Etiquette

Job interviews and business meetings are frequently conducted at breakfast, lunch, or dinner, so be aware of your table manners. To illustrate decisions you might need to make during a business meal, let's eavesdrop on Tom Reed, a job candidate having a meal with several employees of the company he wants to work for. After introductions, the bread is passed to Tom. He places a roll on the small bread-and-butter plate to the right of his dinner plate. Soon, he picks up the roll, takes a bite, and returns it to the plate. Midway through the meal, Tom rises from his chair, places his napkin on the table, and says, "Excuse me; I need to make a potty run." So far, Tom has made four etiquette blunders: The bread-and-butter plate he used belongs to the person seated on his right; his own is to the left of his dinner plate. When eating a roll, he should break off one piece at a time and butter the piece as he is ready to eat it. The napkin should have been placed on his chair, indicating his plan to return. (When departing for good, leave it to the left of your plate.) And finally, the words *potty run* are too casual for a business meal. A simple statement such as, "Please excuse me; I'll be back in just a moment," would be adequate.

There are some additional table manners to keep in mind. Do not begin eating until the people around you have their plates. If you have not been served, however, encourage others to go ahead. To prevent awkward moments during the meal, avoid ordering food that is not easily controlled, such as ribs, spaghetti, chicken with bones, or lobster.

Meeting Etiquette

Business meetings should start and end on time, so recognize the importance of punctuality. Anne Marie Sabath, owner of a firm that provides etiquette training for business employees, says, "We teach people that if you're early, you're on time, and if you're on time, in reality, you're late." Showing up late for any meeting will be viewed as rudeness by coworkers, your boss, and your clients. Do not feel obligated to comment on each item on the agenda. Yes, sometimes silence is golden. In most cases, you should not bring up a topic unless it is related to an agenda item. If you are in charge of the meeting, end it by summarizing key points, reviewing the decisions made, and recapping the responsibilities assigned to individuals during the meeting. Always start and end the meeting on a positive note.[37]

Cell phone contempt surfaces in offices, restaurants, houses of worship, and many other places.

Cell Phone Etiquette

New technologies often bring new annoyances, and the cell phone is no exception. *Cell phone contempt* surfaces in offices, restaurants, houses of worship, and many other places. Cell phone etiquette is based on a few simple guidelines. First, it is not acceptable to use your cell phone at business meetings, in elevators, or at restaurants. If you receive a call at a restaurant, take the call outside the dining area. When making or receiving a call, talk in a normal speaking voice. Too often cell phone users talk louder than normal because they feel the need to compensate for the size of small phones. Try to confine your calls to private areas; it is rude to inflict your conversation on people near you.[38] Finally, if a coworker or friend insists on "staying connected" at all times, and you find this behavior annoying, confront the person. However, choose your words carefully. If a coworker takes a call at a meeting, for example, you might say, "When you answer your cell phone it makes the group feel unimportant and as if we don't have your full attention."[39]

© Rick Gomez/Corbis

Communication technologies can create annoyances. If you are trying to enjoy a meal at your favorite restaurant, you probably do not want to sit next to someone who is talking loudly on their cell phone. If you are making an important presentation at a team meeting, and some members are busy sending out text messages, you will likely feel some frustration. Is anyone listening to me!

Conversational Etiquette

When you establish new relationships, avoid calling people by their first name too soon. Never assume that work-related associates prefer to be addressed informally by their first names. Use titles of respect—Ms., Mr., Professor, or Dr.—until the relationship is established. Too much familiarity will irritate some people. When the other person says, "Call me Ruth" or "Call me John," it is all right to begin using the person's first name.

A conversation that includes obscene language can create problems in the workplace. Although the rules about what constitutes profanity have changed over the years, inappropriate use of foul language in front of a customer, a client, or, in many cases, a coworker is a breach of etiquette. An obscenity implies lack of respect for your audience. Also, certain language taboos carry moral and spiritual significance in most cultures. Obscene language is often cited by persons who file sexual harassment charges.[40]

> ## *Total Person Insight*
>
> **JARED SANDBERG**
> Columnist, *Wall Street Journal*
>
> *"Profanity will always offend someone, but the lack of profanity will never offend anyone."*[41]

Networking Etiquette

Networking—making contact with people at meetings, social events, or other venues—is an effective job search method. Networking is also important to salespeople searching for prospects and to professionals (accountants, lawyers, consultants, etc.) who need to build a client base.

When you meet people at an event, tell them your name and what you do. Avoid speaking negatively about any aspect of your current job or your life. In some cases, you will need to make a date to call or meet with the new contact later. After the event, study your contacts and follow up.

Send a *written* thank-you note if someone has been helpful to you or generous with his or her time. You might also consider sending a newspaper or magazine article as an "information brief," since one goal of networking is information exchange.[42]

We have given you a brief introduction to several areas of etiquette. This information will be extremely helpful as you develop a strong personal brand. Remember that *good etiquette* is based on consideration for the other person. If you genuinely respect other people, you will have an easier time developing your personal approach to workplace manners. You will probably also agree with most of the etiquette "rules" we have been discussing. Nancy Austin, coauthor of *A Passion for Excellence*, says, "Real manners—a keen interest in and a regard for somebody else, a certain kindness and at-ease quality that add real value—can't be faked or finessed."[43] Real manners come from the heart.

Incivility—The Ultimate Career Killer

Civility in our society is under siege. In recent years, we have witnessed an increase in coarse, rude, and obnoxious behavior. Unfortunately, some of the most outrageous behavior by athletes, coaches, politicians, and business leaders has been rewarded with wealth and influence.

As noted in Chapter 1, civility is the sum of the many sacrifices we are called upon to make for the sake of living together. At work, it may involve refilling the copier paper tray after using the machine or making a new pot of coffee after you take the last cup. It may mean turning down your radio so workers nearby are not disturbed or sending a thank-you note to someone who has helped you complete a difficult project. Small gestures, such as saying "Please" and "Thank you" or opening doors for others, make ourselves and others more content. Learning to discipline your passions so as to avoid obnoxious behavior will demonstrate also your maturity and self-control.

Professional Presence at the Job Interview

Professional presence has special meaning when you are preparing for a job interview. In most cases, you are competing against several other applicants, so you can't afford to make a mistake. A common mistake among job applicants is failure to acquire background information on the employer. Without this information, it is difficult to prepare questions to ask during the interview, and decisions about what to wear will be more difficult.

Keep in mind that regardless of the dress code of the organization, it is always appropriate to dress conservatively. If you arrive for an interview wearing torn jeans and a T-shirt, the person conducting the interview may think you are not serious about the job. The expectation of most employers is that the job applicant will be well groomed and dressed appropriately.

Joann Lublin, columnist for the *Wall Street Journal*, says interview etiquette begins the minute you walk in the door. Employers are building a picture of you piece by piece. You will always lose credibility if you are late or if you fail to give your full attention during the interview. Don't even think about peeking at your Blackberry.[44]

LOOKING BACK: REVIEWING THE CONCEPTS

- Explain the importance of professional presence.

Professional presence is a dynamic blend of poise, self-confidence, control, and style. Once acquired, it permits you to be perceived as self-assured and competent. These qualities are quickly perceived the first time someone meets you.

- Understand the importance of a favorable first impression.

People tend to form impressions of others quickly at the time they first meet them, and these first impressions tend to be preserved. The impression you form of another person during the initial contact is made up of assumptions and facts. Assumptions are often based on perceptions of surface language—the pattern of immediate impressions conveyed by appearance. Verbal messages also influence the impression you make on others.

- Define *image* and describe the factors that form the image you project to others.

Image is a term used to describe how other people feel about you. In every business or social setting, your behaviors and appearance communicate a picture that others observe and remember. This picture determines how they react to you. Image is formed by a variety of factors, including manners, self-confidence, voice quality, versatility, integrity, entrance and poise, facial expression, surface language, competence, positive attitude, and handshake.

- List and discuss factors that influence your choice of clothing for work.

Image consultants contend that discrimination on the basis of appearance is a fact of life. Clothing is an important part of the image you communicate to others. Four factors tend to influence your choice of clothing for work: (1) the products or services offered by the organization, (2) the type of person served, (3) the desired image projected by the organization, and (4) the region where you work.

- Understand how workplace etiquette contributes to improved interpersonal relations.

Etiquette, sometimes called *manners* or *protocol*, is tradition based on kindness, efficiency, and logic. Dining, meeting, cell phone, conversational, and networking etiquette are all important in the workplace.

ON THE JOB Q & A: WILL MY INDIVIDUALITY BE LOST?

Q: In the near future I will begin my job search, and I want to work for a company that will respect my individuality. Some companies are enforcing strict dress and grooming codes and other policies that, in my opinion, infringe on the rights of their employees. How far can an employer go in dictating my lifestyle?

A: This is a good question, but one for which there is no easy answer. For example, most people feel they have a right to wear the fragrance of their choice, but many fragrances contain allergy-producing ingredients. In some employment settings, you will find "nonfragrance" zones. Secondhand smoke is another major issue in the workplace because most research indicates that it can be harmful to the health of workers. Rules regarding body piercings, hair length, and the type of clothing that can be worn to work have also caused controversy. There is no doubt that many companies are trying to find a balance between their interests and the rights of workers. Enterprise Rent-A-Car has placed restrictions on the length of an employee's hair and has established more than 25 dress code guidelines for its employees. The company believes employee appearance is crucial to its success. The best advice I can give you is to become familiar with the employer's expectations *before* you accept a job. The company has a responsibility to explain its personnel policies to prospective employees, but sometimes this information is not covered until after a person is hired.[45]

KEY TERMS

professional presence 230
primacy effect 232
assumptions 233
cultural influences 234
image 234
surface language 235
career apparel 236
wardrobe engineering 236
business casual 237
etiquette 241

TRY YOUR HAND

1. Many people complain that interrupting has become a major annoyance. You begin speaking and someone finishes your sentence. Marilyn Vos Savant, author of the "Ask Marilyn" column, recommends a technique that can stop interrupters. When someone interrupts you, stop

speaking abruptly and say "What?" This will highlight the interruption, and the person who interrupts you will be forced to repeat himself or herself too, which is an unpleasant experience. Repeat this method, if necessary, until the offender lets you complete your sentences. Marilyn Vos Savant says you should save this method for *chronic* interrupters.[46]

2. The first step toward improving your voice is to hear yourself as others do. Listen to several recordings of your voice on a cell phone message, tape recorder, or digital recording, and then complete the following rating form. Place a checkmark in the appropriate space for each quality.

QUALITY	MAJOR STRENGTH	STRENGTH	WEAKNESS	MAJOR WEAKNESS
Projects confidence	____	____	____	____
Projects enthusiasm	____	____	____	____
Speaking rate is not too fast or too slow	____	____	____	____
Projects optimism	____	____	____	____
Voice is not too loud or too soft	____	____	____	____
Projects sincerity	____	____	____	____

3. You have assumed the duties of sales manager at a new Lexus automobile dealership that is scheduled to open in three weeks. You will hire and train all salespeople. What types of career apparel would you recommend to members of your sales team? What grooming standards would you recommend?

4. Many employers say that Generation Y job applicants arrive at the job interview with an overblown sense of entitlement—an enhanced view of their self-importance. To avoid sending this message, what behaviors should be avoided during the interview?

INTERNET INSIGHTS

Throughout the past few years, we have seen an increase in the number of etiquette consulting and training companies. These firms will help you develop and initiate dress codes and conduct etiquette-training programs for employees. Contact two of the companies listed below and review the services offered. Then prepare a written summary of your findings. Also, contact the Association of Image Consultants International (*http://www.aici.org*) and Global Protocol, Inc. (*http://www.globalprotocol.com*), to determine what services are offered to members.

The Protocol School of Washington
McLean, VA
http://info@psow.com

Brody Communications
Elkins Park, PA
http://www.brodypro.com

American Management Association
http://www.amanet.org
(Click on Projecting a Positive Professional Image.)

Universal Class
Online Class: Etiquette 101
http://www.theetiquetteinstitute.com

ESP
The Executive Social Presentation Program
http://www.iesp.org

YOU PLAY THE ROLE

After spending a number of years working for a prestigious CPA firm, you established your own company. Cameron, Stanley, and Robert is the area's top accounting firm. You cater to an upscale business clientele who appreciate your outstanding customer service and the quality of your firm's work. Currently, you employ ten associates. The newest member of your accounting firm is Annika Johnson, a young CPA who is proud to be a member of Generation Y. Her intelligence, self-confidence, and image impressed you during the hiring process; however, you are now noticing an image change. Although she is well paid, Annika likes to shop at discount clothing stores, always searching for a great bargain. Very often her clothing and accessories communicate a "thrift store" image that clashes with the upscale image of CSR. You have decided to meet with Annika and try to encourage her to adopt a wardrobe that is more appropriate for the clientele she serves. You will meet with another class member who will assume the role of Annika Johnson.

BELOW THE SURFACE:

Creating Your Own Brand

Branding, a concept introduced at the beginning of this chapter, has recently surfaced as a personal development strategy. Using the principles of successful brand development, many people are positioning themselves to stand for something—to say something important about themselves that will affect how others perceive them. The authors of *Be Your Own Brand* note that the concept of brand in business has a well-defined meaning: "A brand is a perception or emotion, maintained by a buyer or a prospective buyer, describing the experience related to doing business with an organization or consuming its products or services."[47] In a personal context, you can think of it this way: "Your brand is a perception or emotion, maintained by somebody other than you, that describes the total experience of having a relationship with you."[48]

The key to understanding the concept of personal and business branding is understanding the nature and needs of a relationship. L.L. Bean has become a major force in outdoor and casual clothing by implementing business practices that build customer loyalty and repeat business. In addition to selling quality products, this company works hard to build a trusting relationship with its customers.

Personal brand development begins with self-management practices that help you create and strengthen relationships with other people. Early in his career, Jerry Seinfeld decided he would never use profanity in his comedy routines. This personal decision forced him to use more creativity, and he became a stronger comedian. Jeff Bezos, founder of Amazon.com, recalls an early life experience that changed the way he viewed relationships. He made a comment to his grandmother that hurt her feelings. Later, his grandfather met with him privately and said, "You'll learn, one day, that it's much harder to be kind than clever."[49] This insight has helped Bezos in his professional life.

To develop a distinctive brand that will help you in your interactions with others may require making some changes in your life. To become distinctive, you must stand for something. What you stand for relates to your values. Thus, a strong personal brand is generally built from the inside out. But, to some extent, you can also decide what type of image you want these values to project. This may require changes in your manners, dress, voice quality, facial expression, posture or behaviors that reflect your integrity.

QUESTIONS

1. Judith Sills, clinical psychologist who writes a column for *Psychology Today*, says your brand is the professional identity you create in the minds of others. Would you take the time to create your own brand? Explain your answer.
2. If you decide to create your own brand, what personal qualities will give you greater visibility, recognition, and acceptance in the labor market? These qualities should send the message, "Pick me; I'm special."

CLOSING CASE: Make Yourself Memorable

The words *magnetism, charisma, authenticity,* and *class* are used to describe persons who are admired and respected. These special individuals are also memorable. Some say class and charm are fading fast from the American scene, replaced by bad behavior displayed by professional athletes, movie stars, radio and TV commentators, and politicians. Yet, there are some role models worth remembering. The late Paul Newman was a serious actor, a successful racer, and a generous philanthropist. He established Newman's own brand of food and condiments and then directed more than $250 million to charity. He was dedicated to helping make the world a better place for all.[50]

Arthur Ashe was the first African-American male to win the U.S. Open and Wimbledon tennis tournaments and the first African-American on the U.S. Davis Cup team. He was also the first African-American male ranked number one in the tennis world. He displayed a unique combination of grace and class. His life was marked by personal modesty, civility, and generosity. Ashe led an exemplary family and professional life until his untimely death from AIDS, which he had contracted after heart bypass surgery. The late Payne Stewart, killed in the bizarre crash of a Learjet, is remembered as a vicious competitor and a classy hero to many golf fans. Cellist Yo-Yo Ma and talk-show host Oprah Winfrey display magnetism and charm.

The authors of *Make Yourself Memorable* say that memorable people have style. They describe the four interlocking elements of style as *look, conduct, speech,* and *presentation.* Ann Landers, the late advice columnist, used to say that if you had class, success would follow. She described some of the elements of class:[51]

- Class never tries to build itself up by tearing others down.
- Class never makes excuses.
- Class knows that good manners are nothing more than a series of small, inconsequential sacrifices.
- Class is comfortable in its own skin. It never puts on airs.
- Class is real. It can't be faked.

QUESTIONS

1. Some social critics say that too many people these days are rude, crude, and inconsiderate of others. Do you agree? Explain.
2. Make a list of prominent people who, in your opinion, have class. Also, make a list of friends or coworkers who have class. List and evaluate the personal qualities displayed by these individuals you most admire.

3. If you want to become a more memorable person—someone with class—what type of self-improvement program would you undertake? Explain. If you decided to develop a strong personal brand, would class be a major component of your brand?

INTEGRATED RESOURCES

CLASSROOM ACTIVITIES

IRM Application Exercise 11.1
IRM Application Exercise 11.2
IRM Application Exercise 11.3
IRM Application Exercise 11.4
IRM Application Exercise 11.5

PART 4

If We All Work Together . . .

CHAPTER 12
Team Building: A Leadership Strategy

TIP OF THE ICEBERG

CHAPTER PREVIEW

LEARNING OBJECTIVES

After studying Chapter 12, you will be able to

- Explain the importance of teamwork in an organizational setting.
- Identify and explain common types of work teams.
- Explain the behavioral science principles that support team building.
- Describe the team-member skills that employees need.

© PhotoAlto/Odilon Dimier/ Getty Images

NEW FORMS OF TEAM DEVELOPMENT

In today's complex and ever-changing environment, organizations continue to experiment with new forms of team development. Some of the most successful teams bring together employees with different talents and perspectives. A few years ago, the Lexus division of Toyota Motor Corporation decided the brand needed a makeover. Management thought that Lexus cars lacked the necessary luxury cachet to compete with BMW and Mercedes in the "prestige luxury" segment, cars priced above $70,000.

Lexus assembled a team of employees from various departments, including marketing and finance. The team interviewed wealthy car buyers who had previously owned luxury vehicles. These interviews took place during a period of two years and included people from various regions of the country. They discovered that ultra-wealthy buyers like unique experiences inaccessible to the general public; so Lexus tripled the number of special events it holds. For example, it hosted a fashion show with *Vogue* at a vintage car show in California.[1]

Many small companies have embraced the use of teams. At ICU Medical Inc., maker of medical devices, any worker can form a team to tackle a project. Team members define the problem, assign tasks, and create deadlines themselves. Over the years, teams have altered production processes, set up a 401(k) plan, and solved logistical problems in the movement of parts. George Lopez, CEO at ICU, says letting employees form teams has helped him spread out the decision-making and encourages input from people closest to the problems.[2]

Photo by Rusty Jarrett/Getty Images for NASCAR

Every second counts in a NASCAR race. Each team member is responsible for a task or series of tasks. A small mistake can result in the loss of several positions on the race track. Crew training, with emphasis on teamwork, is essential.

As competition increases and work-related problems become more complex, organizations are seeking more input from their employees. However, there is an enormous vacuum in leadership today. Bill George, author of *True North, Authentic Leadership,* and other publications, says too often the wrong people are attaining leadership roles. He states that there are leaders throughout organizations who are waiting for opportunities to lead. Too often these people do not feel empowered to seek leadership roles.[3]

The focus of this chapter is team-building leadership strategies, so it is important to understand the difference between leadership and management. **Leadership** is the process of inspiring, influencing, and guiding employees to participate in a common effort.[4] Stephen Covey, in his book, *The 8th Habit,* says, "Leadership is communicating people's worth and potential so clearly that they come to see it in themselves only."[5] Leaders are made, not born. Leadership is a series of skills that can be acquired through study and practice.

Thanks to the efforts of James Kouzes and Barry Posner, we know a great deal about the practices of exemplary leaders. Kouzes and Posner have summarized and reported on many years of research on this topic in *The Leadership Challenge,* a best-selling book.[6] After a lengthy study of the dynamic process of leadership, they found that the most effective leaders engage in five practices of exemplary leadership (see Figure 12.1).

FIGURE 12.1 Five Practices of Exemplary Leadership

The Leadership Challenge is considered to be the definitive field-guide on leadership. There are over a million copies in print, in fifteen languages. The authors have devised the following five practices of exemplary leadership.

Model the Way. Leaders must model the behavior they expect from others.

Inspire a Shared Vision. The leader's dream or vision is the force that invents the future. It is the employees' belief in and enthusiasm for the vision that motivates them to give their best.

Challenge the Process. Leaders do not accept the status quo. They search for opportunities to innovate, grow, and improve processes.

Enable Others to Act. Effective leaders make people feel confident, strong, and capable of taking action.

Encourage the Heart. Through good times and bad, leaders encourage the heart of their employees to carry on and do their best.

Source: James M. Kouzes and Barry Z. Posner, *The Leadership Challenge*, 3rd ed. (San Francisco, CA: Jossey-Bass, 2002), pp. 13–20.

Management is the process of coordinating people and other resources to achieve the goals of the organization. Most managers focus on four kinds of resources: material, human, financial, and informational.[7] Most leaders achieve their goals by combining effective leadership and management.

Leadership Challenges in a Changing Workplace

The New Economy is characterized by rapid change and demand for increased productivity. As the pace of change quickens and the pressure to work harder increases, the result is greater employee stress and tension. How can a supervisor motivate employees who are tired and frustrated? Some of the most important leadership strategies, such as building trust, empowering employees, and developing the spirit of teamwork, can take many months, even years, to implement. How do managers respond to leaders at the top of the organization who want changes implemented overnight?

Diversity has also become a more prominent characteristic of today's work force. We have seen increased participation in the labor force by women and minorities. Supervising a multicultural and multilingual work force can be very challenging. We are seeing greater use of part-time or temporary workers, who may have less commitment to the organization. And Generation Y workers have been described as the most high-maintenance workforce in the history of America.[8]

Team Building: An Introduction

When you assume the duties of team supervisor, your title is likely to be "team leader" or "team facilitator." The changing role of this new breed of leader is discussed in this chapter. In addition, we discuss ways in which you can become an effective team member.

Can the element of teamwork make a difference between the successful and unsuccessful operation of an organization? Yes, there is evidence that a leadership style that emphasizes **team building** is positively associated with high productivity and profitability. Problems in interpersonal relations are also less common where teamwork is evident. Teamwork ensures not only that a job gets done but also that it gets done efficiently and harmoniously.

There is also evidence that team building can have a positive influence on the physical and psychological well-being of everyone involved. When employees are working together as a team, the leader and members often experience higher levels of job satisfaction and less stress.

Another positive outcome of teamwork is an increase in synergy. **Synergy** is the interaction of two or more parts to produce a greater result than the sum of the parts taken individually.[9] Mathematically speaking, synergy suggests that two plus two equals five. Teamwork synergy is especially important at a time when organizations need creative solutions to complex problems.

Total Person Insight

JOHN DONAHOE
President, eBay

Leadership is a journey, not a destination.
It is a marathon, not a sprint.
It is a process, not an outcome.[10]

Teamwork Doesn't Come Naturally

Many organizations are working hard to get all employees to pull together as a team. Teamwork at a hospital, for example, may begin with acceptance of a common vision, such as providing outstanding health-care services. The only way to make this vision a reality is to obtain the commitment and cooperation of every employee. This will require meaningful employee participation in planning, solving problems, and developing ways to improve health care.

Most jobs today require ongoing interaction between coworkers and managers. The spirit of teamwork helps cement these interpersonal relationships. However, working together as a team does not come naturally. Some people value individualism over teamwork. Team skills often lag far behind technical skills. The good news is that teamwork does flourish under strong leadership.

Common Types of Work Teams

Teams have become popular because they have proven to be effective in such areas as cost reduction, developing innovative new products, and improving quality. This section focuses on two of the most common types of teams: self-managed and cross-functional.

Self-Managed Teams

Self-managed teams assume responsibility for traditional management tasks as part of their regular work routine. Examples include decisions about production

Employees formerly concerned only with their own jobs suddenly become accountable for the work of the total team.

quotas, quality standards, and interviewing applicants for team positions. A typical self-managed team usually has 5 to 15 members who are responsible for producing a well-defined product (such as an automobile) or service (such as processing an insurance claim). Team members usually rotate among the various jobs and acquire the knowledge and skills to perform each job. Each member eventually can perform every job required to complete the entire team task. Employees formerly concerned only with their own jobs suddenly become accountable for the work of the total team.[11] One advantage of this approach is that it reduces the amount of time workers spend on dull and repetitive duties.

Cross-Functional Teams

Cross-functional teams are task groups staffed with a mix of specialists, focused on a common objective.[12] These teams are often temporary units with members from different departments and job levels. The teams are often involved in developing new work procedures or products, devising work reforms, or introducing new technology in an organization. Team members often provide a link among separate functions, such as production, distribution, finance, and customer service.

Hypertherm Incorporated, a metal-cutting equipment maker based in Hanover, New Hampshire, has developed cross-functional teams for each of its five product lines. Team members represent engineering, marketing, production, and sales. Salespeople and marketers know customers best, so they make an important

Bruce Ayres/Stone/Getty Images

What is a flat organization? To answer this question, visit ICU Medical Inc., a small company that makes medical devices. Any worker can create a team to tackle a project. At ICU Medical, decision making is not in the hands of a few top executives. The goal is to involve employees who are closest to the problem.

contribution to new product development. During the hiring process, every effort is made to screen out persons who would not be effective team players.[13]

Virtual Teams

As employees work at locations around the globe, the need for virtual teams has become crucial. **Virtual teams** are composed of employees who are physically dispersed throughout the nation or around the world. Modern Technology makes it possible for employees to collaborate on projects without face-to-face contact. Of course there are significant challenges when virtual team members work in different time zones and different cultures.[14]

Teams Take Time to Develop

Although we are seeing greater use of teams, this approach to employee participation is by no means a quick fix. In the case of self-managed teams, it can sometimes take one or two years for members to learn all the tasks they will perform as they rotate from job to job. It also takes time for a team to mature to the point where it is comfortable making decisions in such areas as work scheduling, hiring, training, and problem solving.

As teams become more popular, we need to increase our understanding of factors that contribute to team effectiveness. If you have ever enjoyed the experience of being part of a great team, then you probably discovered the following determinants of team effectiveness.[15]

People-Related Factors. The team is characterized by mutual trust and respect. Team members know the power of reflection and silence when agenda topics are being discussed. Members listen to each other and welcome a diversity of ideas and viewpoints.

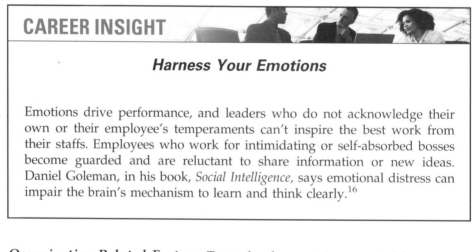

CAREER INSIGHT

Harness Your Emotions

Emotions drive performance, and leaders who do not acknowledge their own or their employee's temperaments can't inspire the best work from their staffs. Employees who work for intimidating or self-absorbed bosses become guarded and are reluctant to share information or new ideas. Daniel Goleman, in his book, *Social Intelligence,* says emotional distress can impair the brain's mechanism to learn and think clearly.[16]

Organization-Related Factors. Team development is supported by management personnel at every level. They are interested in outcomes and provide rewards and recognition of accomplishments.

Task-Related Factors. Each team has clear objectives and project plans. They are given autonomy and assignments that are professionally challenging.

FIGURE 12.2 Five Dysfunctions of a Team

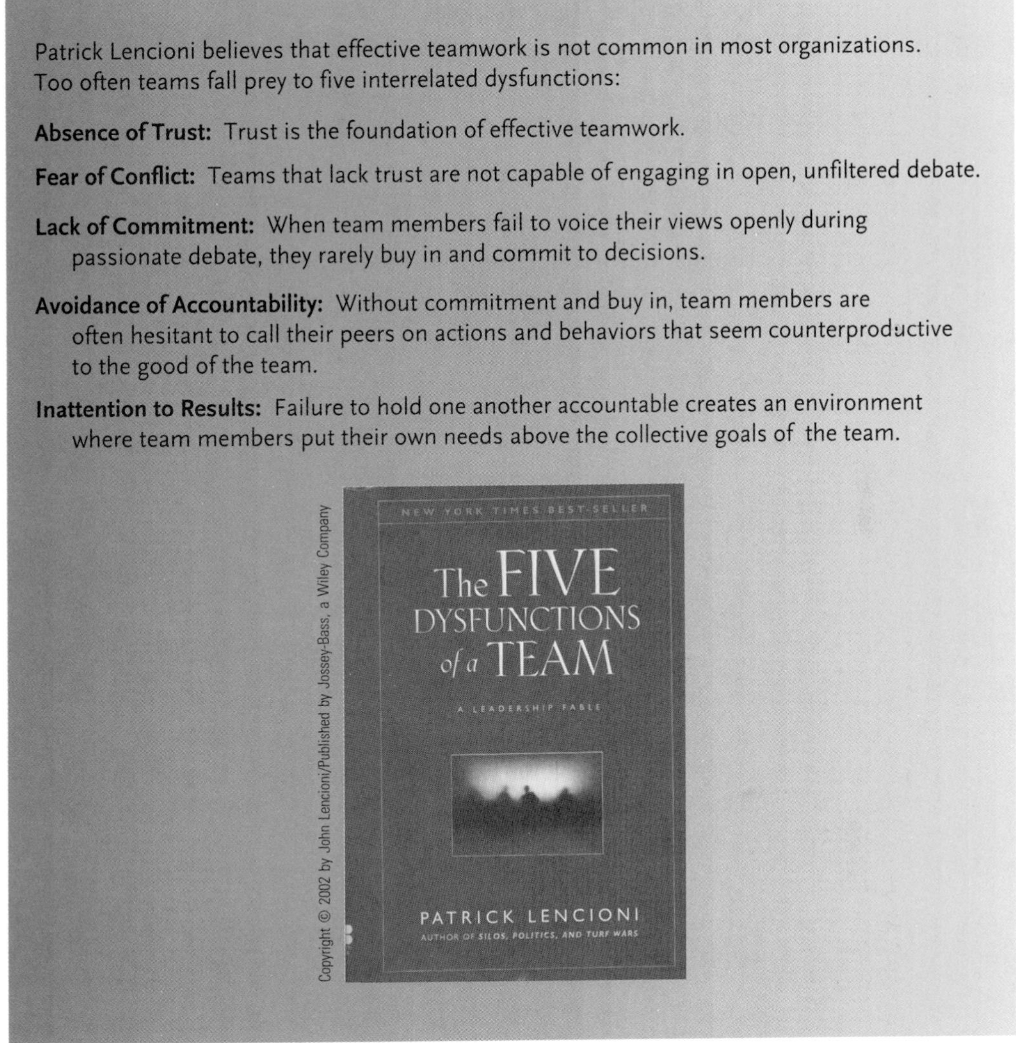

Patrick Lencioni believes that effective teamwork is not common in most organizations. Too often teams fall prey to five interrelated dysfunctions:

Absence of Trust: Trust is the foundation of effective teamwork.

Fear of Conflict: Teams that lack trust are not capable of engaging in open, unfiltered debate.

Lack of Commitment: When team members fail to voice their views openly during passionate debate, they rarely buy in and commit to decisions.

Avoidance of Accountability: Without commitment and buy in, team members are often hesitant to call their peers on actions and behaviors that seem counterproductive to the good of the team.

Inattention to Results: Failure to hold one another accountable creates an environment where team members put their own needs above the collective goals of the team.

Source: Patrick Lencioni, *The Five Dysfunctions of a Team* (San Francisco, CA: Jossey-Bass, 2002), pp. 187–190. Reproduced with permission of John Wiley & Sons, Inc.

Patrick Lencioni, author of *The Five Dysfunctions of a Team,* has spent many years researching factors that contribute to unproductive teams. In his best-selling book, he provides a five-part model that explains how teams typically hurt themselves (see Figure 12.2).

Behavioral Science Principles Supporting Team Building

One approach to the study of leadership is examining the careers of successful leaders who demonstrated their ability to develop teamwork. A second approach to the study of leadership is reviewing the findings of scholars who have identified the characteristics of successful leaders. What do successful leaders have in common? See in the sections that follow, how Douglas McGregor, Robert Blake, Jane S. Mouton, and Robert K. Greenleaf have answered this question.

McGregor's Influence

In the late 1950s, a book by Douglas McGregor entitled *The Human Side of Enterprise* presented convincing arguments that management had been ignoring certain important facts about people. The author said that managers often failed to recognize the potential for growth of most workers and their desire for fulfillment.

He identified several characteristics of an effective work team.[17]

1. The atmosphere of the workplace tends to be informal, comfortable, and relaxed. It is a working environment in which people are involved and interested.
2. There is a lot of discussion about work-related issues. Virtually everyone participates, but contributions remain pertinent to the task of the group. The members listen to one another.
3. The tasks or objectives of the group are well understood and accepted by the members.
4. There is disagreement. The group is comfortable with this and shows no signs of having to avoid conflict.
5. People freely express their feelings as well as their ideas, both on the problem and on the group's operation. There is little avoidance, and there are few "hidden agendas."

McGregor's views on the characteristics of effective work teams, represent "classic" thinking. His thoughts continue to have merit today.

Total Person Insight

Patrick Lencioni
Author, *The Five Dysfunctions of a Team*

"It is teamwork that remains the ultimate competitive advantage, both because it is so powerful and so rare."[18]

The Ohio State Model

The wide range of types of leadership positions may cause you to ask: Do people in these positions have much in common? Will team-building strategies work in most situations? The answer to both questions is yes. A great majority of successful leaders share certain behavior characteristics. Two of the most important dimensions of supervisory leadership–*consideration* and *structure*—have been identified in research studies conducted by Edwin Fleishman at Ohio State University[19] and validated by several additional studies. By making a matrix out of these two

FIGURE 12.3 Basic Leadership Styles from the Ohio State Study

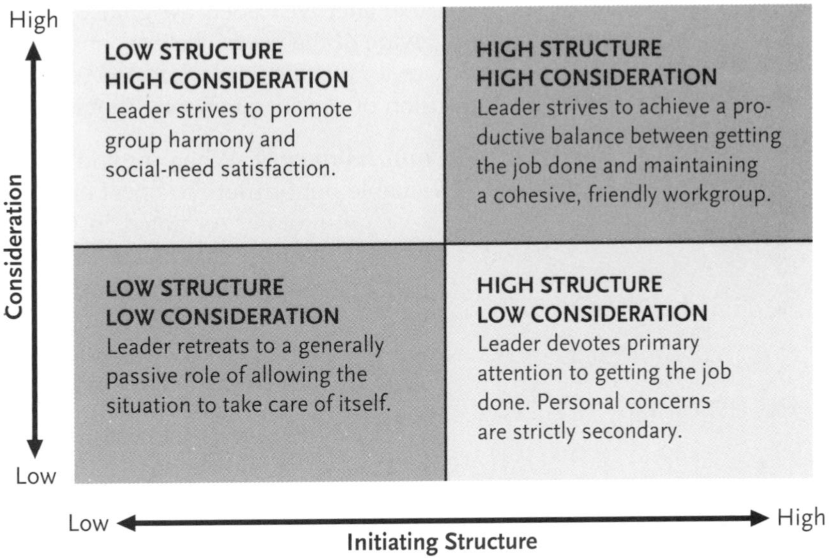

	Low Initiating Structure	High Initiating Structure
High Consideration	**LOW STRUCTURE HIGH CONSIDERATION** Leader strives to promote group harmony and social-need satisfaction.	**HIGH STRUCTURE HIGH CONSIDERATION** Leader strives to achieve a productive balance between getting the job done and maintaining a cohesive, friendly workgroup.
Low Consideration	**LOW STRUCTURE LOW CONSIDERATION** Leader retreats to a generally passive role of allowing the situation to take care of itself.	**HIGH STRUCTURE LOW CONSIDERATION** Leader devotes primary attention to getting the job done. Personal concerns are strictly secondary.

This matrix is similar to the Leadership Grid (formerly called the Managerial Grid) developed by Robert Blake and Jane Mouton. The Leadership Grid is based on two leadership style dimensions: concern for people and concern for production.

Source: James M. Kouzes and Barry P. Posner *The Leadership Challenge*, 3rd ed. (San Francisco, CA: Jossey-Bass, 2002), pp. 13–20.

independent dimensions of leadership, the researchers identified four styles of leadership (see Figure 12.3).

Consideration

The dimension of **consideration** reflects the extent to which a leader's relationships with subordinates are characterized by mutual trust, respect for the employees, consideration of their feelings, and a certain warmth in interpersonal relationships. When consideration is present, the leader–subordinate relationship is characterized by a climate of good rapport and two-way communication.

Structure

The dimension of **structure** reflects the extent to which a leader is likely to define and direct his or her role and the roles of subordinates toward goal attainment. Individuals who incorporate structure into their leadership style actively direct group activities by planning, setting goals, communicating information, scheduling, and evaluating performance. People who work under the direction of a highly structured leader know what is expected of them.

It is interesting to note that the dimensions of consideration and structure are independent of each other. A leader may be well qualified in one area but lack competence in the other. Anyone who assumes a leadership role can consciously work to develop competence in both areas.

Improving Consideration Skills

Brian Tracy says that effective leaders are guided by the *law of empathy*: "Leaders are sensitive to and aware of the needs, feelings, and motivations of those they lead."[20] This is good advice for anyone who wants to become an outstanding leader. To improve the dimension of consideration, one should adopt the following practices:

Recognize Accomplishments. When individual achievements are overlooked, leaders miss a valuable opportunity to boost employee self-confidence and build morale. As noted in Chapter 10, people need recognition for good work, regardless of the duties they perform or the positions they hold. Of course, recognition should be contingent on performance. When recognition is given for mediocre performance, the leader is reinforcing a behavior that is not desirable.

A supervisor should provide each employee with as many opportunities to succeed as possible.

Provide for Early and Frequent Success. According to an old saying, "Nothing succeeds like success." A supervisor should provide each employee with as many opportunities to succeed as possible. The foundation for accomplishment begins with a carefully planned orientation and training program. Supervisors and managers should review job duties and responsibilities, organizational policies and procedures, and any other pertinent information with their employees early in the relationship. Successful leaders are successful teachers.

Take a Personal Interest in Each Employee. Everyone likes to be treated as an individual. Taking a personal interest means learning the names of spouses and children, finding out what employees do during their leisure time, asking about their families, and acknowledging birthdays. The more you learn about the "whole person," the better you will be able to help employees balance their work lives with the rest of their lives.

Establish a Climate of Open Communication. To establish a climate of open communication, the leader must be available and approachable. Employees should feel comfortable talking about their fears, frustrations, and aspirations. Communication is closely linked to employee morale—morale is directly linked to productivity. Therefore, efforts to improve the communication process represent a good use of the supervisor's time and energy.

Therefore, efforts to improve the communication process represent a good use of the supervisor's time and energy.

CRITICAL THINKING CHALLENGE:

Analyze It

Reflect on your work experience and experiences in high school or college. Recall situations when you felt like a member of an effective team. What did the supervisor, manager, teacher, or coach do to develop the spirit of teamwork? Once you have reviewed the behaviors of these team leaders, assign each person one of the five leadership styles developed by Blake and Mouton (see Figure 12.4).[21]

Discover Individual Employee Values. Today's lean, flatter organizations offer employees fewer opportunities for promotion, smaller raises, and less job security. As a result, many workers no longer feel secure or identify with the company. Leaders should encourage employees to explore their values and determine whether there is a match between what matters most to them and the work they are doing. If a value conflict turns up, determine whether it is possible to redesign the job or give the employee a new assignment.[22]

Improving Structure Skills

The leader who incorporates structure into his or her leadership style plays an active role in directing group activities. The team builder gives the group direction, establishes performance standards, and maintains individual and group accountability. The following practices can be used to develop the dimension of structure:

Communicate Your Expectations. Members of the group or team must possess a clear idea of what needs to be accomplished. The law of expectations, according to Brian Tracy, states, "Whatever you expect, with confidence, becomes your own self-fulfilling prophecy."[23] Leaders must effectively formulate their expectations and then communicate them with conviction.

Bob Hughes, a consultant in the area of team building, suggests establishing baseline performance data so progress can be assessed.[24] In an office that processes lease applications, where accuracy and speed are critically important, the baseline data might include the number of error-free lease applications the team processes in one day. In an ideal situation, team members will be involved in setting goals and will help determine how best to achieve the goals. The goal-setting process is described in Chapter 4.

Provide Specific Feedback Often. Feedback should be relevant to the task performed by the employee and should be given soon after performance. Feedback is especially critical when an employee is just learning a new job. The supervisor should point out improvements in performance, no matter how small, and always reinforce the behavior she or he wants repeated. The most relevant feedback in a self-managed work team usually comes from coworkers, because team members are accountable to one another.

A person can make a mistake and still be a valuable employee.

Deal with Performance Problems Immediately. As a leader, you must deal quickly with the person who does not measure up to your standards of performance. When members of the group are not held accountable for doing their share of the work or for making mistakes, group morale may suffer. Other members of the group will quickly observe the poor performance and wonder why you are not taking corrective action.

To achieve the best results, focus feedback on the situation, issue, or behavior, not on the employee. A person can make a mistake and still be a valuable employee. Correct the person in a way that does not create anger and resentment. Avoid demoralizing the person or impairing his or her self-confidence.[25]

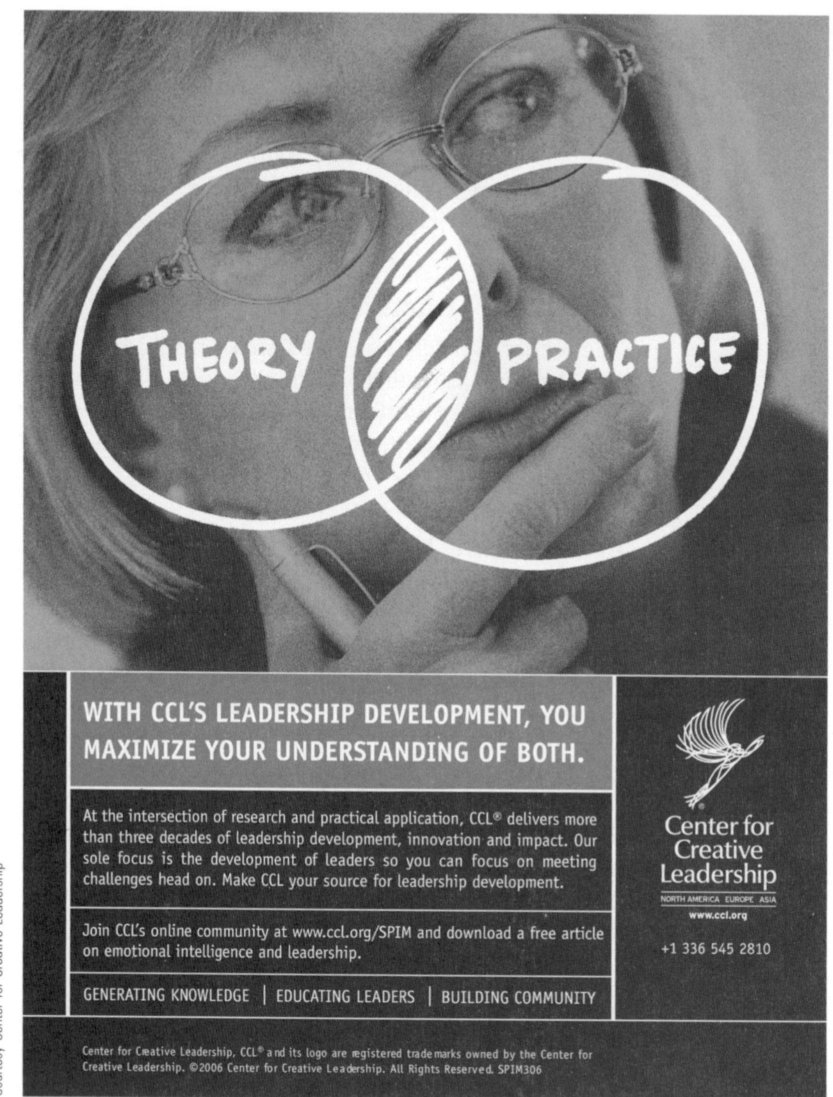

Courtesy Center for Creative Leadership

Effective leaders never stop learning. Programs offered by the Center for Creative Leadership help managers and executives learn how to work more effectively with people.

Coaching for Peak Performance. When performance problems surface, leaders must assume the role of coach. **Coaching** is an interpersonal process between the leader and the employee in which the leader helps the employee improve in a specific area. The coaching process involves four steps. *Step one* involves documentation of the performance problem. *Step two* involves getting the employee to recognize and agree that there is a need to improve performance in a specific area. Leaders should never assume the employee sees the problem in the same way they do. *Step three* involves exploring options. At this point, it is often best to let the employee suggest ways to improve performance. *Step four* involves getting a commitment from the employee to take action.[26]

Skill Development: Apply It

Assume you are the manager of the record-keeping department at a credit union. Three of the employees are responsible for sorting and listing checks and keeping personal and commercial accounts up-to-date. A fourth employee handles all inquiries concerning overdrafts and other problems related to customer accounts. List four specific behaviors you would develop that would contribute to the leadership quality described as *consideration* and four behaviors that would contribute to the quality described as *structure.*

The Leadership Grid

In the early 1960s, Robert Blake and Jane Mouton authored a popular book entitled *The Managerial Grid* (*http://www.gridinternational.com*). The **Leadership Grid®** (formerly called the Managerial Grid®) is a model based on two important leadership-style dimensions: concern for people and concern for production[27] (see Figure 12.4). Where work is physical, concern for production may take the form of number of units assembled per hour or time needed to meet a certain production schedule. In an office setting, concern for production may take the form of

FIGURE 12.4 Blake and McCanse's Leadership Grid®

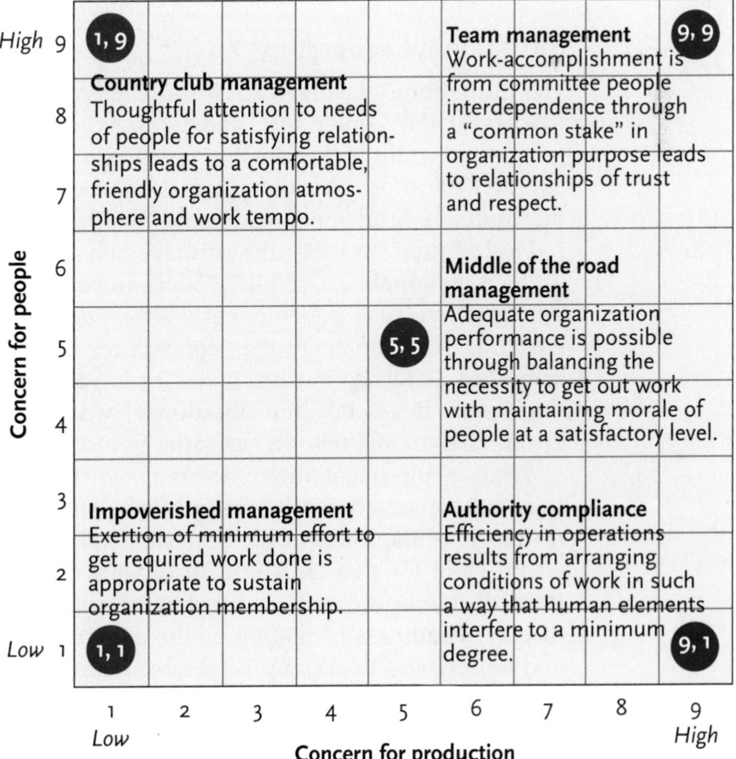

Source: Robert Kreitner, *Management* (11e), (Boston: Houghton Mifflin Harcourt Publishing Company, 2009), p. 408.

document-preparation volume and accuracy. Concern for people can be reflected in the way a supervisor views work and safety conditions, compensation, recognition for a job well done, and awareness of employees' need to be treated with respect. The Grid helps clarify how these two dimensions are related and establishes a uniform language for communication about leadership styles and patterns. Although there are many possible leadership styles within the Grid, five encompass the most important differences among managers. Blake and Mouton developed descriptive names for each.[28]

Using the scale from 1 to 9 as marked on each axis, the five styles emerge as follows:

9, 1 style: primary concern for production; human elements are secondary

1, 9 style: primary concern is people; production secondary

1, 1 style: minimum concern for either production or people

5, 5 style: moderate concern for both people and production

9, 9 style: major concern for both people and production

Blake and Mouton devoted more than 30 years to the study of the team-building leadership style. They maintain that this style is the one most positively associated with productivity and profitability, career success and satisfaction, and physical and mental health. The term *one best style* is used by the authors to describe this orientation. This style, they state, achieves production through a high degree of shared responsibility coupled with high participation, involvement, and commitment—all of which are hallmarks of teamwork.[29]

Situational Leadership

The **Situational Leadership Model**, developed by Paul Hersey and his colleagues at the Center for Leadership Studies (*http://www.situational.com*), offers an alternative to the Leadership Grid. **Situational leadership** is based on the theory that the most successful leadership occurs when the leader's style matches the situation. Situational leadership theory emphasizes the need for flexibility.[30]

Paul Hersey says that the primary behaviors displayed by effective managers in the Situational Leadership Model can be described as *task behavior* and *relationship behavior*. Task behavior, as Hersey describes it in his book *The Situational Leader*, is very similar to the "concern for production" dimension of the Leadership Grid. And relationship behavior is very similar to the "concern for people" dimension. In essence, the situational leader and the person who uses the Leadership Grid model rely on the same two dimensions of leadership.[31]

What is the major difference between these two leadership models? Hersey says that, when attempting to influence others, you must (1) diagnose the readiness level of the follower for a specific task and (2) provide the appropriate leadership style for that situation. In other words, given the specific situation, you must decide how much task behavior and how much relationship behavior to display. Readiness is defined as the extent to which an employee has the ability and willingness to accomplish a specific task. If an employee has the experience and skill to perform a certain task or activity, this information will influence the leader's style. However, the leader must also consider the employee's confidence level, commitment, and motivation to accomplish the task or activity. Hersey reminds us that readiness levels often vary greatly among members of the work group.[32]

HUMAN RELATIONS IN ACTION

Servant Leadership

One of the most important leadership principles is the idea of *servant leadership,* a concept developed by Robert K. Greenleaf. He said, "The servant-leader is servant first. It begins with the natural feeling that one wants to serve, to serve first." Greenleaf believed that true leadership emerges from those whose *primary* motivation is a deep desire to help others. Servant-leadership encourages collaboration, trust, and the ethical use of power and empowerment.[33]

Additional Leadership Qualities

In addition to consideration and structure skills, leaders need some additional qualities (see Figure 12.5). One of these is character. As noted in Chapter 5, character is composed of personal standards of behavior, including honesty, integrity, and moral strength. Effective leadership is characterized by honesty, truthfulness, and straight dealing with every person.[34] Without character it is impossible to build a trusting relationship with the people you lead.

A second important quality is emotional intelligence, a concept that was discussed in Chapter 9. Emotional intelligence is a much more powerful predictor of leadership success than IQ, because it gives you the ability to monitor your own and others' emotions and deal with them effectively.[35] A leader with high emotional intelligence is more likely to detect friction and eliminate conflict among team members. This leader is also more flexible, and therefore better able to use situational leadership.

Character and emotional intelligence are leadership qualities that can be developed. Leaders create themselves—they are not born. One very important key to growth in both of these areas is self-awareness. Without self-awareness we may behave in ways that are potentially ineffective.[36]

Teamwork: The Employee's Role

Each member should assume an active part in helping the work unit achieve its mission. This means that every member of the work group can and should be a

FIGURE 12.5 Additional Leadership Qualities

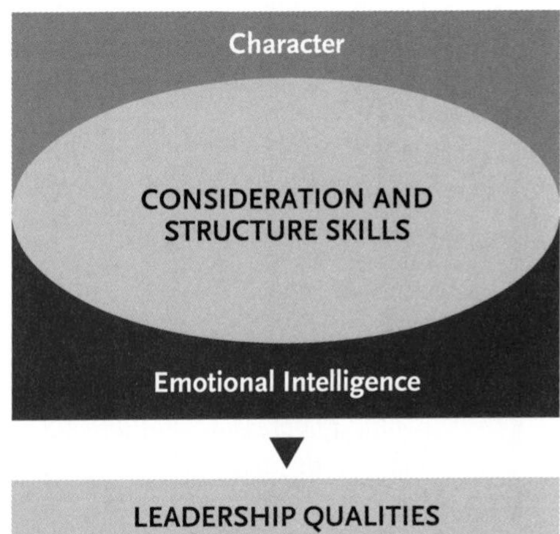

team member and a team builder. These dual roles are achieved when employees assume greater responsibility for the success of the work unit. Today's most valued employees are those who are willing to assume leadership responsibilities.

Employees as Leaders

In traditional organizations, there were leaders and followers, and the followers were not expected to develop leadership skills. Today, some of the most effective leaders are helping their work-team members develop leadership skills so that the team's success will not ride on one person. At a time when most organizations are attempting to compete in a complex, ever-changing global market, there is real merit in establishing a diversity of leadership within the work group. If we are willing to expand our definition of leadership, we can see leaders everywhere.[37]

- The quiet "worker bee" frequently serves as a leader when the issue is how to get the work done during a crisis situation.
- The "corporate counselor," who informally guides coworkers through stressful problems by merely listening, is an emotional leader.
- The rigid "rule follower" keeps our creativity from becoming irresponsible.

Will the "employees as leaders" approach catch on? J. Oliver Crom, CEO of Dale Carnegie & Associates, Inc., is optimistic. He says that leadership skills are needed at all levels of the organization and adds that, "Every employee is a leader" might well be today's business slogan.[38]

Becoming a Valued Team Member

Throughout your working life, your success is very likely to depend on your ability to be an effective team member. Here are some tips on how to become a respected team member in any organizational setting.[39]

1. *Avoid becoming part of a clique, or subgroup within the team.* As a member of a clique, you are very likely to lose the trust and respect of other team members.
2. *Avoid any action that might sabotage the team.* By engaging in frequent criticism of other team members, gossip, or other unconstructive behaviors, you undermine team efforts.
3. *Keep in mind that effective team membership depends on honest, open communication among team members.* Use the fundamentals of constructive self-disclosure discussed in Chapter 8.
4. *As a team member, do not feel the need to submerge your own strong beliefs, creative solutions, and ideas.* If the team members are about to make a decision that in your opinion is not "right," do not hesitate to speak up and express your views.

> ## *Total Person Insight*
>
> **John C. Maxwell**
> Author, *The 17 Essential Qualities of a Team Player*
>
> *"Great challenges require great teamwork, and the quality most needed among teammates amid the pressure of a difficult challenge is collaboration... Each person brings something to the table that adds value to the relationship and synergy to the team."*[40]

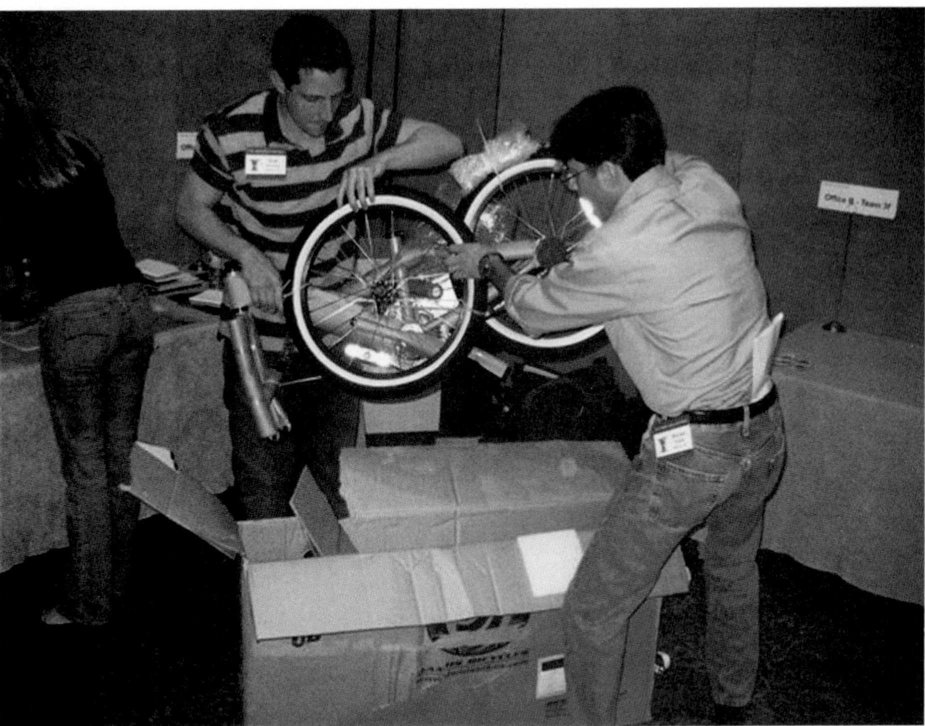

Courtesy of PricewaterhouseCoopers LLP (PwC)

PricewaterhouseCoopers LLP (PwC) has created a culture that fosters collaboration and knowledge sharing. The company is also committed to making a difference in the communities in which it does business. A training program involving team-based bicycle building helps new hires learn valuable teamwork skills. Employees work together in groups to build bikes for children and adults. The completed bikes are donated to area youth organizations, senior-care facilities, and other nonprofits.

Teamwork can be a very satisfying experience. It can generate positive energy and contribute to a sense of optimism about the future. As a team member, you have the opportunity to assume a very important leadership role.

Managing the Relationship with Your Boss

The idea that you should manage the relationship with your boss may sound a little unusual at first. But it makes a lot of sense when you consider the advantages of assuming this responsibility. When the subordinate and the boss are both working to maintain a good relationship, conflict is less likely to surface. The boss-subordinate relationship is not like the one between parent and child—the burden for managing the relationship *should not* and *cannot* fall entirely on the one in authority.

When you take time to manage the relationship with your boss, he or she will become more effective in performing his or her job. In many cases, managers are no more effective than the combined competence of the people they supervise. Some employees do not realize how much their boss needs assistance and support from them.

How do you go about managing your boss? Here are some general considerations.

Assess Your Own Strengths. The boss represents only one-half of the relationship. The development of an effective working relationship also requires reflecting on your own strengths. As noted in Chapter 4, the first step towards strength building is to discover your greatest talents.

Develop an Understanding of Your Boss. Become familiar with this person's strengths, weaknesses, work habits, communication style, and needs. Spend time studying your boss. In some cases, the direct approach is best. Ask your boss, "How would you like me to work with you?" Try to determine his or her goals and expectations. What is the person trying to accomplish? Does your boss enjoy casual meetings to discuss business matters or formal meetings with written agendas?

Flex Your Communication Style. In terms of communication style, is your boss supportive, emotive, reflective, or director? Once you have answered this question, begin thinking of how to flex your style in ways that will build rapport and avoid unnecessary stress. Remember, style flexing is a temporary effort to act in harmony with another person's preferred communication style (see Chapter 3).

Be Frank and Candid. Suppose that to avoid conflict, you almost never disagree with your boss—even when your boss is obviously wrong. Are you making a contribution to his or her growth and development? Obviously not. And don't hesitate to speak up regarding your contributions. Learn how to point out your accomplishments gracefully. You might say, "I know you're busy, so why don't I send you an e-mail explaining what I'm working on and what I've done?"[41]

As organizations become flatter, with fewer layers of management and more projects carried out by teams, collaboration has become more important. Effective team members are those who collaborate actively with their leader and other members of the team.

HUMAN RELATIONS IN ACTION

Tips for Young Leaders

Wanted: A new breed of boss who can provide strong leadership, handle technology, inspire teamwork, and cope with uncertainty. The person who fits this description may be quite young and inexperienced. Many of today's leaders are no longer molded solely by seniority and experience. Here are some tips for the young manager:

- Keep in mind that watching your own bosses in action is not enough to teach you to be one.
- Never assume that others are motivated by the same things you are.
- Don't ask for suggestions or opinions that you are not seriously prepared to consider.
- Give before you take. Approach relationships (with your employees, your boss, and customers) with what you have to offer, not with what you want.
- Reach out to people with more age and experience.[42]

LOOKING BACK: REVIEWING THE CONCEPTS

- Explain the importance of teamwork in an organizational setting.

Teamwork ensures not only that a job gets done but also that it gets done efficiently. Therefore, successful teamwork can often make the difference between the profitable and the unprofitable operation of an organization. The team-building leadership style is effective because it is suited to the needs of most of today's employees.

- Identify and explain common types of work teams.

Many companies are forming specific types of teams. Two of the most common are self-managed teams and cross-functional teams. Self-managed teams assume responsibility for traditional management tasks as part of their regular work routine. Team members are responsible for producing a well-defined product or service. They usually rotate among the various jobs and acquire the knowledge and skills to perform each one. Cross-functional teams are task groups staffed with a mix of specialists focused on a common objective. These teams are often temporary units with members from different departments.

- Explain the behavioral science principles that support team building.

One way to learn about team building is to study leaders who promote teamwork and scholars who discuss it; examples are McGregor, Blake and Mouton, Greenleaf, and others. Two important dimensions of supervisory leadership contribute to team building. One of these dimensions, *consideration*, reflects the extent to which a supervisor maintains relationships with employees that are characterized by mutual trust, respect, and rapport. The other dimension, *structure*, reflects the extent to which a supervisor is likely to direct group activities through planning, goal setting, communication, scheduling, and evaluating. The Leadership Grid® and the Situational Leadership Model help clarify these two dimensions of leadership. Effective leaders must also develop the qualities of character and emotional intelligence.

- Describe the team-member skills that employees need.

Members of an effective work group should assume effective leadership and membership roles. Each team member helps the group achieve its mission. Everyone assumes the role of team member and team builder. Employees are in a unique position to give guidance and support to their supervisor or manager. Most bosses need this assistance and support to achieve success.

ON THE JOB Q & A: ACHIEVING TEAM MEMBER RECOGNITION

Q: I work for a company that frequently uses cross-functional teams to complete certain projects. Whenever I serve on one of these teams, I feel frustrated. I want to get a promotion, but team assignments seem to hide my talents. How can I make the best of my next team assignment?

A: If your company is having success with these teams, the best way to get the attention of top management is to be an effective team member. When you get your next team assignment, make a quick study of how the group is working together and note any problems that could prevent the team from reaching its goals. Your visibility will increase if you find ways to enhance team performance. You might share important information with team members or offer to help team members develop some specific skills. In most cases it's possible to help your teammates grow while developing yourself.[43]

KEY TERMS

leadership 254
management 255
team building 256
synergy 256
self-managed teams 256
cross-functional teams 257
virtual teams 258
consideration 261
structure 261
coaching 264
Leadership Grid® 265
Situational Leadership Model 266
situational leadership 266

TRY YOUR HAND

1. Business publications such as the *Wall Street Journal, Fortune, BusinessWeek,* and *Fast Company* frequently feature articles describing problem bosses. Managers with high-tech backgrounds (computer science, electrical engineering, mathematics, etc.) sometimes create employee frustration through insensitive or impersonal behavior. These so-called nerd managers are often more focused on technology than on people. They have high IQs but rank low in emotional intelligence, and they lack people skills. The result is often high employee turnover. Let's assume that you are working for a small business and the owner is often described by employees as the "nerd boss from hell." What steps might you take to influence your boss, who seems to spend all his time obsessing about technology and ignoring the needs of his employees? Review the material featured in this chapter, and then develop a plan that would help your boss develop a strong team-building leadership style.[44]

2. There is increasing pressure on organizations to allow employees' personal problems to be brought to the attention of the supervisor or manager. Personal problems that can disrupt people's lives include dealing with a teenager on drugs, coping with the needs of a sick parent, losing a babysitter, or getting a divorce. Schedule an interview with two persons who hold supervisory-management positions and ask these questions:
   a. Do you assume the role of mentor and counselor when an employee brings a personal problem to your attention?
   b. Should you give the person with a serious problem some special consideration, such as time off, less demanding work, or professional help that is paid for by the company?

3. The skills needed to be an effective leader can be developed by anyone who is willing to invest the time and energy. It is possible to practice important leadership skills before you assume the duties of a supervisor or manager. Review the various ways to improve consideration and structure skills discussed in this chapter, and then begin searching for opportunities to practice these skills. Here are some opportunities for practice:
   a. Volunteer assignments in your community
   b. Group assignments at work, at college, or at your place of worship
   c. Involvement in political, professional, or social activities

4. The authors of *The Leadership Challenge* have identified five practices of exemplary leadership (see Figure 12.1). Review these practices and select the two that you feel present the greatest challenge to someone who has been promoted to a leadership position for the first time. Provide a rationale for your choice.

INTERNET INSIGHTS

1. Many companies provide Internet access for employees and allow them to work in virtual teams. Members may work at headquarters, in satellite offices, on the road, and from home. Virtual team members may never meet one another face to face because they communicate via e-mail, conference calls, and other methods. Web-based tools have been designed to help teams work together more effectively. Visit the following websites and review their

services. Then prepare a brief written report on your findings.[45]

WEBSITE	PURPOSE
WebEx *http://www.webex.com*	Let's you conduct online meetings, sales presentations, training sessions, and other online events.
WebOffice *http://weboffice.com*	WebOffice Workgroup combines asynchronous tools such as document sharing and calendaring with real-time Web meeting technology.
ScheduleOnline *http://www.scheduleonline.com*	A group calendar that lets users schedule events, invite people to meetings, and reserve physical resources such as conference rooms or equipment.

2. Several websites provide workers with an opportunity to post complaints about their boss, employer, or coworker. Visit the following website and prepare a brief written report on your findings. The website *http://www.badbossology.com* will help you with difficult boss problems. It offers free access to hundreds of articles on solving problems with difficult bosses.

YOU PLAY THE ROLE

You are currently a computer technician employed by Tech Assistance, Inc. The company provides a wide range of services, including computer system setup, PC and server repairs and upgrades, virus and spyware removal, data recovery services, and Internet security. The company was founded by Erin Wilson about five years ago. You are one of five technicians who make service calls and occasionally work in the repair center when needed. You like your work, but feel a sense of frustration when fellow employees fail to give their best efforts. The owner is very effective in solving technical problems but often displays poor people skills. She simply does not pay attention to employees; to what they are doing, or to how they are feeling. He knows almost nothing about their hobbies, family status, or personal concerns. There are times when you feel like quitting, but you like solving technical problems and helping customers with their computer needs. You have decided to meet with Erin and provide some suggestions on how to become a more effective leader. Use the name Reagan Simpson during the role play.

BELOW THE SURFACE:

Teams in Action

At the beginning of this chapter, you were introduced to two different forms of team development. The Lexus division developed a "super affluent team," nine employees from various departments who traveled the country asking the ultra-rich a series of lifestyle questions. The goal was to learn how to give the Lexus brand an image makeover. Lexus wanted to compete more effectively with European luxury brands. Lexus used the *cross-functional team* format.[46]

ICU Medical, Inc., also introduced at the beginning of the chapter, uses cross-functional teams to foster creativity and solve a variety of problems. ICU allows workers to initiate teams, a practice that is quite rare. George Lopez, CEO of ICU Medical, Inc., basically told his employees (around 1,480) to form teams and come up with ways to boost production. This approach stands in sharp contrast to the "top-down" decision-making approach that is so common in corporate America.[47]

The General Electric (GE) aircraft-engine assembly facility in Durham, North Carolina, provides a good example of a self-managed team. About 200 employees are involved in building huge jet engines the size of a large automobile. The engines are assembled by nine self-managed teams. Team members make a wide range of decisions, such as job assignments, how to improve the manufacturing process, vacation schedules, and the assignment of overtime. If a team member slacks off, members deal with the problem.[48]

QUESTIONS

1. If you were a GE employee and nominated to lead one of the nine self-managed teams, what would you look forward to the most (and what would you fear the most) about the experience?
2. What do you consider to be the major arguments for and against the team development practices used at ICU Medical, Inc.?
3. Looking into the future, do you see growth in the use of the various team formats? Explain your answer.

CLOSING CASE:
Virtual Teamwork: Making It Work

Virtual teams are composed of employees who are physically dispersed throughout the nation or around the world. They are linked by various forms of electronic technology. Face-to-face contact is usually minimal or nonexistent. Virtual teams face several challenges: time zone differences, which make quick information exchanges difficult, and cultural miscues, which can cause misunderstandings. When teams don't meet in person, its less likely they will develop the kind of chemistry common to productive teams that have face-to-face meetings. Many virtual teams are in continuous danger of becoming dysfunctional.[49]

Recent research has identified certain traits and practices common to most virtual teams. Here are a few important rules for making these teams productive.[50]

- Choose a few team members who already know each other. This will speed up the process of building networks among team members. Invest in online resources that help all team members quickly learn about one another.
- Ensure the task is meaningful to team members and the company. Assign only tasks that are challenging and interesting.
- The virtual team should include "boundary spanners," persons who have many connections to useful people outside of the team.
- Develop a team mission statement along with teamwork expectations, project goals, and deadlines.
- Create an online site where team members can collaborate, exchange ideas and motivate one another. The team should have a shared online workspace that all members can access 24 hours a day.
- Encourage frequent communication and try to reach agreement in preferred communication tools.
- If you are a virtual team leader, find ways to mark team progress toward goals.

QUESTIONS

1. Which of the five dysfunctions of a team (presented in Figure 12.2) would be the greatest barriers to virtual team productivity? Defend your answer.
2. What can be done to avoid information overload when the virtual team is made up of 25 to 30 members?

INTEGRATED RESOURCES

VIDEOS:

Turbulent Times: Numis
Managing Equality
Leadership: A Vision for Transformation

CLASSROOM ACTIVITIES

IRM Application Exercise 12.1
IRM Application Exercise 12.2
IRM Application Exercise 12.3

Resolving Conflict and Dealing with Difficult People

TIP OF THE ICEBERG

CHAPTER PREVIEW

LEARNING OBJECTIVES

After studying Chapter 13, you will be able to

- List and describe some of the major causes of conflict in the workplace.
- Use assertiveness skills in conflict situations.
- Understand when and how to implement effective negotiation skills.
- Identify key elements of the conflict resolution process.
- Discuss contemporary challenges facing labor unions.

Do Mandatory Health-Improvement Policies Work?

Workplace changes often become a personal matter for employees. This is especially true when an employer implements a policy that workers fear or dislike. Most organizations are searching for ways to cut medical costs. The starting point is frequently creation of a smoke-free work environment, followed by programs that help employees quit smoking. Today, many wellness programs include free weight-loss and smoking-cessation classes. More than 80 percent of companies with more than 50 employees have wellness programs.[1]

As the cost of health care increases, some companies are replacing voluntary programs with mandatory wellness policies. Employees at Crown Laboratories, in Johnson City, Tennessee, are not allowed to smoke—even at home. The Scotts Company, a giant lawn-care company, forbids employees to smoke on or off the job. The state of Alabama has approved a plan that requires obese employees to lose weight or pay a fine. Starting in January of 2010, state workers will participate in free health screenings. If the screening indicates obesity, they will be given a year to see a doctor at no cost and enroll in a weight-loss program. If the follow-up screening indicates no progress, they will have to pay $25 a month for insurance that is otherwise free. Workers who choose to smoke already pay $24 a month for their health insurance.[2]

Photo by Mario Tama/Getty Images

A growing number of organizations have established a smoke-free work environment. Some have developed programs that help employees to quit smoking. As health care expenses increase, some voluntary wellness programs are being replaced by mandatory policies. These policies often create conflict.

Some wellness policies raise privacy and discrimination issues. How far can an employer intrude into employees' lives? This chapter offers specific guidelines for effectively resolving a wide range of conflicts.

A New View of Conflict

Most standard dictionaries define **conflict** as a clash between incompatible people, ideas, or interests. These conflicts are almost always perceived as negative experiences in our society. But when we view conflict as a negative experience, we may be hurting our chances of dealing with it effectively. In reality, conflicts can serve as opportunities for personal growth if we develop and use positive, constructive conflict resolution skills.[3]

Much of our growth and social progress comes from the opportunities we have to discover creative solutions to conflicts that surface in our lives. Dudley Weeks, professor of conflict resolution at American University, says conflict can provide additional ways of thinking about the *source* of conflict and open up possibilities for improving a relationship.[4] When people work together to resolve conflicts, their solutions are often far more creative than they would be if only one person addressed the problem. Creative conflict resolution can shake people out of their mental ruts and give them a new point of view.

Much of our growth and social progress comes from the opportunities we have to discover creative solutions to conflicts that surface in our lives.

Meaningful Conflict

Too much agreement is not always healthy in an organization. Employees who are anxious to be viewed as "team players" may not voice concerns even when they have doubts about a decision being made. Four years before the first flight of space shuttle Challenger, some NASA engineers discovered problems with the O-ring seals, but these concerns were disregarded. Howard Schwartz, in his book *Narcissistic Process and Corporate Decay*, described the Challenger disaster as a tragic example of the "exportation of conflict."[5] Meaningful conflict can be the key to producing healthy, successful organizations because conflict is necessary for effective problem solving and for effective interpersonal relationships.[6] The problem is not with disagreements, but with how they are resolved.

Finding the Root Causes of Conflict

Throughout this text, we have often compared the challenges of interpersonal relations to an iceberg. The tip of the iceberg is in plain view and readily available for consideration. However, most of the iceberg exists below the surface and can create problems if we choose to ignore it. Let's assume that the owner of your company has initiated a ban on sexual harassment. This behavior has been carefully defined by the company lawyer, and the message seems very clear: employees who are guilty of sexual harassment will be terminated. The Iceberg of Conflict, Figure 13.1, reveals a wide range of factors that will influence each employee's perception of the new company policy.

FIGURE 13.1 Iceberg of Conflict

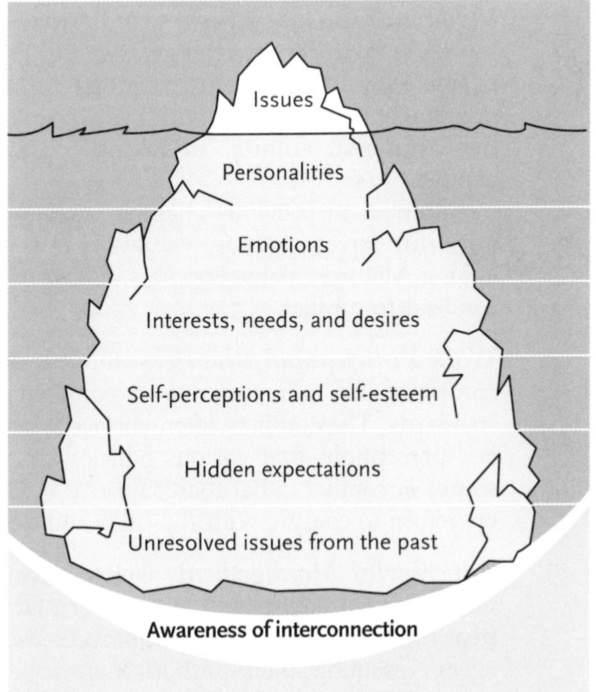

Source: From Kenneth Cloke and Joan Goldsmith, *Resolving Conflicts at Work: A Complete Guide for Everyone on the Job*, pp. 114–116, copyright © 2000 by Jossey-Bass. Reprinted with permission of John Wiley & Sons, Inc.

When you are in conflict, each level of the iceberg represents something that may influence the conflict-resolution process. It is important that we go deep enough to understand the influence of our emotions, self-perceptions, needs, unresolved issues from the past, and other things that exist at each level of the iceberg. The Iceberg of Conflict helps you better understand yourself and your opponent.

Conflict Triggers

A **conflict trigger** is a circumstance that increases the chances of intergroup or interpersonal conflict. If the conflict trigger appears to stimulate constructive conflict, it can be allowed to continue. When the symptoms of destructive conflict surface, steps should be taken to remove or correct the offending conflict trigger.[7]

Organizational Change. Organizational change is one of the seven root causes of conflict. In most organizations, there is tension between opposing forces for stability (maintain the status quo) and change. If management wants to shift more health care costs onto workers, tension may surface. With too much stability, the organization may lose its competitive position in the marketplace. With too much change, the mission blurs and employee anxiety develops.[8]

Ineffective Communication. A major source of personal conflict is the misunderstanding that results from ineffective communication. In Chapter 2, we discussed the various filters that messages must pass through before effective communication can occur. In the work setting, where many different people work closely together, communication breakdowns are inevitable. Achieving effective two-way communication is always a challenge.

Value and Culture Clashes. In Chapter 5, you read that differences in values can cause conflicts between generations, between men and women, and between people with different value priorities. Today's diverse work force reflects a kaleidoscope of cultures, each with its own unique qualities. The individual bearers of these different cultural traditions could easily come into conflict with one another.

As noted in previous chapters, generational influences are among the most powerful forces shaping values in our modern workforce. Value differences among Matures, Baby Boomers, Generation X, and Generation Y (Millennials) can lead to conflict.

Work Policies and Practices. Interpersonal conflicts can develop when an organization has unreasonable or confusing rules, regulations, and performance standards. The conflicts often surface when managers fail to tune in to employees' perceptions that various policies are unfair. Managers need to address the source of conflict rather than suppress it. Conflict also surfaces when some workers refuse to comply with the rules and neglect their fair share of the workload.

Adversarial Management. Under adversarial management, supervisors may view their employees and even other managers with suspicion and distrust and treat them as "the enemy." Employees usually lack respect for adversarial managers, resenting their authoritarian style and resisting their suggestions for change. This atmosphere makes cooperation and teamwork difficult.

Competition for Scarce Resources. It would be difficult to find an organization, public or private, that is not involved in downsizing or cost-cutting. The result is often destructive competition for scarce resources such as updated computerized equipment, administrative support personnel, travel dollars, salary increases, or annual bonuses. When budgets and cost-cutting efforts are not clearly explained, workers may suspect coworkers or supervisors of devious tactics.

Personality Clashes. There is no doubt about it: Some people just don't like each other. They may have differing communication styles, temperaments, or attitudes. They may not be able to identify exactly what it is they dislike about the other person, but the bottom line is that conflicts will arise when these people have to work together. Even people who get along well with each other in the beginning stages of a work relationship may begin to clash after working together for many years.

CAREER INSIGHT

Dealing with Workplace Bullies

Building a civilized workplace involves getting rid of workplace bullies. Workplace bullying can include sarcastic comments, physical threats, social exclusion, or work sabotage. Unlike sexual or racial harassment, this aggressive behavior is not necessarily illegal. But it does violate company policies that prohibit intimidation. Abusive supervisors and coworkers who cause emotional distress should not be tolerated. One of the most underutilized weapons in the arsenal against bullies is telling them the truth about the way they make you feel.[9]

Resolving Conflict Assertively

Conflict is often uncomfortable whether it is in a personal or professional setting. People sometimes get hurt and become defensive because they feel they are under personal attack. Because we have to work or live with certain people every day, it is best to avoid harming these ongoing relationships. But many people do not know how to participate in and manage conflict in a positive way. Many professionals advise going directly to the offending person and calmly discussing his or her irritating behavior rather than complaining to others.[10] Figure 13.2, "Dealing with People You Can't Stand," offers specific strategies you might use. By taking those steps to change *your* behavior, you might facilitate a powerful change in theirs. Keep in mind that some people are unaware of the impact of their behavior, and if you draw their attention to it, they may change it.

Whereas these strategies may be comfortable for some people, such a direct approach may be very uncomfortable for many others. People who attempt to avoid conflict by simply ignoring things that bother them are exhibiting **nonassertive behavior**. Nonassertive people often give in to the demands of others, and their passive approach makes them less likely to make their needs known. If you fail to take a firm position when such action is appropriate, customers, coworkers, and supervisors may take advantage of you, and management may question your abilities.

FIGURE 13.2 Dealing with People You Can't Stand

THE BULLY	Bullies find ways to manipulate or control others. They are pushy, ruthless, loud, and forceful and tend to intimidate you with in-your-face arguments. They assume that the end justifies the means. **Strategy:** Keep your cool. Immediately respond calmly and professionally to let the bully know you are not a target: "When you're ready to speak to me with respect, I'll be ready to discuss this matter." Walk away from a ranting bully. Ask the bully to fully explain what he or she is trying to say or do, and then paraphrase your understanding of the bully's real intentions.
THE BACKSTABBER	They present themselves as your friend but do everything in their power to sabotage your relationships with your supervisors, coworkers, and clients. They use tactics such as withholding information from you and then suggesting to others that you are incompetent, witless, and worthy of demotion. **Strategy:** Once you've discovered your saboteur, tell key people that the person is, in fact, not a friend, which takes power from the backstabber and reveals the smear campaign.
THE WHINER	They wallow in their woe, whine incessantly about the injustices that surround them, and carry the weight of the world on their shoulders. **Strategy:** Listen and write down their main points. Interrupt and get specifics so you can identify and focus on possible solutions. If they remain in "it's hopeless" mode, walk away saying, "Let me know when you want to talk about a solution."
THE JERK	They tend to be self-centered, arrogant, manipulative, and goal-oriented. They trust no one and refuse to collaborate with others. They may take pot-shots at you during meetings, but avoid one-on-one confrontations. They lack empathy, but can be great sweet-talkers to the boss. **Strategy:** They do not respond to normal pleas to change their behavior, so just back off. Do not take their bait, limit your contact with them, avoid conflict when possible, and always be on guard.
THE KNOW-IT-ALL	They will tell you what they know, but they will not bother listening to your "clearly inferior" ideas. Often, they really don't know much, but they don't let that get in the way. They exaggerate, brag, and mislead. **Strategy:** Acknowledge their expertise, but be prepared with your facts. Use "I" statements, such as "From what I've read and experienced . . ."
THE NEBBISH	When faced with a crucial decision, they keep putting it off until it is too late and the decision makes itself, or they say yes to everything but follow through on nothing. **Strategy:** Help them feel comfortable and safe in their rare decisions to move forward, and stay in touch until the decision is implemented. Arrange deadlines and describe the consequences that will result when they complete the tasks and what will happen if they don't.
THE EXPLODERS	They throw tantrums that can escalate quickly. When they blow their tops, they are unable to stop. When the smoke clears and the dust settles, the cycle begins again. **Strategy:** When an explosion begins, assertively repeat the individual's name to get his or her attention, or repeat a neutral comment such as "Stop!" Calmly address what they said in their first few sentences, which usually reveals the real problem. Give them time to regain self-control. Suggest that they take time out to cool down, and then listen to their problems in private.

Source: Figure from *Dealing with People You Can't Stand* by Rick Brinkman and Rick Kirschner. Copyright © 1994 by McGraw-Hill, Inc. Reprinted by permission of The McGraw Hill Companies.

TABLE 13.1 BEHAVIORS EXHIBITED BY ASSERTIVE, AGGRESSIVE, AND NONASSERTIVE PERSONS

	ASSERTIVE PERSON	AGGRESSIVE PERSON	NONASSERTIVE PERSON
In conflict situations	Communicates directly	Dominates	Avoids the conflict
In decision-making situations	Chooses for self	Chooses for self and others	Allows others to choose
In situations expressing feelings	Is open, direct, honest, while allowing others to express their feelings	Expresses feelings in a threatening manner; puts down, inhibits others	Holds true feelings inside
In group meeting situations	Uses direct, clear "I" statements: "I believe that …"	Uses clear but demeaning "you" statements: "You should have known better …"	Uses indirect, unclear statements: "Would you mind if … ?"

Assertive behavior, on the other hand, provides you the opportunity to stand up for your rights and express your thoughts and feelings in a direct, appropriate way that does not violate the rights of others. It is a matter of getting the other person to understand your viewpoint.[11] People who exhibit appropriate assertive behavior skills are able to handle their conflicts with greater ease and assurance while maintaining good interpersonal relations.

Some people do not understand the distinction between being aggressive and being assertive. **Aggressive behavior** involves expressing your thoughts and feelings and defending your rights in a way that *violates* the rights of others. Aggressive people may interrupt, talk fast, ignore others, and use sarcasm or other forms of verbal abuse to maintain control.

Table 13.1 may give you a clearer understanding of how nonassertive, assertive, and aggressive individuals respond when confronted with conflict situations.

How to Become More Assertive

Entire books have been written that describe how to improve your assertiveness skills. Several years ago, the American Management Association (*http://www.amanet.org*) began offering skill-development seminars that focus on assertiveness training, including Assertiveness Training for the New or Prospective Manager and Assertiveness Training for Women in Business.[12] Enrollees have the opportunity to achieve greater credibility by learning how to handle tough situations with composure and confidence. Whether you choose to read the books or participate in assertiveness training, know that you can communicate your wants, dislikes, and feelings in a clear, direct manner without threatening or attacking others. Here are three practical guidelines that will help you develop your assertiveness skills.

In the Beginning, Take Small Steps. Being assertive may be difficult at first, so start with something that is easy. You might decline the invitation to keep the minutes at the weekly staff meeting if you feel others should assume this duty from time to time. If you are tired of eating lunch at Joe's Diner (the choice of a coworker), suggest a restaurant that you would prefer. If someone insists on keeping the temperature at a cool 67 degrees and you are tired of being cold all the time, approach the person and voice your opinion. Asking that your desires be considered is not necessarily a bad thing.

Use Communication Skills That Enhance Assertiveness. A confident tone of voice, eye contact, firm gestures, and good posture create nonverbal messages that say, "I'm serious about this request." Using "I" messages can be especially helpful in cases where you want to assert yourself in a nonthreatening manner. If you approach the person who wants the thermostat set at 67 degrees and say, "You need to be more considerate of others," the person is likely to become defensive. However, if you say, "I feel uncomfortable when the temperature is so cool," you will start the conversation on a more positive note.

Be Soft on People and Hard on the Problem. The goal of conflict resolution is to solve the problem but avoid doing harm to the relationship. Of course, relationships tend to become entangled with the problem, so there is a tendency to treat the people and the problem as one. Your coworker, Terry, is turning in projects late every week, and you are feeling a great deal of frustration each time it happens. You must communicate to Terry that each missed deadline creates serious problems for you. Practice using tact, diplomacy, and patience as you keep the discussion focused on the problem, not on Terry's personality traits.

CRITICAL THINKING CHALLENGE:

Analyze and Synthesize It

List the various conflicts you witnessed among workers within an organization in which you worked as an employee or volunteer. Carefully examine each conflict scenario and go beyond the generally perceived cause for the disagreements. Determine if there was a "root" cause. What did you discover?

Learn to Negotiate Effectively

In the past, the responsibility for negotiating an effective resolution to conflicts was often given to supervisors, department heads, team leaders, shop stewards, mediators, and other individuals with established authority and responsibility. Today, many companies have organized workers into teams and are empowering those workers to solve their own problems whenever possible. This means that every employee needs to learn how to effectively negotiate satisfactory resolutions to conflicts. Danny Ertel, author and consultant in the area of negotiations, says, "Every company, today, exists in a complex web of relationships, and the shape of that web is formed, one thread at a time, through negotiations."[13] Team assignments, compensation, promotions, and work assignments are just a few of the areas where you can apply negotiation skills.

Think Win/Win

There are basically three ways to approach negotiations: win/lose, lose/lose, and win/win. When you use the **win/lose approach**, you are attempting to reach your goals at the expense of the other party's. For example, a manager can say,

Soon after celebrating their 15th wedding anniversary, Elaine and Michael Honig decided to get a divorce. As joint owners of the successful Honig Vineyard, the divorce could have created serious problems. However, they decided to remain friends as well as business partners after the divorce.

"Do as I say or find a job somewhere else!" The manager wins; the employee loses. Although this approach may end the conflict on a short-term basis, it does not usually address the underlying cause of the problem. It may simply sow the seeds of another conflict because the "losers" feel frustrated. (This strategy may be effective in those rare instances when it is more important to get the job done than it is to maintain good human relations among the work force.)

When the **lose/lose approach** is used to settle a dispute, each side must give in to the other. If the sacrifices are too great, both parties may feel that too much has been given. This strategy can be applied when there is little time to find a solution through effective negotiation techniques, or when negotiations are at a standstill and no progress is being made. Union-management disputes, for example, often fall into the lose/lose trap when neither side is willing to yield. In these cases, an arbitrator, a neutral third party, may be called in to impose solutions on the disputing parties.

In general, the win/lose and lose/lose approaches to negotiating create a "we versus they" attitude among the people involved in the conflict, rather than a "we versus the problem" approach. "We versus they" (or "my way versus your way") means that participants focus on whose solution is superior, instead of working together to find a solution that is acceptable to all.

The basic purpose of the **win/win approach** to negotiating is to fix the problem—not the blame! Don't think hurt; think help. Negotiating a win/win solution to a conflict is not a debate

The basic purpose of the win/win approach to negotiating is to fix the problem—not the blame!

FIGURE 13.3

Rob Walker reviewed several of the best-selling books on negotiation, including *Getting to Yes, You Can Negotiate Anything, The Negotiation Tool Kit,* and *The Power of Nice*. He discovered a few basic negotiating tips that recur in these popular advice books:

- Stay rationally focused on the issue being negotiated.
- Exhaustive preparation is more important than aggressive argument.
- Think through your alternatives.
- The more options you feel you have, the better a negotiating position you will be in.
- Spend less time talking and more time listening and asking good questions. Sometimes silence is your best response.
- Let the other side make the first offer. If you are underestimating yourself, you might make a needlessly weak opening move.

Source: Rob Walker, "Take It or Leave It: The Only Guide to Negotiating You Will Ever Need," *Inc.*, August 2003, p. 81.

where you are attempting to prove the other side wrong; instead, you are engaging in a dialogue where each side attempts to get the other side to understand its concerns, and both sides then work toward a mutually satisfying solution. Your negotiations will go better when you shift your emphasis from a tactical approach of how to counter the other person's every comment to discovering a creative solution that simple haggling obscures.[14]

Perhaps the most vital skill in effective negotiations is listening. When you concentrate on learning common interests, not differences, the nature of the negotiations changes from a battle to win, to a discussion of how to meet the objectives of everyone involved in the dispute (see Figure 13.3).

Beware of Defensive Behaviors

Effective negotiations are often slowed or sidetracked completely by defensive behaviors that surface when people are in conflict with each other. When one person in a conflict situation becomes defensive, others may mirror this behavior. In a short time, progress is slowed because people stop listening and begin thinking about how they can defend themselves against the other person's comments.

We often become defensive when we feel our needs are being ignored. Kurt Salzinger, Executive Director for Science at the American Psychological Association, reminds us that conflicts are often caused by unfulfilled needs for things such as dignity, security, identity, recognition, or justice. He says, "Conflict is often exacerbated as much by the process of the relationship as it is by the issues."[15] Determining the other person's needs requires careful listening and respect for views that differ from your own. If you feel you are trapped in a win/lose negotiation and can hear yourself or the other person becoming defensive, do everything in your power to refocus the discussion toward fixing the problem rather than defending your position.

HUMAN RELATIONS IN ACTION

Parable of the Orange

Two people each want an orange, but negotiations drag on without a solution. Finally, they agree to split the orange in half. But it turns out that one person simply wanted the juice, and the other person wanted only the rind. In this case, haggling obscured the solution. If they had engaged in a true dialogue, each side could have gotten what it wanted.[16]

Know That Negotiating Styles Vary

Depending on personality, assertiveness skills, and past experiences in dealing with conflict in the workplace, individuals naturally develop their own negotiating styles. But negotiating is a skill, and people can learn how and when to adapt their style to deal effectively with conflict situations.

Robert Maddux suggests that there are five different behavioral styles that can be used during a conflict situation. These styles are based on the combination of two factors: assertiveness and cooperation (see Figure 13.4). He takes the position that different styles may be appropriate in different situations.

FIGURE 13.4 **Behavioral Styles for Conflict Situations**

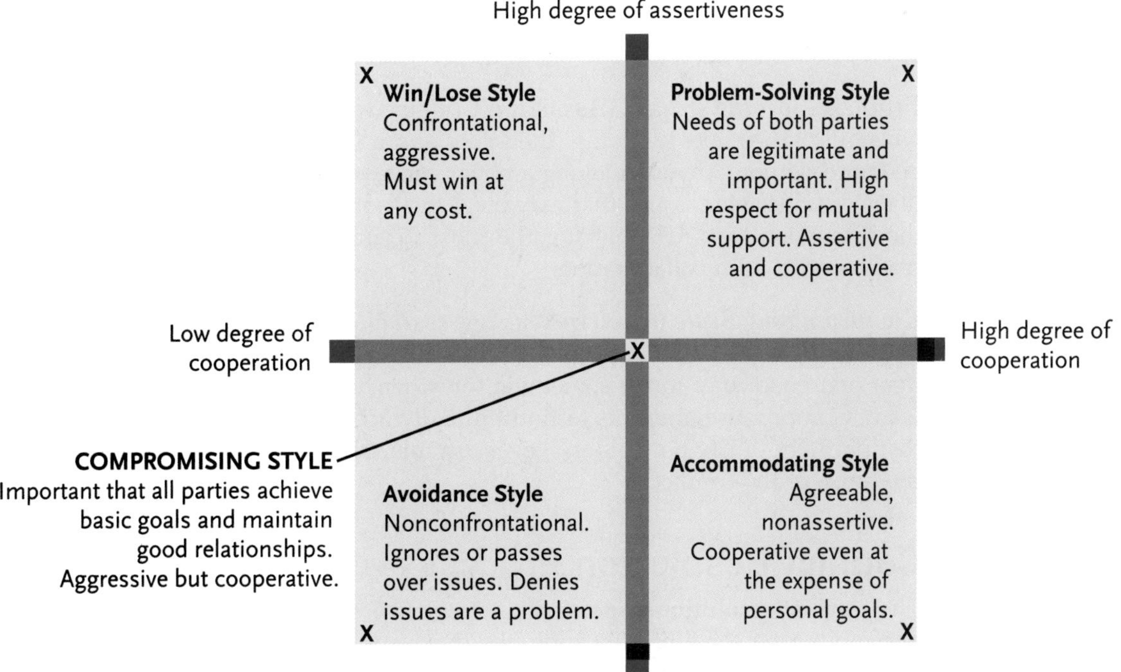

Source: Adapted from Robert B. Maddux's *Team Building: An Exercise in Leadership*, Crisp Publications, Inc., Menlo, CA, 1986, p. 53. Reprinted by permission of the publisher.

Total Person Insight

ROGER FISHER
WILLIAM URY
Authors, *Getting to Yes*

"Any method of negotiation may be fairly judged by three criteria: It should produce a wise agreement if agreement is possible. It should be efficient. And it should improve, or at least not damage, the relationship between the parties."[17]

Avoidance Style (Uncooperative/Nonassertive). This style is appropriate when the conflict is too minor or too great to resolve. Any attempt to resolve the conflict might result in damaging a relationship or simply wasting time and energy. Avoidance might take the form of diplomatically sidestepping an issue or postponing your response until a more appropriate time.

Accommodating Style (Cooperative/Nonassertive). This style is appropriate when resolving the conflict is not worth risking damage to the relationship or general disharmony. Individuals who use this approach relinquish their own concerns to satisfy the concerns of someone else. Accommodating might take the form of selfless generosity or blind obedience to another's point of view.

Win/Lose Style (Uncooperative/Aggressive). This style may be appropriate when the conflict involves "survival of the fittest," when you must prove your superior position, or when your opinion is the most ethically or professionally correct. This power-oriented position allows you to use whatever means seem appropriate when it is time to stand up for your rights.

Problem-Solving Style (Assertive/Cooperative). This style is appropriate when all parties openly discuss the issues and a mutually beneficial solution can be found without anyone making a major concession. Problem solvers attempt to uncover underlying issues that may be at the root of the problem, and then focus the discussion toward achieving the most desirable outcome. They seek to replace conflict with collaboration.

Compromising Style (Moderately Aggressive/Moderately Cooperative). This style is appropriate when no one person or idea is perfect, when there is more than one good way to do something, or when you must give to get what you want. Compromise attempts to find mutually acceptable solutions to the conflict that partially satisfy both sides. Never use this style when unethical activities are the cause of the conflict.

Conflict Resolution Process

The **conflict resolution process** consists of five steps that can be used at work and in your personal life. To apply the five steps requires understanding and acceptance of everything we have discussed up to this point in the chapter: application of assertiveness skills, understanding how to deal with various types of difficult people, support for the win/win approach to conflict resolution, and learning how to negotiate.

Skill Development: Apply It

Identify an instance when you were in a conflict with another person. How was the conflict resolved? How would the conflict resolution have changed had you *intentionally* implemented your avoidance style, your accommodating style, your win/lose style, your problem-solving style, and your compromising style? What does this tell you about your potential conflict resolution skills?

A misunderstanding is a failure to accurately understand the other person's point. A disagreement, in contrast, is a failure to agree, which would persist despite the most accurate understanding.

Step One: Decide Whether You Have a Misunderstanding or a True Disagreement

David Stiebel, author of *When Talking Makes Things Worse!*, says a misunderstanding is a failure to accurately understand the other person's point. A disagreement, in contrast, is a failure to agree, which would persist despite the most accurate understanding. In a true disagreement, people want more than your explanation and further details; they want to change your mind.[18] When we fail to realize the distinction between these two possibilities, a great deal of time and energy may be wasted. Consider the following conflict situation.

As Sarah entered the driveway of her home, she could hardly wait to share the news with her husband Paul. Late that afternoon, she had met with her boss and learned she was the number-one candidate for a newly created administrative position. Sarah entered the house and immediately told Paul about the promotion opportunity. In a matter of seconds, it became apparent that he was not happy about the promotion. He said, "We don't need the extra money, and you do not need the headaches that come with an administrative position." Expecting a positive response,

From *The Wall Street Journal*, permission Cartoon Features Syndicate

"There's no denying the conflict around here, J.B., but a flak jacket?"

Sarah was very disappointed. In the heat of anger, Sarah and Paul both said things they would later regret.

If Sarah and Paul had asked each other a few questions, this conflict might have been avoided. Before arriving home, Sarah had already weighed the pros and cons of the new position and decided it was not a good career move; however, she wanted her husband's input before making the final decision. This conflict was not a true disagreement in which one person tries to change the other person's mind; it was a misunderstanding that was the result of incomplete information. If Sarah and Paul had fully understood each other's position, it would have become clear that a true disagreement did not exist.

Step Two: Define the Problem and Collect the Facts

The saying "A problem well defined is a problem half solved" is not far from the truth. It is surprising how difficult this step can be. Everyone involved needs to focus on the real cause of the conflict, not on what has happened as a result of it.

As you begin collecting information about the conflict, it may be necessary to separate facts from opinions or perceptions. Ask questions that focus on who is involved in the conflict, what happened, when, where, and why. What policies and procedures were involved?

Conflict resolution in the age of information offers us new challenges. As we are faced with information overload, we may be tempted to use the information we already have rather than search for the new information needed to guide a decision.[19]

> ## *Total Person Insight*
>
> MARCI DU PRAW
> Senior Mediator with Resolve
>
> *"If handled well, conflict is an opportunity to work together in a way that brings out strengths."*[20]

Step Three: Clarify Perceptions

Your perception is your interpretation of the facts surrounding the situations you encounter. Perceptions can have a tremendous influence on your behavior. In a conflict situation, it is therefore very important that you clarify all parties' perceptions of the problem. You can do this by attempting to see the situation as others see it. Take the case of Laura, a sales representative who was repeatedly passed over for a promotion although her sales numbers were among the best in the department.

After a period of time, Laura became convinced that she was the victim of gender discrimination. She filed charges with the Equal Employment Opportunity Commission (EEOC), and a hearing was scheduled. When Laura's boss was given a chance to explain his actions, he described Laura as someone who was very dedicated to her family. He said, "It's my view that she would be unhappy in a sales management position because she would have to work longer hours and travel more." He did not see his actions as being discriminatory. Laura explained that she valued the time she spent with her husband and children but achieving a management position was an important career goal.

Step Four: Generate Options for Mutual Gain

Once the basic problem has been defined, the facts surrounding it have been brought out, and everyone is operating with the same perceptions, everyone involved in the conflict should focus on generating options that will fix the problem. Some people, however, do not consider generating options to be part of the conflict resolution process. Rather than broadening the options for mutual gain, some individuals want to quickly build support for a single solution. The authors of the best-selling book *Getting to Yes* say, "In a dispute, people usually believe that they know the right answer—their view should prevail. They become trapped in their own point of view."[21] Group members should be encouraged to generate a wide variety of ideas and possibilities.

Step Five: Implement Options with Integrity

The final step in the conflict resolution process involves finalizing an agreement that offers win/win benefits to those in conflict. Sometimes, as the conflict resolution process comes to a conclusion, one or more parties in the conflict may be tempted to win an advantage that weakens the relationship. This might involve hiding information or using pressure tactics that violate the win/win spirit and weaken the relationship. Even the best conflict solutions can fail unless all conflict partners serve as "caretakers" of the agreement and the relationship.[22]

Establish timetables for implementing the solutions, and provide a plan to evaluate their effectiveness. On a regular basis, make a point to discuss with others how things are going to be sure that old conflict patterns do not resurface.

Alternative Dispute Resolution

At times, you and your coworkers or employer may not be able to reach a satisfactory resolution to your conflicts. You may believe you have been fired without cause, sexually harassed, discriminated against, overlooked for a promotion, or unfairly disciplined. Your only recourse may be to ignore the situation or take your employer to court. Ignoring the situation does not make it go away, and court battles can take years and can be extremely expensive. In some instances, you may have a legitimate complaint but not a legal claim. To help keep valued employees content and out of court, many organizations have created formal Alternative Dispute Resolution programs, or ADRs. A Cornell University study discovered that more than 80 percent of large employers nationwide operate internal ADRs, and all federal departments are required to offer ADR options.[23]

These programs usually involve any or all of the following: an open door policy that allows you to talk confidentially with upper management personnel, a toll-free hot line to which employees can air grievances and get general advice, a peer review panel that investigates and attempts to resolve the problem, a third-party mediator who listens to arguments and attempts to forge a mutually acceptable solution, or an arbitrator who imposes a final and binding solution to the problem.[24]

The Role of Labor Unions in Conflict Resolution

Since the 1930s, labor unions have had the authority to negotiate disputes between union members and management. This arrangement serves as an equalizing factor that allows organized workers the power necessary to challenge

AP Photo/Ron Edmonds

Harvard scholar Henry Louis Gates Jr. returned from a trip and had difficulty opening the door to his home. A passerby thought Gates might be a burglar and called police. Sgt. James Crowley arrived on the scene and a major conflict ensued. The conflict became a national issue when president Obama publicly criticized the police officer. The "beer summit" was an attempt at reconciliation.

managers' decisions. Most management–labor union disputes escalate when the employment contracts that establish the workers' wages, benefits, and working conditions expire and need to be renegotiated. The overwhelming majority of employment contracts are settled through **collective bargaining**, a process that defines the rights and privileges of both sides involved in the conflict and establishes the terms of employment and length of the contract (usually from three to five years). However, if labor and management cannot settle their differences, they may submit their disputes to one of the following:

- **Mediation**—A neutral third party listens to both sides and suggests solutions. It carries no binding authority. Both parties are free to reject or accept the mediator's decision.
- **Voluntary arbitration**—Both sides willingly submit their disagreements to a neutral party. The arbitrator's decision must be accepted by both sides.
- **Compulsory arbitration**—When the government decides that the labor-management dispute threatens national health and safety, or will damage an entire industry, it can appoint an arbitrator who dictates a solution that is binding on both sides and can be enforced in a court of law.

When collective bargaining, mediation, and arbitration are not enough to settle disputes, union leaders may recommend, and members may vote, to go on strike against their employers. A strike generally results in a lose/lose situation in which workers lose paychecks, employers lose sales, customers lose products or services, and communities lose economic stability. In the fall of 2008, the International Association of Machinists and Aerospace Workers staged an eight-week strike against Boeing Company. The strike cost an estimated $100 million a day in deferred revenue and production delays.[25]

Contemporary Issues Facing Labor Unions

Only 12 percent of workers in America are members of a labor union and thus protected by collective bargaining. This is down from 33 percent in the 1950s.[26]

HUMAN RELATIONS IN ACTION

Screaming Managers Take Heed

Some managers think screaming at employees is the best way to motivate them. They should spend time observing Tony Dungy and Lovie Smith, two very successful National Football League coaches. They don't curse, scream, or sarcastically chew out players. These two men—the first African-Americans to lead Super Bowl Teams–believe they can win more games by giving directions calmly and treating players with respect.[27]

Although many organizations have adopted conflict-resolution policies similar to unions' collective-bargaining process, most employees have few choices beyond quitting their jobs and moving on to a friendlier employer if they cannot settle disputes with their current employer.

The future of labor unions and the protection they provide for workers seems to depend on union organizers' ability to attract new members. As workers lose jobs to cheaper offshore workers and take on a larger proportion of their health insurance premiums, thus lowering their take-home pay, it would seem logical that union membership might begin to increase. At the same time, anti-union employers such as Wal-Mart, FedEx, and McDonalds actively strive to keep their workers happy and productive so that they do not perceive a need for what unions have to offer them.[28] Organizations often hire expensive anti-union consulting and legal firms to fend off union attempts to be sanctioned through the long and involved process established by the National Labor Relations Board (NLRB). But there is an alternative that is becoming popular in the global union movement. The "card-check neutrality" process allows union representatives to gather signatures from employees expressing their desire to join a union. If it is able to get signed cards from a majority of eligible workers, the union is authorized to negotiate the employees' next labor contract. Companies organized via the card-check process include Marriott, Freightliner, Cingular, and Rite-Aid.[29]

Labor unions are striving for survival, but they may thrive in the next millennium if they take direct action to address the following needs of the work force:

- Adopt a global mentality. Acknowledge that offshore workers under contract to American-based companies may be eligible for union representation, too, and adjust policies and decisions accordingly.
- Encourage organizations to save money by sending low-wage jobs offshore and then using the additional revenue to create good, higher-paying jobs and fund the necessary re-training for workers who live in the United States.
- Reduce the inequities between executives' million-dollar salaries and employees' declining compensation (in real dollars).
- Provide affordable health care at reasonable rates through whatever avenue is effective, including, but not limited to, socialized medicine.
- Provide membership and corresponding benefits to temporary and contract workers.

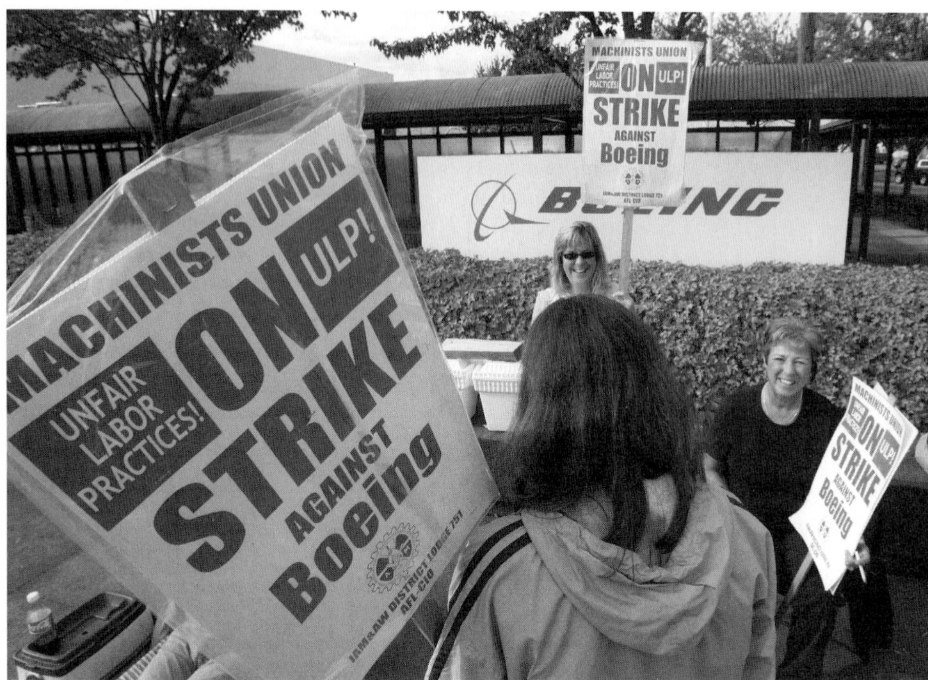

AP Photo/Ted S. Warren

A strike by members of the International Association of Machinists and Aerospace Workers idled several Boeing company factories. Key contract issues were job security and rising health care costs. Company officials say the strike could cost Boeing an estimated $100 million in revenue from delayed airplane deliveries.

LOOKING BACK: REVIEWING THE CONCEPTS

- List and describe some of the major causes of conflict in the workplace.

Conflicts among people at work happen every day and can arise because of changes within the organization, poor communication, values and culture clashes, confusing work policies and practices, competition for scarce resources, or adversarial management. Often, however, conflicts come from coworkers who refuse to carry their fair share of the workload or have a difficult personality. Although unresolved conflicts can have a negative effect on an organization's productivity, a difference of opinion sometimes has a positive effect by forcing team members toward creative and innovative solutions to problems.

- Use assertiveness skills in conflict situations.

Assertiveness skills are necessary when you want to maintain your rights during a conflict with someone else but want to avoid being overly aggressive, which means interfering with others' rights. Begin building assertiveness skills by tackling relatively minor issues first until you gain the confidence to take on those who try to take away your power. Use "I" statements rather than "you" statements so that the other person does not become defensive. Focus on fixing the problem rather than attacking the other person.

- Understand when and how to implement effective negotiation skills.

You can vastly improve your human relations skills when dealing with difficult people by learning when and how to intentionally implement Robert Maddux's five negotiating styles: avoidance style, accommodating style, win/lose style, problem-solving style, and compromising style.

- Identify key elements of the conflict resolution process.

When employees cannot solve their conflicts in an informal manner, many organizations create solutions through a conflict resolution process. The five-step conflict resolution process is described in this chapter. Often, an ADR program can resolve conflicts that might otherwise lead to legal action.

- Discuss contemporary challenges facing labor unions.

Labor leaders and business owners are finding new ways to cooperate with each other rather than negotiating with a nonproductive "us versus them" attitude. They are finding that flexibility and innovation are far more effective than old adversarial styles. If labor and management cannot settle their differences, they may submit their disputes to mediation, voluntary arbitration, or compulsory arbitration. Labor unions, today, must be more responsive to balancing the inequities between executives' salaries and employees' wages, controlling health care costs, retaining "good" high-paying jobs, containing the competition for jobs from cheap offshore laborers, and adjusting to management's trend of hiring temporary and part-time workers as opposed to full-time workers.

ON THE JOB Q & A: IGNORE WARNING SIGNS AT YOUR PERIL

Q: The old adage "Fool me once, shame on you. Fool me twice, shame on me!" has become a reality in my career search. Last year, I accepted a position with an ad agency where the owners did not disclose they were married to each other until after I was on the job. I quit after nine months when I discovered they expected me to provide clients with inaccurate information. I accepted my next job with an event-production company, even though the hiring supervisor made disparaging remarks about the person who had previously held my position. It is now obvious that this supervisor acts condescendingly toward everyone, including me. I should have recognized the clues that indicated I was heading into these bad-boss environments. How can I avoid falling into another bad situation now that I am once again looking for a job?

A: Many applicants ignore warning signs about their prospective supervisors, yet the type of person you will be working with is one of the most important factors you should consider when job hunting. Prepare a list of ideal traits you would want in your next supervisor and keep this information in mind as you ask questions during your interview. Ask your interviewer direct questions such as "What are the characteristics of your most valued employees?" "Give me an example of how an employee's unethical conduct is handled." "During a recent crisis within the organization, who was the 'hero' and why?" "What is your employee retention rate?" Try to obtain complete answers to your questions. Prior to the interview, and throughout the interview, learn as much as possible about the company culture. What types of employees are selected for leadership positions? What leadership behaviors are rewarded within the company?[30]

KEY TERMS

conflict 278
conflict trigger 280
nonassertive behavior 281
assertive behavior 283
aggressive behavior 283
win/lose approach 284
lose/lose approach 285
win/win approach 285
conflict resolution process 288
collective bargaining 292
mediation 292
voluntary arbitration 292
compulsory arbitration 292

TRY YOUR HAND

1. Has there been someone in your life (now or in the past) that you just can't (or couldn't) stand? Explain the behaviors this person exhibits that get on your nerves. Carefully examine Figure 13.2, determine which category fits the person best, and then describe what you might do to help this person change his or her behavior. Be specific.

2. Describe a conflict that is disrupting human relations at school, home, or work. It might involve academic requirements at school, distribution of responsibilities at home, or hurt feelings at work. Identify all the people involved in the conflict, and decide who should be involved in the conflict resolution process. Design a conflict resolution plan by following the steps given in this chapter. Implement your plan and report the results of this conflict resolution process to other class members.

3. To learn more about your level of assertiveness complete the short quiz below. Simply answer "yes" or "no" to each question and then interpret your score.

ARE YOU ASSERTIVE ENOUGH?

Take this short quiz from *The Instant Manager* to find out.

Being assertive is not the same as being aggressive. Assertiveness is confidence translated into action. It is neither bullying nor brow-beating, but simply allowing your convictions to carry a conversation. Honesty combined with a non-confrontational manner will make assertiveness one of the most valuable tools in your managerial tool kit.

Answer "Yes" or "No" to each question. Do you...

Yes☐ No☐ 1. Apologize when you don't have an instant solution to a problem?
Yes☐ No☐ 2. Frequently apologize for your decisions?
Yes☐ No☐ 3. Feel that you do not have the right to change your mind?
Yes☐ No☐ 4. Feel guilty when you make mistakes, even when they can be fixed?
Yes☐ No☐ 5. Automatically say "yes" when someone makes a request?
Yes☐ No☐ 6. Feel foolish asking questions when you do not understand something?
Yes☐ No☐ 7. Follow instructions without question?
Yes☐ No☐ 8. Think your opinion does not count, especially if it differs from the majority?
Yes☐ No☐ 9. Feel that you do not have the right to ask people to change their behavior towards you?
Yes☐ No☐ 10. Feel guilty delegating or deferring tasks?
Yes☐ No☐ 11. Have trouble walking away from an argument?

Total number of "Yes" ☐

HOW TO INTERPRET YOUR SCORE.

If you answered "Yes" to:

8 to 11 of the questions: You need serious improvement. Take an acting or public speaking course, review your accomplishments—whatever will boost your self-confidence.

4 to 7 of the questions: You are just squeaking by. Try some speaking and body-language techniques and learn to keep your cool.

0 to 3 of the questions: You are just about right. Keep it up!

Excepted from *The Instant Manager—More than 100 Quick Tips & techniques for Great Results*, by Cy Charney (AMACOM 2004).

4. To develop your assertiveness skills, find a partner who will join you for a practice session. The partner should assume the role of a friend, family member, or coworker who is doing something that causes you a great deal of frustration. (The problem can be real or imaginary.) Communicate your dislikes and feelings in a clear, direct manner without threatening or attacking. Then ask your partner to critique your assertiveness skills. Participate in several of these practice sessions until you feel confident that you have improved your assertiveness skills.

INTERNET INSIGHTS

1. Go to *http://www.adr.org* to view the website of the American Arbitration Association and review the dispute resolution services available. Also visit *http://www.adr.org/International* to view the related website of the International Center for Dispute Resolution. List the services the ICDR provides. When might you use their services?
2. It is your turn to play investigator; search the Web and see how many sites you can find regarding *Dealing with Difficult People.* Which sites were the most informative and gave you pragmatic skills to transfer this information into the workplace? Support your selections.

YOU PLAY THE ROLE

Assume the role of a business manager for a large hospital. About three weeks ago, you received some incomplete medical records from Ashley Mason, the physician in charge of the emergency room. With a red pen, you marked the areas that were incomplete and sent the forms back to the doctor. You attached a terse note that requested the forms to be returned within 24 hours. Three days passed without a reply, and your anger increased each day. Finally, you sent the doctor an e-mail that basically accused Dr. Mason of incompetence in the area of medical record keeping. The doctor phoned you immediately and said the entire emergency room staff had been extremely busy and did not have a moment to spare. You replied that timely and accurate record keeping is the responsibility of every physician employed by the hospital. Unfortunately, your tone of voice and your selection of words were totally inappropriate. Basically, you treated Dr. Mason like a child who had misbehaved, and the doctor hung up on you. You immediately felt like a fool and regretted your behavior. The next day, the completed forms were returned to you. You have decided to meet with Dr. Mason. Your goal is to repair the damaged relationship and set the stage for effective communications in the future. Before meeting with another class member who will assume the role of Dr. Mason, review the information on the art of apologizing in Chapter 8 and information in this chapter on resolving conflicts.

BELOW THE SURFACE:

Get Healthy…Or Else

At the beginning of this chapter, we noted that workplace conflict often develops when an employer implements a policy that workers fear or dislike. Mandatory health-improvement policies provide a good example. Some employees are required to participate in screenings that will identify problems with blood pressure, cholesterol, or obesity. A Massachusetts man sued The Scotts Company, the giant lawn-care corporation, for loss of his job after a drug test showed nicotine in his urine. The test indicated that he had violated a company policy forbidding employees to smoke on or off the job.[31]

Many companies want their workers to become more aware of their health. However, some employers say mandatory policies go too far. Alan Jay Weiner, founder of Technology 21, says mandatory policies are an invasion of the employee's privacy. He thinks the next step may be denying health insurance to workers who ride a motorcycle.[32] The state of Alabama is cracking down on employees who are overweight. Although state employees can enroll in wellness programs at no charge, some wonder if they will lose their jobs if they fail to achieve weight-loss guidelines. Chegula Motely, a health department employee, says, "It's terrible, some people come into this world big."[33]

In some cases, you may be the person who will make decisions regarding the wellness of your employees or coworkers. A manager met with his staff in a hotel bar during a medical industry conference. A pregnant member of his team ordered a martini. The manager and team members were uncomfortable, but no one expressed their concerns. One of your coworkers drinks too much at after-work get-togethers, and you feel very uncomfortable when she or he gets really drunk. You want to talk to him or her about the problem, but fear it might alienate you from your peers.[34] What should you do?

QUESTIONS

1. Although many organizations are initiating mandatory wellness programs, others are relying on persuasion and rewards to encourage employees to voluntarily improve their health. If you owned a small company with 50 employees, which approach would you choose? Explain your answer.
2. Many organizations are structured around teams. Teams have proven to be effective in many areas such as improving quality, cost reduction, and new product development. Assess how teams might be used to encourage voluntary participation in wellness programs.
3. At some point in your work life, you will likely work for a company that offers no health insurance, or a health insurance program with very limited coverage. For example, some plans require the worker to pay medical bills up to a certain amount—the first $500 or $1,000 for example. Assess what steps you could take to avoid costly health-related problems.

CLOSING CASE: Resolving Marital Conflict

A growing body of research indicates that there is no such thing as a compatible couple. Most couples, whether they are happy or unhappy, tend to argue about the same things: money, expectations as to who should do what around the house, work obligations, kids, insufficient separation from extended family members, differing leisure activities such as a golf game or family outing, or vacation with or without the kids. As a result, marriage therapists are now attempting to help spouses manage, accept, and even honor their discord rather than trying to resolve the irresolvable.[35]

In his book *Don't You Dare Get Married Until You Read This!,* Corey Donaldson says that the majority of issues that cause marital conflict exist before the wedding, but couples are not willing to ask or answer tough questions: Can physical violence by a mate be justified? What will we do if our child is born with a disability? Are you uncomfortable with women in high-paying jobs? Are you comfortable with my religious observance? My family? My desire for wealth?[36]

Of course, asking the right premarital questions does not guarantee a relationship free from conflicts: They will and do occur in even the most solid marriages. Some experts suggest that bickering can be good for relationships. It may be one of the keys to a strong marriage because open conflict improves communication and allows each partner to vent his or her frustrations. But you need to learn how to argue effectively. Dr. Phil McGraw suggests several ways you can make your arguments as constructive as possible.[37]

- Decide what you want before you start an argument. Avoid simply complaining; ask for what you want.
- Keep it relevant. Focus on what you are arguing about. If you stray, the argument will resurface again until the real issue is addressed.
- Make it possible for your partner to retreat with dignity. Avoid calling each other names that linger beyond the argument. Show your partner courtesy and respect, even if he or she is wrong.
- Know when to say when. If you have to give up too much of your life to maintain the relationship, maybe it is not worth it.

Keep in mind that if your objective in an argument is to win, the other person has to lose. This win/lose mind-set will only perpetuate the conflict.[38]

QUESTIONS

1. Have you had a conflict at home that had an effect on your work? Explain.
2. How might the premarital questions suggested in this case have an impact on marital relations? What other questions need to be answered?
3. A growing number of companies are helping employees and their spouses improve their marriage skills. Employers figure that reducing divorce and relationship stress can make workers happier and more productive. If you were developing a marriage relationship training program, what topics would you choose?[39]

INTEGRATED RESOURCES

VIDEOS:

Managing Equality
Informal Organization Structure
Alex and Melinda: Performance Review

CLASSROOM ACTIVITIES

IRM Application Exercise 13.1
IRM Application Exercise 13.2
IRM Application Exercise 13.3

PART **5**

Special Challenges in Human Relations

Chapter 14
Responding to Personal and Work-Related Stress

Chapter 15
Valuing Work Force Diversity

Chapter 16
The Changing Roles of Men and Women

CHAPTER 14

Responding to Personal and Work-Related Stress

© Somos/Veer/Getty Images

CHAPTER PREVIEW

LEARNING OBJECTIVES

After studying Chapter 14, you will be able to

- Understand the stress factor in your life.
- Explain the major personal and work-related causes of stress.
- Recognize the warning signs of too much stress.
- Learn how to identify and implement effective stress-management strategies.
- Identify stress-related psychological disorders and therapy options.

TIP OF THE ICEBERG

Stress So Bad It Hurts

During a recent visit to her doctor, Melinda Beck complained that the muscle injections he was giving her had not relieved her neck and shoulder pain. His response was concise and very direct: "You can't blame me for everything that's hard in your life." Beck burst into tears and immediately started thinking about previous visits to her doctor with bouts of low-back pain, irritable-bowel syndrome, and muscle aches. Plenty of doctors had used the *stress* word while diagnosing her health problems.

Ironically, Melinda Beck knows a lot about the causes of stress and stress management. As a health-journal columnist for the *Wall Street Journal*, she has researched this topic extensively. In one of her columns entitled "Stress So Bad It Hurts—Really," she described an interview with Dr. Christopher L. Edwards, director of the Behavioral Chronic Pain Management program at Duke University Medical Center. He stated that psychological stress can turn into physical pain and illness in a number of ways. Dr. Edwards noted that his clinic is seeing an increase in patients amid the recent economic crisis: "There's a very strong relationship between the economy and the number of out-of-control stress cases we see."[1]

Throughout your career, you will encounter many anxiety-provoking events. We live in a world of continuous change that often creates a heightened sense of urgency. Many organizations are searching for ways to wring more productivity from a smaller number of employees. Tensions build as people work longer hours and live with the possibility that they may be part of the next round of layoffs.

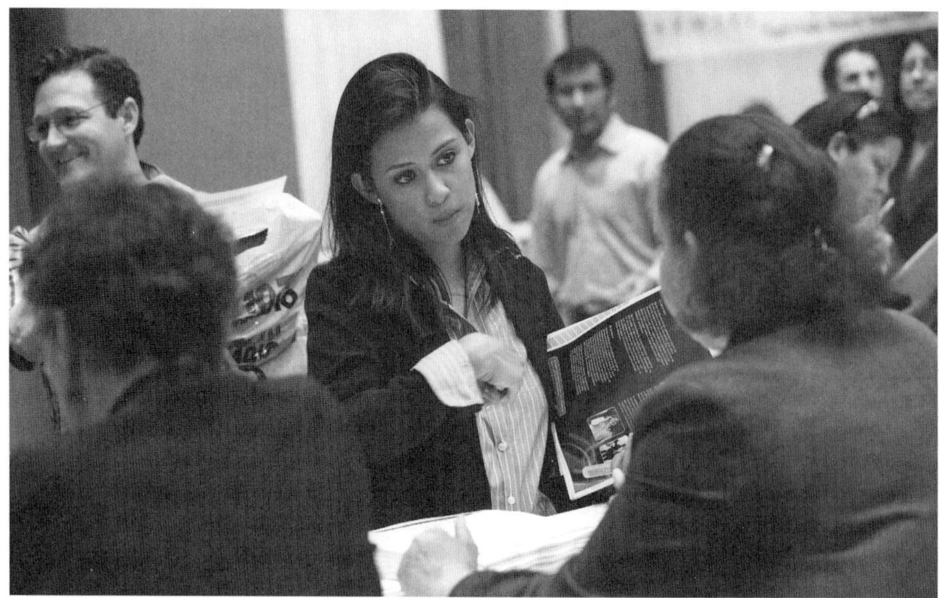
MARK RALSTON/AFP/Getty Images

These job applicants are no doubt feeling a great deal of stress. During a period of high unemployment, the competition for fewer jobs is more intense.

The Stress Factor in Your Life

Stress refers to two simultaneous events: an external stimulus, called a stressor, and the physical and emotional responses to that stimulus (anxiety, fear, muscle tension, surging heart rate, and so on). Stress can come from your environment, your body, or your mind.[2] Environmental stress at work may be caused by noise, safety concerns, windowless settings, long hours, or unrealistic deadlines. Some bodily stress can be attributed to poorly designed workstations that produce eye strain, shoulder tension, or lower-back discomfort. However, the stress that comes from our minds is the most common type of stress.

There can be positive aspects of mental stress. Stress *can* be a powerful stimulus for growth if it motivates you to do your best work. It can build within you the energy and desire needed to perform effectively. It can also promote greater awareness and help you focus on getting tasks completed quickly and efficiently. However, a great deal of the mental stress we encounter every day is caused by our negative thinking and faulty reasoning. For example, someone with large house payments and a great deal of personal debt may begin to worry excessively about the possibility of a layoff; the individual who lacks self-confidence may fear each technology change that is introduced at work; or workers in organizations being merged may mentally anguish over who will be laid off next.

However, a great deal of the mental stress we encounter every day is caused by our negative thinking and faulty reasoning.

Responding to Stress

Stress responses consist of three elements: the event or thought (stressor) that triggers stress, your perception of it, and your response to it.[3] In his book *Stress*

Total Person Insight

Price Pritchett
Ron Pound
Authors, *The Stress of Organizational Change*

"Most people seem to agree that these are high pressure times. Employees complain of being burned out. Used up. Overloaded. Too many of us are just plain tired, overdosed on change, sick of ambiguity and uncertainty."[4]

for Success, James Loehr suggests that as you are exposed to new stressors, you should try to respond in ways that help you establish mental, physical, and emotional balance.[5] Unfortunately, most of us do not take the time to train our minds and bodies so that we build our capacity to handle the stress in our lives.

Our natural response to stress is as old as life itself—adapted by almost all species as a means of coping with threats to survival. When faced with an unexpected or possibly threatening situation, human beings—like animals—instinctively react with the **fight or flight syndrome**: Adrenaline pours into the bloodstream, heart rate and blood pressure increase, breathing accelerates, and muscles tighten. The body is poised to fight or run. Ironically, the same instincts that helped our ancestors survive are the ones causing us physical and mental health problems today.

The human response to stress is not easily explained. Repeated or prolonged stress can trigger complex physiological reactions that may involve several hundred chemical changes in the brain and body.[6] Everyone reacts differently to stress, so there is no single best way to manage it. You must train yourself to

The authors of *The Stress of Organizational Change* note that much of the stress we are feeling these days is self-induced. Many of us resist change and hang on to old habits and beliefs.

respond effectively to the stressors in your personal and professional life so that you will not only survive, but thrive. The first step is to understand what might cause you to become stressed.

Major Causes of Stress

Some say the pace at work is so dizzying that it takes them hours to finally relax after the workday ends.

A study by the National Institute for Occupational Safety and Health found that half the working people in the United States view job stress as a major problem in their lives.[7] Some say the pace at work is so dizzying that it takes them hours to finally relax after the workday ends. Most of us can benefit from learning how to pinpoint the sources of stress in our life. If we can anticipate the stressors, we may be able to respond to them in a more effective manner.

Work-Life Balance

What do workers want most from their job? Many surveys indicate that work-life balance is the most important employment benefit.[8] Unfortunately, an economic downturn forces many workers to defer efforts to strike a better work-life balance. During a recession, workers may feel obligated to work longer hours, take less vacation, or postpone taking a sabbatical.

A few companies are taking steps to help employees achieve more control over their time. Dow Corning has a "No-Meetings Week" once a quarter, an attempt to call a halt to all nonessential internal meetings. IBM has established a companywide "Think Fridays," a block of Friday-afternoon time free of nonessential meetings and interruptions. Some companies encourage workers to schedule family time or time for leisure activities.[9]

Long Hours/Irregular Schedules. The New Economy, sometimes referred to as the 24/7 economy, is a nonstop "We never close" economy. Companies increasingly need employees who can work flexible schedules. Evening shifts, rotating shifts, 12-hour workdays, and weekend work often add stress to workers' lives. Tess Mateo, a director in the CEO's office at PricewaterhouseCoopers, recalls an early morning conference call with eight coworkers who were working in six time zones.[10] Working in a global economy often requires a very flexible work schedule.

In recent years, a growing number of workers call workloads excessive and say that they are bothered by increased pressure on the job. Many of the companies that have slashed their payroll now spread the same amount of work over fewer people. Years of multitasking and workaholism have left workers across the American economic and geographic spectrum feeling exhausted.[11]

Change

Changes in the workplace come in many forms, including the need to do a job faster, to master advanced technology, or to take on a new work assignment. Consider employees who have been accustomed to working alone and now must work with a team, or employees who have held jobs that required little contact with the public and now must spend a great deal of time with clients, patients, or customers. When companies restructure in an attempt to meet demands of the marketplace, they often do not take into consideration the life demands of the employees.

As we look to the future, there are two realities to keep in mind. First, management personnel above you are trying to cope with their own high-pressure responsibilities, so you are not likely to get much emotional handholding from them. Second, the pace of change is not likely to slow down. The authors of *The Stress of Organizational Change* say the secret to coping with high-velocity change is *surrender*: "Surrendering to change does the most to eliminate the stress. It creates the opportunity for break*through* rather than break*down*." They note that much of the pressure we are feeling these days is self-induced stress. Resisting change, or hanging on to old habits and beliefs, requires the investment of a great deal of emotional energy.[12] Surrendering to change demands a higher level of adaptability to our ever-changing workplace.

Multitasking

It's Monday morning, and you just finished a one-hour meeting with a cross-functional team. You promised the team members you would send them an e-mail that summarizes the decisions made during the meeting. As you walk back to your office, you glance at your iPhone and 39 e-mails are waiting for a response. A text message from your boss indicates she wants an updated product shipping report ASAP. Your afternoon includes three meetings, and you must leave the office at 4:30 p.m. to attend your daughter's soccer game.[13] Welcome to the world of multitasking.

Researchers at the University of California found that many workers experience frequent distractions throughout the day, and it often takes up to 25 minutes to return to an abandoned task. Edward Hallowell, author of *Crazy Busy*, compares multitasking to playing tennis with two balls. When we are constantly jumping between tasks, our performance will often suffer.[14]

Although multitasking can be stressful, we must find ways to embrace it. We are now living in a complex, fast-response world, and our challenge is to immediately address whatever task is most critical. The good news is we are able to get someone's attention at a moment's notice. In today's environment, not being able to multitask would probably be highly stressful.[15]

Internet Addiction. Many Internet users become addicted to computer use in the same way that some people become addicted to gambling or alcohol. Research conducted by Stanford University suggests that as many as 6 to 14 percent of Internet users have a dependency on the Internet. Problems associated with Internet addiction include the adoption of a machinelike mind-set that reflects the characteristics of the computer itself; withdrawal from relationships with coworkers, family members, and friends; depression and irritability when not at the computer; and health issues caused by a bad diet and lack of sleep and exercise.[16]

The Computer Workstation. Many employees spend the majority of their time at work sitting at a computer workstation, which may or may not be properly designed for long-term comfort. To keep up with the increasing demands at the office, many continue their work in front of their home computers. Telecommuters and home-based business workers often spend countless hours at their workstations, too, but they often resist spending their personal income to buy professionally designed office furniture and equipment. They may sit in a cast-off chair with little support, in front of an antique desk, and stare at a poorly positioned monitor; or perhaps they are hunched over a laptop on the couch or

HUMAN RELATIONS IN ACTION

Take Back the Weekend

Some companies are taking steps to reduce workloads. At Cummins, based in Columbus, Indiana, teams have been formed to identify and cut out unnecessary work. They search for low-value tasks that create an overload. At CarMax, a Richmond, Virginia, auto retailer, CEO Austin Ligon begins some monthly meetings by asking, "What are we doing that is stupid, unnecessary, or doesn't make sense?" To reduce workloads many companies have eliminated or shortened meetings, reduced internal reports, and removed redundant tasks.[17]

at the kitchen table. Poorly designed computer workstations at the office and in the home can produce major stress when they cause carpal tunnel syndrome (a repetitive stress wrist injury), back pain, spine and neck problems, aching shoulders, sore elbows, and eyestrain. Experts in **ergonomics**—techniques for adapting the work environment to the human body—say that anyone spending hours in front of a computer should get the right equipment and use it properly.[18] Figure 14.1 presents some pointers that might help alleviate some of the effects of workstation-related stress.

Noise Pollution

Noise is unwanted sound, such as the roar of traffic, your neighbor's loud music, or the loud voice of the person who occupies the cubicle nearby. It can increase your stress level without your conscious awareness. It is the uncontrollability of noise, rather than its intensity, that often is the greatest irritant. The noise you can't shut off is likely to have a negative effect on your emotional well being. Persistent exposure to noise can cause headaches, sleep disturbances, anxiety, and depression. Research indicates that noise affects people more than any other work area pollutant.[19] See Figure 14.2.

Skill Development: Apply It

Troubleshoot your computer workstation at home or at work. Evaluate the lighting, noise infiltration, air quality, seating, monitor and keyboard placement, and work surface. Identify ways you could improve it and how those improvements might reduce your stress level.

Incompetent Leaders

Organizations often promote individuals into supervisory positions when they exhibit extraordinary talents in a specific technical field. The most talented electrician becomes maintenance supervisor. The most efficient surgical nurse is promoted to nursing supervisor. The top salesperson is made sales manager. But technical superstars may be poor supervisors. And studies indicate that incompetent supervisors are a major source of stress in the workplace.[20]

FIGURE 14.1 **Suggestions for Alleviating Some of the Effects of Workstation-Related Technostress**

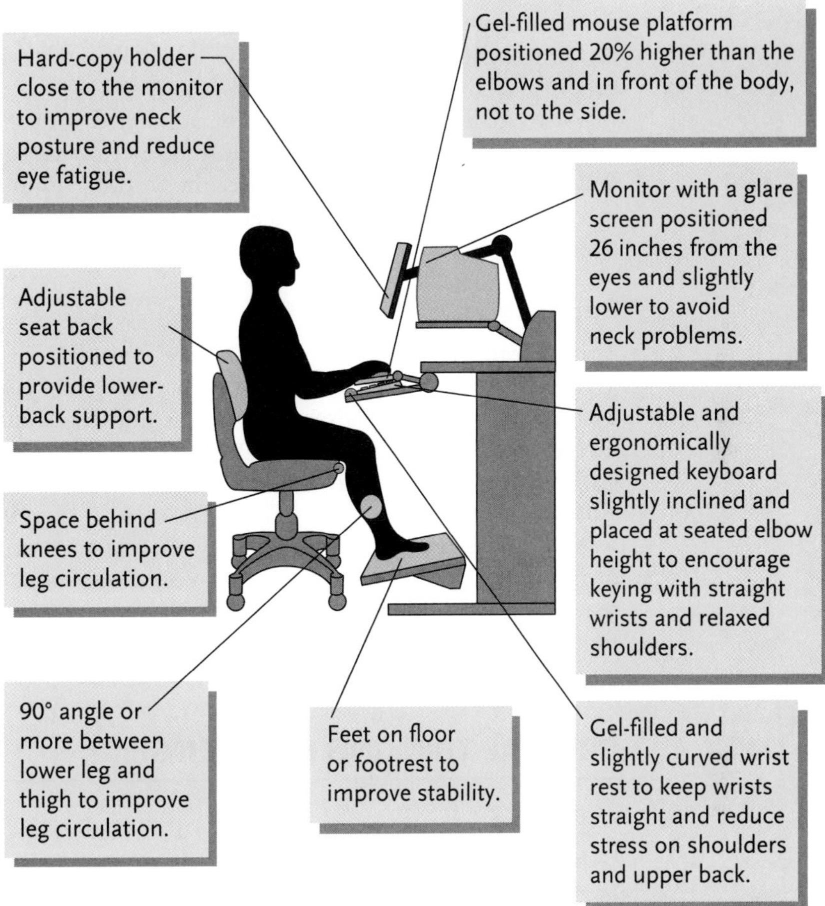
WORKSTATION SPECIFICATIONS
Hard-copy holder close to the monitor to improve neck posture and reduce eye fatigue.
Gel-filled mouse platform positioned 20% higher than the elbows and in front of the body, not to the side.
Monitor with a glare screen positioned 26 inches from the eyes and slightly lower to avoid neck problems.
Adjustable seat back positioned to provide lower-back support.
Adjustable and ergonomically designed keyboard slightly inclined and placed at seated elbow height to encourage keying with straight wrists and relaxed shoulders.
Space behind knees to improve leg circulation.
90° angle or more between lower leg and thigh to improve leg circulation.
Feet on floor or footrest to improve stability.
Gel-filled and slightly curved wrist rest to keep wrists straight and reduce stress on shoulders and upper back.

Source: Gannett News Service. Used with permission.

FIGURE 14.2 **Contributions to Workspace Distractions Overall**

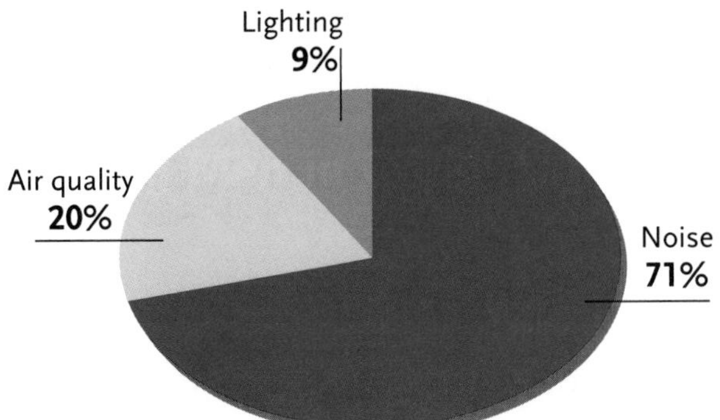
Lighting
9%
Air quality
20%
Noise
71%

Source: Excerpt from "Contribution to Workspace Distractions Overall," American Society of Interior Designers, 1996.

Work and Family Transitions

In our fast-moving world, most of us have learned that certain transitions are inevitable. A **transition** can be defined as the experience of being forced to give up something and face a change. Author Edith Weiner states, "People are now in a constant state of transitioning. It is difficult for anyone to say with any degree of certainty where he or she will be maritally, professionally, financially or geographically five years from now."[21]

When a single person marries or a married couple divorces, the transition can be extremely stressful and can affect job performance. A new baby and the challenge of child care can cause stress in working mothers and fathers. As double-income parents attempt to meet the needs of the family, they often feel guilty about the time spent away from their children.

Rumination

Throughout your career, you will face countless disappointments and defeats. Your boss said she would like to give you a salary increase but didn't have the authority to approve raises. Later, you find that out she lied. You miss a team meeting because of an illness. Later you find out that a team member was highly critical of your work on an important project. Do you confront these foes or suffer in silence?

Most of us revisit personal and work related problems too often. The process of replaying the incident over and over in our mind is referred to in the field of psychology as **rumination.** Ruminative thinking, the recurring intrusion of thoughts about negative events, can result in lose of concentration, loss of sleep, and feelings of depression.[22]

CRITICAL THINKING CHALLENGE:

Analyze It

How would having your stress under control help your interpersonal relationships at work? At home?

Warning Signals of Too Much Stress

In today's stress-filled world, it makes sense to become familiar with the signals that indicate you are experiencing too much stress in your life. Table 14.1 offers information regarding physical, emotional, and relational symptoms that may need your attention. When these symptoms persist, you are at risk for serious health problems because stress can exhaust your immune system, making you more vulnerable to colds, flu, fatigue, and infections. Recent research demonstrates that 90 percent of illnesses are stress related.[23]

Stress-Management Strategies

Ideally, we should do everything in our power to eliminate those elements that cause us stress—lack of work-life balance, change, multitasking, noise pollution, long hours/irregular schedules, incompetent leaders, work/family transitions, and rumination—but this is not generally a realistic option. We can try to reduce

TABLE 14.1 SYMPTOMS OF STRESS

Physical symptoms may result from or be exacerbated by stress.

Sleep disturbances
Back, shoulder, or neck pain
Tension or migraine headaches
Upset or acid stomach, cramps, heartburn, gas, irritable bowel syndrome
Constipation, diarrhea
Weight gain or loss, eating disorders
Hair loss
Muscle tension
Fatigue
High blood pressure
Irregular heartbeat, palpitations
Asthma or shortness of breath
Chest pain
Sweaty palms or hands
Cold hands or feet
Skin problems (hives, eczema, psoriasis, itching)
Periodontal disease, jaw pain
Reproductive problems
Immune system suppression: more colds, flu, and infections
Growth inhibition

Emotional symptoms can affect your performance at work, your physical health, or your relationships with others.

Nervousness, anxiety
Depression, moodiness
"Butterflies"
Irritability, frustration
Memory problems
Lack of concentration
Trouble thinking clearly
Feeling out of control
Substance abuse
Phobias
Overreactions

Relational symptoms are antisocial behaviors displayed in stressful situations and can cause the rapid deterioration of relationships with family, friends, coworkers, or even strangers.

Increased arguments
Isolation from social activities
Road rage
Domestic or workplace violence
Conflict with coworkers or employers
Frequent job changes
Overreactions

Source: Sheila Hutman, Jaelline Jaffe, Robert Segal, Heather Larson, Lisa F. Dumke, "Stress: Signs and Symptoms, Use and Effects," *Helpguide: Expert, Non-Commercial Information on Mental Health & Lifelong Wellness.* [accessed February 22, 2006]. Reprinted with permission from *http://www.helpguide.org*.

them, but eliminating them is often not possible. We can, however, learn ways to manage our reactions to the stressors in our daily lives and minimize their negative impact.

There is no one-size-fits-all way to reduce stress. Some believe that quick fixes such as smoking, alcohol, or food binges will reduce their stress, but these strategies have no staying power and will cease working over time.[24] You have to become aware of what calms you best. Do not wait until you are feeling stressed before you employ stress-management techniques; make them part of your daily routine. Space does not permit an in-depth presentation of all stress-management strategies, but we will describe those that are widely used today.

Everyone should make the effort to put stressful situations into proper perspective and deal with them accordingly. Once you become aware of what creates a stressful response in you (stress is very individualized), begin looking for stress management strategies that will help you cope with the stressful situations.

Sleep

Perhaps one of the most effective strategies for managing the negative aspects of stress is getting enough quality sleep. Growth hormones and repair enzymes are released and various chemical restoration processes occur during sleep. (This explains why children need considerably more sleep than adults.) To train your body so that you can deepen your capacity to handle stress, follow these guidelines to improve your sleep recovery periods:

- Develop a sleep ritual: Go to bed and get up at the same time as often as possible.
- Mentally wind down before going to bed. Avoid stressful activities.
- Avoid central nervous system stimulants such as caffeine, chocolate, alcohol, or nicotine near bedtime.
- Keep your bedroom cool, well ventilated, and dark.[25]

Many workers get less than the recommended amount of sleep (seven to eight hours) at night and therefore experience daytime drowsiness. This problem is so widespread that many employers encourage employees to take a short nap. Most employees are more productive and less apt to make fatigue-induced errors after waking from a short nap.[26]

Exercise

Study after study has proven that exercise, for most people, is the number one treatment for stress and tension. Exercise designed to reduce stress is not necessarily strenuous and may include aerobic exercise such as walking, swimming, low-impact aerobics, tennis, or jogging. Even gentle exercise such as yoga or tai chi will help you manage your daily stress load.

Unfortunately, about 70 percent of Americans do not exercise regularly, and nearly 40 percent are not active at all. A study published in the *New England Journal of Medicine* indicates that by age 18 or 19, a majority of American females engage in virtually no regular exercise outside of their schools' physical education classes.[27] Too many people, men and women, fail to take advantage of the physical and mental benefits of exercise. These benefits include lower cholesterol, weight loss, increased mental alertness, and a stronger heart. Before you begin a strenuous physical exercise program, check with your doctor to be sure it is appropriate for you.

Michael Goldman/Getty Images

Yoga, as practiced by these individuals, can help us manage the stress in our lives. Exercise designed to reduce stress need not be strenuous and may include walking, swimming, jogging, and low-impact aerobics.

HUMAN RELATIONS IN ACTION

Two-Minute Stress Buster

This stress reduction method is perfect for persons who are very busy. You can do it any time of day at virtually any location—your office, car, or commuter train. Sit quietly and focus on your breathing. Inhale slowly through your nose, visualizing your lungs filling with oxygen. As you exhale slowly through your mouth, relax your shoulders; stretch or yawn. Repeat this exercise two or three times.[28]

Deep Breathing

When you participate in deep breathing exercises you are forced to focus on the present moment rather than those things that are causing you stress. In his book *Breathe Smart: The Secret to Happiness, Health, and Long Life*, Aaron Hoopes describes techniques that can effectively calm your body.[29]

Complete Cycle Breathing. Start and end your day with three rounds of a complete cycle of breathing: Inhale, then pause while gently holding the breath in; exhale, then pause while holding the breath out. When you pause with your breath in, it creates a moment of stillness in which the whole body is focused on processing oxygen. When you suspend breathing out for a moment, it allows the

HUMAN RELATIONS IN ACTION

Helper's High

In his research, Arizona State University psychologist Robert Cialdini describes the euphoria experienced by those who frequently give their time and energy to others as the "helpers' high." He states that these good feelings may lower the output of stress hormones. Another study, conducted at Cornell University, found that volunteers were happier than nonvolunteers and had more energy and a greater sense of control over their lives. Some ideas for volunteer opportunities:

- If you are talented in such areas as music, accounting, law, carpentry, sewing, or coping with the health care system, find out where your expertise can be useful.
- Find organizations that know how to put volunteers to good use, such as your local blood bank, library, or museum, and offer them your time.[30]

body to use all the oxygen remaining in your lungs. Normally, we take 14 to 19 breaths a minute while at rest. The goal of deep breathing programs is to lower that rate to under ten.[31]

Abdominal Breathing. Press your abdominal muscles out and down as you inhale, which creates a vacuum that pulls the lungs down, allowing them to expand beyond the typical shallow breath that uses only the top third of the lungs. As you exhale, pull the abdominal muscles up and in so that the lungs empty from the bottom up, which clears the stale air out of your body and brings in fresh oxygen.

Deep breathing is one of the most direct ways to reduce stress. By paying attention to your breathing, you can switch off the stressed part of your nervous system and return to a state of calm.[32]

Meditation

Once the fight-or-flight reaction was fully understood, researchers began searching for a way humans could proactively *respond* to rather than simply *react* to this innate condition. A real breakthrough came when Herbert Benson at Harvard Medical School discovered a simple series of steps that lead toward effective **meditation**, a relaxation technique that slows your pulse, respiration, and brainwave activity and lowers your blood pressure. Meditation is sometimes called the smart person's bubble bath. About ten million Americans say they practice some form of meditation.[33]

Scientific studies show that meditation can have a profound stress-reducing effect because it trains and conditions the mind in the same way exercise trains and conditions the body. Richard Davidson's research at the University of Wisconsin in Madison suggests that through regular meditation, the brain is reoriented from a stressful fight or flight mode to one of acceptance, a shift that increases contentment with the realities of life. The process effectively deactivates the frontal areas of the brain, where sensory information is received and processed. Meditation allows people to quietly and intentionally detach from their

TABLE 14.2 5-MINUTE STRESS BUSTERS

- Take 5 minutes to identify and challenge unreasonable or distorted ideas that precipitated your stress. Replace them with ideas that are more realistic and positive.
- Take a 5-minute stress-release walk outdoors: Contact with nature is especially beneficial.
- Enjoy stress relief with a gentle 5-minute neck and shoulder massage.
- Spend 5 minutes visualizing yourself relaxing at your favorite vacation spot.
- Take a 5-minute nap after lunch.
- Spend 5 minutes listening to a recording featuring your favorite comedian.

emotional reactions so that they can respond appropriately. It allows them to peacefully observe their stress-producing thoughts and then choose to release them.[34]

Most meditation techniques involve these elements:

1. Sit or lie down in a comfortable, quiet place where you are not likely to be disturbed.
2. Intentionally relax the muscles of your body from your toes to your head.
3. Focus on the sound of each breath, using the abdominal breathing techniques mentioned earlier.
4. Train yourself to think about the calm and peaceful present. Mentally place past and potential future stressful events into this calm place. Fully and calmly accept these realities, thus robbing the innate fight or flight reaction of its power. Acknowledge your thoughts, realize which ones do not serve you, and then mentally release them.

To receive the full benefits of meditation, many people find it helpful to be trained by an expert in the field. Meditation classes and facilities are available in schools, hospitals, prisons, law firms, government buildings, airports, and corporate offices throughout the civilized world. Companies such as AOL, Raytheon, and Nortel Networks offer meditation classes to their employees because they acknowledge the possibility that employees who participate will experience sharpened intuition, steely concentration, and plummeting stress levels. They recognize the power in the statement "Don't just do something—sit there!"[35]

Don't just do something – sit there!

In addition to meditation, there are other stress management activities that can be used during brief pauses in your day. Table 14.2 provides some examples.

Laugh and Have Fun

Laughter is a gentle exercise of the body, a form of "inner jogging." When you laugh, your immune system is given a boost, stress-related hormones such as cortisol are reduced, and your respiratory function is improved.[36] Having fun while you are on the job does not exclude being serious about your work and caring about doing a good job, but being serious and caring is very different from being humorless and solemn. It is possible for people to have fun at work without being silly or inappropriate.

Some people are not funny, and not everyone needs to be able to tell a funny story. The goal is to create a positive, fun-loving atmosphere that helps reduce stress levels. When asked how they infused fun into the workplace, employers said:

> *Every month we had client reports due, and most of us dreaded the solitary extra-hours work that the tasks required. So we started planning to stay late one night each month. We went to a deli for snacks and then held a work party. We were all on our own computers in our own offices, but we took regular breaks, helped each other, enjoyed our meals together, and had some laughs in the after-work casual environment.*
>
> *We had been working so hard and had nailed all of our goals for the quarter. I called my team into my office and presented them with movie tickets—for the two o'clock show, that day! It was great. We took off as a group and felt like kids, playing hooky from school. It was so spontaneous, and they loved it.*[37]

Some people have lost touch with what is fun for them. Ann McGee-Cooper, author of *You Don't Have to Go Home from Work Exhausted*, recommends making a list of things that are fun for you and then estimating the time they take.[38] This exercise may help you realize that there is plenty of time for fun things in your life. A walk in the park will require only 20 minutes, and reading the comics takes only 5 minutes out of your day.

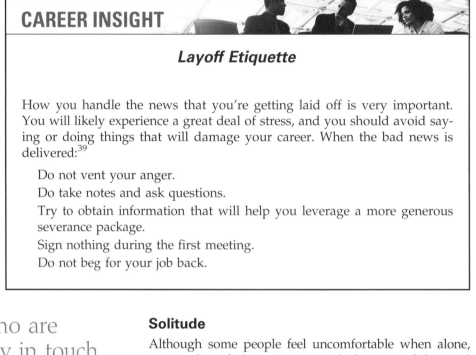

CAREER INSIGHT

Layoff Etiquette

How you handle the news that you're getting laid off is very important. You will likely experience a great deal of stress, and you should avoid saying or doing things that will damage your career. When the bad news is delivered:[39]

Do not vent your anger.

Do take notes and ask questions.

Try to obtain information that will help you leverage a more generous severance package.

Sign nothing during the first meeting.

Do not beg for your job back.

Those who are constantly in touch with others can benefit from the therapeutic effect of solitude.

Solitude

Although some people feel uncomfortable when alone, many others feel "over-connected" because of the need to constantly respond to cell phone, e-mail, Facebook, Twitter, and text messages. Those who are constantly in touch with others can benefit from the therapeutic effect of solitude. Solitude can be viewed as an emotional breather, a restorer of energy, and a form of rest similar to sleep. Ester Buchholz, author of *The Call of Solitude*, says alone-time is a great protector of the self and the human spirit. She also notes that solitude is often required for the unconscious to process thoughts and events.[40] To experience the benefits of solitude, get up twenty minutes earlier in the morning. Use this time for meditation, journal writing, or just sitting in silence. Enjoy this period of solitude free from the current pressures and demands on your life.

Resilience

Resilience means being capable of bouncing back when you are confronted with stressful situations. At 3M's headquarters in Maplewood, Minnesota, more than 7,000 employees have completed a "Resilience at Work" training program that covers such diverse topics as financial planning, time management, and parenting. These topics represent those factors in a person's life that could cause stress if they got out of control. Participants are taught to determine what issues are within their control and how to deal with them when they get out of control.

In many cases, planning ahead is all that is needed to begin the process of taking control of your life. Creating a realistic family budget that leads toward effective financial planning can provide resilience when unexpected, uncontrollable expenses occur. Rework the budget accordingly, and move forward with the new one. If your time management is chaotic, try controlling your schedule by building in ten to fifteen minutes of cushion time so you are less likely to be late for work or late for an appointment.

Many people create their own stress. They may want more leisure time, but they also want that new SUV or flat screen HDTV, so they take on a second job. As they engage in stressful multitasking, put in long days, and use words such as "obsessed" and "overwhelmed," they often begin to think that busyness is a measure of their status. They live in a permanent state of perceived emergency that causes toxins to build up inside them.[41] Programs like the one at 3M help employees learn to let go of things they cannot control.

> ***Total Person Insight***
>
> MATTHEW HUTSON
> Author, *Laughing Stock*
>
> *"A contagious laugh promotes bonding, reduces stress, and spreads the wealth of laughter's physical benefits."*[42]

Coping with Psychological Disorders

In the ideal scenario, when a stressful situation ends, hormonal signals switch off the fight or flight response, and the body returns to normal. Unfortunately, stress does not always let up. If you are under stress day after day and year after year, your hormonal response never shuts down. This can have a hazardous, even lethal, effect on your body and mental health.[43]

Once every ten years, the National Institute of Health (NIH) conducts a national study to assess mental illness in America. The findings of the most recent study, published in 2005, indicate that mental illness, in its many forms, affects one-quarter of the U.S. population.[44] In the final pages of this chapter, we will briefly examine three common psychological disorders and discuss therapy options.

Anxiety

Anxiety is a condition in which intense feelings of apprehension are long-standing and usually disruptive. Millions of Americans struggle with unwanted anxiety, and the cost in terms of suffering and lost productivity is very high. For most people, anxious feelings surface from time to time, but they are neither long-standing nor disruptive. If you have ever been tense before taking an exam or making an oral presentation, you have some idea of what anxiety feels like.[45]

Anxiety becomes a *disorder* only when it persists and prevents you from leading a normal life. Psychiatrists have found that there are several different anxiety disorders. A *phobia,* an irrational fear of a specific object or situation, represents one type of anxiety. Claustrophobia (fear of confined spaces) and agoraphobia (fear of crowds and public places) are two of the many phobias that can have a disruptive effect on a person's daily life.[46]

What is the best treatment for anxiety? Many anxious states are caused by stress, so consider using the stress management methods described in this chapter. Various methods of relaxation, for example, can lessen the severity of anxiety symptoms. However, when self-help methods do not bring the desired results, seek professional help (see Figure 14.3).[47]

FIGURE 14.3 **Getting Professional Help**

Organization	Description
Anxiety Disorders Association of America http://www.adaa.org	The mission of the ADAA is to promote the prevention, treatment, and cure of anxiety disorders and to improve the lives of all people who suffer from them.
Depression and Bipolar Support Alliance http://www.dbsalliance.org	This organization runs local support groups around the country for people coping with depression and bipolar disorder.
National Alliance on Mental Illness http://www.nami.org	NAMI offers support groups and courses to help people with psychiatric disorders, as well as family members living with and caring for the mentally ill.
The Therapy Directory http://therapists.psychology today.com/rms/prof_search.php	*Psychology Today* magazine maintains a searchable database people can use to find a therapist in their area.
The Mental Health Association http://www.depressionscreening.org	The Mental Health Association offers a free depression-screening test, which may help identify depressive symptoms and determine whether a further evaluation by a medical or mental health professional is necessary.
Online Clinics http://www.onlineclinics.com	Online Clinics was created to serve clinics, clinicians, and patients who want to find quality health care services online.

Source: Adapted from Leila Abbound, "Mental Illness Said to Affect One-Quarter of Americans," *Wall Street Journal*, June 6, 2005.

Charles Barsotti/Cartoon Bank

"No, no, that's not a sin, either. My goodness, you must have worried yourself to death."

Depression

Depression is a mood disorder. Nearly 19 million American adults experience it. This psychological disorder costs U.S. businesses nearly $70 billion annually in lost productivity, medical expenditures, and other related expenses. People of all ages can experience depression, but it primarily impacts workers in their most productive years: the 20s through 40s.[48]

When depression seriously affects a person's productivity on the job or in interpersonal relationships, psychiatrists consider that individual to have a depression. Symptoms such as withdrawal, overwhelming sadness, or hopelessness may persist for weeks or months.

In most cases, depression is a treatable disorder, but it often requires a variety of approaches. An important U.S. study on depression found that two-thirds of patients achieve remission if they stick with therapy. Persisting in treatment is very important.[49] Many employers have found that investing in therapy for depressed employees can reduce absenteeism while improving workers' health.[50] To learn more about therapy options, see Figure 14.3.

Burnout

Burnout is a gradually intensifying pattern of physical, psychological, and behavioral dysfunction that evolves in response to a continuous flow of stressors.[51] When you experience burnout, you feel that your energy fuel tank is operating on empty. Just as the engine of a car literally stops running without fuel and oil, a complete mental or physical breakdown can result from burnout. The most common symptoms of burnout include the following:

- Increased detachment from coworkers, customers, or clients
- Increased tardiness, absenteeism, cynicism, and moodiness
- Increased disorientation: forgetfulness or low concentration
- Increased personal problems: drug or alcohol abuse, decreased social contacts, or marital discord

All individuals experience one or two of these symptoms from time to time. But a person experiencing burnout exhibits these behaviors with increasing frequency and intensity. A candidate for burnout is likely to be someone who can't seem to "turn work off," needs to feel in control of their work, puts work before their families and personal lives, and puts in long hours at work.[52]

Popular Therapy Options

Many organizations offer various **employee-assistance programs (EAPs)** aimed at overcoming anxiety, depression, burnout, alcohol abuse, and drug abuse. These programs are designed to address the negative effects of psychological disorders before employees become dysfunctional.

In addition to EAPs, millions of people choose to participate in one or more relevant **twelve-step program** for help with drug and alcohol addiction, eating disorders, and gambling addiction. All twelve-step programs rely on the same fundamentals:

- ***Working the steps.*** This means admitting the problem, recognizing that life has become unmanageable, and turning life over to a higher power.
- ***Attending meetings.*** Meetings of twelve-step programs are held in convenient locations throughout communities across the country. Members describe their own problems and listen to others who have experienced similar problems. In most cases, members form strong support groups.

Web-based counseling is growing in popularity. Some licensed therapists give their clients a choice of face-to-face counseling or online counseling. In addition, there are thousands of support groups organized around various psychological disorders and moderated by therapists—some are licensed, some are not. Web-based therapy may be risky. There is often no guarantee that the self-proclaimed therapist is legitimate or licensed to practice in your state, and no online therapist can promise confidentiality.[53]

LOOKING BACK: REVIEWING THE CONCEPTS

- Understand the stress factor in your life.

Stress refers to two simultaneous events: an external stimulus, called a stressor, and the physical and emotional response to that stimulus. Stress at work may be caused by many factors. Our stress response consists of three elements: the event or thought (stressor) that triggers stress, your perception of it, and your response to it. When individuals cannot adequately respond or successfully adapt to change, stress is usually the result.

- Explain the major personal and work-related causes of stress.

When individuals cannot adequately respond or successfully adapt to change, stress is usually the result. Major causes of stress include failures to achieve work-life balance, long hours and irregular schedules, multitasking, change, Internet addiction, poorly designed computer work stations, noise, incompetent leaders, work and family transitions, and rumination.

- Recognize the warning signs of too much stress.

Some stress in life can have a positive effect as it helps keep people motivated and excited. Therefore, the goal is not to eliminate stress, but to learn how to manage various stressors and reduce their negative effects on the body and the mind. Table 14.1 provides information regarding physical, emotional, and relational symptoms that may need your attention.

- Learn how to identify and implement effective stress-management strategies.

You are more likely to handle the ever-increasing stress of today's demands when you maintain a sleep routine and exercise program, practice the relaxing effects of deep breathing and meditation, laugh and have fun, seek out moments of solitude, and learn how to physically and mentally recover once the stress is reduced or ended.

- Identify stress-related psychological disorders and therapy options.

When stress becomes persistent and overwhelming, it can lead to debilitating psychological disorders such as anxiety, depression, and burnout. While self-management techniques sometimes help, there may come a time when medication and one-on-one or group therapy with a licensed therapist is necessary. Employee assistance programs at work and community-based twelve-step programs may offer additional support.

ON THE JOB Q & A: COPING WITH WORK OVERLOAD

Q: I work for a large company and enjoy my job. However, the recent recession has forced my company to reduce its workforce. Because of downsizing, all of us in the office are working 60-hour weeks to get the work done. I take work home and do the work two people used to do. By the end of the week, my mind is numb, my productivity is down, and I am exhausted. This not only is hard on my family, but it seems that if the work can't be handled during a normal workweek, then we need to hire more people to do the job. What do you suggest?

A: If you can get another job that is less stressful, then consider starting a job search. However, if you feel lucky to have your job, then let your boss know that you need help. Talk with your colleagues to find out if they share your concerns, conduct your own research on the impact that unrelenting stress has on worker productivity, and then report your findings to your employer. There is ample evidence that working on too many projects at one time (multitasking) can reduce worker effectiveness. Explain that on-the-job productivity is enhanced when you are able to shift your focus by going home, being with your family, or socializing. Then, try not to accept unreasonable amounts of work that forces you to take work home or work on weekends. Be prepared to offer a positive solution to the work-overload problem. To reduce workloads, your company might eliminate or shorten some meetings, reduce internal reports, or remove redundant tasks.[54]

KEY TERMS

stress 304
fight or flight syndrome 305
ergonomics 308
transition 310
rumination 310
meditation 314
resilience 317
anxiety 318
depression 319
burnout 319
employee-assistance programs (EAPs) 320
twelve-step program 320

TRY YOUR HAND

1. Determine what circumstances are causing the most stress in your life. For example, are you trying to work too many hours while going to school? Are you experiencing parental or peer pressure? Do you feel burdened with things you cannot control? Then answer the following questions:
   a. What aspects of the situation are under your control?
   b. Are there any aspects of the situation that are out of your control? Explain.
   c. What steps can you take to help eliminate the stress?
   d. What individual stress management strategies could you use to counteract the effects of this stress?
2. Consider the following company-sponsored stress management programs. List them in order from most beneficial to you to least beneficial. Explain your reasoning.
   a. Access to on-site exercise facilities or company-sponsored health club membership
   b. A workshop on stress management sponsored by the company
   c. A cafeteria where healthy, nutritionally balanced foods are served
   d. Access to a soundproof audiovisual room for viewing relaxing videotapes, listening to soothing music, or taking a nap
3. Stress often increases as we struggle with time management. How well do you manage your time? Take a few minutes and answer each question below. Then spend time developing a time management program that meets your individual needs.
   a. Do you develop a daily "to do" list that indicates the activities you hope to work on?
   b. Do you maintain a planning calendar—a single place to record daily appointments, deadlines, and tasks?
   c. Do you have a series of personal and professional goals that guide you in setting priorities for use of your time?
   d. Have you learned to say no to proliferating requests for your participation in team activities, projects, social activities, and so on, that may complicate your life?
4. Try a one-day "news fast." Do not read, watch, or listen to any news for a day and see how you feel.

INTERNET INSIGHTS

1. Go to *http://www.Monster.com*, the online jobs database, and enter *fun* or *humor* into the search box. Are there any organizations in your area that promote a "fun" working environment? Search East Coast (example: New York City), West Coast (example: San Diego), and Midwest (example: Kansas City) locations. Which region exhibits more fun opportunities than the others? What semantics are used to describe the fun working environment?
2. Go to *http://www.netaddiction.com/resources/internet_addiction_test.htm* and take the 20-question Internet Addiction Test. Determine your score, and then do as the test's creator suggests when it comes to time to evaluate your responses to specific questions.

YOU PLAY THE ROLE Assume you are the spouse of Terry, a call-center customer-service representative. Terry routinely comes home from work stressed out and in a surly mood. Each representative at the center handles up to 120 calls per day and faces more frequent personal attacks than workers in most other occupations, with little or no opportunity to respond. The management of the organization is inflexible when it comes to accommodating its customers' needs, so the call-center personnel have little power to make the customers happy. Many times they are forced to refuse the customers' requests and respond, "It's corporate policy." Terry has become irritable, impatient, and emotionally unavailable to you and your three elementary-school-aged children. The job pays better than any other opportunities in the area, and your family has become dependent on Terry's income. Upon returning home from work today, Terry walked past you and the kids, went into your bedroom, closed the door, turned on the TV, and began rapidly consuming a cold beer. You've had enough! Rather than escalate the stress by mentioning the divorce option, you have decided to try to talk with Terry about reducing the stress in your lives. Role-play this discussion with one of your classmates, who will play the role of Terry.

BELOW THE SURFACE:

Surviving Workplace Stress

At the beginning of this chapter, we discussed the stress-related problems experienced by Melinda Beck, health columnist for the *Wall Street Journal*. She visited her doctor seeking relief for neck and shoulder pain. Millions of people in America experience the physical, emotional, and relational symptoms of stress. Table 14.1 provides a description of typical symptoms in each category. Beck learned that psychological stress can turn into physical pain and illness in a number of ways.[55]

From day one, Leander Hasty, video game software engineer at Electronic Arts, began working exhausting schedules. An 85-hour work week was not uncommon. Stress created health-related problems for Leander. It triggered an allergic reaction that resulted in stomach problems and chronic headaches.[56]

Stress can take a physical toll on many body systems. The result may be a weakened immune system, increased blood pressure, digestive problems, muscle aches, and a feeling of exhaustion. Stress, when ignored, may result in health problems that are very serious, such as depression or burnout.

Everyone should develop a stress management plan that limits its more damaging effects. A well-rounded plan includes exercise, relaxation, time management, and support from family members, friends, and co-workers.[57]

QUESTIONS

1. If a friend or coworker complains about feeling uptight and unable to relax, what relaxation methods would you recommend?
2. You are currently the human resources manager at a medium-size law firm that includes 18 lawyers, 10 legal assistants, and 5 support staff. Many of the younger lawyers seem to feel the need to prove themselves by staying late in the office. Three of your experienced lawyers are battling depression, and two others are problem drinkers. Most of the lawyers feel pressure to achieve billable-hour quotas set by the partners who own the firm. Research conducted at the University of Arizona indicates that your employees are displaying behaviors that are typical. Depression, problem drinking, and lack of work-life balance are common among attorneys.[58] Evaluate what steps would be appropriate to help your employees cope with overwork conditions, mental-health problems, and lack of balance. Prepare a list of resources in your community that might be available to assist you with these issues.

CLOSING CASE:
Achieving a More Balanced Life

Katherine Garrigan has worked full time at a Chicago museum for almost two years. During that time, the 24-year-old has taken just two short vacations totaling about eight days.[59] Jacqueline Platt, a 26-year-old account executive at PJ Inc., a New York–based public-relations firm, described her upcoming trip to Barcelona: she plans to spend time at the beach, eat tapas, see the sights, and party until 5 a.m. Unfortunately, she has to squeeze it all into one weekend. Her work schedule does not allow for a longer vacation.[60]

Many Americans have adopted a demanding work ethic that leaves little time for a well-rounded life. U.S. workers tend to work long hours and spend less time on vacation than do workers in many other industrialized countries. Long hours at work usually result in loss of leisure time and less time with family and friends. Consider these characteristics of the U.S. workforce:

- A full 35 percent of the employed workers are not taking all of their paid vacation days. During one recent year, Americans failed to take 438 million days of paid vacation.[61]
- McDonalds Corporation offers salaried employees an eight-week paid sabbatical for every ten years of employment. Sabbaticals, which originated in academia, provide employees time for rest and reflection—a break from 50-hour work weeks. Yet, only 5 percent of American companies offer paid sabbaticals.[62]
- Some companies discourage use of sick days. Nearly half of the full-time workers in America do not have paid sick days and those who do have this benefit are often discouraged from using it.[63]

Most workers want to succeed and advance at work, yet schedule time for family, friends, and leisure activities. Many fail in their attempt to achieve this level of work-life balance.

QUESTIONS

1. Many workers do not use all of the paid vacation time they have earned. Assess which factors may influence workers to make this decision.
2. Some companies feel vacation can have a positive effect on the personal health of their workers. They believe that workers asked to do more with fewer resources may need their vacation time more than ever. Argue whether employers should require workers to take all of their paid vacation days. Why or why not?
3. Several companies, including Accenture, Cisco Systems, and Wells Fargo, offer paid sabbaticals to employees who want to work for a nonprofit and education-related organization, for example. Evaluate the advantages and disadvantages of this approach to sabbaticals.

INTEGRATED RESOURCES

CLASSROOM ACTIVITIES

IRM Application Exercise 14.1
IRM Application Exercise 14.2
IRM Application Exercise 14.3

Valuing Work Force Diversity

TIP OF THE ICEBERG

CHAPTER PREVIEW

LEARNING OBJECTIVES

After studying Chapter 15, you will be able to

- Define the primary and secondary dimensions of diversity.
- Discuss how prejudiced attitudes are formed.
- Develop an awareness of the various forms of discrimination in the workplace.
- Understand why organizations are striving to develop cultures that value diversity.
- Identify ways in which individuals and organizations can enhance work force diversity.
- Discuss the current status of affirmative action programs.

Diversity on a Global Scale

Diversity at IBM is not just a matter of doing the right thing; it is a business imperative. IBM is truly a global enterprise, with 355,000 employees serving more than 170 countries. Success depends on engaging people at every level to work effectively together across different countries, time zones, languages, and cultures.[1]

IBM has become a leader in eliminating traditional barriers that exist because of race, gender, sexual orientation, disability, age, or language. The goal has been to build a culture that is respectful and inclusive.[2]

Building a culture of diversity can pay big dividends in the form of recruitment and retention of talent. Throughout recent years, IBM has been recognized as one of the top 50 companies for diversity by *Diversity Inc. Magazine*. The company has also received the Corporate Equality Index award given by the Human Rights Campaign (HRC). HRC is America's largest civil rights organization working to achieve lesbian, gay, bisexual, and transgender equality.[3]

Diversity can be a source of competitive advantage in the marketplace. It gives organizations an enhanced ability to understand the needs of different market segments. At PepsiCo, new products inspired by members of its diverse workforce include a wasabi-flavored snack aimed at Asian Americans; guacamole-flavored Doritos Chips aimed at Hispanics; and Mountain Dew Code Red, which appeals to African Americans.[4]

Photo by Shekhar Ghosh/The India Today Group/Getty Images

Diversity at IBM is truly a global enterprise. Employees are located in more than 170 countries. This IBM training session is being held in Daksh in Gurgaon, Haryana, India.

Work Force Diversity

America has always served as host to a kaleidoscope of the world's cultures, and the diversity movement is likely to continue. Growing minority and immigrant populations will contribute to increased racial and ethnic diversity. The American work force is becoming more racially and ethnically diverse, increasingly female, increasingly older, and increasingly nonwhite.[5]

Valuing diversity means appreciating everyone's uniqueness, respecting differences, and encouraging every worker to make his or her full contribution to the organization. Organizations that foster the full participation of all workers will enjoy the sharpest competitive edge in the expanding global marketplace.

Dimensions of Diversity

There are primary and secondary dimensions of diversity. The **primary dimensions** are core characteristics of each individual that cannot be changed: age, race, gender, physical and mental abilities, ethnic heritage, and sexual orientation (see Figure 15.1). Together they form an individual's self-image and the filters through which each person views the rest of the world. These inborn elements are interdependent; no one dimension stands alone. Each exerts an important influence throughout life. Marilyn Loden and Judy Rosener describe individual primary dimensions in their book *Workforce America!* They say, "Like the interlocking segments of a sphere, they represent the core of our individual identities."[6]

The greater the number of primary differences between people, the more difficult it is to establish trust and mutual respect. When we add the secondary dimensions of diversity to the mix, effective human relations become even more difficult. The **secondary dimensions** of diversity are elements that can be

FIGURE 15.1 Primary and Secondary Dimensions of Diversity

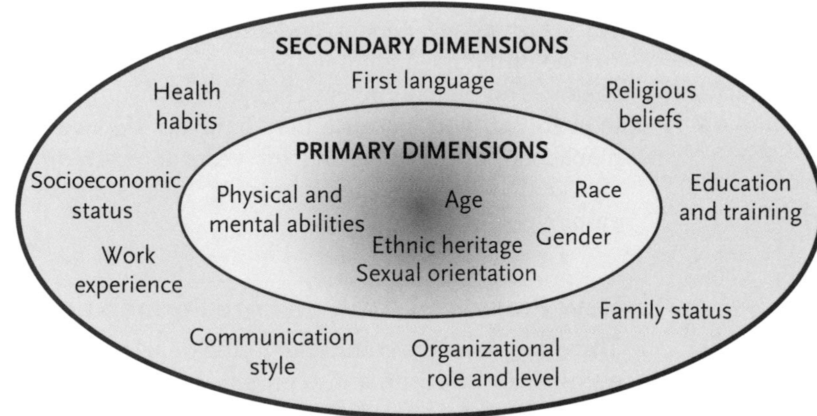

changed, or at least modified. They include a person's work experience, health habits, religious beliefs, education and training, first language, family status, organizational role and level, communication style, and socioeconomic status (see Figure 15.1). These factors all add a layer of complexity to the way we see ourselves and others. The blend of secondary and primary dimensions adds depth to each person and helps shape his or her values, priorities, and perceptions throughout life.[7]

The greater the number of primary differences between people, the more difficult it is to establish trust and mutual respect.

Each of us enters the work force with a unique perspective, shaped by these dimensions and our own past experiences. Building effective human relationships is possible only when we learn to accept and value the differences in others. Without this acceptance, both primary and secondary dimensions of diversity can become roadblocks to further cooperation and understanding.

Prejudiced Attitudes

Prejudice is a premature judgment or opinion that is formed without examination of the facts. Throughout life, we often prejudge people in light of their primary and secondary dimensions. Rather than treat others as unique individuals, prejudiced people tend to think in terms of **stereotypes**—perceptions, beliefs, and expectations about members of some group. In most cases, a stereotype involves

Total Person Insight

Rev. Joseph Lowery
Minister, United Methodist Church

Rev. Joseph Lowery mocked racial stereotypes while delivering the closing prayer at President Barack Obama's inauguration. He prayed for a day "when black will not be asked to get back, when brown can stick around, when yellow will be mellow, when the red man can get ahead, man, and when white will embrace what is right."[8]

the false assumption that all members of a group share the same characteristics. The most common and powerful stereotypes focus on observable personal attributes such as age, gender, and ethnicity.[9]

One of the most common stereotypes in the workplace has been labeled "singlism." This stereotype is based on the assumption that singles have lots of time to spend at work because they have no life away from work. Human-resources managers have been trying for years to discredit the notion that heavy travel, weekend work, and overbearing jobs should be reserved for unmarried employees.[10]

How Prejudicial Attitudes Are Formed and Retained

Three major factors contribute to the development of prejudice: childhood experiences, ethnocentrism, and economic conditions.

Childhood Experiences. Today's views toward others are filtered through the experiences and feelings of childhood. Children watch how their family members, friends, teachers, and other authority figures respond to different racial, ethnic, and religious groups. As a result, they form attitudes that may last a lifetime, unless new information replaces the old perceptions. Prejudicial attitudes are not unalterable. Whatever prejudice is learned during childhood can be unlearned later in life.[11]

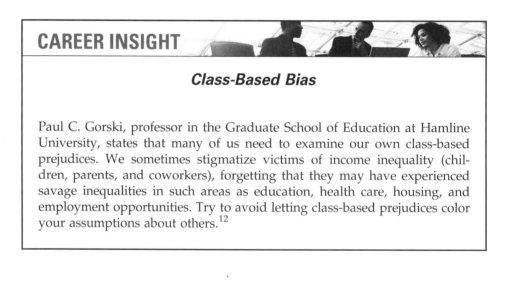

CAREER INSIGHT

Class-Based Bias

Paul C. Gorski, professor in the Graduate School of Education at Hamline University, states that many of us need to examine our own class-based prejudices. We sometimes stigmatize victims of income inequality (children, parents, and coworkers), forgetting that they may have experienced savage inequalities in such areas as education, health care, housing, and employment opportunities. Try to avoid letting class-based prejudices color your assumptions about others.[12]

Ethnocentrism. The tendency to regard our own culture or nation as better or more "correct" than others is called **ethnocentrism**. The word is derived from *ethnic,* meaning a group united by similar customs, characteristics, race, or other common factors, and *center.* **Ethnicity** refers to the condition of being culturally rather than physically distinctive.[13] When ethnocentrism is present, the standards and values of our own culture are being used as a yardstick to measure the worth of other cultures.

In their book *Valuing Diversity*, Lewis Brown Griggs and Lente-Louise Louw compare ethnocentrism in an organization to icebergs floating in an ocean. We can see the tips of icebergs above the water level, just as we can see our diverse coworkers' skin color, gender, mannerisms, and job-related talents and hear the words they use and their accents. These are basically "surface" aspects of a person that others can easily learn through observation. However, just as the enormous breadth of an iceberg's base lies beneath the water's surface, so does the childhood conditioning of people from different cultures. As icebergs increase in number and drift too close together, they are likely to clash at their base even though there is no visible contact at the water's surface.[14] As organizations increase the diversity of their work force, the potential for clashes resulting from deep-seated cultural conditioning and prejudiced attitudes also increases.

Economic Factors. When the economy goes through a recession or depression, and housing, jobs, and other necessities become scarce, people's prejudices against other groups often increase. If enough prejudice is built up against a particular group, members of that group may be barred from competing for jobs. The recent backlash against immigrants can be traced, in part, to a fear that the new arrivals will take jobs that would otherwise be available to American workers. Prejudice based on economic factors has its roots in people's basic survival needs, and, as a result, it is very hard to eliminate.

Increasingly, income and wealth inequality in America is viewed by many as a serious barrier to racial harmony. Ronald Walters, University of Maryland political scientist, says, "You can only have meaningful racial reconciliation when people of roughly equal socioeconomic status can reach across the divide of race."[15] The gap in well-being between whites and nonwhites barely changed throughout the booming 1990s and remains huge. The racial divide in wealth (value of all assets) and income shows no sign of narrowing.[16]

Unconscious Prejudices. Many people have biases that they don't know they have. These *implicit biases* are acquired over a lifetime, absorbed from our culture, and work automatically to color our perceptions and influence our choices. A massive national study, *Project Implicit*, measures the pervasiveness of implicit (implied or inferred) social bias toward race, gender, sexual orientation, age, ethnicity, weight, and religion.[17]

Research results based on several million participants in the study were carefully studied before the 2008 presidential election. Findings indicate white voters have an implicit negativity toward African Americans and the elderly. Senator McCain (age 72) and Senator Obama (African American) both had handicaps during the campaign. Obama's promise of change, and other personal qualities, may have led voters to move beyond their own implicit biases related to age and race.[18]

CRITICAL THINKING CHALLENGE:

Analyze It

In an ideal world, everyone would be free of prejudiced attitudes and would avoid thinking in terms of stereotypes. However, childhood experiences can shape attitudes that are difficult to change. Do you carry any prejudices that are obvious carryovers from your childhood or adolescence? Are you doing anything to overcome these prejudices? Explain.

The Many Forms of Discrimination

Discrimination is behavior based on prejudiced attitudes. If, as an employer, you believe that overweight people tend to be lazy, that is a prejudiced attitude. If you refuse to hire someone simply because that person is overweight, you are engaging in discrimination.

Discrimination is behavior based on prejudiced attitudes.

Individuals or groups that are discriminated against are denied equal treatment and opportunities afforded to the dominant group. They may be denied employment, promotion, training, or other job-related privileges on the basis of race, lifestyle, gender, or other characteristics that have little or nothing to do with their qualifications for a job.

Gender

Discrimination based on gender has been, and continues to be, the focus of much attention. The traditional roles women hold in society have undergone tremendous changes in the past few decades. Women enter the work force, not only to supplement family income, but also to pursue careers in previously all-male professions. Men have also been examining the roles assigned them by society and are discovering new options for themselves. Most companies have recognized that discrimination based on gender is a reality and are taking steps to deal with the problem. Chapter 16 is devoted to an in-depth discussion of overcoming gender bias.

Age

People who make up today's work force are working longer and living longer. Meaningful employment is a source of well-being for many of these workers. In light of our extended life span, it's time to rethink the concept of age. Tom Lowry, author of a *BusinessWeek* article entitled "Extreme Experience" says, "If 60 is the new 40, then 80 is the new 60." He describes 25 persons, who range in age from 75 to 100, who run their companies or wield real influence in the business world.[19] CVS Caremark, a large drugstore chain, is currently recruiting baby boomers and other older workers. Stephen Wing, director of CVS workforce initiatives, says, "When you're in your 50s and 60s, you're in your prime."[20]

Of course not every organization has adopted an enlightened view of age. Some companies fail to understand that workers in their 50s and 60s are productive, cost-effective employees. During the recent recession, age-discrimination

Sally Forth © King Features Syndicate

HUMAN RELATIONS IN ACTION

Generational Tension

Many of today's younger workers are hoping older Americans will retire and make room for them. Many older workers have seen their retirement funds disappear in the wake of the stock market collapse, and they can't afford to retire. In addition, many of the older workers who lost their jobs during the recent recession face discrimination getting new ones. Add to this complex picture thousands of baby-boomer generation workers who are more interested in *renewal* than *retirement*. They want to secure work with social value... work they can feel proud of. An expanded AmeriCorps may be the answer for some of these people.[21]

complaints processed by the Equal Employment Opportunity Commission (EEOC) reached a record high. Some companies replace older workers with younger workers in order to reduce compensation expenses.

Age bias is still pervasive in hiring. Older workers should anticipate the most common fears employers have about older workers and defuse them. This means showing plenty of energy, flexibility, reasonable pay expectations, and up-to-date skills.[22]

Race

Few areas are more sensitive and engender more passion than issues surrounding race. **Race** denotes a category of people who are perceived as distinctive on the basis of certain biologically inherited traits, such as skin color or hair texture.[23] Because people cannot change these inherited traits, they can easily become victims of discrimination.

Throughout American history, we have seen attempts to place people in racial categories and judge them as racial symbols rather than as unique individuals. During World War II, many Americans of Japanese ancestry were confined in concentration camps because they were considered a security threat, merely because of their racial heritage. Until the mid-1960s, some African Americans were not allowed to drink from public water fountains, to sit anywhere but in the rear of public transportation, or to attend public schools established for white children only. Because of the war on terrorism, today's "racial" targets often include immigrants from Pakistan, Iraq, and other Middle Eastern countries, as well as their American-born children.

There is as much genetic variability between two people from the same "racial group" as there is between two people from any two different "racial" groups.

The Myth of Race. Critics of racial categories view them as social inventions that intensify and reinforce racist beliefs and actions. They believe that one way to break down racial barriers and promote a race-free consciousness is to get rid of traditional racial categories. A growing number of geneticists and social scientists reject the view that "racial" differences have an objective or scientific foundation.[24] The American Anthropological Association (AAA) has taken the official position that "race" has no scientific justification in human biology. The AAA position is

Photo by Pete Souza/White House via Getty Images

President Barack Obama and golf champion Tiger Woods both have multiracial backgrounds. They share America's changing geography of race, culture, and identity. Millions of Americans have mixed racial origins.

that, "There is as much genetic variability between two people from the same 'racial group' as there is between two people from any two different 'racial' groups."[25]

It is important to keep in mind that some race categories include people who vary greatly in terms of ethnicity. The Asian label includes a wide range of groups, such as Vietnamese, Filipino, Chinese, and Korean, with distinct histories and languages. The label "African American" does not take into consideration the enormous linguistic, physical, and cultural diversity of the peoples of Africa.[26]

Because interracial relationships are now much more common than they were before, millions of Americans are of mixed races that do not fit the usual general categories. Golf champion Tiger Woods (his father is African American and his mother is from Thailand) is proud of his multiracial background. President Barack Obama, son of a black man and a white woman, has revived a national conversation regarding multi-ethnic people.

HUMAN RELATIONS IN ACTION

The Macaca Incident

George Allen served one term as governor of Virginia and then he was elected to the U.S. Senate. While seeking re-election to the Senate, he used the term "Macaca," an unfamiliar ethnic slur, to describe a dark-skinned man of Indian descent seated in the audience. The use of this sarcastic word triggered an extraordinary fall from political grace. He lost the election.[27]

Race as Social Identity. Although races are not scientifically defensible, they are "real" socially, politically, and psychologically. Race and racism affect our own self-perception and how we are treated by others. Groups that are working to build ethnic pride, such as Native Americans, oppose efforts to get rid of the traditional racial categories, which they consider part of a positive identity.

Religion

Discrimination based on a person's religious preference has been an issue throughout history. Religion has always had the power to fracture and divide people of faith. Members of various denominations often lack tolerance for beliefs that differ from their own.

Charges of religious discrimination in the workplace have increased in recent years according to EEOC reports.[28] Muslims face unique challenges as they attempt to balance their prayer schedule with inflexible work schedules. Misunderstandings occur frequently over relatively minor issues, such as Muslim women's right to wear head scarves and Muslim men's right to maintain facial hair.

Readers of *Spirituality & Health* magazine frequently voice concerns regarding lack of tolerance among members of the three major faith groups: Judaism, Christianity, and Islam. Rabbi Rami Shapiro, who writes the "Roadside Assistance for the Spiritual Traveler" column for this publication, offers us this timely advice:[29]

> *We need to understand all three levels of religion and promote the voices of the ethicists and mystics within each faith, rather than the shrill and fearful screams of fanatics who hew to the tribal vision of their religion.*

Total Person Insight

YONAT SHIMRON
Staff Writer, *News & Observer*

"American religion is startlingly complex and diverse, the authors of a Baylor University study say. Though Americans may agree that God exists, they do not agree on much else."[30]

Disability

The Americans with Disabilities Act (ADA) sets forth requirements for businesses with 15 or more employees. It bans discrimination against workers and customers with disabilities and requires employers to make "reasonable accommodations" so that the disabled can access and work in the workplace.

The National Sports Center for the Disabled's mission is to positively impact the lives of people with any physical or mental challenge. Today, the NSCD is one of the largest outdoor therapeutic recreational agencies in the world. Thousands of lessons are provided each year.

It covers a wide range of disabilities, including learning impairments, AIDS, alcoholism, visual impairments, and physical impairments that require use of a wheelchair (visit *http://www.adata.org*). Although legal protection is in place, the employment rate for people with disabilities ages 21 to 64 is only 38 percent.[31]

Disabled people who want to work face several problems. Many of the jobs performed by people with disabilities are being outsourced abroad. Doug Schalk lost his position as a call-center customer representative at Vanguard Car Rental USA Incorporated when it transferred his job to India. Many of the low-paying service-sector jobs often filled by those with disabilities do not provide adequate health benefits to meet the needs of disabled workers.[32]

The U.S. Department of Justice is moving on two fronts to expand businesses' obligations to accommodate disabled people. Congress is working on legislation that broadens the number of people entitled to employment rights under the ADA. It is also seeking expansion of disabled-access requirements. Needless to say, businesses are worried about the cost increases that will accompany these changes.[33]

Several companies are setting a good example with major programs to accommodate both employees and customers with disabilities (see Table 15.1). In addition, many corporate diversity training programs include sessions on disability awareness and employment.

TABLE 15.1 ENABLING THOSE WITH DISABILITIES

COMPANY	TYPE OF ASSISTANCE
Crestar Bank	Provides voice-activated technology for disabled customer service representatives. Makes special services available to customers with disabilities.
Honeywell	Participates in Able to Work program, a consortium of 22 companies that find ways to employ disabled persons. Uses its high-tech innovations to assist employees with disabilities.
Johnson & Johnson	Has established a comprehensive disability management program that tailors work assignments to employees returning to work after an injury.
Caterpillar	Serves as a model of high-tech accessibility for the disabled; sponsors Special Olympics.
America OnLine	Has agreed to work with the National Federation of the Blind to ensure that AOL content is largely accessible to the blind.

Source: John Williams, "The List—Enabling Those with Disabilities," *BusinessWeek*, March 6, 2000, p. 8; and "The New Work Force," *BusinessWeek*, March 20, 2000, pp. 64–74.

Sexual Orientation

Discrimination based on a person's sexual orientation is motivated by *homophobia*, an aversion to homosexuals. Not long ago, gays and lesbians went to great lengths to keep their sexuality a secret. But today many gays and lesbians are "coming out of the closet" to demand their rights as members of society. Indeed, many young people entering the work force who are used to the relative tolerance of college campuses refuse to hide their orientation once they are in the workplace.

HUMAN RELATIONS IN ACTION

Meeting Someone with a Disability

Here are a few suggestions for making a good impression. If the person …

… is in a wheelchair. Sit down, if possible. Try to chat eye to eye. Don't touch the wheelchair. It is considered within the boundaries of an individual's personal space.

… has a speech impediment. Be patient, actively listen, and resist the urge to finish his or her sentences.

… is accompanied by a guide dog. Never pet or play with a guide dog; you will distract the animal from its job.

… has a hearing loss. People who are deaf depend on facial expressions and gestures for communication cues. Speak clearly and slowly. Speak directly to the person, not to an interpreter or assistant if one is present.[34]

HUMAN RELATIONS IN ACTION

The Pain of Growing Up Gay

At age 14, Mitchell Gold harbored a secret that he felt would forever ruin his chances of happiness and success in life. He was gay and afraid his family would disown him if they knew his secret. Today he is owner of a fast-growing furniture company located in Taylorsville, North Carolina, and he is working hard to make sure no other teenager has to experience what he did. He has launched an educational campaign called Faith in America to combat religion-based prejudices directed toward the gay community. The centerpiece of his campaign is a book entitled *Crisis: 40 Stories Revealing the Personal, Social and Religious Pain and Trauma of Growing Up Gay in America*. These personal stories describe the pain being inflicted on many gay teens.[35]

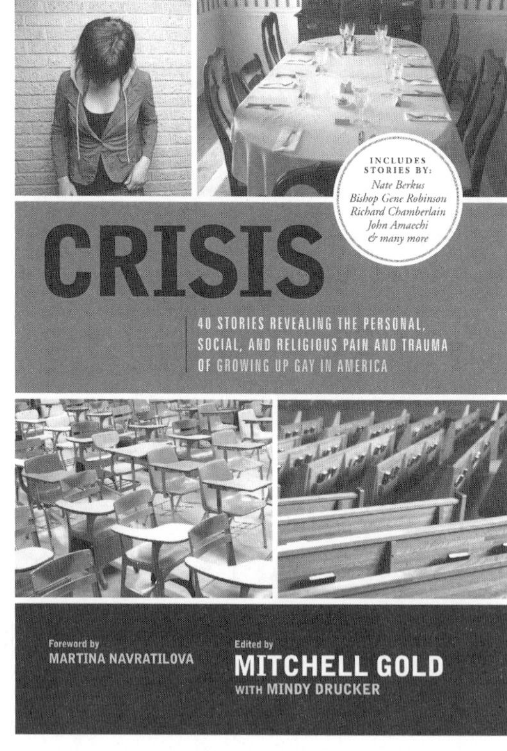

Courtesy of Greenleaf Book Group LLC

Source: Yonat Shimron, "Passion for Justice," *News & Observer*, November 20, 2008, p. D1. For additional information, visit *http://www.crisisbook.org*.

Gay rights activists are working hard to create awareness that discrimination based on sexual orientation is no less serious than discrimination based on age, gender, race, or disability. Activist groups, such as the Human Rights Campaign, the Interfaith Alliance, and the Southern Poverty Law Center, are also working to rid the workplace of antigay behaviors, such as offensive jokes, derogatory names, or remarks about gays. An atmosphere in which gays and lesbians are comfortable about being themselves is usually more productive than an atmosphere in which they waste their time and energy maintaining alternate, and false, personalities.

In recent years, we have witnessed several workplace trends favorable to gay and lesbian employees. More than 80 percent of *Fortune* 500 companies include sexual orientation in their antidiscrimination policies, and some companies have established lesbian and gay resource groups—known in some companies as affinity groups—that provide a point of contact for previously invisible employees. Also, a majority of the nation's top 500 companies now extend medical benefits to same-sex partners.[36]

There is no federal law that expressly forbids workplace discrimination against lesbian, gay, bisexual, and transgender people. However, many employers and state and city governments have enacted policies and laws to address discrimination based on sexual orientation.[37] Policies aimed at preventing verbal and physical harassment of students based on sexual orientation have been adopted by many public schools and colleges. In some cases, these initiatives have generated considerable controversy. Some religious and conservative groups have actively opposed these violence-prevention efforts, believing that they promote homosexuality.[38]

Subtle Forms of Discrimination

A person who feels he or she has been the victim of discrimination based on gender, age, race, abilities, or sexual orientation can take legal action by filing a complaint with his or her state's office of the Equal Employment Opportunity Commission. However, although many state and federal laws protect individuals from discrimination based on these issues, they do not specifically protect workers from the more subtle forms of discrimination. For example, those who graduated from an Ivy League college may treat coworkers who graduated from state-funded colleges as inferior. Overweight employees might experience degrading remarks from coworkers. Those who speak with a distinct regional accent may hear snickers behind their back at work. People who do not value differences often equate a difference with a deficiency.

Valuing diversity requires us to think about many human differences that might cause discrimination in the workplace. Examples include politics, personal history, and socioeconomic status. Because there are no laws regarding these issues, employees need to understand the negative impact of these subtle forms of discrimination and take responsibility for creating an atmosphere where they are not tolerated.

What Can You Do?

What should you do if you discover you are the target of some form of subtle, unprotected discrimination because you are different from others at work? If you want to stay in the organization, you will need to determine whether the "difference" is something you can change—your weight, the way you dress, your manner of speaking. If the difference is something you cannot or choose not to change, you may need to address the situation directly. Review the assertiveness skills you studied in Chapter 13. Your assertiveness may help change other people's attitudes and in turn alter their discriminatory behaviors. Another powerful method of eliminating subtle discrimination is to compensate for it by excelling in your work. Become an expert on the job, and work to increase your skills and your value to the organization. As your colleagues gain respect for your talents, they will likely change their attitudes toward you. But if your future appears blocked, investigate other workplaces where management may be more

HUMAN RELATIONS IN ACTION

Tools for Tolerance: Workplace

- Hold a "diversity potluck" lunch. Invite coworkers to bring foods that reflect their cultural heritage.
- Suggest ways to overcome any barriers that might prevent people of color and women from succeeding.
- Value the input of every employee. Reward managers who do.
- Push for equitable leave policies. Provide paid maternity and paternity leave.
- Start a mentoring program that pairs employees of different ages, such as seniors with entry-level workers.
- Vary your lunch partners. Seek out coworkers of different backgrounds, from different departments, and at different levels in the company.[39]

open to diversity. The important point is that you should refuse to allow discrimination to limit your personal and professional success.

The Economics of Valuing Diversity

The new millennium has brought greater understanding that diversity can be a source of competitive advantage. This occurs when a company makes full use of the ideas, talents, experiences, and perspectives of all employees at all levels of the organization. Joe Watson, a recruiter of minorities, believes that if you want to satisfy clients and customers from diverse backgrounds, you need a diverse mix of employees who are more likely to understand them. People from various cultural and ethnic backgrounds can offer different perspectives and stimulate creativity. "This type of inclusion," says Watson, "isn't about joining hands and singing 'Kumbaya.' This is about improving corporate performance."[40]

A study conducted by the Society for Human Resource Management revealed diversity initiatives within organizations can affect an organization's bottom line by reducing costs associated with turnover, absenteeism, and low productivity. In addition, efforts to value workers' and customers' diversity reduce complaints and litigation and improve the organization's public image.[41] Organizations that pursue diversity and make it part of their culture usually outperform companies that are less committed to diversity.

> The price tag for *not* helping employees learn to respect and value each other is enormous.

The price tag for *not* helping employees learn to respect and value each other is enormous. Many highly skilled and talented employees will leave an organization that does not value diversity. A comment, gesture, or joke delivered without malice but received as an insult will create tension among workers and customers alike.

Managing Diversity

Managing diversity is the process of creating an organizational culture where the primary and secondary dimensions of diversity are respected. This process

> ### *Total Person Insight*
>
> Stephen R. Covey
> Author, *The Seven Habits of Highly Effective People*
>
> *"Without diversity, there can be no synergy. It's only because there are differences that can be courageously expressed by the different parties that you can create a third-alternative solution to problems. If two agree, one is unnecessary."*[42]

can be a challenge now that the work force is composed of so many different nationalities. Managers at some Marriott Hotels work with employees from 30 different countries. The employees who are part of the Toyota Formula 1 race team represent 27 nationalities. Even some small retail stores have become a kind of United Nations. The Kroger supermarket in Durham, North Carolina, has employees from ten countries. The issue is further complicated when an organization's diverse work force is in global satellite offices separated by thousands of miles. Microsoft's research unit, for example, is staffed by 700 multinational scientists and engineers working in six laboratories on three continents.[43]

What Individuals Can Do

People tend to hang on to their prejudices and stereotypes. If certain white people believe people of color are inferior, they are likely to notice any incident in which a person of color makes a mistake. But when a person of color exhibits competence and sound decision-making abilities, these same white people may not notice, or they may attribute the positive results to other circumstances. You cannot totally eliminate prejudices that have been deeply held and developed over a long time. But you can take steps to change those attitudes and behaviors that may have a negative impact on your employer's efforts to enhance diversity.

Learn to look critically and honestly at the particular myths and preconceived ideas you have been conditioned to believe about others.

1. *Learn to look critically and honestly at the particular myths and preconceived ideas you have been conditioned to believe about others.* Contact among people of different races, cultures, and lifestyles can break down prejudice when people join together for a common task. The more contact there is among culturally diverse individuals, the more likely it will be that stereotypes based on myths and inaccurate generalizations will not survive.
2. *Develop sensitivity to differences.* Do not allow gender-based, racist, or antigay jokes or comments in your presence. If English is not a person's native language, be aware that this person might interpret your messages differently from what you intended. When in doubt as to the appropriate behavior, ask questions. "I would like to open the door for you because you are in a wheelchair, but I'm not sure whether that would offend you. What would you like me to do?"
3. *Develop your own diversity awareness program.* The starting point might be creation of a "diversity profile" of your friends, coworkers, and acquaintances. How much diversity do these individuals have in terms of race? Ethnicity?

Skill Development: Apply It

Career success often depends on your ability to work effectively with people who differ from you in age, gender, race, physical traits, sexual orientation, and other dimensions of diversity. Assume that you are the owner of a small business and have decided to develop your own diversity awareness program. What activities would you include? Be specific.

Religion? Assess the cultural diversity reflected in the music you listen to and the books you read. Visit an ethnic restaurant and try to learn about more than the food. Study Islam, Buddhism, and other faiths that may be different from your own.[44]

What Organizations Can Do

A well-planned and well-executed diversity program can promote understanding and defuse tensions between employees who differ in age, race, gender, religious beliefs, and other characteristics. Programs that are poorly developed and poorly executed often backfire, especially in organizations where bias and distrust have festered for years. A comprehensive diversity program has three pillars:[45] organizational commitment, employment practices, and training and development (see Figure 15.2).

Organizational Commitment. Catalyst, a research and advisory group, conducted a survey of 106 global companies to determine why these companies use

FIGURE 15.2 Three Pillars of Diversity

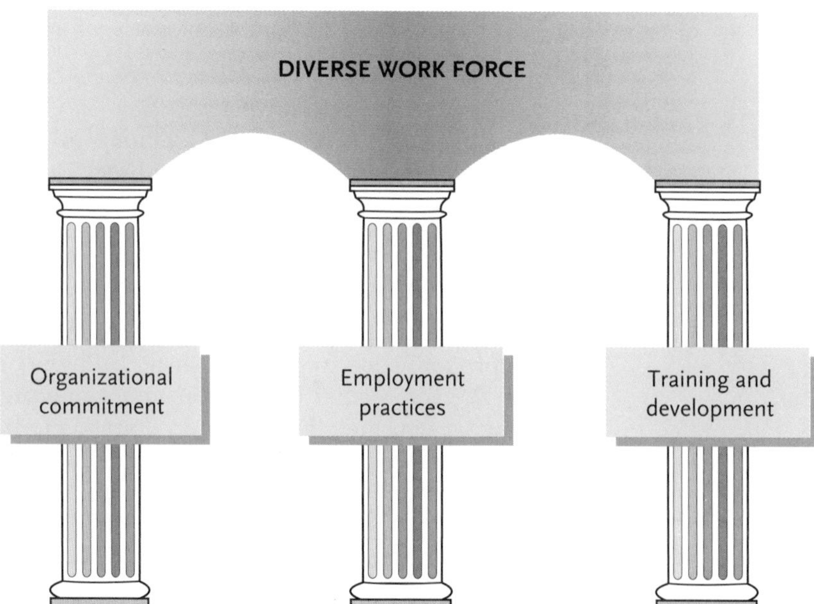

diversity strategies as part of their overall business plan. Nearly 90 percent said their diversity program was designed to help them gain a competitive advantage.[46] When the objective of the diversity initiative is to achieve a stronger competitive position, the commitment is usually quite strong.

Companies that see diversity programs as a quick-fix *event*—a one-day workshop that promotes the advantages of a diverse work force—often create greater, not less, divisiveness among workers. Companies that see diversity programs as a *process* know that the key to a successful diversity program is long-term commitment.

At Consolidated Edison, responsibility for diversity extends to the entire management team. Each of the 2,100 officers and managers is reviewed and compensated in part for their success in hiring, promoting, and retaining minorities. PepsiCo, the soft drink maker, links bonuses to diversity performance. Both of these companies made the "America's 50 Best Companies for Minorities" list published by *Fortune*.[47]

To achieve work force diversity, organizations need to design a plan that actively recruits men and women of different ethnicities, family situations, disabilities, and sexual orientations. Diversity should not be limited to race and gender.

Employment Practices. To achieve work force diversity, organizations need to design a plan that actively recruits men and women of different ethnicities, family situations, disabilities, and sexual orientations. Diversity should not be limited to race and gender. One approach is to make a special effort to plug into networks that are often ignored by corporate recruiters. Many communities have established groups such as the Center for Independent Living for those with limited abilities; the Family Service League for displaced homemakers and single parents; and Parents, Families, and Friends of Lesbians and Gays. All of these groups can help identify employees.

Organizations must also foster a climate for retention. Newly hired people who are different from the majority must often contend with an atmosphere of tension, instability, and distrust and may soon lose the desire to do their best work. Subtle biases often alienate these employees and create unnecessary stress.

Training and Development. To develop a culture that values and enhances diversity, organizations need training programs that give managers and employees the tools they need to work more effectively with one another regardless of their backgrounds. Unfortunately, most of the diversity training efforts at American companies are ineffective for these reasons:

- Mandatory programs, often undertaken mainly to avoid liability in discrimination lawsuits, are frequently ineffective and may even be counterproductive. Voluntary diversity training, undertaken to advance the organization's goals, is more effective.[48]
- Middle managers, who play a key role in hiring, development, and promotion decisions, often do not support diversity efforts. To overcome this roadblock, top management must champion diversity and model ideal behaviors to middle management. They should also reward middle managers who take steps to enhance diversity initiatives.[49]

Done well, diversity training programs can promote harmony, reduce conflict, and help give the organization a competitive advantage. Participants should learn which specific behaviors will not be condoned and the basic rules of civil behavior. We may not be able to stop people from bringing their prejudices to work, but they can learn to act as though they have none.

Affirmative Action: Yesterday and Today

The Civil Rights Act of 1964 marked the beginning of antidiscrimination employment legislation. In an attempt to make up for past discrimination in the workplace, Title VII of this act forbids discrimination in all areas of the employment relationship. The intent of Title VII is to ensure that employment decisions are made on the basis of an individual's qualifications rather than on the basis of personal biases. Discrimination on the basis of sex, race, color, religion, or national origin is illegal under this law.[50] Over the years, various laws have been passed to expand the list of *protected* individuals. Examples include:

- Age Discrimination in Employment Act
- Vietnam Era Veterans Readjustment Assistance Act
- Pregnancy Discrimination Act
- Americans with Disabilities Act
- Civil Rights Act of 1991

The Equal Employment Opportunity Commission (EEOC) is charged with enforcing Title VII and several other employment-related laws. One recent EEOC lawsuit filed against Lockheed Martin Corporation illustrates the high cost of discrimination. Charles Daniels, an African American electrician at the company, said he was subjected to racial harassment by coworkers on a daily basis and death threats once he complained to supervisors. After a long trial, Mr. Daniels was awarded $2.5 million. The EEOC received nearly 7,000 racial-discrimination complaints during 2007.[51]

Affirmative Action

Affirmative action involves intentionally seeking and hiring employees from groups that are under-represented in the organization.[52] Affirmative action began in 1961, when President Kennedy issued an executive order declaring that federal contractors should "take affirmative action" to integrate their workforce. The initiative was broadened to include policies that favored women and minorities in hiring and promotion at work and in college admissions.

Although affirmative action has stirred controversy for many decades, there is no doubt that this initiative has helped minorities gain access to large corporations and top universities. The number of African Americans at the nation's top 50 colleges and universities has doubled in recent decades. Women have also benefited, especially in the 1970s and 1980s when they began breaking into traditionally male-dominated fields.[53]

The courts have played an important role in several affirmative action events. In 1978, the Supreme Court ruled in favor of a white man who was denied admission to medical school. This opinion upheld the use of race in choosing among qualified applicants but ruled that inflexible hiring quotas are unconstitutional. In 1986, the Supreme Court forced a union to give membership to minorities. In 2003, the Supreme Court ruled that use of racial preferences to ensure diversity at the University of Michigan was legal. Three years later, Michigan voters approved an anti-affirmative action referendum. Now admissions officers cannot know an applicant's race or gender when reviewing an application.[54]

Affirmative Action Issues. Many people say it is time to rethink affirmative action or even eliminate it. Recent political and legal interpretations of affirmative action have stimulated a nationwide debate over the merits of any program that grants preferential treatment to specific groups. The following are common arguments voiced by those who want to end or change preferential policies:[55]

- *Preferences are discriminatory.* They tend to discriminate against those who are not members of the "right" race or gender, such as white men. Preferential policies often give a leg up to those who have suffered no harm, while holding back those who have done no wrong.
- *Preferences do not make sense, given changing demographics.* The population eligible for affirmative action continues to grow several times faster than the "unprotected" population. Hugh Davis Graham, author of *Collision Course,* believes the future of affirmative action programs is threatened because of the explosive growth in the number of people immigrating to the United States. Recent immigrants are eligible for affirmative action programs originally designed to empower minorities.[56]
- *Socioeconomic status as an indicator of need.* Race may not be the best indicator of need for affirmative action. Some argue that the factors that go into creating educational disadvantages, for example, transcend race. Consider the recent high school graduate who has to work 30 hours a week to support her three siblings because her mother is sick and her father is deceased.[57]

Those who say affirmative action causes companies to hire and promote less qualified people fail to realize that the hiring process usually goes beyond the abilities, knowledge, and skills of the job candidate and includes additional merit-based factors, such as education and experience. When these factors are included in the hiring process, recipients of affirmative action are less likely to feel stigmatized. The way people react to a preferential selection procedure will often depend on how well it is structured and implemented.[58]

LOOKING BACK: REVIEWING THE CONCEPTS

- **Define the primary and secondary dimensions of diversity.**

Primary dimensions of diversity include gender, age, race, physical and mental abilities, sexual orientation, and ethnic heritage. Secondary dimensions include religious beliefs, work experience, communication style, organizational role and level, family status, socioeconomic status, first language, and education and training.

- **Discuss how prejudiced attitudes are formed.**

Prejudice is a premature judgment or opinion based partly on observation of others' differences and partly on ignorance, fear, and cultural conditioning. Prejudiced people tend to see others as stereotypes rather than as individuals. Prejudicial attitudes are formed through the effects of childhood experiences, ethnocentrism, and economic factors. Many people have unconscious prejudices, biases they don't know they have.

- **Develop an awareness of the various forms of discrimination in the workplace.**

Discrimination is behavior based on prejudicial attitudes. Groups protected by law from discrimination in the workplace include people who share characteristics such as gender, age, race, disability, religion, and sexual orientation. More subtle discrimination can arise when individuals have different appearances or educational backgrounds. These subtle forms of discrimination may not be illegal, but they are disruptive to a productive work force.

- **Understand why organizations are striving to develop cultures that value diversity.**

The issue of valuing diversity is an economic one for most organizations. The work force will soon be made up of a minority of white men and a majority of women, people of color, and immigrants. To remain competitive, organizations must value the contributions of all of their diverse workers and make full use of their ideas and talents. Only then will they be able to understand their equally diverse customers' needs. Valuing diversity is not just a nice idea, but a business imperative.

- **Identify ways in which individuals and organizations can enhance work force diversity.**

Individuals can enhance diversity by letting go of their stereotypes and learning to critically and honestly evaluate their prejudiced attitudes as they work and socialize with people who are different. They will need to develop sensitivity to differences and their own personal diversity awareness programs. Organizations must commit to valuing individual differences and implementing effective employment practices that respect and enhance diversity. Their diversity training programs should be an ongoing process rather than a one-time event. They need to seek out, employ, and develop employees from diverse backgrounds.

- **Discuss the current status of affirmative action programs.**

Affirmative action involves intentionally seeking and hiring employees from groups that are underrepresented in the organization. Affirmative action guidelines have helped bring fairness in hiring and promotion to many organizations. Today, however, some people believe these guidelines are discriminatory because they allow preferential treatment for the people they were designed to protect. These preferences may no longer make sense, critics say, given the changing demographics of today's work force.

ON THE JOB Q & A: IS SPEECH TRAINING THE ANSWER?

Q: I am a call-center associate for a global company whose headquarters is in Seattle, Washington. We take calls from customers all over the world who are asking for help solving a product or service problem. Although we have been trained to use simple semantics as we try to assess callers' situations and offer them advice accordingly, it is not uncommon for customers to get irritated and verbally abusive when they cannot understand some of my instructions. I was born in India but have lived in the United States for many years. Some callers think I am based in a foreign country, not the States. I have a master's degree from an American university, but admittedly I do have a slight accent. My boss says that handling customers' rude behavior is part of a call-center associate's job. He also suggested I consider accent-reduction training. Is this a realistic option?

A: Your employers have a vested interest in keeping their external and internal customers happy. A display of rude behavior in any form can have a major adverse effect on their competitive advantage in the global marketplace. Rest assured; they want to solve this problem. Talk with them and ask for training that will help you handle callers who may be making judgments about your competence before you are allowed to exhibit your knowledge and expertise. In recent years, demand for accent-reduction training has grown as foreign-born workers fill many jobs in the United States. If you have a heavy accent, consider enrolling in an accent-reduction program. The English language has sounds not present in other languages, so you may benefit from accent modification.[59]

KEY TERMS

valuing diversity 326
primary dimensions 326
secondary dimensions 326
prejudice 327
stereotypes 327
ethnocentrism 328
ethnicity 328
discrimination 330
race 331
managing diversity 338
affirmative action 342

TRY YOUR HAND

1. The "managing diversity" movement has raised the discussion of equal employment opportunity and affirmative action to a higher level. Consider the following comments by R. Roosevelt Thomas, Jr., which appeared in a *Harvard Business Review* article entitled "From Affirmative Action to Affirming Diversity":

   > *Managers usually see affirmative action and equal employment opportunity as centering on minorities and women, with very little to offer white males. The diversity I'm talking about includes race, gender, creed, and ethnicity but also age, background, education, function, and personality differences. The objective is not to assimilate minorities and women into a dominant white male culture but to create a dominant heterogeneous culture.*[60]

   What does "dominant heterogeneous culture" mean to you? Consider your former or current workplace. Assess how the atmosphere at work would be different if Roosevelt got his wish. Be specific.

2. For one week, keep a journal that records instances in which you see actions or hear comments that reflect prejudicial, negative stereotypes. For example, watch a movie or TV show and observe whether the actors are predominantly of a particular race or ethnic group. Listen to your friends' conversations, and notice any time they make irrational judgments about others based on stereotypes. Finally, reflect on your own attitudes and perceptions. Do you engage in stereotyping?

   Share your experiences with a class member, and propose what steps you can take to help rid the environment of negative stereotyping.

3. Arrange a meeting with someone who is a member of a racial or ethnic group different from your own, and attempt to build a relationship by discussing the things that are important to each of you. Perhaps it is another student, coworker, or member of your community. As you get to know this person, become aware of his or her beliefs and attitudes. Try not to be diverted by accent, grammar, or personal appearance; rather, really listen to the person's thoughts and ideas. Search for things you and your new acquaintance have in common, and assess how your differences could be opportunities for personal growth.

INTERNET INSIGHTS

1. Before, during, and after the terrorist attacks and the war in Iraq, Muslims became victims of discrimination throughout the world, merely because of their religious beliefs and stereotyped physical appearance. Some people from other cultures and religions were afraid to be in their presence, and some Muslims were verbally, if not physically, abused by those who could not see beyond the terrorist stereotype. Just as Americans discriminated against the Japanese before, during, and after World War II, Muslims will probably face the same behaviors in the years to come—unless individuals take the responsibility to learn more about their culture. Visit the Muslim Public Affairs Council website at *http://www.mpac.org,* the Muslim American Society at *http://www.masnet.org,* or *http://www.Islam101.net,* an introductory guide for non-Muslims. What did you learn that would help you respond to someone who displays a bias against Muslims in your presence?

2. Go to the website of the National Organization on Disability (NOD) at *http://www.nod.org.*

The NOD is dedicated to closing the employment gap that exists between people with disabilities and those without, and thereby helping to strengthen the nation's work force. It brings opportunities for employers to tap into new sources of creativity, to find loyal employees, and to expand work force and consumer diversity. Click on the Economic Participation icon, and then on Featured Articles. Read the article of your choice and share the information you learn with your classmates.

YOU PLAY THE ROLE

You are currently supervising 15 employees. Until recently, the work group was working as a productive team and was free of any serious interpersonal relationship problems. Last week, Deaven Erhardt, a relatively new hire, posted an article from the *New York Times* supporting gay marriage on the workroom bulletin board. The article emphasized freedom of marital choice, which some of your senior colleagues find morally offensive. A week later, Erhardt posted another article from the *San Francisco Chronicle* supporting same-sex marriage and a petition to endorse gay marriage in your state. Needless to say, the workroom was becoming a politically contentious environment and was no longer free of interpersonal relationship problems. You explained the situation to your manager, and he suggested that you meet with Erhardt and request that no more articles be displayed in the work area. You will meet with another class member who will assume the role of Deaven Erhardt. Try to convince your role-play partner that these politically sensitive articles are inappropriate in a work setting.

BELOW THE SURFACE:

PepsiCo Opens Door to Diversity

PepsiCo's diversity program was briefly introduced at the beginning of this chapter. Today's emphasis on diversity is part of the company's game plan to better understand the wide range of tastes of new consumers around the world. In recent years, the soda and snacks giant has enforced aggressive hiring and promoting rules. Half of all new hires have to be either women or ethnic minorities. Managers earn bonuses in part by how well they recruit and retain new employees. Today, 25 percent of PepsiCo's managers are women and 6 of its top 12 executives are now women or minorities.[61]

The CEO of PepsiCo is Indra Nooyi, who was raised in a middle-class family in India. She moved to America in 1978 for graduate school at Yale University. From day one, she has worked hard to create a more diverse workplace.[62]

PepsiCo has been a pioneer in the area of diversity. In the early 1940s, the "Cola Wars" involved two major players: Coca-Cola and Pepsi-Cola. Walter S. Mack, the astute president of the underdog Pepsi-Cola Company, believed the black consumers were largely ignored. At the end of World War II, he developed a full department of black salesmen with a budget for advertising and promotion tools. Ms. Nooyi recently recognized the success of the earliest minority hires: "This inspiring team of African American professionals were far ahead of their time and set the standard for passion, determination and connecting with our customers and consumers. They also established the economic value of diversity long before 'affirmative action' was conceived."[63]

QUESTIONS

1. David Thomas, senior associate dean at Harvard Business School, says diversity is the bridge between the workplace and the marketplace. Do you agree with his point of view? Defend your response.
2. At PepsiCo, managers earn bonuses in part by how well they recruit and retain employees. Do you feel this policy has merit? Support your answer.

CLOSING CASE: Coping with Bigotry

Bigots are people who are strongly partial to their own group, religion, race, lifestyle, and so on and intolerant of those who differ from them. Bigotry, prejudiced attitudes expressed through intolerant behaviors, has long been a part of American history, as witnessed by slavery, antigay hate crimes, anti-Semitism, and terrorist stereotyping. Bigoted ideas do not arise spontaneously; they are learned. If they are learned, they can be changed.

The "No Place for Hate" campaign in the Houston, Texas, schools was designed to help young people respect diversity. The hope is that if children learn this lesson early enough, they will reject bigotry for life and thereby rid the world of this historical baggage. Jordan's Queen Rania attended an English school in her native Kuwait that had children from Europe, Africa, the Far East, and the United States. She acknowledges that her interactions with the children from various cultures helped her realize that those things that make everyone similar far outweigh those things that make them different. At the end of the day, everyone wants the same thing out of life.

Research shows that prejudiced attitudes are fluid and that when we become conscious of our bigotry, we can take active and successful steps to combat it. In experiments, researchers have discovered that as people become consciously aware of their prejudices, they feel guilty and try harder to rid themselves of them. Once you become aware of your bigoted tendencies, feel guilty about them, and have the desire to overcome them, the cure is meaningful contact with and knowledge about different cultures.

Today it is easy to obtain information about different countries and cultures through the Internet, TV news, and journalists' reports from various regions of the world. As neighborhoods are integrated with various cultures from around the world, people learn to live with and respect their neighbors' traditions. Biases are more likely to change when members of racially mixed groups cooperate to accomplish shared goals.[64]

QUESTIONS

1. Do any of your family members exhibit bigotry? If so, where do you believe those attitudes originated? Do you share the same beliefs? Why or why not? Evaluate your responses.
2. Is racial profiling a form of bigotry? Support your reasoning.
3. What would the workplace be like if we could end bigotry? What would the world be like? Where do we start this process?

INTEGRATED RESOURCES

VIDEO:

Diversity: More Than Just a Policy

CLASSROOM ACTIVITIES

IRM Application Exercise 15.1
IRM Application Exercise 15.2

CHAPTER 16

The Changing Roles of Men and Women

TIP OF THE ICEBERG

CHAPTER PREVIEW

LEARNING OBJECTIVES

After studying Chapter 16, you will be able to

- Describe how the traditional roles of men and women are changing.
- Understand problems facing women and men as a result of gender bias in organizations.
- Discuss ways to cope with gender-biased behaviors.
- Explain the forms of sexual harassment and learn how to avoid being a victim or perpetrator of them.

Day of Vindication for Lilly Ledbetter

Lilly Ledbetter did not know about pay discrimination laws until late in her career. The Alabama woman was just 26 when Title VII of the Civil Rights Act of 1964 was passed to enforce equality in the workplace. Ledbetter worked for two decades in the not-so-friendly ranks of Goodyear Tire and Rubber's plant in Gadsden, Alabama. It was not until someone left an anonymous note in her mailbox that she realized she was paid much less than the men at Goodyear—in fact, $6,000 less than men doing the same work, including those who were the lowest paid in their job duties.

More than ten years after first filing a gender discrimination claim with the Equal Employment Opportunity Commission, the beaming retired 70-year-old grandmother stood in the East Room of the White House and watched the President of the United States sign a landmark piece of pay-equity legislation bearing her name.

"I cannot begin to describe how honored and humbled I feel today," Ledbetter said. "When I filed my claim ... never, never did I imagine the path that it would lead me down."

Barack Obama signed the Lilly Ledbetter Fair Pay Act in January 2009. Obama said, "This bill will send a clear message that making our economy work means making sure it works for everybody. It is fitting that with the very first bill I sign we are upholding one of the nation's first principles that we are all created equal and each deserve a chance to pursue our own version of happiness."[1]

SAUL LOEB/AFP/Getty Images

President Obama signes his first bill into law. The Lilly Ledbetter Fair Pay Act provided vindication for a grandmother from Alabama who had faced years of pay-based discrimination. Ms. Ledbetter was able to join the president at the signing of this landmark piece of legislation.

Obama signed the bill not only in honor of Ms. Ledbetter, but also in honor of his own grandmother, "who worked in a bank all of her life, and even after she hit that *glass ceiling*, kept getting up again," and for his daughters, "because I want them to grow up in a nation that values their contributions, where there are no limits to their dreams."[2]

Ms. Ledbetter will not see any money as a result of the legislation Mr. Obama signed into law. "Goodyear will never have to pay me what it cheated me out of," she said, "In fact, I will never see a cent. But with the President's signature today, I have an even richer reward."[3]

Women and men often face injustices as the result of gender stereotyping in the workplace. Throughout this chapter we will examine these and other gender issues that create human relations problems at work and at home.

Traditional Roles Are Changing

All cultures promote one set of behaviors for boys and a separate set for girls. Children generally learn their socially acceptable roles by the time they are five years old, but these roles are often continually reinforced throughout the life cycle by teachers, parents, authority figures, and the media. These traditional roles can be harmful to both men and women. For instance, the expectation that men should be aggressive and unemotional stifles their sensitivity and creativity. The assumption that women are emotional and weak hinders them in reaching leadership positions. Although men and women will always be different, their roles can and should be more nearly equal.

Gender bias (also known as **sexism**) is discrimination on the basis of gender. When employers base employment, promotion, job-assignment, and compensation decisions on a person's gender, human relations and productivity suffer. Gender bias is no longer a female-only issue, and many organizations are making the necessary adjustments.

Changes in the Role of Women

In the past, children were more likely to see their mothers as homemakers and their fathers as breadwinners. This has dramatically changed with women joining the work force in record numbers. The recent economic downturn has accelerated this trend. A growing number of women have assumed the role of breadwinner.

The women's movement that began in the 1960s with Betty Friedan's book, *The Feminine Mystique,* has helped women make tremendous strides toward equality with men in the workplace.[4] In addition, women receive more than 55 percent of both the bachelor's and the master's degrees awarded by U.S. colleges. Women are rapidly closing the MD and PhD gap and comprise almost half of law school graduating classes.[5] Although women make up more than half of America's labor force, as of 2009, only 15 *Fortune* 500 companies (3 percent) and 25 *Fortune* 1000 companies have women CEOs or presidents. Three newcomers to the *Fortune* 500 list are Ellen Kullman, DuPont; Laura Sen, BJ's; and Carol Bartz, Yahoo.com.[6]

The impact of women in the workplace has been described as the "revolution that won't quit." As more and more women spend time and money on their education and postpone marriage and motherhood, we will no doubt see women's participation in the work force increase even more. Many women receive important financial and intrinsic rewards from their work, but they also face many challenges. Those who choose to have children must decide if and when to leave the work force and for how long. Women who leave their jobs to start a family wonder if their education and skills will be obsolete by the time they return to work. There is the very real possibility that during these women's absence, the types of jobs they were trained for will disappear.

When new mothers return to work, they often find it difficult to find jobs with schedules that are flexible enough to allow for the demands of a family. They actively seek out organizations that are not only female-friendly in hiring and promotion, but also family-friendly in their employment practices. It has been more than 40 years since the National Organization for Women (NOW) was formed to fight business policies and behaviors that discriminate against women, and there is reason for women to celebrate their progress. Women are now more likely than men to hold managerial and professional jobs, reflecting a 25-year pattern of gains in education and job status. However, women still lag behind men at the higher levels of the organization.[7]

Women have made significant gains in a wide range of traditionally male-dominated areas such as finance, marketing, law, medicine, and computer technology. However, some problem areas persist. Studies indicate that men continue to dominate craft, repair, and construction jobs, whereas women hold only a small percentage of these skilled trade jobs. The good news is that research shows that men and women are increasingly moving into, and succeeding in, nontraditional careers. If fewer than 25 percent of the workforce is of one gender, a career is considered nontraditional.[8]

Achieving success in the 21st century will require women to take risks that could lead to failure in their personal as well as their professional lives. Yet many women today are impelled by fearless confidence that they can achieve anything they choose. They embrace these risks as opportunities for success, recognition, and financial security.

Changes in the Role of Men

Many boys have been conditioned from their early years to be competitors and to win. They have been urged to be aggressive, to learn teamwork, to select traditional male pastimes such as sports and cars, and to enter a masculine profession such as sales, automotive repair, management, engineering, or law. A boy was taught to withstand physical pain and to push his body to the limits. Above all, he was not to act like a girl, to take up interests that were considered feminine, or to show any tendencies that could be considered homosexual. A girl could be a tomboy, but a boy could not be a "sissy." Whereas a woman's worth was measured in terms of her physical attractiveness, a man's was measured by his ability to compete and achieve his goals. This traditional man's world attached great value to independence and autonomy and less value to relationships and connection. If women have been viewed as "sex objects," perhaps men have been seen as "success objects." Robert Bly, author of *Iron John,* says it is time for men to question the images of manhood conveyed by popular culture.

> *We are living in an important and fruitful moment now, for it is clear to men that the images of adult manhood given by the popular culture are worn out; a man can no longer depend on them. By the time a man is thirty-five he knows that the images of the right man, the tough man, the true man, which he received in high school do not work in life.*[9]

A man is under constant pressure to prove himself and keep moving up the ladder.

The Burden of Stress

Psychologists have become increasingly aware that we have neglected the stress associated with being male throughout the generations. The 1950s "organization man" assumed the role of breadwinner—a role accompanied by a great deal of self-imposed as well as societal stress. The pressure to achieve in the workplace was intense, but he was still expected to be the head of the household at home. His male identity often revolved around being the sole provider of the family's income because the woman's place was in the home. Men were reluctant to leave a bad job because they feared losing their family's only paycheck. The 1980s baby boomer men were likely to equate success with high income, movement up the career ladder, and the accumulation of material things such as a nice home and a nice car. Long hours at work often meant that men were emotionally and physically absent from friends and family members, which resulted in a great deal of guilt.[10]

The men of the 21st century are discovering that the strong, unemotional, in-control image supported by previous generations is not healthy or realistic.

The men of the 21st century are discovering that the strong, unemotional, in-control image supported by previous generations is not healthy or even realistic. Many have learned to define the kind of life they want to lead, rather than being restricted to traditional gender-role stereotypes.

Where Is the Balance? As men reexamine their role in society, they face conflicting role messages, even as women entering the work force do. Both men and women often discover that the joy of parenting can be just as satisfying as the achievement of career goals. But such feelings are confusing. Men and women alike are often expected to maintain aggressive attitudes toward their careers while being attentive husbands or wives and fathers or mothers. Those who were brought up in homes with a single parent, who struggled to make ends meet, have had few role models from whom to learn how to balance career and family life. Is it any wonder they feel frustrated?

CRITICAL THINKING CHALLENGE:

Analyze It

1. Do members of your immediate family hold traditional or nontraditional gender roles? If so, have any of these roles undergone changes during the past decade? Examine why there have been changes.
2. Before marriage, each partner should understand the other partner's expectations with regard to careers, family responsibilities, and priorities. What are your expectations of your spouse (if you are married), or what do you imagine they would be (if you are not)?

Problems Facing Women in Organizations

When women pursue careers, they often face three major challenges: the wage gap, the glass ceiling, and balancing career and family. Many employers are making changes that will accommodate the needs of the growing number of working women and mothers, but more needs to be done.

The Wage Gap

Men start their career with a slight earning edge over women. The salary difference eventually mushrooms to several thousand dollars.[11] The Equal Pay Act was passed in 1963, but women, overall, are substantially lagging behind men in pay (see Figure 16.1).[12]

The ramifications of the wage gap persist even after women leave the workforce. "If a woman is paid less, her Social Security payments are lower when she retires, and her pension is lower," explains Rep. Jan Schakowsky (D-Ill). "That's of huge concern as the population ages."[13]

Many nontraditional careers pursued by women, however, lead to greater annual earning than women typically average. Compare the annual salary of a teacher at $43,000 to a pharmacist at $75,000. According to Warren Farrell, author of *Why Men Earn More: The Startling Truth Behind the Pay Gap—and What Women Can Do About It*, more than 80 occupations provide women the opportunity to earn from 5 percent up to 43 percent more than men holding down the same jobs.[14]

FIGURE 16.1 Earnings Gap

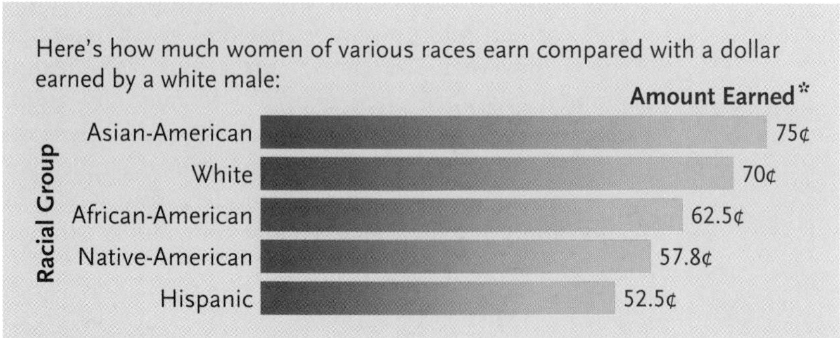

Source: Carol Hymnowitz, "On Diversity, American Isn't Putting Its Money Where Its Mouth Is," *Wall Street Journal*, February 25, 2008, p. B1. Bureau of Labor Statistics collected in 2005.

Although discrimination is partly to blame for wage disparities, other factors also contribute to this problem. Today, women are more committed to building a career, but many women still take time off to have children. This works against them, because continuous work experience tends to increase both productivity and pay in many employment settings.[15]

Research indicates that some women are willing to accept lower pay than men, and that women are less apt to haggle when offered a starting salary or a pay raise. Women, as well as men, need to acquire as much information as possible about their value in the open market and use their negotiation skills to achieve equity in compensation.[16]

American women are a majority of the population, a majority of the electorate, and comprise half the workforce They earn more than half the bachelor's and master's degrees, a level of educational achievement far exceeding that of women in developing countries. In the short term, the U.S. economy is experiencing a downturn, but the long-term picture is quite positive for well-educated women. The number of workers needed to cover job growth and replace retiring baby boomers will be very large.[17]

The Glass Ceiling

There is a condition in the workplace that gives women a view of top management jobs but blocks their ascent. It is often referred to as the **glass ceiling**. Catalyst, a women's advocacy group that has studied women in business for more than 40 years, has documented widespread limits on female career advancement to the highest levels of our nation's largest corporations. Nearly all of the *Fortune* 500 companies have male CEOs, as stated earlier in this chapter. Although we are seeing some positive change at the middle-management ranks, women are still being held back by some widely held misconceptions. Top male executives say the major barrier for women is a lack of significant general management and line experience and less time in the "pipeline." Women in senior management positions say the *real* problems are (1) preconceptions of women held by men and (2) exclusion of women from informal networks of communication.[18]

FIGURE 16.2 Nicking the Glass Ceiling

Year	Percent of Top Level Positions
1998	11.2%
2005	16.4%
2006	15.6%
2007	15.4%
2008	15.7%

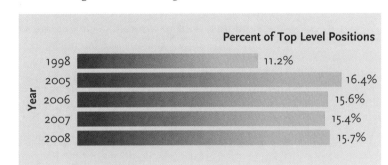

Data: Catalyst; *Fortune* 500 companies.

While women make up 59.6 percent of the labor force, the number of top-level corporate officers remains small.

> *At a time when Americans are congratulating themselves for having a diverse field of political candidates, their business leadership still doesn't equally value diverse employees and managers. In fact, progress for women and minorities in terms of both pay and power has stalled or regressed at many of the nation's biggest companies. This inequality shapes perceptions about who can or should be a leader.*[19]

More top-level positions are available to women today than at any other time in history. However, many women do not take advantage of these opportunities because they have been socially conditioned to first satisfy the needs of their family members: husbands, children, elderly parents, and others. Women who pursue top-level positions must often cope with jobs structured to accommodate the lives of men with wives who do not have full-time careers. They also must cope with the social pressure to fulfill more traditional, "feminine" roles.[20]

Why should we be concerned about the dominance of men in top leadership positions? Cultures that are totally masculine often lack compassion and give rise to rigid, intolerant practices since they lack the intuitive, empathic qualities more common among women. In some cases, a highly competitive masculine culture encourages greed and corruption. The male-dominated hierarchy at Enron, WorldCom, Bernard L. Madoff Investment Securities LLC, and Tyco, for example, fostered unethical practices on a grand scale.

Total Person Insight

Claire Shipman
Katty Kay
Authors, *Womenomics*

"Professors at Pepperdine University conducted a massive 19-year survey of 215 Fortune *500 companies. By every measure of profitability, the study found that companies with the best records for promoting women to executive positions outperform the competition."*[21]

Macho leadership styles can also alienate women. The idea is not to push men off the stage but to get more women onto the stage with them. In an ideal situation, women and men will share the stage and create a culture where everyone is able to express the full range of his or her talents.[22]

Balancing Career and Family Choices

Women today know that they will probably be working for pay for part or all of their adult lives. This expectation is quite a departure from previous generations, when most women assumed the responsibilities of wife and mother. The challenge of performing multiple roles, however, can be stressful and tiring. A majority of the women in two-income families not only contribute significantly to their family's income, but also do most of their family's household chores. Lily Tomlin once said, "If I'd known what it was like to have it all, I would have settled for a lot less."[23] Many women in America no doubt share this thought.

As we look for ways to help women balance career and family, we should not overlook the rewards that are experienced by women who work. Many women who hold both work and family roles treasure the friendships they develop at work and enjoy the intellectual challenges that work provides. Yet a large number of women who try to balance work and family roles say "work is no haven." They feel frustrated because many long-standing work and family problems remain unresolved. These include a lack of quality, affordable child care, inflexible work schedules, and time management problems.[24]

The "Mommy Track" and Other Options. The term **Mommy Track** is used to describe the lifestyle of women who choose a career path that allows a mother flexible or reduced work hours and tends to slow or block advancement. It is a lifestyle that many choose in order to pursue childbearing.

HUMAN RELATIONS IN ACTION

Ways Women Can Hold Their Own in a Male World

- *Make sure women are valued.* Check to see whether the company values women, and if they are represented on the board and in leadership positions.
- *Identify alpha and beta males.* Separate the two types of men in the office and engage in conversations accordingly. Alpha males have a "get it done" mindset, and beta males are more concerned with "collaboration and partnership."
- *Find a mentor.* Look for a female employee at the company with direct experience in a male-dominated workplace.
- *Speak assertively.* Eliminate the phrase "I'm sorry" from your vocabulary. Apologizing for a situation that you are not responsible for demonstrates weakness. Do not begin a phrase, "I think," as it demeans what you are saying.
- *Socialize with the boys.* Make your best effort to socialize with your male coworkers in formal and informal situations.
- *Do not assume stereotypical roles.* Let others "clean up" after your coworkers and bring coffee to meetings.[25]

SALLY FORTH

Sally Forth © King Features Syndicate

Women who follow this lifestyle number in the millions, and they are incredibly important to families and to our society, yet they are often underappreciated and frequently do not earn respect in the workplace. These are women who know in their hearts that staying home to raise their children is the right choice for the whole family. Some do it from the outset of their marriages, while others make the difficult transition from career-driven women to homemakers. Either way, it is a choice that is incredibly rich and rewarding, not to mention challenging, according to Dr. Laura Schlessinger in her book *In Praise of Stay-at-Home Moms.*[26]

Many women want to expand their life choices but are uncertain about the options available. If you are a woman who wants both career and family, then consider the following[27]:

- Choose a career that will give you the gift of time. Some careers provide more flexibility and are more forgiving of interruptions such as parental leave.
- Choose a partner who supports your goal of having a career and family.
- Choose an employer who has given work/life balance a high priority. Be prepared for some disappointments as many corporate leaders are still unwilling to respond to work/life issues.
- Be prepared to use your negotiation skills to push for policies and practices that are favorable to employees with children. If your employer does not provide job-protected leave or flexible work schedules, use your assertiveness skills to press for policy changes.

According to Judith Warner who wrote *Perfect Madness—Motherhood in the Age of Anxiety*, mothers who try to achieve work/family balance (I'm a great mom and a great worker) often feel a sense of frustration as they try to "do it all."[28]

Problems Facing Men in Organizations

Many men are beginning to realize that they have been as rigidly stereotyped in their role as women have been in theirs. Men encounter resistance from their family, coworkers, and friends when they attempt to break out of their stereotypes. The changes a man makes to alter traditional masculine role characteristics can be threatening to others and can cause serious problems in his relationships. Yet the stress men are under today to conform to the expectations of society often leads to heart disease and other health problems. Many wonder if upholding the male image is worth the price.

Men Working with Women

Male attitudes toward female ambitions have changed over the years. One reason for this change is the dramatic increase of female college classmates. Men have learned that they will be competing with these smart and ambitious women in the workplace. They are also learning that women can be excellent coworkers, team members, and leaders. Those men who are secure in their talents and abilities welcome the opportunity to work beside equally self-assured women. Those men who are threatened by powerful, talented women need an attitude adjustment.

Balancing Career and Family Choices

Henry David Thoreau observed that "the mass of men lead lives of quiet desperation." Does this dire observation apply to men who are pursuing careers and assuming family roles today? The answer is a qualified yes. Men, like women, now have more choices regarding marriage and family life and face many barriers to achieving work/life balance.

- The long-term trend toward wage equality gives families more choices regarding who should assume the roles of breadwinner, child-care provider, and housekeeper. One wife in four now out-earns her husband. Because of their upbringing, most men are often ill suited to staying at home with their children while their wives become the breadwinners.[29]
- Men often seek a "package deal" in life that includes four elements: marriage, fatherhood, employment, and homeownership—not necessarily in that order. Yet these goals often conflict. Many men express the desire to be closer to their children than their traditional fathers were to them, but they get caught in the traditional cycle of working long hours to pay for a nice home for the wife and kids.[30] Unfortunately, men are often reluctant to talk openly about personal pressures created by these work/family conflicts, and the cycle continues.
- Working fathers who want to take paternity leave or time off to help raise their children often experience discrimination in the workplace. Women who choose these options are generally seen in a more positive light. Many men still feel that taking parental leave will unofficially penalize them.[31] Just as women struggle with this issue, men must also step forward and encourage employers to commit to family-friendly workplace policies and practices.
- Men are less likely than women to adopt a healthy lifestyle and seek health care when it is needed. As a result, they lead in each of the ten leading causes of death and have a life span shorter than that of their female counterparts.[32]

During life's most stressful transitions, such as divorce or loss of a job, men often spend more time reflecting on things they value in life. Those who feel that their male identity is dependent on what is accomplished at work and that success is measured by the size of their paycheck sometimes reestablish their priorities. In a *Wall Street Journal* article entitled "Who's the New Guy at Dinner? It's Dad ...," one dad explains his transition following the loss of his managerial job at AOL. He says he told his young twin daughters, "I'm going to find a new job doing something I love that makes people happy." When he was hired as a fifth-grade teacher, his children were thrilled, and so was he. He can now spend more time with his children.[33]

TABLE 16.1 STRIKING A BALANCE

If You Are the at-Home Partner

- Own the choice you've made while recognizing that traditional gender roles don't always correspond with a couple's actual competencies.
- Inoculate yourself against the loss of identity you may feel, or the isolation you may experience, by forging a strong community of other professionals who have made similar decisions to head home.
- Understand that your partner's work, while providing time away from child-care duties and household chores, is not vacation.
- Talk clearly with your partner about what's going to work for a two-year period, not just for the moment. Recognize that your current arrangement is not forever.

If You Are the Breadwinner

- Some resentments are unavoidable and can convey important information about yourself.
- Be sensitive to your partner's loss of professional identity. Don't take work inside the home for granted.
- Give your partner time to adjust to new duties before swooping in to correct their parenting behavior or housekeeping style.
- Do not assume that because you earn the money, you hold greater decision-making status in your relationship.

Source: Two People, One Breadwinner, sidebar: "Striking a balance" by Deborah Siegel from *Psychology Today*, July/August 2007. Reprinted with permission from *Psychology Today* Magazine (Copyright © 2007 Susex Publishers, LLC.).

Challenges and Opportunities for Working Men and Women

As men and women struggle with their career and family choices, many progressive organizations are gearing up to meet the needs of their employees in the 21st century. They are recognizing the demands placed on working parents and are attempting to address the problems associated with quality child care. At the same time, they realize they must provide flexible work schedules that adjust to the changing roles of men and women.

Eighty percent of employers report that child care problems force employees to lose work time.

The Challenge of Child Care

The need for affordable, quality child care has never been greater. Mothers and fathers alike face forced overtime and unpredictable hours as their employers attempt to cut costs while improving productivity. At the same time, many day-care providers shut their doors at 6 p.m. and on weekends. Workers who cannot balance the demands of work with available child care are often disciplined or fired.

Some companies provide on-site day-care centers and find this fringe benefit a strong factor in retaining valuable employees who are also parents. Eighty percent of employers report that child care problems force employees to lose work time.[34]

Many of *Fortune*'s 100 Best Companies to Work For have made the list because of their sensitivity to the needs of workers with children; consequently, they have

HUMAN RELATIONS IN ACTION

The Family and Medical Leave Act

The Family and Medical Leave Act (FMLA) guarantees continuation of any paid health benefits, plus a return to the same or an equivalent job, for employees (men as well as women) who take up to 12 weeks' unpaid time off—all at once or intermittently—so that they can care for themselves or an ailing family member such as a parent, child, or spouse during a serious health condition, or for childbirth or adoption. (Some states are considering providing financial compensation during part or all of the employee's time off.)

To qualify, you must work for an employer with 50 or more employees and at a location with at least 50 employees within 75 miles. Your employer can deny leave if you have not worked there for at least 12 months and for at least 1,250 hours during the past year. You also may be ineligible for protection if you are among your employer's top 10 percent of employees, based on pay. If you feel you have a legitimate family leave dispute, contact the Wage and Hour Division of the United States Department of Labor (*http://www.wageandhour.dol.gov*).[35]

provided programs and activities that meet workers' needs. Aflac, 26 on the list of the 100 Best Companies to Work For in 2009, has the largest onsite corporate day care in the state of Georgia. Unique among Aflac's day care structure is that the hours for day care extend to 11:30 p.m. so that second-shift employees can benefit also.[36]

Keep in mind, however, the resentment that may build among child-free employees who see employees with children receiving special treatment. Child-free workers are often asked to work overtime, the night shift, or weekends while their coworkers who are parents arrive late or leave early to accommodate the needs of their children. To prevent this potential human relations problem, employers should considering offering flexible schedules to all employees. (See Figure 16.3.)

Flexible Work Schedule Opportunities

Men and women who are concerned about balancing personal and work lives say that flexible work schedules rank very high on the list of desired benefits. As a result,

FIGURE 16.3 A Two-Way Street

To make flexible scheduling more fair for working parents and child-free employees alike, some employers are:

- Allowing all employees to apply for flexible schedules
- Requiring proposals that outline how the flexible schedule will impact work that must be completed in a timely manner
- Evaluating flexible setups regularly
- Making scheduling a team responsibility
- Cross training workers so that they can take over their coworkers' responsibilities when necessary

Source: Figure adapted from Sue Shellenbarger, "A Two-Way Street," *Wall Street Journal*, November 17, 2005, p. D1.

FIGURE 16.4 Flextime in Action

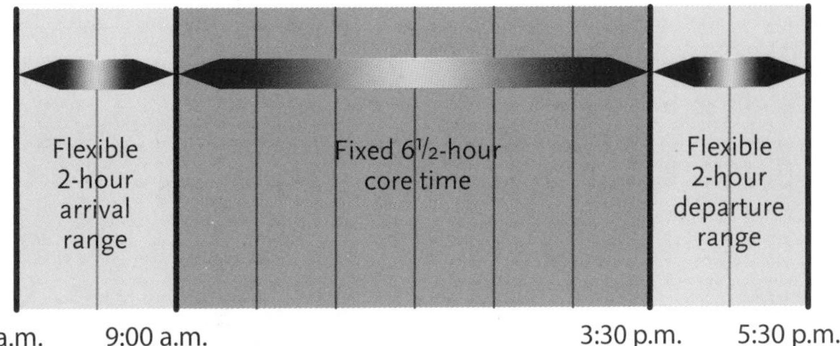

Source: Robert Kreitner, *Management*, 9th edition (Boston: Houghton Mifflin Company, 2004). Reprinted by permission of The Houghton Mifflin Company.

many organizations allow various scheduling options so that they can recruit and retain the top talent in the labor market. Indeed, in the current recession, more employers are using flexible setups to save money. On the basis of an April 2009 survey by Towers Perrin of 700 employers, 21 percent to 32 percent are either implementing or considering part-time shifts of four-day workweeks, as a cost-cutting tool.[37]

Flextime. **Flextime** typically includes a core time when all employees work, usually between 9:00 a.m. and 3:30 p.m. Employees can determine their own arrival and departure times within certain limits, which may mean arriving at 7 a.m. or leaving at 5:30 p.m. (see Figure 16.4).[38]

Compressed Workweek. Typically, a **compressed workweek** consists of four 10-hour days—for example, Monday through Thursday or Thursday through Sunday. Employees may be given the opportunity to adjust their work schedules to fit their lifestyle. One of the newest compressed workweek schedules, often called the 9/80, is growing in popularity. Employees work one extra hour each day for nine days, a total of 80 hours in two weeks, and receive a three-day weekend every other week.[39]

Virtual Assistant. A **virtual assistant** is someone who takes care of activities that most employers are not interested in doing. It allows them freedom to focus on the things that are important and bring the most long-term benefit, and it allows them to increase effectiveness. Among the numerous personal or work-related tasks of a virtual assistant are transcription, event planning, presentations, market research, online marketing, etc. It's about simplification.[40]

Skill Development: Apply It

Being able to determine whether an organization is a good "fit" for you and your family's needs is an important skill to develop. Consider the organizations in your area that might be considered "family friendly." Describe the benefits working mothers receive. Do these benefits apply to working fathers, too? If you are choosing to be child-free, what benefits are important to you as you strive to balance your work/life? Explain.

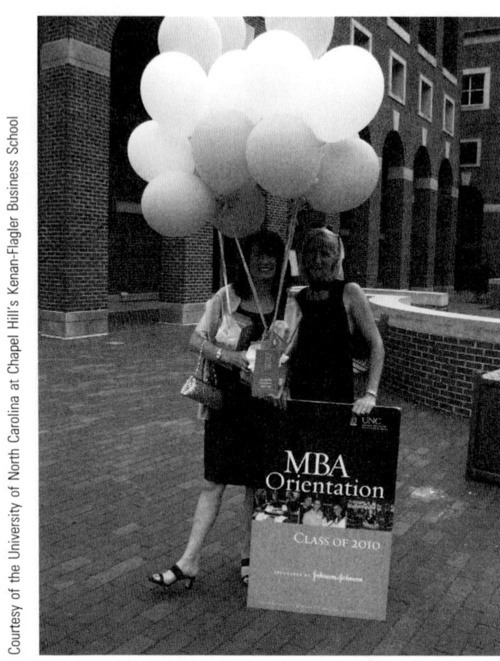

Courtesy of the University of North Carolina at Chapel Hill's Kenan-Flagler Business School

On Mondays, Tuesdays, and half of Wednesdays, Anna Miller is the MBA program associate director at the University of North Carolina Kenan-Flagler Business School. The rest of the time, she is home with her four children. Meghan Gosk has a similar schedule but in reverse. When faced with the option of reducing work hours or sacrificing something in the family schedule, Miller and Gosh chose a flexible job sharing arrangement.

Job Sharing. With **job sharing**, two employees share the responsibilities of one job. For example, one employee might work the mornings and the other employee might work the afternoons. In some cases, each job sharer works two days alone and one day overlapping with the other person. This means the job is fully covered, and each job sharer knows what the other is doing.[41] Job sharing is growing in popularity.

Telecommuting. The availability of powerful home-office computer and communication technologies, the large-scale use of temporary workers as the result of massive downsizing, and the demands of workers who want to blend work and family have fueled an increase in **telecommuting**—employees working at home at a personal computer linked to their employer's computer. The number of corporate telecommuters in 2009 was 8.7 million. Work-at-home employees confer savings on real estate and office costs. Employers who are equipped to measure output against costs often discover that an efficient telecommuter is an asset.[42]

ROWE (Results-Only Work Environment). Employees can leave the office whenever they please. They do not have to tell anyone where they are going or why. If an employee chooses to share the fact that he or she is taking the afternoon off to go to a baseball game, no one is allowed to make muttered comments about his or her work ethic. It is no surprise that this system has boosted morale; perhaps more significant, it has improved productivity as well.[43]

CAREER INSIGHT 

"Does a Flexible Work Schedule Make You a Target for Layoffs?"

As the economy continues to fluctuate, employees who have chosen flexible work options often fear loss of job security. Maintaining a flexible work schedule during a recession requires planning—and luck. In an uncertain workforce climate, many employers focus on those employees who are there 9-to-5 and whom they see on a daily basis. Other employers evaluate costs and view an efficient part-timer or telecommuter as an asset. In a nontraditional work environment where you have chosen a flexible work option, "you need to be realistic, be flexible, and deliver results." Your schedule may be scrutinized, so it is important to attend meetings and come into the office on a day off. "To improve your survival chances, ask yourself, 'What's most important to my company right now, and how do I make sure I'm contributing to that, and that my achievement is visible to my boss?'"[44]

How to Cope with Gender-Biased Behavior

Traditional attitudes, beliefs, and practices are not changed easily. If you are a man or a woman breaking into a nontraditional role, you may encounter resistance. In addition, you may be confused about how to act or you may be overly sensitive about the way others treat you. As a result, if you are choosing a new role for yourself, you may have to adopt new behaviors and be prepared to confront some of the very real obstacles you will encounter.

Sexual Harassment in the Workplace

One of the most sensitive problems between men and women in organizations is **sexual harassment**, unwelcome verbal or physical behavior that affects a person's job performance or work environment. Employers have a legal and moral responsibility to prevent sexual harassment, which can occur from men harassing

HUMAN RELATIONS IN ACTION 

Four-Star General Ann E. Dunwoody

Ann E. Dunwoody achieved the rank of four-star General, a position never before reached by a woman in the US military. Even though General Dunwoody was nominated and decorated (a significant break through in the glass ceiling), women in the military still face serious obstacles. The rate of rape and sexual assault in the military continues to be high and unreported—perhaps as much as 80 percent. General Dunwoody has a gender-biased issue to deal with that could be career altering for both sexes in the next decade.[45]

women, women harassing men, or same-sex harassment. As men and women work together on teams, more employers are becoming acutely aware of the increased potential for misinterpreted comments and actions between the genders. When sexual harassment is present in the workplace, the cost of increased absenteeism, staff turnover, low morale, and low productivity can be high.

The number of reported incidents of sexual harassment directed toward men is increasing, according to the US Equal Employment Opportunity Commission (EEOC). "There are positive changes taking place in the workplace that are allowing and encouraging men to report these claims," said Danny Baker, of the Washington-based Gender Public Advocacy Coalition. "This is also related to an increasing dialogue about what we call male-on-male sexual harassment."[46]

Forms of Sexual Harassment. Under the law, sexual harassment may take one of two forms. The first is **quid pro quo** (something for something), which occurs when a person in a supervisory or managerial position threatens the job security or a potential promotion of a subordinate worker who refuses to submit to sexual advances. These kinds of threats are absolutely prohibited, and employers are liable for damages under the Fair Employment Practices section of the Civil Rights Act. These behaviors can take the form of comments of a personal or sexual nature, unwanted touching and feeling, or demands for sexual favors.

The second form of sexual harassment involves the existence of a **hostile work environment**. Supreme Court decisions have held that sexual harassment exists if a "reasonable person" believes that the behavior is sufficiently severe or pervasive to create an abusive working environment, even if the victim does not get fired or held back from a promotion. A hostile work environment exists when supervisors,

Sexual harassment against men is a growing problem in the workplace. Few people take this problem seriously, but it is indeed becoming a serious issue.

HUMAN RELATIONS IN ACTION

Pregnancy Discrimination

Discrimination against pregnant women in the work force has increased 23 percent in the past ten years. It is one of the fastest-growing categories of charges filed with the EEOC.

The charges are coming from women in entry-level jobs as well as executives. Pregnant women claim they have been unfairly fired, denied promotions, and in some cases urged to terminate pregnancies in order to keep their jobs. Several factors may be behind this trend.

- More pregnant women are staying in the workplace rather than quitting their jobs as in previous generations.
- Pregnancy is expensive for employers. The result is a squeeze on maternity leave pay and time off by employers.
- Stereotypes about pregnant women persist. Mounting research indicates that men and women alike view pregnant women as less competent.
- Employers are making honest mistakes or are confused by conflicting laws. Many states have protections for pregnant women that go beyond the federal law, which allows for twelve weeks or unpaid leave.[47]

coworkers, vendors, or customers use sexual innuendo, tell sexually oriented jokes, display sexually explicit photos in the work area, discuss sexual exploits, and so on. Unlike quid pro quo harassment, hostile work environment claims tend to fall in a gray area: What is offensive to one person may not be offensive to another. The bottom line is that most kinds of sexually explicit language, conduct, and behavior are inappropriate in the workplace, regardless of whether such conduct constitutes sexual harassment within the legal meaning of the term. (See Table 16.2.)

How to Address Sexual Harassment

Ever since Professor Anita Hill accused Supreme Court Judge nominee Clarence Thomas of lewd and overbearing conduct toward her, the country has been trying to determine the difference between innocent comments and sexual harassment.

TABLE 16.2 SEXUAL BOUNDARIES 2.0

20 YEARS AGO	TODAY
Sexually explicit remarks	Sexually explicit emails, IMs
Lewd one-on-one talk	Raunchy office banter
Inappropriate touching	Inappropriate joking
Violating office romance policies or dating subordinates	Violating office company-imposed relationship pacts, aka love contracts

In many workplaces, the definition of harassment has become more nuanced.

Source: Michelle Conlin, "Indiscretions: Harassers in High Places," *BusinessWeek*, November 13, 2006, p. 44. Reprinted by special permission. Copyright © 2006 by The McGraw-Hill Companies, Inc.

The key word is *unwelcome.* Victims of sexual harassment need to tell the harasser, in no uncertain terms, that his or her behavior is inappropriate. Meanwhile, victims should record the occurrence in a journal that includes the date and details of the incident. They should also talk with coworkers who can provide emotional support and help verify instances of harassment. Chances are, if one person is being harassed, others are as well. If the harasser continues the behavior, the victim should go to a higher authority such as the harasser's supervisor or the organization's human resources division. Under the law, companies are legally liable if they do not immediately investigate the situation and take action to eliminate the offensive behaviors. These actions can include reprimand, suspension, or dismissal of the harasser.

The Supreme Court has given employees and employers help in understanding the legal aspects of sexual harassment. The court handed down two landmark rulings that included the following guidelines:[48]

- Companies can be held liable for a supervisor's sexually harassing behavior, even if the offense was never reported to management.
- An employer can be liable when a supervisor threatens to punish a worker for resisting sexual demands—even if such threats are not carried out.

The court also offered employers advice on how to avoid costly legal fees. A company can deflect sexual harassment charges by developing a zero-tolerance policy on harassment, communicating it to employees and making sure victims can report abuses without fear of retaliation. If the employer can show that an employee failed to use internal procedures for reporting abusive behavior, the company will be protected in a court of law.

Although the courtroom doors are open for individuals to protect themselves from unwanted behavior, pressing a sexual harassment charge is a lengthy, expensive, and psychologically draining experience. Before you file charges, be sure you have used all the remedies available to you through your employer.

Learn to Understand and Respect Gender Differences

As mentioned in Chapter 2, gender bias often acts as a filter that interferes with effective communication between men and women. In recent years, popular books/videos such as *You Just Don't Understand: Women and Men in Conversation* and *Talking 9-5* by Deborah Tannen and *Men Are from Mars, Women Are from Venus* by John Gray have heightened awareness of the differences between women's and men's communication styles. These differences, according to Tannen, are due to linguistic style. **Linguistic style** refers to a person's speaking pattern and includes such characteristics as directness or indirectness, pacing and pausing, word choice, and the use of such elements as jokes, figures of speech, stories, questions, and apologies. Linguistic style is a series of culturally learned signals that we use to communicate what we mean.[49] Communication experts and psychologists have made the following generalizations concerning gender-specific communication patterns:

- Men tend to be more direct in their conversation, whereas women are more apt to emphasize politeness.

- Men tend to dominate discussions during meetings and are more likely to interrupt.
- Women prefer to work out solutions with another person; men prefer to work out their problems by themselves.
- Men tend to speak in a steady flow, free of pauses, interrupting each other to take turns. Women tend to speak with frequent pauses, which are used for turn taking.
- Male-style humor tends to focus on banter, the exchange of witty, often teasing remarks. A woman's style is often based on anecdotes in which the speaker is more likely to mock herself than she is to make fun of another person.
- Women are likely to downplay their certainty; men are likely to minimize their doubts.[50]

Does linguistic style really make a difference? Let's assume that two employees, Mary and John, are being considered for promotion to a management position. The person who must make the decision wants someone who displays a high degree of self-confidence. If John is regularly displaying the "male" communication patterns described previously, he may be viewed as the more confident candidate. But if the person making the promotion decision is searching for someone who is sensitive, an attentive listener, and a consensus builder, Mary may win the promotion. We know that people in positions of power tend to reward linguistic styles similar to their own, so the candidate (male or female) with the greatest versatility may get the promotion.[51] In Chapter 3, we defined *versatility* as acting in ways that earn social acceptance.

A Few Words of Caution

Differences do exist: Most men are somewhat more competitive, assertive, and task focused, and most women are more sensitive, cooperative, and people-focused than most men. However, our stereotypes about men and women are often too strong and too inflexible.[52] When we place too much emphasis on the ways in which women and men differ, we stop viewing them as individuals. As noted in Chapter 3, it is tempting to put a label on someone and then assume the label tells you everything you need to know about that person.

Once you understand the concept that men and women communicate in different ways, you can begin to flex your style. Refer to Table 16.3 for more specific suggestions on how to communicate better with the opposite gender. Keep in mind, however, that an overextension of a strength *can* become a weakness. It is interesting to note that some men who have worked with women on a regular basis for many years and have successfully adjusted their communication style accordingly may find it difficult to communicate in a male environment. The same may be true for women who have worked for years in a male environment. They may find it difficult to transfer into a new work setting that is dominated by women.

Men and women have so much to learn from each other. NYU psychologist Carol Gilligan offers this metaphor: "One can think of the oboe and the clarinet as different, yet when they play together, there is a sound that's not either one of them, but it doesn't dissolve the identity of either instrument."[53]

TABLE 16.3 WORKPLACE TIPS FOR AVOIDING GENDER-SPECIFIC LANGUAGE BARRIERS

MEN CAN ...
• think about women as fellow employees rather than sexual objects. • recognize that, within their gender group, women are as unique as men. • communicate with women based on their individuality rather than on the characteristics of a stereotyped group. • use general humor, not sexual humor. • remember that even when intentions are good, the impact of your communication may be bad. • follow this rule: When in doubt, do not make the statement or act out the thought.
WOMEN CAN ...
• stay calm when expressing feelings to avoid being labeled as overemotional. • express feelings verbally rather than nonverbally. Men are not always good at reading behavior. • avoid male bashing. • use general humor, not self-effacing humor. • say what needs to be said concisely, without excessive apologies or disclaimers. • recognize that a man may not understand the impact of his sexually related comment. When something is offensive, say something right away.

Source: From Anita Bruzzese's, "Working Toward a Truce in the Battle of the Sexes," Springfield *News Leader*, August 9, 1994, p. b1. Reprinted by permission.

Total Person Insight

ALICE SARGEANT
Author, *The Androgynous Manager*

"Men and women should learn from one another without abandoning successful traits they already possess. Men can learn to be more collaborative and intuitive, yet remain result-oriented. Women need not give up being nurturing in order to learn to be comfortable with power and conflict."[54]

Learn New Organization Etiquette

As women enter into upper levels of management and men begin to work in support positions, the ways in which men and women deal with each other change subtly. Does this change require new rules of etiquette? In some cases, yes. The following guidelines may help you understand how to act in these new situations:

1. When a woman visits a man's office, he should rise from his desk to greet her. When a man enters a woman's office, she should rise from her desk to greet him.
2. Whoever has a free hand (could be a small woman) should help anyone carrying too heavy a load (could be a large man).

3. Women resent being "go-fers." Meeting participants should not expect a woman to take notes, answer the phone, or type material. Men and women should rotate such clerical duties. A woman should not leap to serve coffee when it is time for a break.
4. Whoever arrives first at a door should open it, and whoever stands in the front row in the elevator should get off first.
5. Whoever extends an invitation to lunch or dinner should in most cases, pay the tab.
6. Training materials, memos, and so on should be written in gender-free language. Clerical and secretarial personnel should not be referred to only as "she" or "her" and management personnel only as "he" or "him."

The new etiquette provides a means to overcome old stereotypes and traditional ways of setting men and women apart solely on the basis of gender. By practicing these points of etiquette and adopting a positive, helpful attitude toward each other, men and women can help ease the transition from traditional to nontraditional roles. Women and men both will be winners.

LOOKING BACK: REVIEWING THE CONCEPTS

- Describe how the traditional roles of men and women are changing.

The traditional roles assigned to both genders limit their opportunities to choose careers and lifestyles best suited to their abilities and true interests. Many men and women are breaking out of these traditional roles. During the past few decades, women have entered the job world in increasing numbers and in professions previously considered all male. As a result, men and women have a wider range of choices regarding marriage and children than ever before. Organizations are beginning to offer their employees options such as job sharing, flextime, job redesign, and telecommuting so that they can better handle the demands of work and family.

- Understand problems facing women and men as a result of gender bias in organizations.

Women are still subject to a wage gap, earning less than men receive for similar work, but the gap is narrowing. Moreover, the glass ceiling gives women a view of top-level jobs, but blocks their ascent. They are making progress, however, in the mid-management ranks. The real problems seem to be the preconceptions men have of women and the exclusion of women from the informal networks of communication. Men are working to dispel the myth that men must always be in control, emotionally unexpressive, logical, and achievement oriented. They realize that the rigid male role has had adverse effects on their relationships with their families. Many men are choosing more personally rewarding careers that allow time for family responsibilities even if they must sacrifice some material gain to do so.

- Discuss ways to cope with gender-biased behaviors.

Methods of coping with gender-biased behaviors include understanding remedies available through the organization's sexual harassment policy, learning how to effectively communicate with the opposite gender, and observing the new rules of etiquette in the workplace.

- Explain the forms of sexual harassment and learn how to avoid being a victim or perpetrator of them.

Sexual harassment may be a problem for men as well as women. It may take on two forms: quid pro quo, a threat to job security or promotion if sexual favors are not granted, or sexually explicit language, photos, or innuendo that create a hostile work environment. Most organizations have developed guidelines to help employees avoid harassment or fight it when it occurs.

ON THE JOB Q & A: ENTREPRENEURSHIP

Q: Many of us who are enrolled in this Human Relations course are considering becoming entrepreneurs. Are there tests, assessment tools, or mentors who could guide us in this career decision-making process?

A: Good for you! In these uncertain economic times, it is important to explore all of your options. Yes, there are numerous tests to help people determine whether they are good candidates for starting a business. But whether a test can really determine who does or does not make a capable entrepreneur is debatable. There are some personality traits common among successful entrepreneurs, like the tendency to have a higher risk tolerance, drive, and resiliency to overcome failure than the general population according to experts.

Author Bill Wagner offers an *Entrepreneur IQ* test at his Web site, *http://TheEntrepreneurNextDoor.com*, which compares your answers to others. A Harvard University professor developed a psychological profile of entrepreneurs that is available, free of charge, at the *Wall Street Journal's http://Startup.Journal.com/sidebar/20020430-mancuso-quiz-doc.html*. In addition, there are the Strong and MBTI tests used to assess entrepreneurial aptitude.

Many communities have an organization called SCORE (Service Corps of Retired Executives), which includes retired executives who are willing to guide and share their experiences with entrepreneurs and small businesses nationwide.

There are extroverts and introverts, and people with all types of educational and experiential backgrounds, who become successful entrepreneurs. The only real distinguishing trait seems to be self-efficacy (as discussed in Chapter 4)—confidence that you can build a successful business.[55]

KEY TERMS

gender bias (sexism) 350
glass ceiling 354
Mommy Track 356
flextime 361
compressed workweek 361
virtual assistant 361
job sharing 362
telecommuting 362
sexual harassment 363
quid pro quo 364
hostile work environment 364
linguistic style 366

TRY YOUR HAND

1. The following situations represent either quid pro quo or hostile environment forms of sexual harassment in the workplace. Identify the form represented by each situation, and explain your reasoning. Describe the actions you might take if you were the potential victim in each incident.

   a. Julie thinks David is very handsome. She often stares at him when she thinks he is not looking. David is aware of Julie's staring and is very uncomfortable but is too shy and embarrassed to say anything to her.
   b. While sitting at her desk, Karen receives the following electronic message from her boss on her computer screen: "Can we discuss your possible promotion over dinner this evening?"
   c. At a convention reception, one of Joan's most important clients invites her out for cocktails and dinner. She politely declines. He announces loudly, "She won't go out to dinner with me, and I'm her best customer!" Under

his breath he says, "Honey, if you want my business, you'd better cooperate." Joan's boss insists she go to dinner with the client.

2. On a sheet of paper, list and explain the various choices you would make when attempting to balance your career and family responsibilities. For example, will marriage be a part of your future? Will you have children? When? How will you provide care for these children while you and your spouse are at work? Would you prefer home-based work? Which flextime options would you consider valuable? Do you want to work for someone else or own your own business?

3. During a period of one week, analyze your verbal and nonverbal communications with people who are of the opposite gender. Try to determine whether any linguistic style differences are apparent during conversations. If you discover style differences, try to determine if they serve as a barrier or aid effective communication.

INTERNET INSIGHTS

1. If you are thinking about starting a business or becoming an entrepreneur, visit any or all of these sites and discover the support and advice they offer: *http://www.entrepreneurs.about.com*, *http://www.sba.gov/smallbusinessplanner/index*, the U.S. Small Business Administration's Online Women's Business Center (*http://www.onlinewbc.gov*), and Center for Women & Enterprise (*http://cwionline.org*).

2. Those who would like to examine various flexible work-schedule options can visit *http://www.workoptions.com*. Write an analysis of how the information available on this site might help individuals make an educated decision about their personal and professional life choices.

YOU PLAY THE ROLE

If you are looking to use flexible work schedule options (review the different options listed in this chapter) at your place of work, you need to be prepared when asking for permission. Your supervisor may initially say "no"; however, be prepared with counter arguments. Write a business proposal discussing the benefits of your plan to you and the company. If you select telecommuting, describe the arrangements that you have made for your designated home workspace, the logistics of how often you will "check in" with your supervisor, and a vehicle for feedback to assess your performance. You must show enthusiasm for this approach. Finally, be a good listener and try to determine the major objections to your proposal. Flexible work schedule options, specifically telecommuting, may be new to this workplace and require additional education and adjustments. Select a class member to play the role of your supervisor as you present your proposal.

BELOW THE SURFACE:

Insuring Pay Equality for Women Everywhere

In the opening vignette of this chapter, we described the signing of the Lilly Ledbetter Fair Pay Act of 2007 into legislation. Initially, on May 27, 2007, the Supreme Court handed down a 5-4 ruling that would make it much harder for women and other

(*continued*)

workers to sue their employers for pay discrimination. A lower court jury ruled in favor of Ledbetter, but the U.S. Supreme Court overturned the judgment and told the 69-year-old Jacksonville, Alabama, resident that, despite any discrimination that occurred, her wait of more than 180 days after the first occurrence of pay discrimination was too long for her to sue, even if she *didn't know* how much more her colleagues were being paid. In a vigorous dissenting opinion, Supreme Court Justice Ruth Bader Ginsburg urged Congress to quickly pass a law correcting this damaging decision. During the summer of 2007, the House and Senate passed the Lilly Ledbetter Fair Pay Act of 2007, which would allow an employee to file a claim within 180 days of the *last* discriminatory paycheck, not the *first*. The White House, however, vetoed the bill.

It was not until President-elect Obama signed the bill in January, 2009, that the bill finally became law.[56]

QUESTIONS

1. Many members of Congress did not support the Ledbetter Fair Pay Act, saying that government should not play such a powerful role in the private enterprise system. Substantiate your support or nonsupport of their position.
2. Predict the impact of the Lilly Ledbetter Fair Pay Act in terms of other women's issues discussed in this chapter.
3. What inferences are inherent in this bill in a down economy when more families have to make choices as to who will be the breadwinner in the family?

CLOSING CASE: A Saner Workplace

Companies everywhere are starting to retool. "The one-size-fits-all workplace doesn't work," says the Alfred P. Sloan Foundation's Christensen. "The idea that you will work full-time year in and year out, that you will be on a career trajectory that is a straight line, is vanishing. Employees increasingly feel more entitled to say: 'I need and I want to work in a certain way'."

In their book, *Womenomics: Write Your Own Rules for Success,* broadcasters Claire Shipman and Katty Kay cite studies that show the increasing impact of professional women on companies' bottom lines and give practical advice on how to create "a more sane" work life. Women may be driving the workforce revolution, but men are realizing the benefits, too.

At Capital One Financial, Judy Pahren, director of human resources, realized that *flexibility* was not just a "woman initiative" but, rather, a need across an entire employee base. "We had thought that maybe it was gender-based; however, it was true of the men who worked at Capital One Financial also." A few months later, The Flexible Work Arrangements program was implemented for the entire company. The program allows employees to determine their work schedules with their immediate supervisors; options are flextime, telecommuting, a compressed workweek, or part-time employment.

More and more workers of *both* sexes are willing to scale back career goals, according to Families & Work Institute data. In focus groups, employees say things like "I need to make these choices because my family is a priority" or "I need to make these choices to make my life work."

According to Brenda Barnes, CEO of Sara Lee, "Today's business environment provides the opportunity for work-life balance. This doesn't mean employees work less; instead, it means empowering employees to do their work on a schedule that works for them. So if they want to work from their kitchen table at 3 a.m., as long as the work gets done, who cares when or where they are doing it? Companies need to recognize that this kind of *flexibility* offers employees the ability to manage and balance their own career and lives, which improves productivity and employee morale."[57]

QUESTIONS

1. On the basis of your personal and professional needs, design a Flexible Work Arrangement that would allow you to have work-life balance in your career.
2. Predict the implications of a Flexible Work Arrangement program for the future. Evaluate the impact on business/industry, management, employees, and consumers. Is the Capital One Financial's Flexible Work Arrangement program a realistic option for employees who work in retailing? Manufacturing? The hospitality industry? Explain your answer.
3. Capital One thought work *flexibility* was a key issue only for female employees. They realized, with additional inquiry, that it was true for the men employees as well. Analyze why both sexes are willing to scale back career goals and the implications their decisions will have on their career and life choices.

INTEGRATED RESOURCES

VIDEOS:

Alternative Work Arrangements at HP
Managing Equality

CLASSROOM ACTIVITIES

IRM Application Exercise 16.1
IRM Application Exercise 16.2
IRM Application Exercise 16.3

PART 6

You Can Plan for Success

Chapter 17
A Life Plan for Effective Human Relations

© Jupiterimages/Comstock Images/ Getty Images

CHAPTER 17

A Life Plan for Effective Human Relations

TIP OF THE ICEBERG

CHAPTER PREVIEW

LEARNING OBJECTIVES

After studying Chapter 17, you will be able to

- Learn how to cope with the forces that influence the work/life balance.
- Define success by standards that are compatible with your needs and values.
- Discuss the meaning of *right livelihood*.
- Describe four nonfinancial resources that can enrich your life.
- Provide guidelines for developing a healthy lifestyle.
- Develop a plan for making needed changes in your life.

Chad Smith Prepares for a New Career

After graduation from high school, Chad Smith hit the ground running. He held some well-paying construction jobs before going to work in the auto industry. Chad was earning more than $50,000 a year and life looked good. He was happily married and the father of three sons. Then he was laid off from his night-shift job at a Chrysler assembly plant. When Chrysler closed its third shift, more than 1,000 employees were thrown out of work. Returning to construction work was not an option because home building in the Rockford, Illinois, area had slowed dramatically and offered few jobs.

At age 29, Chad Smith is back in the classroom as part of a federal retraining program. He is studying software development and computer networking at Rock Valley College, a community college in Rockford, Illinois. He enjoys his coursework and is already thinking about earning a bachelor's degree: "I love school, because I've seen the other side."

Chad Smith and his wife Brandi are making ends meet with his unemployment checks and her part-time job as a nurse at a local hospital. Brandi is now the breadwinner and assumes responsibility for the family's health insurance.[1]

As the United States shifts toward a service economy, many new jobs cannot match the wages workers once earned in factories. The recent economic downturn has forced many people to defer dreams of striking a better work-life balance.

Sally Ryan for The Wall Street Journal

After graduation from high school, Chad Smith landed a well-paying construction job. Later, he began working the night shift at a Chrysler assembly plant. When employment opportunities in both of these areas disappeared, he decided it was time to go back to school.

Achieving Balance in a Chaotic World

In this chapter, we help you construct a life plan that will enhance your relationships with people in your personal life and in your work life. This plan will also help you to better manage the relationship you have with yourself. We discuss the meaning of success and suggest ways to cope with major disappointments that will surface in your work life. You will learn how to avoid being trapped by a lifestyle that offers financial rewards but little else. This chapter also helps you define your relationship with money and describes four nonfinancial resources that give meaning to life. Finally, you will learn how to develop the mental and physical fitness needed to keep up in today's frantic, fast-paced world.

Redefining Our Work Lives

In Chapter 1, we noted that the labor market has become a place of churning dislocation caused by the heavy volume of mergers, acquisitions, business closings, bankruptcies, and downsizings. We also noted that changing work patterns have created new opportunities and new challenges. Millions of American workers are self-employed, working as independent consultants, contractors, landscape gardeners, and financial consultants. Thousands of new small business firms have created rewarding careers for owners and their employees.

It is important to visualize a future filled with sharp detours and several redefinitions of our work lives. Tom Peters, noted author and consultant, was one of the first observers to recognize that a typical career path is no longer linear and is not always upward. He says, "It's more like a maze, full of hidden turns, zigs, and zags that go in all sorts of directions—even backwards sometimes, when that makes sense."[2] The dream of finding job security and knowing that we have "arrived" is obsolete.

Toward a New Definition of Success

Most of us have been conditioned to define success in narrow terms. Too frequently we judge our own success, and the success of others, by what is accomplished at work. Successful people are described as those who have a "good job," "make good money," or have "reached the top" in their field. Bill George, author of books entitled *True North* and *Authentic Leadership*, suggests we forge an *integrated life* that blends work with such things as family, friends, community service, exercise, church, and whatever else matters in your life.[3]

From early childhood on, many people are taught to equate success with pay increases and promotions. Too often, unfortunately, people who try to achieve these career goals are forced to give up everything else that gives purpose and meaning to their lives. Po Bronson, author of *What Should I Do with My Life?*, says more people need to search for work they are passionate about. His best-selling book profiles 55 people who struggled to find their calling. One of the persons he interviewed was Ann Miyhares, a Cuban-American who made her family proud by becoming a senior vice president at a bank but lost their respect when she exchanged her banking career for that of a social worker.[4]

From early childhood on, many people are taught to equate success with pay increases and promotions.

> ### *Total Person Insight*
>
> **Joan Gurvis**
> Co-Author, *Finding Your Balance*
>
> *"Having employees whose work and personal lives are balanced has tangible benefits—both for the employees and the organization overall—including an increased ability to attract and retain skilled people and higher production, satisfaction, and morale."*[5]

The Need for New Models of Success

In recent years, a growing number of people are angry, disillusioned, and frustrated because they have had to abruptly change their career plans. They gave their best efforts, worked long hours, and then the company eliminated their jobs. A variety of economic, social, and demographic forces have combined to create a high level of career distress among all age groups. Young workers, often burdened with student loans, face the prospect of being unemployed or underemployed. Older workers, nearing retirement, have seen the value of their 401 (k)s decrease by as much as 50 percent. Many of these baby boomers are postponing retirement, thus creating a "gray ceiling" that impedes the advancement of younger workers.

One-Dimensional Model. The traditional success model defined success almost exclusively in terms of work life. The model emphasized working long hours, reaching work-related goals, and meeting standards often set by others.

"I really didn't enjoy working five days a week, fifty weeks a year for forty years, but I needed the money."

The old model of success required us to be "one-dimensional" people for whom work is the single dimension. In the life of such a person, everything that has meaning seems to be connected to the job. When a person defines himself or herself by a job and then loses that job, what does that person have left? Of course, the loss of a job encourages some people to search for meaning beyond their work.

Total-Person Model. Some of the most successful organizations in America create a culture that satisfies both personal and work-related needs. They realize the ideal work environment embraces the *total person* (see Chapter 1).

When Jeff Soderberg founded Software Technology Group (*http://www.stgutah.com*), a technology consulting business based in Salt Lake City, he created a new model of success. His company provides employees with plenty of time to have a life. He does not believe there is a correlation between time spent at work and success. He refuses to hire workaholics, and, in an industry where 80-hour workweeks are common, he tells new hires, "We expect a 40-hour workweek." Soderberg sets a good example by frequently taking time off during the week to enjoy rock climbing in the nearby canyons.[6]

Zappos.com has been described as an e-commerce juggernaut—the decade's most innovative start-up. The company started in 1999 as an online shoe store and has since expanded into a wide range of goods. Tony Hsieh, founder of Zappos.com, makes a lot of money, but that is not his goal in life. He wants to unlock the secrets of human happiness, and his company is his research center. His single-minded focus on happiness has resulted in several "best places to work" awards. The 1,300 employees of Zappos have great admiration for the company and Tony Hsieh. Hsieh is not buying his employees' loyalty. The average hourly worker earns just more than $23,000 a year, and they do not receive the perks offered by many companies.[7]

Loss of Leisure Time

Throughout history, Americans have burdened themselves with a very demanding work ethic. They spend more time on the job than employees in any other industrialized nation. What's more, downsizing efforts have left fewer people to do the same amount of work; therefore, many people are working even harder. Most of these workers yearn for more leisure time. U.S. workers not only work long hours, but they spend less time on vacation than do workers in most other industrialized countries.

Developing Your Own Life Plan

The goal of this chapter is to help you develop a life plan for effective relationships with yourself and others. The information presented thus far has, we hope, stimulated your thinking about the need for a life plan. We have noted that personal life can seldom be separated from work life. The two are very much intertwined. We have also suggested that it is important for you to develop your own definition of success. Too frequently, people allow others (parents, teachers, counselors, a spouse) to define success for them. Finally, as you begin work on your life plan, keep in mind the following advice from Jack Canfield, author of *The Success Principles:*

> *If you want to be successful, you have to take 100% responsibility for everything that you experience in your life. This includes the level of your achievements, the results you produce, the quality of your relationships, the state of your health and physical fitness, your income, your debts, your feelings—everything!*[8]

Because work is such an important part of life, we will now move to a discussion of items that will help you in your career planning. We will discuss the concept of "right livelihood."

CRITICAL THINKING CHALLENGE:

Analyze It

For most people, true success is a combination of achievements. These achievements might relate to such things as leisure time, earnings, job status, health, or relationships. On a piece of paper, describe your personal definition of success.

Toward Right Livelihood

Ann Rea studied fine arts in college. She enjoyed painting and drawing but put those interests aside in order to pursue a career in information technology. This was a practical choice because jobs in this field were available. However, IT work was not rewarding. While working as an IT project management consultant in Davis, California, she met pop artist Wayne Thibaud, who urged her to start

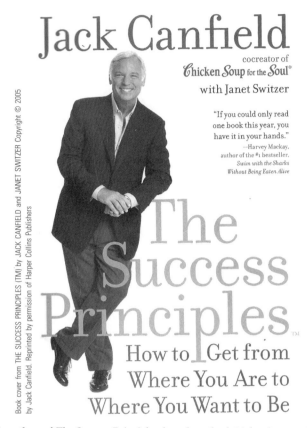

Jack Canfield, author of *The Success Principles,* has described 64 fundamentals of success in his best-selling book. These timeless principles have been used by successful men and women throughout history.

painting again. Later, she worked on another project management job under the supervision of a terrible boss, a "real jerk" in her words. That experience motivated her to try to make a living as a painter. Today she is widely known for her paintings of California vineyards.[9]

Ann Rea, like many other people, has been searching for "right livelihood." The concept of right livelihood is described in the core teachings of Buddhism.[10] In recent years, the concept has been described by Michael Phillips in his book *The Seven Laws of Money* and by Marsha Sinetar in her book *Do What You Love … The Money Will Follow.* **Right livelihood** is work consciously chosen, done with full awareness and care, and leading to enlightenment. Barbara Sher, contributor to *New Age* magazine, says right livelihood means that you wake up in the morning and spend all day working at something you really want to do.[11]

For Stephen Lyons, the search for right livelihood began when he fell on hard times—divorce, unemployment, and bankruptcy. He came from a family of blue-collar tradesmen, none of whom had attended college. He trained as an electrician and had steady work until a recession created large-scale unemployment in the San Francisco area. Finally, he convinced a small college that he could repair their cranky air-conditioning system and ended up with a job and

After graduating from the Cleveland Institute of Art, Ann Rea embarked on a "practical" career in investments and IT project management. After seven miserable years, time spent mostly in corporate cubicles, she opted for a major career makeover and started painting full time.

the opportunity to earn a business degree at the school. With more education, he felt confident to start a business installing home solar-power systems. Creating renewable energy has turned out to be a form of right livelihood for Lyons.[12]

There are three characteristics to right livelihood: choice, emphasis on more than money, and personal growth.

Right Livelihood Is Based on Conscious Choice

Marsha Sinetar says, "When the powerful quality of conscious choice is present in our work, we can be enormously productive."[13] She points out that many people have learned to act on what others say, value, and expect and thus find conscious choice very difficult:

> *It takes courage to act on what we value and to willingly accept the consequences of our choices. Being able to choose means not allowing fear to inhibit or control us, even though our choices may require us to act against our fears or against the wishes of those we love and admire.*[14]

To make the best choices, you must first figure out what you like to do, as well as what you are good at doing—your strengths. What you like doing most is often not obvious. It may take some real effort to discover what really motivates you. Students often get help from career counselors or explore a career option during a summer internship. If you are employed, consider joining a temporary project team. A team assignment provides an opportunity to work with persons who perform very different types of duties. You might also consider reassignment within your organization.

Right Livelihood Places Money in a Secondary Position

People who embrace right livelihood accept that money and security are not the primary rewards in life. Michael Phillips explained that "right livelihood has within itself its own rewards; it deepens the person who practices it."[15] For example, people who work in the social services usually do not earn large amounts of money, but many of them receive a great deal of personal satisfaction from their work. You may need to trade some income for self-expression, mental rewards, or some other form of personal satisfaction. Ann Rea, painter, may not make large sums of money as a painter, but the work provides enormous personal satisfaction.

Many people who once viewed success in terms of wealth, material possessions, and status are realizing that something is missing from their lives. They do not *feel* successful. They once felt pressured to "have it all" but now feel disappointed that their achievements have not brought them real happiness.

Right Livelihood Recognizes That Work Is a Vehicle for Personal Growth

Most of us spend from 40 to 60 hours each week at work. Ideally, we should not have to squelch our real abilities, ignore our personal goals, and forget our need for stimulation and personal growth during the time we spend at work.[16] Most employees know intuitively that work should fulfill their need for self-expression and personal growth, but this message has not been embraced by many leaders. Too few organizations truly empower workers and give them a sense of purpose. When employees feel that the company's success is their own success, they will be more enthusiastic about their work.

The search for right livelihood should begin with a thoughtful review of your values. The values clarification process (see Table 5.1) should be completed *before* you interview for a job. Frank Harrington spent 13 years climbing the ranks at a California-based semiconductor maker. Throughout that period, he gradually realized he hated his job, so he changed careers. Preparing for a new career took years, but today he is a nurse and much happier.[17]

Most employees know intuitively that work should fulfill their need for self-expression and personal growth, but this message has not been embraced by many leaders.

When a job fails to fulfill your expectations, consider changing jobs, changing assignments, or changing careers. If the job is not right for you, your body and your mind will begin sending you messages. When you begin feeling that something is lacking, try to answer these basic questions: What is making me feel this way? What, exactly, about my current position is unpleasant? Choosing a satisfying career and lifestyle requires understanding what contributes to your job satisfaction. Self-exploration and continual evaluation of your needs, goals, and job satisfaction are important. Don't wait for a crisis (layoff) to clear your vision.[18]

Total Person Insight

Pamela York Klainer
Founder, *Power and Money LLC*

"Plain talk about our experiences with money remains the last taboo to break in our society.... Part of becoming an effective, happy person is making old money messages current and bringing hidden money messages out into the open."[19]

Defining Your Relationship with Money

Money is a compelling force in the lives of most people. It often influences the selection of a career and the commitment we make to achieve success in that career. Sometimes we struggle to achieve a certain economic goal only to discover that once we got what we wanted, it did not fulfill us in the way we had hoped. Money does not create or sustain happiness. Happiness comes from social relationships, enjoyable work, fulfillment, a sense that life has meaning, and membership in civic and other groups.[20]

The way we choose to earn, save, and spend our money determines, in large measure, the quality of our lives.

Many people struggle with money management decisions and seem unable to plan for the future. The personal savings rate in America is at a record low, and the household debt burden is at a record high. Many people are ill prepared to cope with the financial drain that comes with the loss of one's job or a serious health problem that is not covered by medical insurance. We are also a nation of hyperconsumers, "living way beyond our means and seemingly helpless to save ourselves," according to Geoffrey Colvin, senior editor of *Fortune* magazine.[21]

True Prosperity. The way we choose to earn, save, and spend our money determines, in large measure, the quality of our lives. For example, if you think that having *more* money is going to produce happiness or peace of mind, will you ever earn enough? Shakti Gawain, author of *Creating True Prosperity*, says that more money does not necessarily bring greater freedom, fewer problems, or security. Rather, "prosperity is the experience of having plenty of what we truly need and want in life, material and otherwise." Gawain says, "The key point to understand is that prosperity is an *internal* experience, not an *external* state, and it is an experience that is not tied to having a certain amount of money."[22] Many of us go through life unconscious of our own real needs and desires. We must learn to predict more accurately what will give us lasting pleasure instead of short-term pleasure.[23] How do we do this? Steven Reiss (see Chapter 7) says that nearly everything we experience as meaningful can be traced to one of sixteen basic desires or to some combination of those desires (see Figure 7.1). Now would be a good time to revisit this list of basic desires and identify the five or six that seem most important to you. This review may help you understand your relationship with money.

Mature Money Management. Many people do not have a mature relationship with money. They spend everything they earn and more, and then they have bouts of financial anxiety. People who are deep in debt often experience symptoms of depression. Money issues continue to be the number one cause of divorce in the United States.[24] Space does not permit a comprehensive examination of money management, but here are some important suggestions from Jonathan Clements, an expert on financial planning:[25]

- *Develop a personal financial plan.* With a financial plan, you are more likely to achieve your financial goals. A key element of your plan is determining where your income is going. With a simple record-keeping system, you can determine how much you spend each month on food, housing, clothing, transportation, and other things. Search for spending patterns you may want to change.
- *Spend less than you earn.* Many people constantly strive to raise their standard of living by purchasing a better car, a bigger house, or expensive clothes. Academics refer to this as the *hedonic treadmill.* Credit comes easy, so its hard to discipline yourself against going into debt. The cost of credit is often much more than we realize. A three-year auto loan (for a $35,195 loan) at a 5.89 percent rate has $3,287 in financing costs. Extend this loan to five years, and the financing cost will exceed $5,000.[26]
- *Maintain a cash cushion.* If you lost your job today, how long could you live on your current cash reserves? Financial consultants suggest that cash reserves should be equal to the amount you earn during a two- or three-month period.

Achieving Wedded Bliss. Many people do not think about financial compatibility before or after marriage. When couples talk about financial issues and problems, the result is usually less conflict and smarter financial decisions. David Bach, author of several books on financial planning, helps couples achieve financial compatibility. He has the partners start by writing down what is most important to each of them—their five top values. They are also instructed to write down what the purpose of money is. He says, "Smart financial planning is more than a matter of numbers; it involves values first and stuff second."[27]

HUMAN RELATIONS IN ACTION

Painless Ways to Save

Let's assume you have decided to develop a three-year savings plan for a major purchase. The following "incidental expenses" provide some saving options.

	SAVINGS
Take lunch to work three days per week and save $6.50 per day.	$3,000
Rent your movies instead of going to the theater.	$450
Skip the coffee shop and brew your own at home.	$4,000
Buy frozen gourmet pizza instead of ordering delivery.	$1,500
Total Savings	$8,950[28]

> ### *Total Person Insight*
> **Julie Connelly**
> Contributing Editor, *Fortune*
>
> *"Keep in mind that there is no harder work than thinking—really thinking—about who you are and what you want out of life. Figuring out where your goals and your skills match up is a painful, time-consuming process."*[29]

Defining Your Nonfinancial Resources

If you become totally focused on your financial resources, then chances are you have ignored your **nonfinancial resources**. And it is often the nonfinancial resources that make the biggest contribution to a happy and fulfilling life. A strong argument can be made that the real wealth in life comes in the form of good health, peace of mind, time spent with family and friends, learning (which develops the mind), and healthy spirituality. Paul Hwoschinsky, author of *True Wealth*, makes this observation about nonfinancial resources: "If you are clear about who you are, and clear about what you want to do, and bring your financial and nonfinancial resources together, it's extraordinary what can happen. I encourage people to really honor their total resources, and magical things happen. New options occur."[30]

If you focus most or all of your attention on work and you suffer a major work-related disappointment, then the result is likely to be feelings of depression and despair. Thoughts such as "Now I have lost everything" can surface when you fail to get a promotion, find out that you were not selected to be a member of a special project team, or learn that your job has been eliminated. But if you fully understand the power of your nonfinancial resources, then work-related disappointments are easier to cope with. The starting point is to realize that *most* of your resources are nonfinancial. During periods of great uncertainty, it is especially important that you think about your nonfinancial assets and consider ways to enhance them. We briefly discuss four nonfinancial resources that can enrich your life: physical and mental health, education and training (intellectual growth), leisure time (time for family, socializing, recreation), and healthy spirituality (see Figure 17.1).

Physical and Mental Health

Is the statement "Health means wealth" just a worn-out cliché, or is this slogan a message of inspiration for people who want to get more out of life? If good health is such an important nonfinancial asset, then why are so many people flirting with self-destruction by eating the wrong foods, drinking too much, exercising too little, and generally choosing unhealthy lifestyles? The answer to the second question may be lack of awareness of the benefits of physical fitness. Here are a few benefits of a modest exercise program.[31]

- There is an interrelationship between health and outlook on life. For example, when the physical body is fit, toned, and strong, this condition has a positive effect on the mind. We are more likely to experience higher levels of self-esteem, feel a greater sense of self-confidence, and have a more positive outlook on life.

FIGURE 17.1 Put Balance in Your Life

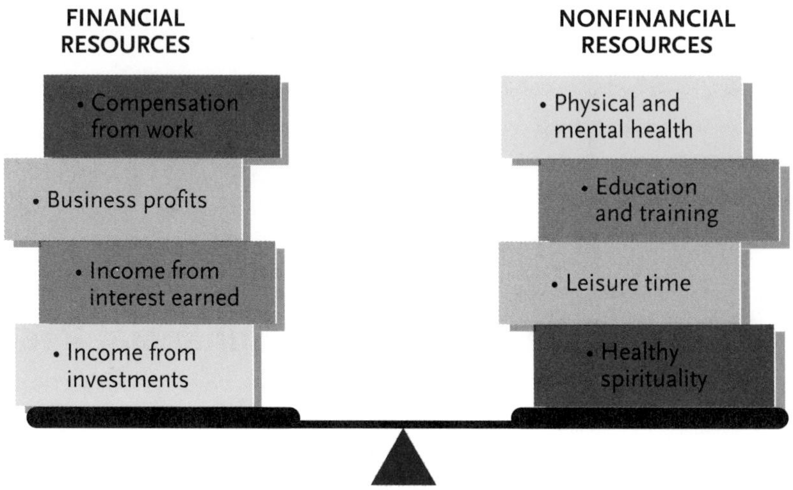

- Regular exercise and a healthy diet produce greater mental clarity, a higher energy level, and a more youthful appearance. Even low-intensity exercise such as walking can result in weight loss and reduction in the death rate from coronary artery disease and stroke.

More than 80 percent of the companies with 50 employees have wellness programs. Healthy employees file fewer insurance claims and are less likely to call in sick.[32] Increasingly, incentives are being used to encourage employee participation in various programs.

Education and Training (Intellectual Growth)

The New Economy thrives on a well-educated and well-trained work force. It rewards workers who take personal responsibility for their learning. The need to continually update, train, and develop yourself involves becoming a *career activist*, someone who writes your own script rather than waiting for someone else to write it for you.[33]

- *Think of yourself as a unique brand.* In Chapter 11, we noted that branding can play a crucial role in your career success. Developing a strong personal brand requires giving attention to several things, one of which is staying competent. To do this you must clarify, confirm, and build your strengths (see Chapter 4). The authors of *What Every Successful Woman Knows* say, "Build your brand and toot your own horn—a lot."[34]
- *Be selective in what you learn.* Learning often requires large amounts of time and energy, so consider carefully what knowledge or skill will generate the most improvement.
- *Take advantage of various learning pathways.* It helps to think of your job as a learning resource. Take full advantage of instructional programs offered by your employer. Volunteer for team assignments that will provide new learning opportunities. Peter Senge, author of *The Fifth Discipline*, says the fundamental learning unit in any organization is a team.[35] And look outside the company at community college classes or programs offered by Toastmasters, Dale Carnegie, or other organizations.

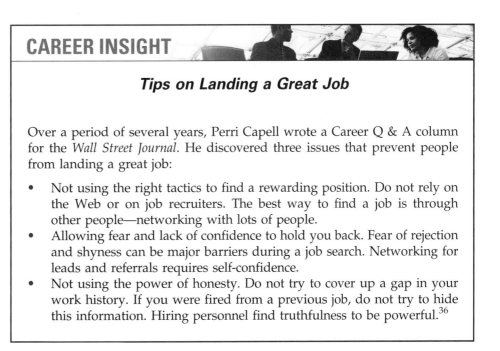

CAREER INSIGHT

Tips on Landing a Great Job

Over a period of several years, Perri Capell wrote a Career Q & A column for the *Wall Street Journal*. He discovered three issues that prevent people from landing a great job:

- Not using the right tactics to find a rewarding position. Do not rely on the Web or on job recruiters. The best way to find a job is through other people—networking with lots of people.
- Allowing fear and lack of confidence to hold you back. Fear of rejection and shyness can be major barriers during a job search. Networking for leads and referrals requires self-confidence.
- Not using the power of honesty. Do not try to cover up a gap in your work history. If you were fired from a previous job, do not try to hide this information. Hiring personnel find truthfulness to be powerful.[36]

Leisure Time

Leisure time can provide an opportunity to relax, get rid of work-related stress, get some exercise, spend time with family and friends, or simply read a good book. Many people cherish leisure time but experience schedule creep. *Schedule creep* is the tendency of work to expand beyond the normal work schedule and replace available leisure time. It often surfaces in small symptoms—an extra hour or two here, a weekend worked there.[37]

If you are working for a workaholic, someone who may have given up all or most of his or her leisure time, you may be pressured to work at the same pace. If your boss is constantly trying to meet impossible deadlines and deal with last-minute rushes, you may feel the need to give up time for recreation or family. If this happens, try to identify the consequences of being overworked. Look at the situation from all points of view. If you refuse to work longer hours, what will be the consequences for your relationship with the boss, your relationship with other employees, or your future with the organization?[38]

Is it worth taking some risks to protect the leisure time you now have? Should you increase the amount of leisure time available in your life? Consider the following benefits of leisure time:

- As we noted previously in this text, maintaining social connections with friends and family can be good for your health. A growing number of studies show that if you have strong and fulfilling relationships, you may live longer, decrease your chances of becoming sick, and cope more successfully when illness strikes.[39] Time spent with friends and family can be a powerful source of mental and physical renewal.
- One of the best ways to feel satisfied about your work is to get away from it when you begin to feel worn out. People who take time off from work often return with new ideas, a stronger focus, and increased energy. When you

discover that end-of-the-week exhaustion is still hanging around Monday morning, it is time to take some vacation or personal days.[40]

- A growing body of research indicates that the American trend toward skipping vacations is hazardous. People who skip vacations have a higher risk of death from heart disease and other serious health problems.[41]
- Find some quiet time for yourself each day. You might use it to meditate, take the dog for a walk, or just sit quietly. Use this time to nourish yourself and bring balance to your life.

If you want more leisure time, then you must establish your priorities and set your goals. This may mean saying no to endless requests to work overtime or rejecting a promotion. Sometimes you must pull back from the endless demands of work and "get a life."

Healthy Spirituality

Healthy spirituality is receiving greater attention in education and in the workplace. More business and professional schools are offering courses dealing with spirituality and *personal fulfillment*. Patricia Aburdene, author of *Megatrends 2010*, says the number one megatrend is spirituality. She defines a megatrend as the large, overarching direction that shapes our lives. Aburdene explains how integrity, trust, doing good deeds, and giving back can translate into high performance and healthy profits.[42]

Spirituality can be defined as an inner attitude that emphasizes energy, creative choice, and a powerful force for living. It involves opening our hearts and cultivating our capacity to experience reverence and gratitude. It frees us to become positive, caring human beings.[43]

Spirituality encompasses faith, which can be described as what your heart tells you is true when your mind cannot prove it. For some people, faith exists within the framework of a formal religion; for others, it rests on a series of personal beliefs such as "Give others the same consideration, regard, kindness, and gentleness that you would like them to accord you."[44] Many people think of spirituality as a remote, abstract concept. But traditional teachings suggest that spirituality is directly connected to the most ordinary human activities.[45]

An understanding of the many aspects of spirituality can give us an expanded vision of what it means to be human. Although spirituality is often associated with religion, it should be viewed in broader terms. Robert Coles, of Harvard Medical School, likes a definition of spirituality given to him by an 11-year-old girl:

> *I think you're spiritual if you can escape from yourself a little and think of what's good for everyone, not just you, and if you can reach out and be a good person—I mean live like a good person. You're not spiritual if you just talk spiritual and there's no action. You're a fake if that's what you do.*[46]

An understanding of the many aspects of spirituality can give us an expanded vision of what it means to be human.

The words of this young girl remind us that one dimension of spirituality involves showing concern and compassion for others. Thomas Moore, author of the best selling book *Care of the Soul*, says, "To be spiritual means to mature to a point beyond limited self-interest and anxiety about self."[47] Healthy spirituality involves acts of generosity, sharing, and kindness.

Total Person Insight

THE DALAI LAMA
Co-Author, *The Art of Happiness*

"Spirituality I take to be concerned with those qualities of human spirit—such as love and compassion, patience, tolerance, forgiveness, contentment, a sense of responsibility, a sense of harmony—which bring happiness to both self and others."[48]

Spirituality at Work. In many ways, large and small, work can be made more spiritual. The philosophy of Worthington Industries is expressed in a single sentence: "We treat our employees as we would like to be treated."[49] Herr Foods Inc. promises, "An atmosphere that enhances the moral and spiritual integrity of each individual."[50]

Research indicates that the new generation of workers, Generation Y, will be looking deep inside companies to see what makes them tick. The person with a passion for environmental issues will be drawn to companies like outdoor apparel maker Patagonia, which contributes 1 percent of sales to environmental causes.[51]

Many activities can be considered spiritual. Visiting an art gallery, listening to a concert, or walking near the ocean can stimulate healthy spirituality. Table 17.1 describes some ways to begin your journey to healthy spirituality.

For many people, a commitment to a specific religion is an important dimension of spirituality. Active membership in a religious group provides an opportunity to clarify spiritual values and achieve spiritual direction. It also provides social connections—an extended family that you can depend on for social support.[52]

Total Person Insight

T. BOONE PICKENS
Chairman, BP Capital Management

"I encourage every one of my employees to get fit. We have nearly 100 percent participation in our corporate wellness program. Our $2.5 million gym nearly paid for itself in healthcare savings. Even at 80, I'm no exception."[53]

Developing a Healthy Lifestyle

Earlier in this chapter, we noted that a healthy lifestyle can provide a higher energy level, a greater sense of self-confidence, and, generally, a more positive outlook on life. People who maintain good health usually have more endurance, spend less time feeling tired or ill, and miss less work than persons who are not healthy. Good health is receiving greater attention today because many Americans are investing more time and energy in their work. They are being asked to work longer hours and to do more in less time. Good health can help combat stress and tension at work and at home. In this section, we offer guidelines that form the framework for a good diet and a good exercise program.

TABLE 17.1 WAYS TO ACHIEVE HEALTHY SPIRITUALITY

As interest in healthy spirituality grows, people are searching for ways to become more spiritual. The following spiritual practices draw our focus away from ourselves and the anxieties in our lives.

- *Meditation* Oprah Winfrey described the powerful influence of meditation this way: "There is no greater source of strength and power for me in my life now, than going still, being quiet, and recognizing what real power is." (See Chapter 14 for a step-by-step guide to meditation.)
- *Prayer* Dr. Larry Dossey, physician and author of numerous books on the role of spirituality in medicine, says prayer can be a powerful force in our lives. Prayer groups have been established at many organizations.
- *Spiritual Reading* In addition to sacred readings, consider *Healing and the Mind* by Bill Moyers, *The Soul of a Business* by Tom Chappell, and *The Hungry Spirit* by Charles Handy.
- *Time with Nature* Spiritual contemplation during a walk in the woods or a visit to a quiet lake can help us balance mind, body, and spirit.

Sources: David Elkins and Amanda Druckman, "Four Great Ways to Begin Your Spiritual Journey," *Psychology Today*, September/October 1999, p. 46; Larry Dossey, M.D., "Can We Change the World?" *The Inner Edge*, June/July 2000, pp. 22–23.

Guidelines for a Healthy Diet

Eating the right foods can improve your health, boost your energy level, and, in some cases, extend your life. We will review several important dietary guidelines.

Maintain a Diet That Is Balanced and Varied. The U.S. Department of Agriculture (USDA) published the MyPyramid, an individualized approach to improving diet and lifestyle (see Figure 17.2). A new USDA website (*http://www.mypyramid.gov*) allows consumers to enter their age, sex, and activity level and get back a tailored personal diet. For example, here are the daily recommendations for a 30-year-old female who gets less than 30 minutes of exercise a day:

Grains	6 ounces	(Make half your grains whole.)
Vegetables	2.5 cups	(Vary your veggies.)
Fruits	1.5 cups	(Select fruits for meals and snacks.)
Milk Products	3 cups	(Consume milk, yogurt, and cheese.)
Meat & Beans	5 ounces	(Go lean with protein.)
Oils	5 teaspoons	(Select healthy oils.)

This customized plan is based on an estimated requirement of 1,800 calories a day. Everyone should monitor their body weight to determine whether they need to adjust calorie intake.[54]

Eating a variety of foods is important because you need more than forty different nutrients for good health: vitamins and minerals, amino acids (from

FIGURE 17.2 U.S. Department of Agriculture's MyPyramid

Note: The MyPyramid has six vertical stripes, each one representing a different food group. The width of each band suggests how much food a person should choose from each group.

Source: United States Department of Agriculture.

proteins), essential fatty acids (from fats and oils), and sources of energy (calories from carbohydrates, fats, and proteins). The number of servings you need each day depends on your total calorie intake. The type of foods you eat is also very important. Whole grains should be substituted for refined grains, and dark greens such as broccoli and kale represent a preferred vegetable food group. These foods help reduce the risk of developing diabetes and heart disease and help with weight maintenance.

Reduce Calorie Intake. More than 65 percent of Americans are overweight, and these added pounds increase the risk of heart disease, cancer, and diabetes. Inactivity combined with diets high in calories, salt, and fats can result in serious health problems. Americans are putting on extra pounds much earlier and faster than they did in previous generations. Control of weight is fundamentally simple—*calories in versus calories out*. If you eat 100 more calories a day than you burn, you gain about one pound in a month, or, about ten pounds in a year.[55] Recent research conducted by the National Institute of Health indicated that reduced-calorie diets can be a very effective weight-loss regimen.[56]

Cut Down on Fatty Foods. The foods that are popular with many Americans are relatively high in fat, especially saturated fat, which contributes to high blood cholesterol levels. Many restaurant foods are high in fat because it gives menu items the flavor people often seek when eating out. A large tuna melt at Quiznos has 2,090 calories and 175 grams of fat.[57] Heart disease and certain kinds of cancer are byproducts of foods that contain highly saturated fats. Avoid foods that

TABLE 17.2 LOW-FAT SNACK CHOICES

	SATURATED FAT (GRAMS)	SODIUM (MILLIGRAMS)	CALORIES
Quaker Lightly Salted Rice Cakes	0	15	35
Barbara's Rite Lite Rounds (crackers)	0	200	70
Healthy Choice Microwave Popcorn	1.5	140	100
Mariani Sweetened Dried Cranberries	0	0	100

Note: Read labels carefully. Be sure to notice the portion sizes and be realistic about what you actually consume.

Source: University of California, *Berkeley Wellness Letter*, May 2001, p. 6; The Quaker Oats Company, Chicago, Ill. Barbara's Bakery, Petaluma, CA; Mariani Packing Company, Vacaville, CA.

include partially hydrogenated oils—better known as *trans fats*. These artery-clogging fats can be very harmful to your health.

Eat Foods with Adequate Starch and Fiber. Foods high in starch, such as breads made with whole grains, dry beans and peas, and potatoes, contain many essential nutrients. High-fiber diets can help reduce the odds of getting cancer of the colon. Some cereals and most fruits and vegetables are good sources of fiber.

Avoid Too Much Sodium. A common byproduct of excess sodium is high blood pressure. In the United States, where sodium-rich diets are very common, the average person consumes about 3,400 milligrams of sodium each day—well beyond the 2,300 milligrams recommended by the U.S. Dietary Guidelines.[58] Table 17.2 includes some examples of foods that are low in sodium and saturated fats.

If You Drink Alcohol, Do So in Moderation. Alcoholic beverages are high in calories and low in nutrients and cause serious health risks when used in excess. Excessive alcohol consumption has been linked to liver damage, certain types of cancer, and high blood pressure.

With the help of these healthy diet guidelines, you can develop your own plan for achieving a healthful diet. Keep in mind that good nutrition is a balancing act. You want to select foods with enough vitamins, minerals, protein, and fiber but avoid too much fat and sodium. You want to consume enough calories to maintain the energy level required in your life but avoid weight gain.

Improving Your Physical Fitness

"Sedentary living is so dangerous that it is simply not an option." This is the conclusion of research conducted at Duke University. An inactive life style (sedentary sickness) results in an array of risk factors such as weight gain, increases in bad cholesterol and blood sugar levels.[59]

Physical fitness can be defined as the ability to perform daily tasks vigorously and have enough energy left over to enjoy leisure activities. It is the ability to endure difficult and stressful experiences and still carry on. Physical fitness, which involves the performance of the lungs, heart, and muscles, can also have a positive influence on mental alertness and emotional stability. Research indicates that even a moderate level of physical activity can have a surprisingly broad array of health benefits on virtually every major organ system in the body.[60] For most people, a program that involves regular physical activity at least three or four times a week and includes sustained physical exertion for 30 to 35 minutes during each activity period is adequate.[61] This modest investment of time and energy will give you a longer and healthier life.

To achieve lifesaving benefits from exercise, start slowly with an aerobic fitness activity you feel you will enjoy. Walking, swimming, running, low-impact aerobics, and jogging are aerobic exercise. When we engage in aerobic exercise, the body is required to improve its ability to handle oxygen.[62] These exercises strengthen the heart, burn up calories, increase stamina, and help release tension.

If you are younger than 35 and in good health, you probably do not need to see a doctor before beginning an exercise program. If you are older than 35 and have been inactive for several years, consult your doctor before engaging in vigorous exercise.[63]

Skill Development: Apply It

A major purpose of this chapter is to help you create a plan for effective relationships with yourself and others. Take time to reflect on your life and identify the specific behaviors that you want to develop. List these behaviors on a piece of paper and then describe when and how you will develop these behaviors.

Planning for Changes in Your Life

Throughout this book, we have emphasized the concept that you can control your own behavior. In fact, during these turbulent times, changes in your behavior may be one of the few things under your control. What are some behaviors you can adopt (or alter) that will make an important positive change in your life? Once you have identified these behaviors, you can set goals and do what is necessary to achieve them.

At the end of Chapter 1, you were encouraged to complete the Human Relations Abilities Assessment (HRAA) Form that is on your textbook website. If you completed this form, then you no doubt gained awareness of your strengths and a better understanding of the abilities you want to improve. Now would be a good time to complete the form a second time and determine if your *Xs* have moved to the right on the various scales. Completion of the HRAA Form will help you identify the behaviors you want to change.

The Power of Habits

Before we discuss specific goal-setting methods, let us take a look at the powerful influence of habits. Some habits, like taking a long walk three or four times a week, can have a positive influence on our well-being. Simply saying "Thank you" when someone does a favor or pays a compliment can be a habit. Other habits, such as smoking, never saying no to requests for your time, feeling jealous, or constantly engaging in self-criticism, are negative forces in our lives. Stephen Covey, author of *The 7 Habits of Highly Effective People*, makes this observation: "Habits are powerful factors in our lives. Because they are consistent, often unconscious patterns, they constantly, daily, express our character and produce our effectiveness … or ineffectiveness."[64]

Breaking deeply embedded habits, such as impatience, procrastination, or criticism of others, can take a tremendous amount of effort. The influences supporting the habit, the actual root causes, are often repressed in the subconscious mind and forgotten.[65] How do you break a negative habit or form a positive habit? The process involves five steps.

Motivation. Once you are aware of the need to change, you must develop the willingness or desire to change. After making a major commitment to change, you must find ways to maintain your motivation. The key to staying motivated is to develop a mind-set powerful enough that you feel compelled to act on your desire to change.

Knowledge. Once you clearly understand the benefits of breaking a habit or forming a new one, you must acquire the knowledge you need to change. Seek information, ask for advice, or learn from the experiences of others. This may involve finding a mentor, joining a group, or gathering sufficient material and teaching yourself.

Practice. Information is only as useful as you make it. This means that to change your behavior you must *practice* what you have learned. If you are a shy person, does this mean you need to volunteer to make a speech in front of several hundred people? The answer is no. Although there is always the rare individual who makes a major change seemingly overnight, most people find that the best and surest way to develop a new behavior is to do so gradually.

Feedback. Whenever you can, seek feedback as you attempt to change a habit. Dieters lose more weight if they attend counseling sessions and weigh-ins. People who want to improve their public speaking skills benefit from practice followed by feedback from a teacher or coach. Everyone has blind spots, particularly when trying something new.

Reinforcement. When you see yourself exhibiting the type of behavior you have been working to develop—or when someone mentions that you have changed—reward yourself! The rewards can be simple, inexpensive ones—treating yourself to a movie, a bouquet of flowers, a favorite meal, or a special event. This type of reinforcement is vital when you are trying to improve old behaviors or develop new ones.

The Goal-Setting Process

Goals should be an integral part of your plan to break old habits or form new ones. You will need an assortment of goals that address the different needs of your life. After a period of serious reflection, you may be facing many goal-setting possibilities. Where do you begin? We hope that reading the previous chapters in this book, completing the HRAA Form, and reviewing the material in this chapter will help you narrow the possibilities.

The goal-setting process was described in Chapter 4. The major principles of goal setting are outlined in Table 4.1. These time-tested principles can help you achieve any realistic goal.

The Choice is Yours

Are you ready to develop a life plan for effective human relations? We hope the answer is yes. One of the positive aspects of personal planning is that you are making your own choices. You decide what kind of person you want to be and then set your own standards and goals. The results can mean not only career advancement and financial benefits, but also the development of strong, satisfying relationships with others. These relationships may be the key to future opportunities, and you in turn, may be able to help others reach their goals.

In the opening chapter of this text, we talked about the total person approach to human relations. By now, we hope you realize that you are someone special! You have a unique combination of talents, attitudes, values, goals, needs, and motivation—all in a state of development. You can decide to tap your potential to become a successful, productive human being however *you* understand those terms. We hope this book helps you to develop your human relations skills and to become what you want to be. You can turn the theories, concepts, and guidelines presented here into a plan of action for your own life and career. We wish you the best!

LOOKING BACK: REVIEWING THE CONCEPTS

- Learn how to cope with the forces that influence the work/life balance.

The labor market has become a place of great uncertainty due to the heavy volume of mergers, acquisitions, business closings, and downsizing. There is increasing pressure to work harder, work longer hours, and give up more leisure time. Learning how to cope with the forces that influence work/life balance has never been more challenging.

- Define success by standards that are compatible with your needs and values.

The traditional definitions of success that most of us know are too confining. They describe success almost entirely in terms of measurable job achievements. These definitions leave out the intangible successes to be had in private and professional life. Many people today are discovering that true success is a combination of achievements.

- Discuss the meaning of *right livelihood.*

Achieving right livelihood is a very important dimension of success. Right livelihood is work consciously chosen and done with full awareness and care that leads to enlightenment. Right livelihood recognizes that work is a vehicle for self-expression, and places money in a secondary position.

- Describe four nonfinancial resources that can enrich your life.

A person's nonfinancial resources often make the biggest contribution to a happy and fulfilling life. Each of us has four nonfinancial resources that can enrich our lives: physical and mental health, education and training (intellectual growth), leisure time (time for friends and family, socializing, recreation), and healthy spirituality.

- **Provide guidelines for developing a healthy lifestyle.**

Many Americans are working to achieve healthy lifestyles. Healthy lifestyles can give us a higher energy level, a greater sense of self-confidence, and, generally, a more positive outlook. People who maintain good health usually have more endurance, spend less time feeling tired or ill, and miss less work than those who are not physically fit.

- **Develop a plan for making needed changes in your life.**

Planning for changes in your life often requires breaking negative habits or forming positive habits. The process of breaking habits and forming new ones involves five steps: motivation, knowledge, practice, feedback, and reinforcement. Goal setting is also an integral part of a successful plan to make changes. Chapter 4 deals with goal setting in detail.

KEY TERMS

right livelihood 382
nonfinancial resources 387
spirituality 390
physical fitness 395

TRY YOUR HAND

1. The concept of *right livelihood* is based on conscious choice, placing money in a secondary position, and work as a vehicle for personal growth. Take time to reflect on the past six months and evaluate if *right livelihood* principles have guided you in your decision making. If so, discuss the influence of the concept, and if not, evaluate its importance in future decision making.

2. Throughout this chapter you were encouraged to take control of your life and establish your own definition of success. This chapter has a strong "all development is self-development" theme. Can we really control our own destinies? Can we always make our own choices? Mike Hernacki, author of the book *The Ultimate Secret of Getting Absolutely Everything You Want*, says yes:

   > *To get what you want, you must recognize something that at first may be difficult, even painful to look at. You must recognize that* you alone *are the source of all the conditions and situations in your life. You must recognize that whatever your world looks like right now, you alone have caused it to look that way. The state of your health, your finances, your personal relationships, your professional life—all of it is your doing, yours and no one else's.*[66]

   Do you agree with this viewpoint? Take a position in favor of or in opposition to Hernacki's statement. Prepare a short one- or two-paragraph statement that expresses your views.

3. There are many ways to deepen and extend your spirituality. One way is to begin placing a higher value on silence, tranquility, and reflection. If your life is extremely busy, you may not be taking time for thought or reflection. If you are accustomed to living in the presence of noise throughout the day, quiet times may make you feel uncomfortable at first. During a period of one week, set aside a few minutes each day for your own choice of meditation, prayer, contemplation, or reflection. Try to find a quiet place for this activity. At the end of the week, assess the benefits of this activity, and consider the merits of making it part of your daily routine.[67]

INTERNET INSIGHTS

1. At some point in your life, full-time employment will become less appealing. You will begin thinking about part-time work that will give you time to pursue a personal interest,

start a family, become an independent consultant, earn a degree, or simply enjoy more leisure time. Several Internet sites can help you acquire information:

NAME	URL	SERVICES
Aquent	*http://www.aquentpartners.com*	Helps find work for health care, finance, marketing, and other areas.
Manpower	*http://www.manpower.com*	Finds assignments in a wide variety of fields.
Monster	*http://www.monster.com*	Allows searching for jobs by title and location: US or International. Also provides Career Tools: **1.** Career Snapshots: explore your options; **2.** Career Benchmarking: how you compare to your peers; **3.** Career Mapping: helps you understand your options in building your career plan; and **4.** Career Services: speed up your job search.

Visit two of these websites and study the information provided. Prepare a written summary of your findings.

2. Visit *http://www.mypyramid.gov* and request a personalized MyPyramid health plan. Simply key in your age, gender, and physical activity level. Review the recommendations you receive and compare these to your current diet and exercise level.

YOU PLAY THE ROLE

Ambry Waller, one of your closest friends, used to go fishing quite often, and he loved to hike in the mountains. After getting married, his life changed dramatically. He and his wife purchased a new home, and soon they were raising a family. Once the bills started piling up, he abandoned his leisure-time activities and started working long hours at his job. He eagerly volunteered for overtime in order to increase his earnings. As the years passed, Ambry and his wife adopted many trappings of middle-class life: a big house, two cars, a huge flat screen TV in the family room, and a motorboat that sits idle for most of the year. One afternoon, you meet Ambry for a beer at a local bar. The conversation quickly turns serious as Ambry describes his frustration: "I love my wife and children, but I am so tired of working long hours and worrying about my financial obligations. My credit-card debt is now over $7,000."

In this role-play activity, you will meet with another class member who will assume the role of Ambry Waller. Your goal is to help Ambry identify some ways he can achieve greater work/life balance. Your name for this role play will be Corey Cell.

BELOW THE SURFACE:

Unemployed, Unretired, and Unhappy

At the beginning of this chapter, we introduced Chad Smith who had no interest in going to college after graduation from high school: "When you're making $55,000 at 18 years old, it's hard to tell yourself to go to school; you've got the world by the tail." Ten years later he was married, the father of three children, and earning good pay at a Chrysler assembly plant. Then he was laid off and facing an uncertain future.[68]

A few years ago, Paul Nelson gave up his long career in the defense industry for peaceful retirement in Tucson, Arizona. The weather was mild, and he had plenty of time to volunteer and work in the garden. Then his wife of 46 years died unexpectedly. He tried to swap his house for a smaller one and lost part of his retirement savings in the process. Then the stock market took a nosedive, wiping out most of his remaining savings. At age 71, Paul Nelson hopes to be unretired soon.[69]

Chad Smith is currently enrolled in a federal retraining program and Paul Nelson is looking for work at local hardware stores and Home Depot. Like thousands of other retirees, he is low on money and looking for work.

Joining the unemployed and the underemployed are thousands of workers who are employed but do not find their jobs rewarding. In 2002, Richard Binder quit his job as a software engineer to become a "pen doctor." He repairs fountain pens sent to him from customers around the world. His gross income is less than what he earned as a software engineer, but he is happier. He says, "Basically, I get my pleasure from making people happy with their pens." For Richard Binder, the search for right livelihood is over.[70]

QUESTIONS

1. Given the changes taking place in our economy, you may need to return to the classroom at age 30, 40, or 50. How would you feel about the prospect of becoming a middle-aged student?
2. Mary Lou Quinlan spent 20 years climbing the ladder in the field of advertising. Finally she became CEO of N.W. Ayer, a successful advertising company. She achieved "success" but she was not happy. She then decided to become an entrepreneur. That decision was made after completing the following steps:

   > *I got a piece of paper and divided it in half. On the left side, I wrote down what I love to do and what I'm good at, and on the right side, I wrote down what I don't like to do and what I stink at. Unfortunately, what I don't like to do and what I stink at were my job descriptions as CEO.*[71]

   Quinlan founded a consulting company named Just Ask a Woman, a firm that helps companies market to women. Evaluate the advantages and disadvantages of the decision making model used by Quinlan.
3. Many companies are reducing the contribution made to employee retirement programs and others are eliminating these contributions. Briefly describe the retirement program you would like to establish and maintain during the years ahead. Predict the major barriers to achieving your goal.

INTEGRATED RESOURCES

CLASSROOM ACTIVITIES

IRM Application Exercise 17.1
IRM Application Exercise 17.2

Notes

Chapter 1

1 Thomas Moore, "Finding Life at Work," *Spirituality & Health*, March/April 2008, p. 12.

2 Thomas Moore, *A Life at Work* (New York: Broadway Books, 2008), pp. 8–11.

3 Edward M. Hallowell, *Connect* (New York: Pantheon Books, 1999), pp. 1–14.

4 John Seely Brown and Paul Duguid, *The Social Life of Information* (Boston: Harvard Business School Press, 2000), pp. 2–13.

5 Gerhard Gschwandtner, "The Magic Formula for Sustainable Success," *Selling Power*, June 2006, p. 10.

6 Ronald Alsop, "How to Get Hired," *Wall Street Journal*, September 22, 2004; Marshall Goldsmith, "Nice Guys Can Finish First," *Fast Company*, November 2004, p. 123.

7 Monica Langley and Jefferey McCracken, "Ford Taps Boeing Executive as CEO," *Wall Street Journal*, September 6, 2006, p. A1.

8 Joann S. Lublin, "Mergers Often Trigger Anxiety, Lower Morale," *Wall Street Journal*, January 16, 2001, pp. B1, B4; Daniel Roth, "How to Cut Pay, Lay Off 8,000 People, and Still Have Workers Who Love You," *Fortune*, February 4, 2002, pp. 63–68.

9 James O'Toole and Edward C. Lawler III, "A Piece of Work," *Fast Company*, June 2006, p. 88; Mike Brewster, "The Freelance Conundrum," *Inc.*, December 2004, p. 38.

10 Jeffrey Pfeffer, *The Human Equation* (Boston: Harvard Business School Press, 1998), p. 293.

11 Jeff Pettit, "Team Communication: It's in the Cards," *Training & Development*, January 1997, p. 12.

12 Excerpt adapted from Ronald Alsop, "Back on Top," *Wall Street Journal*, July 21, 2005, p. A.1.

13 Rachel Emma Silverman, "Working on Your Marriage—at Work," *Wall Street Journal*, May 31, 2007, p. 1.

14 William M. Bulkeley, "IBM to Help Pay for Plans to Curb Childhood Obesity," *Wall Street Journal*, October 24, 2007, p. D4.

15 Anne Fisher, "Success Secret: A High Emotional IQ," *Fortune*, October 26, 1998, p. 293.

16 Adapted from Marshall Goldsmith, "Nice Guys Can Finish First," *Fast Company*, November 2004, p. 123.

17 Robert Kreitner, *Management*, 9th ed. (Boston: Houghton Mifflin, 2004), p. 304.

18 Allan A. Kennedy, interview by, in "The Culture Wars," *Inc.*, 20th Anniversary Issue, 1999, pp. 107–108.

19 Anita Raghavan, Kathryn Kranhold, and Alexei Barrionuevo, "How Enron Bosses Created a Culture of Pushing Limits," *Wall Street Journal*, August 26, 2002, p. B1.

20 Suein L. Hwang, "Workers' Slogans Find New Home This Side of the Great Wall," *Wall Street Journal*, October 16, 2002, p. B1.

21 Brian Tracy, *The 100 Absolutely Unbreakable Laws of Business Success* (San Francisco: Berrett-Koehler Publishers, Inc., 2000), p. 121.

22 Sue Shellenbarger, "Along with Benefits and Pay, Employees Seek Friends on the Job," *Wall Street Journal*, February 20, 2002, p. B1.

23 "Great Expectations," *Fast Company*, November 1999, p. 224.

24 Betsy Jacobson and Beverly Kaye, "Balancing Act," *Training & Development*, February 1993, p. 26.

25 Sue Shellenbarger, "Job Candidates Prepare to Sacrifice Some Frills and Balance—For Now," *Wall Street Journal*, November 21, 2001, p. B1; Stephanie Armour, "Workers Put Family First Despite Slow Economy, Jobless Fears," *USA Today*, June 6, 2002, p. 38.

26 Rochelle Sharpe, "Labor Letter," *Wall Street Journal*, September 13, 1994, p. 1.

27 Alan Farnham, "The Man Who Changed Work Forever," *Fortune*, July 21, 1997, p. 114; Cynthia Crossen, "Early Industry Expert Soon Realized a Staff Has Its Own Efficiency," *Wall Street Journal*, November 6, 2006, p. B1.

28 James Baughman quote from Frank Rose, "A New Age for Business?" *Fortune*, October 8, 1990, p. 162.

29 Bradley J. Rieger, "Lessons in Productivity and People," *Training & Development*, October 1995, pp. 56–58.

30 "A Field Is Born," *Harvard Business Review*, July/August 2008, p. 164.

31 Jim Collins, "The Classics," *Inc.*, December 1996, p. 55.

32 John A. Byrne, "The Man Who Invented Management," *BusinessWeek*, November 28, 2005, pp. 97–106.

33 Thomas J. Peters and Robert H. Waterman, Jr., *In Search of Excellence: Lessons from America's Best-Run Companies* (New York: Harper & Row, 1982), p. 14; Tom Peters, "Tom Peters' True Confessions," *Fast Company*, December 2001, p. 80.

34 Adapted from Ryan Underwood, "A Field Guide to the Gurus," *Fast Company*, November 2004, p. 104.

35 Stephen R. Covey, *The Seven Habits of Highly Effective People* (New York: Simon & Schuster, 1989), pp. 66–67.

36 Richard Koonce, "Emotional IQ, A New Secret of Success," *Training & Development*, February 1996, p. 19; Cary Cherniss and Daniel Goleman, eds., *The Emotionally Intelligent Workplace* (San Francisco: Jossey-Bass, 2001), pp. 13–26.

37 Denis Waitley, *Empires of the Mind* (New York: Morrow, 1995), p. 133.

38 Michael Crom, "Building Trust in the Workplace," *The Leader*, October 1998, p. 6; Ron Zemke, "Can You Manage Trust?" *Training*, February 2000, pp. 76–83.

39 Harold H. Bloomfield and Robert K. Cooper, *The Power of 5* (Emmaus, Pa.: Rodale Press, 1995), p. 61.

40 Louis S. Richman, "How to Get Ahead in America," *Fortune*, May 16, 1994, pp. 46–54; Ronald Henkoff, "Winning the New Career Game," *Fortune*, July 12, 1993, pp. 46–49.

41 Jack Canfield, *The Success Principles* (New York: Harper Collins, 2005), pp. 3–18.

42 Thomas Moore, *A Life at Work* (New York: Broadway Books, 2008), pp. 7–11.

43 Barry Salzberg, "Why Mentoring Matters in a Hypercompetitive World," *Harvard Business Review*, July–August 2008, p. 154.

44 Kelly K. Spors, "What Makes a Great Place to Work?" *Wall Street Journal*, October 1, 2007, pp. R1–R6.

45 Malcolm Flescher, "World Wide Winner—The UPS Story," *Selling Power*, November/December 2001, p. 58.

46 Simona Covel, "Tapping the Creativity of Downtime," *Wall Street Journal*, July 24, 2008, p. B5.

47 Thomas Petzinger, Jr., "The Front Lines," *Wall Street Journal*, May 21, 1999, p. B1; Lucy McCauley, "Relaunch!" *Fast Company*, July 2000, pp. 97–108; Liz Stevens, "In the Race, America Has the Most Rats," *The News and Observer*, November 21, 1999, p. E3; Julie Gordon, "Teaching Selling Skills to the Financial World," *Denver Business Journal*, November 3, 2000, p. 10B.

Chapter 2

1 Maggie Jackson, *Distracted: The Erosion of Attention and the Coming Dark Age* (New York: Prometheus Books, 2008), p. 14.

2 "Maggie Jackson's Call for Focus—Fighting Back in an Age of Distractions," *A Buzzflash Interview*, June 30, 2008 [cited 30 June 2008]. Available from http://blog.buzzflash.com/interviews/115; INTERNET.

3 David Robinson, "What Were We Talking About?" *Wall Street Journal*, June 12, 2008, p. A15.

4 David Shenk, *Data Smog—Surviving the Information Glut* (San Francisco: Harper Edge, 1997), p. 54.

5 John Stewart and Gary D'Angelo, *Together—Communicating Interpersonally* (New York: Random House, 1988), p. 5.

6 Kerry J. Sulkowicz, "The Corporate Shrink," *Fast Company*, September 2006, p. 103.

7 For more information on the components of communication, see Scot Ober, *Contemporary Business Communication*, 5th ed. (Boston: Houghton Mifflin, 2003), pp. 5–9.

8 Carol Hymowitz, "Mind Your Language: To Do Business Today, Consider Delayering," *Wall Street Journal,* March 27, 2006, p. B1.

9 Cai Shaoyao, "Cyberlingo—A Jargon Not for General Use," *Shanghai Star*, January 6, 2005 [cited 26 October 2005]. Available from http://app1.chinadaily.com.cn/star/2005/0206/vo2–3.html; INTERNET; Julie Martin, "Cyberlingo! BRB? ROTFL? LOL? It's Greek to Me" [cited 26 October 2005]. Available from http://www.goodchatting.com/articles/archives/000006.php; INTERNET.

10 Sarah E. Needleman, "Informal Lingo Might Put Off Job Recruiters," *The News & Observer*, August 3, 2008, p. 49.

11 Matthew McKay, Martha Davis, and Patrick Fanning, *Messages: The Communication Skills Book* (Oakland, Calif.: New Harbinger, 1995), p. 108.

12 Deborah Tannen, *You Just Don't Understand: Men and Women in Conversation* (New York: Ballantine Books, 1990), pp. 24–25, 85.

13 Jena McGregor, "Customer Service Champs," *BusinessWeek,* March 3, 2008, p. 37.

14 Don Clark, "Communication and Leadership," July 17, 2005, pp. 9, 10 [cited 27 October 2005]. Available from http://www.nwlink.com/donclark/leader/leadcom.html; INTERNET.

15 Ibid., p. 7.

16 William B. Gudykunst, Stella Ting-Toomey, Sandra Sudweeks, and Lea Stewart, *Building Bridges: Interpersonal Skills for a Changing World* (Boston: Houghton Mifflin, 1995), pp. 315–316. "Playing Keepaway," *Psychology Today,* June 2007, p. 15.

17 Clark, "Communication and Leadership," p. 8.

18 Sssh! Listen Up! *High Gain Inc. Newsletter*, June 2003, p. 3.

19 Excerpt adapted from "Ask Annie," *Fortune,* July 19, 1999. Copyright © 1999 Time Inc. All rights reserved.

20 Susan Scott, *Fierce Conversations: Achieving Success at Work and in Life, One Conversation at a Time* (New York: Viking, 2002), pp. 156–157.

21 Michael Toms, "Dialogue—The Art of Thinking Together—Sparks Spirit of 'Aliveness' in Organizations," *The Inner Edge,* August/September 1998, p. 462.

22 Leigh Buchanan, "The Office," *Inc.* October 2006, p. 140.

23 Stephen R. Covey, *The Seven Habits of Highly Effective People* (New York: Simon & Schuster, 1989), pp. 240–241.

24 C. Glenn Pearce, "Learning How to Listen Empathically," *Supervisory Management*, September 1991, p. 11.

25 Robert Epstein, "Waiting," *Psychology Today*, September/October 2001, p. 5.

26 Susan Scott, *Fierce Conversations* (New York: Viking, 2002), pp. 156–157. Chapter 7 is entitled "Let Silence Do the Heavy Lifting."

27 Jared Sandberg, "Ruthless Rumors and the Managers Who Enable Them," *Wall Street Journal*, October 29, 2003, p. B1.

28 Tammy Galvin, "Nothing Ventured," *Training*, February 2004, p. 4.

29 Robert Kreitner, *Management*, 10th ed. (Boston: Houghton Mifflin Company, 2007), p. 349.

30 Ibid., p. 355.

31 Suzy Wetlaufer, "The Business Case Against Revolution," *Harvard Business Review*, February 2001, p. 119.

32 Adapted from "The 10 Commandments of E-MAIL," *Harvard Communications Update,* Vol. 2, No. 3, March 1999, pp. 7–8; Carolyn Kleiner, "Online Buffs Hit or Miss on Manners," *U.S. News & World Report,* March 22, 1999, p. 60; "Etiquette with Office Gadgets," *Training,* January 1999, p. 24; p. 49; "Telephone Tips," *The Office Professional,* see http://www.hardatwork.com; INTERNET.

33 John Derbyshire, "To: Emailers, Subject: Etiquette," *Wall Street Journal,* March 21, 2007, p. P10; Robert Kreitner, *Management*, 10th ed. (Boston: Houghton Mifflin, 2007), p. 362.

34 "Etiquette with Office Gadgets," *Training*, January 1999, p. 24.

35 Marina Krakovsky, "Caveat Sender—The Pitfalls of E-mail," *Psychology Today*, March/April 2004, pp. 15–16.

36 Marcia Jedd, "Rethinking Instant Messaging," *Sales & Marketing Management,* November/December 2007, p. 19; Carola Mamberto, "Instant Messaging Invades the Office," *Wall Street Journal,* July 24, 2007, p. B1.

37 Tippi Rasp, "Text Messaging Becoming Most Popular Form of Communication," http://www.EnidNews.com, August 16, 2008.

38 "Twitter," http://en.wikipedia.org/wiki/Twitter, August 2, 2009.

39 Joann S. Lublin, "You Blew the Interview, But You Can Correct Some of the Blunders," *Wall Street Journal*, December 5, 2000, p. B1; Anne Faircloth, "How to Recover from a Firing," *Fortune,* December 7, 1998, p. 239; Chris Serres, "They Want to Get Inside

Your Head," *News & Observer*, May 6, 2001, p. 1E; "Ask Annie; Knowing When It's Time to Quit, and False Promises," *Fortune*, February 7, 2000, p. 210.

40 This exercise is based on information taken from Scott, *Fierce Conversations*, pp. 117–118.

41 A Buzzflash Interview, "Maggie Jackson's Call for Focus—Fighting Back in an Age of Distraction." June 30, 2008.

42 Jean P. Fisher, "Surgical Tools Cleaned Improperly" [cited 4 November 2005]. Available from http://www.newsobserver.com/new/health_science/story/2581297p-8376237c.html; INTERNET; Jeff Molter, "Duke Provides Additional Information to Patients Exposed to Hydraulic Fluid," August 4, 2005 [cited 4 November 2005]. Available from http://www.dukemednews.org/news/article.php?id=9189; INTERNET; Sarah Avery, New Firm to Track Duke Patients," *The News & Observer*, August 26, 2005, p. A1.

43 Eric Ferreri, "Patients Try to Tie Ailments to Duke," *The News & Observer*, August 13, 2007, p. B1.

Chapter 3

1 Walt Mossberg and Kara Swisher, "Scenes From a Marriage," *Wall Street Journal*, June 9, 2008, p. R4.

2 Robert Bolton and Dorothy Grover Bolton, *People Styles at Work* (New York: AMACOM, 1996), p. 10.

3 Camille Wright Miller, "Mirroring Others Helps You Connect with Them," *The Roanoke Times*, August 24, 2005.

4 Tony Alessandra, *Behavioral Profiles: Participant Workbook* (San Diego: Pfeiffer & Company, 1994), p. 12.

5 Robert Bolton and Dorothy Grover Bolton, *People Styles at Work* (New York: AMACOM, 1996), pp. ix–x.

6 Robert Bolton and Dorothy Grover Bolton, *People Styles at Work* (New York: AMACOM, 1996), p. x.

7 Robert J. Sternberg, *Thinking Styles* (New York: Cambridge University Press, 1997), p. 8.

8 Robert Bolton and Dorothy Grover Bolton, *People Styles at Work* (New York: AMACOM, 1996), p. x.

9 P. Christopher Earley and Elaine Mosakowski, "Cultural Intelligence," *Harvard Business Review*, October 2004, p. 3 of reprint R0410.

10 David W. Johnson, *Reaching Out—Interpersonal Effectiveness and Self-Actualization* (Englewood Cliffs, NJ: Prentice-Hall, 1981), pp. 43–44. The dominance factor was described in an early book by William M. Marston, *The Emotions of Normal People* (NewYork: Harcourt, 1928). Research conducted by Rolfe La Forge and Robert F. Suczek resulted in the development of the Interpersonal Check List (ICL), which features a dominant–submissive scale. A person who receives a high score on the ICL tends to lead, persuade, and control others. The Interpersonal Identity Profile, developed by David W. Merrill and James W. Taylor, features a factor called "assertiveness." Persons classified as high in assertiveness tend to have strong opinions, make quick decisions, and be directive when dealing with people. Persons classified as low in assertiveness tend to voice moderate opinions, make thoughtful decisions, and be supportive when dealing with others.

11 Christopher Caggiano, "Psychopath," *Inc.*, July 1998, pp. 77–85.

12 "Assertiveness Training" [cited 30 August 2008]. Available from http://www.amanet.org/seminars; INTERNET.

13 For more information, see Robert Bolton and Dorothy Grover Bolton, *People Styles at Work* (New York: American Management Association, 1996).

14 The research conducted by La Forge and Suczek resulted in identification of the hostile/loving continuum, which is similar to the sociability continuum. Their Interpersonal Check List features this scale. L. L. Thurstone and T. G. Thurstone developed the Thurstone Temperament Schedule, which provides an assessment of a "sociable" factor. Persons with high scores in this area enjoy the company of others and make friends easily. The Interpersonal Identity Profile developed by Merrill and Taylor contains an objectivity continuum. A person with low objectivity is seen as attention seeking, involved with the feelings of others, informal, and casual in social relationships. A person who is high in objectivity tends to be indifferent toward the feelings of others. This person is formal in social relationships.

15 For more information, see Robert Bolton and Dorothy Grover Bolton, *People Styles at Work* (New York: American Management Association, 1996).

16 Jay Dixit, "Reading Between the Lines," *Psychology Today*, July/August 2007, p. 78.

17 "On the Human Side," *Time*, February 19, 1979, p. 75.

18 "A Global Profiling Tool" (Wilson Learning Corporation: Eden Prairie, Minn., 1999); Tom Ritchey, *I'm Stuck, You're Stuck* (San Francisco: Berrett-Koehler, Inc., 2002), p. 5.

19 Robert Bolton and Dorothy Grover Bolton, *People Styles at Work* (New York: AMACOM, 1996), p. 87.

20 Ibid.

21 "Ask Dr. E," *Psychology Today*, January/February 2000, p. 28.

22 Greg Hitt, "Spin Doctors Prescribe Dose of Self-Deprecation for Howard Dean (Yeeeaaah!)," *Wall Street Journal*, January 23, 2004, p. B1.

23 David W. Merrill and Roger H. Reid, *Personality Styles and Effective Performance* (Radnor, Pa.: Chilton Book, 1981), p. 88.

24 Wilson Learning Corporation, *Growth Through Versatility* (Eden Prairie, Minn.: Wilson Learning Corporation), p. 4.

25 "Versatility: The Key to Sales Performance" (Edina, Minn.: Wilson Learning Worldwide, 2004), pp. 1–4.

26 Bob Reeves, "It Takes All Types," *Lincoln Star*, May 24, 1994, p. 11.

27 Kerry J. Sulkowicz, "The Corporate Shrink," *Fast Company*, January/February 2006, p. 104.

28 Brian Grow, "Out at Home Depot," *BusinessWeek*, January 15, 2007, pp. 56–62.

29 Gary A. Williams and Robert B. Miller, "Changing the Way You Persuade," *Harvard Business Review*, May 2002, pp. 65–67.

30 Judith Sills, "When Personalities Clash," *Psychology Today*, November/December 2006, pp. 61–62.

31 Stuart Atkins, *The Name of Your Game* (Beverly Hills, Calif.: Ellis & Stewart, 1981), pp. 49–50.

32 Ibid, p. 51.

33 Chris Lee, "What's Your Style?" *Training*, May 1991, p. 28.

34 Michael Kaplan, "How to Overcome Your Strengths," *Fast Company*, May 1999, p. 225.

35 Barry L. Reece and Gerald L. Manning, *Supervision and Leadership in Action* (New York: Glencoe, 1990); Camille Wright Miller, "Working It Out," *Roanoke Times & World-News*, July 17, 1994, p. F-3.

36 Joel Spolsky, "How Hard Could It Be?" *Inc.*, July 2008, p. 73.

37 Robert A. Guth, "Ballmer Aims to Find Microsoft's Balance," *Wall Street Journal*, June 27, 2008, p. B5.

Chapter 4

1 Patrick J. Sauer, "Redemption Doesn't Come Easy—How I Did It," *Inc.*, May 2006, p. 107.

2 Ibid.

3 "Vickie Stringer." Available at http://www.com?authors/vickie_stringer.htm; INTERNET.

4 [Accessed 17 November 2000]. Available at http://www.es.emory.edu/mfp/efficacynotgiveup.html; INTERNET; Dave Shiflett, "Sad Song, Sweet Ending," *Wall Street Journal*, August 19, 2007, p. 8.

5 Douglas A. Bernstein, Louis A. Penner, Alison Clarke-Stewart, and Edward J. Roy, *Psychology*, 7th ed. (Boston: Houghton Mifflin, 2006), p. 557.

6 Nathaniel Branden, *The Six Pillars of Self-Esteem* (New York: Bantam, 1994), p. 7.

7 Robert Reasoner, "The True Meaning of Self-Esteem," National Association for Self-Esteem, Normal, Il. [cited April 30, 2003]. Available at http://www.self-esteemnase.org; INTERNET.

8 Phillip C. McGraw, *Self Matters* (New York: Simon & Schuster, 2001), pp. 69–70.

9 Sharon Begley, "Follow Your Intuition: The Unconscious You May Be the Wiser Half," *Wall Street Journal*, August 30, 2002, p. B1; Sharon Begley, "How Do I Love Thee? Let Me Count the Ways—and Other Bad Ideas," *Wall Street Journal*, September 6, 2002, p. B1.

10 Douglas A. Bernstein, Louis A. Penner, Alison Clarke-Stewart, and Edward J. Roy, *Psychology*, 7th ed. (Boston: Houghton Mifflin, 2006), pp. 450–505.

11 Marilyn Elias, "Short Attention Span Linked to TV," *USA Today*, April 5, 2004, p. A1; Lyric Wallwork Winik, "The Toll of Video Violence," *Parade*, July 22, 2004, p. 15.

12 Douglas A. Bernstein, Louis A. Penner, Alison Clarke-Stewart, and Edward J. Roy, *Psychology*, 7th ed. (Boston: Houghton Mifflin, 2006), pp. 490–491.

13 Ibid, pp. 490–491.

14 Robert Epstein, author of *The Case Against Adolescence*, believes that teens should have more options in areas such as work, owning property, signing contracts, and making decisions regarding health care. He believes these options would help teens move to adulthood faster.

15 Emmett Miller, *The Healing Power of Happiness* (Emmaus, Pa.: Rodale Press, 1989), pp. 12–13.

16 Lacey Beckmann, "One More Thing Money Can't Buy," *Psychology Today*, November/December, 2002, p. 16.

17 Amy Saltzman, *Downshifting* (New York: HarperCollins, 1990), pp. 15–16.

18 Emmett Miller, *The Healing Power of Happiness* (Emmaus, Pa.: Rodale Press, 1989), pp. 12–13.

19 Phillip C. McGraw, *Self Matters* (New York: Simon & Schuster, 2001), p. 73.

20 Don Miguel Ruiz, *The Four Agreements* (San Rafael, Calif.: Amber-Allen Publishing, 1997), p. 12.

21 Robert Reasoner, "The True Meaning of Self-Esteem," National Association for Self-Esteem, Normal, Il. [cited April 30, 2003]. Available at http://www.self-esteemnase.org; INTERNET.

22 Arthur H. Goldsmith, Jonathan R. Veum, and William Darity, Jr., "The Impact of Psychological and Human Capital on Wages," *Economic Inquiry*, October 1997, p. 817.

23 Hyrum W. Smith, *The 10 Natural Laws of Successful Time and Life Management* (New York: Warner Books, 1994), p. 178.

24 Oprah Winfrey, "You Are the Dream," *O, The Oprah Magazine*, March 2001, p. 39.

25 Annie Gottlieb, "The Radical Road to Self-Esteem," *O, The Oprah Magazine,* March 2001, pp. 101–102.

26 Don Miguel Ruiz, *The Four Agreements* (San Rafael, Calif.: Amber-Allen Publishing, 1997), pp. 47–61.

27 James J. Messina and Constance M. Messina, *The SEA's Program Model of Self-Esteem* [cited 9 November 2005]. Available from http://www.coping.org/selfesteem/model.htm; INTERNET.

28 Nathaniel Branden, *The Six Pillars of Self-Esteem* (New York: Bantam, 1994), p. 33.

29 Matthew McKay and Patrick Fanning, *Self-Esteem*, 2nd ed. (Oakland, Calif.: New Harbinger, 1992), p. 42.

30 Phillip C. McGraw, *Self Matters* (New York: Simon & Schuster, 2001), pp. 209–212.

31 Arnold A. Lazarus and Clifford N. Lazarus, *The 60-Second Shrink* (San Luis Obispo, Calif.: Impact Publishers, 1997), p. 40.

32 Marcus Buckingham, *Go Put Your Strengths to Work* (New York: Free Press, 2007), p. 19.

33 Marcus Buckingham and Donald O. Clifton, *Now, Discover Your Strengths* (New York: Free Press, 2001), p. 8.

34 Ibid., pp. 28–35.

35 Ibid., pp. 28–31.

36 Nanette Byrnes, "Start Search," *BusinessWeek*, October 10, 2005, p. 74.

37 Chip R. Bell, "Making Mentoring a Way of Life," *Training*, October 1996, p. 138; Lin Standke, review of *Managers as Mentors: Building Partnerships for Learning*, by Chip R. Bell, *Training*, April 1997, pp. 64–65.

38 Carol Hymowitz, "Today's Bosses Find Mentoring Isn't Worth the Time and Risks," *Wall Street Journal,* March 13, 2006, p. B1.

39 Fiona Haley and Christine Canabou, interviews by, "The Mentors' Mentors," *Fast Company*, October 2003, p. 59.

40 Thomas J. DeLong, John J. Gabarro, and Robert J. Lees, *Harvard Business Review,* January 2008, p. 117.

41 Cindy Krischer Goodman, "Novice Workers Offer Lessons," *News & Observer,* April 30, 2006, p. 8E.

42 Ginger Adams and Tena B. Crews, "Telementoring: A Viable Tool," *Journal of Applied Research for Business Education*, Vol. 2, No. 3, 2004, pp. 1–4.

43 Stan Goldberg, "The 10 Rules of Change," *Psychology Today*, September/October 2002, pp. 38–44.

44 Andrew Weil, "Images of Healing," *Dr. Andrew Weil's Self Healing*, November 2003, p. 3; Amy Dockser Marcus, "Heart Surgeons Try Using the Power of Suggestion," *Wall Street Journal*, February 20, 2004, p. D1.

45 Rami Shapiro, "What Do You Think of 'The Secret'?" *Spirituality & Health*, May/June 2007, p. 17.

46 James Bauman, "The Gold Medal," *Psychology Today*, May/June 2000, pp. 62–68.

47 Will Schutz, *The Human Element* (San Francisco: Jossey-Bass Publications, 1994), p. 43.

48 See McGraw, *Self Matters*, for comprehensive coverage of how internal dialogue influences our self-concept.

49 Matthew McKay and Patrick Fanning, *Self-Esteem*, 2nd ed. (Oakland, Calif.: New Harbinger, 1992), p. 42.

50 Julie Morgenstern, "Fire Your Inner Critic," *O, The Oprah Magazine*, August 2004, pp. 75–77.

51 Herb Kindler, "Working to Change Old Habits," *Working Smart*, May 1992, p. 8.

52 Jack Canfield and D. D. Watkins, *Jack Canfield's Key to Living the Law of Attraction* (Deerfield Beach, Fl: Health Communications, 2007), pp. 31–34.

53 Phillip C. McGraw, *Self Matters* (New York: Simon & Schuster, 2001), pp. 204–205.

54 Roy J. Blitzer, Colleen Petersen, and Linda Rogers, "How to Build Self-Esteem," *Training & Development*, February 1993, pp. 58–60.

55 Messina and Messina, *The SEA's Program Model of Self-Esteem*, p. 9.

56 Marcus Buckingham, *Go Put Your Strengths to Work* (New York: Free Press, 2007), pp. 130–134.

57 Patrick J. Sauer, "Redemption Doesn't Come Easy How I Did It," *Inc.,* May 2006, p. 108.

58 "Vickie Stringer." Available at http://www.inc.com/magazine/20060501/ga-stringer.html; INTERNET.

59 Ibid.

60 Shoshana Zuboff, "Only the Brave Surrender," *Fast Company,* October 2004, p. 121.

Chapter 5

1 Jane Stancill, "Penalties Stand for Duke Cheaters," *The News & Observer*, June 2, 2007, p. B1.

2 Charlotte Allen, "Their Cheatin Hearts," *Wall Street Journal,* May 11, 2007, p. W11. For additional information regarding the Duke Business School scandal see Michelle Conlin, "Cheating—or Postmodern Learning?" *BusinessWeek*, May 14, 2007, p. 42 and David Crary, "Students Lie, Cheat and Steal," *The News & Observer,* December 1, 2008, p. 5A.

3 David Gergen, "Candidates with Character," *U.S. News & World Report*, September 27, 1999, p. 68. The importance of honesty in leadership positions is discussed in James M. Kouzes and Barry Z. Posner, *The Leadership Challenge,* 3rd ed. (San Francisco: Jossey-Bass, 2002), pp. 27–28.

4 Patrick Smith, "You Have a Job, But How About a Life?" *BusinessWeek*, November 16, 1998, p. 30.

5 Nathaniel Branden, *Self-Esteem at Work* (San Francisco: Jossey-Bass, 1998), p. 35.

6 Stephen R. Covey, *The Seven Habits of Highly Effective People* (New York: Simon & Schuster, 1989), p. 92.

7 Roy Chitwood, "Still Trying to Slip Past Gatekeepers? Forget it!" *Value-Added Selling* 21, December 26, 2003, p. 1.

8 Hyrum W. Smith, *The 10 Natural Laws of Successful Time and Life Management* (New York: Warner Books, 1994), pp. 14–15.

9 J. David McCracken and Ana E. Falcon-Emmanuelli, "A Theoretical Basis for Work Values Research in Vocational Education," *Journal of Vocational and Technical Education*, April 1994, p. 4.

10 Sue Shellenbarger, "Some Top Executives Are Finding a Balance Between Job and Home," *Wall Street Journal*, April 23, 1997, p. B1. Anne Mulcahy was named CEO of the year in 2008 by *Tech Her.*

11 Katharine Mieszkowski, "FitzGerald Family Values," *Fast Company*, April 1998, p. 194.

12 Rebecca Ganzel, "Book Reviews," *Training*, June 2000, pp. 76–77.

13 Jack Canfield, *The Success Principles* (New York: HarperCollins, 2005), pp. 20–29.

14 Adapted from Jack Canfield, *The Success Principles* (New York: HarperCollins, 2005), pp. 32–33.

15 Neil Howe and William Strauss, "The Next 20 years: How Customers and Workforce Attitudes Will Evolve," *Harvard Business Review,* July/August 2007, pp. 41–52.

16 Jeffrey Zaslow, "The Latest Generation Gap: Boomers Are Often Unfairly Lumped Together," *Wall Street Journal*, July 8, 2004, p. 1; Shirley Holt, "Generation Gaps in the Workplace," *The Roanoke Times*, March 27, 2005, pp. 1, 3; Karen Auby, "A Boomer's Guide to Communicating with Gen X and Gen Y," *BusinessWeek,* August/September 1, 2008, p. 63.

17 Douglas A. Bernstein, Louis A Penner, Alison Clarke-Stewart, and Edward J. Roy, *Psychology*, 7th ed. (Boston: Houghton Mifflin, 2006), pp. 491–505.

18 Toms, "Investing in Character," *The Inner Edge,* June/July 2000, pp. 5–8.

19 Chris Lee and Ron Zemke, "The Search for Spirit in the Workplace," *Training*, June 1993, p. 21.

20 "By the Numbers," *Corporate Responsibility Officer,* November/December 2007, p. 18.

21 Character Counts! National Office at http://www.charactercounts.org [cited 12 January 2003]. Available from http://www.charactercounts.org; INTERNET.

22 Linda Formichelli, "Programming Behavior," *Psychology Today*, January/February 2001, p. 10.

23 Morris Massey, *The People Puzzle* (Reston, Va.: Reston Publishing, 1979).

24 O. C. Ferrell, John Fraedrich, and Linda Ferrell, *Business Ethics*, 5th ed. (Boston: Houghton Mifflin, 2002), pp. 123–135.

25 Jancee Dunn, "Now What Do I Do?" *O, The Oprah Magazine,* March 2008, p. 89.

26 Paul B. Brown, "What I Know Now," *Fast Company,* November 2005, p. 108.

27 John Hollon, "Drucker Knew Best," *Workforce Management*, November 21, 2005, p. 58.

28 Sue Shellenbarger, "In Cataclysmic Times, Workers Need Room to Rethink Priorities," *Wall Street Journal*, September 19, 2001, p. B1.

29 Toddi Gutner, "A Balancing Act for GenX Women," *BusinessWeek*, January 21, 2002, p. 82; "Generational Truths," *Training,* June 2007, p. 13.

30 John Beebe, "Conscience, Integrity and Character," *The Inner Edge*, June/July 2000, pp. 9–11.

31 Jane Porter, "Using Ex-Cons to Scare MBAs Straight," *BusinessWeek*, May 5, 2008, p. 58.

32 "Making Sense of Ethics" [cited 13 January 2003]. Available from http://www.josephsoninstitute.org/MED/MED-1makingsense.htm; INTERNET.

33 Craig Mindrum, "Business Ethics—Moral Intelligence and Workforce Performance," *Workforce Performance Solutions*, March 2006, pp. 28–32.

34 Price Pritchett, *The Ethics of Excellence* (Dallas, Tex: Pritchett & Associates, n.d.), p. 28.

35 William J. Bennett, "Educating for National Leadership: A 20 Year Anniversary Seminar," *Imprimis*, November 2002, p. 4.

36 "CyberSource® Joins with Association of Certified Fraud Examiners to Support 2002 National Fraud Awareness Week," July 29, 2002 [cited 13 January 2003]. Available from http://www.cybersource.com/news_and_events/view.xml?page_id5949; INTERNET. Raymund Flandez, "Stop That Thief," *Wall Street Journal*, June 16, 2008, p. R6.

37 "Making Sense of Ethics" [cited 13 January 2003]. Available from http://www.josephsoninstitute.org/MED/MED-1makingsense.htm; INTERNET.

38 Ed Emde, "Employee Values Are Changing Course," *Workforce*, March 1998, p. 84 [cited 18 November 2005]. Available from http://www.workforce.com/archive/article/21/97/39.php?ht5values%20values; INTERNET.

39 Jennifer Reingold, "Walking the Walk," *Fast Company*, November 2005, pp. 81–85.

40 Dan Rice and Craig Dreilinger, "Rights and Wrongs of Ethics Training," *Training & Development*, May 1990, p. 105.

41 Susan Scherreik, "A Conscience Doesn't Have to Make You Poor," *BusinessWeek*, May 1, 2000, pp. 204–206.

42 Jack Welch and Suzy Welch, "The Real Verdict on Business," *BusinessWeek*, June 12, 2006, p. 100.

43 Ben W. Heineman, Jr., "Avoiding Integrity Land Mines," *Harvard Business Review*, April 2007, pp. 100–108.

44 Andrew Stark, "What's the Matter with Business Ethics?" *Harvard Business Review*, May/June 1993, p. 38.

45 "Tom Chappell—Minister of Commerce," *Business Ethics*, January/February 1994, p. 17.

46 Ferrell, Fraedrich, and Ferrell, *Business Ethics*, pp. 182–183.

47 Patrick M. Lencioni, "Make Your Values Mean Something," *Harvard Business Review*, July 2002, pp. 5–9.

48 Julia Stewart, "The Pancake Pusher," *Fortune*, October 15, 2007, p. 48.

49 Joshua Hyatt, "How to Hire Employees," *Inc.*, March 1990, p. 2. For more information on the importance of cultural fit read Ari Weinzweig, "Ask Ari Weinzweig," *Inc.*, December 2007, p. 84.

50 Anne Fisher, "How Can You Be Sure We're Not Hiring a Bunch of Shady Liars?" *Fortune*, May 26, 2003, p. 180.

51 Michelle Reece, "Business Ethics and the Pharmaceutical Industry," *SPBT Focus*, Fall 2005, p. 24.

52 Jennifer Merritt, "Welcome to Ethics 101," *BusinessWeek*, October 18, 2004, p. 90; Ronald Alsop, "Right and Wrong," *Wall Street Journal*, September 17, 2003, p. R9.

53 Terry Kabachnick, "Why Aren't You Hiring People Who Love What They Do?" *Retailing Issues Letter*, Center for Retailing Studies, Texas A&M University, College Station, TX, Vol. 19 No. 2, 2008, p. 5.

54 Richard Lacayo and Amanda Ripley, "Persons of the Year," *Time*, December 31, 2002, pp. 32–33.

55 Paula Dwyer and Dan Carney, with Amy Borrus and Lorraine Woellert in Washington and Christopher Palmeri in Los Angeles, "Year of the Whistleblower," *BusinessWeek*, December 16, 2002, pp. 107–108; Michael Orey, "WorldCom-Inspired 'Whistle-Blower' Law Has Weaknesses," *Wall Street Journal*, October 1, 2002, p. B1; R. Scott Oswald and Jason Zuckerman, "Protecting the Whistleblower," *Corporate Responsibility Officer*, January/February 2008, p. 49.

56 Sarah Jay, "Corruption Issues: A View from Shanghai," *International Business Ethics Institute*, Vol. 1, No. 1, November 1, 1997 [cited 27 November, 2005]. Available from http://www.business-ethics.org/newsdetail.asp?newsid531; INTERNET.

57 Chris Hill and Toby Hanlon, "26 Simple Ways to Change How You Feel," *Prevention*, August 1993, p. 126.

58 Sue Shellenbarger, "How and Why We Lie at the Office: From Pilfered Pens to Padded Accounts," *Wall Street Journal*, March 24, 2005, B1; Jared Dandberg, "Hard to Rein in Office Pilfering," *The News & Observer*, November 23, 2003, p. E12; Jared Sandberg, "Office Sticky Fingers Can Turn the Rest of Us into Joe Fridays," *The News & Observer*, November 19, 2003, p. B1.

59 Deborah Solomon, "For Financial Whistle-Blowers, New Shield Is an Imperfect One," *Wall Street Journal*, October 4, 2004, p. A1.

60 "Fraud Busters: Eight Who Made a Difference," Taxpayers Against Fraud [cited 30 November 2005]. Available from http://www.taf.org/whistleblower bios.pdf; INTERNET.

Chapter 6

1 Philip Kotler and Gary Armstrong, *Principles of Marketing*, 12th ed. (Upper Saddle River, NJ: Prentice Hall, 2008), pp. 20–21; "Supermarket and Other Grocery Stores"[cited 1 October 2008]. Available from http://www.answers.com/topic/stew-leonards; INTERNET.

2 Douglas A. Bernstein, Louis A. Penner, Alison Clarke-Stewart, and Edward J. Roy, *Psychology*, 6th ed. (Boston: Houghton Mifflin, 2006), pp. 686–687.

3 Hyrum W. Smith, *The 10 Natural Laws of Successful Time and Life Management* (New York: Warner Books, 1994), p. 48.

4 Stew Leonard, "Love Your Costumer," *Newsweek*, June 27, 1988, two unnumbered pages; Katherine Davis Fisherman, "The Disney World of Supermarkets," *New York Magazine*, March 11, 1985; B. L. Ochman Public Relations, "Stew Leonard's Fact Sheet" (New York: B.L. Ochman Public Relations).

5 Price Pritchett, *New Work Habits for the Next Millennium* (Dallas, Tex.: EPS Solutions, 1999), p. 2.

6 John Hollon, "The Cult of Welch," *Workforce Management*, October 10, 2005, p. 74.

7 Daniel H. Pink, *A Whole New Mind* (New York: Riverhead Books, 2005), pp. 48–63.

8 Laura Landro, "Compassion 101: Teaching M.D.s to Be Nicer," *Wall Street Journal*, September 28, 2005, p. D1.

9 Daniel H. Pink, *A Whole New Mind* (New York: Riverhead Books, 2005), p. 154.

10 Jerome Kagan, *Psychology: An Introduction* (New York: Harcourt Brace Jovanovich, 1984), p. 548.

11 Kurt Mortensen, *Maximum Influence: The 12 Universal Laws of Power Persuasion* (New York: AMACOM, 2004), pp. 62–68.

12 Douglas A. Bernstein, Louis A. Penner, Alison Clarke-Stewart, and Edward J. Roy, *Psychology*, 6th ed. (Boston: Houghton Mifflin, 2006), pp. 688–689.

13 "At Your Service," *Fast Company*, October 2004, p. 81.

14 William F. Schoell and Joseph P. Guiltinan, *Marketing*, 5th ed. (Boston: Allyn & Bacon, 1992), pp. 166–167; William M. Pride and O. C. Ferrell, *Marketing* (Boston: Houghton Mifflin, 2000), p. 211.

15 Andy Serwer, "Starbucks Hot to Go," *Fortune*, January 26, 2004, p. 68.

16 Bobbie Gossoge, "And There Was Happiness in Aqualand," *Inc.*, August 2007, pp. 96–101.

17 Jeffrey M. O'Brien, "A Perfect Season," *Fortune*, February 4, 2008, pp. 62–66.

18 Kellye Whitney, "New-Hire Failure Linked to Interpersonal Skills," *Chief Learning Officer Magazine* [cited 5 October 2005]. Available from http://www.clomedia.com; INTERNET.

19 Nathaniel Branden, *Self-Esteem at Work* (San Francisco: Jossey-Bass, 1998), pp. 94–97; "Adjusting an Attitude," *San Jose Mercury News*, August 20, 1997, p. G6.

20 His Holiness the Dalai Lama and Howard C. Cutler, *The Art of Happiness* (New York: Riverhead Books, 1998), pp. 16–17.

21 Tal Ben-Shahar, *Happier* (New York: McGraw-Hill, 2007), p. 33.

22 Tom Butler-Bowdon, *50 Success Classics* (London: Nicholas Brealey, 2004), pp. 168–171.

23 Tal Ben-Shahar, *Happier* (New York: McGraw-Hill, 2007), p. 107.

24 Ibid.

25 Alison Stein Wellner, "Are You Sales Phobic? Alas, the Cure Is to Sell More Often," *Inc.*, March 2007, pp. 52–56.

26 Tal Ben-Shahar, *Happier* (New York: McGraw-Hill, 2007), p. 111.

27 Patricia Sellers, "Now Bounce Back!" *Fortune*, May 1, 1995, p. 57.

28 His Holiness The Dalai Lama and Howard C. Cutler, *The Art of Happiness* (New York: Riverhead Books, 1998), p. 37.

29 Martin Seligman, *Learned Optimism* (New York: Knopf, 2001), p. 4.

30 Redford Williams and Virginia Williams, *Anger Kills* (New York: Harper Perennial, 1993), p. 12.

31 Patricia Kitchen, "If the Job Is a Lemon, Make Lemonade," *The News & Observer*, October 5, 2008, p. 8e.

32 Bob Wall, *Working Relationships* (Palo Alto, Calif.: Davies-Black, 1999), pp. 11–12.

33 Ibid., p. 17.

34 Brian Tracy, *The 100 Absolutely Unbreakable Laws of Business Success* (San Francisco: Berrett-Koehler 2000), pp. 67–70.

35 Nathaniel Branden, *Self-Esteem at Work* (San Francisco: Jossey-Bass, 1998), pp. 111–112.

36 Harry E. Chambers, *The Bad Attitude Survival Guide* (Reading, Mass.: Addison-Wesley, 1998), pp. 6–7.

37 Weekly online news from *Workforce Week Management* distributed to subscribers November 29, 2005.

38 Hamilton, "Net Work," p. EB117.

39 Quoted in Nancy W. Collins, Susan K. Gilbert, and Susan Nycum, *Women Leading: Making Tough Choices on the Fast Track* (Lexington, Mass.: Stephen Greene Press, 1988), p. 1.

40 "100 Best Companies to Work For," *Fortune*, February 4, 2008, pp. 75–94.

41 Joann S. Lublin, "Getting Your Company to Take You Back After a Dot-Com Fling," *Wall Street Journal*, June 5, 2001, p. BI.

42 "Stew Leonard's" [cited 1 October 2008]. Available from http://www.answers.com; INTERNET.

43 Robert Levering and Milton Moskowitz, "100 Best Companies to Work For," *Fortune*, January 20, 2003, p. 152.

44 Philip Kotler and Gary Armstrong, *Principles of Marketing*, 12th ed. (Upper Saddle River, NJ: Prentice Hall, 2008), p. 20.

45 Robert Levering and Milton Moskowitz, "And the Winners Are…," *Fortune*, February 2, 2009, p. 77.

46 George F. Will, "The Perils of Bad Promises," *The Washington Post*, January 16, 2005, p. B7; Associated Press, "Fed Pension Agency Could See $71 Billion Deficit," June 9, 2005 [cited 9 December 2005]. Available from http://www.msnbc.msn.com; INTERNET; Associated Press, "Verizon Ends Manager Pension Contributions" [cited 7 December 2005]. Available from http://www.abcnews.go.com; INTERNET; "Dr. Spencer Johnson" [cited 7 December 2005]. Available from http://www.spencerjohnsonpartners.com; INTERNET; Spencer Johnson, *Who Moved My Cheese?* (New York: G. P. Putnam's Sons), 1998.

Chapter 7

1 "Attack on the World Records" [cited 14 October 2008]. Available from http://www.nbolympics.com; INTERNET.

2 "Michael Phelps" [cited on 14 October 2008]. Available from http://en.wikipedia.org/wiki/Michael_Phelps; INTERNET.

3 Vicki Michaelis, "Built to Swim, Phelps Found a Focus and Refuge in Water" [cited on 14 October 2008]. Available from http://www.usatoday.com; INTERNET.

4 Douglas A. Bernstein, Louis A. Penner, Alison Clarke-Stewart, and Edward J. Roy, *Psychology*, 7th ed. (Boston: Houghton Mifflin, 2006), pp. 397–398.

5 Jack Canfield, *Key to Living the Law of Attraction* (Deerfield Beach, Fl: Health Communications, Inc., 2007), p. 54.

6 M. G. Lord, "Raison McÊtre," *New York Times Book Review*, August 18, 2002, p. 13.

7 Jim Carlton, "Wild Horses, Couldn't Drag Them Away from Stones Shows," *Wall Street Journal*, November 22, 2002, p. A1.

8 Robert Kreitner, *Management*, 10th ed. (Boston: Houghton Mifflin, 2007), pp. 381–382.

9 Brittany Hite, "Employers Rethink How They Give Feedback," *Wall Street Journal*, October 13, 2008, p. B5. See *The Trophy Kids Grow Up*, by Ron Alsop, for a detailed discussion of how the Millennial generation is changing the workplace.

10 Data were collected by use of the Reiss Profile, a standardized psychological test used to measure 16 desires.

11 Steven Reiss, "Secrets of Happiness," *Psychology Today*, January/February 2001, pp. 50–56. To learn more about the Reiss Profile, see *Who Am I: The 16 Basic Desires That Motivate Our Happiness and Define Our Personalities* (New York: Berkley Books, 2000).

12 Cynthia Berryman-Fink, *The Managers' Desk Reference* (New York: AMACOM, 1989), pp. 156–157.

13 "California Teen Sets Everest Record," *The News & Observer,"* May 20, 2007, p. 13A.

14 Robert Kreitner, *Management*, 10th ed. (Boston: Houghton Mifflin, 2007), pp. 378–380.

15 "Belonging Satisfies Basic Human Need," *The Menninger Letter*, August 1995, p. 6.

16 Frederick Herzberg, Bernard Mausner, and Barbara Black Snyderman, *The Motivation to Work* (New York: Wiley, 1959).

17 C. R. Snyder, "Hope Helps," *Psychology Today*, November/December 1999, p. 20. Expectancy Theory is discussed in Robert Kreitner, *Management*, 10th ed. (Boston: Houghton Mifflin, 2007), pp. 382–383.

18 Richard Barrett, "The Power of Purpose," *The Inner Edge*, August/September 1999, p. 20.

19 Robert Kreitner, *Management*, 10th ed. (Boston: Houghton Mifflin, 2007), p. 385.

20 Ibid., p. 403; Ron Zemke, "Toxic Energy Dumps," *Training*, January 2001, p. 18.

21 Berryman-Fink, *The Manager's Desk Reference*, pp. 156–157.

22 "Management Glossary" [cited 27 December 2005]. Available from http://www.management.about.com; INTERNET; Brigitte Blobel, "If You Have Class, Then You Are Just as Good as Your Guests," *Audi Magazine*, December 2001, pp. 72–75.

23 Karen Auby, "A Boomer's Guide to Communicating with Gen X and Gen Y," *BusinessWeek*, September 1, 2008.

24 Kelly K. Spors, "Top Small Work Places," *Wall Street Journal*, October 13, 2008, p. R5.

25 Shelly Banjo, "A Perfect Match," *Wall Street Journal*, October 13, 2008, p. R9.

26 Patrick J. Sauer, "Open-Door Management," *Inc.*, June 2003, p. 44.

27 Janice Love, review of *The Set-Up-to-Fail Syndrome*, by Jean-Francois Manzoni and Jean-Louis Barsoux, *Training*, April 2003, p. 49; Sharon Begley, "Expectations May Alter Outcomes Far More Than We Realize," *Wall Street Journal*, November 7, 2003, p. B1.

28 Ibid.; Ann C. Humphries, "Motivating Generation X" [cited 27 December 2005]. Available from http://www.christianwomentoday.com/workplace/genx; INTERNET. Karen Auby, "A Boomer's Guide to Communicating with Gen X and Gen Y," *BusinessWeek*, September 1, 2008, p. 63.

29 Peter Doskoch, "The Winning Edge," *Psychology Today*, November/December 2005, pp. 42–45.

30 Ibid., pp. 46–47.

31 M. Scott Peck, *The Road Less Traveled* (New York: Simon & Schuster, 1978), pp. 18–20; Christine B. Whelan, "The Road Is Heavily Traveled Now," *Wall Street Journal*, October 7, 2005, p. W13.

32 G. Pascal Zachary, "The New Search for Meaning in 'Meaningless' Work," *Wall Street Journal*, January 9, 1997, p. B1.

33 Robin A. Sheerer, *No More Blue Mondays* (Palo Alto, Calif.: Davies-Black Publishing, 1999).

34 Carol Kleiman, "The Move to Telecommuting," *San Jose Mercury News*, April 16, 2000, p. PC1; Carol Kleiman, "Work/Life Programs Now Essential, Not a Frill, Consulting Firm Says," *San Jose Mercury News*, April 2, 2000, p. PC1.

35 Peter Doskoch, "The Winning Edge," *Psychology Today*, November/December 2005, p. 50.

36 Lynne Cox, Swimming to Antarctica, Editors' Pick, *Mercedes*, Winter 2004, p. 72. "The Barnes & Noble Review" [cited 24 March 2004]. Available from http://www.barnesandnoble.com; INTERNET.

37 Michael Specter, "The Long Ride," *New Yorker*, July 15, 2002, pp. 48–58, p. 172. "Management Theory? Management Madness," *Psychology Today*, March/April 1997, pp. 58–62.

38 George Anders, "At Office Retreats, Tales of Adversity Fire Up the Staff," *Wall Street Journal*, October 13, 2006, pp. A1–A2.

39 Ibid.

Chapter 8

1 "5 Stories of Quantum Change," *Spirituality & Health*, January/February 2008, pp. 41–43. Note: Within this article is a story titled "When I Surrendered" by Jim Teeters.

2 "Now Go Out and Lead!" *BusinessWeek*, January 8, 2007, p. 73.

3 Martha Beck, "True Confessions," *O, The Oprah Magazine*, June 2002, pp. 183–184.

4 Aviva Patz, "Go Ahead—Get Mad," *Health & Healing*, June 2003, pp. 95–97.

5 Daniel Goleman, "What Makes a Leader?" *Harvard Business Review*, November/December 1998, p. 95.

6 Cary Cherniss and Daniel Goleman, *The Emotionally Intelligent Workplace* (San Francisco: Jossey-Bass, 2001), p. 258.

7 David Stewart, "Talk at Work: Do You Dialogue?" *Health & Healing*, Vol. 5, No. 6, 2002, p. 2.

8 Bill George, Peter Sims, Andrew N. McLean, and Diana Mayer, "Discovering Your Authentic Leadership," *Harvard Business Review*, February 2007, pp. 129–138.

9 Jack Welch and Suzy Welch, "Get Real, Get Ahead," *BusinessWeek*, May 14, 2007, p. 100.

10 Karen Wright, "In Search of the Real You," *Psychology Today*, May/June 2008, pp. 70–77.

11 Roy M. Berko, Andrew D. Wolvin, and Darlyn R. Wolvin, *Communicating* (Boston: Houghton Mifflin, 1995), p. 46.

12 *Communication Concepts—The Johari Window* (New York: J. C. Penney Company, Consumer Affairs Department, 1979). Roy M. Berks, Andrew D. Wolvin, Darlyn R. Wolvin, *Communicating—A Social and Career Focus*, 8th ed. (Boston: Houghton Mifflin Company, 2001), pp. 73–75.

13 Thomas Moore, "Finding Freedom in Forgiveness," *Spirituality & Health*, May/June 2008, p. 12.

14 Parker J. Palmer, "Life on the Mobius Strip," *Inner Edge*, August/September 2000, pp. 22–23.

15 Marshall Goldsmith, "How to Learn the Truth About Yourself," *Fast Company*, October 2003, p. 127.

16 Maury A. Peiper, "Getting 360 Feedback Right," *Harvard Business Review*, January 2001, pp. 3–7; William C. Byham, "Fixing the Instrument," *Training*, July 2004, p. 50.

17 "The Path of a Heart-Centered Leader," *Spirituality & Health*, May/June 2005, pp. 53–55.

18 Jared Sandberg, "Do You Hear What I Hear? Telling Off a Colleague—Silently," *Wall Street Journal*, October 23, 2007, p. B1.

19 Beverly Engel, "Making Amends," *Psychology Today*, July/August 2002, pp. 40–42.

20 Ibid.

21 Sharon Nelton, "The Power of Forgiveness," *Nation's Business*, June 1995, p. 41.

22 Lazarus and Lazarus, *The 60-Second Shrink* (San Luis Obispo, Calif.: Impact, 1997), pp. 76–79.

23 Joann S. Lublin, "Talking Too Much on a Job Interview May Kill Your Chance," *Wall Street Journal*, October 30, 2007, p. B1.

24 Margery Weinstein, "Office Trust Busters," *Training*, July 2006, pp. 10–11.

25 Bob Wall, *Working Relationships* (Palo Alto, Calif.: Davies-Black, 1999), p. 166.

26 David Kiley, "The Flight for Ford's Future," *BusinessWeek*, August 11, 2008, pp. 40–43.

27 Joyce Brothers, "The Most Important People We Know ... Our Friends," *Parade Magazine*, February 16, 1997, pp. 4–6; Sue Shellenbarger, "Ovulating? Depressed? The Latest Rules on What Not to Talk About at Work," *Wall Street Journal*, July 21, 2005, p. D1.

28 John Murawski, "Stray Remarks Can Hunt Your Job Searchers," *News & Observer*, April 30, 2006, p. E1.

29 Stephen M. R. Covey, *The Speed of Trust* (New York: Free Press, 2006), pp. 5–10.

30 Jack Welch and Suzy Welch, "The Blame Game—Forget It," *BusinessWeek*, March 5, 2007, p. 92.

31 Blaine Hartford, "Trust Your Surgeon? Mate? Friends? Colleagues? What Makes Up a Feeling of Trust?" *Health & Healing*, June 2000, p. 36.

32 Ron Zemke, "Can You Manage Trust?" *Training*, February 2000, p. 78; Ron Zemke, "A Matter of Trust," *Training*, December 2002, p. 12.

33 Aubrey C. Daniels, *Bringing Out the Best in People* (New York: McGraw-Hill, 1994), p. 41.

34 Jack R. Gibb, *Trust: A New View of Personal and Organizational Development* (Los Angeles: Guild of Tutors Press, 1978), p. 29.

35 Susan Scott, *Fierce Conversations* (New York: Viking, 2002), pp. 198–201.

36 Excerpt adapted from Camille Wright Miller, "Self-Evaluation Painful, But It's Valuable," *The Roanoke Times*, November 16, 2003, p. B1.

37 See Kerry Patterson, Joseph Grenny, Al Switzer, and Ron McMillan, *Crucial Conversations* (New York: McGraw-Hill Companies, 2002).

38 Sarah Boehle, "Crafting a Coaching Culture," *Training*, May 2007, pp. 22–24.

39 Stephen M. R. Covey, *The Speed of Trust*, p. 1.

40 Ibid., pp. 13–17.

41 "The Five Dysfunctions of ATeam: Book Review" [cited 3 March 2008]. Available from http://www.social-media-university-global.org; INTERNET.

42 Ibid.

43 Jeffrey T. Polzer, "Making Diverse Teams Click," *Harvard Business Review*, July-August 2008, pp. 20–21.

Chapter 9

1 Linda Tischler, "Hospitality, Sweet," *Fast Company*, September 2006, p. 29.

2 Ibid., p. 30.

3 Douglas A. Bernstein, Louis A. Penner, Alison Clarke-Stewart, and Edward J. Roy, *Psychology*, 7th ed. (Boston: Houghton Mifflin, 2006), pp. 429–430.

4 Carol S. Pearson, "The Emotional Side of Workplace Success," *The Inner Edge*, December 1998/January 1999, p. 3.

5 Daniel Goleman, *Emotional Intelligence* (New York: Bantam Books, 1995), pp. 34 and 43; Stephen R. Covey, "Questions for Covey," *Training*, July/August 2007, p. 40.

6 Daniel Goleman, *Working with Emotional Intelligence* (New York: Bantam Books, 1998), pp. 24–28; Robert Kreitner, *Management*, 10th ed. (Boston: Houghton Mifflin, 2007), p. 447.

7 John Selby, *Conscious Healing* (New York: Bantam Books, 1989), p. 32.

8 James Georges, "The Not-So-Stupid Americans," *Training*, July 1994, p. 90.

9 Joan Borysenko, *Inner Peace for Busy People* (Carlsbad, Calif. Hay House, Inc., 2001), p. 83.

10 Tim Sanders, *Love Is the Killer App* (New York: Crown Business, 2002), pp. 17–18.

11 Ibid., p. 23.

12 Ron Zemke, "Contact! Training Employees to Meet the Public," *Service Solutions* (Minneapolis: Lakewood Books, 1990), pp. 20–23.

13 Peter J. Frost, *Toxic Emotions at Work* (Boston: Harvard Business School Press, 2007), pp. 5–7.

14 Ibid., p. 3.

15 Bernstein et al., *Psychology*, p. 473.

16 Ibid.

17 Ibid., p. 399.

18 Jason Zweig, "How to Control Your Fears in a Fearsome Market," *Wall Street Journal*, July 19, 2008, p. B1.

19 William C. Menninger and Harry Levinson, *Human Understanding in Industry* (Chicago: Science Research Associates, 1956), p. 29.

20 Joan Borysenko, *Guilt Is the Teacher, Love Is the Lesson* (New York: Warner Books, 1990), p. 70.

21 Anthony Balderrama, "Finding a Job Using Uncommon Search Tactics," *The News & Observer*, November 30, 2008, p. F1.

22 Visit the Wikipedia (http://www.wikipediea.org) or Businessballs (http://www.businessballs.com) Web sites for a comprehensive overview of TA Theory.

23 Bernstein et al., *Psychology*, p. 23.

24 P. Christopher Earley and Elaine Mosakowski, "Cultural Intelligence," *Harvard Business Review*, October 2004, p. 139.

25 *Outsourced* [accessed 8 December 2008]. Available from http://www.netflix.com; INTERNET.

26 P. Christopher Earley and Elaine Mosakowski, "Cultural Intelligence," pp. 141–142.

27 Ibid., p. 141.

28 Harold H. Bloomfield and Robert K. Cooper, *The Power of 5* (Emmaus, Pa.: Rodale Press, 1995), p. 334; Redford Williams and Virginia Williams, *Anger Kills* (New York: HarperCollins, 1993), p. 3; Redford Williams, "Why Anger Kills," *Duke Medicine Healthline*, Winter 2007, p. 11.

29 Kimes Gustin, *Anger, Rage, and Resentment* (West Caldwell, N.J.: St. Ives' Press, 1994), p. 1.

30 Art Ulene, *Really Fit Really Fast* (Encino, Calif.: HealthPoints, 1996), pp. 170–174.

31 Pemna Chödrön, "The Answer to Anger and Other Strong Emotions," *Shambhala Sun*, March 2005, p. 32.

32 Jared Sandberg, "Shooting Messengers Makes Us Feel Better But Work Dumber," *Wall Street Journal*, September 11, 2007, p. B1.

33 Rolland S. Parker, *Emotional Common Sense* (New York: Barnes & Noble Books, 1973), pp. 80–81.

34 Pema Chodron, "The Answers to Anger and Other Strong Emotions," *Shambhala Sun*, March 2005, p. 32.

35 Les Giblin, *How to Have Confidence and Power in Dealing with People* (Englewood Cliffs, N.J.: Prentice-Hall 1956), p. 37.

36 "Workplace Violence: An Employer's Guide" [accessed 12 December 2008]. Available from http://www.workviolence.com; INTERNET.

37 Carol Hymowitz, "Bosses Have to Learn How to Confront Troubled Employees," *Wall Street Journal*, April 23, 2007, p. B1.

38 Jennifer J. Laabs, "Employee Sabotage: Don't Be the Target," *Workforce*, July 1999, pp. 32–42; Michelle Conlin and Alex Salkever, "Revenge of the Downsized Nerds," *BusinessWeek*, July 30, 2001, p. 40.

39 Laabs, "Employee Sabotage," pp. 32–42.

40 Anne Fisher, "How to Prevent Violence and Work," *Fortune*, February 21, 2005, p. 42.

41 Pete Carey, "Economic Instability May Lead to Danger," *The Roanoke Times*, November 28, 2008, p. 8.

42 Hale Dwoskin, *The Sedona Method* (Sedona, Ariz.: Sedona Press, 2003), p. 30.

43 Walton C. Boshear and Karl G. Albrecht, *Understanding People: Models and Concepts* (San Diego: University Associates, 1977), pp. 41–46.

44 Chris Hill and Toby Hanlon, "Twenty-Six Simple Ways to Change How You Feel," *Prevention*, August 1993, p. 63.

45 Bloomfield and Cooper, *The Power of 5*, p. 368; Jill Neimark, "Open Mind Open Heart," *Spirituality & Health*, May/June 2008, p. 14.

46 Erin White, "Review Went Badly? Stay Cool, Find a Fix or Look to Move On," *Wall Street Journal*, May 23, 2006, p. B7.

47 Jill Hamburg Coplan, "Getting Mad at Work Is a Male Prerogative," *BusinessWeek*, April 21, 2008, p. 18.

48 Joan Borysenko, *Minding the Body, Mending the Mind* (New York: Bantam Books, 1987), pp. 164–165.

49 Don Miguel Ruiz, *The Four Agreements* (San Rafael, Calif.: Amber-Allen Publishing, 1997), p. 111.

50 Daniel Goleman, Editor *Healing Emotions* (Boston: Shambhala Publications, Inc., 1997), p. 33.

51 Sam Keen, *Fire in the Belly—On Being a Man* (New York: Bantam Books, 1991), p. 242.

52 Gerard Egan, *You and Me* (Monterey, Calif.: Brooks/Cole, 1977), p. 73.

53 Arnold A. Lazarus and Clifford N. Lazarus, *The 60-Second Shrink* (San Luis Obispo, Calif.: Impact, 1997), pp. 10–11.

54 Borysenko, *Minding the Body, Mending the Mind*, p. 169.

55 Ellen Safier, "Our Experts Answer Your Questions," *Menninger Letter*, May 1993, p. 8.

56 Leo F. Buscaglia, *Loving Each Other* (Thorofare, N.J.: Slack, 1984), p. 160.

57 Keen, *Fire in the Belly*, p. 242.

58 Excerpted from Marilyn Vos Savant, "Ask Marilyn," *Parade*, February 18, 2009.

59 Linda Tischler, *Fast Company*, pp. 29–30. "Danny Meyer Walks into a Pub" [accessed 14 December 2008]. Available from http://nymog.com; INTERNET.

60 "Setting the Table" [accessed 3 December 2008]. Available from http://books.google.com; INTERNET.

61 Carol Hymowitz and Joann S. Lubin, "Many Companies Look the Other Way at Employee Affairs," *Wall Street Journal*, March 8, 2005, p. B1; Aleksandra Todorova, "Romancing a Colleague," *The News & Observer*, February 27, 2005, p. E9; Carol Hymowitz, "Managing Your Career," *Wall Street Journal*, November 18, 1997, p. B1; Hal Lancaster, "Managing Your Career," *Wall Street Journal*, September 23, 1997, p. B1; Jennifer J. Salopek, "You Don't Have to Play Cupid, Exactly," *Training & Development*, December 1998, p. 60.

Chapter 10

1 Kelly K. Spors, "Top Small Workplaces," *Wall Street Journal*, October 13, 2008, pp. R1 and R8; "Workplace Awards" [accessed 28 December 2008]. Available from http://www.winningworkplaces.org; INTERNET; "Our Story" [accessed 29 December 2008]. Available from http://www.newbelgium.com; INTERNET.

2 Judith Orloff, "Accessing Sacred Energy," *Spirituality & Health*, May/June 2004, pp. 48–51; Judith Orloff, *Positive Energy* (New York: Harmony Books, 2004), pp. 1–15, 288. More information regarding positive energy can be found in Barbara Frederickson, *Positivity* (New York: Random House, Inc., 2009).

3 Scott McCartney, "How U.S. Airways Vaulted to First Place," *Wall Street Journal*, July 22, 2008, p. D3.

4 Justine Willis Toms, "A Baby Step Toward Better Community," *New Dimensions*, May/June 1999, p. 2.

5 Kip Tindele, "The Professional Organizer," *Fortune*, September 3, 2007, p. 26.

6 Kenneth Blanchard and Spencer Johnson, *The One Minute Manager* (New York: Morrow, 1982), p. 43.

7 Douglas A. Bernstein, Louis A. Penner, Alison Clarke-Stewart, and Edward J. Roy, *Psychology*, 7th ed. (Boston: Houghton Mifflin, 2006), p. 206.

8 Phred Dvorak, "Hotelier Finds Happiness Keeps Staff Checked In," *Wall Street Journal*, December 17, 2007, p. B3.

9 Tom Rath and Donald O. Clifton, *How Full Is Your Bucket?* (New York: Gallup Press, 2004), pp. 31–33; "Employee Engagement" [accessed 3 December 2008]. Available from http://www.gallup.com; INTERNET.

10 Holly Dolezalek, "Don't Go," *Training*, July/August 2003, p. 52; Rath and Clifton, *How Full Is Your Bucket?*, pp. 39–40.

11 David Dorsey, "Happiness Pays," *Inc. Magazine*, February 2004, pp. 89–94.

12 For a comprehensive introduction to positive reinforcement, see Aubrey C. Daniels, *Other People's Habits—How to Use Positive Reinforcement to Bring Out the Best in People Around You* (New York: McGraw-Hill, 2001).

13 Tom Rath and Donald O. Clifton, *How Full Is Your Bucket* (New York: Gallup Press, 2004), p. 15.

14 Ron Alsop, "The Trophy Kids Go to Work," *Wall Street Journal*, October 21, 2008, pp. D1 and D4. Profiles of several Generation Y employers can be reviewed in "Cool, Determined, and Under 30," *Inc.*, October 2008, pp. 97–105.

15 Sheldon Lewis, "Another Reason to List What You're Grateful For," *Spirituality & Health*, March/April 2008, p. 27. To learn more about the powerful influence of gratitude, read *Thanks! How the New Science of Gratitude Can Make You Happier*, by Robert Emmons (Boston: Houghton Mifflin, 2007).

16 "Have a Nice Day," *American Way*, January 1, 2007, p. 18.

17 Joann S. Lublin, "Notes to Interviewers Should Go Beyond a Simple Thank You," *Wall Street Journal*, February 5, 2008, p. B1.

18 David Stewart, "Talk at Work: Do You Dialogue?" *Health & Healing*, Vol. 5, No. 6, 2002, p. 2.

19 Jon R. Katzenbach, *Why Pride Matters More Than Money* (New York: Crown Business, 2003), pp. 23–24.

20 Gary Kelly, "The Winning Spirit," *Spirit*, November 2008, p. 4.

21 John A. Byrne, "How to Lead Now," *Fast Company*, August 2003, pp. 62–70.

22 Deepak Chopra, *The Seven Spiritual Laws of Success* (San Rafael, Calif.: Amber-Allen, 1994), pp. 30–31.

23 *Random Acts of Kindness* (Berkeley, Calif.: Conari Press, 1993), pp. 1, 54, 68, and 91.

24 Malcolm Boyd, "Volunteering Thanks," *Modern Maturity*, May/June 1997, p. 72.

25 Bob Nelson, *1001 Ways to Reward Employees* (New York: Workman, 1994), p. ix.

26 Ibid., p. xv.

27 "Rich DeVos Remarks—Delta Pi Epsilon Distinguished Lecturer," *Delta Pi Epsilon Journal*, Fall 1995, pp. 221–223.

28 "How to Run an Incentive Program," *Incentive*, July 1990, p. 2.

29 Kelly K. Spors, "Top Small Workplaces," p. R8.

30 Stephen J. Dunbar, "The Freaky Side of Business," *Training*, February 2006, p. 8.

31 Joel Spolsky, "Employees Will Always Game Incentive Plans—Because the Geniuses Who Design Them Don't Anticipate How Employees Will Respond," *Inc.*, October 2008, p. 85.

32 Dave Murphy, "If You Want Gold, Give Them a Goal," *San Francisco Chronicle*, April 14, p. J1; Jeff Barbian, "Golden Carrots," *Training*, July 2002, p. 18.

33 Jared Sandberg, "A Modern Conundrum: When Work Is Invisible, So Are the Satisfactions," *Wall Street Journal*, February 19, 2008, p. B1.

34 Cedric B. Johnson, "When Working Harder Is Not Smarter," *The Inner Edge*, April/May 2000, pp. 18–21.

35 Ibid., p. 19.

36 Daniel H. Pink, *A Whole New Mind* (New York: Riverhead Books, 2005), pp. 48–53.

37 Mitchell Schnurman, "Kissing Up: It Works…But Only if You Mean It," *Roanoke Times & World-News*, September 28, 1993, p. E1.

38 Anne Fisher, "Show Off, Without Being a Blowhard," *Fortune*, March 8, 2004, p. 68.

39 Kelly K. Spors, "Top Small Workplaces," p. R4.

40 Ibid., p. R8.

41 John A. Byrne, "How to Lead Now," *Fast Company*, August 2003, pp. 62–70; Katzenbach, *Why Pride Matters More Than Money*, pp. 13–19, 47–67; Dorsey, "Happiness Pays," pp. 89–94.

Chapter 11

1 Joann S. Lublin, "High-End Helps for Job Hunters: Does It Pay?" *Wall Street Journal*, January 6, 2009, pp. D1 and D4.

2 Philip Kotler and Gary Armstrong, *Principles of Marketing*, 12th ed. (Upper Saddle River, NJ: Prentice Hall, 2008), p. 141; pp. 230–239.

3 David McNally and Karl D. Speak, *Be Your Own Brand—A Breakthrough Formula for Standing Out from the Crowd* (San Francisco: Berrett—Koehle Publishers, Inc., 2002), p. 112.

4 Stephen R. Covey, *The Seven Habits of Highly Effective People* (New York: Simon & Schuster, 1989), pp. 22, 34.

5 Susan Bixler, *Professional Presence* (New York: G. P. Putnam's Sons, 1991), p. 16. For more information on professional presence see Judith Sills, "Becoming Your Own Brand," *Psychology Today*, January/February 2008, p. 62.

6 Ann Demarais and Valerie White, *First Impressions* (New York: Bantam Books, 2004), pp. 22–23.

7 Ibid., p. 16.

8 Ibid.

9 Gordon Anders, "Hey, Not So Fast," *Wall Street Journal*, January 11, 2005, p. D9.

10 Danielle Sacks, "The Accidental Guru," *Fast Company*, January 2005, pp. 69–70.

11 Judith Sills, "Becoming Your Own Brand," *Psychology Today*, January/February, 2008, p. 62.

12 Jeffrey Zaslow, "First Impressions Get Faster," *Wall Street Journal*, February 16, 2006, p. D4.

13 Ann Demarais and Valerie White, *First Impressions* (New York: Bantam Books, 2004), p. 22.

14 Leonard Zunin and Natalie Zunin, *Contact—The First Four Minutes* (New York: Ballantine Books, 1972), p. 17.

15 Clyde Haberman, "No Offense," *New York Times Book Review*, February 18, 1996, p. 11.

16 Norine Dresser, *Multicultural Manners: Essential Rules of Etiquette for the 21st Century* (Hoboken, NJ: John Wiley and Sons Inc., 2005). This book provides comprehensive coverage of multicultural etiquette.

17 Susan Bixler and Nancy Nix-Rice, *The New Professional Image*, 2nd ed. (Avon, Mass: Adams Media Corporation, 2005), p. 311; Susan Bixler and Lisa Scherrer Dugan, *5 Steps to Professional Presence* (Avon, Mass: Adams Media Corporation, 2001), pp. 4–8.

18 Suein L. Hwang, "Enterprise Takes Idea of Dressed for Success to a New Extreme," *Wall Street Journal*, November 20, 2002, p. B1.

19 "GPA Licensee Certification/Train-the-Trainer" [cited 16 January 2006]. Available from http://www.globalprotocol.com; INTERNET. See "Overview of Image Consulting" [cited January 14,

2009.] Available from http://www.aici.org; INTERNET.

20 Dave Knesel, "Image Consulting—A Well-Dressed Step Up the Corporate Ladder," *Pace*, July/August 1981, p. 74.

21 Cora Daniels, "The Man in the Tan Khaki Pants," *Fortune*, May 1, 2000, p. 338; Susan Bixler and Nancy Nix-Rice, *The New Professional Images*, 2nd ed. (Avon, Mass: Adams Media Corporation, 2005), pp. 133–144.

22 Christina Binkley, "Business Casual: All Business, Never Casual," *Wall Street Journal*, April 17, 2008, pp. D1 and D8.

23 Karen Auby, "A Boomer's Guide to Communicating with Gen X and Gen Y," *BusinessWeek*, August 25/September 1, 2008, p. 63.

24 Deborah Blum, "Face It!" *Psychology Today*, September/October 1998, pp. 34, 69.

25 Susan Bixler, *The Professional Image* (New York: Perigee Books, 1984), p. 217; Susan Bixler and Lisa Scherrer Dugan, *5 Steps to Professional Presence* (Avon, Mass: Adams Media Corporation, 2001), pp. 8–10.

26 Susan Bixler, *The Professional Image* (New York: Perigee Books, 1984), p. 219.

27 Heather Won Tesoriers, "At Vioxx Trial, Fast Talkers Challenge Court Stenographer," *Wall Street Journal*, October 25, 2005, p. B1.

28 Joann S. Lublin, "To Win Advancement, You Need to Clean Up Any Bad Speech Habits," *Wall Street Journal*, October 5, 2004, p. B1.

29 Ibid.

30 Lydia Ramsey, "You Never Get a 2nd Chance," *Selling*, October 2003, p. 3.

31 Adapted from Zunin and Zunin, *Contact*, pp. 102–108; "Handshake 101," *Training & Development*, November 1995, p. 71.

32 Susan Bixler and Lisa Scherrer Dugan, *5 Steps to Professional Presence* (Avon, Mass: Adams Media Corporation, 2001), p. 65.

33 Cynthia Crossen, "Etiquette for Americans Today," *Wall Street Journal*, December 28, 2001, p. W13.

34 Gwendolyn Bounds, "Handyman Etiquette: Stay Calm, Avert Eyes," *Wall Street Journal*, May 10, 2005, p. B1.

35 Barbara Pachter and Mary Brody, *Complete Business Etiquette Handbook* (Englewood Cliffs, NJ: Prentice-Hall, 1995), p. 3.

36 Amy Gamerman, "Lunch with Letitia: Our Reporter Minds Her Manners," *Wall Street Journal*, March 3, 1994, p. A14.

37 Ann Marie Sabath, "Meeting Etiquette: Agendas and More," *DECA Dimensions*, January/February 1994, p. 8; "Is Etiquette a Core Value?" *Inc.*, May 2004, p. 22.

38 Leila Jason, "Are There Rules of Etiquette for Cell-phone Use?" *Wall Street Journal*, September 10, 2001, p. R16; Dana May Casperson, "Tactfully Respond to Cell Phone Intrusion," *Selling*, April 2005, p. 5.

39 Dana May Casperson, "Break Those Bad Cell-phone Habits," *Selling*, January 2002, p. 9.

40 Gene Veith, "Curse of the Foul Mouth," *Wall Street Journal*, January 24, 2003, p. D1; Tara Parker-Pope and Kyle Pope, "When #@%&@ Is—and Isn't—Appropriate," *Wall Street Journal Sunday*, featured in *The News & Observer*, January 21, 2001, p. D4.

41 This quote was attributed to Rand Corporation. See Jared Sandberg, "In the Workplace, Every Bleeping Word Can Show Your Rank," *Wall Street Journal*, March 21, 2006, p. B1.

42 Barbara Moses, *Career Intelligence* (San Francisco: Berrett-Koehler, 1997), p. 175.

43 Nancy K. Austin, "What Do America Online and Dennis Rodman Have in Common?" *Inc.*, July 1997, p. 54.

44 Joann S. Lublin, "Interview Etiquette Begins the Minute You Walk in the Door," *Wall Street Journal*, August 1, 2006, p. B1.

45 "How Much Can Employer Dictate Your Lifestyle?" *San Jose Mercury News*, May 2, 1993, pp. 1 PC and 2 PC; Susan Barciela, "Looks and Dress Still Count, Though the Lawyers Might Argue," *Roanoke Times & World-News*, June 19, 1993, p. D2; Susan Bixler, "Your Professional Presence," *Training Dimensions*, Vol. 9, No. 1, 1994, p. 1.

46 Marilyn Vos Savant, "Ask Marilyn," *Parade*, May 30, 2002, p. 19.

47 David McNally and Karl D. Speak, *Be Your Own Brand* (San Francisco: Berrett-Koehler, 2002), p. 4.

48 Ibid.

49 "The Right Words at the Right Time," *O, The Oprah Magazine*, May 2002, p. 202.

50 Joe Morgenstern, "Paul Newman: So Much More Than Just a Pretty Face," *Wall Street Journal*, September 30, 2008, p. B17; Mark Vaughn, "Paul Newman 1925–2008," *Autoweek*, October 6, 2008, p. 43.

51 Stephanie G. Sherman, *Make Yourself Memorable* (New York: American Management Association, 1996), pp. 3–4; "People in the News," *U.S. News &*

World Report, November 8, 1999, p. 12; Ann Landers, "If You've Got Class, Nothing Else Matters," *The News & Observer,* July 11, 1998, p. E2; Carlin Flora, "The Superpowers," *Psychology Today,* May/June 2005, pp. 40–50.

Chapter 12

1 Gina Chon, "To Woo Wealthy, Lexus Attempts Image Makeover," *Wall Street Journal,* March 24, 2007, pp. A1 and A12.

2 Erin White, "How a Company Made Everyone a Team Player," *Wall Street Journal,* August 13, 2007, p. B1.

3 Bill George (with Peter Sims), *True North* (San Francisco: John Wiley & Sons, Inc., 2007), p. xxiv.

4 Robert Kreitner, *Management,* 11th ed. (Boston: Houghton Mifflin, 2009), p. 402.

5 "Stephen Covey Talks About the 8th Habit: Effective Is No Longer Enough," *Training,* February 2005, pp. 17–19.

6 James M. Kouzes and Barry Z. Posner, *The Leadership Challenge,* 3rd ed. (San Francisco: Jossey-Bass, 2002), pp. 3–12.

7 William M. Pride, Robert J. Hughes, and Jack R. Kapoor, *Business,* 8th ed. (Boston: Houghton Mifflin, 2005), p. 198.

8 Nadira A. Hira, "You Raised Them, Now Manage Them," *Fortune,* May 28, 2007, pp. 38–46.

9 Robert Kreitner, *Management,* 11th ed. (Boston: Houghton Mifflin, 2009), p. 182.

10 Bill George (with Peter Sims), *True North* (San Francisco: John Wiley & Sons, Inc., 2007), p. 3.

11 Robert Kreitner, *Management,* 11th ed. (Boston: Houghton Mifflin, 2009), pp. 353–354.

12 Ibid., pp. 482–483.

13 Scott Thurm, "Teamwork Raises Everyone's Game," *Wall Street Journal,* November 7, 2005, p. B8.

14 Lynda Gratton, "Working Together...When Apart," *Wall Street Journal,* June 16, 2007, p. R4.

15 Robert Kreitner, *Management,* 11th ed. (Boston: Houghton Mifflin, 2009), pp. 386–388; David Stewart, "True Teamwork," *Health & Healing,* Vol. 6, No. 1, 2003, p. 2.

16 Carol Hymowitz, "Business Is Personal, So Managers Need to Harness Emotions," *Wall Street Journal,* November 13, 2006, p. B1.

17 Adapted from a list in Douglas McGregor, *The Human Side of Enterprise* (New York: McGraw-Hill, 1960), pp. 232–235, 21.

18 Patrick Lencioni, *The Five Dysfunctions of a Team* (San Francisco: Jossey-Bass, 2002), p. vii.

19 These two dimensions can be measured by the *Leadership Opinion Questionnaire* developed by Edwin A. Fleishman and available from Pearson Performance Solutions. Available from http://www.pearsonps.com; INTERNET.

20 Brian Tracy, *The 100 Absolutely Unbreakable Laws of Business Success* (San Francisco: Berrett-Koehler, 2000), pp. 138–139.

21 A description of these five styles appears in Robert Kreitner, *Management,* 11th ed. (Boston: Houghton Mifflin Harcourt Publishing Company, 2009), p. 408.

22 "Making a Nickel Do a Dime's Work," *Training,* April 1994, p. 12.

23 Brian Tracy, *The 100 Absolutely Unbreakable Laws of Business Success* (San Francisco: Berrett-Koehler, 2000), pp. 19–20.

24 "Tips for Teams," *Training,* February 1994, p. 14.

25 David G. Baldwin, "How to Win the Blame Game," *Harvard Business Review,* July/August 2001, pp. 1–7 (Reprint RO107C).

26 Kenneth R. Phillips, "The Achilles' Heel of Coaching," *Training & Development,* March 1998, p. 41; Anne Fisher, "In Praise of Micromanaging," *Fortune,* August 23, 2004, p. 40.

27 The Leadership Grid® from *Leadership Dilemmas—Grid Solutions* by Robert R. Blake and Anne Adams McCanse (formerly of the Manager Grid Figure by Robert R. Blake and Jane S. Mouton). Gulf Publishing Company, p. 29. Copyright © 1991 by Scientific Methods, Inc. Reprinted by permission.

28 Text list of Blake/Mouton descriptive names for leadership styles in grid. From *The New Managerial Grid,* by Robert R. Blake and Jane Srygley Mouton (Houston: Gulf Publishing Company). Copyright © 1978, p. 11. Reprinted by permission of Scientific Methods. Scientific Methods now operates as Grid International, Inc. For information regarding Grid International see "A Proud Legacy of Success" at http://www.gridinternational.com.

29 Robert R. Blake and Jane Srygley Mouton, "How to Choose a Leadership Style," *Training & Development,* February 1982, pp. 41–42.

30 Robert Kreitner, *Management,* 11th ed. (Boston: Houghton Mifflin, 2009), p. 409.

31 Paul Hersey, *The Situational Leader* (Escondido, Calif.: Center for Leadership Studies, 1984), pp. 29–30. To obtain current information on the Situational Leadership Model, visit http://www.situational.com.

32 Ibid., pp. 29–45.

33 "What Is Servant Leadership?" [cited 11 February 2009]. Available from http://www.greenleaf.org/whatissl/index.html; INTERNET.

34 Brian Tracy, *The 100 Absolutely Unbreakable Laws of Business Success* (San Francisco: Berrett-Koehler, 2000), p. 121.

35 Cary Cherniss and Daniel Goleman, *The Emotionally Intelligent Workplace* (San Francisco: Jossey-Bass, 2001), pp. 22–23.

36 Will Schutz, *The Human Element* (San Francisco: Jossey-Bass, 1994), pp. 237–238.

37 Margaret Kaeter, "The Leaders Among Us," *Business Ethics*, July/August 1994, p. 46.

38 J. Oliver Crom, "Every Employee a Leader: Part One," *The Leader*, April 1997, p. 6.

39 Peter Koestenbaum, *Leadership—The Inner Side of Greatness* (San Francisco: Jossey-Bass, 1991), pp. 179–183; Stephen Covey, "Why Is It Always About You?" *Training*, May 2006, p. 64.

40 John C. Maxwell, *The 17 Essential Qualities of a Team Player* (Nashville, Tenn.: Thomas Nelson Publishers, 2002), pp. 13–14.

41 Rachel Leibrock, "Manage Your Manager, Keep Your Job," *News & Observer*, October 12, 2008.

42 Dimitry Elias Legger, "Help! I'm the New Boss," *Fortune*, May 29, 2000, p. 281.

43 Timothy D. Schellhardt, "To Be a Star Among Equals, Be a Team Player," *Wall Street Journal*, April 20, 1994, p. B1.

44 Michaele Weissman, "Nerd Alert!" *Wall Street Journal*, May 14, 2001, p. R14; Peter Frost and Sandra Robinson, "The Toxic Handler: Organizational Hero—and Casualty," *Harvard Business Review*, July/August 1999, pp. 97–106.

45 Eleena de Lisser, "Firms with Virtual Environments Appeal to Workers," *Wall Street Journal*, October 5, 1999, p. B2; Gina Imperato, "Real Tools for Virtual Teams," *Fast Company*, July 2000, p. 382.

46 Gina Chon, "To Woo Wealthy, Lexus Attempts Image Makeover," pp. A1 and A12.

47 Erin White, "How a Company Made Everyone a Team Player," p. B1. For more information on putting employees in charge see Heather Green, "How Meetup Tore Up the Rule Book," *BusinessWeek*, June 16, 2008, p. 88.

48 Paul Roberts, "Live from Your Office! It's…," *Fast Company*, October 1999, p. 180; Vicki Lee Parker, "Durham Plant Is GE's 'Go-To,'" *The News & Observer*, April 22, 2004, p. D1.

49 Lynda Gratton, "Working Together…When Apart," *Wall Street Journal*, June 16, 2007, p. R4.

50 Ibid.

Chapter 13

1 Dee Gill, "Get Healthy…Or Else," *Inc.*, April 2006, p. 36.

2 Dee Gill, "Get Healthy…Or Else," *Inc.*, pp. 35–37; Michelle Conlin, "Get Healthy—Or Else," *BusinessWeek*, February 26, 2007, pp. 58–69; Phillip Rawls, "Alabama: Lose Weight or Pay Up," *News & Observer*, August 22, 2008, p. 14A.

3 Dudley Weeks, *The Eight Essential Steps to Conflict Resolution* (New York: G. P. Putnam's Sons, 1992), p. 7.

4 Ibid., pp. 7–8.

5 Adam Hanft, "The Joy of Conflict," *Inc.*, August 2005, p. 112; Adam Hanft, "Down with Bossocracy," *Inc.*, April 2004, p. 126.

6 Susan M. Heathfield, "Fight for What's Right: Ten Tips to Encourage Meaningful Conflict" [cited 7 February 2006]. Available from http://www.about.com; INTERNET.

7 Robert Kreitner, *Management*, 11th ed. (Boston: Houghton Mifflin Harcourt Publishing Company, 2009), p. 444.

8 Robert Kreitner, *Management*, 9th ed. (Boston: Houghton Mifflin Harcourt Publishing Company, 2004), pp. 529–530.

9 "Lawyers and Employers Take Fight to 'Workplace Bullies,'" *Wall Street Journal*, August 4, 2008, p. B6; Kerry Sulkowicz, "Analyze This," *BusinessWeek*, February 18, 2007, p. 16.

10 Carol Kleiman, "How to Deal with a Co-worker Who's Getting on Your Nerves," *San Jose Mercury News*, October 3, 1999, p. PC1.

11 "Assertiveness: More Than a Forceful Attitude," *Supervisory Management*, February 1994, p. 3.

12 American Management Association, *Catalog of Seminars* (New York: American Management Association) [cited 1 January 2006]. Available from http://www.amanet.org; INTERNET.

13 Danny Ertel, "Turning Negotiation into a Corporate Capability," *Harvard Business Review*, May/June 1999, p. 3.

14 Rob Walker, "Take It or Leave It: The Only Guide to Negotiating You Will Ever Need," *Inc.*, August 2003, pp. 65–77.

15 Kurt Salzinger, "Psychology on the Front Lines," *Psychology Today*, May/June 2002, p. 34.

16 Rob Walker, "Take It or Leave It: The Only Guide to Negotiating You Will Ever Need," *Inc.*, August 2003, p. 77.

17 Roger Fisher and William Ury, *Getting to Yes* (New York: Penguin Books, 1981), p. 4.

18 David Stiebel, *When Talking Makes Things Worse!* (Dallas: Whitehall & Nolton, 1997), p. 17.

19 Roger Fisher and Alan Sharp, *Getting It Done* (New York: Harper Business, 1998), pp. 81–83.

20 Marci Du Praw, "Cut the Conflict with Consensus Building," *Training*, May 2006, p. 8.

21 Roger Fisher and William Ury, *Getting to Yes* (New York: Penguin Books, 1981), p. 59.

22 Dudley Weeks, *The Eight Essential Steps to Conflict Resolution* (New York: G. P. Putnam's Sons, 1992), p. 228.

23 University of North Texas-Dallas: Alternative Dispute Resolution Certificate Brochure, updated 25 March 2002 [cited 22 February 2003]. Available from http://www.unt.edu/unt-dallas/brochures/adresd.htm; INTERNET.

24 Toddi Gutner, "When It's Time to Do Battle with Your Company," *BusinessWeek*, February 10, 1997, pp. 130–131.

25 Rory Marshall, "Boeing Factories to Get Back to Work," *The News & Observer*, November 3, 2008, p. 5A.

26 "Does America Still Need Labor Unions?" *Parade*, February 22, 2009, p. 14.

27 Carol Hymowitz, "Two Football Coaches Have a Lot to Teach Screaming Managers," *Wall Street Journal*, January 29, 2007, p. B1.

28 Andy Meisler, "A High-Stakes Union Fight: Who Will Fold First?" *Workforce Management*, January 2004, p. 28.

29 Ibid., p. 38. Also see Moira Herbst, "Big Labor's Big Chance," *BusinessWeek*, September 8, 2008, p. 26.

30 Excerpt adapted from Joann S. Lublin, "Before You Say Yes, Look for the Signs of a Bad Boss Ahead," *Wall Street Journal*, November 29, 2005, p. B1.

31 Sacha Pfeiffer, "Employee Fired for Smoking Off Work Sues," *News & Observer*, December 1, 2006, p. D1.

32 Alan Jay Weiner, "None of Your Business," *Inc.*, June 2006, p. 22.

33 Phillip Rawls, "Alabama: Lose Weight or Pay Up," *News & Observer*, August 22, 2008, p. 14A.

34 "Ask Inc.," *Inc.*, February 2007, p. 57; Kevin Sulkowicz, "(Not) the Life of the After-Work Party," *BusinessWeek*, 2007, p. 43.

35 Hilary Stout, "The Key to a Lasting Marriage: Combat," *Wall Street Journal*, November 4, 2004, p. D1.

36 Jeffrey Zaslow, "Ready to Pop the Question? Hold Off Until You've Done the Interrogation," *Wall Street Journal*, February 6, 2003, p. D1.

37 Phillip C. McGraw, "Couples Combat: The Great American Pastime," *O, The Oprah Magazine*, August 2002, p. 43.

38 Ibid.; "How To," *Training & Development*, April 1998, p. 10; Jeffrey Zaslow, "Divorce Makes a Comeback," *Wall Street Journal*, January 14, 2003, pp. D1, D10; Zaslow, "Ready to Pop the Question?" p. D1.

39 Rachel Emma Silverman, "Working on Your Marriage," *Wall Street Journal*, May 31, 2007, p. D1.

Chapter 14

1 Melinda Beck, "Stress So Bad It Hurts—Really," *Wall Street Journal*, March 17, 2009, p. D1.

2 Bruce Cryer, Rollin McCraty, and Doc Childre, "Pull the Plug on Stress," *Harvard Business Review*, July 2003, pp. 1–2.

3 Richard Laliberte, "Lighten Up," *New Choices*, June 2001, p. 65.

4 Price Pritchett and Ron Pound, *The Stress of Organizational Change* (Dallas: Pritchett, LP, 2005).

5 James E. Loehr, *Stress for Success* (New York: Times Books, 1997), p. 4.

6 Harold H. Bloomfield and Robert K. Cooper, *The Power of 5* (Emmaus, Pa.: Rodale Press, 1995), p. 18.

7 Cora Daniels, "The Last Taboo," *Fortune*, October 28, 2002, p. 138.

8 "Work-Life Balance Tops Pay," *USA Today*, March 13, 2008, p. 1B.

9 Sue Shellenbarger, "Another Casualty Emerges from the Crisis: Family Time," *Wall Street Journal*, October 15, 2008, p. D1; Sue Shellenbarger, "Time-Zoned: Working Around the Round-the-Clock Workday," *Wall Street Journal*, February 15, 2007, p. D1.

10 Sue Shellenbarger, "Time-Zoned: Working Around the Round-the-Clock Workday," p. D1.

11 Sonja Steptoe, "Ready, Set, Relax!" *Time*, October 27, 2003, pp. 38–41; Sue Shellenbarger, "Are Saner Workloads the Unexpected Key to More Productivity?" *Wall Street Journal*, March 10, 2000, p. B1.

12 Price Pritchett and Ron Pound, *The Stress of Organizational Change* (Dallas, Tex.: Pritchett, 2005), pp. 3–8.

13 This hypothetical example was adapted from Mary Donato, "Workplace Stress: A Survival Guide," *Sales & Marketing Management*, November/December 2006, p. 24.

14 David H. Freedman, "Why Interruption, Distraction, and Multitasking Are Not Such Awful Things After All," *Inc.*, February 2007, pp. 67–68.

15 Ibid., p. 68.

16 Lee Gomes, "Excessive Internet Use Has Features in Common with Some Addictions," *Wall Street Journal*, October 24, 2006, p. B3; Lisa M. Kreiger, "Addiction to Web Is Growing Problem," *News & Observer*, October 20, 2006, p. 3A.

17 Sue Shellenbarger, "Taking Back the Weekend: Companies Help Employees Cut Back on Overwork," *Wall Street Journal*, May 18, 2006, p. D1.

18 Karin Rives, "Home Workers Feel the Pain," *The News & Observer*, July 18, 2004, p. E1; Albert R. Karr, "An Ergo-Unfriendly Home Office Can Hurt You," *Wall Street Journal*, September 30, 2003, p. D6.

19 "Sound Bites," *UC Berkeley Wellness Letter*, September 2004, pp. 6–7; Jane Spencer, "Behind the Music: iPods and Hearing Loss," *Wall Street Journal*, January 10, 2006, p. D1; Steve Thompson, "Straight Pipes and Street Civility," *Autoweek*, March 20, 2006, p. 10.

20 Kenneth Labich, "Psycho Bosses from Hell," *Fortune*, March 18, 1996, p. 123; Vanessa Ho, "Companies Get the Message That Happy Workers Help Bottom Line," *Roanoke Times & WorldNews*, November 13, 1995, p. E6.

21 Edith Weiner, "The Fast Approaching Future," *Retail Issues Letter*, July 1994, p. 3.

22 Douglas A. Bernstein, Louis A. Penner, Alison Clarke-Stewart, and Edward J. Roy, *Psychology*, 7th ed. (Boston: Houghton Mifflin, 2006), pp. 515 and 605.

23 Art Ulene, *Really Fit Really Fast* (Encino, Calif.: HealthPoints, 1996), pp. 56–58.

24 John Carpi, "Stress: It's Worse Than You Think," *Psychology Today* [cited 16 February 2006]. Available from http://www.psychologytoday.com; INTERNET.

25 Loehr, *Stress for Success*, pp. 179, 183; Eilene Zimmerman, "Sleep Less, Feel Better," *Sales & Marketing Management*, June 2004, p. 49.

26 Arlene Weintraub, "Napping Your Way to the Top," *BusinessWeek*, November 27, 2006, pp. 97 and 99.

27 Robert Tomsho, "Exercise Levels Drop for Teenage Women," *Wall Street Journal*, September 5, 2002, p. D3; "What's News," *Wall Street Journal*, April 8, 2002, p. A1.

28 Adapted from Aggie Casey, "A Breath of Peace," *Health*, January/February 2004, p. 94.

29 Jennifer Derryberry, "The Joy of Breathing," *Spirituality & Health*, July/August 2004, pp. 78–79.

30 "Doing Well by Doing Good," *Wellness Letter*, University of California, Berkeley.

31 Robert J. Davis, "Breathing and Hypertension," *Wall Street Journal*, April 27, 2004, p. D4.

32 Frederic Luskin, "Just Relax," *Parade*, September 24, 2006, p. 16.

33 Joel Stein, "Just Say Om," *Time*, August 4, 2003, p. 50; Katherine Ellison, "Mastering Your Own Mind," *Psychology Today*, September/October, 2006, pp. 70–77.

34 Ibid., pp. 47–56; Richard J. Davidson et al., "Alterations in Brain and Immune Function Produced by Mindfulness Meditation," *Psychosomatic Medicine*, received for publication December 2002 [cited 16 February 2006]. Available from http://www.psychosomaticmedicine.org; INTERNET; "Mindfulness Meditation," *Spirituality & Health*, March/April 2004, p. 74; Michelle Conlin, "Meditation," *BusinessWeek*, August 30, 2004, pp. 136–137.

35 Michelle Conlin, "Meditation," *BusinessWeek*, August 30, 2004, pp. 136–137.

36 Megan Satosus, "No Fun of Any Kind," *CIO Magazine*, May 2, 2005 [cited 16 February 2006]. Available from http://www.cio.com; INTERNET.

37 Beverly Kaye and Sharon Jordan-Evans, "Ain't We Got Fun?" *Fast Company, Talent & Careers Resource Center* [cited 16 February 2006]. Available from http://www.fastcompany.com; INTERNET.

38 Ann McGee-Cooper, *You Don't Have to Go Home from Work Exhausted* (New York: Bantam Books, 1992), pp. 52–53.

39 "Anger Can't Prevent a Layoff," *The News & Observer*, April 5, 2009, p. 6E.

40 Ester Buchholz, "The Call of Solitude," *Psychology Today*, January/February 1998, pp. 50–54; "Loners May Not Fear Others, They Just Need Some Solitude," *Wall Street Journal*, Thursday, March 1, 2007, p. B7.

41 Kim Wright Wiley, "Reaching Your Peak," *Selling Power*, March 2004, pp. 56–61.

42 Matthew Hutson, "Laughing Stock," *Psychology Today*, May/June 2008, p. 53.

43 Sheila Hutman, Jaelline Jaffe, Robert Segal, Heather Larson, and Lisa Dumke, "Stress: Signs and Symptoms, Causes and Effects" [cited 11 February 2006]. Available from http://www.helpguide.org/mental/stress_signs.htm; INTERNET.

44 Leila Abbound, "Mental Illness Said to Affect One-Quarter of Americans," *Wall Street Journal*, June 7, 2005, p. D1.

45 Douglas A. Bernstein, Louis A. Penner, Alison Clark-Stewart, and Edward J. Roy, *Psychology*, 7th ed. (Boston: Houghton Mifflin, 2006), pp. 589–590.

46 Ibid.

47 To learn about specific ways to control your fears see Jason Zweig, "How to Control Your Fears in a Fearsome Market," *Wall Street Journal*, July 19, 2008, p. B1.

48 Paul Raeburn, "Mental Health: Better Benefits Won't Break the Bank," *BusinessWeek*, December 17, 2001, p. 100; Elyse Tanouye, "Mental Illness: A Rising Workplace Cost," *Wall Street Journal*, June 13, 2001, p. B1.

49 Sharon Begley, "New Hope for Battling Depression Relapses," *Wall Street Journal*, January 6, 2004, p. D1; Avery Johnson, "Treatment Works for Two-Thirds of the Depressed," *Wall Street Journal*, November 1, 2006.

50 Lindsey Tanner, "Treating Workers' Depression Pays," *News & Observer*, September 26, 2007, p. 4A.

51 Douglas A. Bernstein, Louis A. Penner, Alison Clark-Stewart, and Edward J. Roy, *Psychology*, 7th ed. (Boston: Houghton Mifflin, 2006), p. 495.

52 Dana Mattioli, "When Devotion to Work Becomes Job Obsession," *Wall Street Journal*, January 23, 2007, p. 88.

53 Rebecca Segall, "Online Shrinks: The Inside Story," *Psychology Today*, May/June 2000, pp. 38–43; Joshua Rosenbaum, "The Typing Cure," *Wall Street Journal*, September 16, 2002, p. R10.

54 Based on Ann Landers, "Maybe It's Time to Change Jobs," *Roanoke Times & World-News*, September 1994; Camille Wright Miller, "'Prime' Is Performance, Attitude Issue," *The Roanoke Times*, September 22, 1996, p. B2.

55 Melinda Beck, "Stress So Bad It Hurts—Really," p. D1.

56 Nicole C. Wong, "Fiancee's Blog Spurs Suit Against Game Firm," *News & Observer*, May 7, 2006, p. 3E.

57 Ricky W. Griffin, *Principles of Management* (Boston: Houghton Mifflin Company, 2007), pp. 238–239.

58 Sue Sellenbarger, "Even Lawyers Get the Blues: Opening Up About Depression," *Wall Street Journal*, December 13, 2007, p. D1.

59 Erin White, "For Young Workers, Taking Time Off Can Be Stressful," *Wall Street Journal*, March 27, 2007, p. B10.

60 Anjoli Athavaley, "Vacation Deflation: Breaks Get Shorter," *Wall Street Journal*, August 15, 2007, p. D1.

61 Anjoli Athavaley, "Vacation Deflation: Breaks Get Shorter"; Howard Shapiro, "Vacation Time Going Unused," *News & Observer*, February 17, 2008, p. 8G.

62 Michael Arndt, "Nice Work if You Can Get It," *BusinessWeek*, January 9, 2006, pp. 56–57.

63 Molly Selvin, "Taking Sick Days Often Discouraged," *News & Observer*, May 27, 2007, p. 5E.

Chapter 15

1 Ronald C. Glover, "Diversity on a Global Scale" [cited 11 April 2009]. Available from http://www.ibm.com/ibm/glbt; INTERNET.

2 Ibid.

3 "The 9th Annual 2009 DiversityInc Top 50 Companies for Diversity" [cited 9 April 2009]. Available from http://www.diversityinc.com; INTERNET; "Awards and Recognition Archive" [cited 13 April 2009]. Available from http://www.ibm.com/ibm/glbt; INTERNET.

4 Carol Hymowitz, "The New Diversity," *Wall Street Journal*, November 14, 2005, pp. R1–R3.

5 Connor Dougherty, "Nonwhites to Be Majority in U.S. by 2042," *Wall Street Journal*, August 14, 2008, p. A3.

6 Marilyn Loden and Judy B. Rosener, *Workforce America!* (Homewood, Ill.: Business One Irwin, 1991), pp. 114–115. Information on primary and secondary dimensions of diversity can also be found in Marilyn Loden, *Implementing Diversity* (Burr Ridge, Ill.: McGraw-Hill, 1996).

7 Ibid., p. 21.

8 Jonathan Kaufman, "Celebration Stirs a New Racial Optimism," *Wall Street Journal*, January 21, 2009, p. R7.

9 Douglas A. Bernstein, Louis A. Penner, Alison Clarke-Stewart, and Edward J. Roy, *Psychology*, 7th ed. (Boston: Houghton Mifflin, 2006), p. 692.

10 Sue Shellenbarger, "The Stereotypes Behind 'Singlism' Persist," *Wall Street Journal*, December 9, 2008, p. D5.

11 D. Stanley Eitzen and Maxine Baca Zinn, *In Conflict and Order* (Boston: Allyn & Bacon, 2001), p. 237.

12 Paul C. Gorski, "The Question of Class," *Teaching Tolerance,* Spring 2007, pp. 26–29.

13 D. Stanley Eitzen and Maxine Baca Zinn, *In Conflict and Order* (Boston: Allyn & Bacon, 2001), p. 237.

14 Lewis Brown Griggs and Lente-Louise Louw, *Valuing Diversity* (New York: McGraw-Hill, 1995), pp. 3–4, 150–151.

15 Ibid., p. 151.

16 Yochi J. Dreazen, "U.S. Racial Wealth Gap Remains Huge," *Wall Street Journal,* March 14, 2000, p. A2.

17 June Kronholz, "How the Unconscious Affects the Truth," *Wall Street Journal,* August 2, 2008, p. W6; "General Information—Project Implicit" [cited 13 April 2009]. Available from http://www.projectimplicit.net; INTERNET.

18 Ibid.

19 Tom Lowry, "Extreme Experience," *BusinessWeek,* September 8, 2008, p. 46.

20 Joseph Weber, "This Time, Old Hands Keep Their Jobs," *BusinessWeek,* February 9, 2009, p. 50.

21 Ellen Goodman, "Working Longer, with Pride," *News & Observer,* March 21, 2009, p. 15A.

22 Sue Shellenbarger, "Work & Family Mailbox," *Wall Street Journal,* April 13, 2006, p. D4.

23 Craig Calhoun, Donald Light, and Suzanne Keller, *Sociology,* 6th ed. (New York: McGraw-Hill, 1994), p. 241.

24 Nicholas D. Kristof, "Is Race Real?" *New York Times,* July 11, 2003; Robert S. Boynton, "Color Us Invisible," *New York Times Book Review,* August 17, 1997, p. 13.

25 Stephen Magagini, "A Race Free Consciousness," *The News & Observer,* November 23, 1997, pp. A25–A26.

26 Carol Mukhopadhyay and Rosemary C. Henze, "How Real Is Race? Using Anthropology to Make Sense of Human Diversity," *Phi Delta Kappan,* May 2003, p. 675.

27 Frank Bruni, Kim Severson, and Grant Barrett, "Buzzwords Are Catchy—and Caustic," *News & Observer,* December 25, 2006, p. 3A.

28 Phred Dvorak, "Religious–Bias Filings Up," *Wall Street Journal,* October 16, 2008, pp. B1–B2.

29 Rabbi Rami Shapiro, "Can We Reconcile Faiths? Did Jesus Walk on Water?" *Spirituality & Health,* November/December 2007, p. 16.

30 Yonat Shimron, "God as Fearsome Father," *News & Observer,* October 1, 2006, p. 24A.

31 Kris Maher, "Disabled Face Scarcer Jobs, Data Show," *Wall Street Journal,* October 5, 2005, p. D1.

32 Ibid.

33 Elizabeth Williamson and Kris Maher, "Businesses Face Push to Expand Disabled Access," *Wall Street Journal,* June 17, 2008, p. A6.

34 "When Meeting Someone with a Disability." Adapted from "Communication Solutions." Used by permission of Progressive Business Publications.

35 Yonat Shimron, "Passion for Justice," *News & Observer,* November 20, 2008, p. D1. For additional information visit http://www.crisisbook.org.

36 Sue Shellenbarger, "A Mid Gay Marriage Debate, Companies Offer More Benefits to Same-Sex Couples," *Wall Street Journal,* March 18, 2004, p. D1; Barbara Rose, "Policies to Accommodate Gays Draw Scrutiny," *The News & Observer,* July 3, 2005, p. E12; Rachel Emma Silverman, "Wall Street, a New Push to Recruit Gay Students," *Wall Street Journal,* February 9, 2000, p. B1.

37 "Employment and Rights in the Workplace" [cited 16 April 2009]. Available from http://www.lambdalegal.org; INTERNET.

38 Robert Tomsho, "School & Efforts to Protect Gays Face Opposition," *Wall Street Journal,* February 20, 2003, p. B1.

39 "Tools for Tolerance: Workplace," adapted from *101 Tools for Tolerance: Simple Ideas for Promoting Equity and Celebrating Diversity.* Copyright © 2000, Southern Poverty Law Center, Montgomery, AL. Reprinted by permission of Southern Poverty Law Center. *101 Tools for Tolerance* is available free from the SPLC. For more information, visit http://www.splccenter.org or send a fax to (334) 264–7310.

40 Chuck Salter, "Diversity Without the Excuses," *Fast Company,* September 2002, p. 44.

41 Jessica Marquez, "Survey Says Diversity Contributes to the Bottom Line," *Workforce Management,* November 18, 2005 [cited 23 February 2006]. Available from http://www.workforce.com; INTERNET.

42 Stephen R. Covey, "Questions for Covey," *Training,* June 2007, p. 64.

43 Fay Hansen, "Microsoft R & D Seeks Global Tech Talent, Not Bargains," *Workforce Management,* July 2005, p. 39; Kreitner, *Management,* p. 80; "Toyota's Charge Toward the Pinnacle of the Sport," *Canadian Grand Prix Program 2002,* p. 54; Robin Townsley Arcus, "World Market," *The Urban Hiker,* October 2000, p. 34.

44 *101 Tools for Tolerance* (Montgomery, Ala.: Southern Poverty Law Center), pp. 4–7.

45 Gail Johnson, "Time to Broaden Diversity," *Training*, September 2004, p. 16; Adapted from Leone E. Wynter, "Do Diversity Programs Make a Difference?" *Wall Street Journal*, December 4, 1996, p. B1.

46 "Time to Diversify," *Sales & Marketing Management*, May 2002, p. 62.

47 Jonathan Hickman, "America's 50 Best Companies for Minorities," *Fortune*, July 8, 2002, pp. 110–120.

48 Shankar Vedantam, "Forced Diversity Training Fails," *News & Observer*, July 21, 2008, p. 3A.

49 "Diversity Dilemma," *Training*, July/August 2007, p. 10.

50 Ricky W. Griffin, *Principles of Management* (Boston: Houghton Mifflin Company, 2007), p. 195.

51 Kris Maher, "Lockheed Settles Racial-Discrimination Suit," *Wall Street Journal*, January 3, 2008, p. A4.

52 Ricky W. Griffin, *Principles of Management*, p. 195.

53 Jonathon Kaufman, "Fair Enough," *Wall Street Journal*, June 14, 2008, p. A8.

54 Ibid.; Liz Gillian, "Race Can't Be Used as Factor," *The Daily Tar Heel*, January 11, 2007, p. 3.

55 Terry Eastland, "Endgame for Affirmative Action," *Wall Street Journal*, March 28, 1996, p. A15; John J. Miller, "Out of One Set of Preferences, Many ... and Many New Debates," *New York Times Book Review*, March 27, 2002, p. A16; Roger Pilon, "The Complexities of Unfair Discrimination," *Wall Street Journal*, December 13, 2002, p. A17.

56 Miller, "Out of One Set of Preferences," p. A16.

57 "Refocus Affirmative Action," *The Daily Tar Heel*, February 21, 2008, p. 16.

58 Roger O. Crockett, "How to Narrow the Great Divide," *BusinessWeek*, July 14, 2003, p. 104; Sharon S. Brehm, Saul M. Kassin, and Steven Fein, *Social Psychology*, 5th ed. (Boston: Houghton Mifflin, 2002), pp. 478–480.

59 Accent reduction training programs have become very popular in recent years. Select a professional trainer who is a certified member of the American Speech-Language Hearing Association.

60 R. Roosevelt Thomas, Jr., "From Affirmative Action to Affirming Diversity," *Harvard Business Review*, March/April 1990, p. 114.

61 Jia Lynn, "Pepsi's Diversity Push Pays Off," *Fortune*, September 4, 2006, p. 32.

62 Chad Terhune and Joann S. Lublin, "Pepsi's New CEO Doesn't Keep Her Opinions Bottled Up," *Wall Street Journal*, August 15, 2006, pp. B1 and B7.

63 Stephanie Capparell, "How Pepsi Opened Door to Diversity," *Wall Street Journal*, January 9, 2007, pp. B1 and B2. For comprehensive history of PepsiCo's early efforts to achieve diversity see Stephanie Capparell, *The Real Pepsi Challenge: The Inspirational Story of Breaking the Color Barrier in American Business* (New York: Wall Street Journal Books/Free Press, 2007).

64 Elizabeth Schulte, "Can We End Bigotry Through Education?" *Socialist Worker*, July 20, 2001, p. 9; "Bush Marks Black History Month with Call to End Bigotry" [cited 25 February 2006]. Available from http://www.eyewitnessnewstv.com/global/story; INTERNET; Robert Epstein, "In Her Own Words," *Psychology Today*, May/June 2002, pp. 40–42.

Chapter 16

1 Sheryl Gay Stolberg, "Obama Signs Equal-Pay Legislation," *The New York Times*, January 29, 2009.

2 Ibid.

3 Ibid.

4 Wendy Kaminer, "Sexual Politics, Continued," *New York Times Book Review*, March 23, 1997, p. 12.

5 Michelle Conlin, "The New Gender Gap," *BusinessWeek*, May 26, 2003, pp. 75–82.

6 "Fortune 500 CEOs: Women on the Rise," *Fortune* [cited 23 April 2009]. Available from http://postcards.blogs.fortune.cnn.com/2009/04/20/fortune-500-ceo-women-on-the-rise/; INTERNET; John Gettings, David Johnson, Borgna Brunner, and Chris Frantz, "Wonder Women: Profiles of leading female CEOs and business executives." [cited 23 April 2009]. Available from http://www.infoplease.com/spot/womenceo1.html; INTERNET.

7 Sue Shellenbarger, "Number of Women Managers Rises," *Wall Street Journal*, September 30, 2003, p. D1.

8 "The Pros and Cons of Non-Traditional Careers" [cited 21 April 2009]. Available from http://www.quintcareers.com/pros-cons_non-traditional_careers.html; INTERNET.

9 Robert Bly, *Iron John* (Reading, Mass.: Addison-Wesley, 1990), p. iv.

10 Sue Shellenbarger, "For Harried Workers in the 21st Century, Six Trends to Watch," *Wall Street Journal*, December 29, 1999, p. B1.

11 Lyric Wallwork Winik and Meg Massey, "A New Push for Equal Pay," *Intelligence Report*. Available from http://www.Parade.com/intel; INTERNET.

12 Carol Hymowitz, "On Diversity, America Isn't Putting Its Money Where Its Mouth Is," *Wall Street*

Journal, February 25, 2008, p. B1. Bureau of Labor Statistics collected in 2005.

13 Lyric Wallwork Winik and Meg Massey, "A New Push for Equal Pay," *Intelligence Report*. Available from http://www.Parade.com/intel; INTERNET.

14 Linda Lowen, "Non-traditional Jobs Often Pay Women More," *About.com Women's Issues* [cited 21April 2009]. Available from http://www.womenissues.about.com/od/intheworkplace/a/HigherEarnings.htm; INTERNET.

15 "A Salary Gap Remains Between Genders, Census Results Indicate," *Wall Street Journal*, March 25, 2003, p. D1; Charles J. Whalen, "Closing the Pay Gap," *BusinessWeek*, August 28, 2000, p. 38.

16 Gene Koretz, "She's a Woman, Offer Her Less," *BusinessWeek*, May 7, 2001, p. 34.

17 Marie Cocco, "The Glass Ceiling Holds Strong" [cited 26 February 2009]. Available from http://www.realclearpolitics.com/printpage/?url=http; INTERNET; Claire Shipman and Katty Kay, *Womenomics: Write Your Own Rules for Success* (New York: HarperCollins, 2009), pp. 14–17.

18 Gale Duff-Bloom, "Women in Retailing—Is There a Glass Ceiling?" *Retailing Issues Letter*, Center for Retailing Studies, Texas A&M University, May 1996, pp. 1–4; Margaret Hefferman, "The Female CEO," *Fast Company*, August 2002, pp. 60–61.

19 Carol Hymowitz, "On Diversity, America Isn't Putting Its Money Where Its Mouth Is," *Wall Street Journal*, February 25, 2008, p. B1. Bureau of Labor Statistics collected in 2005.

20 Anna Fels, "Do Women Lack Ambition," *Harvard Business Review*, April 2004, pp. 7–8.

21 Claire Shipman and Katty Kay, *Womenomics: Write Your Own Rules for Success* (New York: HarperCollins, 2009), pp. 2–3.

22 "The Emancipated Organization," *Harvard Business Review*, September 2002, pp. 1–3 (Reprint F0209B). (This article features an interview with Kim Campbell, Canada's first female prime minister.)

23 "Women Taking Care of Business," *Roanoke Times & World-News*, May 13, 1995, p. A16.

24 Sally Harris, "Research Finds Work Not 'Haven' from Home," *Spectrum*, February 21, 2003, p. 1.

25 Dana Mattioli, "Ways Women Can Hold Their Own in a Male World," *The Wall Street Journal*, August 25, 2008, p. D4. Reprinted by permission.

26 Dr. Laura Schlessinger, *In Praise of Stay-at-Home Mom* (New York: HarperCollins Publishers, 2009), introduction.

27 Sylvia Ann Hewlett, "Executive Women and the Myth of Having It All," *Harvard Business Review*, April 2002, pp. 5–11; Margaret Heffernan, "The Female CEO," *Fast Company*, August 2002, pp. 58–66.

28 Judith S. Nulevitz "The Mommy Trap," *New York Times Book Review*, February 20, 2005, pp. 1, 12–13.

29 Dorothy Foltz-Gray, "Bread Winning Wives," *Health*, October 2003, pp. 103–107; Sue Shellenbarger, "As Moms Earn More, More Dads Stay Home: How to Make the Switch Work," *Wall Street Journal*, February 20, 2003, p. D1.

30 "Today's Dads: Same Old Parenting Trap," *BusinessWeek*, October 14, 2002, p. 167. (This article summarizes the views of Nicholas Townsend, author of *The Package Deal*, a book about the many life/work conflicts men face.)

31 Jeffrey Winters, "The Daddy Track," *Psychology Today*, September/October 2001, p. 17.

32 David Gremillion, "Men's Health Needs a Heartfelt Change," *The News & Observer*, June 17, 2001, p. A31.

33 Jeffrey Zaslow, "Who's the New Guy at Dinner? It's Dad; Laid-Off Fathers Face Tough Job at Home," *Wall Street Journal*, October 2, 2002, p. D1.

34 Child Care Connections. Available from http://www.childcareconnections.net/employers/indes.shtml; INTERNET.

35 Aaron Bernstein, Ronald Grover, and Cliff Edwards, "Making Family Leave Family Friendly," *BusinessWeek*, September 30, 2002, p. 44; Sue Shellenbarger, "Shaky Job Market Makes Family Leave Riskier Business," *Wall Street Journal*, August 22, 2001, p. D1; Sue Shellenbarger, "A Downside of Taking Family Leave: Getting Fired While You Are Gone," *Wall Street Journal*, January 25, 2003, p. D1; "The Incredible Shrinking Family Leave: Pressed Bosses Are Cutting Into Time Off," *Wall Street Journal*, October 17, 2002, p. D1.

36 *Aflac*, 100 Best Companies To Work For 2009 [cited 20 June 2009]. Available from http://money.cnn.com/magazines/fortune/bestcompanies/2009/napshots/26.html; INTERNET.

37 Sue Shellenbarger, "Does Avoiding a 9-to-5 Grind Make You a Target for Layoffs?" *Wall Street Journal*, April 22, 2009, p. D1.

38 Sue Shellenbarger, "Bob's Mobile Office and Day-Care Center," *Wall Street Journal*, December 26, 2002, p. D1.

39 Kathy Bergen, "Compressed Workweek Pays Off—On 10th Day," *Roanoke Times & World-News*, March 30, 1997, p. B2.

40 "Tips for Working with a Virtual Assistant (and Why You Might Want One)" [cited 11 August 2008]. Available from http://www.zenhabits.net/2008/01/tips-for-working-with-a-virtual-assistant-and-why-you-might-want-one; INTERNET.

41 Carol Kleiman, "Get Two Workers for the Price of One!" *The News & Observer*, February 26, 2003, p. E14.

42 Sue Shellenbarger, "Does Avoiding a 9-to-5 Grind Make You a Target for Layoffs? *Wall Street Journal*, April 22, 2009, p. D1.

43 "Beyond Flextime Trashing the Workweek," *Inc.*, August 2008, pp. 30–31.

44 Sue Shellenbarger, "Does Avoiding a 9-to-5 Grind Make You a Target for Layoffs?" *Wall Street Journal*, April 22, 2009, p. D1.

45 Bob Herbert, "The Great Shame" [cited 21 March 2009]. Available from http://www.nytimes/2009/03/21/opinion/21herbert.html?_r=1; INTERNET.

46 "More Men Report Sexual Harassment in US Workplace" [cited 25 April 2009]. Available from BNET in partnership with mywire; INTERNET.

47 Sue Shellenbarger, "Downsizing maternity leave: Employers cut pay, time off," *Wall Street Journal*, June 11, 2008, p. D1; Sue Shellenbarger, "Government Eases Path for Parents to Sue Employers," *Wall Street Journal*, May 24, 2007, p. D1.

48 Susan B. Garland, "Finally, a Corporate Tip Sheet on Sexual Harassment," *BusinessWeek*, July 13, 1998, p. 39.

49 Deborah Tannen, "The Power of Talk: Who Gets Heard and Why," *Harvard Business Review*, September/October 1995, pp. 129–140.

50 Jayne Tear, "They Just Don't Understand Gender Dynamics," *Wall Street Journal*, November 20, 1995, p. A14; Dianna Booker, "The Gender Gap in Communication," *Training Dimensions* (West Des Moines, Ia.: American Media Incorporated, Fall 1994), p. 1; Jennifer J. Laabs, "Kinney Narrows the Gender Gap," *Personnel Journal*, August 1994, pp. 83–85; Scot Ober, *Contemporary Business Communication*, 5th ed. (Boston: Houghton Mifflin, 2003), pp. 58–59.

51 Tannen, "The Power of Talk," p. 146.

52 Sharon S. Brehm, Saul M. Kassin, and Steven Fein, *Social Psychology*, 5th ed. (Boston: Houghton Mifflin, 2002), pp. 154–156.

53 Anastasi Toufexis, "Coming from a Different Place," *Time*, Fall 1990, p. 66.

54 Alice Sargeant, *The Androgynous Manager* (New York: American Management Association, 1983), p. 37.

55 Small Talk. Available from smalltalk@wsj.com; INTERNET.

56 Sheryl Gay Stolberg, "Obama Signs Equal-Pay Legislation," *The New York Times* [cited 29 January 2009]. Available from http://www.nytimes.com/2009/01/30/us/politics/30ledbetter-web.html?ref=politics; INTERNET; Michelle Diament, "What an Outrage! At the Mercy of the Court," *AARP Bulletin*, September 2007, p. 4.

57 "A Saner Workplace," *BusinessWeek*, June 1, 2009, pp. 066–069.

Chapter 17

1 Amy Merrick and Roger Thurow, "The Jobless Go Back to School and, They Hope, Work," *Wall Street Journal*, February 5, 2009, p. A14.

2 Robert M. Strozier, "The Job of Your Dreams," *New Choices*, April 1998, p. 25.

3 Diane Brady, "Getting to the Corner Office," *BusinessWeek*, March 12, 2007, p. 104.

4 Po Bronson, *What Should I Do with My Life*? (New York: Random House, 2002), p. 365; Patricia Kitchen, "Seeking Your Calling," *The Record*, March 9, 2003, p. D1.

5 Ralph Fiennes, "Success—An Owner's Guide," *O, The Oprah Magazine*, September 2001, p. 51.

6 Ethan Watters, "Come Here, Work, and Get Out of Here, You Don't Live Here. You Live Someplace Else," *Inc.*, October 30, 2001, pp. 56–61; "Why We're Different" [cited 27 April 2009]. Available from http://www.stgutah.com; INTERNET.

7 Max Chafkin, "Get Happy," *Inc.*, May 2009, pp. 67–73.

8 Jack Canfield, *The Success Principles* (New York: HarperCollins, 2005), p. 3.

9 Anne Fisher, "The Practical Painter," *Fortune*, May 14, 2007, p. 124.

10 See His Holiness the Dalai Lama and Howard C. Cutler, *The Art of Happiness at Work* (New York: Riverhead Books, 2003), pp. 157–173.

11 Yvonne V. Chabrier, "Focus on Work," *New Age*, 1998, p. 95.

12 Bronson, *What Should I Do with My Life*? pp. 68–72.

13 Marsha Sinetar, *Do What You Love … The Money Will Follow* (New York: Dell, 1987), p. 11.

14 Ibid., pp. 11–12.

15 Michael Phillips, *The Seven Laws of Money* (Menlo Park, Calif.: Word Wheel and Random House, 1997), p. 9.

16 Sinetar, *Do What You Love*, pp. 14–15.

17 Erin White, "Profession Changes Take Time But May Be Worth Wait," *Wall Street Journal*, November 27, 2007, p. B6.

18 Carole Kanchier, "Dare to Change Your Job and Your Life in 7 Steps," *Psychology Today*, March/April 2000, pp. 64–67.

19 Polly LaBarre, "Money Therapy 101," *Fast Company*, February 2002, pp. 116–119.

20 Suze Orman, "The Pursuit of Cold, Hard Happiness," *O, The Oprah Magazine*, March 2004, pp. 54–56; Sharon Begley, "Wealth and Happiness Don't Necessarily Go Hand in Hand," *Wall Street Journal*, August 13, 2004, p. B1.

21 Geoffrey Colvin, "We're a Nation Helpless to Save Ourselves," *Fortune*, April 18, 2005, p. 52.

22 Shakti Gawain, *Creating True Prosperity* (Novato, Calif.: New World Library, 1997), p. 7.

23 Carlin Flora, "Happy Hour," *Psychology Today*, January/February 2005, p. 48.

24 "Why Money Matters Are a Leading Cause of Divorce," *Spirituality & Health*, November/December 2006, p. 32.

25 Jonathan Clements, "If You Didn't Save 10% of Your Income This Year, You're Spending Too Much," *Wall Street Journal*, December 22, 2004, p. D1; Jonathan Clements, "Rich, Successful—and Miserable: New Research Probes Midlife Angst," *Wall Street Journal*, October 5, 2005, p. D1.

26 Jonathan Clements, "Amid Losses, 12 Financial Truths Persist," *Wall Street Journal*, Sunday, June 18, 2006, p. 7E; Jonathan Welsh, "When a $38,000 Car Costs $44,000," *Wall Street Journal*, May 22, 2007, p. D1.

27 Toddi Gutner, "Talk Now, Retire Happily Later," *BusinessWeek*, April 2, 2001, p. 92.

28 Adapted from "Calculate Your Savings Possibilities," SunTrust Banks, Inc., 2009.

29 Julie Connelly, "How to Choose Your Next Career," *Fortune*, February 6, 1995.

30 Michael Toms, "Money: The Third Side of the Coin" (interview with Joe Dominguez and Vicki Robin), *New Dimensions*, May/June 1991, p. 7.

31 Susan Smith Jones, "Choose to Be Healthy and Celebrate Life," *New Realities*, September/October 1988, pp. 17–19.

32 Dee Gill, "Get Healthy…Or Else," *Inc.*, April 2006, p. 36.

33 *The Career Activist* concept is described in Barbara Moses, *Career Intelligence: The 12 New Rules for Work and Life Success* (San Francisco: Berrett-Koehler Publishers, Inc., 1998).

34 Toddi Gutner, "A 12-Step Program to Gaining Power," *BusinessWeek*, December 24, 2001, p. 88.

35 Ron Zemke, "Why Organizations Still Aren't Learning," *Training*, September 1999, p. 43.

36 Perri Capell, "Major Lessons on Achieving Career Objectives," *Wall Street Journal*, June 3, 2008, p. D5.

37 Sue Shellenbarger, "Working 9 to 2: Taking Steps to Make Part-Time Job Setups More Palatable," *Wall Street Journal*, February 17, 2005, p. D1.

38 Jay T. Knippen, Thad B. Green, and Kurt Sutton, "Asking Not to Be Overworked," *Supervisory Management*, February 1992, p. 6.

39 Art Ulene, *Really Fit Really Fast* (Encino, Calif.: HealthPoints, 1996), pp. 198–199.

40 Marilyn Chase, "Weighing the Benefits of Mental-Health Days Against Guilt Feelings," *Wall Street Journal*, September 9, 1996, p. B1.

41 Sue Shellenbarger, "Slackers, Rejoice: Research Touts the Benefits of Skipping Out on Work," *Wall Street Journal*, March 27, 2003, p. D1.

42 Anne Fisher, "Catch the New MBA Craze: Raoism," *Fortune*, February 8, 2006, p. 36; "The #1 Megatrend in Business Today Is…Spirituality," *Spirituality & Health*, March/April 2006, p. 30.

43 Leo Booth, "When God Becomes a Drug," *Common Boundary*, September/October 1991, p. 30; David N. Elkins, "Spirituality," *Psychology Today*, September/October, 1999, pp. 45–48.

44 Harold H. Bloomfield and Robert K. Cooper, *The Power of 5* (Emmaus, Pa.: Rodale Press, 1995), p. 484.

45 Thomas Moore, "Sacred Time with Children," *Spirituality & Health*, November/December 2007, p. 12.

46 "Making the Spiritual Connection," *Lears*, December 1989, p. 72.

47 Thomas Moore, "Will We Take the Moral Values Challenge?" *Spirituality & Health*, January/February 2005, pp. 10–11.

48 "Teaching Tolerance," Spring 2005, p. 28.

49 "Career Opportunities" [cited 1 May 2009]. Available from http://www.worthingtonindustries.com; INTERNET.

50 "Our Philosophy" [cited 1 May 2009]. Available from http://www.herrs.com; INTERNET.

51 Ann States, "Get Ready for a Pickier Workforce," *BusinessWeek*, September 18, 2006, p. 82.

52 Kevin Helliker, "Body and Spirit: Why Attending Religious Services May Benefit Health," *Wall Street Journal*, May 3, 2005, p. D1.

53 "T. Boone Pickens," *Spirit*, November 2008.

54 Sara Schaefer Munoz, "The Food Pyramid Gets Personalized," *Wall Street Journal*, April 20, 2005, p. D1; "Johanns Reveals USDA's Steps to a Healthier You" [cited 24 February 2006]. Available from http://www.mypyramid.gov; INTERNET.

55 Paul Raeburn, "Why We're So Fat," *BusinessWeek*, October 21, 2002, pp. 112–114; Sara Schaefer Munoz, "New U.S. Diet Guide Focuses on Calories, Exercise," *Wall Street Journal*, January 12, 2005, p. D4; Nancie Hellmich, "Obesity on Track as No. 1 Killer," *USA Today*, March 10, 2004, p. A1.

56 Jennifer Levitz, "Calorie Counters Have It Right, Diet Study Says," *Wall Street Journal*, February 26, 2009, pp. D1 and D2.

57 Michael Orey, "A Food Fight Over Calorie Counts," *BusinessWeek*, February 11, 2008, p. 36.

58 Melinda Beck, "A Salty Tale: Why We Need a Diet Less Rich in Sodium," *Wall Street Journal*, April 21, 2009, p. D1.

59 "Just Move," *Duke Medicine HealthLine*, Winter 2007, p. 6.

60 Robert Langreth, "Every Little Bit Helps," *Wall Street Journal*, May 1, 2000, p. R5; Tara Parker-Pope, "Health Matters," *Wall Street Journal*, August 9, 2004, p. R5.

61 John Swartzberg, "Exercise: It's Not Just Physical," *UC Berkeley Wellness Letter*, November 2002, p. 3.

62 Robert A. Gleser, *The Healthmark Program for Life* (New York: McGraw-Hill, 1988), p. 147.

63 *Fitness Fundamentals* (Washington, DC: Department of Health and Human Services, 1988), p. 2.

64 Stephen R. Covey, *The Seven Habits of Highly Effective People* (New York: Simon & Schuster, 1989), p. 46.

65 James Fadiman, *Be All That You Are* (Seattle: Westlake Press, 1986), p. 25.

66 Mike Hernacki, *The Ultimate Secret of Getting Absolutely Everything You Want* (New York: Berkley Books, 1988), p. 35.

67 Adapted from Bloomfield and Cooper, *The Power of 5*, pp. 492–493.

68 Amy Merrick and Roger Thurow, "The Jobless Go Back to School and, They Hope, Work," p. A14.

69 Heather Green, "The Unretired," *BusinessWeek*, December 15, 2008, pp. 46–48.

70 Kate Bonamici, "Fountain Pen Doctor," *Fortune*, January 23, 2006, p. 40.

71 Mary Lou Quinlan, "Just Ask a Woman," *Fast Company*, July 2003, p. 50.

Name Index

Note: Page numbers in italic type indicate illustrations.

D

E

F

G

H

I

J

K

L

Subject Index

Note: Page numbers in italic type indicate illustrations. Figures and tables are indicated, respectively, by *f* or *t* following the page number.

N

O

P

S

Features Designed to Engage Students

Tip of the Iceberg and Below the Surface Opening and Closing Cases:

These in-depth introductory and concluding cases provide a nice frame to the chapter content. The interconnectivity allows students to think comprehensively about real world and hypothetical examples of chapter concepts. There is also an additional end of chapter case that brings to life the material covered in the chapter.

Total Person Insights

These short boxes share the thoughts, anecdotes, and advice of respected writers, educators, and business leaders.

HUMAN RELATIONS IN ACTION

These boxes provide "how to" tips and examples from the real world.

SKILL DEVELOPMENT: APPLY IT AND CRITICAL THINKING CHALLENGE: ANALYZE IT, SYNTHESIZE IT, OR EVALUATE IT

These boxes ask students to use their critical thinking skills. Emphasis is placed on effective communication and self-development, ways to help students achieve insight, and the relationship skills needed to deal with a wide range of people-related problems.